THE KING IS DEAD

THE KING IS DEAD

Studies in the Near Eastern Resistance to Hellenism
334–31 B.C.

by Samuel K. Eddy

Ye daughters of Israel, weep over Saul,
  who clothed you daintily in scarlet,
  who put ornaments of gold upon your apparel.
How are the mighty fallen
  in the midst of the battle!

2 Samuel i. 24–25

This land is helter-skelter, and no one knows
  the result which will come about.

.   .   .   .

(Then) it is that a king will come, belonging
  to the South, Ameni the Triumphant, his name.

.   .   .   .

And justice will come into its place,
  while wrongdoing is *driven* out.
Rejoice, he who may behold (this) and
  who may be in the service of the king!

from the "Prophecy of Nefer-rohu"

University of Nebraska Press, Lincoln
1961

Publishers on the Plains

UNP

Copyright © 1961 by the University of Nebraska Press.
Library of Congress catalog card number 61–10151.
Manufactured in the United States of America.

Patri matrique

Introduction

The victory of Alexander the Great at Gaugamela in 331 B.C. was his third and final defeat of the Persian armies of Dareios III. Dareios fled eastward across the plains of his dying empire and presently was murdered by his own desperate generals. His successor, the satrap Bessos, reigning as Artaxerxes IV, was relentlessly hunted down and executed by Alexander, who thus brought to an end native Persian kingship. A period of drastic political and social upheaval began for the Orient when the Makedonian conqueror, looking to the consolidation of his conquests, settled Greek and Makedonian veterans in the Near East. Hellenic occupation meant the suppression of native rule and traditional kingship. Under Alexander's successors, Antigonos the One-Eyed, Seleukos, Ptolemy, and Lysimachos, the development of permanent Hellenic occupation of the region was carried to a further stage.

My aim in these studies is to search for evidence of Oriental opposition to Hellenic imperialism, to discover its causes and the ways it was advocated and justified, to show what forms it took, and to find out what effects it had, both immediate and more far-reaching. The resistance, as I hope to show, was justified almost universally in religious terms, especially from the point of view of the Oriental theology about kingship. Kings were believed to be vicegerents of the great high gods, of Ahura Mazdāh, of Yahweh, or of Marduk, or even to be gods themselves, as in Egypt. The law these kings enforced was divine law; therefore, Makedonian and Greek imperialism was an attack on the all-ruling gods of the East. It is for this reason that I shall speak of the "religious resistance" to Hellenism.

The Eastern regions examined are: Persis, the other parts of Iran, Mesopotamia, Syria, Anatolia, Jewish Palestine, the settlements of Jews elsewhere in the ancient world, and Egypt. (India is omitted because evidence of Hellenic occupation there is extremely meagre.) Each of these regions or peoples had its own unique culture, different in greater or lesser degree from all the other civilizations in the Near East. I shall, however, occasionally refer to the inhabitants of these countries as "Orientals"—a generalization intended to differentiate them sharply from their foreign masters.

The relationship of Greek to Oriental was very much altered in 133 B.C. when the first Roman province was organized in Western Anatolia and a new regime came into being. In Asia Minor, for example, in the early part of the first century B.C., a partial alliance existed between Greeks and Asiatics: Mithradates the Great, part-Iranian King of Pontos, created a Greco-Oriental state to oppose the Roman advance. Similarly, in Egypt the famous Kleopatra VII tried to use both Egyptians and Greeks in her anti-Roman activities. Such developments are outside the scope of this book, which deals with the Oriental resistance to Hellenism only during the time when a Greek or Makedonian regime was a power in the East.

The words "Greek" and "Makedonian" are used almost interchangeably. This is not precisely accurate usage, but it is convenient and permissible. With the passage of time the distinction between the two peoples vanished—as, for example, the Makedonian dialect had vanished by 200 B.C. It is impossible to distinguish between a Makedonian and Greek policy of imperialism or even between Greek and Makedonian men except in the case of the Hellenistic kings. Both Greeks and Makedonians belonged to a common Hellenistic culture.

The word "Hellenism" is used in these studies in a very broad sense. It is used to cover all the facets of Greek culture, and therefore embraces not only philosophy, drama, and the rational view of life, but also other Greek and Makedonian values. Many Hellenes were more deeply concerned with the maintenance of armies, the conduct of economic life, the business of the various departments of the Hellenistic monarchies, or the pursuit of high personal status, than with philosophical schools, the theater, or the empirical study of nature and human institutions. The society of the Hellenistic world was much diversified and extremely complex, and this was as true for the Oriental side of it as it was for the Greek. Many scholars who have dealt with some phase of the conflict between West and East during this period have been inclined to interpret it as a struggle between Oriental revealed religion and European humanism, particularly in the case of the Jews. But, in reality, how important was such an ideological battle? Did certain Orientals really think of themselves as defending the City of God against the onslaught of an Army of Men? Or, did they carry on their conflicts with Greeks for simple, unvarnished personal primacy? What particular aspects of Hellenism did Orientals actually hate? The philosophic activity or the immediate ruling circle? To discover answers to these questions, then, will be an important part of the problem before us.

Contents

List of Plates

Map

A map of the Hellenistic Near East precedes page i.

THE KING IS DEAD

ABBREVIATIONS AND SIGNS

Abbreviations of names of ancient authors and their works, of periodicals, and of standard collections of coins, inscriptions, and papyri, conform to the more or less usual practice. I do not give a list of such abbreviations; in case of doubt, consult the bibliography. The only abbreviations which might cause difficulty are:

A.N.E.T.   *Ancient Near Eastern Texts* (ed. J. B. Pritchard).
C.A.H.   *Cambridge Ancient History.*
R.E.   Pauly-Wissowa-Kroll, *Realencyclopädie der classischen Altertumswissenschaft.*

In the quotations of ancient texts, the following signs are used:

. . . .   to indicate matter omitted or missing from the text.
( )   to indicate a word supplied to make the sense of the document clear.
[ ]   to indicate a word supplied to fill a lacuna.

SPELLING OF NAMES

The "Perikles" school of Greek orthography is preferred here because it more nearly reproduces the original Greek spellings than does the "Pericles" school of our fathers. Thus, many Greek proper names are transliterated, e.g., *Antiochos* instead of the Latinized form *Antiochus*. In some cases, however, a proper name is given in its English form if it is very well known, and this has resulted in certain inconsistencies, e.g., *Ptolemy* instead of *Ptolemaios*. The older custom of spelling Greek names "as an intelligent Roman of the age of Augustus would" seems to me wholly arbitrary and artificial; moreover, it generates its own inconsistencies—Ptolemy, for example, should appear as *Ptolemaeus.*

The spelling of names of Near Eastern peoples, places, and things follows what I believe to be the most common practice of Assyriologists or Egyptologists. Where they use a Greek instead of a native form, I have spelled the Greek form in Greek fashion, e.g., *Dareios* instead of *Darius.* Jewish proper names in most cases appear as they are spelled in the Bible; otherwise they are transliterated strictly from the Greek.

Chapter I

The Persians

It was the end of one age and the beginning of a new. Europe had triumphed in her great campaign to conquer Asia. Dareios III, King of the Medes and Persians, was defeated and slain—buried with spectacular rites accorded by the magnanimous victor, Alexander of Makedon. The armies of the former Great King, once numerous and powerful, had been destroyed or dispersed in the fateful battles on the Granikos, at Issos, and near Gaugamela. The Persian Empire, which in its day had comprised by far the vastest and wealthiest parts of the ancient world, lay in fragments unmourned by its several nationalities. Persis, homeland of the Achaemenids and of the Empire's satraps, Persis which once had sent out kings to vanquish most of Asia, had fallen almost without resistance. Its roads had echoed to the tramp of foreign soldiery, and its palaces had been ransacked and looted of the treasures that once had flowed in from all the countries under the heaven of Ahura Mazdāh. The grand capital, Persepolis, had been despoiled, its sacred sculptures insulted and defiled, and then burned—even burned with fire—destroyed by that very element that was the holy manifestation of the Persian fire-god, Atar. Only rubble heaps and a few columns still stood against the sky.

The ravaging of Persis was inspired by the hatred that had burned in Greek hearts since the days of Kyros the Great's conquest of Ionia, a hatred which had been fed by the first Dareios' suppression of the Ionian revolt in 493 and Xerxes' subsequent attempt to overrun Hellas itself. All these years in which Greek soil had been the theater of operations, the heavy burden of feeding the invading host had fallen on the populace. As part of the Persian policy of calculated *Schrechlichkeit*—whose object was to frighten Hellenes out of making any resistance at all—some cities were depopulated. So in 493 Miletos saw many of her inhabitants taken away to Elam for having led the Ionian Revolt against the Great King; and in 490 the people of Eretria were similarly treated for having helped Miletos. Athens, which had aided Ionia, was systematically devastated in 480 and 479, and her

3

Akropolis burned as revenge for the Greeks' having fired Persian-held Sardeis in 499. The horrors of war had been borne especially by Greek temples; they were a source of ready wealth which the Persian commanders could confiscate for the pay of their mercenaries. Thus Demeter's shrine at Eleusis and other holy places throughout Greece and Ionia were pillaged. Apollo of Milesian Branchidai was even carried off a prisoner of war to Susa—an event remembered by Alexander's general Seleukos, who returned the bronze statue to the Milesians along with captured Persian gold. The Great Persian War degenerated into atrocity and counteratrocity: when Artayktes, Persian governor of Sestos, allegedly profaned the Temple of Protesilaos at Elaios, the avenging Greeks led by Xanthippos nailed Artayktes living to a plank and left him to die. And the retreating Persians levelled the city of Olynthos and massacred its people.[1]

It is clear, however, that in this war Persian hatred for Greek religion itself, and Greek for Persian, did not play a primary part. The excesses were the inevitable accompaniment of desperate warfare. The burning and destruction of Greek, or Babylonian, temples by the Persians did not come about out of the conviction that foreign cults or foreign deities were necessarily evil, but because temple spoilation was a source of easy treasure and because deity-kidnapping was universally practiced in the East to undermine the local will, even the ability, to resist. When Xerxes destroyed Babylon, he levelled the city and sent Marduk off to Persia, because Marduk represented the supernatural first cause of hostility to Persian rule. The temples destroyed in Greece were temples of states that put up the strongest resistance— Eretria, Athens, Miletos, and the cities along the Propontis which had been lukewarm to Dareios' impressment for his raid into Skythia. On the other hand, we know the Persians sometimes enlarged non-Iranian temples, as in the case of the Temple of Ammon at Hibis in Egypt. Nor did Persians have any objection to specifically Greek rites or Greek religious personnel: when Xerxes captured Athens in 480, he ordered the restored Athenian exiles with him to offer sacrifice Hellenic-style on the Akropolis, and many years later Kyros the Younger kept an Ambrakiot soothsayer in his retinue.[2]

But the Persians never ceased trying to recover the parts of western

[1] Miletos: Herod. vi. 18, 20; Eretria: *ibid.*, vi. 102; Athens: *ibid.*, viii. 53; Ktes., *Persika*, Epit., 26; temples in general: Aisch., *Pers.* 809–12; Herod. vi. 102; vi. 9, 13, 32–3, 102; vii. 8; viii. 53; R. Ghirshman, *Iran* (1954), 150; Apollo: Paus. i. 16. 3; C. B. Welles, *Royal Correspondence in the Hellenistic Period* (1934), No. 5, ll. 38–41, pp. 33–40; Artayktes: Herod. vii. 33; viii. 127; ix. 116.

[2] Xerxes and Babylon: Herod. i. 183; iii. 150; Ktes. *Persika*, Epit., 52–3; Diod. ii. 9. 4; A. T. Olmstead, *H.P.E.* (1948), 236–7; 237, n. 23; temple destruction in Greece:

Anatolia that were taken from them by the Delian League of Greek city-states, nor did the Hellenes ever stop trying to create trouble for Persia in her Egyptian province. Because Persian gold frequently was a force in Greek international politics, the leaders in the city-states and later in Makedonia never were able to escape from a fear of Persian meddling or aggression. Hatred of Persia was kept alive through warfare down to the time of Philip, and more than a century's suffering, humiliation, and dread created in many Greeks a desire for violent revenge, which could hardly fail to color their dealings with the conquered Persians after Alexander.

More importantly, occasional easy victories over Persian forces served to create a contempt for Oriental strength and fighting power which remained part of the climate of opinion during the years when a Greco-Makedonian regime replaced the Achaemenids. Xenophon, as a high officer of that remarkable Ten Thousand who fought their way to Hellas from the heart of the Persian Empire, had firsthand acquaintance with the competence of the Persian official class. He accused them of debauchery, cowardice, and physical weakness. The Persian cavalry, once-feared scourge of the plains, was now, he said, recruited from porters, bakers, cooks, cup-bearers, bathroom attendants, butlers, waiters, chamberlains, and beauty-doctors. The supposed archdrunkard Artaxerxes II was said to delight in the skills of a favorite dancer, Zenon of Crete. Ktesias, Artaxerxes' court physician, brought to Greece the story that Annaros, Persian viceroy in Babylon, wore women's garments and jewelry, and never ate his dinner without the company of a hundred female companions. To many other Greeks who witnessed the last years of the expiring Achaemenid empire, deceit and cunning seemed to have replaced manliness and courage, and the cares of state to have been abandoned for drunkenness and revelry.[3] Not that a Greek would feel a fine moral shiver at this evidence of decadence; its significance to him was that a hard-bitten adventurer with well-sharpened weapons and under the proper leader could enrich himself without undue risk.

This picture of Persian weakness acquired the force of authority, a

---

Ktes., *Persika*, Epit., 17; Strabo xiii. 1. 22 (591); Ammon of Hibis: H. E. Winlock, *The Temple of Hibis in el-Khargah Oasis*. Part I: *The Excavations* (1941); E. F. Schmidt, *Persepolis* (1953), i. 26–7; Persian tolerance: Herod. viii. 54–5; Xen. *Anab.*, i. 7. 18; i. 8. 5.

[3] Xenophon's remarks in *Kyro.* viii. 8. 1–27; Artaxerxes' desires are from the same passage and Plut. *Art.*, xxi. 2 and Ktes. *Persika* = Athen. i. 22 C; xii. 530 D. The drunkenness and revelry reported by Ktes. *On the Tributes Paid Throughout Asia;* by Amyntas, *Stathmoi;* and by Baiton, *Stathmoi* in Athen. x. 422 B and Strabo xv. 3. 22 (735); Ephoros, *History* xviii = Athen. xi. 500 C.

prestige which it retained even after the conquest and down to the
time of Strabo. The picture was frequently recolored in the two
decades when the Greeks and Makedonians of Alexander's generation
were growing up. Herakleides of Pontos in Asia Minor accused the
Persians of being more devoted to luxury and pleasure than any other
people; another Herakleides, he of Kumai, thought the royal court
spent its nights trifling with women—Artaxerxes III of all persons
being said to have three hundred harp-playing concubines. Much the
same tale came from Klearchos of Kypriote Soloi. While such gossip
was pure propaganda put out by seemingly knowledgeable eastern
Greeks to win sympathy for a war of liberation, the picture came nonetheless to be believed, and even a man like Aristotle thought of Asiatics
as the pawns of dissipated despots, and all Asia a community of male
and female slaves. Wherefore, he added, the poets sing, "It is meet for
Hellenes to rule over barbarians."[4]

In Greek eyes, then, the Persian Empire was a place of fabled wealth,
of gold, silver, splendid horses, of amazing agricultural fertility, all
possessed by weaklings. Poverty-ridden as Greeks were, their economy
racked by continuing intercity wars, their society threatened by the
presence of sporadically employed, hungry mercenary soldiers, in the
fourth century the Persian Empire seemed an object that they—with
their military and technical superiority—could easily convert into a
source of booty. Contributing to this feeling was the fact that Greeks,
because of their high competence, were holding an increasing number
of military and professional posts in the Empire. After all, as Plato
once observed, the only things a man could really trust were his wisdom and vigor. Had not Isokrates suggested that the ills of Hellas—
social, economic, and political—could be cured by the annexation of
the Great King's western provinces from Kilikia to Sinope and by
colonization of the region with the reckless, desperate exiles and the
turbulent bands of discontented mercenaries in Greek society?[5]

With such notions as these in their heads, and with memories of the

----

[4] Herakleides of Pontos, *On Pleasure* = Athen. xii. 512 AB; date from *R.E.* viii,
Nu. 45, S. 472–5, *c.* 350 B.C. Herakleides of Kumai, *Persian History* i = Athen. xii.
514 B; his date from *R.E.* viii, Nu. 42, S. 469–70, *c.* 350–40 B.C. Klearchos of Soloi,
Lives = Athen. xii. 514 DE; his date *c.* 325 B.C. from *R.E.* xi, Nu. 11, S. 580–3. Aristotle's remarks from the *Polit.* i. 2 (1252 B) ; i. 6 (1255 A) ; iii. 14 (1285 A) .

[5] Greek professionals included the physician Ktesias and the general Memnon
who defended western Anatolia against Alexander himself, aside from the numerous
Greek mercenary soldiers in the army of Dareios III. The existence of Greek stone-
cutters at work on royal buildings goes back to the period of Dareios I (*DSi* 3i–3j,
11. 40–9 in R. G. Kent, *Old Persian* [2nd ed., 1953], 144) . Plato, *1 Alki.* 121 A–123
D. Isokrates' plan outlined in the *Phil.* 119–23.

sufferings Hellas had undergone at Persian hands, Greeks and Makedonians came to Persepolis and watched Alexander sit down under the
golden canopy of Dareios' throne. It was an emotional moment. One
of Alexander's advisors, Demaratos of Corinth, burst into tears and
wept that Greeks of former generations had missed the spectacle of
Alexander in the seat of the vanquished Great Kings. And after
Alexander had marched towards India away from the smoking ruins
of Persepolis, some men he left behind began to help themselves to
Persian wealth. In Media a certain Kleandros plundered temples, ransacked ancient sepulchres, and inflicted outrages on the local inhabitants. At Pasargadai, Polymachos of Pella was accused of having taken
part in robbing the monumental tomb of King Kyros himself.[6]

It would be a mistake to assume that all Greeks regarded the Asiatics
as fair game. Alexander himself had Kleandros and Polymachos and
their accomplices executed when he returned from India. He knew
that the empire he was preparing to consolidate could be ruled in
peace only if such arrogance was ruthlessly forbidden. Perhaps, too,
he had been moved by the verses of Euripides, a poet he was fond of
quoting. Euripides had portrayed Asiatic peoples subject to Greek
tyranny, and showed them capable of shocking revenge, but ultimately
human and deserving of understanding and humane treatment. The
author of the Hippokratic *Airs, Waters, and Places* distinguished between the whipped agricultural slaves of the enervating Asiatic river
valleys and the hardy, warlike freemen of the mountain regions, an
idea that had also occurred to Herodotos. And there were Greek
intellectuals who had learned much from the East, men like Demokritos, who doubtless had interests other than Persian debauchery.
Plato's Academy was fascinated by the dualism of Zoroastrianism, ideas
mediated to them by the *magoi* of Ionia.[7]

It was actually the internationalist point of view that prevailed
among the Makedonians at the beginning of Alexander's regime. True,
Persepolis was burnt as a matter of policy to show Asia that Athens
and, according to W. W. Tarn, the Temple E-sagila in Babylon were
avenged. But aside from this, once the Makedonians had defeated all
organized Persian military resistance and assumed control of the

---

[6] Demaratos from Plut., *Alex.* xxxvii. 4; lvi. 1. Kleandros: Arr. *Anab.*, vi. 27. 3–5;
Polymachos: Plut. *Alex.* lxix. 2.

[7] Euripides' attitude is known from the *Medea, Hecuba,* and *Troades*; see, too,
the comments of Sir Gilbert Murray, *Euripides and His Age* (1913), 51–4; 56–8; 83–8.
Hippokrates, *Airs, Waters, and Places* 16; Herod. ix. 122. For the Platonic Academy
see W. Jaeger, "Greeks and Jews," *JR* 18 (1938), 129–30; J. Duchesne-Guillemin,
The Western Response to Zoroaster (1958), 70–85.

former bureaucracy, their official treatment of the beaten Persians was
by ancient standards remarkably lenient and humane. Not only did
Alexander continue to employ many of the provincial governors in his
own administration of Asia, he also behaved according to the customs
prescribed for an Achaemenian monarch, recruited noble Persians for
his army and gave them high rank and privilege, and undertook to
marry his generals to aristocratic ladies of Iran. Alexander's policy
of fusion of East and West found its most impressive expression in his
celebration at Opis, where Greek and Persian consummated together a
sacrificial communion meal, while Alexander the Idealist prayed that
homonoia, "like-mindedness, concord," might be created and made
to last between his European and Asiatic subjects. Greek seers and
Persian *magoi* together conducted rites to solemnize this attempted
marriage of East and West.[8]

But to the rank and file of the Greco-Makedonian forces all this
mixing seemed senseless. The Persian Empire had been won by the
spear, and by the laws of war was theirs to deal with as they pleased.
Had not Alexander himself taken 180,000 talents of Dareios' bullion
from Susiana and Persis? Should the soldiers and settlers and government officials do less among the vanquished? For them to associate on
equal terms with barbarians was an insult to Hellenes. Consequently,
when Alexander's restraining hand relaxed with his death, the old
prejudices reasserted themselves. Of the eighty marriages with Iranian
ladies, only one, that of Seleukos and Apama, lasted.

Seleukos by 312 B.C. had begun the consolidation of an empire that
covered most of Asia, including Persis. This process involved him, as
well as his successors, in a series of wars against other Greco-Makedonian kingdoms rising in the Oriental part of Alexander's empire. In
such circumstances, the Seleukids required an efficient army and
bureaucracy to exercise close economic supervision in the state if they
and their kingdom were to survive. The new dynasty inevitably had to
depend on numbers of technologically proficient and practical-
minded Greeks who ambitiously emigrated eastwards to escape the

[8] On the destruction of Persepolis see Arr. *Anab.* iii. 18. 11–2; Curt. v. 7. 3–5;
Diod. xvii. 72. 1–2; Kleitarchos = Athen. xiii. 576 DE; Plut. *Alex.* xxxviii. 1. The
act has been discussed by W. W. Tarn, *Alexander the Great* (1948–50), i. 54; ii.
47–8.

Alexander's Persian customs: Ephippos, *On the Passing of Alexander and Hephaistion* = Athen. iv. 146 C; Douris [*Histories*] = Athen. i. 17 F; Plut. *Alex.* xlv.
1–3; xlvii. 3–4; li. 1; lxix. 1. Provincial governors in Tarn, *op. cit.,* i. 137; the army,
ibid., i. 111, 115–6. The marriages: Chares of Mitylene, *History of Alexander* x =
Athen. xii. 538 B-F; Plut. *Eum.* i. 3; Arr. *Anab.* vii. 4. 4–6. For the feast at Opis and
its meaning see W. W. Tarn, *op. cit.,* ii. 434–49 and literature there cited.

hard conditions in Hellas. Only by giving them the political, social, and economic control of Asia could the Seleukids compete with other states organized along efficient Greco-Makedonian lines.

Many of these immigrants were adventurous and self-reliant types, like Eumenes of Kardia, intent on making new lives for themselves in the conquered East, and determined to grow powerful through loyalty to the Makedonian regime, cost what it might to the former overlords of Persis. As a result, however enlightened Seleukos I may have intended his regime in Iran to be, however humane many of his officials, like Peukestas at Persepolis, undoubtedly were, still, many of the immigrants were animated by ideas of Greek superiority and Greek imperial rights, and looked upon their holding positions in the satrapies and hipparchies of Iran as an excuse to grow rich. Such men were Kleandros and Polymachos.[9]

Persian resistance to the Makedonians, therefore, never lacked for provocation, and in fact never stopped after the death of Dareios. Some of the satraps Alexander had retained in service turned out to be halfhearted in their support of the new regime, and some actually rebellious to it. Those who remained loyal to the idea of native Iranian rule were gradually eliminated and replaced by Europeans. The failure of guerilla resistance like that of Spitamenes in Sogdiana,[10] however, showed the Persians that the immense technical and organizational superiority of the Europeans made further attempts at open military resistance as vain as the deployment of the huge armies of the Great King. But if physical resistance was impossible, religious resistance was not. It was even natural to the ideals of Persian civilization.

Since the existence of a Persian monarchy, preferably Achaemenian, was part of the right order of this world created by Ahura Mazdāh, hopes for the resurrection of a specifically Persian state were in part religiously inspired. (This will be discussed more fully in the following chapter.) Ahura Mazdāh, like Marduk or Asshur, was an imperial deity who, having created the earth, set human beings to rule it as he wanted it ruled. As immortal and beautiful Ahura Mazdāh continued to live, so his state must continue to survive. The re-creation of a native Persian state was critically important to the former notables

---

[9] Eumenes began life as the son of a dispossessed waggoner, became secretary to Alexander, and eventually governor of Kappadokia. His career is recorded by Plutarch and Diodoros. Peukestas is mentioned by Arr. *Anab.* vi. 30. 2–3 and Diod. xix. 14. 4–5.

[10] Arr. *Anab.* iv. 3. 1; 6. 7; 17. 7; iii. 28. 10; 19. 6.

of the vanquished Persian Empire for material reasons as well. The secular aristocracy was a governing military class, holding widespread lands and positions of authority from the Great King. Similarly, the *magoi*, the most influential of the various priests, were powerful because of their relationship to the kings. By 323 B.C., however, only two Iranian satraps were still in power, neither of them Persian, Oxyartes in Paropanisidai and Phrataphernes in Parthia-Hyrkania.[11] The continuing influence of the Iranian aristocracy was clearly in jeopardy from the new Alexandrian and Seleukid states.

Two ideas—the displacement of the notables, and the interruption of the divinely ordained state and kingship—underlie all the Persian religious literature of resistance. One example of this is to be found in that fascinating collection of protest *The Sibylline Oracles*.[12] It is agreed among scholars that the third book is the work of a Jew who around 140 B.C. pieced together Hellenic and Oriental oracles as propaganda against the Greeks in general and the Seleukid Empire in particular. The Seleukids were then attempting to extirpate the recently organized Jewish State of the Maccabees in Palestine.

The compiler's disguise as a Sibyl was admirably suited to his purpose, for Sibylline literature was widely known in all the ancient world, and was revered for its authority and antiquity. The earliest Greek author to mention a Sibyl was Herakleitos of Ephesos in the late sixth century. A Sibyl was a divinely inspired woman who uttered prophecies of amazing and usually disastrous things to come. Such disasters could be avoided by some change along lines laid down by the prophetess. Several places we know to have been the seats of these Kassandras; in Ceasar's time ten separate places were known to Varro alone, including Persis. He even says that the Persian was the oldest of all, deriving this information from Aristotle's adopted son Nikanor, who was on Alexander's staff until his return to Hellas in 324.[13]

Now, prophecy by inspired women was extremely well known in the Near East. The Witch of Endor was one such mentioned in the Old

---

[11] Diod. xviii. 3. 1–4; 39. 6.

[12] Literature on *The Sibylline Oracles:* J. Geffcken, *Die Oracula Sibyllina* (1902); H. C. O. Lanchester, "The Sibylline Oracles," in *The Apocrypha and Pseudepigrapha of the Old Testament* (ed. R. H. Charles, 1913), ii. 368–406; H. N. Bate, *The Sibylline Oracles, Books III-V* (1918); T. Zielinski, *La Sibylle* (1924); E. R. Bevan, *Sibyls and Seers* (1928); A. Kurfess, *Sibyllinische Weissagungen* (1951).

[13] Herakleitos, frag. 12 (Bywater) = Plut. *On the Pythian Oracles* 6 (397 A); Nikanor quoted by Varro quoted by Lac. *Div. Inst.* i. 6; and *s.v.* "Nikanor" in *R.E.* xvii. 1, Nu. 4, S. 267–8.

Testament; in late Assyrian times the Assyrian kings themselves attached considerable importance to prophecy. A similar institution flourished among the Persians. Strabo mentions water-diviners, dream-diviners, and the *magoi,* who prophesied in much the same way as the late Assyrian prophetesses.[14]

The Sibyls, as far as our extant collection is concerned, universally prophesied in Greek; yet of the ten listed by Varro, three—the Trojan, Phyrgian, and Persian—and a fourth identified elsewhere as the Babylonian[15] must have prophesied in local Greek dialects or eastern tongues. That their material could survive in the common Greek, however, is deduced by analogy from the surviving *koinē* oracles coming from Aramaic-speaking Jewish and Christian Sibyls, who disguised themselves as Hellenic, and issued their direful warnings in *koinē* Greek, the lingua franca of the Hellenistic world. Their purpose was to make appeal to Gentiles more forceful as seeming to come from a Gentile source. So in like manner the Persian or Chaldean Sibyls could survive as oracles translated into Greek. Their manifest hostility to their Greek rulers would have made their position treasonable, and consequently they would have sought to hide their eastern origin.

Nikanor's inclusion of information about the Persian Sibyl in his lost biography of Alexander can only mean that there was Persian Sibylline propaganda, no doubt hostile to Alexander. We know that there was Greek Sibylline propaganda in favor of him. Kallisthenes, Aristotle's nephew who accompanied Alexander as a historian of the campaign until his death in 330, wrote that both Apollo of Didyma and the Erythrean Sibyl had prophesied Alexander's coming kingship.[16] Whether Kallisthenes' statement was true or untrue makes no difference. Such contemporaries as Aristoboulos and Ptolemy, the future king, admitted that the gods were behind Alexander's great successes. Kallisthenes simply said what pro-Makedonian people of this age wanted to believe: that the gods had also predicted that his career would be successful. In these circumstances it would be natural to expect a Persian Sibyl to attack him with counter propaganda. Now, there is evidence that our extant collection of Sibylline Oracles contains a Persian prophecy in Book iii, lines 388–395. It accepts the actuality of Alexander's kingship of all Asia, but it predicts his early

[14] Examples of Assyrian prophetesses in *A.N.E.T.,* 449–51; the Persian diviners in Strabo xvi. 2. 39 (762).

[15] Paus. x. 12. 9; Schol. on Plato, *Phaid.* 244 B.

[16] Kallisthenes = Strabo xvii. 1. 43 (814); xiv. 1. 34 (645).

death at the hands of coming Oriental successors of the Achaemenids on account of his injustice and cruelty.[17]

Scholars have been divided in interpreting this oracle: some say it is Persian referring to Alexander, others Jewish referring to Antiochos IV Epiphanes. It seems, however, that Bousset's suggestion is the only possible one, that a Jewish writer altered an old Persian oracle to fit Antiochos IV by adding lines 396–400.[18] Lines 388–395 must be Persian and old, since they refer undoubtedly to Alexander. The man who comes to Asia wearing a purple cloak must be a king already when he leaves Europe; this was not true of Antiochos Epiphanes. Furthermore, this man is said to subdue all Asia, which was true only of Alexander, and of no one after his time. Antiochos exercised power in Asia along with the Attalids of Pergamon, various small kingdoms in Anatolia and Armenia, but most of all with the Arsakids of Parthia and the Euthydemids of Baktria. Antiochos did not leave a tree with ten branches, that is, a line of ten succeeding kings, although Alexander was followed by the Seleukid dynasty, of whom, counting from Alexander, Antiochos IV was the tenth king. There is, too, a similarity here with the picture of Alexander in the Sassanian work *Arda Viraf Namak*, in which Alexander wreaks havoc, destruction, and slaughter in Persia, and then, annihilated, flees to hell.[19] Since Sassanian knowledge of even the Arsakid period was quite scanty, some tradition of the earlier

[17] My translation of iii. 388–400 as follows:

> One day shall come to Asia's wealthy land an unbelieving man,   388
> Wearing on his shoulders a purple cloak,
> Wild, despotic, fiery. He shall raise before himself
> Flashing like lightning, and all Asia shall have an evil
> Yoke, and the drenched earth shall drink in great slaughter.
> But even so Hades care for him completely overthrown.
> He shall be utterly destroyed by the race of the
> Family he wishes utterly to destroy.   395

> After he has sent forth a root, whom the Enemy of man shall kill,
> He shall leave another tree of ten branches. He shall slay
> The warrior ancestor of the purple race
> And he shall die by the hand of his own grandsons in Ares' way;
> And then a parasite branch shall rule.   400

[18] W. Bousset, "Oracula Sibyllina," *ZNTW* 3 (1902), 23ff. H. H. Rowley in *Darius the Mede and the Four World Empires* (1935), 115–9, favors identification with Epiphanes. Lanchester, Bate, and Kurfess are undecided. A. Bentzen, *IOT* (2nd ed., 1952) ii. 241–2, says that Book iii contains Persian oracles on Alexander but does not specify what verses they are.

[19] *Arda Viraf Namak* i. 1–16; K. F. Geldner, "Awestalitteratur," in *Grundriss der iranischen Philologie* (1904), ii. 34; E. G. Browne, *Literary History of Persia* (2nd ed., 1951) i. 118.

Makedonian period must have survived, for the view of Alexander in Medieval Persia was by no means generally hostile.

It is possible to say something further about the probable source of this oracle. It must be remembered that the Persians of the Empire lived in other places besides Persis itself. There was a sort of Persian Dispersion, made up of small settlements of Persian soldiers, administrators, and priests. These settlements were made between the second half of the sixth and the end of the fifth century, so that by Alexander's day many were well established. Many of them were located in western Asia Minor. (I shall go more fully into this question in Chapter III.)

Now, the king in lines 390–391 is said to be wild and fiery; he rouses up flashes of lightning. There was a famous picture of Alexander that would have suggested exactly these qualities to a Sibyl. It was painted by Apelles, whose brilliant work was much admired in antiquity because it was graphically lifelike. Apelles painted several pictures of Alexander; his most famous portrait showed Alexander holding a thunderbolt, the king no doubt posing as Zeus, striding forward and about to hurl the bolt like the statue of the god in the National Museum in Athens. So realistically was the picture done that both the fingers of the hand and the lightning bolt seemed to stand out from the canvas.

The extraordinary coincidence is that this picture was displayed in the Temple of Artemis at Ephesos, and therefore it was known to Persian priests. The cult of Artemis at Ephesos was syncretic, that is, Artemis was identified with the Persian Anahita, and there were Persian *magoi* connected with the cultus. One of the *magoi,* incidentally, was even painted by this same Apelles. Pliny the Elder says that this painter flourished between 332 and 328 B.C., and this date probably is pretty close to that of the prophecy we are considering.[20]

That Ephesos was the source of this pro-Persian oracle is probable since lines 388–395, and its second century epilogue, lines 396–400, are followed by a long section, 401–473, which deals almost exclusively with other places in Asia Minor: Phrygia, Lykia, Rhodes, Samos, and places in the Troad.

The evidence for a date around 325 B.C. is the consideration that the prophecy was probably a reply to that propaganda concerning the divine nomination of Alexander's kingship that turns up in Kallisthenes. As already said, Nikanor around this time knew of Persian

[20] Apelles from Plut. *Alex.* iv. 1–2; Pliny, *N.H.* vii. 125; xxxv. 79–96.

Sibylline utterances. Furthermore, the oracle predicted Alexander's death, which did occur in 323, and knew no other subsequent event.

There was other Persian religious propaganda of presumably early date. While it has left no trace in classical authors, it has left traditions in the Avesta and the Pahlevi translations of Arsakid and early Sassanid times. The *Dinkard* states that Alexander invaded Iran and, impelled by an evil destiny, almost destroyed Persian religion. Only two copies of the Avesta were then in existence, and Alexander destroyed one when he burned Persepolis. The other was stolen from a certain fortress and removed to Greece for translation, never to be returned to Iran.[21] A. T. Olmstead and E. E. Herzfeld have maintained that this story was fabricated in late Parthian or early Sassanid times to explain the then lack of written sacred literature. H. S. Nyberg condemned literal belief in this tradition and called it a phantasy. On the other hand, it has been accepted as generally trustworthy by a number of scholars, among them K. F. Geldner, A. V. W. Jackson, and W. B. Henning.[22] I think that the latter view is correct, because we can show that a written Persian sacred literature existed, and can safely suppose that Persepolis contained copies of it. Hermippos of Smyrna, who lived in the second half of the third century B.C., says that the works of Zoroaster, amounting to 100,000 verses, had been written down. Pausanias, of the middle of the second century A.D., says that he had seen *magoi* reading an hourlong ritual from a non-Greek book. W. B. Henning has published a Manichean text reporting a statement of Mani, the well-known Iranian prophet of the third century of our era. Mani insisted that the disciples of Zoroaster had written down their teacher's words, and that these manuscripts were the basis of the Sassanid Avesta.[23]

---

[21] *Dinkard* iii. 3–5; iv. 23–4.

[22] A. T. Olmstead, *H.P.E.* (1948), 476; E. Herzfeld, *Archeological History of Iran* (1934), 53; H. S. Nyberg, *Die Religionen des alten Iran* (1938), 424–5. K. F. Geldner, "Awestalitteratur," in *Grundriss der iranischen Philologie* (1904), ii. 32–6; A. V. W. Jackson, "Die iranische Religion," *ibid.*, ii. 691; *Zoroastrian Studies* (1928), 169–70; W. B. Henning, "The Disintegration of the Avestic Studies," *TPS* (1942), 40–56. Henning's arguments were accepted by F. Altheim, "Awestische Textgeschichte," *Hallische Monographien* 9 (1949), 18, 28. Earlier scholars who also accepted the tradition included M. Haug, *Essays on the Religion of the Parsis* (3rd ed., 1884); M. N. Dhalla, *Zoroastrian Civilization* (1922), 40; *History of Zoroastrianism* (1938), 293; and E. G. Browne, *History of Persian Literature* (2nd ed., 1951), i. 97.

[23] Hermippos, for what it is worth, is called "a careful writer" by Jos., *A. Ap.* i. 163. He lived towards the end of the third century: *R.E.* viii, Nu. 6, S. 845–52. His information on Persian religion is cited in Pliny, *N.H.* xxx. 1 and Diog. Laer. i. 8. Pausanias: v. 27. 6. Strabo: xv. 3. 14–5 (733). Henning's text is the *Kephalaia*, p. 7,

It would, after all, have been the usual thing for Persepolis, the religious center of the Persian Empire, to have maintained a library of religious literature. We know through excavation that all the other Oriental capitals did so. And it could be safely assumed that this library was destroyed when Persepolis was fired and the buildings fell in, particularly if the writing had been done on perishable material. The *Arda Viraf Namak,* which reports Alexander's flight to hell, repeats the tradition that he burned the Avesta, and adds that it was written in gold ink on cowhides. Hermippos, again, said, probably in his lost book entitled *On the Magoi,* that the 100,000 verses of Zoroaster were written on oxhides. The cowhides of the Persian source and the oxhides of the Hellenistic Greek source mean the same thing, simply leather, the material we now know to have been used for most of the Dead Sea Scrolls. We know, too, that the Achaemenid Persian government used parchment and leather as a writing material for its correspondence, and that from Dareios I on, cattle and sheep were raised for the purpose, among others, of providing skins for making material for correspondence. We have recently come into possession of a small cache of Persian official documents written on leather, dating from the end of the fifth century B.C., in Egypt. What the Persian chancery could do, so could also the devotees of Persian religion.[24]

In view of the above I am inclined to accept the tradition of the *Dinkard* as a late version, exaggerated as to the number of copies of the Avesa then in existence and as to the removal of one copy to Greece, of what was once an active accusation of the anti-Makedonian religious resistance: Alexander's conquest threatened to bring about the end of Persian religion through the destruction of the religious capital and an important archive, a destruction spectacular enough and sufficiently well known to be used as effective propaganda. One would expect, too, some kind of exhortation to resist, perhaps some comment on the noxious character of the Makedonians, but no such remarks exist in the *Dinkard.*

Besides these poor, broken fragments we have versions of a Persian anti-Hellenic religious text that came to have great influence all over

27–33, and is discussed in his "The Disintegration of the Avestic Studies," *TPS* (1942), 47.

[24] *Arda Viraf Namak* i. 16; Hermippos *apud* Pliny, *N.H.* xxx. 1; Diog. Laer. i. 8. Dareios I from *DB* lxx. 4. 89, in R. G. Kent, *Old Persian* (2nd ed., 1953), 132 and Ktes. *Persika* = Diod. ii. 32. 4. The Egyptian find in J. Kutscher and J. Potolsky, "An Aramaic Leather Scroll of the Fifth Century B.C.," *Kedem* 2 (1945), 66–74; E. G. Kraeling, *The Brooklyn Museum Aramaic Papyri* (1953), 16–7, and n. 65.

Western Asia. Certain Persians prophesied that the hated European would be expelled from Iran and from Asia by divine intervention and that the Orient would be restored to its former primacy. This idea circulated clandestinely for several centuries. We know of it in more than one version: in the Old Testament Book of Daniel; in fragments of an *Oracle of Hystaspes* quoted by Lactantius as late as A.D. 300; and in a Medieval translation from Persian into Pahlevi, the *Bahman Yasht.*

This last-named document, when shorn of the numerous accretions of Sassanid and even later periods, is the archetype of this propaganda. J. W. Swain has ingeniously argued that the Jewish prophecies in Daniel 2 and 7, which discuss a progression of kingship over the Orient from Assyria to Media to Persia to Makedonia towards the imminent intervention of a longed-for divine monarchy, are derived from a Persian source. This thesis sustained the earlier opinions of E. Meyer and F. Cumont.[25] In brief, Swain's argument is as follows. Daniel's highly selective interpretation of the historical sequence of rule in the East—Assyria-Media-Persia-Makedonia—exactly conforms with that known to two Roman writers, Ennius and Aemilius Sura,[26] who lived before the Romans knew anything of the Jews, and even before Daniel was published in its present form. This idea could not have come to Rome from either Egyptian or Chaldean sources, because the empires of the Egyptian XVIIIth and XIXth Dynasties and of Chaldean Nebuchadnezzar are omitted from the list. Since the Romans of Ennius' and Sura's day, before 171 B.C., had no contact with or detailed knowledge of Palestine, Syria, or the more easterly parts of Asia, and since the Greeks were ignorant of the idea, their knowledge of it must have come from Asia Minor. The only localities there that could have known such a tradition of world-rule were the numerous Persian settlements and holy places. The Iranian background of the notion is suggested by the fact that both Media and Persis are allotted places in the progression. Swain has conjectured that the Romans heard of the doctrine from anti-Hellenic Persian clergy of Artemis Persika, that is, Anahita, at Hiera Kome, a holy precinct just in the rear of the Roman armies operating against the

---

[25] J. W. Swain, "The Theory of the Four Monarchies: Opposition History under the Roman Empire," *CPh* 35 (1940), 1–21; E. Meyer, *Ursprung und Anfänge des Christentums* (1921), ii. 191–4; F. Cumont, "La fin du monde selon les mages occidentaux," *RHR* 103 (1931), 50–1, 67. Swain's conclusions have been accepted by H. L. Ginsberg, *Studies in Daniel* (1948), 5.

[26] Sura *apud* Vel. Pat. i. 6. 6; Ennius, *Ann.* 501 (ed. Vahlen).

Makedonian king Antiochos III during the campaign of Magnesia in 190 B.C.

Before proceeding to consider the close parallels between the *Bahman Yasht* and the second, fourth, and seventh chapters of Daniel, I shall argue that the present text of the yasht stems from a Hellenistic original. E. Meyer forty years ago suggested this idea, partly because the text itself says that it has been compiled from four necessarily earlier—but now lost—texts. Therefore, although our manuscripts of the document are no earlier than the thirteenth century, commentators have agreed that the yasht was composed at least as early as the Sassanid period, and that it has been rewritten several times since.[27]

Now, this document has been repeatedly and badly re-edited to describe Byzantine, Muslim, and Turkish invasions of Iran. To remedy the resulting confusion, it was necessary several times to gloss the text. I think, however, that it was glossed already in the Sassanid period.[28] This implies that the original text was pre-Sassanid. Furthermore, it conceives of the coming of a divine hero descended from an ancient ruling dynasty, a being sometimes called Peshyotanu, sometimes Saoshyans, and sometimes Hushedar, who will expel the invaders. It says in effect, therefore, that there is no Persian king on the throne, so that there is no human military leader to drive out the enemies of Iran. This was not the case during Sassanid times, when the powerful dynasty of that name not only held sway in Iran, but even challenged the Byzantine Empire for control of both Syria and Anatolia. This requires a post-Sassanid date—universally rejected— or a pre-Sassanid date for the time of the original composition of this

[27] E. Meyer, *Ursprung und Anfänge des Christentums* (1921), ii. 190. The four earlier sources are mentioned in *Bahman Yasht* i. 1, 6. For the manuscript tradition see M. Haug, *Essays on the Religion of the Parsis* (3rd ed., 1884), 213–4; E. G. Browne, *History of Persian Literature* (2nd ed., 1951), i. 169; H. S. Nyberg, *Die Religionen des alten Iran* (1938), 36. There is a detailed discussion of the text with English translation and notes in E. W. West, *Pahlevi Texts* i (*Sacred Books of the East* v [1880]), pp. l–lix, 189–235.

[28] The text of *Bahman Yasht* iii. 14 mentions the name of the coming hero. It reads: "It is his father, a prince of the Kayan race, (who) approaches the women, and a religious prince is born to him; he calls his name Bahram the Vargavend. . . ." Bahram was a Sassanid king. But the verse actually has a variant on this, and concludes, "some have said Shapur." Shapur was another Sassanid king, so that it appears that this gloss was made in Sassanid times.

An even greater number of glosses appears on verse iii. 19, which reads: "Quite innumerable are the champions, furnished with arms and with banners displayed some have said from Sagastan, Pars, and Khurusan, some have said from the Lake of Padashkhvargar, some have said from the Hiratis and Kihistan, some have said from Tapiristan."

apocalypse. This brings us to either the Arsakid or the Hellenistic era, a time during which non-Persians controlled Persis and the other parts of Iran.

The detailed conceptions of at least one section of the *Bahman Yasht* certainly did exist in the first century A.D. or first century B.C., that is, long before the accession of Ardashir I, who founded the Sassanid dynasty in A.D. 226. The proof of this lies in the extraordinary similarity of parts of the *Bahman Yasht* and parts of the *Oracle of Hystaspes,* which existed in the first century B.C. or A.D.[29] They have ideas in common which are so similar that the *Bahman Yasht* has to have this pre-Sassanid source behind if it is not pre-Sassanid itself. These similarities include the idea of the loss and resumption of world empire by Iran,[30] war to bring about the expulsion of foreigners,[31] the barrenness of earthly life during the period of alien domination, with neither rain from the sky nor water from the springs in the earth,[32] the affliction of fields by both excessive heat and by cold,[33] so that while crops may flower they will not ripen.[34] Both foresee widespread death of animals,[35] the darkening of the sun,[36] the shortening of the year, month, and day,[37] and evil portending for children;[38] mankind hates living and desires death,[39] and is diminished to a tenth of its former number.[40] The foreigners rule without law, justice, or mercy,[41] and the end of their rule is signalled when an object falls from heaven.[42]

The very close similarities between the two apocalypses include such unique conceptions as mankind's reduction to a tenth, the shortening of year, month, and day, the budding but not the ripening of crops, and the alternation of excessive heat and excessive cold on the earth. These images are not drawn from natural experience, but

---

[29] The date of the *Oracle of Hystaspes* is discussed below.

[30] *Bahman Yasht* i. 3–5; iii. 21–3; *Oracle of Hystaspes* frag. 13 = Lac. *Div. Inst.* vii. 15.

[31] *Bahman Yasht* iii. 18–23; *Oracle of Hystaspes,* frag. 13 = Lac. *Div. Inst.* vii. 19.

[32] *Bahman Yasht* ii. 31, 41; *Oracle of Hystaspes,* frag. 14 = Lac. *Div. Inst.* vii. 16.

[33] *Bahman Yasht* ii. 42; *Oracle of Hystaspes,* frag. 14 = Lac. *Div. Inst.* vii. 16.

[34] *Bahman Yasht* ii. 31; *Oracle of Hystaspes,* frag. 14 = Lac. *Div. Inst.* vii. 16.

[35] *Bahman Yasht* ii. 43; *Oracle of Hystaspes,* frag. 14 = Lac. *Div. Inst.* vii. 16.

[36] *Bahman Yasht* ii. 31; *Oracle of Hystaspes,* frag. 14 = Lac. *Div. Inst.* vii. 16.

[37] *Bahman Yasht* ii. 31; *Oracle of Hystaspes,* frag. 14 = Lac. *Div. Inst.* vii. 16.

[38] *Bahman Yasht* ii. 44; *Oracle of Hystaspes,* frag. 15 = Lac. *Div. Inst.* vii. 17.

[39] *Bahman Yasht* ii, 44; iii. 2; *Oracle of Hystaspes,* frag. 14 = Lac. *Div. Inst.* vii. 16.

[40] *Bahman Yasht* ii. 31, 47; *Oracle of Hystaspes,* frag. 14 = Lac. *Div. Inst.* vii. 16.

[41] *Bahman Yasht* ii. 28; *Oracle of Hystaspes,* frag. 15 = Lac. *Div. Inst.* vii. 17; cf. *Sib. Or.* iii. 388–95.

[42] *Bahman Yasht* iii. 15; *Oracle of Hystaspes,* frag. 15 = Lac. *Div. Inst.* vii. 17.

are instead visions of a supernatural world, and as such would hardly occur identically and independently to two individuals.

If these arguments be admitted, it must follow that at least a part of the *Bahman Yasht,* the detailed picture of the apocalyptic conditions brought about by a successful invasion of Iran by foreigners, existed before the time of Ardashir I. But the *Bahman Yasht* must therefore also have said something of the invasion. In fact it does, and twice names its leader as Alexander the Great. He was not at all a threat to Sassanid prophets living more than half a millennium after his death. The name Alexander, then, is further evidence of Hellenistic date. He is called "Destroyer of the Religion" and "Invader."[43] The first epithet is a parallel to the tradition preserved in the *Dinkard,* the second to the Sibylline Oracle. Furthermore, the rank and file of the aggressors are once identified as *Yunan,* which is ancient Near Eastern usage for "Greeks," derived from the word for "Ionians." This word is a Pahlevi vocalization equivalent to Old Persian *Yaunā,* Elamite *Iauna,* Hebrew *Yāwān,* and Hindu *Yavanā.* Sassanid writers, however, usually referred to Greeks as *Rūmi.*[44]

It is true that the *Bahman Yasht* sometimes says that the invaders come from *Rum.* That is Sassanid editing. It sometimes indicates that they are Muslims. That is post-Sassanid editing. The apocalypse normally refers to them by the cryptic title, "The Demons with Dishevelled Hair of the Race of Wrath." This, from the old Persian point of view, was a good characterization. The appearance of the Great King, Dareios or Xerxes, in the Persepolis reliefs was with neatly marcelled hair and beard and attended by attentive and docile courtiers. On the other hand, the portrait coins of Alexander, the bust by Lysippos, and the statue attributed to Euphranor show him with his hair madly tousled, and we can imagine the impression made by his rough-and-ready Makedonian soldiers recruited from a people whom the Greeks of the age of Demosthenes accused of wearing bearskins as their usual clothing. There was even an ancient tradition in Greek that Alexander had the nature of a wild beast and very sharp teeth, and that his hair was like the mane of a lion.[45]

---

[43] *Bahman Yasht* ii. 19; iii. 34.

[44] *Bahman Yasht* iii. 5. Old Persian: R. G. Kent, *Old Persian* (2nd ed., 1953), 204; Elamite: Persepolis Treasury Tablet 21, in G. G. Cameron, *Persepolis Treasury Tablets* (1948), 119. Hebrew and Hindu from C. C. Torrey, "'Yāwān' and 'Hellas' as Designations of the Seleucid Empire," *JAOS* 25 (1904), 302–11.

[45] (Ps. -) Kal. i. 13. 3. The Greek kingdom in Daniel vii. 7 is a beast, "terrible and dreadful and exceedingly strong; and it had great iron teeth; it devoured and broke in pieces, and stamped the residue with its feet."

With this strong evidence of Hellenistic date in mind, we can now pass to a consideration of the parallels which exist between the *Bahman Yasht* and Daniel, which certainly is of Hellenistic date. If we can show that Daniel was dependent on the Persian document, we shall have established our case.

The *Bahman Yasht* may be summarized as follows. Zarathushtra sees in a dream a tree root whose branches are gold, silver, bronze, and something (the word is missing from the text) mixed with iron. Ahura Mazdāh explains that the first three noble metals are symbolic of three Persian kings and the fourth of the Evil Race of Wrath. Then follows a long description of the calamities Iran will undergo—including those listed above—in this final period of wicked and godless rule by the foreign invaders. In its glorious conclusion, the yasht predicts that Iran will be restored to true religion and Iranian rule by the victory of a militant messiah named Peshyotanu and his army of innumerable cavalry.[46]

The similarities of this with Daniel are striking. In Daniel 2, the prophet tells of a dream in which a statue made of four metals symbolizes the successive sovereignties of four imperial kingdoms. These metals are gold, silver, bronze, and iron mixed with clay. The choice of identical metals by two writers working independently to represent a progression of rule is doubtful; what makes it really impossible is that the metals in both cases appear in dreams, and that in both the last metal is mixed with something else instead of being pure. In both cases the fourth kingdom is wiped out by a fifth kingdom whose origins are divine. In Daniel 4, Nebuchadnezzar sees a vision of a tall tree whose roots are bound with a band of iron and bronze. This represents the king himself, who does not recognize that God is the real ruler of men. The tree is cut down and its branches hewn off. This is interpreted to mean that Nebuchadnezzar must lose his sovereignty and graze like an ox. In the *Bahman Yasht,* one of the signs of the end is that a shrub loses its leaves, and this is interpreted to stand for the destruction of the Race of Wrath, which knows not Iranian religion.

In Daniel 7, the prophet has a nightmare. He sees four horrendous monsters coming out of the sea one after another. These are interpreted to be four kings (vii. 17) of which the last is a Greek. This demonic being is slain, and its place taken by a messianic figure who rules a new fifth monarchy in righteousness and forever.

Of course it is possible that the *Bahman Yasht* was influenced by

[46] For an approximation of the original text see Appendix, pp. 343–349, below.

Daniel instead of the other way around. What is the evidence that Judah was influenced by Persian thought in Hellenistic times? The opinion of modern scholars is that between the third and first centuries B.C. Judaism received several fresh conceptions from Iran. These included the notion of a dualism in the divine order of things, that is, between a Righteous God and an Evil Devil; the existence of an angelic hierarchy; and the inevitability of a Last Judgment with heavenly rewards for good people and hellish punishments for wicked. The climate of opinion in Judah, therefore, definitely favored assimilation of some Iranian conceptions.[47]

There is unmistakable Persian influence in the text of Daniel itself. It contains Persian loan-words; J. A. Montgomery lists seventeen of them, of which all but three are included in the Aramaic portion of the book, chapters 2–7, including *apadana* at v. 45, the Persian word for a royal pavilion. A Persian title appears in Daniel; in chapter 2 the prophet addresses the Chaldean king Nebuchadnezzar by the Persian title "King of Kings." This was not at all Hebrew usage; the only other place it occurs in the Old Testament is in Ezra, which quotes a letter written in Aramaic from King Artaxerxes to the Jewish people.[48] The existence of Daniel 2, 4, and 7 in Aramaic and not in Hebrew is itself suggestive, for Aramaic was the international language of commerce and diplomacy in the Persian Empire.

The progression of empire in Daniel 2 and 7 is nowadays interpreted to refer to the successive rule of the Assyrians, Medes, Persians, and Greeks in the Near East.[49] But if these two chapters were native Jewish, it would be difficult to explain why the Median kingdom would appear. The Jews themselves had never experienced Median rule. The historical progression was Assyria, Chaldea, Persia, and Greece.

The *Bahman Yasht* seems also to have influenced another Jewish prophet. Shortly after 165 B.C., when Daniel had reached its present

[47] There is an extensive literature on this subject; I shall cite only a few recent works. G. Widengren, "Quelques rapports entre juifs et iraniens à l'époque des Parthes," Supplement to *Vetus Testamentum* 4 (1956), 197–241; W. F. Albright, *From the Stone Age to Christianity* (Anchor ed., 1957), 361–3; J. Duchesne-Guillemin, *Ormazd et Ahriman* (1953), 71–84; *The Western Response to Zoroaster* (1958), 86–96.

[48] On Persian loan-words in Daniel see J. A. Montgomery, *A Critical and Exegetical Commentary on the Book of Daniel* (1927), 21 and *passim;* J. C. Dancy, *A Commentary on I Maccabees* (1954), 29; G. Widengren, *op. cit.* (1956), 223; A. Jeffery, "Daniel," *The Interpreter's Bible* (1956), 349. The title "King of Kings" in Dan. ii. 37; Ezra vii. 12.

[49] For a discussion of the identities of the metals and beasts see H. H. Rowley, *Darius the Mede and the Four World Empires* (1935); and H. L. Ginsberg, *Studies in Daniel* (1948).

PLATE I

1. Head of the "Alexander Rondanini," now in the Glyptothek, Munich (No. 298). This statue is sometimes attributed to the sculptor Euphranor, sometimes (probably in error) to Lysippos. There is no certain evidence as to who did sculpt it, and the statue may have been made by a third (and unknown) man. Euphranor, for what it may be worth, is said by Pliny (*N.H.* xxxv. 128) to have been the first to represent heroic figures in imposing style. Certainly the treatment of this statue follows this tradition. Alexander is portrayed vigorously, with powerful neck and shoulders and a large head. The hair is executed with a profusion of locks falling here and there to create dramatic differences of light and shadow. This technique, contrasted with the much smoother rendering of the neck and shoulders, accentuates and calls attention to Alexander's hair. Such a rendering of Alexander was more or less common, as we know from the bust by Lysippos and the "Pergamene Head." (Photograph supplied by the authorities of the Glyptothek.)

2. Tetradrachm of about 317–290 B.C. The obverse depicts Alexander as the hero Herakles wearing the lion-scalp headdress associated with the legend of the savage lion of Nemea. The reverse shows Zeus enthroned holding sceptre and eagle and has the legend "ALEXANDROU BASILEŌS [Of King Alexander]." This probably led Orientals to suppose that the obverse portrait was simply Alexander himself. The reverse also carries the monogram ΔI, indicating that the coin was struck in some eastern mint (cf. *Syl. Num. Graec.* [Copenhagen, 1943], *Macedonia*, Vol. 2, Nos. 851–2). Very similar coins were struck in other eastern mints, including Ekbatana and Babylon, so that Persians must have been familiar with them. The lion's mane, of course, takes the place of the hero's human hair; it should be compared with the Persian royal portraits in Plate III. The dignified appearance of the Achaemenids is much in contrast with the wild look, and shows that the Persians could conceive of Alexander as the "Evil Demon of the Race of Wrath, Who Has Dishevelled Hair." (From the author's collection.)

1.

2.

PLATE I. IMPRESSIONS OF ALEXANDER THE GREAT

PLATE II. PERSIANS AND MAKEDONIANS IN COMBAT

PLATE II

The "Alexander Mosaic," from the House of the Dancing Faun at Pompeii. Although this mosaic was probably made a good deal later than the age of Alexander, most art historians agree that it closely follows a painting of the late fourth or early third century B.C. Alexander is shown at the head of his army leading a charge in the Battle of Issos. The Makedonian king at the extreme left, hair flying in the rush of his attack, almost succeeds in coming right up with Dareios III, who attempts to retreat in his cumbrous, large-wheeled chariot; the Great King is saved by one of his noblemen, who interposes his body to receive Alexander's savage spear thrust. The artist has captured the feeling Alexander's victories produced: the irresistibility of the young conqueror and the horror and helplessness of the Persians before his onslaught. The sloping spears in the background suggest marching men and communicate a sense of great events in progress.

I cannot resist quoting the adjectives that A. Maiuri (*Roman Painting* [1953], 70) has used to describe this Alexander, since they closely reproduce words and impressions that appear in the Persian anti-Hellenic literature. He calls Alexander "fiery" (cf. *Sib. Or.* iii. 389), with "hair streaming in the wind like a young god's." This second epithet, of course, is approving of Alexander from a European point of view. If, with M. Swindler (*Ancient Painting* [1927], 282), we sympathize with the Persians' "disquietude, pain, and terror," we see how they could call Alexander's invading host the demons of the "Race of Wrath." (Photograph supplied by the authorities of the Museo Nazionale, Naples.)

form, a series of prophecies was produced that goes under the name
1 Enoch. The book was dependent not only on Daniel, but on other,
similar material. It prophesies an imminent last age during which
sinners flourish. The supernatural signs of the period will be the
shortening of the year, the failure of rain, a dearth of crops, and, I
presume, excessive heat, since the sun is predicted to shine very
brightly. 1 Enoch also says that the stars will not move properly,
perhaps based on the *Bahman Yasht* statement that a star will fall to
earth to signal the end of the time of troubles.[50]

The possibility that the Jews invented these conceptions and gave
them to the Persians may be safely dropped. It may be taken as
generally true that a great imperial people like the Persians, with
their memory of Empire over the whole of the ancient Near East,
would be more likely to develop such a prophecy and influence third-
rate states like Judah, than the reverse. There is actually no evidence
of Jewish influence in Hellenistic Iran. Jerusalem, Yahweh, his people,
and his priests were in the Persian mind only minor names in a
faraway province called simply "Across the River."

A point of difference between the *Bahman Yasht* and Daniel 2 is
the meaning attached to the metals, kings in the first case, kingdoms
in the second. Daniel 4 and 7, however, still refer to kings. This difference can be explained. Since the *Bahman Yasht* speaks of the progression of rule from monarch to monarch, it represents a version of the
propaganda intended primarily for Persia itself. But in the Anatolian
version that Sura knew, as in Daniel 2, national kingdoms replaced
the kings. This change took place when the Persians carried the idea
abroad; Persian kings did not have the same appeal for the East as a
whole as they did in Persis; on the other hand, rule by a series of
Oriental dynasties meant a great deal more to the East.

There is evidence that the Achaemenid kings did not always insist
on being known as specifically "Persian." We have fifty-seven inscriptions surviving in Old Persian from the whole of the Achaemenid
dynasty. Of the fifty-seven, only eight contain the phrase "King of
Persia" in the titulary. The latest case of the use of the title is by
Xerxes, who died around 465 B.C. Of his four successors whose inscriptions survive, none used it. They were content to call themselves
"Great King, an Achaemenid." But even the earlier kings were seldom
called "Persian." Dareios I in the three Old Persian inscriptions he
cut near Suez in Egypt only once called himself "Persian." Of the

---

[50] For literature on 1 Enoch see p. 243, n. 70 below. The places in 1 Enoch referred to here are lxxx. 2–3, 5–6; the *Bahman Yasht* passages are ii. 31, 41–2; iii. 15.

eighteen inscriptions of the same king from Susa, located in ancient Elam, the gentilic occurred in only one case. Dareios' one surviving Greek inscription calls him simply "King of Kings." Normal usage among the Greeks was to say that people who were pro-Persian "Mede-ized"; they did not "Persian-ize." In cuneiform business documents from Babylon, until there were signs that Babylon was preparing a revolt, Xerxes appeared simply as "King of Babylon, King of Lands"; when it was necessary to assert his sovereignty, he used the title "King of Persia, Media, King of Babylon and the Lands." Even in this case he still employed an imperial, catholic titulary. In the Old Testament the Jews, it is true, often exactly identify Persian kings as Persians. But the remarkable thing is that even in Ezra and Nehemiah, books about men who were in intimate contact with the Great Kings, Kyros and Artaxerxes are each once called "King of Babylon." Dareios is three times called a Mede in Daniel. The Achaemenids were inter-nationally minded. In Kyros' audience hall at Pasargadai and even on Xerxes' foundation tablets at Persepolis itself, the Persian kings had inscriptions written in the three imperial languages: Old Persian, Elamite, and Akkadian.[51] People other than Persians had to be im-pressed.

The internationalizing of the prophecy occurred when it left Persis and went into the world. The Persians who felt the loss of empire most keenly meant to make trouble for the Makedonians wherever they could, and the spread of this propaganda was a good way to encourage anti-Hellenism among non-Persian peoples, many of whom had supported the Empire in the past. The message of hope was car-ried by Persian *magoi,* who formed an already established net in many of the old provinces of the shattered Achaemenid state. The role of this clergy is discussed more at length in Chapter III. Suffice it to say here that around 400 B.C. Artaxerxes II established a cult of the Per-sian goddess Anahita at Babylon,[52] and we may suppose that *magoi* accompanied her thither to supervise the cult, and that they settled there and maintained their Persian identity as we know they did in other places outside Iran. In Babylon, then, the *magoi* taking ac-count of the local religious pageantry of this cosmopolitan center

---

[51] The Old Persian inscriptions are published in R. G. Kent, *Old Persian* (2nd ed., 1953) ; Dareios' Greek inscription in E. L. Hicks and G. F. Hill, *A Manual of Greek Historical Inscriptions* (2nd ed., 1901) , No. 20; Greek usage from Herodotos and Thoukydides, *passim.* Xerxes' Babylonian titulary in G. G. Cameron, "Darius and Xerxes in Babylonia," *AJSL* 58 (1941) , 323–4. Ezra v. 13; Neh. xiii. 6; Dan. v. 31; ix. 1; xi. 1. The trilinguals in R. G. Kent, *op. cit.*

[52] Berossos, *Chaldaika* iii = Clem. Alex. *Protrep.* v. 65.

of Oriental civilization, altered their native five-monarch prophecy
into a more internationally palatable five-monarchy prophecy. It was
in this version that it became known to Sura in Asia Minor and the
Jews of Babylonia.

We must posit transmission through Babylonia, for the background
of the prophecies in Daniel is Perso-Babylonian. The Jews undoubtedly further altered the Persian version so that the theology of Daniel
is Jewish. But the milieu of the book is thoroughly Babylonian; much
takes place at the court of Nebuchadnezzar, King of Babylon, or of
Belshazzar, supposed King of Babylon, or in the surrounding countryside. Daniel himself has the Babylonian name Belteshazzar.[53] He acts
like a dream-divining *magos*. While dreams and visions were not unknown to Hebrew prophets as a means of revelation, they were rare
and sometimes distrusted as too similar to foreign methods.

There are unmistakable elements of Babylonian cultus in Daniel 7.
E. Kraeling has shown that the imagery of this chapter is not native
Hebrew, but based on the mythic ritual of the Mesopotamian New
Year Festival. The salient points are the placing of several thrones
for a divine judgment, a victory of a Son of Man over the nations of
the earth, and his receiving rule over them as a reward for it. The
nations are also symbolized by fantastic monsters. The image of the
judgment thrones was suggested by the Babylonian image of the gods
sitting in council at the *Akitu*-festival determining the fates of
kings and kingdoms for the coming year; the victory of the Son of
Man and his subsequent reward were inspired by the re-enthronement
of the king, the representative on earth of the god Marduk, because
of his victories over foreign foes. The symbols of the horrendous
beasts, standing for kingdoms, came from the descriptions of the unspeakable monsters assisting Tiamat, the enemy of good order, as
portrayed in the epic *Enuma elish*. A winged lion like the one of
Daniel vii. 4 was shown in the reliefs at Persepolis. J. Duchesne-Guillemin has suggested that the figure of the old man with beard white
as snow presiding at the judgment may have been taken from the
bearded bust mounted on a winged disk used in Mesopotamia to represent Marduk and Asshur, and, I might add, at Persepolis to represent
Ahura Mazdāh.[54]

I do not believe that the local Chaldean clergy had much to do

[53] Dan. i. 7; ii. 26; iv. 8, 9, 19; v. 12; x. 1.

[54] E. Kraeling, "Some Babylonian and Iranian Mythology in the Seventh Chapter
of Daniel," *Oriental Studies in Honour of Cursetji Erachji Pavry* (1933), 228–31.
The winged lion in E. F. Schmidt, *Persepolis* (1953), i, Pl. 114, 116. J. Duchesne-
Guillemin, *Ormazd et Ahriman* (1953), 73, n. 1.

with the alterations of the Persian prophecy, at least in any far-reaching way. While we know that some of them were hostile to the Greek regime and were enjoying a native religious revival,[55] still the omission of a Babylonian state in the progression of monarchies known to Sura or to Daniel shows that they did not influence the alterations.

There was a considerable Jewish colony in Mesopotamia, and it must have been through these people that the Jews of Palestine came to learn Persian conceptions. We know that there was communication between the Babylonian Diaspora and the Main Body in Palestine. The notable figures of Ezra and Nehemiah came from the East in the Persian period, and in the first century b.c., Hillel. In Herodian days, a period for which we have more abundant information than for the third or second centuries, there was a good deal of pilgrimage from Babylonia to Jerusalem, and Herod even settled six hundred Babylonian Jews at Trachonitis. No doubt these persons brought more with them than the pious hope to behold Zion. As a result of the finding of the Dead Sea Scrolls, some scholars have suggested that the Massoretic text of the Old Testament came into Palestine during the Hellenistic period. It is almost a certainty that both Tobit and the "Story of the Three Guardsmen" in 1 Esdras were imported from Babylonia. These folk tales both show a strong coloring of Iranian elements. Acceptance of these and possibly other Persian ideas may have been assisted in Palestine by contacts with Samaritans, who in the second century b.c., according to Josephos, still claimed descent from Medes and Persians.[56]

If native Persians felt anguish for the destruction of their Empire and suffered from the loss of the influential positions they held in it, so, too, perhaps, did some Jews, men who, like Ezra and Nehemiah, performed official commissions for the Great Kings. And there were other reasons for Jews to sympathize with the Persians of Babylonia. In the very first days of Makedonian rule there the Jewish colony was

[55] The role of the Chaldean clergy is covered on pp. 106–115, 125–128, below.

[56] Ezra vii. 6, 13–4, 25; Neh. i. 1–3, and on these passages the comments of M. Noth, *The History of Israel* (1958), 319, 329. On Hillel and pilgrimage generally see G. F. Moore, *Judaism in the First Three Centuries of the Christian Era* (1927), i. 4, 77–9; S. W. Baron, *S.R.H.J.* (2nd ed., 1952), i. 213–4, 392, n. 3–5. For the Massoretic text see F. M. Cross, *The Ancient Library of Qumran* (1958), 143, and literature cited there.

Settlement at Trachonitis in Jos. *Ant.*, xvii. 23–31.

Iranian descent of Samaritans in Jos. *Ant.*, xii. 257.

On Tobit see p. 191, below. For the "Story of the Three Guardsmen" see C. C. Torrey, *The Apocryphal Literature* (1945), 48–54; G. Widengren, "Quelques rapports entre juifs et iraniens à l'époque des Parthes," Supplement to *Vetus Testamentum* 4 (1956), 197–241.

presented with demands made by the new regime. Some of them were pressed for the corvee, presumably to rebuild the Temple of Marduk destroyed by Xerxes around 480 B.C. They refused to perform the work, and were exempted from it by Alexander himself.[57] Consequently, from the earliest period of Greek occupation, both the Jews of Babylonia and the remnants of the Persian imperial class could find grounds to hate their Hellenic overlords.

The exact circumstances whereby a Persian idea or a Babylonian image came to find a place in the writings ascribed to Daniel is unknown. But we can show now that the composition of Daniel was not a simple process. That is to say, we now know something of the sources that stand behind Daniel. Among the Qumran manuscripts is a scrap of leather nowadays called "The Prayer of Nabonidus." It is parallel to the account of Nebuchadnezzar's madness described in Daniel 4. In the Qumran fragment, instead of Nebuchadnezzar, Nabonidus, King of Babylon from 555 to 538, is praying after having recovered from some affliction sent by God on account of his impiety. He says that a prophet—no name is given—told him that the reason for his sickness was that he had worshipped idols made of "silver and gold, of bronze, or iron, of stone, of clay. . . ."[58]

To revert, now, to religious resistance in Persis itself, we ought to show that the *Bahman Yasht* has affinities with the religious conceptions of Achaemenid times. We may begin with a discussion of the Persians' use of a tree, encircled by a vine, as a symbol of the imperial monarchy. Herodotos before 430 B.C. knew of a Persian legend that connected the idea of a tree with their universal kingship. He says that Mandane, daughter of Astyages, King of the Median Empire, was married to Kambyses, a Persian noble. In the first year of this union, Astyages dreamed that a vine, issuing from Mandane's womb, covered all Asia. She subsequently gave birth to Kyros, who became King of the Persians, King of the Medes, and eventually King of All Lands in Asia. A variant on this legend was preserved by Ktesias, writing about two generations before Alexander. He says that when war broke out

---

[57] Hekataios of Abdera = Jos. *A. Ap.*, i. 192.

[58] A translation of the "Prayer" is in M. Burrows, *More Light on the Dead Sea Scrolls* (1958) , 400; see, too, Burrows' remarks *ibid.*, 169, 173–4, 247–8. D. N. Freedman, "The Prayer of Nabonidus," *BASOR* 145 (1957), 31–2; J. T. Milik, " 'Prière de Nabonidus' et autres écrits d'un cycle de Daniel," *RB* 63 (1957), 407–15.

In his book *The Ancient Library of Qumran* (1958), 123–4, F. M. Cross suggests that the "Prayer" may be only a development out of traditions common to both it and canonical Daniel, without actually being a source; W. F. Albright in a review of Cross' book in the book review section of *The New York Times*, April 20, 1958, 12, says that it *is* one of the literary sources of Daniel.

between Kyros and Astyages, the latter fled to his palace in Ekbatana, where he found his daughter Amytis hiding a tree in the upper rooms of the palace. After Kyros won the war and took over the Median Empire, he married Amytis. Thus, in both Herodotos and Ktesias, well before the conquest of Alexander, the notion of a Persian's winning imperial rule was associated with the idea of a vine or tree.[59]

There is a good deal of evidence that the Achaemenids after Kyros took trees very seriously, and invoked some sort of arboreal cult connected with the idea of kingship. On his way to protect the imperial frontier against the Greeks, Dareios was given a plane tree and vine of gold by a wealthy Lydian named Pythios. The latter's name suggests some relationship with a cult, since Pythia, the feminine form of the name, was the title of Apollo's priestess at Delphi. One of the places that contributed elements to the figure of the classical Apollo was probably Anatolia. A decade after Dareios, Xerxes rewarded Pythios with seven thousand gold staters, and on his campaign against Hellas, at Kallatebos, on the road from Phrygia to Sardeis, found a plane tree so beautiful, says Herodotos, that he presented it with gold ornaments and put it under the care of one of the Immortals, the royal household troops. The importance of this act was such that apparently some Athenian, after Xerxes had been repulsed, went to the trouble of making up a tale about another Phrygian tree. Pliny the Elder preserves a note that when Xerxes arrived at Laodikeia, a plane tree changed miraculously into an olive tree.[60]

At the Persian court was a golden plane tree kept as a permanent fixture. It was decorated with a mass of jewels imported from parts of the Empire, and it was worshipped and hymned by the Persians. The king held court under it. This tree and a vine of gold, sometimes kept in the bedroom of the Great King, were seen by the Makedonians at Persepolis. It is likely that the two were a single composition, since

[59] Herod. i. 108 and Just. i. 4–5. There is more evidence here of Jewish borrowing of Persians' legends for their own purposes. Herodotos also says (i. 107) that previous to the dream of Astyages given in the text, he had had a like vision in which water issued from Mandane and overflowed all Asia. In the nationalist Jewish apocalypse 4 Ezra iv. 24–6, dating from about A.D. 75, the eventual victory over Rome by the Jews is foretold, and the Jewish people likened to a growing vine and a flowing river chosen by God.

Ktes. *Persika*, Epit. 2–3.

[60] Dareios: Herod. vii. 27; on Apollo see W. K. C. Guthrie, *The Greeks and Their Gods* (1951), 73–87. Xerxes: Herod. vii. 31; Pliny, *N.H.* xvii. 242.

Herodotos also says (viii. 99; see, too, Aristoph., *Wasps* 860–2) that when the first news of Xerxes' victory reached Susa, the Persians there strewed myrtle branches in the streets of that capital, and burnt incense, an expensive commodity whose use suggests a religious rite.

the Greek of Plutarch and Diodoros actually mentions a climbing vine. It must have climbed on something. What became of it we do not know. It is last reported in the hands of Antigonos Monophthalamos at Susa in 316 B.C. The activities of Antigonos both before and after seizing the tree invest it with royal meaning. He had first gone to Persis, where he was hailed King of Asia by the notables, and then having exercised kingship by appointing satraps for districts in Iran, he went to Susa and laid hands on the tree-vine.[61]

The role the tree played is suggested by its portrayal in the Persepolis sculptures, along with the ubiquitous palmette decorations. It is likely that the Persians adopted the palmette device from Egypt, and used it, therefore, in a sense akin to the Egyptian. The flower borrowed—the sedge—was the heraldic symbol of Upper Egypt, whence the great Asiatic empire of the New Kingdom had been governed. Tree-worship is depicted on the façades of the monumental stairways at Persepolis, where the winged Ahura Mazdāh disk appears over trees being touched by winged sphinxes whose paws are raised in the Persian attitude of worship. The buildings themselves were shot through with tree symbolism, for the roofs of the Gateway of All Lands, the great entrance to the whole terrace, the Apadana and the Throne Hall were supported by columns which represented stylized trees, perhaps palms. Thus the columns of these buildings were symbolic, apparently, of sacred groves. Four seals recovered from the ruins of Persepolis show palm trees in fruit receiving adoration. The winged disk symbol of deity floats above the tree.[62]

The above motifs, like so much in Persian art, have roots in Assyro-Babylonian culture. We possess numerous examples of late Assyrian seal cylinders showing the winged Asshur disk floating above deities who touch a tree with their hands. Sometimes these deities are re-

---

[61] The tree—or vine—is described by Xen. *Hell.* vii. 1. 38, which is a speech by Antiochos of Arkadia, reporting on his sojourn in Persia; Phylarchos, *Histories* xxiii = Athen. xii. 539 CD; Chares of Mitylene, *History of Alexander* v = Athen. xii. 514 F; Amyntas, *Stathmoi* = Athen. *ibid.* See, too, A. T. Olmstead, *H.P.E.* (1948), 520.

That the tree and vine were a single composition is suggested by L. Pearson, *The Lost Histories of Alexander the Great* (1960), 58, n. 34. The Greek passages— ἡ χρύση ἀναδενδράς—are Plut., *fort. Alex.,* 11 (342 B) and Diod. xix. 48. 7.

The goings of Antigonos in Diod. xix. 48. 1–7.

[62] The palmettes: E. F. Schmidt, *Persepolis* (1953), i. 224–5; Pl. 127; H. I. Frankfort, *Kingship and the Gods* (1948), 27. Persepolis reliefs: E. F. Schmidt, *op. cit.,* i. Pl. 16 B, 17 A, 19, 22, 127, 160. The columns at Persepolis are described *ibid.,* i. 68, 79–80, 132, Figs. 28, 54. They are interpreted by A. U. Pope, "Persepolis as a Ritual City," *Arch.* 10 (1957), 127–8. The Persepolis seals in E. F. Schmidt, *Persepolis* (1957), ii. 10, 27–9; Pl. 8, Nos. 24–7.

placed by priests or sphinxes. This scene, copied by the Persians, represents the veneration of the Tree of Life. This ancient Oriental conception existed already in Sumer and Akkad, where Trees of Life were cultic objects—sometimes decorated with metal bands—standing in temple gardens. The gardener of the Tree was the king. This belief continued into Assyrian times. Pliny says that the most famous of all palm trees ever known were those kept at Babylon in a garden within the precincts of a royal court, and that they were reserved for the kings of Persia alone. The Tree was symbolic of life itself, and, moreover, the Tree of Life was the king. In Zarathushtra's vision, the four branches of the root of the Tree represent three Persian kings and the rule of the Race of Wrath, that is, Alexander the Invader. In Daniel 4, the Tree is Nebuchadnezzar, and the roots of the Tree are bound in the style of old-time religion with metal fillets.[63]

The Persian kings existed to govern mankind—they sat under the gold tree to dispense justice; to be the enemy of lying religion—there was an Iranian belief that a certain tree was a supernatural enemy of impiety; and to protect the state from its enemies—Dareios and Xerxes and the plane trees of the Greek campaigns. Like other Near Eastern monarchs, they ruled as proxies for their high god, Ahura Mazdāh, creator of sky and earth and all therein.[64] The Persepolis Tree of Life, with which the Great Kings were so intimately involved, represented the rightful, proper continuity of Achaemenid government under Ahura Mazdāh, which had come to Kyros when he overthrew Astyages. Did not Kyros the vine issue from Mandane the Mede? And so in the *Bahman Yasht* a tree is the symbol of royal government and the succession of royal government. The yasht is no departure from, but rather a development of Old Persian religious beliefs. There is only the substitution of the spiritualized tree in Zarathushtra's dream, whose first root is gold, for the real gold tree kept in Persepolis.

The conception of the transfer of imperial rule in Asia from Assyria to Media to Persia is also Old Persian. When exactly this idea of history originated we do not know. It was probably in the fifth century. The reverse order of rule appears in the Babylonian titulary

[63] Examples of Assyrian seals in W. H. Ward, *The Seal Cylinders of Western Asia* (1910), 226–33, Fig. 689–96. On the Tree of Life see S. Smith, "Notes on 'The Assyrian Tree,'" *BSOS* 4 (1926), 69–76; G. Widengren, *The King and the Tree of Life in Ancient Near Eastern Religion* (1951). The identification of tree and king discussed on pp. 42–8. Pliny: *N.H.* xiii. 41.
Persian kings as roots: *Bahman Yasht* i. 3–5; cf. Dan. iv. 21–2.
[64] The role of the king and of Ahura Mazdāh in governing the earth is covered in Chapter II. The tree which fights impiety is mentioned in the *Rashn Yasht* x. 17 and *Videvdād* xxvi. 1.

of Xerxes at the very time when he destroyed E-sagila, the important Temple of Marduk at Babylon. Then local documents stopped calling him simply "King of Babylon, King of Lands," and started naming him "King of Persia, King of Media, King of the Lands." The last phrase stands for Mesopotamia, that is, "Assyria." Possession of Babylon had been for some time an important ideological asset for Oriental kings. Many Assyrian monarchs had journeyed annually to Babylon to "take the hands of Marduk" in order to renew their kingship in the eyes of Western Asia. When Xerxes destroyed E-sagila, he also deported Marduk to Iran, and removed, therefore, not only the necessity of going to Babylon, but also the symbol of sovereignty itself. Thus, Empire had truly been transferred to Persia. Herodotos, writing about 430 B.C. on the rise of the Persian Empire, mentions the same order of sovereignty in Asia as does Aemilius Sura and the book of Daniel: Assyria, Media, and Persia. And he says that he learned his Persian history from Persian sources.[65]

The great denouement towards which the *Bahman Yasht* says human history is moving, the advent of a savior who defeats evil and restores religion and the kingdom, was also a development out of beliefs of Achaemenid times. According to the Gathas, Zarathushtra at first seems to have thought of himself and his immediate followers as saviors; but after his death, this idea was altered to belief in a single, unique individual yet to come. Hence the arrival of Peshyotanu as prophesied in the *Bahman Yasht* is not a new conception. Also in the Gathas, the functions of the savior are connected with the last judgment of Ahura Mazdāh. He fights against Evil and is the Foe of Fury and Upholder of Righteousness. In one hymn the savior's coming is said to be accompanied by miracles to identify him. Peshyotanu's advent will be signalled by a falling star. The Gathas also say that at the Judgment there will be an apocalyptic battle, fought by the Army of Good and the Army of Evil with real weapons. In the same way, Peshyotanu leads an army of cavalry against the Demons of the Race of Wrath.[66] Dareios III, who lived between the development of the

[65] On Xerxes' titles see G. G. Cameron, "Darius and Xerxes in Babylonia," *AJSL* 58 (1941), 323–4. On the significance of Babylon: A. T. Olmstead, *History of Assyria* (1923); E. J. Bickermann, "Notes on Seleucid and Parthian Chronology," *Berytus* 8, fasc. 2 (1944), 75; and G. G. Cameron, *loc. cit.*

Herodotos i. 95, 130. See, too, Ktes. in Diod. ii. 1–34; Just. i. 2, 6; xi. 15.

[66] On the savior of the Gathas see Yasna xxxi. 16; xlv. 11; xlvi. 3–4; xlviii. I have used the translations and commentary of J. Duchesne-Guillemin, *The Hymns of Zarathustra* (1952); see, too, J. H. Moulton, *Early Zoroastrianism* (1913), 158–9, and n. 1; A. T. Olmstead, *H.P.E.* (1948), 100.

The miracles in Yasna xliv. 16; cf. *Bahman Yasht* iii. 13, 15. The apocalyptic battle Yasna xxxi. 18; xliv. 14–6; cf. *Bahman Yasht* iii. 19–20.

Gathas and the period of the *Bahman Yasht,* may have interpreted the approaching battle of Issos in 331 B.C. in similar cosmic terms. Curtius reports the sense of a speech he made on the eve of the fight. It may be genuine, as was remembered by a hired Greek soldier in his army and preserved in the "Mercenary Source" of the history of Alexander's invasion of Asia. Not only does the speech put the battle in a theological setting, but the characterization of Alexander is like that of the *Dinkard* and *Bahman Yasht,* and the description of the Hellenic army like that of the Demons of the Race of Wrath. Dareios is made to say that the Greeks are madmen struck with frenzy whom the gods of the Persian Empire are about to defeat, and that Alexander is like a wild beast rushing upon destruction.[67]

Thus the *Bahman Yasht* in Pahlevi is intimately connected with the Achaemenid period of Iranian religious development. It is vaguely parallel to a *Bahman Yasht* in Persian, a ritual invocation of Ahura Mazdāh against the power of the *daevas,* who are led by Ahriman. The Pahlevi yasht would be a reasonable extension of this, substituting Greeks for *daevas* and Alexander for Ahriman. Although the Persian religious literature that has come down to us is much concerned with the problem of the struggle between Ultimate Evil and Ultimate Good—that is, Ahura Mazdāh and Ahriman—Persians did occasionally translate the cosmic battle into mundane political terms. This is shown by a remark of Plutarch's that preserves a Persian belief of the fourth century B.C. The information comes from Theopompos, who in turn learned it from *magoi.* For six thousand years Ahura Mazdāh and Ahriman will fight, and Ahriman will cause pestilence and famine. The *Bahman Yasht* predicts that famine will mark the rule of the Race of Wrath. At the end of the period, Good will win, and people will adopt one manner of life and become one state ($\mu\acute{\iota}\alpha\nu\ \pi o\lambda\iota\tau\epsilon\acute{\iota}\alpha\nu$) in which all men speak the same language.[68] I might add, too, that the Persians before Alexander thought of the conflict of Good and Evil taking place within Time—Zervan. This was developed, perhaps, into a conception of the temporary triumph

---

[67] The "Mercenary Source" is an account of the Perso-Makedonian campaign from Granikos to Issos left by a Greek soldier hired for Dareios' service, according to W. W. Tarn, *Alexander the Great* (1950), ii. 71–5, 128–30; but see the doubts of its existence in L. Pearson, *The Lost Histories of Alexander the Great* (1960), 78–82.
Dareios' speech: Curt. iv. 13. 12–4; specific points: the frenzy: cf. *Bahman Yasht* i. 5; ii. 24–6; *Dinkard.* iii. 3–5; Yasna xlviii. 12; divine intervention in battle: *Bahman Yasht* iii. *passim;* Yasna xxx. 8; xxxi. 16; xlv. 11; the army: *Bahman Yasht* iii. 17, 19–20, 22; Yasna xxxi. 16–8; xliv. 14–6.
[68] The Persian *Bahman Yasht* in J. Darmesteter, *The Zend Avesta* ii (*Sacred Books of the East* xxxii [1883]), 21, 31–4. Plutarch, *Isis and Osiris* 47 (370 BC); J. Duchesne-Guillemin, *Ormazd et Ahriman* (1953), 65–6.

of the Evil Race of Wrath taking place at the end of a succession of human governments, which exist in mundane time, before the ultimate victory of Good brought about by the victory of Peshyotanu, a royal savior and agent of Ahura Mazdāh.[69]

All the foregoing points to an early date for the Persian apocalypse, and its original version must antedate Daniel 2, which is dependent on it. Since H. L. Ginsberg has argued convincingly that this chapter dates from around 250 B.C.,[70] the Persian original must be placed around 300 B.C., soon after Alexander's conquest and the Seleukid occupation of Iran. Perhaps it was composed directly after Antigonos Monophthalamos laid hands on the golden tree at Susa in 316.

The final example of Persian religious literature hostile to Hellenic rule of the fallen Achaemenid Empire is in the fragments of the *Oracle of Hystaspes*. This is known only from paraphrased portions used by the Latin writer Lactantius. What we have of the oracle says that from the beginning of time to the final judgment of humanity by fire there will be a period of six thousand years. As the last age begins its approach, wickedness increases: this age we are living in now says the oracle. The cause of evil is Rome, and since Rome is shortly to be removed from earth the rule of the Empire will revert to Asia. There will be a series of apocalyptic battles which will accomplish this. During the period of Roman rule, important cities (Persepolis?) will be destroyed, and supernatural chaos will make life unbearable for mankind. The description of these calamities closely follows that given in the *Bahman Yasht*. But when things have become truly terrible, then the Good People will gather on a mountain and an Evil One will appear to fight against them. The Good will call upon a god—Juppiter, in the Latin of Lactantius—and he will send a King who defeats the Evil One. The latter flees only to be caught and cast into hell. A Last Judgment occurs, in which the Good are purified by fire and the Evil consumed in it. A new Age of Gold then settles over the earth.

Scholars are agreed that this oracle is Persian in origin, and have

---

[69] On Zervan see: H. S. Nyberg, *Die Religionen des alten Iran* (1938), 380–8; A. Christensen, *Études sur le Zoroastrianisme de la Perse antique* (1928), 45–59; J. Duchesne-Guillemin, *Ormazd et Ahriman* (1953), 120–3; *The Western Response to Zoroaster* (1958), 58–9; "Notes on Zervanism in the Light of Zaehner's *Zurvan*, with Additional References," *JNES* 15 (1956), 108–12; R. C. Zaehner, *Zurvan* (1955), 20, 134, 237–8, 448–9; M. Boyce, "Some Reflections on Zurvanism," *BSOAS* 19 (1957), 304–8.

[70] H. L. Ginsberg, *Studies in Daniel* (1948), 8–9. Based on the résumé of Ptolemaic and Seleukid relationships in Daniel ii. 43–4, which refers to the marriage of Berenike and Seleukos II in 253 B.C.

dated it in the period 100 B.C.–A.D. 50 because the author denounces Rome as the oppressor of the world, and because the earliest dateable citation of it is by Justin Martyr of the middle of the second century A.D.[71] Nonetheless, it can be shown, I think, that our version is a redaction of an earlier version of the third century B.C.

There is a very close similarity between this oracle and the *Bahman Yasht*. F. Cumont thought that the two probably went back to a common source.[72] Be that as it may, the similarities have already been mentioned above. This evidence points to direct copying, and tends to show a more or less common date. Internal evidence points directly at a third century date. Hystaspes is identified as the king converted by Zarathushtra—the same king who is the branch of gold in the yasht. If we can date Hystaspes, we can also date the fictive time in which the oracle was supposedly given, and calculate therefrom when it was supposed to come true, that is, find the period in which it was actually written. Originally, the oracle must have been said to have been revealed long before the time of the end, since Hystaspes received it from a boy seer, and six thousand years were to elapse before the last age. The oracle also says that the final times are already come upon man, so that the six millennia actually must be understood to be almost completed.[73] This is reminiscent of Daniel, too, a book supposedly written in the sixth century B.C., but actually written in the second and intended for the second, when the events it foretells are already past or already moving towards fulfillment. The Jewish prophet was ordered to keep secret the words of the revealing angel until it was time for the world to know them.[74] Now, the age in which Hystaspes was supposed to have lived is known from the date given Zoroaster in Greek tradition. This tradition was undoubtedly come by from Persian sources. Hermodoros, a pupil of Plato's, says that Zoroaster, and therefore his convert Hystaspes, lived five thousand years before the Trojan War. This is the same date given by Hermippos, a man whose information on Zoroastrianism, as we have seen,

---

[71] The fragments are collected and published with a commentary by J. Bidez and F. Cumont, *Les mages hellénisés* (1938), ii. 359–76. On the *Oracle* see, too, H. Windisch, *Die Orakel des Hystaspes* (1929); G. Widengren, "Quelques rapports entre juifs et iraniens à l'époque des Parthes," Supplement to *Vetus Testamentum* 4 (1956), 199, 214; J. Duchesne-Guillemin, *The Western Response to Zoroaster* (1958), 90–1.

Denunciation of Rome and citation by Just. Mar., *Apol.* i. 20, 44.

[72] F. Cumont, "La fin du monde selon les mages occidentaux," *RHR* 103 (1931), 67.

[73] *Oracle of Hystaspes*, frag. 2, 4, 10–13.

[74] Dan. xii. 4.

seems actually to reflect then current Persian practice and belief.[75]
Employing the calculation of Eratosthenes, a contemporary of Hermippos, for the date of the Trojan War, we find that Hystaspes should
have lived around 6,190 B.C. Therefore, the final outcome in the
struggle for Asia's Empire would be predicted for 190 B.C. Assuming
that the originator of the prophecy lived within one generation of the
culmination of the time of the end, one arrives at a date 230–190 B.C.
for its composition. This puts the *Oracle of Hystaspes* within the same
century as the *Bahman Yasht*. This date also fits the reign of Antiochos III, the Seleukid king who campaigned extensively in Iran, and
probably in Persis, in order to recall the Eastern provinces to obedience.

There is also a passage whose ideas are common to the oracle and
the section of Daniel written around 165 B.C. The Persian prophecy
says that when the Impious One comes up with his army in the
last days, the Good People standing on a mountain will implore God
for assistance, and that then God will send them a "Great King" who
defeats the Impious One and has him roasted in hellfire. In Daniel
it is foretold that the King of the North—meaning Antiochos IV, a
man impious towards Yahweh if ever such there was—will make war
on the Jews and will pitch camp between the sea and the glorious,
holy mountain, that is, Jerusalem. But at this point, a "Great Prince,"
Michael, will appear and a war follow with Antiochos whom Michael
will defeat. Then comes Judgment, which as we have seen was a Persian idea imported into Judaism, with rewards and punishments.[76]
The section of Daniel in which these things are forecast occurs immediately at the point in the eleventh chapter where the accurate
history of the Seleukid kings suddenly becomes inaccurate prophecy.
I see no reason why the Jews of those troublous Maccabean days,
when Antiochos was fighting not only them but also preparing an
invasion of Iran once more to attempt the recovery of the lost Seleukid
provinces there, should not have incorporated Iranian oracles as
worthy of belief. After all, both St. Justin and Lactantius believed
that Hystaspes' oracle was accurate and inspired. Why not a Jew of

---

[75] Hermodoros = Diog. Laer. *proem.* i; Hermippos = Pliny, *N.H.* xxx. 1; Plut.,
Isis and Osiris 46 (369 E).

[76] *Oracle of Hystaspes*, frag. 15–8 = Lac. *Div. Inst.* vii. 17–24; Dan. xi. 45–xii. 1.
Mountain imagery also occurs in Dan. ii. 35: the statue of four metals is crushed by
a stone hewn from a mountain which turns into a mountain itself; this represents
the kingdom to come of the righteous Jewish people.

The destruction of the Evil One, here a king, is reminiscent of the flight of
Alexander in *Arda Viraf Namak* i. 1–16; having first wreaked destruction in Iran,
he eventually came to grief in hell.

the second century? After all, Persis had won free of Hellenic control.

That the *Oracle of Hystaspes* was only rewritten for an appearance in the Roman period is shown by the fact that it is concerned with Asia's loss of the seat of the Oriental empire to Europe. This did not occur in Roman times, for when the legions appeared in the East, the empire was already Makedonian, and it had no single Asiatic seat. As Daniel and the *Bahman Yasht* put it, the empire was iron mixed up with clay—it was not a unity. In 190 B.C., the first time a Roman military force appeared in Asia, rule there was shared by the Seleukids, Euthydemids, Arsakids, and Attalids. Only when Alexander beat Dareios III and destroyed Persepolis could *the* seat of empire be said to have been lost by Asia. The originator of the apocalypse was thinking in these terms, for after mentioning the loss of the imperial seat, he next mourns the fact that established cities—Persepolis, perhaps? —will be destroyed by iron and fire.[77] All this points to historical events taking place in the Makedonian period. Therefore, the oracle was originally anti-Makedonian.

It must still be explained why this oracle is not cited by a Greek or Latin writer earlier than Justin. Since the oracle originally appeared in an Oriental language, it was inaccessible to almost all Europeans until it was translated. It would hardly have been immediately translated into the language of its enemies, because literature of this sort was treasonable from the Greek point of view, and secret and holy from the Asiatic. What would make Greek translation desirable would be a period of cultural syncretism, a period in which not only Orientals but Greeks as well longed for supernatural revenge on a common foreign oppressor. This condition did not obtain until after the growing Roman annexations in Anatolia beginning in 133 B.C. Italian looting of the occupied areas then provoked the fanatic hatred of Greeks and Persians culminating in King Mithradates VI of Pontos, who waged a series of frantic wars and frightful massacres against Rome from 90 to 63 B.C. We know that Iranian Mithradates circulated oracles in Greek and ostentatiously took part in Persian cults to make propaganda against Italy.[78] Since Oriental methods of literary production generally tended less towards the composition of fresh works than the rewriting of ancient truths, it is likely that the oracle was translated into Greek about the time of Mithradates' expiring efforts or the period of further annexations by Pompey. It is to the period around 50 B.C. that H. Windisch and F. Cumont attributed it. The

---

[77] Both seat and cities in *Oracle of Hystaspes*, frag. 13–4.
[78] This point is discussed on pp. 178–181, below.

only important change that it would have been necessary to make in our fragments is the substitution of *Romaiōn* for an original *Makedoniōn* in fragment thirteen. After the translation, the text would have been available to Greeks hostile to the Romans, and such people appear with the advent of the anti-imperial elements in Christianity.

This same process occurred in the case of an Egyptian prophecy, the *Oracle of the Potter*, dating from around 200 B.C. It originally existed in Egyptian, but is extant in Greek translations of the third and fourth centuries of the Christian era, when both Egyptians and Greeks in Egypt were hating the Roman yoke. Many of the ideas of the *Oracle of the Potter* were used in the syncretic Greco-Egyptian *Hermetic Corpus,* in the "Little Apocalypse" of the treatise called *Asklepios.* This literature is first cited by Lactantius, around 300 B.C., although the basic concepts he cites do go back to the *Oracle of the Potter,* and even to the earlier apocalyptic literature of the pharaonic period of Egyptian history.[79]

[79] This point is discussed on p. 292, below; see, too, A. D. Nock and A. J. Festugière, *Corpus Hermeticum* (1945) , ii. 326–31, 379–83, nn. 201–26.

Chapter II

The Persian Kingship

The principal cause of the Persian resistance was the loss of the Persian Empire. This is clearly stated in both the *Bahman Yasht* and the *Oracle of Hystaspes*. Both apocalypses prophesy the return of rule to Persia. One does not, I suppose, watch the accumulation of fourteen years of tribute from twenty-five non-Persian provinces disappear in the pack trains of a foreign conqueror without feeling a pang of hunger for revenge. Resentment at the loss of empire is not stated in crass economic terms, however, but in terms of apostasy from true religion and a loss of true kingship, a function which Alexander and the Seleukids were not fulfilling. The Persian resistance came from the articulate elements of Persian society, that is, from those people who had been a part of or close to the dynasty, the aristocrats of both the landholding military and religious classes. Their positions of high status were in danger. As far as Iranian culture as a whole was concerned, there were far too few Greeks in Iran seriously to modify it. Those Europeans who did settle in Iran were in course of time entirely assimilated by intermarriage.

This upper-class background of the literature is apparent from internal evidence. The authors foretell the near total collapse of Iranian society. They hope for a renaissance of much-neglected Iranian religion, and most of all for the restoration of the Achaemenid kingship in a messianic form. The Sibylline Oracle protests against the man who is king without *the* faith, who has ruled unjustly. There is the exaggerated tradition that Alexander destroyed the Avesta, which is to be understood as symbolic of Persian religion. The long prophecies lament the destruction of the Empire and physical damage to all Iran, and the antireligious Last Day which was believed to be beginning. But none of this is an accurate description of conditions in Iran in the Hellenistic period. The third century was prosperous, and Iranian sanctuaries remained wealthy.[1] What it does reflect is the

[1] R. Ghirshman, *Iran* (1954), 228, 237; M. I. Rostovtzeff, *S.E.H.H.W.*, i. 541.

resentment of a dispossessed imperial nobility. The bare fact of European control in Iran threatened the dominance of only the military and religious aristocracy.

Hellenic customs did come into Iran with Greek settlers, armies, and government officials, and were practiced alongside the older Iranian customs. When some Persians began to adhere to Hellenic customs in general and religious practices in particular, the most anti-Hellenic of the Iranians reacted strongly against this cultural treason. Indeed, we might almost call this cultural apostasy, since ancient Oriental societies were conceived of as arising from religious causes— a covenant, for example. Kingship involved religious functions as well as political duties. Other phases of human activity were closely linked with religious belief. And the Persians, with their strongly henotheistic faith in Ahura Mazdāh, thought in terms of heresy and apostasy where we would think in terms of treason or nonconformism. Dareios and Xerxes thought of revolt as a theological issue. The Zarathushtrian Gathas condemn many acts as displeasing to God. And in the Hellenistic period, denunciation of heterodox practices among the Iranians, both secular persons and priests, is strongly stated in the *Oracle of Hystaspes* and the *Bahman Yasht*.

We know that some religious customs of the Greeks and Persians differed and that these differences were important to some Iranian people. The early Persians, as known from both classical writers and the results of archeology, did not erect temples to house cult-statues nor use images themselves, and they condemned persons who did so. Towards the end of the Achaemenid dynasty, Artaxerxes II set up cult-images of Anahita for the first time at Susa, Babylon, Ekbatana, Damaskos, and Sardeis. This was a break with the past. It should be noted, however, that neither Pasargadai nor Persepolis was included in this list and that these places were the homeland of Achaemenid traditions. The usual form of Persian religious architecture was the simple fire-temple, which contained no cult-image.[2]

A most important point of difference lay in methods of disposal of

[2] For an enumeration and discussion of excavated Old Persian sites see L. Vanden Berghe, *Archéologie de l'Iran ancien* (1959), and the literature cited. For Persepolis itself, there is E. F. Schmidt, *Persepolis* i (1953) and ii (1957).

The whole corpus of classical references to Iranian religion is set forth with commentary in C. Clemen, *Die griechischen und lateinischen Nachrichten über die persische Religion* (1920). Herodotos (i. 131–40) gives a succinct account of fifth-century Achaemenid religion as understood by a Greek. Strabo (xv. 3. 13–22 [732–6]) gives a picture showing later modifications.

The prohibition against images in Herod. *loc. cit.* and Cic. *Repub.* iii. 9. 14. Cult statues of Artaxerxes: Berossos, *Chaldaika* iii = Clem. Alex., *Protrep.* v. 65.

the dead. Greeks sometimes cremated, and usually interred their dead, customs that strict followers of Magian practices did not observe. We are told by both Herodotos and Ktesias that the Persians considered cremation unlawful, which indeed the *Videvdād* of Hellenistic date calls a sin without atonement, for cremation was the defilement of holy fire, Atar, with an unclean corpse.[3]

The appeal of Hellenism stemmed from two sources. There was the intrinsic attraction of Hellenism as the culture of a high civilization. It was also the way of life of a victorious ruling class, which occupied almost all the desirable, lucrative, and powerful positions in government, and in some cases, the wealthy parts of the country, being concerned with the efficient exploitation of agriculture and grazing. The Persian aristocrats were subject to natural tendencies to imitate their new rulers' ways, both from a desire to ingratiate themselves and make themselves more efficient, and from a fascination with the manners and customs of people who were obviously successful. While most remained staunchly hostile, many others at least collaborated, and a few became cultural converts.

When the Makedonian satrap of Media, Nikanor, was sent by Antigonos to undo Seleukos' occupation of Babylon, the former's forces included a contingent of Persians. They deserted to Seleukos when their commanding officer Evagoras, satrap of Areia, was killed, because they objected to Antigonos' regime in Iran. This episode shows that some Persians were at least willing to cooperate with whatever Greek power seemed least likely to be a burden to Persis. Similarly, during the winter of 317–316 B.C., when Antigonos was attempting a surprise attack on the forces of Eumenes of Kardia, the natives of Gabiene cooperated with Eumenes by warning him of the approach of hostile soldiers.[4] If such loyalty was forced and half-hearted, yet continued practice must in time have led some Persians to go further, and to become dependent on the Makedonian regime for the maintenance of their political, economic, and social status. In the third century, we hear of high officers in the Seleukid provincial government. Aribazos was governor of Kilikia in 246/5 B.C., and another similarly named person, who may be the same man, was governor of Sardeis under Antiochos III. There were several important officers in the Seleukid army, and some whole military formations,

---

[3] Herod. iii. 16; Ktes. *Persika*, Epit. 57; *Videvdād* i. 17; for the date of the *Videvdād* see p. 79, n. 34, below.

[4] Persian contingent: Diod. xix. 48. 2; 92. 3–4; Gabiene: *ibid.*, xix. 37. 6; Plut. *Eum.* xv. 4.

mostly cavalry, who would have to represent the nobility and its retainers. These men had contact with Greek ways and Greek religion. Acceptance in part was inevitable. Of course this was not a one-way affair, for Europeans adopted Iranian gods and rites, too, and thus a Greco-Iranian class with syncretic religious practices came into being.[5] The protests of the religious resistance were directed against this class, apostates from the true faith, and the new hangers-on from the Greek world.

This cultural interchange was natural; there is no evidence that the Makedonians consciously sought to change the Persians' religion or to diminish the authority of Persian sanctuaries or persecute the priesthoods, or in any way interfere with Persian religious beliefs. Rather, we know that Iranian holy places remained wealthy under Seleukid rule, and retained extensive estates and villages inhabited by their serfs who worked the land.[6]

Nor is there evidence that resistance was a peasant movement against Hellenic economic exploitation as was the case in Egypt and Palestine. The Seleukid regime hardly touched the peasantry at all, and probably no great change was apparent to them. The Makedonian kings theoretically owned all noncity and all nontemple land in Iran; but it was actually held by the aristocracy, in most cases the old families of Achaemenid times. These persons in the main continued their old methods of dealing with the rural classes. Nor did the peasantry suffer from the oppression of a Hellenized bourgeoisie, as was the case in Syria. We know of few *poleis* in Iran. Such as existed were in the eastern part, in the Greco-Bactrian kingdom of the Euthydemids; cities in great numbers were organized in Mesopotamia and the west, but in Iran proper, few, in Persis only two.

Iranian propaganda was directed, then, against cultural apostasy only in the highest persons in society and had behind it people of the same class. And if the Greco-Makedonians occasionally outraged the religious ideas of some Persians by following their European customs, it was only in matters of detail. The most important religious issue was their replacing the Achaemenid dynasty by that first of Alexander, and

[5] Aribazos: Polybios vii. 17. 1; E. R. Bevan, *The House of Seleucus* (1902), i. 91, n. 1; ii. 7. Military officers in Polyainos iv. 15; vii. 40; M. I. Rostovtzeff in *C.A.H.* vii. 170–1. Persians: Livy xxxvii. 40; Polybios xxx. 25; W. W. Tarn, *The Greeks in Bactria and India* (2nd ed., 1951), 32, n. 3. Greek acceptance of Iranian ideas: E. H. Minns, "Parchments of the Parthian Period from Avroman in Kurdistan," *JHS* 35 (1915), 22–65; even in Mesopotamia: M. I. Rostovtzeff, *S.E.H.H.W.* ii. 862; Pl. xcvii. 1–2. There is also the case of Mithrism.

[6] M. I. Rostovtzeff in *C.A.H.* vii. 181; *S.E.H.H.W.* i. 509, 516; R. Ghirshman, *Iran* (1954), 231–9.

then of Seleukos. The fact of Hellenic kingship and rule itself was the issue. For in Persia, the dynasty of Kyros and Dareios I through long custom and tradition had established its right to rule, which right was a part of theology. The kingship carried with it certain sacral responsibilities and obligations which a Makedonian could not possibly fulfill, even if he had willed it, because Europeans simply were not Persians. The King of the Medes and Persians had to be of Iranian family, owning Persian customs and religion, and submitting to a Persian pattern of royal taboos. He had to be chosen by Ahura Mazdāh, and he could not be chosen to rule unless he fulfilled all prerequisites. This is reflected in the literature of resistance. The Sibylline Oracle predicts the coming of a faithless, unjust king to rule in Asia, and foresees his destruction by the dynasty which he seeks to destroy. The two apocalypses are concerned with the idea of kingship, predicting eschatological conflict between an illegitimate foreign king, and the new Persian prince sent from heaven. Kingship is the theme in the propaganda, and must be dealt with in detail; to do so will first entail investigation of Persian concepts of kingship in pre-Alexandrian times.

Analysis of the royal titulary in the Old Persian inscriptions shows the nature of the office of king, and on what qualifications it was held. The texts almost without exception begin with the formula, "I am X, Great King, King of Kings, son of Y, an Achaemenid."[7] Somewhere in the body of the texts it is stated that the office has been bestowed through the favor of Ahura Mazdāh or that the man became king because the god bore him aid.[8] These constantly reiterated phrases are the kings' own statements of the nature of their office and why they held it. They held it because of the divine nomination of Ahura Mazdāh. That is the theological explanation, whatever may be the mundane facts of peaceful inheritance from a father or the violent success of usurpation. In any culture there is a cleavage between ideal

[7] Old Persian royal inscriptions as follows (page numbers refer to R. G. Kent, *Old Persian* [2nd ed., 1953]) : *AmH* i. 1–4, p. 116; *AsH* i. 1–4, p. 116; *CMb*, p. 116; *DPa*, p. 135; *DPb*, p. 135; *DPe* i. 1–5, p. 136; *DPh* i. 1–3, pp. 136–7; *DNa* ii. 8–15, pp. 137–8; *DSb*, p. 141; *DSc*, p. 141; *DSd*, p. 141; *DSf*, ii. 5–8, pp. 142–3; *DE*, ii. 11–20, p. 147; *DH*, i. 1–2, p. 147; *XPa*, ii. 6–11, pp. 147–8; *XPb*, ii. 11–21, p. 148; *XPc*, ii. 6–9, p. 149; *XPd*, ii. 8–14, p. 149; *XPe*, p. 149; *XPf*, ii. 8–15, pp. 149–50; *XPh*, ii. 6–13, pp. 150–1; *XPj*, p. 152; *XSa*, p. 152; *XE*, i. 1–11, p. 152; *XV*, ii. 9–16, p. 152–3; *A¹Pa*, ii. 9–16, p. 153; *D²Sb*, p. 154; *A²Sa*, p. 154; *A³Pa*, ii. 8–21, p. 146.

[8] *Ibid.*, *AmH*, ii. 4–9, p. 116; *AsH*, ii. 5–14, p. 116; *DB*, lxii. 4. 59—lxiv. 4. 69, pp. 129–32; *DPd*, i. 1–5, pp. 135–6; *DPe*, ii. 5–18, p. 136; *DPh*, ii. 3–10, pp. 136–7; *DNa*, i. 1–8, pp. 137–8; *DNb*, viii. 45–9, pp. 138–40; *DSa*, ii. 3–5, p. 141; *DSf*, iii. 8–22; pp. 142–4; *DSi*, ii. 2–4, p. 144; *DSm*, ii. 3–11, p. 145; *DSp*, p. 146; *DZc*, i. 1–4, p. 147; *DE*, i. 1–11, p. 147; *XPh*, iii. 13–6, pp. 150–1; iv. 28–35, *ibid.*; *A¹Pa*, i. 1–8, p. 153; *A²Hc*, iii. 15–20, p. 155.

and practice. Like the Assyro-Babylonian kings whose spiritual successors they were, the Persian kings were kings through the physical
reality of their occupation of the throne. Success was the outward
manifestation of the inner grace of selection by Ahura Mazdāh.

The office that the king occupied was that of Great King, or King
of Kings. The monarch was the supreme legitimate earthly ruler.
Ahura Mazdāh, the god of Persis, could bestow such office because he,
the god, had achieved ecumenical status through the Persian military
conquest of the Near East. He was the universal high god, at least in
Persian eyes, "who created this earth, who created yonder sky, who
created man, who created happiness for man, who made X king."
The god had the right as Creator to dispose of the world to his own
candidate, and, as the Persian said, the god chose to have one Great
King, "One king of many, one lord of many."⁹

Persian religious thought was well suited to such a doctrine. For of
all the peoples of the Orient, with the single exception of the Hebrews,
only they developed a rigidly henotheistic belief and an eschatology
which saw human and divine affairs moving inexorably towards the
predetermined divine and universal victory of Ahura Mazdāh. The
conflict of the god and his enemy Ahriman in Zoroastrian thought was
to be concluded by the victory of the God of Light and Truth over
the Power of Evil. This was a purely religious conception. It was
paralleled by an Achaemenid political and religious conception of the
victory of the dynasty, eternal and everlasting on earth, from whose
efforts a universal state emerged in Asia as the agent of the high god's
rule.

Single monarch and single monarchy—this theology was well known
to Greeks. Aischylos makes one of his characters say that Zeus, his translation of Ahura Mazdāh, had made it a kind of natural law that one
man should rule all Asia, and that Kyros had fulfilled the divine will.
This principle of imperial sway over all the peoples of the East was
known to Herodotos and Xenophon as well.¹⁰

In actual practice, the god's ukase was observed in the Draconian
protocol of the Achaemenid court. For any man, save the legitimate
choice, to sit on Ahura Mazdāh's throne for any reason was an offence
punishable by death. The throne itself was covered with gold—sym-

---

⁹ *Ibid.*, *DNa*, i. 1–8, pp. 137–8; *DNb*, vii. 1–5, pp. 139–40; *DSb*, p. 141; *DSe*, i.
1–7, pp. 141–2; *DSs*, p. 146; *DZc*, i. 1–4, p. 147; *DE*, i. 1–11, p. 147; *XPa*, i. 1–6, pp.
147–8; *XPb*, i. 1–11, p. 148; *XPc*, i. 1–5, p. 149; *XPd*, i. 1–8, p. 149; *XPf*, i. 1–8, pp.
149–50; *XPh*, i. 1–6, pp. 150–1; *XE*, i. 1–11, p. 152; *XV*, i. 1–9, pp. 152–3; *A¹Pa*, i.
1–8, p. 153; *A²Hc*, i. 1–7, p. 155; *A³Pa*, i. 1–8, p. 156.

¹⁰ Aisch. *Pers.* 762–70; Herod. i. 4; vii. 8; ix. 116; Xen. *Kyro.* viii. 7. 11.

bolic of immortality and deity—and was fitted up with feet of lion's paws—symbolic of strength. From representations of it in the Persepolis reliefs, it is evident that it was copied from thrones used by the gods of Assyria.[11] Thus, the Persian king graphically represented the rule of Ahura Mazdāh on earth. This doctrine of unitary Persian rule, long defended by the Achaemenids in the teeth of numerous revolts, was expressed architecturally in Xerxes' Gate of All Lands at Persepolis. Through it passed foreign embassies on their way to transact business with the Great King. The monumental propylaea were guarded by human headed winged bulls, the divine cherubim of Western Asia, wearing feathered crowns and bearded like gods. By them were engraved the words, "By the favor of Ahura Mazdāh, I (Xerxes), made this Gate, 'All Lands.' "[12]

By virtue of his selection, the Persian king was a unique individual. He reflected the awesome power and august majesty of the Persian high god, and held by virtue of his office a position supernatural. He was, if less than a god, still more than a man. Aischylos in the *Persians* calls Dareios, the dead king and father of the reigning sovereign Xerxes, *isotheos,* "equal to the gods," *theion,* "divine," *theomestor,* "divine in council," *theos Persais,* "the Persians' god." He also calls him *akakos,* "guileless, knowing no wrong," a characteristic of godlike beings; this last epithet echoes Dareios' own Behistun inscription, where he boasts that he was not a doer of wrong. The poet also calls Xerxes a being equal to God, sprung from a golden race. Atossa, Xerxes' mother and Dareios' wife, is called wife of the Persians' god, and mother bringing forth the god.[13] Aischylos' evidence cannot be taken literally, for it comes from a source—Greek tragedy—which had to fulfill its own religious canons and include the appearance of a god, here played by Dareios. Yet Aischylos could use the Persian dynasty in this way; if he did not think them gods, at least he could represent them so and expect to be understood.

Other Greeks described the Persian monarchs as having a divine *daimon,* or spirit. Plutarch, dependent upon Persis-dwelling Ktesias

[11] The prohibition: Herod. vii. 16; Curt. viii. 4. 17; Front. *Strat.* iv. 6. 3; the throne itself: Xen. *Hell.* i. 5. 3; Demos. *A. Timo.* 129 (741); Herakleides of Kumai, *Persian History* i = Athen. xii. 514 C; Philos. *Ima.* ii. 31 (385); E. F. Schmidt, *Persepolis* (1953), i. Pl. 98–9, 105, 108–9. The Assyrian parallels in W. H. Ward, *The Seal Cylinders of Western Asia* (1910), 239, Fig. 718; 241, Fig. 722.

[12] The Gate in E. F. Schmidt, *op. cit.,* i. 65, 68; Pl. 9–12; A. T. Olmstead, *H.P.E.* (1948), 286. The quotation is *XPa,* iii. 11–17, in R. G. Kent, *op. cit.,* 148.

[13] Dareios: Aisch. *Pers.* 651, 654–5, 671, 711, 857; cf. *DB* xliii. 4. 61–7 in R. G. Kent, *op. cit.,* 129–32; Atossa: Aisch. *Pers.* 79–80, 157. On these verses see A. S. F. Gow, "Notes on the *Persae* of Aeschylus," *JHS* 48 (1928), 133–58.

for information, describes an argument between Persian courtiers. The royal eunuch Sparamizes ends the debate with the wish that those present may revere the *daimon* of the king. This information matches what fourth-century Theopompos says: that the Persian nobility offered a table heaped with food at all meals for the same *daimon* of the king. This Greek picture of the king's *daimon* is a reasonable interpretation of the Persian belief in the *fravashi*, or "soul," of the monarch. I do not mean to imply that there was a formal cult of the king; but there was reverence or veneration paid by Persians to the august *fravashi* of the human Great King.[14]

The king was a select vessel of the god, poured full of special powers, and surrounded by special magical effects. Persian artists tried to depict this quality simply by making the Persian king bigger than any other man they showed. This technique was pursued in reliefs at Behistun, Naqsh-i-Rustam, and Persepolis. In the Council Hall reliefs at Persepolis the seated king is as tall as the crown prince standing behind him, who, in turn, is larger than the ordinary mortals before them both.[15]

The accoutrements of the king, and special precautions taken with his person, show the same thing. Just as Ahura Mazdāh in the reliefs never touches the ground but always floats in the air, the Persian king never touched the ground. He alighted from his chariot on a gold stool, which a stool-bearer was specially detailed to carry, and he was not touched by anybody's helping hand. He never went on foot outside the palace, and even in it wherever he walked, he walked on Sardeis carpets, which anyone else was forbidden to tread upon. His crown—the *kidaris*—was a tall hat absolutely unique as pictured among the headgear in the Persian reliefs. It is virtually identical, however, with the *kidaris* worn by Ahura Mazdāh.[16]

[14] The argument: Plut. *Art.* xv. 5; Theopompos, *Histories* xviii = Athen. vi. 252 B. L. R. Taylor, "The 'Proskynesis' and the Hellenistic Ruler Cult," *JHS* 47 (1927), 53–62; "The Daimon of the Persian King," *JHS* 48 (1928), 6; W. W. Tarn, "The Hellenistic Ruler Cult and the Daemon," *JHS* 48 (1928), 206–19; F. Cumont, "Nouvelles inscriptions grecques de Suse," *CRAI* (1930), 217–8; A. D. Nock, "Notes on Ruler-Cult, I–IV," *JHS* 48 (1928), 21–43; review: "Taylor: The Divinity of the Roman Emperor," *Gnomon* 8 (1932), 513–8.

[15] F. Sarre and E. Herzfeld, *Iranische Felsreliefs* (1910), Pl. III, IV, XXIII, XXIV, XXXV; E. F. Schmidt, *Persepolis* (1953), i. Pl. 77, 116–7; J. B. Pritchard (ed.), *The Ancient Near East in Pictures* (1954), Pl. 462–3.

[16] The stool: Deinon [*Persian History*] = Athen. xii. 514 AB; E. F. Schmidt, *op. cit.*, i. Pl. 119, 121–3. The carpets: Herakleides of Kumai, *Persian History* i = Athen. xii. 514 C; Chares of Mitylene [*History of Alexander*] = Athen. xii. 514 C; Plut. *Alex.* xxxvii. 4; *Them.* xvi. 2 mentions a parasol that always protected the king from the sun's rays. The *kidaris*: E. F. Schmidt, *op. cit.*, i. 163–4; Pl. 104, 107, 119, 121;

Uniformly, the Persian king and crown prince wear square-cut, beautifully marcelled beards, worn by no other mortal in the reliefs, but shared with Ahura Mazdāh and the cherubim of Persepolis.[17] The king's robe was uniquely his. An aetiological legend known to Xenophon related that Kyros received its prototype when he married the Median king's daughter. When he subsequently became king she presented him with crown and robe. These were the primary symbols of kingship. A similar garment in later times was called the Robe of Kyros. It possessed supernatural powers. It was first worn by a king during his coronation rites at Pasargadai. Plutarch calls these rites *teletē*—a Greek term for a mystery rite—which implies that the king underwent a metamorphosis. For the robe was a talisman: when Kyros the Younger plotted to kill his just-crowned brother, he refused to let the blow be struck while Artaxerxes was wearing the coronation robe.[18] The significance of this garment as a manifestation of true kingship is the key to understanding a story that Herodotos tells of Xerxes' robe, the gift of his wife Amestris. Xerxes is prevailed upon by a mistress, Artaynta, to promise her any boon she may name. When she asks for the robe, Xerxes tries to get her to take in exchange cities, gold, an army. She refuses, holds him to his word, and gets the robe. The result is that Amestris mutilates the girl's mother and Masistes, Artaynta's husband. Masistes seems to have been aiming for the kingship; the robe was essential for this. Thus, the royal robe in Persian eyes was a treasure passing understanding. It conferred extraordinary powers even when worn out. There was the instance of Teribazos, a nobleman, who got Artaxerxes' robe and put it on. Even though the garment had a tear in it, this act was a terrible thing, absolutely forbidden.[19] According to Curtius it was purple and white, and the costume worn with it included a tunic of cloth of gold emblazoned with hawks, by which we might understand the winged Ahura Mazdāh symbol. Ktesias mentions a vermilion garment, which may be included in the robe ensemble; he says that it struck an almost religious awe (θαυμαστόν) in the Persians.[20] All this explains why Alexander insisted on wearing "Median dress," in an effort to convince the

---

Plut. *Art.* xxvi. 2; Arr. *Anab.* vi. 29. 3. These texts indicate that getting the *kidaris* was tantamount to becoming king. Like the robe, the crown was a sign.

[17] E. F. Schmidt, *op. cit.,* i. 116; Pl. 75–6.

[18] Kyros-legend: Xen. *Kyro.* viii. 5. 18; Kyros the Younger: Plut. *Art.* iii. 1–4.

[19] Artaynta-Amestris: Herod. ix. 108–13; Teribazos: Plut. (from Ktes. ?) *Art.* v. 2.

[20] Curt. iii. 3. 17; Esth. viii. 15; Philos. *Ima.* ii. 31 (385) . Ktes. [*Persika*] = Aelian, *Nat. An.* iv. 46. 1.

Persians that he had the attributes of Persian kingship. The robe
seems still to have had significance to the Seleukid monarchs: when
Antiochos IV was dying, he is said to have given his royal robe to the
regent responsible for the raising of Antiochos V.[21]

The Persian kings were regularly honored with *proskunēsis,*
"obeisance," an act of adoration as understood by the Greeks.[22] The
Persian kings lived in almost godlike seclusion. Poseidonios says that
it had been impossible for persons to see him unless they first washed
and then dressed in white clothing. No one was allowed to eat meals
with the king except his wife and mother, until Artaxerxes II changed
this long-followed custom, also allowing the company of royal brothers.
The king dined behind a veil through which he could see his guests,
but through which he could not be seen. Royal servants, furthermore,
had to wash and put on white clothing before waiting upon him, an
act which probably had some sacral significance. He consumed special
food—as did his son the heir apparent, too—a special barley and
wheaten cake, special water, and special wine drunk from an egg-
shaped gold cup. This cup had religious properties, and was used to
pour libations and also in some way to receive signs sent by the gods.[23]
Thus, the Persian king was not the riotous drunkard of fourth-century
Greek writers, but a being who led a life restricted by numerous religious taboos. He lived apart, ate a prescribed diet, never touched the
ground, and was accompanied everywhere by his protecting parasol
and throne.

The best evidence that the Persian king was a being charged with
divine powers is the worship or adoration accorded him after death.
Ktesias knew of a nobleman named Bagapates who dwelt for seven
years at the tomb of Dareios I. Aristoboulos has left a description of
the tomb of Kyros at Pasargadai, as it was when Alexander visited it.
In a grove of trees stood a small tower, richly furnished with funerary
equipment. Here the *magoi* stood guard, sacrificing a horse each

---

[21] Alexander: Ephippos of Olynthos, *On the Death of Alexander and Hephaistion*
= Athen. xii. 537 DE. Antiochos IV: 1 Macc. vi. 15.

[22] *Proskunēsis:* Herod. vii. 136; Just. vi. 2; Plut. *Art.* xxii. 4; Aelian, *Var. Hist.* i.
21. The act is probably the one performed in the Throne Hall reliefs pictured in
E. F. Schmidt, *Persepolis* (1953), i. Pl. 98–9. The Greek verb προσκυνέω does not
have to mean "prostration"; *s.v.* προσκυνέω. in Liddell and Scott, *Greek-English
Lexicon* (9th ed., 1953).

[23] Seclusion: Xen. *Ages.* ix. 1; Just. i. 9; Poseidonios = Athen. i. 28 D. Dining:
Plut. *Art.* v. 3; Esth. i. 6; Herakleides of Kumai, *Persika* ii = Athen. iv. 145 A–F.
Food: Agathokles, *On Kyzikos* iii = Athen. xi. 515 A; Deinon, *Persian History*
iii = Athen. xi. 503 F. The cup: Hermippos = Athen. xi. 478 A.

month to the hero. The horse was regarded throughout Iran as sacred to the sun, a manifestation of Ahura Mazdāh.[24]

The holiness of the Persian king is well established by this host of restrictions and honors intended to conserve the supernatural powers of the king, and to venerate them. He needed them, for as the select governor of Ahura Mazdāh, much was expected of him. His functions were essentially twofold, the standard duties of Oriental kingship: defense of the state from enemies without, and the maintenance of divine law within. Persian law was thought to be immutable and hence divine; as the Jews said it, the law of the Medes and Persians changed not. While law was the king's law, it was the king's only in the matter of enforcement, for its ultimate source was Ahura Mazdāh. Royal enforcement of law was right-doing for the king; nonenforcement was wrong-doing. Right-doing was also rewarding the right, punishing the wrong, sustaining the weak, restraining the strong.[25]

Military defense of the empire from enemies both foreign and domestic was a prime function. The preservation of the integrity of the state in the name of Ahura Mazdāh was the theological rationale behind the suppression of the Ionian revolt, and behind Dareios' and Xerxes' campaigns against European Greece. These campaigns were not so much wars of aggression with the aim of loot, in theory, as the fulfillment of Ahura Mazdāh's will that there be a single, peaceful state in Asia. The Persian kings frequently boasted of their successes in this critically important duty of maintaining Empire-wide respect for this god. Any state or party which revolted did so because another god raised a would-be imperial head. In the inscriptions suppression of rebellion is called the Destruction of the Lie.[26] The maintenance of

[24] Bagapates: Ktes. *Persika*, Epit. 19. Kyros' tomb: Aristoboulos = Arr. *Anab.* vi. 29. 4–11 and Strabo xv. 3. 7 (730) ; Plut. *Alex.* lxix. 1–2; Curt. x. 1. 30. E. F. Schmidt, *Persepolis* (1953), i. 11–2. The horse: Herod. vii. 40; Xen. *Anab.* iv. 5. 34; Strabo xi. 8. 6 (513) ; Just. i. 10; Curt. iii. 3. 11.

[25] Greek understanding: Aisch. *Pers.* 767–70; Jews: Dan. vi. 8, 12, 15. Source: Old Persian inscriptions (page numbers refer to R. G. Kent, *Old Persian* [2nd ed., 1953]), *DB* vii. 1. 17—viii. 1. 20, pp. 117–9; *DNa* iii. 13—iv. 37, pp. 137–8; *DNb* viii. 21–4, pp. 139–40; *DSe* iv. 3–41, pp. 141–2; *XPh* iv. 46–56, pp. 151–2.

Right-doing: *ibid.*, *DB* viii. 1. 20–4, pp. 117–9; lxiii. 4. 61–7, pp. 129–32; *DNb* viii. 5–21, pp. 138–40; *DSe* iv. 30–41, pp. 141–2; *DPd* iii. 12–24, pp. 135–6.

[26] Military defense: *ibid.*, *DB passim*, pp. 116–34; *DPd* iii. 1–24, p. 136; *DPe* iii. 18–24, p. 136–7; *DNa* iv. 30–47, pp. 137–8; *DNb* viii. 31–45, pp. 139–40; *DSj* iii. 4–6, pp. 144–5; *XPh* iv. 28–35, pp. 150–1; *A³Pa* iv. 23–6, p. 156.

Destruction of the Lie: *ibid.*, *DB* x. 1. 26–35, pp. 117–9; xiv. 1. 61–71, pp. 118–20; lii. 4. 2—lvii. 4. 80, pp. 128–32; lxxii. 5. 14–20, pp. 133–4; *DSf* iii. 15–20, pp. 142–4; *XPh* iv. 15–56, pp. 150–2.

the state was the same thing as the maintenance of the primacy of the national god of Persis, and the maintenance of the rightness, the natural supreme existence, of Persian religion, and, of course, the notables of Persis.

In this cult, the most important participant was the king. While the *magoi* assisted him in the supremely important rite of sacrifice,[27] the king himself carried out the sacrifices on the most important occasions: to mark his return to the capital after a journey abroad, to enquire of the divine will in matters pertaining to the succession, and in the conduct of military operations. At Thermopylai, for example, the king himself poured libations. In the Naqsh-i-Rustam reliefs, Dareios I is pictured in the attitude of leading the state fire cult. He is dressed in full regalia, clasping the bow that defends the state in his left hand, while his right is raised in the typical Persian gesture of adoration. At the right is the fire altar, while overhead floats the symbol of the great god Ahura Mazdāh. In the west doorways of the Throne Hall at Persepolis, and in the west doorway of the Main Hall of Dareios I, the royal hero is shown dispatching a sacrificial bull.[28]

The practice of royal sacrifice, especially in the fire cult, was maintained for centuries in Iranian tradition. Mithradates of Pontos in the cult of Zeus Stratios, as Appian specifically says, carried on in the manner of the ancient Achaemenid cult at Pasargadai. The king himself built a fire, carried wood to the altar, poured a libation of milk, honey, oil, and incense, and fired the holy bundles.[29] The maintenance of the state cults was absolutely essential to the continuity of the state itself. So, too, was that of the cults within the state, over which the Great King could exercise control. Artaxerxes intervened in the dispute between his governor Tattenai and the elders of the Jews. Dareios II authorized the keeping of the Festival of Unleavened Bread by his Hebrew mercenary soldiers at Elephantine. The satrap Pherendates, an officer of Dareios I, supervised the appointment of priests for the Egyptian god Khnum.[30] Hence, on religious grounds

[27] The role of the *magoi* is discussed on pp. 65–67, below.

[28] King's return: Xen. *Kyro.* viii. 5. 21, 26; 7. 1; on the succession: Ktes. *Persika*, Epit. 11–2; military campaigns: *ibid.*, 19; at Thermopylai: Herod. vii. 223. Fire cult: A. T. Olmstead, *H.P.E.* (1948), 229; Pl. 30. Sacrificing the bull: E. F. Schmidt, *Persepolis* (1953), i. 136, Pl. 117, 144.

[29] App. *Mith.* ix. 66.

[30] Tattenai: Ezra v–vi; Dareios II and the Feast: A. Cowley, *Aramaic Papyri of the Fifth Century B.C.* (1923), No. 21; a new translation in *A.N.E.T.* (1950), 491; Pherendates: E. G. Kraeling, *The Brooklyn Museum Aramaic Papyri* (1953), 30 and n. 21.

alone, the king was the most important single person in the Empire. The royal Persian fire cult seems to have been the cult of state. The twin fire temples at Pasargadai and at Naqsh-i-Rustam were stylized representations of a fortified hill town. The town was represented as within walls, which were the walls of the shrine, and the hill was symbolized by three wide, low platforms on which the structure stood. Within the shrine, structures represented the town's buildings, and the temple wall had false doors and windows standing for real doors and arrow slots.[31] The fire would seem to have been the soul of the state, with the kings its chief nourishers. In the Hellenistic period, the Persian dynasts near Persepolis employed the title *frātadāra*, "Keeper of the Fire," to describe their function.

The Achaemenid kings, like all Mesopotamian kings before them, were the chief source of divine knowledge, since they were in contact with deity through dreams and other media. One is inevitably reminded of the well-known dreams of Gudea of Lagash, who learned of his god Ningirsu's will that a temple be built in the city.[32] Herodotos says that Xerxes was prompted to begin the invasion of Greece by dreams. Herodotos also says that he learned this from a Persian source so that it is probably entirely accurate—at least as propaganda. Even if these stories are not literally true, they must show what Persians thought about their monarchs' ability to receive important messages from the state god. In Xerxes' dream, a tall, beautiful, winged man stood over him, and commanded him to begin the invasion. The vision can be safely identified with Ahura Mazdāh, who was depicted as human-headed and winged. When Artabanos, a Persian nobleman close to the throne, wore the king's robes and went to sleep in his bed, the same vision came to him. Thus the contention concerning the magical powers of that most important article in the legitimate king's wardrobe are proved. At another time, says Herodotos, Xerxes dreamed that he was crowned with the branches of an olive tree, which spread from his head to cover the whole earth. The interpretation of the *magoi* was that Xerxes would become king of the whole earth when he invaded Greece. This dream uses the symbol of a tree for the earthly state that we have already seen in the legend concerning Kyros and Mandane and in the *Bahman Yasht*. There are also traditions in classical writers of important dreams coming to Kyros the Great. And during the campaign against the invader Alexander, Dareios III had

---

[31] A. T. Olmstead, *H.P.E.* (1948), 64–5, Pl. XI; R. Ghirshman, *Iran* (1954), Pl. 19a.
[32] Discussed in H. I. Frankfort, *Kingship and the Gods* (1948), 255–7.

dreams which were indicative, or so interpreted, of Ahura Mazdāh's will that the king expel the foreigners from his domain.[33]

Not only was divine revelation received through the medium of royal dreaming, it came also through extraordinary phenomena interpreted by the kings with the assistance of the *magoi*. The solar eclipse of 481 B.C. was interpreted by Xerxes to presage disaster for the Greeks, since the sun stood for Hellas and the moon for Persia.[34]

The Persian king, then, was able to discharge his function as the agent of Ahura Mazdāh because he knew the divine will better than anyone else. This was most important for his role in the state cults—not only as a sacrificer, but as a worker of magic—which preserved the army and the state from danger and chaos. During the dangerous crossing of the Hellespont in 480 B.C., Xerxes offered special prayers to the gods who watched over the Persian Empire. These are not named in the text of Herodotos, but in 400 B.C. and subsequently they included Ahura Mazdāh, Mithra, and Anahita, she who was worshipped by *magoi* at Ephesos and whose cult was carried on at Hiera Kome in the rear of the Roman army during the campaign of 190/89 B.C. The bridges across the Hellespont were strewn with the branches of trees, and spices were burned upon them. The king stood by waiting for the light of the sun, and as its disk rose over the eastern horizon, he poured a libation from a golden goblet, which he then threw into the water along with a gold bowl and a Persian sword, thus consecrating the Persian army to the service of Ahura Mazdāh.[35]

Previous to this rite, says Herodotos, Xerxes had commanded that the heads of the bridge carpenters be chopped off. While the Greeks believed that this was only another instance of the monumental *hubris* of an Oriental despot, it is quite likely, if the story is true at all, that it was a case of human sacrifice. Such an extreme measure the Persians may have thought necessary because of the supreme dangers awaiting the massive and irreplaceable armament that Xerxes was taking into lands never before conquered by Persians at an almost legendary distance from Persis. We know that other human sacrifices were performed on royal order during the campaign. The same Pythios whom we have

[33] Xerxes—Artabanos: Herod. vii. 19; Xerxes—olive tree: *ibid.*, i. 108; cf. *Bahman Yasht* i. 3–5. Kyros: Deinon, *Persian History* = Cic. *Div.* i. 23. 46. Dareios III: Curt. iii. 3. 3–6; Cic., *op. cit.*, i. 52. 121; Plut. *Alex.* xviii. 4.

[34] Herod. vii. 37; W. W. How and J. Wells, *A Commentary on Herodotus* (1912), ii. 144–5.

[35] Anahita and Mithra: Old Persian inscriptions (page numbers refer to R. G. Kent, *Old Persian* [2nd ed., 1953]), *A²Sa*, p. 154; *A²Sd*, pp. 154–5; *A²Ha*, p. 155; *A²Hb*, p. 155; *A³Pa*, iv. 23–6, p. 156. Xerxes' activities in Herod. vii. 53–4.

seen giving Dareios I a gold plane tree and a vine of gold had one of his sons taken from him and sacrificed as a scapegoat. The son was the man's eldest; he was cut in two, one half placed on each side of the road, and the army marched between them. Similar war magic was employed by the Romans to cleanse the army by transferring its sin to the slain being. In Greece, Xerxes had buried alive nine boys and nine maidens at Nine Ways. And his wife Amestris was supposed at another time to have buried seven noble Persian boys alive.[36]

Probably the most important part the king played in religion was that of the hero in the Persian equivalent of the Babylonian New Year Festival. If the king was responsible for the safe conduct of military operations, he also kept the state immune from supernatural dangers acted out probably annually in a religious ritual; and at the same time he participated in a sacred marriage intended to reinvigorate the fruitfulness of the earth. Part of what was probably a ritual is depicted in the reliefs at Persepolis, wherein the king fights with various monsters symbolizing forces of Chaos. There is no evidence literary or epigraphic that proves the scenes are actually part of a ritual; but they are so similar to the Mesopotamian pictures of Marduk in combat with Tiamat and her demoniac confederates, a fight which was ritually enacted, that I am confident the Persepolis material represented the same sort of thing to the Persians and was also acted out in some rite, in which the king played the leading part.

The hero in the reliefs, and on several seal cylinders as well, must represent the king, for the victor figure always wears the long square curled beard of the undoubted royal reliefs. On the seals, the hero is similarly shown, and, in addition, seven of the thirteen seals showing battle between man and monster are inscribed with the names of Dareios or Xerxes, usually followed by the title "King." Even with this evidence, E. F. Schmidt and G. G. Cameron were not absolutely certain that in all cases the figure is the king, but feel that in most cases it is.[37] In the reliefs the king, then, sometimes fights and dispatches a lion, stabbing it in the stomach with a sword. The usual beast that the monarch grapples is a monster with the head, body, and forelegs of a lion, the body feathered and winged, with taloned hind legs and a scorpion's tail. There is some slight variation in detail in this genus of monumental monster as displayed at Persepolis. On the

[36] Bridge carpenters: Herod. vii. 35. Pythios' son: *ibid.*, vii. 38–40. The other sacrifices: *ibid.*, vii. 114.

[37] Reliefs: E. F. Schmidt, *Persepolis* (1953), i. 136; Pl. 114–7. Seals: E. F. Schmidt, *The Treasury of Persepolis* (1939), 38–41; *Persepolis* (1957), ii. 18–24, Nos. 1–13, Pl. 3–5. G. G. Cameron, *Persepolis Treasury Tablets* (1948), 55–8.

PLATE III

Relief from the main courtyard of the Treasury of Persepolis, still in position on the south wall. The Great King, Dareios I, is seated on the throne of the Persians, while behind him stands the Crown Prince Xerxes. Dareios is shown with his hair and his long, square-tipped beard carefully groomed in alternate bands of curls and waves. This treatment is common to all Persian reliefs of the Achaemenids, and was copied from the usage of ancient Near Eastern royal reliefs. Compare, for example, the renderings of kings in late Assyrian, Babylonian, and Canaanite art.

Before the king stand two incense burners, usually presumed to be holding frankincense (cf. the *magoi* in Matt. ii. 11). In front of them stands a Median dignitary, with short, pointed beard, who raises his hand to his lips and bows slightly, probably in the rite of *proskunēsis*. The Mede and the other nonroyal figures are made somewhat shorter than Xerxes, and even he, who is standing on the royal dais, is only equal in height to Dareios, who is seated. If the king were to stand up, he would be at least half again taller than the Mede. This convention of portraying kings was used all over the Orient to show that kings were more than mere men. Xerxes' hand, too, is raised in the same gesture that Dareios uses before the sacred fire in the reliefs at Naqsh-i-Rustam.

Both king and crown prince wear the distinctive *kidaris*, although the tops have been destroyed. Dareios holds a sceptre, symbolic of world rule, which was originally tipped with gold (cf. Esth. iv. 11; v. 2), now torn away by Alexander's soldiers. He and Xerxes hold lotus blossoms, symbolic of the Tree of Life. The royal throne stands on feet carved like a lion's, and the throne itself is raised above the level of the common ground by a dais. The king's feet are lifted above the dais by a footstool, whose feet are like a bull's. The king's eye has been gouged out, no doubt by the Makedonians, who thus showed their hatred and contempt for the Persian monarchy. (Photograph supplied by the Oriental Institute of the University of Chicago.)

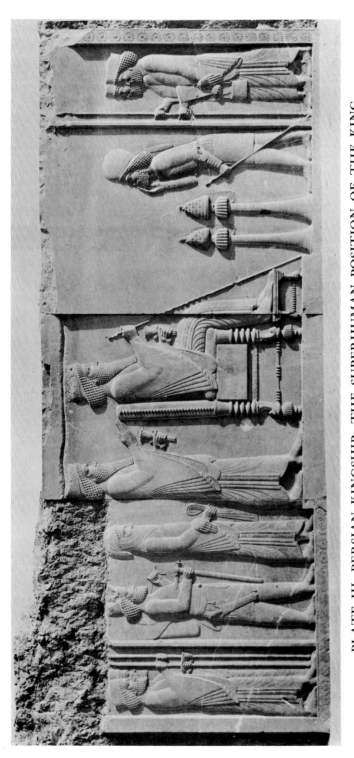

PLATE III. PERSIAN KINGSHIP: THE SUPERHUMAN POSITION OF THE KING

PLATE IV. PERSIAN KINGSHIP: THE COSMIC ROLE OF THE KING

PLATE IV

Relief in the eastern doorway of the Main Hall of the Harem of Xerxes at Persepolis, still *in situ*. On the right is a royal figure, as shown by his royal beard. Some authorities are loath to identify this figure with the king, but such an identification seems highly probable to me. He is engaged in combat with a Death Demon, whom he grasps by a horn with one hand and dispatches by a thrust of his sword with the other. The demon, which stands erect like a man, has a horned head and front paws of a lion, a lion's body feathered and winged, hind feet of a bird, and the tail of a scorpion. It possibly is derived from the dragons and evil monsters described in *Enuma elish,* the Babylonian epic, which were fashioned by Tiamat, the Chaos-figure par excellence. She is said to have created Roaring Dragons, mighty Lion-Demons, Dragon-Flies, and Scorpion Men. This relief, then, could be simply a composite of horrors, and would therefore personify Death itself. The monster certainly owes much to Babylonian conceptions, as comparison with Plate V will show.

This relief is similar to several others at Persepolis, all of them in doorways of the Palace of Dareios I and the Throne Hall. They must, therefore, refer to royal acts, and the figure must be the king's. The figure's headgear, however, is a low round cap, not the royal *kidaris.* Perhaps this should be taken to mean that the combat with the demon was a prerequisite to kingship, or that the king was fighting to regain the kingship in some annual ritual. This interpretation is strengthened by the fact that the reliefs were placed in the doorways of these important buildings: before the king could enter high royal office, Chaos had to be dispelled. (Photograph supplied by the Oriental Institute of the University of Chicago.)

seals, the animals are roughly the same, sometimes lion-headed, sometimes human-headed, usually bull-bodied and winged, perhaps
feathered.[38] Nightmare animals similar to these are known from the
Babylonian *Enuma elish*, the description of the hero-god Marduk's
fight against the devils of Tiamat, and are portrayed on late Assyrian
seal cylinders which show the conflict of the god Asshur with the
same winged, leonine animal. Other seals show a hero or a god fighting
against bulls, or sacrificing them, and lion-gryphons, all very much
like the scenes at Persepolis.[39] A. U. Pope thinks that at Persepolis the
lion figure represents the sun, and that the beast must be slain so that
the earth will not be burnt up. This would be a ritual. Be that as it
may, J. Duchesne-Guillemin and R. C. Zaehner have suggested that a
lion-headed deity in the Mysteries of Mithras probably represented
Ahriman. Therefore the Persepolitan lion-gryphons might represent
the same evil. Certain it is that Alexander's coinage of around 330 B.C.
sometimes showed a winged lion, occasionally bird-headed—a lion-
gryphon—not only being killed by but also killing Persians. Therefore,
whatever name we give to the lion symbol, there is agreement that it
is identical with a Spirit of Death of some sort.[40] The king, therefore,
as protector of the state was obliged to slay it. Since such fantastic
leonine beings did not really exist, there is no possibility that the
sculpture merely shows hunting scenes. Rather, it must be symbolic
of some supernatural concept, and some sort of ritual must have
therefore been necessary to cope with a supernatural Spirit of Death.

What seems to be true on first view from this monumental and
archaeological evidence is that there was a continuity at Persepolis
with the Assyro-Babylonian New Year Festival. There is corroboratory
evidence that the Persians did indeed celebrate such a festival, and
that as in Mesopotamia, the king played the central part. If this is
true, it merely complements what is already known of Persian borrowing of other elements of Mesopotamian religion. The basis of the
New Year Festival was the renewal of state and nature by ritual,
religious means. To the Persian, this would have included the maintenance of the province's loyalty to him. E. E. Herzfeld, A. T. Olmstead,
and E. F. Schmidt have said that the reliefs on the Persepolis stairways

[38] Reliefs: E. F. Schmidt, *Persepolis* (1953), i. 137 and Pl. 116; 257 and Pl. 196;
226 and Pl. 145. Seals: E. F. Schmidt, *Persepolis* (1957), ii. 18–24, Nos. 1–13, Pl. 3–5.

[39] *Enuma elish* i. 125–45; iii. 15–36; W. H. Ward, *The Seal Cylinders of Western
Asia* (1910), 197–210, Figs. 564, 571–2, 615, 620–2, 635.

[40] A. U. Pope, "Persepolis as a Ritual City," *Arch.* 10 (1957), 128–9. J. Duchesne-
Guillemin, *The Western Response to Zoroaster* (1958), 79. G. F. Hill, "Alexander
the Great and the Persian Lion-Gryphon," *JHS* 43 (1923), 156–61.

showing tribute delegations from the provinces depict an important part of this annual celebration.[41]

As for the rest of the Festival, we have no explicit literary source which describes it. But Xenophon describes a procession and celebration of the Persians, which he seems to imply was held regularly, and his account of the procession generally matches the entourage sculptured on the Apadana stairway.[42] First comes a body of men with lances, then bulls to be sacrificed, and horses. Then a chariot sacred to Ahura Mazdāh, followed by two others, one for Mithra and one probably for Anahita. Next a portable fire-altar and the king in full regalia in his chariot. The rest of the procession is made up of cavalry, mace-bearers, and a vast throng of nobility. There are differences in the Greek account and the Persian reliefs. There are no sacrificial bulls at Persepolis, nor the portable fire-altar, although the use of both is well attested in general Persian usage. And, on the other hand, Xenophon does not mention explicitly the tribute delegations. But these may be understood to be included in his general summary statement that there were thousands of men following the king. The number of chariots is two at Persepolis, one for the god, one for the king, and four in Xenophon. But Xenophon's account of three chariots for deities comes from the fourth century, after the reforms of Artaxerxes II, who invoked the deities Ahura Mazdāh, Mithra, and Anahita in his inscriptions, whereas the Persepolis reliefs were carved in the reigns of Xerxes and Dareios, who invoke only Ahura Mazdāh in their inscriptions. That difficulty vanishes. What is remarkable is that there are points of comparison between Xenophon and the reliefs, both in the elements described and in the order in which they are described. Thus it would appear that Xenophon has given us a very short and somewhat blurry account of the procession of the New Year Festival. This being so, may not the other remarks Xenophon makes of the purpose of the entourage and of the events which took place after it had reached its destination have peculiar value as a partial description of the mythic drama which was the heart of the whole proceeding?

According to Xenophon, then, the procession marched to the sanctuaries to offer sacrifice. This was performed by the king himself in honor of Ahura Mazdāh and Mithra. Offering the victims was omitted if the king was absent. Next, Xenophon describes a series of

[41] E. E. Herzfeld, "Notes of the Quarter: Recent Discoveries at Persepolis," *JRAS* (1934), 321; A. T. Olmstead, *H.P.E.* (1948), 180; E. F. Schmidt, *Persepolis* (1953), i. 82.

[42] Xen. *Kyro.* viii. 3. 1–4; E. F. Schmidt, *Persepolis* (1953), i. Pl. 19, 27–52.

acts which purport to be historical events that occurred uniquely in
Kyros' reign, but which actually must represent ritual elements of the
annual drama. These were, then, contests—horse races—which the
king won, and he carried off the chief prize, a bull. This rite would
seem to be one in which the virility and prowess of the king were
tested symbolically, or one which was symbolic of the king's military
victories. Perhaps we could connect this winning of a bull with those
Persepolis portrayals of the royal hero sacrificing a bull. Certainly,
winning the bull stood for winning some great thing, for the contests
were followed by a great victory feast. During this episode, the great
men of the state gave presents to the poor, and may actually have
changed places with them. The celebration ended when the king rewarded the notables with gifts for faithful service, and then participated in a sacred marriage.

All this is very similar to the basic elements in the *Akitu*-festival
of Mesopotamia. There is the great procession, including the king and
the gods of the state. There is the testing of the king, his victory, and
the celebration of his renewal in office. There seems to be the period
when the classes of society are turned topsy-turvy, to symbolize the
chaos the rites are intended to avert, and are then restored aright, as
the whole world is supposed to be aright. There is the sacred marriage
and the formal recognition that the state will proceed as it has in the
past. While there are differences in detail, these may readily be accounted for as the modifications the Persians had necessarily to make
when they assimilated Babylonian rites to their own native ideas. In
essence, the rites are the same: rites of renewal of the state and of
nature for the coming year. The king is tested and found whole, and
his vicegerency for Ahura Mazdāh is renewed. The king acting for
Ahura Mazdāh then performs the same service for his nobility, rewarding them for their good behavior and service to the state. The
whole series of rites ends with a piece of magic, the *hieros gamos,*
whereby the king provides for the general fertility of the realm. Thus,
state and nature are renewed. All this is intimated in the inscription
of Xerxes which accompanies the great Apadana reliefs of the annual
procession:

> A great god is Ahura Mazdāh, who created this earth, who
> created yonder sky, who created man, who created happiness for
> man, who made Dareios king, one king of many, one lord of
> many.[43]

[43] For location of inscription: E. F. Schmidt, *Persepolis* (1953), i. 82; the text
itself is *XPb*, i. 1–8 in R. G. Kent, *Old Persian* (2nd ed., 1953), 147–8.

As the god gives happiness or welfare to man, so, too, the Great King distributed presents to his court.[44]

A rite closely connected with the New Year was the Festival of the Mithrakina, which was a primitive form of war magic. It was celebrated annually, probably in September-October. This time of year was the Old Persian month called *Bāgayādish,* "God-Worship-Month." Since the Pahlevi and New Persian name for the same month is *Mihr,* "Mithra," it must have been originally consecrated to Mithra, god of contracts, of treaties, and of war.[45] The fall of the year was a likely time for a month consecrated to this god, since it was the post-harvest campaigning season, a time too when the heat of the Iranian countries lessens and makes fighting more comfortable. And certainly, a Mithra festival would be celebrated during the god's own particular month. During the Festival, the Persian king, high priest of the state cults and leader in war, was made drunk on *haoma,* and when filled with divine passion, danced the "Persian," a military dance in armor, while the *Mithra Yasht* was recited.[46] The purpose of the rite was to induce possession by king and army of the warlike power and prowess of Mithra, so that warfare would be successful.[47]

[44] Herod. ix. 110; Thou. ii. 97; Xen. *Kyro.* viii. 5. 21; 7. 1; Esth. ii. 18.

[45] Annual celebration: Strabo xi. 14. 9 (530). The kings of Persia received 20,000 colts on the occasion of the rite; perhaps the festival included the sacrifice of horses. The identification of month with Mithra: G. G. Cameron, *Persepolis Treasury Tablets* (1948), 44–5; R. G. Kent, *Old Persian* (2nd ed., 1953), 160–3, 199.

[46] Festival and drunkenness mentioned by Ktes. [*Persika*] = Athen. x. 434 E; Douris, *Histories* vii = *loc. cit.* There is no evidence in either Greek writer that *haoma* was used. *Haoma,* however, was certainly an intoxicant, was certainly full of holiness, and was certainly prepared at Persepolis.

Furthermore, on the use of *haoma* and on the probable chanting of the *Mithra Yasht,* I think the yasht itself is the evidence for both. The yasht is an invocation to Mithra and contains numerous statements to the effect that the army fighting without Mithra is lost. The liturgical nature of this fifth-century hymn is shown, I think, by the constantly repeated refrain in it, which includes the following statement: (*Mithra Yasht* 6 and *passim*): "We worship Grass-Land Magnate Mithra with *Haoma* containing milk and Barsman twigs, with skill of tongue and magic-word, with speech and action and libations, and with correctly uttered words." To speak this sentence must actually be to recite the magic-word with skill of tongue and careful utterance. If this yasht isn't the ritual itself, I can't imagine what could be. I have used the translation of I. Gershevitch in *The Avestan Hymn to Mithra* (1959).

I feel safer in interpreting this yasht as cultic in view of M. Mole's very recent thesis that the Gathas themselves are cultic, much in the manner of the Old Testament Psalms (mentioned in J. Duchesne-Guillemin, *The Western Response to Zoroaster* [1958], 103). Unfortunately, I have not been able to see Mole's book.

[47] It is tempting to identify the *Mithrakina* with a part of the Persian New Year Festival. There was a Near Eastern rite called the *Sakaia,* mentioned by four classical authors: Berossos and Ktesias (Athen. xiv. 639 C); Strabo (xi. 8. 4. [512]); and Dio

Thus, the Persian king was supremely important to the welfare of Persis. He was the agent whereby success at arms, success with agriculture, success against supernatural danger were magically or religiously assured. Without the king, intermediary between Ahura Mazdāh and man, Persis would suffer from the victory of forces real and supernatural. This is exactly what the *Bahman Yasht* and the *Oracle of Hystaspes* say has happened: the evil demons of the Race of Wrath are in occupation of Persis, for the king of bronze is dead; the Tree of Life itself has withered; apostasy is occurring; normal ties between people have disappeared; the working of nature is out of order; an age of chaos has come. Similar results from the loss of kingship are recorded in late Assyrian texts. One says that because the king was afflicted with war and disease the country is in a state of social upheaval and all natural bonds between people have collapsed on account of his distress. Another tells a tale of insurrection and assassination of a king; after a period of calm the gods send a round of fresh civil wars and plague in consequence.[48]

This is all a borrowing of Babylonian ideas, and is indicative that the Persians between the time of Kyros and the reign of Artaxerxes II adopted the essence of Mesopotamian concepts of kingship and adapted them to their own cultural tradition. The Persians even in the reign of Dareios I were comparatively recent immigrants in the Near East, having settled in Iran in the course of the ninth century. When they entered Iran they were barbarians; when three centuries later they ruled the East, they were people with a sophisticated view of

---

Chrysostomos (*Or.* iv. 66–7). Dio and Strabo agree that this was a Persian rite. Berossos says it was Babylonian, unfortunately for my thesis here. Ktesias doesn't say, for Athenaios merely states that he mentioned the *Sakaia* in book ii of his *Persian History*. (Did he discuss its coming to Persis from Babylonia?)

Nonetheless, Berossos, a native Babylonian, in attributing a Babylonian nature to the rite, could be acting as a cultural nationalist, or could be referring to a Persian celebration in Babylon, considering that, as mentioned above, Berossos is also authority for our knowledge that a Persian cult of Anahita came to Babylon in the reign of Artaxerxes II, that is, 150 years before Berossos. Dio says, as does Berossos, that the festival included a feast, during which a prisoner was allowed to sit on the king's throne dressed in royal clothes. This activity would definitely identify the *Sakaia* with the New Year Festival. Strabo says that the festival began among the Persians in commemoration of their destruction of a tribe of Sakai, and that the festival was annual, in honor of Omanos (i.e., Ahura Mazdāh), Anaitis (Anahita), and Anadatos (?). This would give the rite a military aspect, but, unfortunately, where is Mithra in this list? Does he lurk in "Anadatos"?

On the *Sakaia*, see S. Langdon, "The Babylonian and Persian Sacaea," *JRAS* (1924), 65–72.

[48] K. 4541 and K. 7861 cited by C. J. Gadd, *Ideas of Divine Rule in the Ancient East* (1948), 70–1.

their role. To have achieved so much in so short a time indicates that they borrowed heavily from their predecessors; and a mass of evidence proves that they undoubtedly did. Architecture and sculpture were taken from late Babylonian and Assyrian models. Even Zoroastrianism, a conglomeration of beliefs tending towards monotheism and a greater emphasis on ethics and the spiritualization of material things, developed along lines already anticipated in Mesopotamia. As far as their concept of kingship was concerned, the Persians of the fourth century vaguely remembered that it was borrowed from the Medes, their immediate predecessors as rulers of Western Asia. Xenophon says that much of the detail of Persian kingship—the use of cosmetics to inspire awe and symbolize high religious office, the wearing of elevator boots and jewelry, the marcelled hair arrangements, and the magic robe—was taken by the Persians from the Medes. A remark he puts in the mouth of Kyros, that the duties of a good king were like those of a good shepherd, to make his people happy, sounds like a paraphrase of the prologue of the Code of Hammurapi.[49]

Aside from borrowing from their kinsmen the Medes, the Persians also were deeply influenced by direct contact with the Babylonians from the time of Kyros until the end of their independence. No doubt the Persians acquired firsthand knowledge of Mesopotamian concepts of rule when they became the lords of the East through Kyros' conquest of Babylon. The "Cyrus Cylinder" is a document issued in Babylon after the Persian occupation, issued in the name of Kyros by the priests of Marduk. However much the priests had to do with the composition of the text, nonetheless Kyros must have been familiar with, and have assented to, its contents. Here was a most intimate contact between a Persian king and the world of Babylonian ideas. Two decades after this episode, we have from the Old Persian inscription at Behistun, statements of a doctrine of kingship much in accord with Mesopotamian theory. Indeed, part of the "Cyrus Cylinder" sounds very much like section fourteen of Dareios' Behistun text.[50] Strabo says

[49] Xen. *Kyro.* i. 3. 2; viii. 1. 40–1; 2. 14; and see, too, the explicit statement of Strabo xi. 13. 9 (525).

[50] For the "Kyros Cylinder" see A. L. Oppenheim in *A.N.E.T.*, 315–6. In this document Kyros speaks of his rule in behalf of Marduk: "I strove for peace in Babylon and in all his (other) sacred cities. As to the inhabitants of Babylon [they say their] hearts con[tent] (because) [I abolished] the yoke which was against their social standing. I brought relief to their dilapidated housing, putting (thus) an end to their (main) complaints."

Behistun inscription xiv. 1. 55–71 (from R. G. Kent, *Old Persian* [2nd ed., 1953], 118–20); Dareios speaks of his rule in behalf of Ahura Mazdāh: "I restored to the people the pastures and the herds, the household slaves and the houses which

very explicitly that Persian royal usages were taken over from the
Medes. Thus, Achaemenid theory was partly native and partly Babylonian, some influence coming direct, and some coming through the
agency of the Medes. This was symbolized by the decoration on the
Persian king's chariot. According to Curtius' "Mercenary Source," two
gold statuettes were mounted on its yoke, one of Ninos and one of
Belos, the mythical founder-kings of Babylonia-Assyria.[51] With this
recollection of the long continuity of divine rule in the East, the
Persians thought of themselves as chosen by the gods to rule the Orient.

All the above is set forth to indicate the extraordinary importance
of legitimate kingship to the Persians. The king was military commander-in-chief, and also the priest who invoked the gods of war. He
was the head of state in the broadest sense; and he effected the continuity of the state through his control of and participation in the state
cults. It was unimaginable that the Persian society could function
without his presence, which, in a few words, ensured the proper
order of things.

We come now to the crux of the issue. The Persians, having lost
their native dynasty, found Makedonian substitutes unacceptable.
Why? This must be answered in their own terms. There is no evidence that they thought of their loss in terms of economic exploitation.
Rather, they made a magical and religious interpretation of a political
issue. Did not Xerxes call the suppression of revolt dealing with "The
Lie"? He was the chosen of Ahura Mazdāh. For a Babylonian to revolt, or a Baktrian to rebel, or a satrap to cast off his allegiance to the
Great King was for these persons to challenge Ahura Mazdāh's chosen
king. This king was irreplaceable as manipulator of matters divine.
The Makedonians, we are repeatedly assured by the propaganda, were
not legitimate kings. They were not, so far as we know, worshippers of
Ahura Mazdāh; they worshipped the gods of Hellas or Mesopotamia
or Asia Minor. They proclaimed their respect for Zeus and for Apollo
on their coinage. They did not rule in the interest of Ahura Mazdāh;
they introduced Greek law. They even burned the god's capital. The

---

Gaumata the Magian took away from them. I reestablished the people on its
foundation, both Persia and Media and the other provinces. As before, so I brought
back what had been taken away. By the favor of Ahura Mazdāh, this I did."

[51] Strabo xi. 13. 9 (525); Curt. iii. 15. 16. Herodotos said (i. 135) in the fifth
century that no nation was more eager to adopt foreign customs than the Persians.
On the Babylonization of Persian kings, see H. S. Nyberg, *Die Religionen des
alten Iran* (1938), 347–8, 355; C. J. Gadd, *Ideas of Divine Rule in the Ancient
East* (1948), 90–1.

orientation of the new empire was to serve Greek and not Persian interests. None of this could fulfill Ahura Mazdāh's prerequisites of election. A Makedonian, furthermore, whatever his character, his kindness, his solicitude for things Iranian may have been, could not in the eyes of a Persian strictly following his own tradition be Great King, because the Makedonian was not an Aryan, not a Persian, not an Achaemenid. This did not, on the Persians' view, stem from an idea of racial superiority conceived along modern biological lines, but from a feeling that Europeans did not have the ability, the power which modern writers call *mana*, to serve as the choice of Ahura Mazdāh. The Persians undoubtedly felt culturally superior to the Europeans; and this cultural superiority Persians thought of in terms of religious superiority. They believed in their own excellence because they had seen that their high god had given them the rule of the Near East for over two centuries of time. This was considered to be a part of the order ot things. The Persian propaganda conceived of a return of the Achaemenid regime as the given condition from which an argument against the European regime might proceed. The *Bahman Yasht* says that Peshyotanu is a descendant of Hystaspes, whom I identify with the Hystaspes who was the father of Dareios I. The Sibylline Oracle prophesies the victory of the house Alexander is seeking to destroy. The extant fragments of the *Oracle of Hystaspes* do not state who the savior to come will be, but they do call him "Great King." And I suspect that if we had the lost original version, we should find it stated that he was to be a descendant of Hystaspes, and stated in clearer terms than the Pahlevi *Bahman Yasht* uses. Hystaspes does not play any part in the extant fragments; he does not originate the oracle; it is said that he merely listens to it from the lips of a seer. What other role, then, could this ancestor of Dareios play but to sire the coming savior?[52] All of the Persian propaganda says that Alexander—the Evil Invader—was a man without true religious ideas. There is no statement that he polluted Iranian religious sanctuaries. He is presented as an Anti-King. Therefore, the true religion that he had undone was the theology of Achaemenid kingship held immediately before his attack on the Empire. One can scarcely imagine a new doctrine of kingship springing up in Iran in the centuries of Hellenic domination. There is no evidence, moreover, that one did. On the other hand, there is evidence of the continuity of Achaemenid ideas of kingship

---

[52] *Bahman Yasht* iii. 14 and my note on this verse, p. 348, below. *Sib. Or.* iii. 388–95. *Oracle of Hystaspes*, frag. 10, 13.

between Old Persian and Sassanid times.[53] Consequently, the kingship ideas in the propaganda must be interpreted along lines that existed in the Old Persian period.

During that era Ahura Mazdāh always chose kings—as the constantly repeated phrase in the titulary of the Great Kings states—who were of the family of Achaemenes, Persians, of Aryan descent. This was a prerequisite for legitimate kingship. Dareios took pains not to say that his unsuccessful rival Gaumata was Achaemenid, Persian, and Aryan. He was said only to have been a brother of Kambyses and son of Kyros the Great.[54] He was, therefore, of Achaemenid lineage, but this was not stated.

In pre-Alexandrian Persis only an Achaemenid might be king, and only a small, select circle of the highest nobility might marry into the royal family. Hence, all Makedonians were illegitimate rulers. The Persians, Babylonian-like, might have argued that when Alexander defeated Dareios III, Zeus had defeated Ahura Mazdāh, and that therefore there was a new overseer in heaven to enforce the rules of kingship on earth. But we know from the propaganda that they did not think that way, for there is not the slightest hint in any of it that any god but the old god holds sway. There is nothing of any cosmic conflict, of a displacement of one god by a new Marduk, of the overruling of a Nanna by an Enlil, or even of the slumbering of a Ba'al while a Yahweh worked.[55] The *Oracle of Hystaspes* says that when the worshippers of Ahura Mazdāh call upon him from the mountain they will be answered in no uncertain terms. Many Persians were too deeply committed to the idea of the lordship of Ahura Mazdāh, not only as ruler of Asia but also as inspirer of their own private lives, to conceive of another god's supplanting him. That is certainly the feeling of the Zarathushtrian Gathas and of the royal inscriptions. Therefore, in the Hellenistic period, many Persians went on believing in Ahura Mazdāh, and in the theology about his kingship they had always believed, and

---

[53] On this point see C. J. Gadd, *Ideas of Divine Rule in the Ancient East* (1948), 90–1. For the pictorial evidence that Gadd cites see now L. Vanden Berghe, *Archéologie de l'Iran ancien* (1959), 23 and Pl. 25b; 24 and Pl. 28c. At Naqsh-i-Radjab (Pl. 25b), Ardashir receives his crown from Ahura Mazdāh depicted Achaemenid-style, while his son Shapur raises his hand as Dareios had raised his centuries earlier in the Persian gesture of adoration. The Sassanids, too, of course, claimed to be the inheritors of Achaemenid traditions.

[54] *DB* xi. 1. 35–43 in R. G. Kent, *Old Persian* (2nd ed., 1953), 117–20.

[55] Marduk supplants Ea and the divine assembly in *Enuma elish* ii. 88—iv. 30; Nanna, god of Ur, is drastically overruled with dire consequences for his city by Enlil in the "Lament over the Destruction of Ur." Ba'al is said to be asleep or off travelling somewhere by Elijah during the contest on Mt. Carmel: 1 Kings xviii. 27.

the idea of a Makedonian's being his choice never took hold.

It was abundantly clear to them on the basis of custom and tradition that Ahura Mazdāh chose with great consistency an Aryan, a Persian, an Achaemenid. The origins of this rule of selection lie in the victory of Kyros the Great and his family, and could be better understood if we had more data from sixth-century Persia. But to the Persian, the importance of the victory lay not in the circumstances that surrounded it, but in the fact that it took place. In course of time, through the long possession of the kingship by the Achaemenid family, Achaemenid kingship came to be accepted as a truth, a part of the order of things, by the many aristocrats who were close to the dynasty. What information we have of the parentage of the Persian kings shows that the principle in its entirety was this: first, that the king's father be Achaemenid, second that his mother also be Achaemenid, and third, if the mother were not of the royal family, she must at least be of the blood of one of the Seven Very Noble Families.

Herodotos says that when seven members of the aristocracy were planning to oust Gaumata from the kingship, they agreed beforehand that the one who founded the new line of Persian kings would not select wives from outside their own families.[56] The success of the Seven eventuated in Dareios, an Achaemenid, becoming king, and as far as we can check his marital record, he lived up to this stricture.

These regulations later partially broke down, and towards the end of the fifth century B.C. and in the fourth, were sometimes rejected by some persons, but only with the most serious consequences—civil war among the aristocracy. The ideal, however, continued to survive, and the institution of the Seven Very Noble Families was much later a part of the Parthian court. The regulation against a simple member of the aristocracy becoming king was observed during the Civil War of 401 B.C. After the would-be usurper Kyros the Younger, himself of Achaemenid blood, had been slain in his bid for the crown, his followers offered to switch their allegiance to the nobleman Araios. But Araios declined the offer on the grounds that he would be unacceptable to the aristocracy as a whole, although he had at his back the undefeated and invincible Ten Thousand Greeks of Xenophon's account.[57] The king had to be Achaemenid, as much Achaemenid as possible. Herodotos has included in his book a bit of propaganda once used against Kambyses. It is to the effect that Kambyses was the son of Kyros the Great and an Egyptian princess called Neitetis. In Persian

[56] Herod. iii. 84, 88.
[57] Xen. *Anab.* ii. 2. 1.

eyes, this issue of a Persian and a foreigner was automatically a bastard.[58]

The importance of the queen mother's bloodline explains how Xerxes became king in 486 B.C. When his father's successor was mooted, the two leading candidates were Artobazanes, the eldest son of Dareios, whose mother was a commoner, and Xerxes, a younger son, whose mother was Atossa, daughter of Kyros, an Achaemenid. Xerxes became king. Herodotos' explanation that this happened because Xerxes was born to Dareios while the latter was king, whereas Artobazanes was born before his coronation, is not correct. It ignores the matter of Atossa's parentage, and is inconsistent with the later case of Artaxerxes II and Kyros the Younger. The former became king, accepted by the majority of Persians, although he had been born before his father Dareios II became king; Kyros was passed over, although he had been born while Dareios II was king. According to Xenophon, Kyros never claimed legitimacy on the above grounds.[59]

In view of these considerations of parentage, then, the Persian royal family closely interbred, and we hear from two contemporary Greek authors, among others, that the kings bred children with their sisters. This was a recognized institution of royalty in parts of the Orient; brother-and-sister marriage was also practiced among the Egyptians and Elamites.[60] When Artaxerxes I died, his son by Queen Damaspia was recognized as Xerxes II, but he was assassinated by a half-brother, Sekoundyanos, whose mother was a mere Babylonian concubine. This led to civil war between Sekoundyanos and another son of Artaxerxes I, named Ochos, also having a Babylonian woman as mother. Ochos, however, won the civil war, because he rallied the greater number of the aristocrats, and therefore the army, to his side; he had the virtue of being married to one Parysatis, who was a daughter of Achaemenid Xerxes. Again, when the succession was disputed after the death of Artaxerxes II, it was the man with the closest connection with the royal family through his wife who won. The issue was fought between the eldest son of Artaxerxes, Dareios, and the youngest, another

---

[58] Herod. iii. 2.

[59] Xerxes: Herod. vii. 2–3; *XPf* iii. 15—iv. 43 in R. G. Kent, *op. cit.,* 150; Ktes. *Persika,* Epit. 51. Artaxerxes II: Xen. *Anab.* i. 1. 1–4.

[60] Kambyses: Ktes. *Persika,* Epit. 43–4; Artaxerxes II: Plut. *Art.* xxiii. 4; Dareios II: Ktes., *loc. cit.,* 44; Dareios III: Plut. *Alex.* xx. 1; Curt. iii. 8. 12. In general: Antisthenes, *On the Kyroses* ii = Athen. v. 220 C. For the Egyptians and Elamites A. T. Olmstead, *H.P.E.* (1948), 87 and literature cited. On the Persians: E. Kornemann, "Zur Geschwisterehe im Altertum," *Klio* 19 (1925), 355–61.

Ochos. The latter, who married Artaxerxes' wife and daughter, his own half sister Atossa, was victor.[61]

In the reign of Dareios II the old rules were partially obscured through the increasing Babylonization of the court and nobility of Persis. This was the inevitable result of the less sophisticated Persians' being constantly in touch with the highly civilized Mesopotamians with their ancient memories of greatness and achievement. The symptoms are the increasing numbers of Babylonian women found bearing princes in Persia, the changes in religious usage under Artaxerxes II, that is, the use of images outside Persis, and the alteration of some of the protocol of kingship mentioned above. These changes must have created a cleavage in the ranks of the society—those willing to support the newer cosmopolitan ideas, and those clinging to older ideas of strict virtue according to the custom of the ancestors.

All this indicates the importance of queen mothers in the making of a Great King. One must also remember the legend concerning the birth of Kyros the Great: the vine that grew from his mother's womb symbolized his rule. Plato says that Achaemenid princesses were closely watched and regulated to preserve the purity of their blood. Since, therefore, they had such an exalted position, Persian queens, like the Great King, were highly honored and much protected because deity was so close to them. Only a Persian queen or queen mother could sit at table with the king, until Artaxerxes II changed the rules around 400 B.C. The queen, furthermore, before his reign had always gone abroad from the palace shielded from the gaze of the vulgar. The normal honor paid the queen by her servants was *proskunēsis,* the same honor rendered the king by one and all.[62]

Insistence on the value of the queen's blood explains why the Seleukids, who had inherited Persis, alone of Alexander's successors maintained close marital relations with Iranian royalty. Seleukos' wife, Apama, was the daughter of the Baktrian nobleman Spitamenes, who likely had Achaemenid blood in his veins. Hence, their son Antiochos I

[61] Ochos (1): Ktes. *Persika,* Epit. 44–8; A. T. Olmstead, *H.P.E.* (1948), 355–6. Ochos (2): Plut. *Art.* xxvi. 1–2; xxvii. 4–5; xxx. 1.

[62] Plato, *I Alki.* 120 E—121 C; Plut. *Art.* v. 3; Deinon, *Persian History* = Athen. xiii. 556 B. The Achaemenid practice of brother-sister marriage between beings touched specially by deity is strongly reminiscent of the mythical Yama-Yami marriage of ancient Indian literature. From these beings came the human race. It would appear, then, that the Achaemenids may have been acting in the role of progenitor of life when they married their sisters, a role which is suggested by the sacred marriage of the New Year Festival and the general charge they exercised over human life in behalf of Ahura Mazdāh.

was half-Iranian certainly, and possibly part Achaemenid. Unfortunately for the Seleukids, they felt that marital commitments to the
Ptolemies of Egypt and the Antigonids of Makedon were more important for their international policy than marriage with the subju-
gated Iranian nobility was internally. After the time of Seleukos I,
one goes down to Antiochos III before there is another instance of
Seleukid marriage with an Oriental lady. Antiochos III married a
daughter, Laodike, of Iranian Mithradates II of Pontos. He later
called the lady "Queen and Sister." This Antiochos was deeply concerned, as his eastern anabasis showed, for the loyalty of the Iranian
provinces. By Laodike he had a son, Antiochos, and a daughter, another Laodike; they married, and Antiochos became king. Like his
father, he planned extensive operations to secure the tranquility of his
Iranian territory.[63] But neither king was really Achaemenid.

So much for Persian kingship and religion, and the Makedonian
nonfulfillment thereof.

[63] Apama: Arr. *Anab.* vii. 4. 6; E. R. Bevan, *The House of Seleucus* (1902), i. 7,
74; W. W. Tarn, "Queen Ptolemais and Apama," *CQ* 33 (1929), 139–40. Antiochos
I married Seleukos' second wife, and Seleukos, who was still alive, filed a public
disclaimer, saying, "It is not the customs of the Persians and other peoples that I
impose upon you, but a law common to all, by which that is always just which is
decreed by the king" (App. *Syr.* x. 61).

Antiochos III: C. A. Kincaid, "A Persian Prince—Antiochos Epiphanes," *Oriental
Studies in Honour of Cursetji Erachji Pavry*, 209. The title "Queen and Sister" from
O.G.I.S. 224. This inscription comes from Lydia, a place where Persian colonies
existed. Antiochos IV: App. *Syr.* iv. 1.

Chapter III

The *Magoi* and Hellenistic Persis

Up to this point, the authors of the propaganda and the means by which it was spread have not been discussed in detail. That it was developed and spread by *magoi,* a priestly clan in the service of the Achaemenid kings, can be shown.

The *magoi* were an exceedingly old group of priests, who probably existed when the Medes and Persians settled in Iran in the course of the ninth century. They were by no means the only priests, for the Gathas mention others called Karapan priests, Usij priests, and Manthra-speakers. Strabo knew also of necromancers, fish-diviners, and water-diviners. The *magoi* lived under a special law which, like the Holiness Code of Leviticus, maintained the ritual purity of a select group; consequently, they maintained their separate identity far into the historical period, living apart from the rest of society in their own groups, which were concentrated in Media. Deinon included them with the Medes and Persians as a distinct tribe. While a Median dynasty held imperial authority in Asia the *magoi* remained in Media, but the subsequent victory of the Achaemenids caused some of them to go to Persis. By the Roman period, Strabo recognized them as a separate tribe there. Within the tribal group there may have been a head *magos;* in A.D. 200 Diogenes Laertios knew a succession from Zoroaster to Alexander.[1]

It is possible that the *magoi* were a once kingly tribe like the Achaemenids, for in historical times we find them closely attached to royal service and able to do many of the things that the king himself could do. Thus, the *magoi* conducted sacrifices, divined the future through dreams and other media, and carried the sacred fire in royal

[1] Other priests: Yasna xli; xlvii; Strabo xvi. 2. 39 (762). The special law: Amm. Marc. xxiii. 6. 35; and see p. 79 and n. 34, below.

As a tribe: Herod. i. 101; Amm. Marc. xxiii. 6. 34; Deinon [*Persian History*] = Clem. Alex. *Strom.* vi. 3; Strabo xv. 3. 1 (727). I. Gershevitch, *The Avestan Hymn to Mithra* (1959), 17–8.

The succession: Diog. Laer. *proem.* 2.

processions. Like Persian kings they practiced marriage with their sisters.[2] The hypothesis of royal origins goes far to explain how Gaumata the *Magos* was able successfully to revolt against the Achaemenid Kambyses, and how Dareios found it difficult to suppress him. Thirty-seven years after the fall of Astyages the *magoi* rebelled against Kambyses while he was absent in Egypt, and fortunately for them, he was accidentally killed on his way home. The magian king Gaumata was a former officer of the royal government. He established himself and his government in Media, the province in which the *magoi* were most thickly settled.[3] He was able, apparently with little or no trouble, at once to lay hands on the government, to transmit orders to at least some of the imperial satraps, and to remit taxes and military service owed by various persons and communities in the Empire. This fact is agreed upon by Greek writers and at least tacitly by Dareios in the doctored account of the affair he later had inscribed at Behistun.[4] The important fact is that the immediate reaction of many of the political officials was to obey Gaumata. The satrap in western Anatolia, Oroites, was one who cooperated with it. This evidence is valuable because Oroites was far enough away from Media to be able safely to resist Gaumata if the *magos* was merely a revolutionary, as Dareios says. But Oroites did not resist. We do hear of resistance, but only by the Achaemenid clan and their retainers. The feeling that one derives from Herodotos' account of the transactions is that the change in government was effected by a Median group who had some right to the position. It is undeniable that the *magos* had a large following. Herodotos says that after he was killed by Dareios all Asia mourned his death.[5] All this points to the strong probability that the government of the *magoi* had some right to exist, since they belonged to an old royal clan that had been deposed from royal rank.

The festival called "The Slaughter of the *Magoi*" shows the great importance the Persian kings attached to the priests subsequently. It was annually celebrated on the anniversary of Gaumata's death, 10th Bāgayādi, and Herodotos says that no *magos* was allowed to show himself during the day. Perhaps during the ritual the king was on

[2] Similar functions: Herod. i. 131; Deinon = Cic. *Div.* i. 23. 47; Amm. Marc. xxiii. 6. 32–5. Marriage: Herod. iii. 31; Xanthos = Clem. Alex. *Strom.* iii. 11; Sotion = Diog. Laer. *proem.* 7; Strabo xv. 3. 20 (735).

[3] Herod. iii. 61; *DB* xi. 1. 35—xii. 1. 48 in R. G. Kent, *op. cit.*, 117–20.

[4] Herod. iii. 67; Ktes. *Persika*, Epit. 39–45; Just. i. 9; *DB* xxi. 1. 48—xiv. 1. 71 in R. G. Kent, *op. cit.*, 117–20; A. T. Olmstead, *H.P.E.* (1948), 92–3.

[5] Oroites: Herod. iii. 126; Herodotos' feelings: *ibid.*, iii. 65, 73, 75; the mourning: *ibid.*, iii. 67.

trial before Ahura Mazdāh for reinstatement, and feared having a *magos* with royal rights at large to take advantage of them during some critical phase of the religious ceremonies.[6]

We have a great deal of information from Greek writers concerning the intimate cooperation between the *magoi* and the Achaemenids in the period after Dareios I. They accompanied the king, performed sacrifices along with him, supervised his own sacrifices, and chanted invocatory hymns to the gods as the king did to safeguard royal undertakings. The *magoi* had the right of advising the Great King in religious affairs, and were charged with the responsibility of educating royal children, imparting knowledge of things profane and sacred. After the death of a king, they kept watch at his tomb and maintained his cult.[7]

The royal prerogatives of the *magoi* and the very close association of these priests with the Persian dynasty show that they were the source of the obviously religious propaganda and prophecies. Since all of it deals with the re-establishment of the Persian kings as representatives of Ahura Mazdāh, it must have been the work of a group deeply interested in kings and Ahura Mazdāh. Furthermore, since similar Persian propaganda appears in Anatolia, Babylonia, and Judah, it must have been disseminated by Persians who had a common background of ideas and interests and who were at the same time located in these places. The only Persians who could have met these prerequisites were the *magoi*.

The *magoi*, moreover, seem actually to have been interested in proselytizing. Yasna 42 comes from the Achaemenid period. It ends by saying that loyal Persians sacrifice for the safety of the *magoi*, "as they go from afar to those who seek righteousness in the lands." Religious conversion was already known in the Gathas of the sixth century. The fifth-century *Mithra Yasht* predicts that the Mazdayasnian religion will come to pervade Iran. And the *magoi* in St. Matthew's gospel are seeking the savior-to-come so that people may know and worship him through them.[8]

[6] The festival: Herod. iii. 79; Ktes. *Persika*, Epit. 15; the date from W. B. Henning, "The Murder of the Magi," *JRAS* (1944), 133.

[7] Sacrifices and hymns: Herod. i. 131; vii. 133–4; Xen. *Kyro.* vii. 5. 35, 57; iv. 5. 51; viii. 1. 23–4; Curt. iii. 3. 10; v. 1. 22; Amm. Marc. xxiii. 6. 32–6. Advice and education: Xen. *Kyro.* iv. 5. 51; vii. 5. 35, 57; viii. 1. 23–4; Plato *I Alki.* 122 A; Plut. *Art.* vi. 3; Strabo xv. 1. 68 (718); 3. 18 (733). Cult: Aristoboulos = Arr. *Anab.* vi. 29. 7–11. And see pp. 46–47, and n. 24, above.

[8] Yasna 42 in A. T. Olmstead, *H.P.E.* (1948), 476. The Gathic passage is xlvi. 5–6; see, too, H. S. Nyberg, *Die Religionen des alten Iran* (1938), 231, 236. *Mithra Yasht* 96. Mt. ii. 7–9.

The dispersion of the *magoi* is well attested. Only a century after the end of the Hellenistic period, Pliny the Elder listed, from his research in books of the Hellenistic period, the lands where the *magoi* were settled: Persis, Arabia, Ethiopia, and Egypt. Many other countries can be added from contemporary Hellenistic sources. *Magoi* are known to have been located in Koile Syria, Babylonia, Kappadokia, western Anatolia generally, Ephesos, and Elephantine in Egypt. In addition, we may cite as highly probable Susa in Elam, Ekbatana in Media, Damaskos in Syria, Sardeis in Lydia, northern Mesopotamia, and Phrygia.[9] Our certain knowledge indicates that they covered all the Mediterranean's eastern littoral. Only they had the community of interest, ideas, cult, and wide dispersion to have disseminated the *Bahman Yasht* in its versions to western Anatolia through Babylon. Only they could have spread the *Oracle of Hystaspes* into Kappadokia and Pontos, whence it found its way in Greek eventually into the hands of Lactantius, or circulated the Sibylline Oracle on Alexander, which found its way probably from Ephesos into the Sibylline collection of an Alexandrian Jew. Indeed, these *magoi* made a deep impression as they went about spreading the good news of the coming liberation of the East from evil European kings. And the impression was etched on the folk-memory of the eastern Mediterranean peoples. These Persian priests inspired the birth legends of the Savior Jesus in the Gospel According to Matthew, which dimly echoes the *Bahman Yasht*. Three *magoi* from the East appear in Judah seeking the king who is to come, bearing royal gifts of gold, frankincense, and myrrh. They are threatened with extinction by the wicked, Hellenized king, played by Herod. But led by a star in the east which heralds the savior's birth, they find him attended by his mother.[10] That this story is Iranian is proved by the similarity of detail between Matthew and the *Bahman Yasht;* the star motif cannot have been conceived by anyone native to Palestine, because if the *magoi* of Matthew had really followed a star seen in the eastern sky (ἐν τῇ ανατολῇ), they would have begun their journey in the Mediterranean Sea.

[9] Pliny, *N.H.* xxv. 13. Koile Syria: J. H. Moulton, *Early Zoroastrianism* (1913), 187–9, based on Jer. xxxix. 3, 13 and Ezek. viii. 16–8; Babylonia: p. 23, above; Kappadokia: Strabo xv. 3. 15 (733); western Anatolia: *ibid.*, xv. 3. 14 (732); Ephesos: Thou. viii. 109; Cic. *Div.* i. 23. 47; Plut. *Alex.* iii. 4; Elephantine: *P. Brook. Ar.* 4.

Susa, Ekbatana, Damaskos, and Sardeis: F. Cumont, *The Mysteries of Mithra* (1903), 9–10; Berossos, *Chaldaika* iii = Clem. Alex. *Protrep.* v. 65; northern Mesopotamia: Plut. *Luc.* xxiv. 5–7; Phrygia: Diogenes the Tragedian, *Semele* = Athen. xiv. 636 AB.

[10] Mt. ii. 1–12; cf. *Bahman Yasht* iii. 13–8.

That the *magoi* hated Alexander himself seems certain. A fragment of a Manichean-Sogdian manuscript, evidently a translation from a still earlier Middle Persian or Parthian document, ascribes the murder of the *magoi,* the one mentioned above which became a state festival, not to Dareios I who had actually carried it out, but to King Alexander, who certainly was not responsible for it.[11] This lie must be Hellenistic —it could not have been created in later times when Alexander's victory no longer mattered. Either the priests created this phantasy themselves, or some other persons created it for them, a thing most unlikely. In either case this fragment is evidence that the *magoi* had reason to loathe Alexander. In other words, the historic fact of Dareios' slaughter was wilfully distorted to show that these priests, or a number of them, despised the Makedonian conqueror. Although these priests had suffered violence from the Persian dynasty, it should occasion no surprise that they were willing to keep alive its memory in Hellenistic times and even hope for its return. The prophets of Judah had had to struggle with the House of David there, but in the Persian and Greek periods continued to insist that the messiah would come from David's line.

It must not be imagined, of course, that all these priests did side together against the Greeks. Such people never do. Nor should it be thought that the magian propaganda caused all other Persians enthusiastically to hate the Greeks. In Iran, as in the other countries of the Near East, there was never a resistance to Hellenism that involved the whole population. Some people always collaborated. It would be a grave mistake to regard any of these regions as completely unified, for they never had been before Alexander, and they never were after him.

Differences existed between the various religious groups in Persis, and these differences diminished the strength of the resistance movement. In the period before Alexander's victory there were three main groups of religious persons which, it is true, were loosely connected with one another. But in the reign of Dareios I these groups had had important differences. First, there was the Achaemenid group, concerned with the state-cult of the high gods and the theology of kingship. They were apparently also attempting to reconcile the Zarathushtrian concepts of deity with their own and the magian. Second, there were the *magoi,* concerned with the kingship and with assisting the king, but also smarting from the recent destruction of Gaumata

[11] The fragment, TM 393, mentions Alexander in 11. 24–9. It is published and translated by W. B. Henning, "The Murder of the Magi," *JRAS* (1944), 133–44

and his priestly allies. They also differed from the Achaemenids in important points of detail arising from their "Holiness Code." Third, there were the Zarathushtrians, concerned with the theological development of the nature of Ahura Mazdāh.

I have already had a good deal to say about Achaemenid and magian religion. No complete essay on the differences of the two is intended here, only enough to demonstrate that the differences were quite important. The Achaemenid kings practiced inhumation; the *magoi* did not, relying on exposure of corpses. They considered burial a sin without atonement. There was little the *magoi* could do in protest against what they considered a grave religious wrong; hence, they accepted the difference in return for the favored position they enjoyed at the side of the Great Kings, a status far above that of all other priestly sects. But this matter of burial custom was something that would hold them apart from other Persians in the Makedonian period, and there is evidence of Persian burial in Persis during this time.[12] While the Zarathushtrian and magian groups had grown together in the fifth and fourth centuries, it seems that a complete fusion had not been obtained. Nonconformity to magian practices, either by supporters of the royal party or by those people who were the ideological descendants of Zarathushtra would partly account for the denunciations of Iranian apostasy in both the *Bahman Yasht* and the *Oracle of Hystaspes*.[13] There probably continued to exist a few Zoroastrians rather like the prophetic reform party in Judah. Such a group disliked monarchy and its paraphernalia of animal sacrifice that the *magoi* around the king performed. The Gathas show that Zarathushtra and his followers objected strongly to the royal and sacrificial aspects of Persian religion. Yasna 46 condemns in a single sweeping sentence "the sacrificers and sorcerer princes," who bind mankind to the yoke of their will. The hymn concludes that Ahura Mazdāh's retribution will surely follow them. "May good rulers, not

---

[12] Achaemenid burial: Ktes. *Persika*, Epit. 9, 41, 55; Herod. i. 140; iii. 35; vii. 114, 117; Strabo xv. 3. 3 (728); E. F. Schmidt, *Persepolis* (1953), i. 55; J. H. Moulton, *Early Zoroastrianism* (1913), 202–3. Magian practice: *Videvdād* i. 13; A. D. Nock, "Cremation and Burial in the Roman Empire," *HTR* 25 (1932), 342, n. 102; 343; J. H. Moulton, *op. cit.*, 202–3.

Hellenistic Persian burial: E. F. Schmidt, *op. cit.*, i. 55–7; R. Ghirshman, *Iran* (1954), 270 and Pl. 30.

[13] For the fusion of Zarathushtrian and *magos* see: H. S. Nyberg, *Die Religionen des alten Iran* (1938), 301; A. D. Nock, "The Problem of Zoroaster," *AJA* 53 (1949), 277–85; J. Duchesne-Guillemin, *The Western Response to Zoroaster* (1958), 54–7; I. Gershevitch, *The Avestan Hymn to Mithra* (1959), 13–22.

The Hellenistic denunciations are *Bahman Yasht* ii. 45–7; *Oracle of Hystaspes*, frag. 15.

bad, rule over us," laments Yasna 48. The Gathas explain that the evil of rulers is that they prevent mankind's acquisition of Good Mind by royal sacrifice of oxen to Ahura Mazdāh and by the king's laying waste the fields of the righteous. There was strong hostility to the *haoma* ritual as well.[14] All this would have separated the *magoi* and strict Zarathushtrians as much as Zarathushtrians and Achaemenids. While royal participation in both sacrifice and *haoma* rites stirred the Zarathushtrians, there may have been more than that behind the Avestan denunciations of the kings. Like the royal religious party in Judah, the royal party in Iran usurped the place of Ahura, "The Lord," when they adopted Mesopotamian concepts of kingship and made the king intermediate between god and man. The important fact is usually overlooked that Zarathushtra was a contemporary of that supremely important event, the beginning of the Babylonization of Iran, which involved a hitherto simple, pastoral folk in the stream of world thought and development. Thus, there would be a close parallel between the religious situation in Judah in the tenth-eighth centuries and Iran in the six-fourth centuries.

It might be added that there is no real evidence that the Achaemenids ever were Zarathushtrians. The use of a few similar words and phrases about the gods in the Gathas and the Old Persian inscriptions only shows that individuals of the same basic Iranian culture used basically the same concepts. Dareios' name, in Old Persian *Dārayauvahu,* is not Zarathushtrian, meaning, "Who sustains Good Thought," as averred by A. T. Olmstead; both H. S. Nyberg and R. G. Kent agree that it means, "He Who Holds Firm the Good," a quite general meaning. Thus, there is no connection between the *Vohumanah* of the Zarathushtrians and the Achaemenid king. Nor is there any need, particularly, to identify the Vishtaspa of the Gathas with the father of Dareios. Vishtaspa (Hystaspes) may have been a common name in aristocratic circles; it may have been the name of a half-legendary culture-hero, a person like Moses or Lykourgos. Furthermore, the Lie that Dareios and Xerxes refer to in their inscriptions is not a Zarathushtrian religious heresy; it is the political Lie of a province's denial of Achaemenid kingship, the Lie of a rival imperial cult. That is abundantly clear from the context of the inscriptions. The use of the ritual intoxicant *haoma* by *magos* and king is well-attested at Persepolis, and as we have noticed, this practice was hated by Zarathushtrians.

[14] Yasna xlvi. 1, 2, 11; cf. Yasna xliv. 20. Yasna xlviii. 5. Royal sacrifice and laying waste of fields: Yasna xxxii. 9–12. *Haoma* ritual: xliv. 20.

The common people were peasants far removed from these struggles and pursued their usual old-time religion of fertility cult and other ritual exercises.[15] From the foregoing emerges the fact that there was no complete unity among religious groups in Iran. This was of obvious importance: in Hellenistic Persis the various sects could not work together to oppose the Greeks wholeheartedly.

As for the degree to which the secular aristocracy opposed Hellenism in cooperation with the clergy, we must turn to the history of Persis in the third and second centuries. Our information concerning this time is exceedingly meagre. After the murder of Dareios III by his warrior nobles, Alexander executed Bessos, the head of the conspiracy, who ruled for a few months as Artaxerxes IV, last of the Great Kings. The region was then organized as a province of the new Makedonian empire. The first satrap was the Persian Orxines, but after a regime lasting about six years he was hanged on the false charge of having plundered royal tombs. He had been an enormously rich man, descended, it was said, from Kyros. He was accused of having actually rifled Kyros' tomb and of having executed Persians without cause, by another Persian named Bagoas. This incident shows that opportunism was more important than noble solidarity. During the process that led to Orxines' execution the magian attendants of the tomb were put under torture at Alexander's order to make them reveal the guilty persons. They could tell nothing, and the king had to call off his tormentors.[16] This perhaps was the origin of the tale that Alexander was responsible for the Slaughter of the *Magoi*. The new satrap was the Makedonian Peukestas, appointed on account of his personal bravery and his willingness to adopt Persian dress and other customs. This move was probably intended not only to assert Hellenic rule but also to make it as palatable as possible through a show of respect for native tradition. If Greek historians may

[15] Dareios' name: R. G. Kent, *Old Persian* (2nd ed., 1953), 189; for the Lie see the Old Persian inscriptions (page numbers refer to R. G. Kent, *op. cit.*), DB lxii. 4. 59—lxiv. 4. 69, pp. 129–32; DNa v. 47—vi. 30, pp. 137–8; DNb viii. 5–21, pp. 139–40; XPh iii. 13—iv. 41, pp. 150–1. On Persepolitan *haoma:* G. G. Cameron, *Persepolis Treasury Tablets* (1948), 5–7; Tablet No. 11, p. 101; "Persepolis Treasury Tablets Old and New," *JNES* 17 (1958), 162–3; R. T. Hallock, "New Light from Persepolis," *JNES* 9 (1950), 239–40; E. F. Schmidt, *Persepolis* (1957), ii. 55–6. Common people: J. Duchesne-Guillemin, *The Western Response to Zoroaster* (1958), 50–1, 64; R. Ghirshman, *Village Perse-Achéménide* (1954), 29–31.
A discussion of the differences between Achaemenid and Zarathushtrian will be found in H. S. Nyberg, *Die Religionen des alten Iran* (1938), 346–56, 362; J. Duchesne-Guillemin, *op. cit.*, 53–4, 103–4; I. Gershevitch, *The Avestan Hymn to Mithra* (1959), 15–6.
[16] Orxines: Aristoboulos = Arr. *Anab.* vi. 29. 8—30. 2 and Strabo xv. 3. 7 (730); Curt. x. 1. 22–38. The *Magoi:* Arr. *Anab.* vi. 30. 2–3.

be believed, Peukestas' regime was popular with the inhabitants of Persis. He kept order with a force including 10,000 Persian archers and slingers, 3,000 hoplites recruited from every country under heaven, 600 Greek and Thrakian horse, and 400 Persian cavalry. This speaks well for the general sense of Greek statements, and shows that there were numerous Persians willing to support the regime.[17]

When Antigonos Monophthalamos captured Persis in 316 B.C., he was granted the honor of the kingship by the local nobility. This may have been the gesture of a browbeaten aristocracy attempting to ingratiate themselves with their new ruler. Antigonos had shown himself stern by removing Peukestas and substituting his own man, and when the Persian Thespios, one of the most distinguished of the notables, protested that the Persians would obey no one but Peukestas, he was straightway executed. Yet Antigonos continued to receive half-hearted support in Persis, and when his new satrap Nikanor appeared to fight Seleukos in 312 B.C., he brought several thousand Persian troops with him. But by battle's end, these troops deserted to Seleukos the victor, perhaps because the removal of Persophile Peukestas and the death of Thespios caused the Persian military class to lose interest in the continuance of Antigonos' regime.[18] This victory gave Seleukos control of Persis, and the large satrapy became a part of the Seleukid state.

There must have been cooperation between at least some Persian nobles and the new regime, some sincere, a great deal halfhearted. There are a number of indications that this was so. This collaboration is the only way in which we can account for a curious legend concerning Alexander's parentage which appears in Middle Persian literature. It is hard to believe that the story does not go back to some Hellenistic tradition, because it tells a good deal about the Makedonian principals in it, Alexander and Philip, which would have been most difficult for a Persian to have acquired after the end of the ancient world on account of the language barrier. The story appears in the *Shah nameh* of Firdausi, who flourished around A.D. 1000, and also in the tenth century Muslim historiographer Tabari, but the version known to them can be traced back at least to the fourth Christian century.[19]

---

[17] Arr. *Anab.* vi. 30. 2–3; Diod. xviii. 3. 3; xix. 14. 4–5; 17. 7; 21. 2—22. 3; Plut. *Eum.* xiv. 3.

[18] Peukestas—Thespios: Diod. xix. 48. 1–5; Nikanor—Seleukos: Diod. xix. 92. 3–4.

[19] A. G. Warner and E. Warner, *The Shahnameh of Firdausi* (1912), vi. 19. Already in Pseudo-Kallisthenes is the notice that the rulers of Kappadokia had sent a man-eating colt to Philip II. Kappadokia was an area with many *magoi* in it (Strabo xv. 3. 15 [733]). This colt grows up to become Boukephalos (Ps.-Kal. i. 13. 6–7; 17. 1).

The legend itself is *Shah nameh* xviii. 3–4.

The extreme antiquity of the legend is indicated by the statement that Alexander's birth was said to synchronize with that of a white mare. Horses played a role in Old Persian folklore, being associated with kings. We know that horses were sacrificed at the tomb of Kyros the Great; and Herodotos knew a Persian legend that told how Dareios I became king because his horse was first to neigh at the rising sun. The chariot of the Great King, moreover, was always preceded by a number of Nisean horses.[20] Hence, it would appear that Firdausi's story has ultimately an extremely ancient oral tradition behind it.

The legend of Alexander's birth could have been developed to soften the blow of Makedonian occupation by making it seem that the Makedonians were at least part Achaemenid after all. According to the legend, Alexander was the child of Dareios III and a Makedonian princess, whom the king married after defeating her father Philip in battle. The princess, however, had such bad halitosis that Dareios was forced to send her back to Philip, and she returned home pregnant with Alexander. Alexander upon growing to manhood conquered the Persian Empire.

While this story has a whiff of disapproval for the Makedonians, yet it also accepts them. This acceptance was certainly not unanimous. But by the time of Alexander, certain of the nobility had developed a considerable tradition of hostility to the Achaemenids dating from the last quarter of the fifth century. It reached its largest proportions in the Satrap Wars of the fourth century. During this period the royal family was torn by rivalries within it, not only for the kingship, but also for the queenship. The slaughter of one royal candidate after another in battle heavily involved the nobility too, since the opposing candidates for the throne naturally had to make use of the warrior aristocracy as the spearhead of their military forces. The success of Artaxerxes II against Kyros the Younger, for example, was bought only at the price of a bloody fight; the loyal nobles had to oppose a large army of insurgents which included the Ten Thousand mailed hoplites of Xenophon's *Anabasis*. This involved heavy losses for the loyal aristocrats. The whole period must have severely tried the loyalty of numerous noble families. The desire to escape from involvement in the civil wars of the Achaemenids played its part in inducing the satraps, who were drawn from the aristocratic levels of Persian society, to make themselves independent of the Great King by adopting Greek techniques of statecraft and hiring Greek mercenary soldiers,

[20] Sacrifice of horses: Aristoboulos = Arr. *Anab.* vi. 29. 4–11; Dareios-legend: Herod. iii. 86; Nisean horses: *ibid.*, i. 189; viii. 115; E. F. Schmidt, *Persepolis* (1953), i. 83.

as they did in the fourth century. That movement, of course, led to the Satrap Wars.

What is more, these wars killed many nobles who were the prime upholders of the old traditions of Persis, at the very time that the royal family, especially, was being culturally diluted by Babylonian influences in the form of numerous Babylonian women in the royal, and we may guess in aristocratic, harems. These women bore and brought up children who had high rank, and even in some cases became Great Kings. Artaxerxes II was a half-Mesopotamian king; it was he who introduced the state worship of the nature-goddess Anahita, a deity with many similarities to Babylonian Ishtar. We can only speculate on what the nobility thought specifically of this. Yet this was the age in which the Persians' loyalty to their kings began to fade. Numerous assassinations of kings, and increasingly frequent defeats of royal armies at the hands of Greek, Egyptian, and satrapal armies all combined to bring about a much lessened conviction on the part of the aristocracy that the prevailing religious concepts of kingship had real meaning. The royal theology never died out entirely; such an idea seldom did in the ancient Near East. No doubt many still believed. But it can only be, as shown by our evidence of cooperation of some Iranians with Hellenes, that many had given up the idea of Achaemenid divine rule in Persis by the time of Alexander. Many others gave up their idea of a material Achaemenid kingship, but substituted for it the new spiritualized kingship of the messianic prophecies produced in Hellenistic times. Thus, loyalty to the idea of native kingship lost ground, in a mundane sense, only to gain ground in a religious, spiritual sense. The result was the Fifth Monarchy theory of the magian priesthood.

Turning from these general considerations let us briefly review the history of Persis in Hellenistic times. About 280 B.C., a family, doubtless of ancient lineage, became hereditary independent dynasts with headquarters at and around Persepolis. How this happened we do not know. J. de Morgan has suggested from the names used by some of them—Dareios and Artaxerxes—that they may have belonged to a branch of the Achaemenid family, but this is most uncertain. We have no evidence that they ever claimed descent from Achaemenes.[21] They were a mixture of Hellenic and Iranian loyalties, the latter predominating. Their known proximity to the decaying monuments of

[21] J. de Morgan, *T.M.G.R.* (1933), 341–2; E. T. Newell, *The Coinage of the Eastern Seleucid Mints* (1938), 160–1.

vanished Persian glory heightens the morbid impression one forms of them from portraits on their coinage.

These princes tried to put together as much as they could of the ruins that remained to them. Around 300 B.C., someone searched through the remains of the Treasury at Persepolis.[22] What implication this has for the history of the family is unknown. The dynasty unfortunately did not leave any inscriptions at Persepolis; there is a complete gap between the Old Persian inscriptions of Dareios I and his successors and the graffiti of Sassanid times. At the Persepolis Spring Cemetery and also near Istakhr, burials of Hellenistic date have been found, but the scantiness of the remains and the small number actually found show that the area was small and poor. Istakhr itself was a small place, probably the mint of the Persepolitan dynasts. There was no other town in the immediate region.[23]

Actual construction by these little dynasts included a fire temple northwest of the Platform designed in traditional Iranian style; Greek inscriptions found in the ruins equate Persian and Hellenic gods. Sculpture recovered depicts a prince and princess of the family in normal Persian dress and attitude. Palace H on the Terrace itself was built early in the post-Alexandrian period. This poor little palace was connected with a pavilion, and the two buildings were fortified. They were embellished with inscriptions originally cut by Artaxerxes I and III and decorated with reliefs made for Artaxerxes I showing the tribute procession on New Year's Day.[24] Thus, the dynasts attempted to keep alive something of the past tradition of Persian greatness.

They struck a series of coins beginning about 275 B.C. Like the fire temple inscriptions, the coins show a mixture of Hellenistic and Iranian ideas. The reverses usually display a fire temple, which could be a picture of the shrine at Naqsh-i-Rustam, the cemetery of the great Achaemenid kings. At the same time, the coinage is executed in very fine Hellenic style under the first of the dynasts, and oc-

[22] In room 13 of the Treasury, three Alexander-drachms have been found: one struck around 325 B.C., two about 312 B.C.: E. F. Schmidt, *Persepolis* (1953), i. 170; (1957), ii. 113 and Pl. 84.

[23] Burials: E. F. Schmidt, *Persepolis* (1953), i. 56–7; (1957), ii. 117–23. Istakhr: *ibid.*, ii. 122; *The Treasury of Persepolis* (1939), 16 and n. 2; 105; G. C. Miles, *Excavation Coins from the Persepolis Region* (1959), 19–23.

[24] Fire temple: E. F. Schmidt, *Persepolis* (1953), i. 50–1, 56; Fig. 16–7; R. Ghirshman, *Iran* (1954), 231–5; E. E. Herzfeld, "Notes of the Quarter: Recent Discoveries at Persepolis," *JRAS* (1934), 232; *Archeological History of Iran* (1935), 45–7. Palace H: E. F. Schmidt, *op. cit.*, i. 43, 62, 264, 279–82; Pl. 200–5; Strabo xv. 3. 3 (728). Reliefs and inscriptions: E. F. Schmidt, *op. cit.*, i. 279–82; the inscriptions are A^1Pa and A^3Pa, *c* and *d*.

casionally pictures a deity, probably Ahura Mazdāh, modelled and tricked out as a Grecian Zeus. The dynasts did not assume the title of king, but called themselves *frātadāra*, "Keeper of the Fire," and *bagān*, "Divine."[25] The last should be taken in the sense that the Achaemenids were divine: not gods but men charged with supernatural powers.

The portraits of the first kings are quite Hellenic, indicating the presence of Greek engravers at Istakhr and orientation of policy towards the Seleukids. The first *frātadāra*, Bagadates, around 275 B.C. appears on Attic-standard tetradrachms wearing a Persian headdress but without the Oriental beard. The reverses show the prince enthroned with a sceptre like a European ruler or European god; his local coinage—drachms and obols—has an Iranian fire temple. The reverses in either case have an engraved symbol almost certainly the labarum of the Achaemenid kings.[26] Towards the end of the century the coins of Autophradates I show engraving less precise, more careless, with poorly shaped flans, issues much in contrast with the scrupulous work that began the series. There is increasing use of Persian religious symbolism on the reverses. All the coinage for the first time shows the princes with the labarum before a Persian fire temple over which floats the old symbol of Ahura Mazdāh. This no doubt points to a definite break with pro-Seleukid policy.[27] The existence of these partly Hellenized *frātadāra* at this time fits well with the statements in the two long apocalypses. These complain that no real kings, only demons, reign in Iran, but look forward hopefully to the coming of one sent by Ahura Mazdāh to end apostasy and drive out the forces of evil.

But it was Seleukid Antiochos III who intervened and around 205 B.C. recovered control of Persis. He installed a satrap and attempted to consolidate his domination of the region by refounding the two cities of Laodikeia and Antiocheia-in-Persis. The first was situated near

[25] J. de Morgan, *T.M.G.R.* (1935), iii. 379–81; G. F. Hill, *B.M.C. Arabia, Mesopotamia and Persia* (1922), clxv–clxvi; E. E. Herzfeld, *Archeological History of Iran* (1935), 47; E. F. Schmidt, *Persepolis* (1953), i. 56.

[26] J. de Morgan, *T.M.G.R.* (1935), Nos. 1–2, iii. 396–8, Pl. xxvii. 1, 5 for international coins; Nos. 3a, b, c and 4a, b, c, iii. 398–9, Pl. xxvii. 2–4, 6 for local denominations. Labarum: compare the reproductions in *ibid.* iii. Pl. xxvii. 1, 2, 5 with the literary descriptions in Xen. *Anab.* i. 10. 12; *Kyro.* vii. 1. 3. See, too, W. W. Tarn in *C.A.H.* ix. 594–5.

[27] J. de Morgan, *T.M.G.R.* (1935), Nos. 9–14, iii. 400–2, Pl. xxvii. 14, 17–9; xxviii. 5. Allotte de la Fuye, "L'oiseau légendaire des monnaies de la Perside," *Arethuse* (1926), 103–6.

Pasargadai, a town Pliny says was full of *magoi;* Antiochos may have intended to check their influence. Nothing is really known about these *poleis,* since neither has been excavated, except that the latter certainly had Greek civic institutions.[28]

With the defeat of Antiochos III by Rome in 189, about the time the Five Monarchy Prophecy was known in Anatolia, Persis broke off tribute payments and resumed its independence. The Persepolitan coinage struck off along new lines. The title *malik*—king—was assumed by the dynasts. This and a set of facial characteristics quite different from those of Bagadates and his successors indicate that a new family was in power at Persepolis. The headdress worn by the kings is no longer the sacred bonnet of the previous fire-cult; it is Parthian-inspired. The fire temple is so wretchedly engraved that it might almost be mistaken for a geometrical abstraction. Greek influence, as seen in such execution of the dies, was continuing undoubtedly to wane.[29] War presently broke out between Persis and Antiochos IV. Noumenios, Seleukid Satrap of Messene, had to defend himself against Persians coming both by land and by sea. Around 164 B.C. Antiochos himself invaded Persis in order to loot a wealthy temple there; he was repulsed.[30]

Yet soon after the Persepolitans successfully defied Seleukid attacks the threat of Parthian invaders drove them temporarily back into a policy of cooperation with the Greeks. Around 140 B.C., during the campaign of Demetrios II against the Parthians, the Seleukid was joined by a Persian contingent.[31] The campaign was a disaster; a few years later Parthian Mithradates II captured Persis, and the second series of coins was supplanted by a third directly modelled on that of Parthia. The fire temple vanishes to be replaced by a simple altar,

---

[28] Alexander: J. de Morgan, *T.M.G.R.* (1935), iii. 384–5; E. T. Newell, *The Coinage of the Eastern Seleucid Mints* (1938), 160–1.

Laodikeia: Pliny, *N.H.* vi. 115–6; W. W. Tarn, *H.C.* (3rd ed., 1952), 152; A. Aymard, "Du nouveau sur Antiochos III d'après une inscription grecque d'Iran," *RÉA* 51 (1949), 327–45. L. Vanden Berghe, *Archéologie de l'Iran ancien* (1959), 90–1; Pl. 116. Antiocheia-in-Persis: *O.G.I.S.* 233; M. I. Rostovtzeff in *C.A.H.* vii. 189; A. H. M. Jones, *The Cities of the Eastern Roman Provinces* (1937), 251.

[29] J. de Morgan, *T.M.G.R.* (1935), iii. 368–9, 364–5; see especially Nos. 22–5, pp. 404–5, Pl. xxix. 7, 9.

[30] Persian independence: Jos. *Ant.* xii. 294; Pliny, *N.H.* vi. 152; E. R. Bevan, *The House of Seleucus* (1902), ii. 158–9; A. Bouché-Leclerq, *Histoire des séleucides* (1913), i. 22; W. W. Tarn in *C.A.H.* ix. 578–9; R. Ghirshman, *Iran* (1954), 245.

Antiochos' invasion: 2 Macc. ix. 1–2; N. C. Debevoise, *A Political History of Parthia* (1938), 21.

[31] Just. xxxvi. 1; N. C. Debevoise, *op. cit.,* 25; W. W. Tarn in *C.A.H.* ix. 580.

with a crescent above it. The *malik* affects an Arsakid tiara, and his portrait faces to the left, eastern style, instead of to the right as in all preceding issues.[32]

Henceforth, the dynasts of Persis, while they retained their title, *malik,* had to endure three centuries of continuing Arsakid domination. In the coinage Greek influence slowly died away, while Parthian influence became more and more pronounced.[33] Since the Greek threat was dead, the Persians attacked the Arsakids with religious propaganda much as they had the Seleukids. Thus, their emphasis on anti-Hellenic propaganda was dissipated. We have an example of their anti-Parthianism; it is the first chapter of the *Videvdād,* dated around 140 B.C. or a little later.[34] This chapter was included with the bulk of the *Videvdād,* the Magian Holiness Code, as a catalogue of Unholiness in non-Persian Iran. In the list of countries one district is omitted. That is Persis. The named districts included the kingdoms of the Parthians, the Medes, and the tottering state of the Greco-Baktrians. The text says that while Ahura Mazdāh created a good for each district, Ahriman followed him up and countercreated a corresponding evil. Parthian areas are especially singled out: Nisaia, where the early Parthian kings were buried, was guilty of the sin of unbelief;[35] Margiana had indulged sinful lusts;[36] Hyrkania was guilty of some unnatural sin for which there was no atonement;[37] Rhagai, renamed Parthian Arsakeia, had committed another sin without atonement, the sin of utter unbelief.[38] Chorasmia had burned corpses, yet another sin without remedy.[39] The Parthians, as will be shown in the next chapter, did not follow the magian religious prescriptions, for they both burned and buried the dead; and they also committed the heresy of dominating Persis. After these recitations of evil, the text concludes that "There are still other lands and countries, beautiful

[32] J. de Morgan, *T.M.G.R.* (1935), iii. 359–60, 369–70; Nos. 26–7, p. 406, Pl. xxix. 22; W. W. Tarn in *C.A.H.* ix. 580, 586.

[33] J. de Morgan, *T.M.G.R.* (1935), iii. 368–9; Strabo xv. 3. 3, 24 (728, 736).

[34] Translated by J. Darmesteter, *The Zend-Avesta* i (*Sacred Books of the East* iv [1880]), 1–10. Date: K. F. Geldner, "Awestalitteratur" in *Grundriss der iranischen Philologie* (1904), ii. 36; A. Christensen, *Études sur le Zoroastrianisme de la Perse antique* (1928), 43–4; H. S. Nyberg, *Die Religionen des alten Iran* (1938), 6, 314, 471 n. 1; E. E. Herzfeld, *Zoroaster and His World* (1947), ii. 744–5; A. T. Olmstead, *H.P.E.* (1948), 16–7, 130–2.

[35] *Videvdād* i. 8; burial site in W. W. Tarn in *C.A.H.* ix. 575.

[36] *Videvdād* i. 6.

[37] *Videvdād* i. 12.

[38] *Videvdād* i. 16.

[39] *Videvdād* i. 17.

and deep, desirable and bright, and thriving."[40] Thus, the Persians fought their Parthian master. The king from the East whom they had hoped would extirpate the Makedonians turned out unhappily for them to be an Arsakid. The resistance of the Persians against the West had to redirect itself against the Orient.

What effects the Persian propaganda had in the whole Hellenistic period are hard to assess. In Persis itself, it did not lead to a grand revolt against the full tide of Hellenism. But it likely had something to do with the gradual third-century break with the Seleukids. Archaeological and numismatic evidence is overwhelming that Persis remained essentially Persian. While Hellenism is apparent here and there in matters of detail, nonetheless the Iranian element remained heavily predominant and Hellenism made no great impression. After five centuries of struggle, in Iran the Persians created the strongly nationalist Sassanid Persian Empire, consciously trying to continue Achaemenid Persian traditions. The resistance doubtless served to help keep alive native traditions, and by opposing Hellenism helped to keep it from deeply touching Iranian life. The Makedonians, except in Baktria, never succeeded in persuading Iranians to cooperate with them. The hostility of our texts towards the invaders must have had something to do with the conservation of pre-Alexandrian ways of life.

In the East as a whole, the propaganda made an impression which has left traces in the religious beliefs of others. So much effectiveness the magian movement demonstrably had. The idea of the messianic King-Who-Is-to-Come contributed to the messianic movement that was growing all over the Near East in the last century of the pre-Christian era. The idea, with Persian motifs, even touched Christianity, and colored the stories about the Christ.

[40] *Videvdād* i. 21.

Chapter IV

The Other Iranians

There is no evidence of Oriental religious resistance to Hellenism in the non-Persian parts of ancient Iran. None of the important parts of it—Parthia, Baktria, or Media—resented the Makedonian occupation to such a degree that people resorted to active propaganda. What reaction there was shows only that the conflicts of Hellenes and Iranians were rivalries between dynastic groups competing for some economic or strategic advantage. There was no feeling of intense cultural rivalry at all, and no resort to religious propaganda. In this chapter, I shall explain why.

In each of the three areas, local circumstances made the specific attitude towards the Europeans vary. Each area had its own unique cultural tradition. Therefore, when confronted by the exact variant of Hellenism represented by the local regime, each responded in an individual way. All of them, however, went farther in their acceptance of Hellenism than Persis. None of them had, like Persis, an immediate memory of world rule. Therefore, the great issue that the Persians fought for was missing. Only Media had ever been the seat of eastern empire, and that not since 559 B.C. The two centuries that elapsed between the overthrow of Astyages by Kyros of Persis and the coming of the Makedonians seem to have been sufficient to have obliterated any Median desire for an imperial renascence.

Both Parthia and Baktria had always been subject and tributary provinces of either the Median or Persian Empire. Hence, if the victories of Alexander the Great were in one sense a conquest, in another and very real sense they were a liberation.

1. THE PARTHIANS

The Parthian dynasty ruled a state in which there was no cultural unity, such as was to be found in Persis or in Egypt. Successive waves of migration into central Iran had effectively prevented any such thing. There were the Iranian aborigines, by Alexander's time much intermarried with Indo-Europeans who immigrated in the ninth century. The historic Parthians themselves were a still later group—part of a nomadic, barbarous horde called the *Dahai* by Greek writers. One of the *Dahai* tribes was that of the *Parnoi,* and this group furnished the aristocracy—the Parthians—the culturally dominant class in Hellenistic Parthia and Hyrkania.[1]

The Parthians were never connected with the Achaemenid Empire. It means nothing that the name of the founder of their dynasty, Arsakes, is known from Old Persian times. The *Parthyaioi* whom Arrian and Curtius list among the Persian troops at the Battle of Gaugamela were, we are explicitly told, not the Parthians of later times.[2] The early, pre-*Parnoi* Parthians were a people whose name derived from the same geographic district as the name of the *Parnoi* of Hellenistic times. It is probably true, however, that the similarity in names between the Old Persian and Arsakid peoples does show a vague cultural affinity.

The *Parnoi* Parthians migrated into Iran proper in the first half of the third century B.C., fresh from the Eurasian steppe. To escape the military forces of Diodotos of Baktria, they moved into the Seleukid Parthian-Hyrkanian satrapy around 250 B.C. There they killed the Seleukid governor in battle, and succeeded, because of Seleukid pre-occupation with the terrible Third Syrian War, in gaining enough time to make their occupation permanent.[3] Hence, the original independence of the *Parnoi* nobility was not an anti-Hellenic reaction of native Iranism at all, but simply the work of a seminomadic people fighting for its life.

The confusion of ethnic groups in Parthia is further illustrated by what we know of the ruling class in northern Iran between 323 and 250 B.C. Phratapherenes, an Iranian aristocrat who led the Hyrkanian-Parthian cavalry at Gaugamela, was appointed by Alexander to be satrap of the area. He worked well with the Makedonians, being one of two Iranians who were retained in office for a period of many years. We have four issues of his coins, which are Hellenic in character, obverses showing a Greek Zeus or a city-goddess, reverses Athena or a

---

[1] W. W. Tarn in *C.A.H.* ix. 574–5; E. E. Herzfeld, *Archeological History of Iran* (1935), 53; B. P. Lozinski, *The Original Homeland of the Parthians* (1959).

[2] Arsakes: Aischylos mentions (*Pers.* 995–6) a Persian cavalry commander Arsakes, and the name also appears in Old Persian form, *Arshaka,* on a seal recovered from Persepolis (R. G. Kent, *Old Persian* [2nd ed., 1953], 157, 171). *Parthyaioi:* Arr. *Anab.* iii. 11. 4; Curt. iv. 12. 11.

[3] Strabo xi. 9. 3 (515); App. *Syr.* xi. 11. 65; W. W. Tarn in *C.A.H.* vii. 720; N. C. Debevoise, *A Political History of Parthia* (1938), xxxvii; R. Ghirshman, *Iran* (1954), 243–4.

hero in armor driving a quadriga and about to be crowned by a Victory. Phrataphernes was killed fighting Eumenes. Around 315 B.C., a European named Philotas governed Parthia. He was put to death by the Makedonian satrap of Media, Pithon, whose brother Eudamos took his place. Then, around 300 B.C. in northeastern Iran, the Iranian Vahshuvar ruled. He issued Orientalized Greek coins, with portraits executed by Greek craftsmen and with Oriental inscriptions.[4]

No government's control was either long-lived or very firm in this quarter of the world. Indeed, Strabo says that in 250 B.C. the country was full of brigands and nomads, and that wide regions were deserted. The Seleukids were too hotly engaged elsewhere to pacify and develop it, so that in consequence, he laments, it was never properly exploited.[5] Hence, in Parthia-Hyrkania there never was thorough Hellenic occupation or even government consistently in the hands of Makedonians. The inhabitants had only an occasional European satrap to deal with, their own feudal lords, and the half-nomadic wandering peoples. There never was, therefore, much basis for an anti-Hellenic movement. Furthermore, what we know of the *Parnoi* of Arsakid times shows that while their state and social structure were much influenced by Iranian culture, there were Greek currents present as well. The Parthians were unsophisticated immigrants, and their culture was at too low a level technically to compete with the Europeans without some borrowing and adaptation taking place. This, too, helped destroy any basis for real anti-Hellenism.

Parthian social organization resembled the Persian; the king had a status remote from all except an immediate circle of the nobility. The latter held most of the land, and worked it by means of the native Iranian peasantry, whose status was that of serfs. The Arsakids claimed descent from the Achaemenid Artaxerxes II and attempted to rule in the fashion of his dynasty. But only in the reign of Parthian Mithradates II (121–88 B.C.) did they begin to use the ancient title "King of Kings."[6] There is no reason to see in any of this a pan-

---

[4] Phrataphernes: Arr. *Anab.* v. 20. 7; vi. 27. 3; Just. xii. 4; G. F. Hill, *B.M.C. Arabia, Mesopotamia and Persia* (1922) , pp. clvii–clviii; Nos. 1–4, p. 193; Pl. xxviii. 1–3.

The Makedonians: Diod. xix. 14. 1–3; Vahshuvar: G. F. Hill, *op. cit.,* Nos. 1–2, p. 194; Pl. xxviii. 4, 6.

[5] Strabo xi. 7. 2 (509) .

[6] Parthian society: Plut. *Cras.* xxi. 1–2; Just. xli. 2; C. B. Welles and M. I. Rostovtzeff, "A Parchment Contract of Loan from Dura-Europos on the Euphrates," *YClS* 2 (1931) , 52; N. C. Debevoise, *A Political History of Parthia* (1938) , xxxvii–xxxix; R. Ghirshman, *Iran* (1954) , 262–3. Achaemenid descent: F. Justi, "Geschichte Irans," *Grundriss der iranischen Philologie* (1904) , ii. 483;

Iranic, anti-Hellenic propaganda; rather, these measures were more an attempt to conciliate the gentry who were not Parthian than to embarrass the Greeks. The Seleukid dynasty was, after all, genuinely half-Iranian, and the Parthian regime frequently had to face the resistance and hostility of real native Iranians.

Achaemenid ideas of kingship were gradually adopted, as we know from the evidence we have of Persis-like protocol at court. The king lived in semiseclusion. His table was elevated and set apart from the others', and at dinner he sat upon a high couch. His *daimon* was honored, for the Arsakid was more than man, if less than god. Yet to these Persian ideas a Greek flavoring was added. The most important associates of the monarch were termed *philoi* after Makedonian usage, and the titulary on the coinage included the Hellenic epithets *epiphanes* and *theopator*. Of course these terms could also be understood in a Persian sense. The Arsakids and their women formed a closed corporation. The kings married their half sisters, and we have some parchments and a clay tablet from Uruk dated by the regnal year of both king and queen.[7]

While this program had some Persian origins, it did not carry on the older tradition for its own sake alone. No doubt the Parthians were conscious of the Persian past in Iran and used this knowledge to gain a hold on the natives. But they took on the forms without taking on the substance of Old Persian kingship. To use Achaemenid ideas of royal rule was a good way for the Arsakids to stiffen their control over the warrior gentry in Iran, and to create a more centralized, Hellenistic state. Such did not exist in third-century Parthia. Even in the first century and later, Greeks told how the Parthian kings took pride in sharpening and notching the points of their arrows with their own hands, and how they discharged most of their public and private business from horseback.[8] While these Greek canards are not real evidence of contemporary Arsakid customs, they do nevertheless give a picture of what the Parthians came from. The customs of the Parthian kingship were copied from an institution that these late children of the

---

W. W. Tarn, "Queen Ptolemais and Apama," *CQ* 33 (1929), 138–40. The title from coins in W. Wroth, *B.M.C. Parthia* (1903), 24–37.

[7] Court protocol: Poseidonios, *Histories* v = Athen. iv. 152 F—153 A; xvi = *ibid.*, iv. 153 AB; Lucan, *Pharsalia* viii. 404–5; W. W. Tarn in *C.A.H.* ix. 588–9. The documents are in E. H. Minns, "Parchments of the Parthian Period from Avroman in Kurdistan," *JHS* 35 (1915), 28–32 and A. T. Clay, *Babylonian Records in the Library of J. Pierpont Morgan,* Part II: *Legal Documents from Erech* (1915), No. 53, pp. 13, 33, 87.

[8] Plut. *Dem.* xx. 2; Just. xli. 3.

steppe used as a readily accessible and understandable model of centralized society. In the highly organized and competitive society of the
second and first centuries of the pre-Christian era, the Arsakids required centralization and concentration of effort, and, as the
Japanese were later to do, they adopted the methods of cultures they
deemed their superiors.

Royal centralization was necessary in view of the position held by the
gentry, some of whom, like Crassus' opponent Surenas, were extraordinarily powerful in thier own right. Surenas was of high lineage—
his family had the right of crowning the king. He was enormously
wealthy; his property included at least two hundred waggons and a
thousand camels. He was able from his own resources to outfit a force
of a thousand mailed horsemen. It seems likely that Surenas, after his
startling success against the Romans, was put out of the way by King
Orodes to prevent him from aiming at the kingship. From Orodes'
point of view men like Surenas belonging to the Seven Very Noble
Families of the society should be bent to the royal will. From Surenas'
point of view his class should maintain the habit of independence implied by Surenas' coronation rights and by the existence of a council
of nobles which had the right of advising the king.[9] Some of the *Parnoi*
must have opposed the centralizing policy of the kings, and this fact
must be kept in mind when we discuss the role of the captured Greek
cities in the Parthian state. The kings required some force to balance
their own feudal army drawn from the aristocracy. It is symbolic of
the nature of the state that its capital, Hekatompylos, was originally a village road center, refounded as a Greek *polis* by Alexander,
and, in the third century, occupied by Parthians.[10]

The Parthian royal court included Greek elements. The titles *philos,*
"Friend," and *suggenes,* "Kinsman," were used by Makedonians.
Furthermore, love of Hellenism was consciously and overtly advertised
by the dynastic coinage. The term *philhellenos* makes its first
appearance under Mithradates I around 140 B.C. Since this king also
did a great deal to diminish the area of Seleukid control in western
Iran and eastern Mesopotamia, his propaganda cannot be taken at
full face value. Nonetheless, the use of the term itself means that the
Parthians did not undertake a campaign of anti-Hellenic propaganda
as the Persians did. One might mention, too, the tradition that Orodes

[9] For Surenas and the Parthian nobility: Plut. *Cras.*, especially xxi. 5–7; Just. xli.
1–4; C. B. Welles and M. I. Rostovtzeff, *op. cit.*, 52 ff.; W. W. Tarn in *C.A.H.* ix.
588–9; R. Ghirshman, *Iran* (1954), 264. Council of nobles: Strabo xi. 9. 3 (515).
[10] Strabo xi. 9. 1 (514); Polyb. x. 28. 1; Curt. vi. 2. 15.

was watching a scene from the *Bacchai* of Euripides when Roman Crassus' head reached him at Ktesiphon.[11] The tradition at least shows what might be believed of the Parthians of 50 B.C.

The tetradrachms and drachms of Mithradates I—his theophorous name honored Iranian Mithra—pictured on their reverses a number of Hellenic gods and goddesses—Zeus, Demeter, Nike, and Herakles. The portraits of the king seem to have been modelled on a Seleukid representation of Zeus. His successor Phraates II issued coins copied from those of Seleukids Demetrios I and II. On first-century coins the monarch appears much less a Greek: he wears his hair marcelled in Persian fashion, and the typical Parthian headgear now predominates. The usual reverse, however, is Arsakes enthroned like a Zeus with a *nikē* extending a palm of victory towards him.[12] The title *philhellenos* continues to be employed and under Orodes I (80–76/5 B.C.) is constantly reiterated. With Mithradates II numerous and large issues of drachms gradually displaced Seleukid silver in Iran—but not until 40 B.C. were Parthian tetradrachms issued annually to advertise Parthian prestige. By that date the Seleukid Empire was already twenty years defunct, although her coinage continued to circulate alongside Parthian for a while longer in Mesopotamia.[13] By that time Parthia's rival was Rome.

Parthian philhellenism, as known from the coins, was carefully propagated. At first the term did not appear on drachms, which generally were intended for local Iranian circulation, until the reign of Mithradates II. Similarly, the title *Basileus Basileōn* was not used on the tetradrachms, which were intended for international use, but it did appear on the drachms. Only in the reign of Orodes II (*c.* 57–37/6 B.C.) were these legends used indiscriminately.[14] While these facts show that much of the wheat of Parthian philhellenism was mixed

[11] Titles: Poseidonios, *Histories* v = Athen. iv. 153 BC; Strabo xi. 9. 3 (515); W. W. Tarn in *C.A.H.* ix. 588–9. *Philhellenos:* A. de Markoff, *Catalogue des monnaies Arsacides, Subarsacides, Sassanides, Dabweihides* (1889), 3–7; W. Wroth, *B.M.C. Parthia* (1903), No. 48, p. 12. The *Bacchai:* Plut. *Cras.* xxxiii. 2.

[12] Coinage of Mithradates I in W. Wroth, *B.M.C. Parthia* (1903): Zeus: Nos. 51–4, p. 13; No. 57, p. 14; No. 61, p. 15; Nike: No. 29, p. 10; Demeter: No. 29, p. 10; Herakles: No. 48, p. 12; Nos. 55–6, p. 14. For the portrait: No. 48, p. 12; Nos. 58–60, p. 15; A. de Markoff, *op. cit.*, pp. 3–7.

Phraates II: M. Dayet, "Un tétradrachm arsacide inédit," *Arethuse* (1925), 63–6. First-century coins: W. Wroth, *B.M.C. Parthia* (1903): with Mithradates II (123–88/7 B.C.), pp. 24–37 and Pl. vi–viii compare Artabanos II (*c.* 128–124/3 B.C.), pp. 38–41; Pl. viii, ix. A. de Markoff, *op. cit.*, 7–9.

[13] W. Wroth, *B.M.C. Parthia* (1903): Orodes I, Nos. 2–247, pp. 68–96. R. H. McDowell, *Coins from Seleucia on the Tigris* (1935), 203–4.

[14] R. H. McDowell, *op. cit.*, 166–7; R. Ghirshman, *Iran* (1954), 266.

with chaff, they also show that the Arsakids qualified their philiranism as well. Thus Mithradates II, who consolidated the Parthian conquest of Seleukid Mesopotamia, made a dedication to Asklepios at Delos in 110 B.C. Orodes II moved the capital from Iranian Hekatompylos to part-Greek Ktesiphon located in Mesopotamia. He did this without depopulating nearby Seleukeia to provide manpower for the city, as Seleukeia had already depopulated adjacent Babylon.[15] The Parthian kings were all things to all men.

A portrait head of Mithradates I found in Mesopotamia shows mixed Greek and Oriental styles. This is important evidence, since portraits were made to show a character that the king wanted people to accept. In like manner, a head of a Parthian queen made at the end of the first century B.C. or the beginning of the first Christian century shows Hellenic motifs. It was found at Susa in Elam, and had been executed by the Greek Antiochos, son of Dryas. Elements of Grecian architectural styles are evident in Parthian palaces. Even at Kuh-i Khvadjah in eastern Iran a Parthian governor's residence was decorated with meander patterns and akanthos leaves and a fresco of Eros or Dionysos riding an animal.[16] While Seleukeia-on-Tigris was under Parthian control there was no break in the Hellenic style of house architecture until towards the beginning of the Christian era. More important, there was no Parthian interference in the cult of Apollo Komaios. The Greek language also held its own in Parthian Mesopotamia. The legends on the coins show a particularly sharp decline in spelling and form of letters only at the end of the last century B.C. But as late as A.D. 121 at Doura on the upper Euphrates a parchment contract of loan was written in good, idiomatic Attic Greek.[17] Greek methods of finance, Greek law, Greek culture in general con-

[15] The dedication: *O.G.I.S.* 430; Ktesiphon: Amm. Marc. xxiii. 6. 23; N. C. Debevoise, *A Political History of Parthia* (1938), 41.

[16] Mithradates I: D. M. Robinson, "A Graeco-Parthian Portrait Head of Mithradates I," *AJA* 31 (1927), 338–44; the queen: F. Cumont, "Portrait d'une reine parthe trouvé a Suse," *CRAI* (1939), 330–41. But see, too, the *caveat* filed on excessive belief in Hellenizing Parthian art by M. I. Rostovtzeff, "Dura and the Problem of Parthian Art," *YClS* 5 (1935), 294–7.

Kuh-i Khvadjah: L. Vanden Berghe, *Archéologie de l'Iran ancien* (1959), 16–7; Fig. 5; Pl. 16.

[17] Architecture: L. Waterman, *Second Preliminary Report upon the Excavations at Tel Umar, Iraq* (1933), 1–31; N. C. Debevoise, "When Greek and Oriental Culture Met at Seleucia," *Asia* 38 (1938), 746–51; A. Godard, "L'Art de l'époque Séleucide et Parthe," *La Civilisation Iranienne* (1952), 111–5; M. I. Rostovtzeff, "Dura and the Problem of Parthian Art," *YClS* 5 (1935) stresses Orientalizing currents.

Apollo Komaios: Amm. Marc. xxiii. 6. 24. Greek: C. B. Welles and M. I. Rostovtzeff, *op. cit.*, 4; the parchment is Doura No. 10.

tinued to flourish in Parthian-controlled cities, both in Doura in northwestern Mesopotamia and at Avroman in Kurdistan. Greeks still held honored positions in Babylonia and western Iran, and Hellenized Iranians also, as late as the second century of the Christian era. At the same time, however, Pahlevi documents began to appear, showing not an Arsakid policy of cultural repression, but time and a preponderance of Oriental women slowly undermining the continuity of Hellenism.[18]

It was a necessity for the Parthians to treat their Greek subjects with consideration. From the very inception of the dynasty in the middle of the third century, the Arsakids were inevitably involved in international warfare, which had as its aim the aggrandizement of one ruling house or another. Especially after the Arsakids undertook an offensive towards the West in 160 B.C., they were fully and continuously involved in world power politics. Only recent converts from an unsophisticated steppe culture, they had to adopt Hellenic ways if they were successfully to compete, first with the Seleukids, later with the Romans.

Hence, one finds the philhellenic Parthians making use of Greeks in their government and of Greek organizational methods, all inherited from the Seleukids. The Parthian state was divided into Greek eparchies, and administered its cities with *epistatēs* and its provinces with *stratēgoi*. As late as A.D. 135 one Lousias, son of Lousianos, the son of Seleukos, was *epistatēs* at Doura. We know of Seleukid-type *arabarches,* who were employed to keep order along the important trade routes between cities. Surenas' army included two half-breed Greeks used as interpreters. The survival of Hellenistic states rested on their administrative and military efficiency and therefore the loyalty of their inhabitants. A trained personnel was a *sine qua non*. Only the Greeks had the training. As graphically shown by the coinage, there was a dichotomy in Parthia—an Iranian half, rural and traditional, and an Hellenic half, commercial and technically up-to-date. Both were distinct and had no more community of interest with one another than common loyalty to the ruling dynasty. The kings heeded the cities whence Greeks came, and had to treat them well.

This can be readily seen from what we know of the history of Seleukeia-on-Tigris. This city was captured by Mithradates I around 141 B.C. It was permitted to continue an autonomous coinage, which

[18] C. B. Welles, "The Population of Roman Dura," *Studies in Roman Economic and Social History* (1951), 233; M. I. Rostovtzeff in *C.A.H.* vii. 168; C. B. Welles and M. I. Rostovtzeff, *op. cit.,* 35; R. Ghirshman, *Iran* (1954), 230.

right was not revoked except for a two- or three-year period around 40 B.C., until A.D. 24, long after the Hellenistic period had ended. The city was also an important mint for the Arsakid kings. They did not have their own technical personnel to cut dies for the respectable international currency necessary for trade in the vital western regions of the empire. The Greeks could supply them. Similarly the artists, engineers, traders, craftsmen, and entertainers of Seleukeia were necessary for the maintenance of the social and economic life of the area. In 140 B.C., commerce was carried on by Greeks and Hellenized Babylonians. The Parthians did not wish to disrupt the prosperity and way of life of their own state. Seleukeia, an immense city, had great potentialities for armed revolt, and could not, therefore, be harshly dealt with. On the other hand, the Seleukeians had no desire to become involved in a war with the Parthians, for that would only inhibit commerce and disrupt their personal lives. Hence, the two sides adopted a policy of mutual cooperation to secure their own interests.[19]

Seleukeia-on-Eulaios, the ancient Susa of the Elamites, resembled her sister city in Babylonia. The numerous inscriptions recovered by excavation show Greek magistrates continuing to function in Seleukid-created offices. They administered city and countryside in an autonomous republic responsible to a Parthian *stratēgos*.[20] The lack of hostility between Greek townsmen and Parthian king shows that the latter did not adopt an anti-Hellenic attitude. The Seleukeians in both towns probably accepted the Arsakids from the beginning also out of despair of recent Seleukid history. The policy of Antiochos IV Epiphanes, intended to create a Greco-Oriental state and to expand it eastward, is usually thought of in terms of its effects on Judah or other Oriental regions, but seldom for what it meant for the Hellenes in it: competition with Orientals on a more nearly equal basis, a regime of higher taxation, and a time of more intensive military service. All this was toward an end which in 165 B.C. must have appeared unattainable to many responsible persons. For the Seleukid Empire was falter-

[19] Government: C. B. Welles and M. I. Rostovtzeff, *op. cit.*, 46–57 and n. 66b; 33–4 and n. 57; W. W. Tarn, *Seleucid-Parthian Studies* (1930), 24–6. Lousias: F. Cumont, *Fouilles de Doura-Europos* (1926), i. No. 134. Interpreters: Plut. *Cras.* xxxi. 1.

Seleukeia: G. H. Hill, *B.M.C. Arabia, Mesopotamia, and Persia* (1922) cxiv–cxv, 140–6; Pl. xxiii. 3–21; R. H. McDowell, *Coins from Seleucia on the Tigris* (1935), 94–5, 98–100, 158, 205, 220–1. See, too, the remarks of W. W. Tarn in *C.A.H.* ix. 591.

[20] *S.E.G.* vii. 1, 6, 12, 13; F. Cumont, "Nouvelles inscriptions grecques de Suse," *CRAI* (1930), 208–20; "Inscriptions grecques de Suse," *CRAI* (1931), 233–50; 278–92; "Une lettre du roi Artabanus III à la ville de Suse," *CRAI* (1932), 238–60.

ing, and against Rome in 192–89 it suffered a series of great disasters. Between 189 and 175 the northern and eastern provinces in Iran were lost a second time, lost when they had only just been recovered at great cost by Antiochos III. Now a Parthian state stronger than before was stirring, and there were profound rumblings of discontent from Persian and Jew, from Parthian and Mede. So the Greeks called Antiochos IV *Epimanes*—"madman." Events between 165 and 140 showed the growing weakness of the House of Seleukos and the growing power of the dynasty of Arsakes. Greek townsmen in Iran and western Mesopotamia could depend on the Parthians at least to keep order. There was always a threat of hillmen or nomads raiding a city, even perhaps destroying it as had happened in the third century to Herakleia and Alexandreia-in-Margiana.[21] The Parthian regime was certainly no more demanding than Antiochos', and probably less. Its yoke was easy and its burden light, for Greeks became important figures in the Hellenized Parthian state. Certain unnamed Greek historians of the first century even glorified the prowess of the Arsakids at the expense of Rome, a condition which certainly implies acceptance of Parthian government.[22]

The available evidence indicates that in the middle of the second century B.C. the Parthians began to build up a thorough organization of their state, and that by the time of Orodes II, around 40 B.C., Hellenic notions of centralized administration, rational expansion, and economic development were the order of the day. In this program the Parthians enjoyed a great measure of success. They had not suffered a loss of independence and empire as Persis had, but rather had been consistently victorious against Greek military forces. These successes kept the Parthians from feeling dominated by the Makedonians as the frantic Maccabees did. Thus the conquest of Mesopotamia coming when the Seleukid state was sliding into dissolution brought about the Hellenization of the Arsakid state and destroyed any basis for an anti-Hellenic religious movement. When a people involves itself deeply with hopes of messianic intervention, it is a sure sign that they are unable to cope with their problems in a normal human way.

The Parthian state never attained the homogeneity, the rigorous centralization that obtained in Ptolemaic Egypt. It was the true successor of that heterogeneous patchwork the Seleukid Empire. Individual communities had individual obligations to the king. Persis was a subordinate kingdom; Parthia-Hyrkania was the heartland, controlled

[21] Pliny, *N.H.* vi. 47–8.
[22] Livy ix. 18. 6.

by the king and his great landholding aristocrats. Mesopotamia was a collection of Greek cities, autonomous to greater or less degree. This patchwork quality, the subordination of divers small ethnic and cultural units was actually a source of weakness to Parthia. In the first century of the Christian era Pliny the Elder called the Parthian provinces *regna*, "kingdoms," thus showing the attitude of an outsider towards this complicated kingdom. To preserve loyalty among their subjects the Arsakids allowed considerable local autonomy, for there was always a threat of secession. In the second century A.D., this tendency resulted in the independence of Hatra, a district in eastern Mesopotamia.[23] In view of the foregoing, one may see why the Parthians were never intolerant of alien ideas and never supported one group to the exclusion of others.

There is no evidence that the Parthians were the conscious guardians of Iranism in Hellenistic times. Their real principle was to safeguard Arsakid interests. When Elam took the part of Demetrios II in his campaign against Mithradates I, the Arsakid paid back Elymaïs with violence, sacking the temples there exactly as the Seleukids had done before him, and relieving them of ten thousand talents. At the same time, Mithradates suppressed the short-lived independence of Media and Persis and added them to his empire.[24]

The position of the Parthian kings in respect to the religions of Iran is incompletely known. That they were neither Magians nor Zoroastrians is, however, plain enough, since they had themselves buried, practiced blood sacrifice, and supported the rise of Anahita to a more prominent place in the pantheon. The evidence of theophorous names is hard to interpret, but it is true that Mithra does not appear until around 160 B.C. as a part of a king's name. This appearance about a century after the Parthians came into Iran seems to show that the religion of the dynasty was only gradually oriented towards Iranian beliefs as a result of natural syncretism. This interpretation finds support from the Parthian bas-relief in the Bakhtyar Mountains of the first Christian century. Here Parthian figures take part in a sacrifice led by a *magos*. At the same time, however, one of the inscriptions from Susa shows Parthian belief in a *theos pankrator,* an epithet having nothing in common with Ahura Mazdāh's, but similar to those applied to Grecian Zeus or Hebrew Yahweh in the Septuagint translation of

---

[23] Pliny, *N.H.* vi. 112 and Amm. Marc. xxiii. 6. 14. Hatra: *s.v.* "Hatra" in *R.E.* vii. 2516–23.

[24] Elam: Strabo xvi. 1. 18 (744) ; Just. xxxvi. 1; xli. 6; A. Bouché-Leclerq, *Histoire des séleucides* (1913) , i. 364; R. Ghirshman, *Iran* (1954) , 246. Media and Persis: W. W. Tarn in *C.A.H.* ix. 579–80.

the Old Testament. Therefore, when A. V. W. Jackson says the Arsakids were Zoroastrians, using the evidence of names like Artabanos, Mithradates, and Orthagenes, the fact that a perpetual fire burned at Arsakeia, and the use of fire altars as a coin type, he is incorrect. This was simple Iranism. The very Zoroastrian Sassanids later glossed over the Parthian period as one in which the true and undefiled religion was eclipsed.[25] While we know they took part in a cult of fire, their coinage at the same time portrayed Greek gods. While we hear of a council which included *magoi*, the Parthians nonetheless profaned holy earth by their burials.[26] It seems that, as in other facets of their imperial life, the Arsakids were Arsakids: whatever they did was an accommodation of local traditions.

There was thus neither a need nor a basis for the Arsakids to develop religious activity against Hellenism from the time they came into Parthia-Hyrkania until the close of the Hellenistic period. The only case of anti-Greek action in northern Iran occurred in 210 B.C., when Arsakes III was defeated by Antiochos III. At that time, the Iranian population of Sirunka massacred the Greek population in the city while it was besieged by Antiochos. But this action is not necessarily Parthian; we know so little of the whole affair, the circumstances surrounding it, and the degree to which the story may be taken seriously that little significance can be attached to this isolated circumstance.[27]

2. THE BAKTRIANS

A peculiar set of circumstances influenced the relationship that existed between Baktrian and Makedonian. As with the Parthians, there is no evidence for an anti-Hellenic movement. Indeed, scholars have been in general agreement that of all the parts of Iran, Baktria was the most willing to cooperate with the Greco-Makedonian regime.

[25] Arsakids not Zoroastrians: H. S. Nyberg, *Die Religionen des alten Iran* (1938), 406; W. W. Tarn in *C.A.H.* ix. 575, 588; R. Ghirshman, *Iran* (1954), 268–70. The bas-relief: M. I. Rostovtzeff, "Dura and the Problem of Parthian Art," *YClS* 5 (1935), 171–2; *theos pankrator:* F. Cumont, "Inscriptions grecques de Suse," *CRAI* (1931), 244.
A. V. W. Jackson, *Zoroastrian Studies* (1928), 170–1. Sassanid attitude: *Shah nameh* xxi. 2; F. J. Foakes-Jackson, "The Influence of Iran upon Early Judaism and Christianity," *Oriental Studies in Honour of Cursetji Erachji Pavry* (1933), 174.
[26] Strabo xi. 9. 3 (515) ; W. W. Tarn in *C.A.H.* ix. 588, 593–4; M. N. Dhalla, *History of Zoroastrianism* (1938), 294; R. Ghirshman, *Iran* (1954), 264.
[27] M. Holleaux in *C.A.H.* vii. 140–1.

Hostility was wanting for several reasons. In the first place, the Baktrians did not have, as the Persians did, or even the Medes, a tradition of independent rule. Baktria had been a usually docile province of the Achaemenid Empire, only occasionally even meditated revolt, and seldom actually drew the sword against the Great King. It had remained loyal to the central government during the widespread disorders attendant upon Dareios' seizure of the kingship in 522 B.C., and as a loyal province was thereafter assessed the relatively low tribute of 360 talents. Under Xerxes, however, there seems to have been considerable unrest. At the beginning of his reign, his own brother Ariamenes raised a Baktrian force to contest the succession, but his expedition never fought the royal forces since Xerxes won him over with presents. But Xerxes recalled in an inscription that Baktria was a restless land. Herodotos says that another revolt was planned by Masistes, satrap of Baktria, Xerxes' brother, as revenge for the mutilation of his wife by the queen. Masistes was killed, however, before the revolt broke out. Rebellion did actually begin in 465 when Xerxes was assassinated, but it was quickly suppressed.[28]

Very much later, after more than a century of tranquility, the Baktrian satrap Bessos, supported by the Baktrian cavalry in the army of the Great King, arrested and slew Dareios III during the last months of the Empire's existence and made himself Artaxerxes IV.[29] The history of the province shows, then, that Baktria ignored the Achaemenid theology of kingship when expedient, although it never was dangerously disloyal.

The occupation of Baktria-Sogdiana by the Greeks, while it represented a victory of non-Iranian forces, was more a change of masters than an eclipse of empire. Alexander not only married Baktrian Roxane, he also destroyed a settlement of Persians at Kyra, established by Kyros as a garrison to consolidate his conquest. Diodoros says plainly that the Makedonian regime of satrap Stasanor was popular locally because of his consideration for local interests.[30] Hellenic penetration of Baktria, furthermore, was very slight. I mean that settlement of Europeans in northeastern Iran was on a very small scale, and the cities that Alexander founded were heavily populated with

[28] Under Dareios: *DB* xxxviii. 3. 9—xxxix. 3. 21 in R. G. Kent, *Old Persian* (2nd ed., 1953), 125–7; Herod. iii. 92. Xerxes-Ariamenes: Plut. *Sayings of Kings:* Xerxes 1 (173 B); *On Brotherly Love* 18 (488 D); *Them.* xiv. 3; *XPh* iv. 28–35 in R. G. Kent, *op. cit.,* 151. Xerxes-Masistes: Herod. ix. 112–3. Revolt in 465: Ktes. *Persika,* Epit. 31.

[29] Arr. *Anab.* iii. 21. 1, 4–5; 25. 3; Curt. iv. 6. 2–3; v. 9. 2, 10, 16.

[30] Kyra: Strabo xi. 11. 4 (500), Diod. xix. 48. 1.

Baktrians. Thus there was no threat of economic, social, or cultural upheaval, such as occurred in Hellenistic Palestine.

When Baktria broke away from Seleukid control, a gradual withdrawal finally consolidated by the Greek Euthydemos, the new royal dynasty hastened to ally itself with the baronial, landholding military class, in order to resist the attempts of the Seleukids to recapture the lost province. Euthydemos employed ten thousand Baktrian cavalry in his forces. These horsemen were drawn from the same Iranian warrior aristocracy as the Baktrian cavalry that fought in the army of the Great King.[31] Therefore, the notables felt no loss of economic position or social prestige as did some of the gentry of Persis, and thus had one less reason to hope for revenge on the Greeks.

The dynasty of the Euthydemids consciously abandoned a pure form of Hellenism for Baktria in favor of cultural and religious eclecticism. The coinage of these kings acknowledged the cult of numerous deities, including Greek Zeus, Herakles, Apollo, Athena, and the Dioskouroi. Artemis was portrayed on a coin of Euthydemos radiate in the fashion of the Anahita of Baktra.[32] Other local gods and goddesses, some of them dressed up and posturing like Hellenic deities, were also honored. Many of them are difficult to identify, but among them appear Mithra and the Indo-Skyth deity Azilises, the latter masquerading as Zeus. Even Indian influence turns up as Buddhist symbols on the currency of Agathokles. Art as a whole in Baktria was Grecized-Iranian in style.[33] It must be emphasized that the pictures of Baktrian deities on the coinage of this remarkable, sprawling kingdom in northeastern Iran, so far from the city-states of distant Hellas, was visible evidence for him who would look that the Euthydemids were protectors of native religion and of native culture.

This close alliance was a necessity for the Baktrians as well as for the Euthydemids, for Baktria was subject to raids by the nomads coming from the northern Eurasian steppe. This was a true frontier of civilization itself, for Greek and Baktrian alike. The Apollo of the dynasty was suitably warlike for this rough region: he stood bravely erect on

[31] Apollodoros, *Parthia* = Strabo xv. 1. 3 (686); Diod. xix. 48. 1; Strabo xi. 9. 2 (515); 11. 1–8 (516–9). A. Bouché-Leclerq, *Histoire des séleucides* (1913), i. 85; M. I. Rostovtzeff, *S.E.H.H.W.* i. 547, 549; W. W. Tarn, *The Greeks in Bactria and India* (2nd ed., 1951), 72–4, 124 and n. 1.

[32] Hellenic deities: M. T. Allouche-Le Page, *L'art monétaire des royaumes bactriens* (1956), 91–119. Artemis: *loc. cit.*, 112–3; W. W. Tarn, *The Greeks in Bactria and India* (2nd ed., 1951), 270–6.

[33] Baktrianizing gods: Allouche-Le Page, *op. cit.*, 119–21; 141–4. Buddhist influence: Allouche-Le Page, 112–5. In general: W. W. Tarn, "Notes on Hellenism in Bactria and India," *JHS* 22 (1902), 270–86.

the coinage armed with bow and arrow. The Seleukid Apollo of contemporary, civilized Antioch was seated on the reverses of the coins, relaxing on a stone bound with a fillet of wool as though presiding over the deliberations of the Amphiktyonic Council at Delphi.[34] The ancients were conscious of the differences of dynastic problems. When Antiochos III drove Euthydemos to the wall in his eastern wars, Euthydemos was able to persuade Antiochos to ease his pressure against Baktria on the grounds that a horde of approaching barbarians was threatening civilized life; the destruction of the Greco-Baktrian state would mean the end of sophisticated culture in Iran. What one race would lose, the other would also lose. The Baktrian had to defend his home. Therefore, the native Baktrians, living in the walled villages or cities that Greek skill and organization had helped to create, cooperated to resist the ravages of barbarism. W. W. Tarn's researches have shown that the only known satrap of this regime was a native Baktrian, and that a Baktrian sat on the council of King Menander's government. In the middle of the second century Eukratides I took the title *Basileus Eukratides Megas,* "Great King Eukratides," a form which was traditional Iranian usage. Aside from these political considerations, there were also biological facts working for likemindedness. We know nothing of Greek or Makedonian women in the cities of Baktria.[35] Hence, we must presume that to the bonds of mutual self-help were added the ties of conjugal affection.

Baktria, therefore, was a region in which Hellenism, in diluted form, and Iranism made common cause and found a common unity. The unity survived until it was submerged by the invasion of Sakan nomads around 128 B.C., which brought to an end the Greco-Baktrian state.[36]

3. THE MEDES

Media reacted uniquely against the Greeks. She was both hostile and docile. Part of the country surrendered to Hellenism; the other eventually rebelled and established its independence.

As in the case of the other non-Persian districts of Iran, Media in 334 B.C. was a province of Dareios III. Media, however, had once held

[34] M. T. Allouche-Le Page, *op. cit.,* 100–1.

[35] Antiochos III: Polyb. xi. 39. 1–6; Strabo xi. 8. 2–4 (511) . The cities: Polyb. x. 49. 1, 15; W. W. Tarn, *The Greeks in Bactria and India* (2nd ed., 1951) , 121–4. Baktrian government and women: W. W. Tarn, *op. cit.,* 125, 422; "Notes on Hellenism in Bactria and India," *JHS* 22 (1902) , 269. The title: M. T. Allouche-Le Page, *L'art monétaire des royaumes bactriens* (1956) , 69.

[36] Common unity: W. W. Tarn, *The Greeks in Bactria and India* (2nd ed., 1951) , 172; R. Ghirshman, *Iran* (1954) , 221–3. Sakan invasion: Strabo xi. 8. 2 (515) ; W. W. Tarn, *Seleucid-Parthian Studies* (1930) , 4; in *C.A.H.* ix. 582–3.

the hegemony of the East. Her imperial dynasty had been ousted by Kyros the Great and Media made into a province in his empire. Twice the Medes staged obstinate revolts against the Achaemenids. In 522 B.C. they revolted under Gaumata's leadership. As soon as this *magos* had been killed and Dareios I had set off to quell Babylon, Media rebelled again, her forces being commanded by Phraortes. After Dareios' suppression of that movement, Media, hitherto a tax-free partner in Persis' Empire of the East, was assessed an annual tribute of 450 talents. Yet for all that, there was a good deal of collaboration between Persians and Medes; even during the rebellions, Median forces had supported Dareios against their own countrymen. During the next century, Medes held high posts in the government, like Datis' command in the Marathon campaign. But, in 409 B.C., late in the reign of Dareios II, Media began a second series of revolts to regain her independence. This uprising was speedily put down, as was another in 404 B.C.[37]

The attitudes of different members of the Median gentry towards the Empire were thus divided: some were imperial and some were patriotic. This dichotomy continued under Alexander. He appointed Atropates satrap of Media. This man arrested Baryaxes, a Mede, who put a crown on his head and gave out that he was the new king of the Medes and Persians; the would-be king and his associates were executed. About the same time Phradates, satrap of Hyrkania, was suspected of aiming at the kingship; he was executed and replaced.[38] Many Medes served in the armies of the Successors. In 317 B.C. Antigonos' forces included the large contingent of 2,000 Median lancers, and some mounted archers in addition, and it is most likely that satrap Nikanor also had Median troops under command. About this time the Mede Orontobates was satrap of Media.[39]

Seleukos Nikator founded a number of Hellenic *poleis* in Media, superimposing a veneer of Greek institutions and language on old places like Rhagai, which he renamed Europos. The Parthians later called it Arsakeia. The old capital Ekbatana became a Seleukid mint, and about 310 B.C. was issuing staters showing Athena wearing a helmet decorated with the Persian lion-gryphon. During the next

---

[37] Dareios I: *DB* xi. 1. 35—xiv. 1. 71; xxiv. 2. 13–7 in R. G. Kent, *Old Persian* (2nd ed., 1953), 117–23; *DNa* iii. 15–30 in R. G. Kent, *op. cit.*, 138. Herod. i. 130; iii. 97. Dareios II: Xen. *Hell.* i. 2. 19; *Anab.* i. 1. 2.

[38] Atropates—Baryaxes: Arr. *Anab.* vi. 29. 2–3; Phradates—Phrataphernes: Curt. viii. 3. 17; x. 1. 39.

[39] Antigonos: Diod. xix. 29. 2; 39. 2; Nikanor: *ibid.*, xix. 92. 3–4; Orontobates: *ibid.*, xix. 46. 5; in general: *ibid.*, xix. 47. 1–4.

century many of the issues depicted a feeding horse, commemorating the stud farms of Media, now supplying Nisean remounts for the Seleukid cavalry. After Nikator's victory at Ipsos in 301, there was a series of silver staters and gold double darics, a seated Hellenized Ba'al on obverse, an Oriental lion and Seleukid anchor on reverse. This money circulated among the population of these towns, where there were few Greeks and many Medes on military service. The Makedonian kings used these cities as military and cultural bastions. The Hellenized Median warriors at Kangavar built a Temple of Anahita along Doric-Corinthian-Ionic lines. At Avroman they sometimes employed Greek in their legal dealings with one another. At the beginning of the Hellenistic period there was a marked tendency for Medes to Grecize.[40]

Yet there was not complete fascination with Greeks and things Greek. Antigonos had to fight his way through the territory of the Kossaians on the fringes of Media on his way to dispose of Eumenes.[41] The hill people retained their stubborn independence which they had similarly exercised in Old Persian days. Civilized governments thought it unprofitable to break them. At the same time, the nobleman Atropates, Alexander's satrap of Media, was making northwestern Media independent of Makedonian control. He succeeded in establishing an Iranian dynasty which maintained its continuity more or less free from even the suzerainty of the Seleukids throughout the Hellenistic period. In periods of Seleukid strength the Atropatids were forced to recognize Seleukid overlords, but when the Makedonians were heavily engaged in other quarters, Atropatene was able to pursue its own course.[42] The history of Media in the Makedonian period therefore resembled the history of Media in the Achaemenid period in that the loyalty of the country towards the central government was divided.

During the greater part of the third century Greater Media seems to have been quiet. But in the reign of Seleukos II a Parthian advance

---

[40] City foundations: Strabo xi. 13. 6 (524–5) ; W. W. Tarn, *The Greeks in Bactria and India* (2nd ed., 1951) , 19, 231; *H.C.* (3rd ed., 1952) , 152, 159 and literature there cited. Ekbatana: E. T. Newell, *The Coinage of the Eastern Seleucid Mints* (1938) : Athena: No. 428, p. 163; Pl. xxxiii. 1; horses: pp. 163–7 and Polyb. x. 27. 1–13; v. 44. 1; staters and darics: Nos. 460–2; pp. 171–5; Pl. xxxv. 6–9. Temples: E. E. Herzfeld, *Archeological History of Iran* (1935) , 50–1, 75; R. Ghirshman, *Iran* (1954) , 231–5; L. Vanden Berghe, *Archéologie de l'Iran ancien* (1959) , 108 and Pl. 134b; 125 and Pl. 160c.

Median military settlers and Avroman: M. I. Rostovtzeff in *C.A.H.* vii. 168, 187.

[41] Diod. xix. 19. 2–8.

[42] Arr. *Anab.* iii. 8. 4; iv. 18. 3; vii. 13. 2, 6; Strabo xi. 13. 1 (523–4) .

into Hyrkania threatened to end his control of the province, especially
after his severe defeat around 230. Seleukos regrouped, doubtless
drawing heavily on Media to re-equip his cavalry and other forces,
and drove the Parthians back temporarily.[43] The enforced necessity
of supplying the Seleukid forces seems to have been a cause of unrest
and unhappiness with the central government, and when Seleukos
died and was succeeded by short-lived Seleukos III and then by
Antiochos III, the Makedonian Molon, satrap of Media, rebelled. The
revolt was the work of Hellenes, at least in large part. Molon's coinage
was a continuation of Seleukid issues, portraying Apollo Kitharoidos
with flowing locks. By 222 the rebel reached Babylonia and claimed
the royal title. His movement, therefore, seems to have aimed at
winning control of Media for the Greeks there. Perhaps he and his
supporters felt they could better deal with the Parthian problem than
could the government at Antioch, which had numerous problems in
Syria and Asia Minor to solve. At any rate, there is not a hint of
Orientalizing in Molon's coinage.[44] Yet there must have been a Median element involved, since there were such people as Median military settlers, and Molon did base himself on Media. Furthermore,
when Antiochos III advanced against him, most of Molon's troops,
who were Greek, deserted him. Molon was caught and crucified, and
his body was publicly displayed in Media as a warning.[45] Since it is
unlikely that Antiochos executed him Persian-style to impress the
troops who had come over voluntarily, he must have done it to impress
the countryside, and this points towards a native Median movement
of however small proportions.

In the reign of Antiochos III Seleukid policy towards the temples
of the East changed. During military operations in Media in 209 B.C.
Antiochos reached Ekbatana. The Temple of Anahita there boasted
gilded columns and silver-plated bricks and had a full treasury. Antiochos stripped the building and coined four thousand talents from
the bullion to finance his grand campaigns in the east.[46] Previously,
the Seleukids had pursued a policy of moderation towards the treas-

[43] E. T. Newell, *The Coinage of the Eastern Seleucid Mints* (1938), 120–2; E. K.
Bickerman, "Notes on Seleucid and Parthian Chronology," *Berytus* 8, fasc. 2 (1944),
73–83.

[44] Coins: R. H. McDowell, *The Coins of Seleucia on the Tigris* (1935), 35; E. T.
Newell, *op. cit.*, Nos. 225–8, pp. 85–6; Nos. 574–87, pp. 205–7; Pl. xlii. 1–4. Molon's
career: Polyb. v. 41. 1; v. 54. 8–10; App. *Syr.* xi. 1. 1.

[45] Polyb. v. 54. 6–7.

[46] The stripping: Polyb. x. 27. 1–13; A. Bouché-Leclerq, *Histoire des séleucides*
(1913), i. 160; M. Holleaux in *C.A.H.* vii. 140, n. 3. The coinage in E. T. Newell,
The Coinage of the Eastern Seleucid Mints (1938), Nos. 604–9, pp. 211–2; 217–8.

uries of eastern deities. Henceforth, through the reign of Antiochos IV, however, there was occasional pillaging and use of armed violence. The motives behind this shift in practice are hard to explain. M. I. Rostovtzeff thought that it was an attempt to insist upon the sovereign rights of the Seleukid kings.[47] Very well, but it would seem this statement does not go far enough. Looting would have been an extraordinary way of securing simple legal rights, and, at all events, would have been unnecessary unless the temples had in some way challenged Makedonian ownership. Undoubtedly, one motive of Antiochos was to acquire precious metals to support his extensive military operations. But still, violence would have been used only to counter violence. It is impossible to prove unequivocally that the Seleukid operated against the temple because the temple was generating resistance to the regime. We have no direct evidence. All that can be said is this: Media was restless under Antiochos III; by his reign the Persian *magoi* had produced and disseminated their anti-Hellenic propaganda; Media was their traditional home; and there were *magoi* at Ekbatana—and the Makedonians attack. Unfortunately, we have no literature from Median sources that might throw light on this problem. */ o / 6 5 9*

Antiochos' campaigns succeeded in pacifying Greater Media and in reducing Atropatene to his authority. But after the Battle of Magnesia in 189 B.C., Media Atropatene became independent again. R. Ghrishman says that Shiz in Atropatene was a great religious center, where the cult of Anahita had great importance, and where *magoi* were particularly concentrated.[48] But again, it must be admitted that we have no certain evidence of the participation of religiously inspired groups in these independence movements.

Antiochos IV was able to re-establish Seleukid authority throughout Media, but with the growing internal problems of the state, which were intensified by his death in 164 B.C., once more Atropatene became independent. In Media proper, the Seleukid satrap Timarchos of Miletos declared himself sovereign in 162/1 B.C. But Timarchos, having cut himself off from Seleukid support, was immediately defeated by Arsakid Mithradates I, and most of Media was promptly annexed to the Parthian state.[49] The Medes, however, reacted sharply to Parthian rule, much as the Persians did, so that when Demetrios II

---

[47] *C.A.H.* vii. 163.
[48] Independence: E. R. Bevan, *The House of Seleucus* (1902), ii. 158–9; R. Ghirshman, *Iran* (1954), 246; Shiz: *ibid.*, 270.
[49] Diod. xxxi. 27a. 1; Just. xli. 6; W. W. Tarn in *C.A.H.* ix. 578–80.

made an offensive into Media against the Arsakids in 140, Medes cooperated with Makedonians. Demetrios was, however, ultimately defeated, and Bakasis became Parthian satrap of Greater Media. Ten years later, the Seleukids tried again; Antiochos VII Sidetes attacked the Parthians and occupied Ekbatana; but on this occasion, the Parthians fomented an irresistible revolt in the Median cities.[50] The Seleukids were driven out for the last time; apparently the Medes had come to prefer the Arsakids.

Perhaps in response to the challenge of this sensitive frontier, the facts of Median collaboration, and a desire to ape the Achaemenids, the Parthians made Ekbatana a summer capital. It now became one of their mints, striking issues intended for Iranian circulation. In Media Atropatene, a vestige of independence of Parthia was maintained. The capital Phraaspa controlled an army which, according to Apollonides, amounted to ten thousand horse and forty thousand foot. We hear of wars between this Media and Armenia and Parthia.[51]

There is certainly little or no evidence that Media resisted Hellenic occupation on religious grounds or through the medium of religion. While there was undoubtedly a beginning of resistance towards the end of the third century, this was quashed by Antiochos III, and thenceforth the growing power of the Parthians made Media an unfortunate region desired by two greater powers. In these circumstances, there could be little justification for offending one or the other of them, and our lack of evidence of anti-Hellenism would seem to confirm the existence of this sensible policy.

All in all, our survey of the non-Persian parts of Iran shows that in these areas, the lack of a tradition of world rule, the lack of cultural uniformity in some parts, and a dependence on the Greeks in one way or another, either as military allies against some kind of alien domination or as technical experts, made opposition to Hellenism unnecessary or undesirable.

[50] Diod. xxxiv. 16–7; Just. xxxviii. 10; xli. 6; W. W. Tarn in *C.A.H.* ix. 579–80; N. C. Debevoise, *A Political History of Parthia* (1938), 33–4; R. Ghirshman, *Iran* (1954), 248.

[51] Ekbatana: Strabo xi. 13. 1 (522); R. H. McDowell, *Coins of Seleucia on the Tigris* (1935), 47. Phraaspa: Apollonides = Strabo xi. 13. 2; Plut. *Luc.* xxvi. 4; *Pom.* xxxvi. 2; *Ant.* xxxviii. 1–2.

Chapter V

The Western Asians to 189 B.C.

The Western Asians lived in the region where Mesopotamian culture or a form of it predominated. This area included Babylonia proper, as well as Elam to the east, Syria to the west, and Kilikia to the northwest. When Alexander overran it, religious resistance to foreign occupation was a weapon already familiar to the Babylonians, as a result of their having been earlier conquered by the Persians. The victory of Kyros the Great in 538 B.C. had finished Babylonia as a world power. She had henceforth only a memory of the ancient glory the gods had given her and was to suffer the misfortune of two centuries of ruinous Persian occupation. Both the Babylonians and the Elamites at first sought to overthrow it. In 522 B.C. the Babylonians revolted, hoping to recover the independence and power they had known under Nebuchadnezzar. According to Herodotos, they fought with great vigor, and when Dareios besieged Babylon, strangled all the superfluous women in the city to keep them from consuming the scant supply of food. But in spite of this legendary ferocity Babylon was retaken by Dareios. Shortly after the Great King left for other disaffected areas, another rebellion broke out, but it was no more successful than the first, and Persian domination of Babylonia began again.[1]

Elam went through a similar anti-Persian reaction with the same lack of success. Pretenders to the old Elamite dynasty arose and attempted to expel the Persian satraps. Unfortunately for the Elamite rebels, their military resistance collapsed owing to their very small numbers, and the revolt was speedily suppressed by pro-Persian elements in Elam.[2] Syria and Kilikia remained quiet.

Dareios' rapid successes in all these areas were probably a cause of

---

[1] *DB* xvi. 1. 74—xx. 2. 5 in R. G. Kent, *Old Persian* (2nd ed., 1953), 118–23; xlix. 3. 76—1. 3. 92, *ibid.*, 126–8; Herod. iii. 150–60.

[2] *DB* xvi. 1. 72–4; xvii. 1. 81–3; xxii. 2. 8—xxiii. 2. 13; lxxi. 5. 1–14 in R. G. Kent, *op. cit.*, 118–34.

their remaining loyal during the remainder of the Persian period. Only Babylon made one further attempt to free itself. Under the Persians economic conditions in Mesopotamia deteriorated as a result of the fiscal policies of the Great Kings. During the fifth century there was a continuing upward trend in prices and a more or less constant level of wages.[3] This probably contributed to the Babylonians' discontent. Soon after the accession of Xerxes in 486 B.C. there was another insurrection, Babylon's last energetic attempt to control its own affairs and to reinstate Marduk as high god of the four world quarters. The Babylonians justified their uprising with the claim that the Persians had sought to remove Marduk from Mesopotamia. They wished, that is, to carry off his statue from the great temple E-sagila, but had not dared to do so until Xerxes plucked up courage. According to Herodotos' version of the Babylonian story, when Xerxes attempted to remove the image, one of the priests forbade him to do so, so Xerxes killed him. The revolt began over this outrage. The Persian satrap was killed, and a man named Belshimanni was recognized as Marduk's true King of the Lands in 482 B.C. The third attempt to throw off Persian control, however, was a greater failure than the first or second, since the Persians recaptured the city and took punitive measures to prevent a recurrence. The walls of Babylon were partially thrown down, its temples either destroyed or damaged, and Marduk was taken away a prisoner to Persia.[4]

Now the Babylonians interpreted such wars between peoples as reflecting on earth a struggle between gods in the sky for rule of the cosmos. This was a part of their highly elaborate doctrine of kingship, which had been the model for Persian ideas concerning the theology of world rule. In brief, the Babylonians believed that all the affairs of men and states were determined by the gods sitting in council, and that one of the gods acting in behalf of the council enforced the decrees of heaven. This god was given effective rule of the world, and the existence of a human empire reflected the primacy of one or the other national gods. The predominant god nominated and supported some human being to be his king, his executor among men. This man remained king as long as he fulfilled the prerequisites of kingship, defending the state from enemies without and maintaining law, order, and a measure of social justice within. He was also expected to perform the functions of high priest of the national god and to protect

[3] A. T. Olmstead, *H.P.E.* (1948), 77–80.
[4] Herod. i. 183; Ktes. *Persika,* Epit. 52–3; Strabo xvi. 1. 5 (738); Arr. *Anab.* vii. 17. 1; R. Ghirshman, *Iran* (1954), 190–1.

and build up his cult. Failure to follow these rules resulted in the deposition of the man, for the gods were thought to sustain the good and punish the evil. It had come to be recognized, however, that the downfall of a man or even of a state was not always due to his own shortcomings, but rather to the arbitrary, even unjust, action of the gods in council. This great realization sometimes led to acts of profound desperation, sometimes to a feeling of even profounder despair. To the Babylonians of the period, then, the victory of the Persians under Kyros was in theory the victory of Ahura Mazdāh over Marduk, a victory made almost total by Xerxes' deportation of the rebellious god of Babylon.[5]

Henceforth, Babylon and the whole area to which its culture had spread remained passive and quiescent under Persian rule. Apparently the failure of three successive revolts by the great, fortified city of Babylon within one generation, and the horrors of Xerxes' treatment of the city, taught the Mesopotamians the futility of continued rebellion in practice against the power of Ahura Mazdāh, his Great King, and the imperial armies. It is likely that the Persians sensed this too, for around 462 B.C. Artaxerxes I partially restored Babylon. He honored the goddess Ishtar with a stele, reinstated the deposed priests of Marduk, and restored their confiscated lands. Yet the Persians took measures to prevent Babylon from becoming a great power again. The Tigris and Euphrates, the main arteries of Mesopotamia, were blocked to long-distance navigation, and they remained blocked until the Makedonians reopened them. From the middle of the fifth century many Persians settled in Babylon, held extensive tracts of land, and occupied numerous positions in local government.[6] This large and influential colony must have had a good deal to do with the continuing tranquility of the province. The Persians did not attempt a complete restoration of the city or of damaged E-sagila, so that when the Makedonians entered Babylon the ruins that Xerxes had made could still be seen.[7] Doubtless the ruins served not only as a reminder of the strength of Persis, but also as a continuing source of anti-Persian feelings.

From the period of Xerxes' action, religious resistance in Babylon

[5] For Babylonian kingship see: I. Engnell, *Studies in Divine Kingship in the Ancient Near East* (1943); C. J. Gadd, *Ideas of Divine Rule in the Ancient East* (1948); H. I. Frankfort, *Kingship and the Gods* (1948); T. Jacobsen in *The Intellectual Adventure of Ancient Man* (ed. H. I. Frankfort, 1946), 125–201.

[6] Strabo xvi. 1. 9, 11 (740–1); A. T. Olmstead, *H.P.E.* (1948), 291, 298; E. F. Schmidt, *Persepolis* (1953), i. 29.

[7] Strabo xvi. 1. 5 (738); E. F. Schmidt, *Persepolis* (1953), i. 29.

commenced. It was not a movement that came from all the people in Mesopotamia alike, however, but was probably confined to a national party grouped around the Marduk clergy. After all, members of the Babylonian commercial oligarchy continued to flourish under the Persians. One wealthy family of Uruk was able to maintain its high position from late Assyrian through the Chaldean and Achaemenid periods.[8] It was possible, then, for persons in the old ruling circles of Babylonia to maintain their status if they cooperated with the Great King, and, judging by the lack of revolt in Babylonia after 482 and the number of Babylonians in high places, there was much cooperation. Not total collaboration, however, for there are traces in Greek literature of Babylonian religious resistance to Persian rule.

This opposition consisted of the circulation of legends venerating old legitimate rulers, rulers after the heart of lord Marduk. Nitokris and Semiramis, the first an entirely imaginary, the second a real though much magnified, queen, were made national heroines. They supposedly had undertaken great works of magnificent construction for the benefit of their people. This was in direct contrast to the destruction of Xerxes. According to another story, Nitokris outwitted Dareios the conqueror even after her death, as he rifled her tomb for its treasures: on opening it he found only an inscription accusing him of greed. Another tradition said that Dareios forced the women of Babylon to become public prostitutes.[9] It is likely that the basis of our Old Testament book of Esther is a Babylonian legend of the fifth century, describing the conflict and vindication of Marduk (Mordecai) and Ishtar (Esther) with Xerxes (King Ahasoueros). The argument supporting the identification of Esther with a lost Babylonian text is given below.

This ineffectual response of the Babylonians to foreign occupation continued into the Makedonian period. The Babylonians remained generally passive under the Hellenic regime, although they did continue to tell stories about an heroic age, and protested feebly against what they considered wrong. Many had become acquiescent toward whatever destiny befell them, although the Makedonian and Greek attitude ranged from condescension towards the aged to outright contempt for womanly cowards.

A certain amount of knowledge of Mesopotamian life and customs

---

[8] A. T. Olmstead, *H.P.E.* (1948), 74.

[9] Nitokris and Semiramis in Herod. i. 184–7; the tale of the prostitution in Plut. *Sayings of Kings*, Xerxes, 2 (173 C). He also, under "Semiramis," credits this queen with fooling Dareios.

was, of course, current among the Greeks of Alexander's generation. Demokritos had written a book *On the Sacred Writings of the Priests of Babylon,* and this mystic or occult information must have appealed to some Hellenes, as things ancient always did. And, too, Babylonian astronomy was a corpus of data the Greeks frankly respected.[10] But the feelings of Herodotos were quite mixed. He noted the extraordinary number of cities in Mesopotamia and thought Babylon the most magnificent of the whole world. He marvelled at the remains of the massive walls and fortifications erected by Nebuchadnezzar and admired the broad streets laid out at right angles, conveniences which no Greek city of his day had. He was impressed by the extreme wealth of Babylonia—said to have been sufficient alone to feed Persia for four months of the year, whereas the remainder of the empire fed her for the other eight. Herodotos duly reported the yield of grain here as two hundredfold. And yet, in spite of all this, his respect for the Babylonians themselves was small. His admiration was for the natural wealth of the region and the monuments of a vanished age; he knew that Greeks without the wealth of the East had been able to stand against the Persian in open combat and defeat him. At Marathon, Salamis, and Plataia, Greek manhood won at odds over the forces of the Great King in the field. The Babylonians suffered three defeats from the same forces, and suffered them while they stood siege within their all-protecting walls. Babylonian soldiers were almost old-womanish. Herodotos thought the widespread institution of temple prostitution shameful evidence that the Babylonians were essentially base and cowardly.[11]

Aristophanes regarded the Mesopotamians as rather second-class people born to serve others; in *The Babylonians* he exhibited them as slaves driving a treadmill under the lash of their master, the Great King. There was also a contemptuous story about the Assyrian king Ninos. He was said to have spent his entire reign indoors, lolling about in self-indulgence, living with his wives and eunuchs. A popular tale insulted the memory of King Sardanapalos. He was supposed to have lived like a woman, his beard shaved close and his face painted with rouge and other cosmetics so that he would not appear to be a man. His arms were bejeweled, he wore a dress, and he combed wool with his mistresses. These two stories were often repeated in the following years; Aristotle used them as stock illustrations of the worst

[10] Demokritos in Clem. Alex. *Strom.* i. 69; ii. 130. For astronomy and science see A. T. Olmstead, *H.P.E.* (1948), 328–42; 480–5.

[11] Herod. i. 178–99; ix. 122.

sort of unmanly living. Much later than the fourth century, Arrian, reflecting on Alexander's conquests in Asia Minor and Mesopotamia, pronounced the judgment that from Semiramis on, woman's rule in Asia was customary.[12]

Hence, the Greco-Makedonians looked forward to an easy conquest of Mesopotamia in their campaign against Persia, and in this expectation they were not disappointed. Alexander entered Babylon without encountering resistance of any kind. The magnates of the city met him before the walls, and eagerly the population hailed their new lord and master. A procession of subjects led him on to the sounds of festal music—first the *magoi* and behind them the *chaldaioi,* as the Greeks called the priests of Marduk.[13] While it is true that the Babylonians had reason to rejoice over the end of Persian rule, still, more than any other of the great peoples of the ancient Near East, they regarded Alexander's coming as a good in itself, and gave the least trouble to the conquerors.

If the Babylonians hastened to flatter Alexander, their new king correspondingly rewarded the metropolis of the East. He gave orders that the Temple of Marduk should at last be restored, and directed that a number of Babylonian priests should follow in his train. A few years later when crossing the Indus, Alexander had himself purified by them after an untoward portent.[14]

In the years between Alexander's triumphal entry into Babylon and his not-so-victorious return from India, resistance by the native clergy seems to have begun. When he was within a few miles of the city, Chaldeans met him and prophesied that if he re-entered the city from the east, he would surely meet with death. Alexander doubted that it was a genuine prophecy, feeling that they spoke for their own advantage and not for the gods, and he rejected their oracle in the words of Euripides, "Prophets who prophesy the best are best." While Alexander did ignore them on the grounds that the road system did not permit him to redeploy his army, there is a widely quoted variant that

[12] Aristoph. *Babylonians* in T. Kock, *Comicorum Atticorum Fragmenta* i. 407–8. Ninos in Ktes. *Persika* iii = Athen. xii. 528 EF; Sardanapalos in Ktes. *loc. cit.;* Aristot. *Nic. Eth.* i. 5. 3 (1095 B, 19–22) ; *Pol.* ii. 6 (1265 A) ; v. 10 (1312 A) ; Douris of Samos [*Histories*] = Athen. xii. 529 A.

The Ninos story was also retailed by Phoinix of Kolophon = Athen. x. 421 D; xii. 530 E—531 A and Aristoboulos *ibid.,* xii. 530 ABC. Arrian's remark in *Anab.* i. 23. 7.

[13] Arr. *Anab.* iii. 16. 4; Curt. v. 1. 19, 22; Diod. xvii. 64. 4.

[14] Restoration: Arr. *Anab.* vii. 17. 1; Strabo xvi. 1. 5 (738) ; priests: Plut. *Alex.* lvii. 3.

he obeyed the Chaldeans and entered Babylon from the direction of Borsippa.[15]

This variant could hardly be a Mesopotamian re-editing of a Greek history; it is far more likely that it is a piece of Makedonian propaganda intended to make Alexander appear to be a friend of the Chaldeans. As I am about to show, there was Chaldean hostility to Alexander, and their cooperation with the regime was naturally desirable. What was at stake for the Chaldeans was the maintenance of their authority as custodians of the cult and doctrines of Marduk, and they were anxious to see whether the Makedonians' regime might be influenced by them or whether it was to be a repetition of the Persians'. The clergy of Babylon still held the beliefs developed in ancient times by the people of Sumer and Akkad, and they still thought in these terms at least until the second century B.C. Diodoros says that Belephantes, chief of the *chaldaioi* at Babylon, tried to protect Alexander by indicating that reconstruction of the tomb of Marduk would avert his predicted death. This sort of work was a traditional function of kingship. There was still life in the old ideas because many Babylonians believed them. Greater and lesser folk named themselves after their ancient gods: Nanna, Anu, Ishtar, Nabu, Marduk. No doubt some of this was the force of tradition; only the empty form remained where the content had vanished. Babylonian law, on the other hand, continued to be administered, and it influenced the law of Greco-Roman Egypt. The Seleukid kings used Mesopotamian titulary: at Borsippa, Antiochos I made himself sound like one of the old shepherds appointed by the gods to rule the Black Headed People:

> I am Antiochos, the Great King, the Legitimate King, the King of the World, King of All Countries, the Caretaker of the Temples Esagila and Ezida, the First (-born) son of King Seleukos, the Makedonian, King of Babylon.

And the ritual of the important *Akitu*-festival was still being studied; it survives in fragments of two copies from Hellenistic Uruk.[16] Working

---

[15] Arr. *Anab.* vii. 16. 5—17. 6; 22. 1. The variant: Plut. *Alex.* lxxiii. 1–3; Diod. xvii. 112. 2–6. xix. 55. 8; Just. xii. 13–4. The verse of Euripides is frag. 963 (Dindorf) = Arr. *loc. cit.*

[16] Belephantes: Diod. xvii. 112. 2–6; the five deities from theophorous names in documents of the Greek period in *A.N.E.T.*, 222. Survival of law: R. Taubenschlag, "Das Babylonische Recht in den Griechischen Papyri," *JJP* 7/8 (1953/4), 169–85; "Keilinschriftrecht im Rechte der Papyri der römischen und byzantinischen Zeit," *Akten des VIII. Internationalen Kongresses für Papyrologie* (1955), 129–37; Antiochos' titles: *A.N.E.T.*, 317. *Akitu*-ritual: *ibid.*, 331.

from these ancient traditions, then, the *chaldaioi* of Babylon continued
to exert a mild pressure on Alexander, not only, I think, to protect
themselves or to earn embellishments for the temples of the state, but
also to win protection for the local population.

For his part Alexander tried to act like a Babylonian king. He
began the restoration of E-sagila and also carried out sacrifices in
honor of Marduk upon the advice and with the instruction of the
Chaldeans. Unfortunately for Alexander, however, his decision
to restore E-sagila required the expenditure of wealth stored in the
temple itself. The priests resented this plan because E-sagila contained
irreplaceable treasure allegedly dating from Assyrian times. The dis-
bursement of Marduk's hoard was exclusively the right of his priests.
Doubtless the clergy would have preferred an allocation of bullion
from the recently liberated Persian storehouses. If Alexander had
destroyed Persepolis to avenge E-sagila, his present proposition would
seem to make him very insincere and grasping. It was scarcely customary to honor a god with his own property. The case became an
important source of friction between King Alexander and the
priests.[17]

Varying accounts of two subsequent episodes during Alexander's
last months in Babylon touch on the matter of his kingship. Since
there survives undoubted Greek propaganda about what happened,
a propaganda with several versions, it must be a counter to what
Marduk's priests said about these events. The first incident occurred
during a voyage Alexander made down the rivers to inspect the old
Persian barrages and the irrigation system. A gust of wind blew away
Alexander's diadem, and it lit in a reedy marsh, supposedly on the
burial mound of some ancient Mesopotamian king. It is doubtful
that the mound was really a tomb; if it really was why isn't the king's
name given? And who but the Chaldeans could say that the mound
was a royal tomb? The flight of the diadem could be interpreted as
the most appalling of portents. It could show the transfer of Alexander's kingship to some ancient dynasty. Two variants in Greek
accounts show how the regime interpreted it. The one in Appian re-
flects obvious later Seleukid propaganda. It says that Seleukos re-
trieved the fillet and returned it to the king. Thus the Seleukids later
justified their destiny as heirs of most of Alexander's empire. But officers don't jump into the water: they send enlisted men.

The second version, given by Arrian, says that a common sailor, a

17 Arr. *Anab.* iii. 16. 4–5; vii. 17. 2–4; 24. 4.

Phoenician, swam to the bush, bound the diadem around his own head to keep it from getting wet, and returned it to the king. Seers (*mantes*) advised Alexander to put the man out of the way. But he did no more than order the man to be given money for his services and flogged for his presumption.[18] This second version must be the more nearly correct account, since the first must have been developed later, when Seleukos was either aiming for the kingship or actually exercising it. Now, who were these seers? They must have been Greeks, or our sources would somewhere call them *chaldaioi*. Why should they recommend the death penalty? Such drastic retribution would be useful only as a warning to someone who wished to interpret the episode in a particularly exciting way. Who would? The Chaldeans. We have no evidence concerning influential Babylonians in this period other than the clergy. The use the Seleukids made of their version of the story shows what might be made of it. The care with which the Greek seers were said to want to handle the event shows that hopes that the gods had abrogated Alexander's kingship in favor of a common Syrian—was not Sargon I the son of a gardener?—could easily arise. The multiple tradition shows the importance of the event itself.

A second incident occurred which was interpreted as an outright threat to Alexander's kingship. Diodoros, Plutarch, and Arrian all relate that one day when he was away a man dressed in royal regalia was found sitting on the king's throne. Arrian says that the *eunouchoi* —that is, the Babylonian chamberlains—did not remove the man, out of respect for "some Persian custom." The identity of the man is variously stated. Plutarch says that he was a Greek, Dionysios of Messenia. Arrian, following Aristoboulos, says only that he was some prisoner under open arrest; Diodoros says he was a Babylonian. That he was the latter is the most probable, since both he and the chamberlains acted in accord with what Aristoboulos called "some Persian custom." What Greek would know or act this way? The custom almost certainly had something to do with the Rites of the Mock King, which formed a part of the Babylonian New Year Festival. It is extraordinary that nowhere in our sources is it said that Alexander ever celebrated this most important ritual in order to renew his kingship for the coming year. Since all three authorities agree in placing this incident shortly before Alexander's death in June, that is, sometime in the spring, it might very well have occurred in April, the

---

[18] App. *Syr.* ix. 56; Arr. *Anab.* vii. 22. 1–5.

month of the *Akitu*. Were certain Babylonians actually involved in a celebration of this rite? If so, it would have been a threat, at least in ideological terms, to the continuity of Alexander's kingship. One of the concepts of Babylonian kingship was that where there was no *Akitu* there was no king. Alexander was certainly missing. The upshot indicates that the Makedonians took the affair in dead earnest, for Alexander had the man put to torture to find out why he had done what he had done. Two versions of his answer exist. Diodoros and Plutarch make him say that the idea had just fallen into his mind. This is probably the official version released after the inquisition was over, intended for public consumption. The other version—Arrian's —quotes him as saying that he had been inspired by Sarapis. This god did not yet exist; therefore, one has again to deal with a specifically Greek misstatement of what was actually said. Yet this second version must be closer to the truth, since a man who sits on another's throne can certainly think of some reason, especially when put to torture, for having done so. What would a Babylonian have said except that Marduk told him to do it? Thus it is quite possible that a celebration of the New Year Festival, with some poor soul nominated Mock King, was undertaken by certain Babylonians claiming to act in behalf of Marduk. Perhaps the real chosen-of-the-god would become known at the proper time. Or perhaps the poor soul was to be the king. Curious things had happened at the *Akitu*-festival in the past. The "Sargon Chronicle" of neo-Babylonian date says that in ancient times, when King Irra-imitti died during the Rite of the Mock King, the substitute, a gardener named Bel-ibni, became king in his stead.[19]

I cannot prove decisively that the episodes of the lost diadem and the enthroned prisoner have a Chaldean plot behind them. Nonetheless, the care of the Makedonians to know exactly what happened in each case, and the fact that both were overlaid with untrue Greek versions of what transpired, show the great importance that contemporaries attached to the events. This probably indicates that certain persons in Babylon entertained doubts of the legitimacy of Alexander's kingship. Since the idea of rule resolves itself in terms of religion, a priestly group must have been involved which could only be the *magoi* or the *chaldaioi*. It must have been the latter, since we have direct evidence that they were displeased with Alexander over the matter of the use of the temple funds, and had also sought to warn him away from Babylon. What these stories tell us, then, is that the

[19] The versions are in Diod. xvii. 116. 1–3; Plut. *Alex.* lxxiii. 3–4; Arr. *Anab.* vii. 24. 1–3. "Sargon Chronicle" in *A.N.E.T.*, 266–7.

Babylonian clergy created at least a feeling of vague menace, which finally culminated in unmistakable hostility in June, 323.

What had Alexander done to deserve this? We know the Babylonians thought he misused temple funds. But there is also the very strong probability that the Makedonians did not observe the *Akitu*-festival. This would have aroused Babylonian hatred. They were extremely sensitive on this score, since execution of the rites was necessary, they believed, for the defeat of the forces of sterility and chaos, both real and supernatural, which annually threatened the extinction of society. The king had to take part in the ritual. Failure on his part to do so in the past had led to the direst consequences for him. There was the case of the Chaldean king Nabonidos (555–538 B.C.), who meddled with the form of the ritual, altering it in favor of his favorite god, Sin of Harran. But later he did not carry out even this amended form, delegating the duty to his son Belshazzar. The Chaldean clergy betrayed Nabonidos to Kyros.[20]

During the last year that Alexander spent in Babylon, there must have been other grumbling against his regime, and the Marduk clergy could have taken advantage of this and tried to guide it. There were persons who disliked the king. Were the thirty thousand Persian youth he had commenced to train for his army really entirely loyal? There were also the Jews who had had to apply for exemption from laboring on E-sagila. There must have been Babylonians who thought the drastic political upheaval in Asia made it a good time to reassert Babylonian independence. Persis was down. Makedonia was a long way off. Alexander had at the most fifty thousand men in and around Babylon, but the city was very big. Some of these troops had even recently mutinied. Confusion in the camp of the enemy! When Alexander fell sick and came close to death a period critical for the continuance of Makedonian rule commenced. The Chaldeans could interpret Alexander's illness as a sign that Marduk was now decisively rejecting him. The Companions of the king asked the priesthood to permit Alexander to lie in E-sagila in hopes the god would undertake a cure. The clergy replied that the god did not think it desirable. Thus they

[20] For Nabonidos and the rituals see the neo-Babylonian documents, particularly the "Verse Account of Nabonidos" in *A.N.E.T.*, 308–6; and the *Akitu*-ritual, *ibid.*, 331–4.

If Alexander's feast at Opis was a celebration in some way of the New Year, it was a much amended form, not only because Alexander announced a program contrary to the norms of Babylonian society, but also because the feast was not held in Babylon, as tradition demanded it should be. If Alexander's feast was not the New Year Rite, then, we have no evidence that he ever celebrated it.

showed that they no longer considered Alexander to be a king worthy
of Marduk. But in fact the clergy had few supporters. Alexander's
government had made a favorable impression on many Babylonians
which improved as time went by. Pompeius Trogus says with some
exaggeration that after Alexander's death all Babylon lamented him.
He eventually made a mark on the folk tradition of the Mesopotamians and came to be identified with the legendary hero Gilgamesh.[21]

In the years immediately following the death of Alexander, conditions in Mesopotamia became rather more difficult for people as the
Diadochoi struggled among themselves for mastery of the East. Babylonia, because of its rich resources, became a main theater of operations, and it bore the brunt of several campaigns. Under these circumstances, the inhabitants were able occasionally to strike back at the
Greco-Makedonians or to take sides in the fight, hoping to help their
most favored general win. When Eumenes moved northwards through
Syria and eastwards into Mesopotamia, people along the upper Tigris
suddenly fell upon his army one night and inflicted loss upon it. Well
might they rebel. Diodoros says that the region was being heavily
plundered, and that by this time canals to the south had silted up.[22]
In 316 B.C., Antigonos began to show signs of intentions to remove
Seleukos from his post of satrap of Babylonia, and Seleukos, in fear
of his life, fled to Egypt. Antigonos' rule in Babylon was rather more
heavy-handed than Seleukos'. In consequence, the Mesopotamians
hated his regime and stirred up public opinion against him. The
chaldaioi prophesied that Antigonos' failure to lay hands on Seleukos
meant that all Asia would be ruled by the latter, and that he would
kill Antigonos in battle.[23]

While one may be skeptical that this prediction has actually survived in its original form, some such oracle was undoubtedly circulated. We have nearly contemporary evidence of the Chaldeans'
preference for Seleukos, and we also know that they resisted both
Alexander before this time, and Antiochos I after it. The evidence
comes from two fragments of a cuneiform *Babylonian Chronicle*,
probably composed in Babylon around 270 B.C. The first fragment

21 The rebuke to the Companions: *Ephemerides* = Plut. *Alex.* lxxvi. 4; Arr. *Anab.*
vii. 26. 2–3. Favorable to Alexander: Just. xiii. 1. Gilgamesh: A. R. Anderson,
Alexander's Gate, Gog and Magog, and the Enclosed Kingdoms (1932), 3; 20, n. 2;
21, n. 1.

22 Diod. xviii. 72. 3–4; xix. 12. 3; 13. 2.

23 *Ibid.*, xix. 55. 5–8; 56. 4; A. Bouché-Leclerq, *Histoire des séleucides* (1913), i.
20.

covers the years 321 to 312 B.C. The chronicler says that Antigonos' successes caused weeping and mourning in the land, because he attacked the Temple of Nabu, plundered the city and countryside, and burned people with fire when he looted the Temple of Nergal. His extensive depredations forced the people of Babylon into the plain to forage. This was the exact opposite of royal behavior: kings were to be shepherds of the people. Therefore the text terms Antigonos simply an army commander, while it calls Seleukos king. The same attitude appeared in a Hellenistic kinglist also coming from Babylon. It was written with a formulary identical to that of the ancient Sumerian kinglists, thus showing the consciousness of the continuity of royal traditions that existed amongst the priests.[24]

The hatred Antigonos inspired in the Babylonians was probably known to Seleukos, for in 312 B.C. the latter felt himself able to attempt his own restoration, setting out from Egypt with a force no larger than eight hundred foot and two hundred horse. Diodoros says Seleukos was confident that the Babylonians would rally to his side, and indeed events proved him right. Our sources, Greek and Babylonian, agree that when Seleukos returned to Babylon in 312, the greater number of the inhabitants met him joyfully, declared themselves on his side, promised to aid him, and carried out these promises. The garrison Antigonos had installed in the citadel, a thousand strong, surrendered when Seleukos prepared to storm it, because the latter had public opinion on his side.[25] Only the genuine preference of the populace for Seleukos could have brought about so speedy and successful a conclusion of this affair. The *Babylonian Chronicle* awards various titles to Seleukos, none of which it had ever applied to Antigonos. It calls him *Shatammu*-priest, Administrator of Nergal, and Satrap of Akkad. It thus underscores the legitimacy of his rule. It notes that he cleared E-sagila.[26] In 305 Seleukos became king in his own right, and was duly recorded as such. Seleukos had an ear for public opinion, and tablets dating from his regnal years show him using the old title "King of Babylon," which had fallen into abeyance at the time of Xerxes. Even Alexander had not used it.[27] It is clear that the

[24] The chronicle: B.M. 36313 in S. Smith, *Babylonian Historical Texts* (1924), 124–5, 136–7, 150. The kinglist: B.M. 35603 in A. J. Sachs and D. J. Wiseman, "A Babylonian King List of the Hellenistic Period," *Iraq* 16 (1954), 202–12.

[25] Diod. xix. 90. 1–91. 5; App. *Syr.* ix. 54–5.

[26] B.M. 34660 in S. Smith, *op. cit.*, 129–30, 134, 142–4.

[27] Recognition: B.M. 35603 in A. J. Sachs and D. J. Wiseman, *loc. cit.* Title: E. J. Bickerman, "Notes on Seleucid and Parthian Chronology," *Berytus* 8, fasc. 2 (1944), 75.

Babylonians preferred Seleukos' rule because it was legitimate, that is, because he showed respect for the forms of kingship, he cleared the country of invaders, and he protected the cult of Marduk and the other gods.

What other evidence we have of Seleukos' regime in Babylon suggests that his rule was in accordance with local traditions, at least at first. Coins struck between 321 and 316 and from 312 to 306 have as their predominant type the Oriental god Ba'al-tar. On the reverse is an Oriental lion. Seleukos' name and portrait were omitted. These coins were based on the standard of the Persian daric, not on a Greek standard. The series was largely supplemented and almost ended by a new Greek issue when Seleukos took the royal title in 306.[28] This numismatic evidence sustains the impression derived from the *Babylonian Chronicle* that Babylonians could feel that Seleukos' government promoted their well being more than the rule of any of the other Successors.

But this feeling did not survive the difficult period of gradually intensified warfare and Hellenization of Mesopotamia that followed Seleukos' return to Babylon. The consolidation and growing strength of Seleukos made him much less dependent on the support of the Babylonians. Around 310 B.C. he repulsed a raid by Demetrios Poliorketes, although the latter carried off much property and half ruined Babylonia. Hellenistic warfare involved large and continuous efforts on the part of the supporting civil population, and commonly caused heavy economic loss for the agricultural population of the regions through which the soldiers marched. A single army usually amounted to twenty or thirty thousand men, perhaps more, seldom less, followed by an approximately equal number of camp followers and hangers-on. Even if a territory was not systematically devastated to make it useless to an opponent, the feeding of such large numbers moving without any real commissariat demanded heavy sacrifices from the local population.[29] No matter how much army commanders may have desired to spare civilians such hardships, methods of that day did not make for easy conditions. It must have been apparent to the Syrians and Mesopotamians that they were being forced to support a

[28] G. F. Hill, *B.M.C. Arabia, Mesopotamia, and Persia* (1922), pp. clxi. 180; Nos. 6–38, pp. 182–7, Pl. xxi. 2—xxii. 3; Nos. 40–1, p. 188; E. T. Newell, *The Coinage of the Eastern Seleucid Mints* (1938), 99–106; M. T. Allouche-Le Page, *L'art monétaire des royaumes bactriens* (1956), 27–8.

[29] Demetrios: Plut. *Dem.* vii. 2–3. Warfare in general: M. I. Rostovtzeff, *S.E.H.H.W.* i. 137, 145–6.

ruinous warfare for the sake of deciding which Makedonian would come to rule them.

Added to the hardships of the Wars of the Successors was the effect of a process of Hellenization proceeding in Mesopotamia and Syria. Near Babylon the new Greek city Seleukeia-on-Tigris was built by Seleukos. It was intended, as Pliny says, to depopulate the older city, a motive possibly prompted by its anti-Hellenism. The priests of Babylon opposed its construction, and since they could not use physical force, they resorted to creating an incident they could use later. Seleukos asked them to indicate what hour and what day would be most auspicious for beginning work, and according to Appian they gave out a false time. But when the real moment the gods desired arrived, so ran the traditions familiar to Appian, a voice from heaven was heard stating that the work should begin. The priests were then requested to explain this astonishing event, and they confessed that they had prophesied a wrong time since they did not wish the new town to overshadow Babylon.[30] It certainly did not take much vision for them to foresee this result and the decline of E-sagila. The priests' fraud did upset the Makedonians, for the Greek tradition is obviously meant to counteract somebody else's propaganda.

The establishment of Seleukeia-on-Tigris fulfilled the worst fears of the Babylonians. The construction of this mighty, sprawling metropolis, which ultimately grew to have a population of half a million people, entailed the moving of Babylon's lower classes to form the menial and working population of the new city. The effect on Babylon, only a few miles away, was literally depopulation. This resulted in the final decline of the once great Oriental capital. By the beginning of the Christian era, the city was mostly deserted, and its great public buildings and religious sanctuaries were fallen mostly into ruins. Of E-sagila only broken parts remained, and in Babylon agriculture and animal husbandry were carried on inside the crumbling walls. In view of this foreseen disaster, the fate of Seleukeia-on-Tigris was frequently forecast in Chaldean astrological tablets of the early Seleukid era. Other towns were founded in Babylonia. Pliny says the Seleukids

[30] Seleukeia and Seleukos' motive: Strabo xvi. 1. 5 (738); Pliny, *N.H.* vi. 122; A. Bouché-Leclerq, *Histoire des séleucides* (1913), ii. 525. The priests: Appian, *Syr.* ix. 58.

Appian acutally calls the priests *magoi*, not *chaldaioi*. I feel, however, that these clergy were actually Chaldeans from Babylon, not Persian priests; by Appian's time (second century A.D.), the two terms had ceased to have ethnic meaning to many writers: cf. Acts viii. 9, which mentions a Jewish *magos*, i.e., magician, in Samaria.

collected Babylonia's population into cities on account of the rich fertility of the soil.[31] What exactly this means is hard to say. Was it to supervise agriculture? Was it to reduce the amount of ground not under cultivation by consolidation of dwelling places? At any event, this process of town-building was something that must have created great inconvenience for the established population.

There was another such case along the upper Euphrates at the time Doura-Europos was built. Its construction meant that an inhabited village was wiped out and at least some of the population forced to undergo a fresh orientation in their way of life. The new city was settled by European military colonists who received grants of land worked by the native peasants. The region came under a regime of Greek law and customs, which must have involved for a time at least inconvenience and confusion. The peasants, however, maintained the worship of their own gods, Hadad, Atargatis, Nanaia, Adonis, and Marduk, while the Makedonians worshipped Zeus and Artemis.[32] In Syria new cities were founded, so many that the region became almost a "New Makedonia," one whole district being renamed Pieria. Seleukos I founded Antioch as the grand capital of his new empire. Its suburb Daphne was built to be the home and playground of the Hellenic ruling class; it was constructed on an already inhabited plateau. The effects were evidently hard on the native population and a cause of discontent, for in later times the East remembered a tradition of cruel rites the Makedonians had celebrated when construction began. As late as A.D. 600 in Egypt the tale was told that the Makedonians had seized all property in the area in order to finance their work. This recollection may or may not be literally true; it must, however, go back to the Syrian population's feeling of misery.[33]

But perhaps not all was evil. Hellenic immigration greatly intensified economic life along the coast and created many new kinds of activities. Perhaps some Syrians were happy to exchange the new life in the bustling towns for their old life in squalid villages. There was

[31] Effects on Babylon: Diod. ii. 9. 9; Strabo xvi. 1. 5 (738) ; Pliny, *N.H.* vi. 121–2; Paus. i. 16. 3; viii. 33. 3. Astrological tablets in T. G. Pinches, *Historical Records and Legends of Assyria and Babylonia* (2nd ed., 1903) , 477. Seleukid policy: Pliny, *N.H.* vi. 117.

[32] M. I. Rostovtzeff in *C.A.H.* vii. 186–7; "Dura and the Problem of Parthian Art," *YCIS* 5 (1935) , 205–10; W. W. Tarn, *H.C.* (3rd ed., 1952) , 148–9; C. B. Welles, *et al.*, *The Excavations at Dura-Europos: The Parchments and Papyri* (1959) , 1–5, 20–1.

[33] Antioch: Paus. of Damaskos = Mal. viii. 255 D—256 A, 260 A; A. Bouché-Leclerq, *Histoire des séleucides* (1913) , i. 33. Daphne: D. N. Wilbur, *Antioch-on-the-Orontes* (1939) , ii. 50. Egyptian tale: John of Nikiu, *Chronicle* lxi. 4–7 (ed. Charles) . In general: A. H. M. Jones, *The Cities of the Eastern Roman Provinces* (1937) , 295.

great expansion in and around Antioch. The population of the plain near the capital, which was also a fortress, arsenal, focus of commerce, and center of literary activity, probably doubled during the Hellenistic period.[34] To chauvinist Greeks this social revolution was bringing the arts of civilization to a backward East. To create a *polis* was to organize men in the best political and social entity ever devised. It would make possible their philosophical education and their moral betterment.[35] It is surprising that there were no strong apocalyptic responses to this treatment.

Many Black Headed People remained passive and uninterested in becoming Hellenized. Although the Greeks made it easy for Syrians, Mesopotamians, and Elamites to become accredited citizens in the new communities, they did not do so on any large scale. They had little or nothing to do with the new Greek civic deities and did not abandon their native gods. In the reign of Seleukos Nikator the cult of Zeus Olympios at Doura included Greek and a few native worshippers. But soon the cult of the Syrian goddess Nanaia began there and became more and more important to the population. It retained its Syrian flavor and attracted numbers of Europeans. What is disturbing from the Hellenic point of view is that there was no corresponding growth in the importance of Greek cults at Doura.[36]

On the whole, however, the Seleukids tried officially to treat Syrians and Babylonians with respect, and they were certainly careful not to offend the religious feelings of their subjects. The inscriptions tell us they reverenced Babylonian gods and occasionally carried out restorations of their temples. In 268 B.C., Antiochos I Soter began repairs to Nabu's temple at Borsippa. In his dedicatory inscription he employed the familiar Babylonian titulary as King of Mesopotamia, and explained that he hoped to rule, with Nabu's help, according to the age-old canons of kingship:

> O Nabu, lofty son, (most) wise among the gods, splendid (and) worthy of all praise, first-born son of Marduk, child of Arua, the queen who fashioned all creation, do look friendly (upon me) and may—upon your lofty command which is never revoked—the overthrow of the country of my enemy, the fulfillment of (all) my wishes against my foes, constant predominance, a kingdom

---

[34] The population of the plain is roughly estimated from the number of mounds surveyed by R. J. Braidwood, *Mounds in the Plain of Antioch* (1937), 20–37: 57 show habitation in the Persian period; 101 in the Hellenistic.

[35] Plut. *Fort. Alex.* 5 (328 C—329 A) ; cf. Soph. *Ant.* 332–72.

[36] M. I. Rostovtzeff in *C.A.H.* vii. 187, 195; "Le Gad de Doura et Seleucus Nicator," *Mélanges Dussaud* (1939), i. 281–95; *S.E.H.H.W.* i. 490–2.

(ruled) in justice (to all), an orderly government, years of happiness, enough progeny be your permanent gift to the (joint) kingship of Antiochos and his son, Seleukos![37]

But at the same time that the Seleukids played the role of Nabu's king for the benefit of the Mesopotamians, they were actually becoming more and more Hellenic-minded. The government, its policies, its personnel, its outlook became more and more European. This quality is shown in the coinage, which in the third century was entirely Greek. None of the coins of the kings of this period ever portrayed an Oriental deity.[38] At the same time a widespread and magnificent royal cult grew up throughout the Seleukid Empire. Actually this worship and the magistracies in some of the autonomous cities charged to preserve the purity of Greek blood were intended to preserve the distinctiveness of the Makedonians. Although the royal cult was sometimes installed in temples hitherto dedicated exclusively to native deities, it met with little acceptance from the Orientals; of course it was not a worship made compulsory for the native people. At Uruk, for example, the king remained absent from the local pantheon, and there is no evidence of Hellenization of the cults. Therefore there is no evidence of resentment of the royal cult among the Mesopotamians.[39]

The Seleukids had to preserve the culture of their Europeans intact, for only Greeks knew Hellenic techniques, and these were necessary for the safety of the state. The widespread immigration of Greeks in the third century was encouraged, and resulted in the foundation of a city-state system for these persons, with the results we have seen. But the influx of Greeks into the East created a group privileged above the natives. These persons had the control of government in their hands, and were also able to enter and dominate the economic life of the region. Thus some members of this European aristocracy acquired astonishing fortunes. Hermias, Karian *dioiketes* of Antiochos III, was rich enough by himself to pay the royal troops when the king was involved with the suppression of Molon's revolt. Dionysios, *episto-*

[37] M. I. Rostovtzeff, *S.E.H.H.W.*, i. 435–8, 512–3; iii. 1427, n. 234. The inscription from *A.N.E.T.*, 317.

[38] P. Gardner, *B.M.C.: The Seleucid Kings of Syria* (1878) : Seleukos I through Antiochos III.

[39] Royal cult: C. B. Welles, *Royal Correspondence of the Hellenistic Period* (1934), No. 36, pp. 157–60; A. T. Clay, *Babylonian Records in the Library of J. Pierpont Morgan* (1913), ii. No. 53, pp. 33–4; M. I. Rostovtzeff, *S.E.H.H.W.* i. 437–8. Genearchs: W. W. Tarn, *H.C.* (3rd ed., 1952), 162; *The Greeks in Bactria and India* (2nd ed., 1951), 38. Uruk: J. C. Dancy, *A Commentary on I Maccabees* (1954), 66, 75–6.

lographos of Antiochos IV, entered one thousand personal slaves in a royal parade, each of them carrying a silver dish valued at a thousand drachms. This did not mean that conditions were unfavorable for the maintenance of the old Babylonian business families. The family at Uruk mentioned above for its wealth in the Persian period was able to maintain its status under the Seleukids and afterwards in Parthian times. Thus there were numbers of rich Orientals, and they formed a group whose members did become at least partially Hellenized citizens of the new *poleis*. These urban Greeks and Hellenized Babylonians worked closely with the ruling dynasty and were very wealthy people, in strong contrast to the unprivileged, propertyless proletariat.[40] But there is no evidence that this condition brought about religious resistance or protest.

Actually, the urban and rural native populations did not lose much if anything under the Seleukid regime. As it had been for centuries, land was in the hands of a relatively small number of Babylonian entrepreneurs. Much was worked as it had always been worked, by peasants owing definite obligations to the landlord, in many cases a native. They were not, therefore, conscious of any profound change in their lot, except in the few cases where they were uprooted to make way for a *polis*.[41] While peasants were no doubt exploited, they seem on the whole to have accepted their fate. There was no movement to free them and no anti-Hellenic resistance along these lines in consequence. Such resistance would not have been, strictly speaking, anti-Hellenic, since the propertied class was both European and Asiatic.

By the time Seleukos I died and was succeeded by Antiochos I in 281 B.C., conditions in Syria, Elam, Mesopotamia, and Kilikia were as sketched above, as they were to remain unchanged for over a century and a half. The state was organized, most of the new Hellenic cities founded, the economic organization functioning, and the social classes well established. At the same time a new series of wars which heavily involved Syria and Babylonia and Kilikia, the Syrian Wars, began between the Seleukids and the Ptolemies. The First Syrian War was waged from around 280 to 272 B.C., and occasioned heavy fighting and considerable civil effort by both sides. The second fragment of the *Babylonian Chronicle* deals with the internal history of Mesopotamia for 276

[40] M. I. Rostovtzeff, *S.E.H.H.W.* i. 517–9; W. W. Tarn, *H.C.* (3rd ed., 1952), 156–7. Uruk family: A. T. Olmstead, *H.P.E.* (1948), 74.

[41] The impact of the *polis* and Greek methods in (Pseudo-) Aristot. *Economica* ii. 2. 34. Society in general from C. B. Welles and M. I. Rostovtzeff, *op. cit.*, 59–60; M. I. Rostovtzeff, *S.E.H.H.W.* i. 467–72, 497–8, 507–16, 538; ii. 1001, 1005; W. W. Tarn, *The Greeks in Bactria and India* (2nd ed., 1951), 25–6, 56–9, 33.

and 275 B.C. For the first time we meet complaints in cuneiform literature against conditions which the Seleukids created.

In 276 Antiochos I was hard pressed by both the Ptolemaic forces
and the Gallic tribes which had just broken into and were now ravaging Asia Minor. He confiscated the land which only four years previously he had given to people in Babylon. Commodities became scarce
because of governmental requisitions, and there was hoarding of silver
money. The author of the *Chronicle* grumbles that because of the
scarcity of silver the unfamiliar "copper coins of Greece" must be
used and that because the country has been stripped of wealth to
support the army there is scabies in the land.[42]

In 275 the war went on, Antiochos defeating the Gauls in a pitched
battle with elephants brought up from Baktria. The civil governor of
Akkad levied taxes against Babylon in money and slaves, instead of
making the usual demand for grain. There was a regulation of coinage:
Babylonian silver staters were valued against an unknown number of
Greek bronzes. This was probably done to check inflation or profits
made by money-changing. There were disease and a shortage of food.
The governor tried to meet this crisis by handing over supplies from
the royal storehouses to the inhabitants of Babylon, Borsippa, and
Kutha. The government also decided to proceed with the long-delayed
reconstruction of E-sagila, and building materials were collected. It is
interesting to speculate why E-sagila was still being rebuilt. Evidently
Seleukos had not carried the work to completion, possibly because he
sensed the hostility of the *chaldaioi* and wished to discipline them,
or possibly because he had need of all resources to build Seleukeia and
to support his victorious campaigns from Ipsos to Koroupedion. Now
during the bad times of a hard defensive war, when the priests of
Marduk could be valuable in preventing food riots, Antiochos threw
them some bricks and bitumen, possibly as a reward. To resume,
Babylonians were being taken to Seleukeia to help populate the still
growing city. The governor of Akkad commandeered cattle intended
to supply Babylon. The *Chronicle* blames these events for bringing
about extreme hardship and even famine in Akkad. It reads, "The
people hired their children for silver. The people died of hunger. In
that year there was much scabies in the country." In November the
price of dates stood at 72 qa, about twice ordinary value. Fortunately

---

[42] Confiscation: M. I. Rostovtzeff in *C.A.H.* vii. 188; scarcity and the *Chronicle*:
B.M. 92689 in S. Smith, *Babylonian Historical Texts* (1924), 156. For the silver
currency see the excellent remarks of E. T. Newell, *The Coinage of the Eastern
Seleucid Mints* (1938), 61–2.

grain was normal at 36; but sesame stood at 21, two and a half times normal price.[43] The *stratēgos* of Akkad gave an ox and twenty sheep to Marduk, and these were duly sacrificed.[44]

From this fragment of native literature it is evident that during the crisis of the war Antiochos first secured the safety of the state and second the welfare of his Mesopotamian subjects. This was natural— any government would have done so. But in Babylonia there was a Greek government ruling a non-Greek population, and the dichotomy between official interests and official responsibilities was perhaps more sharply marked. In periods of crisis the foreign kings would throw all the regime's resources into the struggle. The commandeered land around Babylon was handed back after the war but was later again confiscated by the government.[45] This method of financing war alien- ated the most articulate and perhaps most influential single group in the population—the priests.

Therefore in the early third century we begin to find literary evi- dence of Babylonian religious resistance to Seleukid occupation. A new recension of the legend concerning Queen Semiramis appeared. It will be recalled that Semiramis had been the heroine in anti- Persian stories known to Herodotos. She was said to have executed extensive building programs, including the construction of temples and the enlargement of the irrigation system; but she was not remem- bered for any martial prowess.[46] Now, to understand what the Baby- lonians attempted to do when they created the Hellenistic account it is necessary first to examine a development of the legend which oc- curred in the fifth century B.C. Within two generations of Herodotos' visit to Mesopotamia, the Babylonians provided themselves with a new mythical history of Semiramis, in which her Assyrians and Babylonians were all-conquering and victorious like the Persians. Our knowledge of the version of around 400 B.C. comes from Diodoros' paraphrase of Ktesias' lost *Persika*. It is as follows. Semiramis was the illegitimate child of the Syrian goddess Derketo, who, appalled at her sin, ex- posed the newborn infant in the desert. The child did not die, how-

[43] The events and prices are taken from J. Epping and J. N. Strassmeier, "Baby- lonische Mondbeobachtungen aus den Jahren 38 und 79 der Seleuciden-Ära," *ZA* 7 (1892), 232–4, 238–45.
Quotation: *Babylonian Chronicle* = B.M. 92689 in S. Smith, *op. cit.*, 156–7.

[44] J. Epping and J. N. Strassmeier, *op. cit.*, 229.

[45] C. F. Lehmann, "Noch einmal *Kassu: Kissioi*, nicht *Kossaioi*," *ZA* 7 (1892), 330; A. T. Olmstead, "Intertestamental Studies," *JAOS* 56 (1936), 247.

[46] Herod. i. 184; iii. 155. For the origins and literary development of the Ninos- Semiramis Romance in Greek literature see M. Braun, *History and Romance in Graeco-Oriental Literature* (1938), 6–13.

ever, but was miraculously nurtured by doves until a herdsman found her and raised her as his own child. This beginning of the legend assimilated elements from the sagas of the Akkadian King Sargon I and of the Persian King Kyros, both of whom were supernaturally rescued from death. Semiramis grew up and eventually found her way to Baktria, where she met Ninos the King of Assyria making war against a local prince. Ninos married her, defeated the Baktrians, and then died, leaving Semiramis sole ruler of his empire. The queen then founded Babylon and built the Temple of Marduk. Having visited Egypt, she made war against Media, and having conquered and annexed it, she connected it to Babylon with a military road built by feats of engineering and marked with noble monuments. She then undertook a campaign against India and annexed the territory west of the Indus without a fight. But in an attempt to penetrate east of the river, she was beaten and forced to retreat. She died after a reign of forty-two years.[47] This series of exploits has clearly been copied from the careers of Kyros and Dareios I, the latter being the organizer of Egypt and the conqueror of India west of the Indus. So much for the second edition of the tale.

The Hellenistic "Semiramis Legend" also comes from Diodoros, who inserted the later material into his essentially Ktesian framework. Diodoros himself says that he used several conflicting authorities for his account, including Kleitarchos of the early Hellenistic period.[48] The later embellishments can easily be detected, for just as Semiramis was first modelled on the Kyros-Dareios figure, she was later developed along lines inspired by Alexander the Great. In the Makedonian edition Ninos, husband-to-be of Semiramis, attacks a king of Baktria named Oxyartes. This man has the same name as the Baktrian nobleman of Alexander's time.[49] Semiramis actually fights in this campaign. She stealthily leads a detachment of Ninos' army up a narrow ravine to capture Oxyartes' army on the heights it is holding, as Alexander led an agile contingent of his army up a rocky defile to surprise Baktrian forces entrenched on a high place.[50] Then, in both the "Semiramis Legend" and the Alexander history, the principal person either marries or arranges a marriage in Baktria, Semiramis with Ninos and Alexander with Roxane.[51] The hero then erects a

[47] Diod. ii. 4. 1—20. 5; cf. Just. i. 1–2. Sargon rescued by a gardener, "The Legend of Sargon," *A.N.E.T.*, 119; Kyros by a peasant: Herod. i. 108–30.
[48] Diod. ii. 7. 3; 20. 3, 5.
[49] Diod. ii. 6. 2; Arr. *Anab.* iv. 19. 5; 20. 4.
[50] Diod. ii. 6. 7–8; Arr. *Anab.* iv. 21. 5–6.
[51] Diod. ii. 6. 9–10; Arr. *Anab.* iv. 20. 4; vii. 4. 4.

monument on the Jaxartes River attesting an advance to the outer-most rim of the civilized world.[52] Further, Semiramis, having become sole ruler after the death of Ninos, visits the Oracle of Ammon in Egypt, and receives the pronouncement that she will achieve undying fame.[53] Her campaign against India takes on the coloring of Alex-ander's, since the Mesopotamians construct a bridge and river fleet on the Indus with the help of Kyprian and Phoenician sailors and ship-wrights as the Makedonians actually did.[54] Having been forced to re-treat from India, Semiramis travels through Gedrosia, is conspired against in Babylon, and decides to die. She vanishes to the gods, much as Alexander returned to his father Ammon.[55]

This comparison of Alexander and Semiramis was not invented by a Greek, for Alexander's accomplishments came off a bit smaller than the woman's. The Hellenistic "Semiramis Legend" credits her with the capture of Ethiopia, a conquest that Alexander never made.[56] Greek propaganda hostile to Alexander did not follow such a line; rather it usually gave him full credit for what he had done, and then attacked his character, stressing the deaths of Kallisthenes and Kleitos, and mak-ing him out to be a passionate, reckless drunkard or a wanton and ruthless murderer. The "Semiramis Legend," on the other hand, is a logical extension of previously established native propaganda brought up to date in order to compare Babylonians favorably with Make-donians.

Diodoros got his revisionary material from a source in Greek but it almost certainly did not come from the Babylonian priest Berossos. This man did not exalt Semiramis since he specifically denied the story that she had built Babylon.[57] It is quite likely that Diodoros' source was the romantically exaggerated *History of Alexander* by Kleitarchos of Alexandria, whom Diodoros cited as his authority that Semiramis constructed Babylon. It is not likely that Kleitarchos in-vented his account of Semiramis. He used sources; Onesikritos' won-derful account of India supplied one background for his Alexander to perform against. While Kleitarchos admittedly made Alexander de-sire to do the deeds done by great figures in the past, he never de-tracted from Alexander's prowess in any way. He actually made him extraordinarily efficient; Kleitarchos said that he killed eighty thou-

[52] Pliny, *N.H.* vi. 49.
[53] Diod. ii. 14. 3.
[54] Diod. ii. 16. 6; Arr. *Anab.* v. 7. 1; vi. 1. 6; *Ind.* xviii. 1, 8.
[55] Diod. ii. 20. 1–2.
[56] Diod. ii. 14. 4. Alexander received envoys from Ethiopia (Arr. *Anab.* vii. 15. 4).
[57] Berossos, *Chaldaika* = Jos. *A. Ap.* i. 142.

sand Indians in the Kingdom of Sambos alone.[58] This makes it quite unlikely that Kleitarchos himself invented the Alexandrian motifs in the life of Semiramis. Rather, it would appear that he picked them up from an otherwise unknown Babylonian "Semiramis Legend." The greater he found Semiramis, the greater he could make Alexander. It is certain that Kleitarchos had a deep interest in Eastern affairs, and he was consistently cited by authors of the later Hellenistic and Roman periods as an authority on strange Oriental customs. This may show that he got at least some information from native informants. Perhaps he derived his interest in Orientalia from his father Deinon, who himself wrote a much cited *Persian History*.[59]

The provenance of this legend must be Babylon itself, since that city plays the role of world capital. The date at which the legend was revised cannot be fixed with any accuracy. It must lie between the death of Alexander in 323 and the date of the publication of the history of Kleitarchos around 275 B.C.[60] Let us say, consequently that the new Babylonian version was made between 320 and 280. Perhaps it was revised in response to the feeling of tension that existed in Babylon at the end of Alexander's life, or within the immediately following years when Antigonos controlled the city. Or perhaps it came into being around 290 B.C. when Seleukos was consolidating his kingdom and beginning the construction of Seleukeia.

The "Semiramis Legend" was known, at least in part, to Greeks other than Kleitarchos and Diodoros. Strabo says that Semiramis had been an untiring builder of cities whose ruins could still be viewed. These were called Mounds of Semiramis. Pliny knew much the same thing about her and mentions places from Arabia to eastern Iran that the queen had allegedly founded.[61] Actually, these tels were but mud ruins of very old places whose real origins had been forgotten by the people in the neighborhood. The fact that people were willing to

---

[58] For Kleitarchos see W. W. Tarn, *Alexander the Great* (1950), ii. 45–9, 60, 62; L. Pearson, *The Lost Histories of Alexander* (1960), 231–42. The Indian incident is Kleitarchos in Curt. ix. 8. 15.

[59] Kleitarchos is used as an authority on the Persian tiara (Schol. *in* Aristoph. *Birds* 487); on the gymnosophists (Diog. Laer. i. 6); on the age and cause of death of Sardanapalos (Athen. xii. 530 A); on Phoenician-Carthaginian sacrificial customs (Schol. *in* Plato, *Rep.* 337 A); on Dionysos' adventures in India (Schol. *in* Apol. Rhod. ii. 904). Deinon: Pliny, *N.H.* x. 136.

[60] Kleitarchos' date: W. W. Tarn, *Alexander the Great* (1950), ii. 16–21; L. Pearson, *The Lost Histories of Alexander* (1960), 231–42.

[61] Strabo xvi. 1. 2 (737); Pliny, *N.H.* vi. 92, 145. Pliny also reports Ktesias' statement that the first voyage undertaken in a long ship was made by Semiramis (*ibid.*, vii. 206).

say that the nearby hillock was a construction of the queen's and the several citations of her we have in Greek and Latin authors and other works show that the legend gained a certain circulation. That its mildly anti-Hellenic character was worrisome is probably indicated by the anti-Semiramis story told by Juba, philhellenic king of Mauretania who lived between 50 B.C. and A.D. 23. He asserted in his book that Semiramis had fallen so deeply in love with a horse that she married it.[62]

One Babylonian seems also to have discouraged belief in the "Semiramis Legend," although not necessarily because he loved the Seleukids or the memory of Alexander. Around 275 B.C. the priest Berossos published a history of Babylonia and Assyria covering the period from the creation to his own day. It was based on Mesopotamian tradition, but written in Greek and dedicated to King Antiochos I Soter. In it Berossos attacked the accuracy of historians who said that Semiramis was the founder of Babylon, and when discussing the origins of the world, he identified Babylonian deities with their Greek opposite numbers in the divine hierarchy.[63] But the fact that Berossos took pains to make the myths and history of Mesopotamia available to Greek readers shows his concern that his own culture, religion, and traditions be known and appreciated. In this he was mildly anti-Hellenic and nationalist, and if he denied that Semiramis had founded Babylon, it was because he preferred a Babylonian history that exalted a courageous king instead of a clever, manly-hearted woman. Berossos incorporated in his book a "Nebuchadnezzar Legend" whose hero was made specifically greater than Seleukos, more magnanimous than Alexander, and braver than the Greek hero Herakles. Berossos wrote that when King Nabopolassar died, his son Nebuchadnezzar was campaigning in Phoenicia, Koile Syria, and Egypt. Upon receiving news of his father's death, he settled the affairs of these countries and hurried across the desert to Babylon, accompanied by only a few men. When he arrived in the capital he found the administration of the empire temporarily in the care of the *chaldaioi,* who were dutifully reserving the throne for him.[64] This tale is founded on fact, but it is also exaggerated in order to detract from Seleukos. Nebuchadnezzar was campaigning in the west when his father died, but he never succeeded in settling the affairs of Egypt, al-

---

[62] Juba = Pliny, *N.H.* viii. 155.
[63] P. Schnabel, *Berossos* (1923) is still best authority. Josephos' citation in *A.Ap.* i. 142.
[64] Berossos, *Chaldaika* iii = Jos. *A.Ap.* i. 135–7.

though he did defeat Egyptian armies. Seleukos had an Egyptian problem, too, wanting very badly to include Koile Syria in his empire. Ptolemy I occupied it during the campaign of Ipsos, in which Seleukos played a vital part in the defeat of Antigonos. Hence, Seleukos, far from settling the affairs of Egypt, did not control even Koile Syria and Phoenicia. Seleukos had also crossed the desert between Egypt and Babylonia with about a thousand men in 312; this was no mean feat, for not only were there physical difficulties but there were marauding parties of Arabs too. Nebuchadnezzar was now revealed to have made the crossing first, and with only a few men. When Seleukos reached Babylon he had to scuffle with Antigonos' general in the citadel; Nebuchadnezzar was welcomed by the priests as the legitimate king. The legend did more than belittle Seleukos; it compared Alexander unfavorably with the Chaldean king. Nebuchadnezzar was said to have embellished Babylon with buildings.[65] Alexander had ordered E-sagila to be restored, but little real work was done. Berossos does not directly state that these comparisons were to be made, but they were obvious to him who read with understanding and did not require attention to be called to them. Whether he included any other anti-Makedonian propaganda we do not know. He may have, for there were other incidents in the "Legend" quoted by Greek writers. Nebuchadnezzar was said to have led an army all the way to the Pillars of Herakles.[66] Alexander was supposed only to have planned this expedition. And Nebuchadnezzar was made to compete successfully even with a Greek demigod. Megasthenes reported a tradition that his achievements in Libya and Iberia had exceeded in courage those of Herakles.[67]

The use of Nebuchadnezzar's name for propaganda purposes was not a fresh device in Hellenistic Babylonia. He had been a source of hope in the past. During the two revolts against Dareios, the Babylonian pretenders both took his name. The first claimed also to be the son of the last native king of Babylon, Nabonidos. Thus, Nebuchadnezzar was regarded as an exemplar of legitimate kingship. Both his anti-Hellenic legend and the one about Semiramis deal with the subject of divine rule, comparing the regime of Makedonian kings adversely with Babylonian. Who was responsible for the "Nebuchadnezzar Legend"? I do not suppose that Berossos was directly responsible, considering the dedication of his book, and especially his going

[65] Berossos, *Chaldaika* iii = *op. cit.*, i. 142.
[66] Megasthenes = Strabo xv. 1. 6 (687).
[67] Megasthenes, *Indike* iv = Jos. *A.Ap.* i. 144.

out of his way to deny that Semiramis had built Babylon. He only retailed a story that must have been created by his more anti-Hellenic colleagues among the *chaldaioi* of Babylon. They must have been responsible for it, because Babylon is the great embellished world capital from which expeditions go to the farthest corners of the lands, and where Chaldean priests administer the state in time of interregnum. This tale must have passed into circulation sometime between the Battle of Ipsos and Seleukos' renunciation of a war of revenge against Ptolemy I around 300 B.C., and 275 when Berossos' *Chaldean Affairs* was made public.

About the same time there was an oracle circulating denouncing the kings of Makedonia and predicting their overthrow. It is included in the Sibylline collection.[68] According to the prophecy, Makedonian kings would bring about heavy suffering for Asia and for Europe too. Alexander would capture Babylon, but after this the Makedonian dynasty would utterly perish amid their own follies and become only a memory. This optimistic prediction can be dated around 300 B.C., since it mentions the sufferings not only of Asia but of Europe as well. Thus it refers to the Wars of the Successors in Hellas which began in 323 and continued until Antigonos Gonatas re-established order around 280. Alexander's family itself came to an end with the murder of young Alexander IV by Kassander in 310/9. Some scholars have thought that this oracle is really Persian, depending on the statement of Nikanor that the Persian Sibyl had had something to say of Alexander's life. But since we know there was also a Chaldean Sibyl, and since the locale in the prediction is Babylon, it seems best to assign this little text a Babylonian provenance.[69]

This prophecy, the two royal legends, and the oracles against the foundation of Seleukeia-on-Tigris all are concerned with the activity of the Makedonian kings. They protest against the increasing Hellenization of the country or its organization to serve Seleukid interests. The process seriously threatened to diminish the authority and pres-

---

[68] *Sib. Or.* iii. 381–7. My translation as follows:

Now Makedonia shall bring about dire suffering for Asia,   381
And for Europe, too, shall grow up great misery
From Kronos' race, offspring of bastards and slaves.
It shall capture even the fortified city of Babylon,
And, having been called mistress of every land   385
On which the Sun looks, shall perish amid bitter follies,
Leaving only a name among the wandering children of later ages.

[69] Schol. *in* Plato, *Phaid.* 244 B mentions a Chaldean Sibyl, as does Paus. x. 12. 9. H. N. Bate, *op. cit.*, H. C. O. Lanchester, *op. cit.*, attribute this text to the Persian Sibyl; A. Kurfess, *op. cit.*, to the Chaldean.

tige of certain of the established ruling classes in Babylon by setting Hellenic people in posts that controlled the country's wealth and especially by founding the new royal city of Seleukeia. Had not both Semiramis and Nebuchadnezzar granted especial benefits to Babylon?

Mention should also be made of the entry of the Persian *Bahman Yasht* into Babylonia. If it was originally developed around 300 B.C., and considering that Daniel 2 was written around 250 B.C., it may have reached Mesopotamia around 275 B.C. This general period was a time of Babylonian anti-Hellenism, and 275 itself a year of "much scabies in the country." Perhaps, then, the *magoi* in Babylon amended the apocalypse by adding images inspired by the *Akitu*-festival in order to encourage Chaldean anti-Hellenists. Babylonian motifs are certainly discernible in Daniel 7: the repulse of monsters of chaos rising from the sea to threaten the world, and their judgment by a victorious, enthroned hero sitting in council clearly reflect dependence on *Enuma elish,* the epic account of the annual re-creation of the world.[70] It is impossible to say what influence the Persian apocalypse had on the Mesopotamians; there is no evidence that it had any.

In comparison with Persian apocalyptic literature the Babylonian propaganda was much less vigorous and aggressive. The Persians looked forward to the destruction of the Greeks, and optimistically believed that after they had been destroyed and the rule of the East had been restored to them, the world would be a much pleasanter place. This degree of hate is not apparent among the Babylonians. Except for the Sibylline Oracle, which predicts the end of Alexander's dynasty, the Babylonian resistance passively accepts the present and contemplates an imaginary past full of glory. This literature aimed only at preserving native self-consciousness by creating a wonderful picture of dead kings and queens, and it probably had the effect of inspiring a few Babylonians here and there to hold to the old ways.

There is no doubt that Babylonian civilization enjoyed a last revival under the Seleukids. In a few towns there was a resurgence of native religious literature written in cuneiform. Business contracts, too, were executed according to the ancient forms, not only between Babylonians but in a few cases between Greeks. Only in some aspects of law did

---

[70] See pp. 23–25, above. For Babylonian elements: E. G. H. Kraeling, "Some Babylonian and Iranian Mythology in the Seventh Chapter of Daniel," *Oriental Studies in Honour of Cursetji Erachji Pavry* (1933), 228–30; G. H. Dix, "The Influence of Babylonian Ideas on Jewish Messianism," *JTS* 26 (1925), 250; H. Gressman, "Foreign Influences in Hebrew Prophecy," *JTS* 27 (1926), 253; O. Eissfeldt, *E.A.T.* (1934), 578.

Hellenic concepts immediately make serious headway against Mesopotamian practice.[71] This renaissance can best be seen in all its aspects in the case of Uruk. From 280 B.C. on the priests of the Anu Temple made numerous copies of antique hymns and rituals: the program of the *Akitu*-festival at Babylon; the religious procedure for covering a temple kettledrum; the ritual to be recited when repairing a temple; the schedule for daily sacrifices to the gods of Uruk. This last was said actually to have been copied from the archives of the priests of Susa in Elam and brought back to Mesopotamia. The sacred structures in the precinct of the Temple of Anu were reconstructed by Anu-uballit in 243 B.C., and the Anu and Antum Temples proper by a second Anu-uballit in 201. These restorations were carried out in purely Babylonian style, although Babylonian temples in other ancient towns sometimes were restored with unmistakable Hellenic additions. At Uruk the New Year Festival was celebrated, and the town itself was governed by native magistrates. Their work and the business of the temple priests were entirely autonomous: tablets were not stamped by a Makedonian *chreōphylakion* as they were elsewhere. Clay bullae and the literary texts show that the native gods and goddesses were very important in the lives of the population. Anu remained at the head of the pantheon and received much worship. In this determinedly Babylonian environment Greeks residing in Uruk took on a Mesopotamian veneer. Thus, a certain Demetrios took the second name Nana-iddin.[72]

Similar vitality was shown by the clergy of the old temples of Nippur, Borsippa, and Sippar, but by and large the renascence of Babylonian religious forms was confined to the few places I have mentioned. In parts of Mesopotamia other than these, interculturation was more nearly two-way. A good many Mesopotamians went Hellenic, at least to the extent of having their names translated into Greek. Even at Uruk, the restorers Anu-uballit had Greek second names: Nikarchos and Kephalion. At Borsippa, the gods Nebo and Ishtar be-

[71] M. I. Rostovtzeff in *C.A.H.* vii. 168, 189; and with C. B. Welles, *op. cit.*, 62–4; R. H. McDowell, *Stamped and Inscribed Objects from Seleucia on the Tigris* (1935), 71–3.

[72] The texts in *A.N.E.T.*, 331–45; reconstructions: H. Lenzen, *Vorläufiger Bericht über die . . . . Ausgrabungen in Uruk-Warka* (1956), 11–42. On administration by Urukians and the temple communities: A. Aymard, "Une ville de la Babylonie séleucide," *RÉA* 40 (1938), 5–42; M. I. Rostovtzeff, *S.E.H.H.W.* i. 435–6, 515–6; iii. 427–8, n. 235. Bullae: M. I. Rostovtzeff, "Seleucid Babylonia," *YCLS* 3 (1932). Gods and Orientalized Greeks: A. T. Clay, *Babylonian Records in the Library of J. Pierpont Morgan* (1913), ii. 14, 21, and the texts.

came Apollo and Artemis. At Nippur there were similar changes.[73]
Going Greek could be well worth while. Hellenized Babylonians were
able to hold high office within the European imperial government, as
in the case of Heliodoros, minister of Seleukos IV.[74]

Much the same thing occurred around the temples of the gods of
Susa. Nanaia's house was ransacked about 325 B.C. by Herakon, a
Makedonian officer, but upon complaint of the Elamites he was punished by Alexander. Susa was presently Hellenized by Nikator: it became Seleukeia-on-Eulaios with an imperial garrison and Greek
magistrates, a mint city of the kings. The royal coinage was stamped
with a portrait of Seleukos, but there was also a series of staters with
Ba'al and a lion very much like the ones struck in Babylon. Many
Greeks were attracted to the Elamite gods: the *stratēgos* Apollodoros
made a dedication to the local Ma around 222 B.C. Nanaia, too, was
important, both to Greeks and Orientals, and her temple was regarded
with extraordinary reverence. Slaves were freed by being consecrated
to her service: a Babylonian lady manumitted her girl Sozaia to Nanaia
early in the second century. There is no evidence that the Elamite gods
were anti-Hellenic, and during Molon's revolt Susa-Seleukeia remained loyal to Antiochos III. Governor Diogenes held the citadel
when Molon took the town by force. When Antiochos succeeded in
crushing Molon, he rewarded Diogenes by making him satrap of
Media, and Apollodoros the Ma worshipper became satrap of Susiana.[75]

The Seleukids certainly were not hostile to the vigor shown by the
native gods of the whole region, and they indirectly fostered the religious revival in Babylonia. Antiochos I, as already said, refounded
the Nabu temple at Borsippa. The restorations of the temples at Uruk
were also assisted by royal funds.[76] This revival of native religion was
scarcely a form of resistance at all. While it passively attempted to pre-

[73] Vitality: Pliny, *N.H.* vi. 123; L. Delaporte, *Le Proche-Orient* (3rd ed., 1948),
313–4. Uruk: H. Lenzen, *op. cit.*, 12. Borsippa: Strabo xvi. 1. 7 (739). Nippur: R. H.
McDowell, *Stamped and Inscribed Objects from Seleucia on the Tigris* (1935), 228.
[74] A. Bouché-Leclerq, *Histoire des séleucides* (1913), i. 239–42; J. W. Swain,
"Antiochus Epiphanes and Egypt," *CPh* 39 (1944), especially for Heliodoros, 76, n.
17; 77, n. 19.
[75] Herakon: Arr. *Anab.* vi. 27. 3–5. Coinage: E. T. Newell, *The Coinage of the
Eastern Seleucid Mints* (1938), No. 300, p. 113, Pl. xxiii. 6; Nos. 318–22, pp. 117–22,
Pl. xxiv. 13–17. Apollodoros: *S.E.G.* vii. 10. Nanaia temple: B. Haussoullier, "Notes
sur les inscriptions grecques des fouilles de Suse," *CRAI* (1927), 220; Pliny, *N.H.*
vi. 135; M. I. Rostovtzeff, *S.E.H.H.W.* i. 436–7. Manumission: *S.E.G.* vii. 26; F. Cumont, "Deux inscriptions de Suse," *CRAI* (1933), 261–2. Diogenes: Polyb. v. 48. 14;
54. 12.
[76] Antiochos: *A.N.E.T.*, 317; general: W. W. Tarn, *H.C.* (3rd ed., 1952), 128–9.

serve the forms and content of native religion, the priests did not attempt to rebel or to wipe out the Seleukid government. For Uruk, this can be very clearly seen from documents written at the time Molon and Achaios revolted against Antiochos III. Media, the region Molon first controlled, was called "Guti" in liver omen texts. So was Parthia. The Guti were an ancient horde of barbarians who had wrecked the Dynasty of Agade in the twenty-second century, and whose name had come to stand for barbarian enemies in general. The Seleukid Empire in the same texts was identified with Akkad, the native name for Babylonia and civilization. A priest on April 30, 221 B.C. anxiously enquired of the native gods, "Would the city be destroyed?"[77] Thus the Babylonian clergy, while eager to retain their own culture intact, were equally anxious to retain the Seleukid government at least for their military protection.

The conditions existing in Mesopotamia and Elam in the third and early second centuries B.C. were largely duplicated in Syria and Kilikia. The only difference was that Hellenization in the latter region took root more deeply, so that Oriental self-consciousness grew correspondingly less. Already in the fourth century B.C. the peoples there had begun to become familiar with Hellenism and to adapt themselves to it. The Makedonian invasion and Greek immigration, therefore, were not quite so much of a shock as elsewhere. The Phoenician cities of Tyre and Sidon, a part of the Ptolemaic Empire, were reorganized as Hellenic *poleis* during the latter part of the third century, and they accepted this without protest. Tombs dating from around 200 B.C. show that numerous Sidonians had taken Greek names.[78] Much the same state of things existed in Syria. Numerous cities were begun by Seleukos Nikator on the sites of older towns—places like Antioch, Seleukeia-in-Pieria, Apameia, Laodikeia. All these newly developed places were provided with Greek civic gods and goddesses and took vigorous part in the cult of the Seleukid kings. In only one case do we hear of resistance. When Seleukeia-in-Pieria was started, an inauspicious clap of thunder accompanied the religious rites celebrated to guarantee the future safety of the place.[79] It is likely that this

[77] F. Thureau-Dangin, *Tablettes d'Uruk* (1922), Nos. 1, 3. A. T. Olmstead, "Intertestamental Studies," *JAOS* 56 (1936), 245 and n. 13; "Cuneiform Texts and Hellenistic Chronology," *CPh* 32 (1937), 8.

[78] 2 Macc. vi. 1–11; Strabo xvi. 2. 14 (754); Jos. *Ant.* xii. 258–64; M. I. Rostovtzeff in *C.A.H.* vii. 190–1. Pseudo-Kallisthenes says (i. 35. 9) that even in his day (c. A.D. 300) men still spoke of Alexander's sack as the "Evils of Tyre." This could be Tyrian or it could be Greek.

[79] Strabo xvi. 2. 4–6 (749–50); App. *Syr.* ix. 63; M. I. Rostovtzeff, *S.E.H.H.W.* i. 481, 491. Thunderclap: App. *Syr.* ix. 58.

story represents the attempt of the priests of a local god, Ba'al or
Hadad, to prevent the foundation of the new *polis* much as Marduk's
priests had tried to stop the construction of Seleukeia-on-Tigris.
But we know of no other resistance. We hear of no revolts on the
part of the Syrian or Palestinian populations against the Ptolemaic
or Seleukid regimes. Polybios does say that the Koile Syrians preferred the Ptolemies. But in Syria, even the temple states rebuilt their
shrines along Greek lines, and the gods took Greek names. Thus Bam-
byke became Hierapolis, Halab Beroia, and Hamath Epiphaneia.
Hadad, god of Damaskos, became Zeus of Damaskos. Atargatis, a goddess famous throughout Syria, often became a Greek city goddess.
Teshub and Ba'al likewise frequently became civic Zeuses. There was,
then, respectable Hellenization of some towns of Syria; it had not been
so widespread in Babylonia.[80]

Kilikia generally accepted European ways without demur. The chief
community there was Tarsos, which had retained a good many of its
native characteristics while a part of the Persian Empire. But after
Alexander's victories, Tarsos became, at least on the surface, a Greek
city. There was a great flowering of the Greek genius there, as seen in
its brilliant philosophical schools, especially the Stoic. The city was
provided with a legend explaining that it had really been founded by
Argives. At the same time, however, lower-class elements retained
much of their native culture. Tyana underwent a similar experience,
adding an Hellenic veneer to its native culture. Strabo was told that
the city was situated on a Mound of Semiramis, indicating that Babylonian ways of thinking were still current among some Kilikians. The
whole region was greatly influenced by the long-established temple
states. One of the most famous was at Olbe. Here, as in Syria, the
gods frequently took Greek names. The indigenous Great Mother became Sarpedonian Artemis. Sandon of Tarsos became Herakles.[81]

All in all, then, our survey of Western Asia shows that in the third
century and in the first years of the second there was only the slightest
resistance to Hellenism, and that was almost entirely in the old
imperial capital of Babylon.

[80] E. R. Bevan, *The House of Seleucus* (1902), i. 208–9; J. P. Mahaffy, *The Progress of Hellenism in Alexander's Empire* (1905), 97; Polyb. v. 86. 9–11. Temple states and gods: M. I. Rostovtzeff, *S.E.H.H.W.* i. 511; W. W. Tarn, *H.C.* (3rd ed., 1952), 342–3.
[81] H. Goldman, *Excavations at Gözlü-Tepe, Tarsus* (1950), i. 5, 38–9, 45–6, 152, 172. Strabo xiv. 5. 12–4 (673–5). Tyana: Strabo xii. 2. 7 (537). Olbe: Strabo xiv. 5. 10 (672). Sarpedonian Artemis: Strabo xiv. 5. 19 (676).

Chapter VI

The Western Asians After 189 B.C.

A new era began for the Western Asians after the defeat of Antiochos at Magnesia in 189 B.C. He was forced to levy contributions of bullion against several temple states in order to meet the heavy indemnity that the Romans demanded as a part of the price of peace. This policy was presently responsible for the king's death.

In Elam there was militant resistance against Antiochos around the Temple of Bel. Diodoros says that the king accused the priests in charge of this holy place of declaring war against him, but he gives no details as to why they did this. Perhaps they knew that Antiochos was coming to collect their god's treasure; perhaps they really revolted. Diodoros' brief note is fortunately supplemented by Justin's equally short account of events. He says that not only did the king approach the sanctuary by night with troops, which implies an intended surprise attack, but that he also found a large number of people prepared to resist. This certainly shows that the people here were in a strongly rebellious state. Antiochos attacked, but was killed in the fight, June 4th, 187 B.C. The language of our authorities is unanimous that Antiochos fought people from the countryside: Diodoros calls them *egchōrioi;* Strabo *barbaroi;* Justin *incolae.* It was a native movement. It was not a revolt by a Greek satrap or by the Greeks of a *polis.* The only indication we have of Greek feelings in Elymaïs is that within five years of Antiochos' death a Greek of Seleukeia-on-Eulaios made a dedication to Artemis and Apollo for the health of Seleukos IV and his consort Laodike.[1] What evidence we have, therefore, makes it appear that people of rural Elam did revolt against Antiochos, that these people were led by the priests or supported by the priests of Bel, and that Antiochos was not only intent on taking money from the sacred treasury, but that he was also attempting to punish disloyal

---

[1] Diod. xxviii. 3. 1; xxix. 15. 1; Strabo xvi. 1. 18 (744) ; Just. xxxii. 2. Date: B. M. 35603; A. Aymard, "Du nouveau sur la chronologie des Séleucides," *RÉA* 57 (1955), 108–9. Dedication: *S.E.G.* vii. 17 (183/2 B.C.) .

Elamites. There is no Elamite literary evidence for this affair and no oracles denouncing the regime.

The reign of Seleukos IV (187–175) was a period of consolidation and retrenchment. But Antiochos IV (175–164), younger son of Antiochos III, began a new policy towards the Oriental peoples in his empire, and sought consciously to bring about the existence of a strongly Hellenized eastern state. From his point of view this was absolutely essential for the continuity of the dynasty. Heavy losses of manpower and money had been sustained in the West against Rome between 192 and 189, and they had come after a generation of serious warfare in the East. Seleukid territory was diminished by the subsequent peace treaty of 188, and recruiting soldiers in Asia Minor was specifically forbidden. Antiochos therefore had to find new means to strengthen the state against the Roman peril in the West and the Parthian menace in the East. Realizing the degree to which Hellenism had taken root in Mesopotamia, Syria, and Kilikia, he attempted to create a closer association between the dynasty and both the Hellenic and Oriental elements of the population. Thus, Hellenism would be zealously propagated in order to give the state large numbers of technically proficient persons so that the Seleukid Empire might make headway against its aggressive enemies. On the practical level, Hellenization would be brought about by a close blending of Orientals with Europeans in already existing, as well as in numerous new, *poleis* which could be incorporated from the larger towns in Syria and Mesopotamia. Antiochos' policy resulted from the previous successful Hellenization of Western Asia, as the experience of the Jews in Jerusalem shows. He made use of already Hellenized elements in the native population.[2]

In Antiochos' reign, then, many old native towns became *poleis*, from Ekbatana in Media to Adana in Kilikia. The huge village of Nisibis became Antiocheia, and the people there issued a coinage inscribed "Of the Antiocheans in Mygdonia." Similarly, Mopsouhestia became a Seleukeia. Uruk, its name now vocalized as Orchoi, experienced more intense Greek influence. A Seleukid registrar stamped clay bullae *Chreōphylakikos Orcheōn*, which may imply formal Greek organization, but there is no real evidence that civic institutions were actually installed. Babylon, however, was refounded as a *polis*. There was reconstruction and expansion of the older Greek theater and of

[2] Antiochos' policy: 1 Macc. i. 11–5; 2 Macc. iv. 7–17; M. I. Rostovtzeff, *S.E.H.H.W.* ii. 64–5, 704; W. W. Tarn, *The Greeks in Bactria and India* (2nd ed., 1951), 21; R. Ghirshman, *Iran* (1954), 228–9.

other buildings. A new gymnasium was built probably at this time. Citizen Philippos hailed Antiochos IV founder of Babylon and Savior of Asia. The coinage appeared with the likeness of a new city goddess, the Tyche of Babylon. Older Greek cities like Doura were supported and subsidized.[3] There was much excitement in Western Asia.

The granting of Greek civic institutions to Mesopotamian and Syrian and Kilikian communities involved some changes in their religious life, that is, the Hellenization to greater or lesser degree of their gods. At Doura, Ba'al Shamim was identified with Zeus Olympios and his temple provided with a Syrian-style cella and a Doric propylaion. Gerasa, now Antiocheia-on-Chrysorhoas, received a Temple of Zeus built on a site belonging to an older Semitic deity. Doura's god could be Hellenized without opposition, because there were still descendants of Makedonian settlers in the city and such assimilation therefore tended to be natural. When a part of Jerusalem was reorganized as Antiocheia, Yahweh was not Hellenized; as E. Bickermann has shown, he was instead assimilated to Ba'al Shamim.[4] No descendants of European military settlers lived in Jerusalem, and her treatment was therefore different. But Syrian Ba'al or Grecian Zeus were gods known very widely, and they were religious symbols of the new imperial unity that Antiochos sought to create.

Tinkering with the character of the gods to secure a reorientation of Asiatic allegiances was dangerous. It was responsible for the only known case of militant religious resistance on the part of the Babylonians. A little-known cuneiform document dated to 168 B.C. records events in Babylon during this period of crisis and conflict over political and religious loyalties. Antiochos appointed a new priest, probably a high priest, who handed over gold in the E-sagila treasury to

[3] In general: M. I. Rostovtzeff in *C.A.H.* vii. 188–9; *S.E.H.H.W.* ii. 703; E. R. Bevan in *C.A.H.* viii. 499, n. 1; E. Bickermann, *Der Gott der Makkabäer* (1937), 90.
Nisibis: Strabo xvi. 1. 23 (747); G. F. Hill, *B.M.C. Arabia, Mesopotamia, and Persia* (1922), cviii. Uruk: K. F. Johansen, "Tonbullen der Seleukidenzeit aus Warka," *Acta Arch.* 1 (1930), 41–54; M. I. Rostovtzeff, "Seleucid Babylonia," *YClS* 3 (1932), 90; A. Aymard, "Une ville de la Babylonie séleucide," *RÉA* 40 (1938), 37.
Babylon: *O.G.I.S.* 233; F. Wetzel, *Das Babylon der Spätzeit* (1957), 3–4, 19–20, 25, 72. Doura: C. B. Welles, "The Population of Roman Dura," *Studies in Roman Social and Economic History* (1951), 252.
[4] Doura: M. I. Rostovtzeff, "Le Gad de Doura et Seleucus Nicator," *Melánges Dussaud* (1939), i. 294; F. E. Brown in *The Excavations at Dura-Europos: Preliminary Report of the Seventh and Eighth Seasons of Work* (1939), 218–58; 284–92; "The Temple of Zeus Olympios at Dura and the Religious Policy of the Seleucids," *AJA* 45 (1941), 94.
Gerasa: C. H. Kraeling, *Gerasa, City of the Decapolis* (1938), 30–2. Jerusalem: E. Bickermann, *Der Gott der Makkabäer* (1937), 96–114; V. Tcherikover, *Hellenistic Civilization and the Jews* (1959), 161–9; 404–9.

the government. Several statues of Hellenized gods were made from this gold by the citizens of the *polis* of Babylon. There followed the dedication of these images, which the Babylonian text euphemistically calls "unsuitable," and their erection in the temple, whose holy of holies had been somewhat altered along Hellenic lines. Patriots, called thieves in the text, then attacked the temple and stripped the statues of Uru-gal and Ammani'ta. These persons were then taken by the authorities, tried, condemned to death, and cast into fire.[5]

Events in Babylonia thus paralleled events in Jerusalem during the crisis which led to the Maccabean revolt. While these events are similar generally as to cause, the Babylonian reaction was by no means as widespread or as vigorous or anything like as successful as the Maccabean rising. Yet the riot that occurred in Babylon and resistance to Antiochos in Elam and Kilikia show that there was opposition to Antiochos' program outside of Judah. The implications of 1 Maccabees that no such opposition existed is another case of Jewish propaganda. When Marduk was challenged in his holy of holies he struck back. Defense of his cult against a similar threat had occurred in Babylon in the 540's. When archaizing King Nabonidos had attempted to change the worship in E-sagila by introducing the god Sin, he met with stern resistance from the priests. They even turned disloyal to him when Kyros attacked and helped the Persian capture the city.[6]

What happened to Marduk in Babylon in 168 was similar to what had happened to him in the 540's. The importance of his cult was diminished. To alter Marduk's cult in any way, to associate Marduk with a god which had never been seen in the country before, was to alter Marduk or to jeopardize his position as lord of the world. In theory this would put the whole organization of society in danger of dissolution. In practice it certainly put the priests of Marduk in danger of loss of prestige. No king could legitimately threaten Marduk because a primary function of Babylonian kingship was to serve the gods and increase their well-being. Antiochos was therefore a no-king. Consequently the priests withdrew their loyalty from the king as they had

---

[5] The tablet is translated in T. G. Pinches, *Historical Records and Legends of Assyria and Babylonia* (2nd ed., 1903), 553. See, too, A. T. Olmstead, "Intertestamental Studies," *JAOS* 56 (1936), 247.

[6] 1 Macc. i. 41.

"Verse Account of Nabonidus" i. 19–22 in *A.N.E.T.* 312–5:

[. . . against the will of the g]ods he (Nabonidus) performed an unholy action,
[. . .] he thought out something worthless.
[He had made the image of a deity] which nobody had (ever) seen in (this) country.
[He introduced it into the temple;] he placed (it) upon a pedestal.

from Nabonidos. Marduk in 168 had not been in such danger since he had been deposed and kidnapped by Xerxes. Antiochos' policy must be opposed. Support for Marduk must be organized. Artaxerxes, Xerxes' son, had finally reinstated Marduk and honored Babylonian gods at least with words. The *chaldaioi* accordingly circulated an old legend describing Xerxes' attack and the ultimate vindication of Marduk by Ishtar in the time of Artaxerxes. The faithful would know what they really meant. This myth has survived in the plot of the Jewish book of Esther.

To support this drastic statement of Esther's origins requires extensive argument. We shall begin by examining the book itself. Whatever else Esther is, it is not history. It is a fictional story about the near-execution of the Jew Mordecai; it is an account of the thwarting of a planned persecution of all the Jews in the whole of the Near East; and it is a tale of the enthronement of the Jewess Esther as Queen of the Persian Empire and wife of Ahasoueros, that is, Xerxes. The stated purpose of this phantasy was to give historical justification for celebrating the Feast of Purim.

Now, what was the nature of the material that the author used for his book? Only two alternatives exist. It was either all fiction or it was part fiction and part fact. Actually, Esther shows a sometimes astonishingly detailed and accurate knowledge of the protocol and customs of Xerxes' court of around 475 B.C., as we know it from Greek authors like Herodotos and Ktesias and from the reliefs of Dareios and Xerxes at Persepolis.[7] There is, for example, a good description of a Persian banquet in Esth. i. 6–8. The fact that Esther is partly based on reliable information raises another question. Esther was written around 125 B.C., according to the generally accepted scholarly opinion.[8] How could a man three centuries removed have known these details? Either there was a continuing knowledge of Persian customs among the Jews, or he learned about them from some foreign source. Jewish knowledge of Persian geography, the Persian kings, and Persian history, however,

---

[7] The accurate verses include Esth. i. 6–8, 11, 13–4; iii. 2, 7, 13; iv. 2; v. 2, 6, 14; viii. 4, 10, 15. Details and Greek parallels in L. B. Paton, *A Critical and Exegitical Commentary on the Book of Esther* (1916), 65; R. H. Pfeiffer, *I.O.T.* (2nd ed., 1948), 737; A. T. Olmstead, *H.P.E.* (1948), 128–9, 170, 182–3, 282.

[8] L. B. Paton, *op. cit.* (1916), 154–5; G. H. Box, *Judaism in the Greek Period* (1932), 148–9; O. Eissfeldt, *E.A.T.* (1934), 564–5; R. H. Pfeiffer, *I.O.T.* (2nd ed., 1948), 729–31; H. H. Rowley, *G.O.T.* (1950), 154–5; F. M. Cross, *The Ancient Library of Qumran* (1958), 121. B. W. Anderson, "The Book of Esther," *Interpreter's Bible* (1954), iii. 827–8, admits the evidence for a date at the end of the second century is very good, but does not want to commit himself to it, feeling that H. Gunkel may be correct in preferring an earlier date.

was exceedingly scanty and very much distorted in the late second century. The authors of 1 and 2 Maccabees thought that Persia was the name of several countries east of the Tigris, including Media and Elam, and that the exiles of 586 had been sent to Persia. The editor of Daniel says that King Dareios ruled 120 provinces organized in three "presidencies," whereas the actual number was about 25, and there was no such thing as a "presidency." He calls Dareios a Mede, makes him the son of Xerxes, and says he was a contemporary of Nebuchadnezzar. He was actually a Persian, the father of Xerxes, and began to reign forty years after Nebuchadnezzar died.[9] Esther itself contains lamentable blunders. Xerxes is supposed to rule 127 provinces; the true figure was 27. He is said to have had women brought from all the provinces of this empire in order to choose one to be his wife.[10] This was the exact opposite of Persian custom. Therefore, parts of Esther must have been written from a source normally not known to the Jews. The source probably was fairly old itself in 125 B.C. since it contained authentic information.

The nationality of this source can be determined by the nationality of the principal characters in Esther. Remarkably enough not one of them has a really Jewish name. With the exception of King Ahasoueros, they have the names of Babylonian and Elamite gods. The name Esther is equivalent to Ishtar; the heroine at ii. 7 is even called "Hadasseh," "bride," a standard epithet of the goddess. While this similarity of terminology might be set down to coincidence, other evidence shows that the similarity is due to design. Esther's relationship to Mordecai, whose name is philologically the same as Marduk, is first cousin. This was the relationship of Marduk and Ishtar. This identity shows that Mordecai and Esther are really Babylonians masquerading as Jews. Their enemy Haman can be equated linguistically with Humman, an Elamite god. Vashti, whom Esther ousts as queen of Persia, can be similarly identified with Mashti, an Elamite goddess.[11]

---

[9] 1 Macc. iii. 31; vi. 1; 2 Macc. i. 13, 19. Jos. *Ant.* xii. 354 simply copies these mistakes. Dan. v. 30—vi. 2; ix. 1; xi. 1. For further examples see C. C. Torrey, " 'Medes and Persians,' " *JAOS* 66 (1946), 1–15.

[10] Esth. i. 1; ii. 2–4.

[11] The identifications: H. Zimmern, "Zur Frage nach dem Ursprunge des Purimfestes," *ZATW* 11 (1891), 157–9; P. Jensen, "Elamitische Eigennamen," *Wiener Zeitschrift für die Kunde des Morgenlandes* 6 (1892), 47–9, 209–11; H. Gunkel, *Schöpfung und Chaos* (1895), 313; P. Haupt, *Purim* (1906); L. B. Paton, *op. cit.* (1916), 88; O. Eissfeldt, *E.A.T.* (1934), 561; R. H. Pfeiffer, *I.O.T.* (2nd ed., 1948), 743 and n. 3; S. A. Cook, *Introduction to the Bible* (1950), 53, feels the identifications attractive but does not commit himself; H. H. Rowley, *G.O.T.* (1950), 155,

There is altogether too much identity here for mere coincidence. Rather, the divine names show that the source behind the Old Testament book dealt with a mythic struggle of pagan gods. Since Marduk-Mordecai and Ishtar-Esther win, the legend was created in Babylonia. It may be added that both historical and linguistic evidence indicates that the Feast of Purim itself was probably an importation from Babylonia, whatever its exact nature there may have been.[12] These origins may well be the reason that the book had such poor standing among the Jews. By A.D. 1958 about one hundred of the Dead Sea Scrolls from Qumran had been certainly identified with the various books of the Old Testament. All are represented except Esther. In the early Christian era there was rabbinical opposition against both its inclusion in the canon of inspired literature and the celebration of the Purim festival.[13]

What was the original Babylonian myth? I shall call it for convenience's sake "Proto-Esther." Scholars like H. Gunkel and P. Haupt thought that the original Mesopotamian myth celebrated a political victory of Babylonians over Elamites in the period before the Assyrian Empire of Tiglath-pileser III put an end to warfare between Babylon and Susa.[14] I think, however, that the plot of Proto-Esther actually was developed and took more or less the form of the story in the Old Testament book in the fifth century B.C., after Xerxes punished Babylon and deported Marduk, and about the time Artaxerxes restored the god and his city. The plot of Proto-Esther does remarkably well as a parallel of the political history of those years. The location of the Persian court at Susa is perfectly all right, since the Achaemenids did use this city as an occasional capital, along with Ekbatana and Pasargadai and Persepolis. The use of Elamite gods to represent Per-

---

merely mentions them without comment or acceptance; B. W. Anderson, *op. cit.*, iii. 827–8 admits the possibility of the identifications, but feels that they could not be proved; N. H. Snaith, "The Historical Books," *The Old Testament and Modern Study* (1951), 106, says, "It is difficult to imagine that the choice is wholly accidental."

[12] Purim: H. Zimmern, "Zur Frage nach dem Ursprunge des Purimfestes," *ZATW* 11 (1891), 157–9; B. Meissner, "Zur Entstehungsgeschichte des Purimfestes," *ZDMG* 50 (1896); J. G. Frazer, *The Golden Bough* (1900), ii. 138–40; B. W. Anderson, *op. cit.*, iii. 824–5.

[13] Qumran: F. M. Cross, *The Ancient Library of Qumran* (1958), 31. Rejection: *Megillah* 7a; G. F. Moore, *Judaism in the First Three Centuries of the Christian Era* (1927), i. 242–6; R. H. Pfeiffer, *I.O.T.* (2nd ed., 1948), 64, 746; B. W. Anderson, *op. cit.*, iii. 825.

[14] H. Gunkel, *Schöpfung und Chaos* (1895), 313; P. Haupt, *Purim* (1906); B. W. Anderson, *op. cit.*, iii. 826.

sian gods is not an obstacle to this hypothesis. In the first place a myth of conflict between Marduk and Humman was less likely to arouse the Persians if they discovered it being recited clandestinely than one which hymned Marduk's recovery from the scheme of Ahura Mazdāh outright. In the second place, the *chaldaioi* in the fifth century were undoubted archaizers who interpreted political struggles in ancient language. In the Hellenistic period, the terms "Guti" and "Elam," names for real enemy countries of about 2000 B.C., were still being used by Babylonian omen texts to designate the Parthians. Therefore, Haman-Humman and Vashti-Mashti stood for the Persians' gods. Babylonians of the late sixth, the fifth, and the early fourth centuries certainly had the opportunity to know Persian court usage and ceremonial well, Babylon being a sometime residence of the Achaemenid kings.[15]

As for the fifth-century parallels, Xerxes, a character in the book, did show violence to Marduk and his city, and carried off the god's statue. Mordecai at the beginning of the story is an exalted person brought low and in danger of losing his life. But Esther, meanwhile having married the Persian king, is able to intervene successfully to preserve the life of Mordecai and thwart Haman's plan to persecute the Jews. Esther and Mordecai then are confirmed in highly honored positions, queen and vizier of the empire. These latter events had their analogues in history. Marduk was restored at Babylon and received back his Babylonian property in the reign of Artaxerxes I. The same king also erected a stele in honor of Ishtar in Babylon.[16] The king in the Hebrew version of Esther is, after all, Xerxes; in the Greek version the king is, on the other hand, Artaxerxes. The presence of Esther at a Persian court matches the increasing prominence of Babylonian women in historical Achaemenid harems and also the increasing importance of Anahita as a divine protectress of the Persian

[15] There was a Babylonian named Marduka who had a high official position at the Persian court, either at the end of the reign of Dareios I or at the beginning of the reign of Xerxes. See A. Ungnad, "Keilschriftliche Beiträge zum Buch Esra und Ester," *ZATW* 58 (1940–1), 240–4; *ZATW* 59 (1942–3), 219. B. W. Anderson, *op. cit.*, iii. 826, uses this information to argue that it ends once and for all the mythic theory of Esther's origin. I cannot agree with this reasoning. The information only shows what one would expect: that the widely used name "Marduk" belonged to a Babylonian at the Persian court. It proves nothing of an identity between the historical Marduka and the fictional Mordecai.

[16] Marduk's property: J. N. Strassmeier, "Einige kleinere babylonische Keilschrifttexte aus dem British Museum," *Actes de Huitème Congrès Internationale de Orientalistes* (1893), 2ᵉᵐᵉ Partie, iB, 279–83, No 24. Ishtar: R. Koldeway, "Ausgrabungsberichte aus Babylon," *MDOG* 32 (1906), 5. A. T. Olmstead, *H.P.E.* (1948), 291.

Empire and above all her actual syncretism with Ishtar. The extraordinary size of the gibbet prepared for Mordecai, one fifty cubits high, that is about seventy-five feet, is probably a recollection of the derrick that was rigged to remove Marduk's statue from its shrine in E-sagila.[17]

The book of Esther is also shot through with ideas drawn from Babylonian mythic literature. The idea of the victory of a woman over a foreign king fits the fifth-century Babylonian spirit much more than it does the Jewish mind, the history of Judith notwithstanding. Herodotos retails contemporary legends concerning the valiant queens Nitokris and Semiramis, although he learned nothing of the earlier hero Gilgamesh.[18] There was nothing like this emphasis on female prowess in native Hebrew thought during the Makedonian period; the Maccabees were too masculine to think of it.

Several motifs in Esther closely resemble ideas in traditional Babylonian myths about Ishtar and Marduk. The temporary eclipse of Marduk in the face of deadly danger was well-known; we hear of "mountains of ordeals" and of a grave of Marduk.[19] The motif of the rescue of a god by a goddess was exceedingly popular, the basis of numerous myths of many cultures of the ancient Near East.[20] While early Mesopotamian legends paired Ishtar with Dumuzi or Tammuz, in later times she was connected with the high god Marduk.[21] The marriage of Ishtar to a human king was an important element in the cults of some Mesopotamian states.[22] In the Old Testament book, Esther was threatened by death in her dealings with the Great King, since the author pretended that for her to approach Ahasoueros might lead to his having her killed.[23] Similarly, in the old myths Ishtar was threatened, or even overcome by death, when she descended to the Nether World, from which she eventually emerged victorious.[24] Human sexuality as related to natural abundance is dimly apparent in Esther. As the story opens Ahasoueros and his men hold a feast for

[17] Women at court: Ktes. *Persika*, Epit. 44–8. Anahita as protectress: pp. 50, 53 above; identified with Ishtar: J. H. Moulton, *Early Zoroastrianism* (1913), 238–9; M. N. Dhalla, *History of Zoroastrianism* (1938), 302. The gibbet: Esth. v. 14.

[18] Herod. i. 184–7.

[19] H. I. Frankfort, *Kingship and the Gods* (1948), 322–3; 410, n. 27.

[20] Mesopotamia: "The Descent of Ishtar to the Nether World," *A.N.E.T.*, 106–9; Phoenicia: "Poems about Ba'al and Anath," *ibid.*, 129–32; Egypt: Plut. *Isis and Osiris.*

[21] H. I. Frankfort, *Kingship and the Gods* (1948), 331; S. H. Hooke, *Babylonian and Assyrian Religion* (1953), 24, 30.

[22] H. I. Frankfort, *Kingship and the Gods* (1948), 295–7.

[23] Esth. iv. 11–6.

[24] "Descent of Ishtar to the Nether World," *op. cit.*, Obv. 60–80; Rev. 30.

one hundred eighty days. This period corresponds roughly to the period during which the earth bears crops and animals bear young. Vashti, the then reigning queen, is sent for to enter the banquet hall, apparently naked,[25] but she refuses to do so. She is forthwith deposed and the banqueting apparently stops. For as soon as Ahasoueros marries Esther, it is stated that the king holds a banquet.[26] All this sounds like the prime function of the fertility goddess par excellence—Ishtar. A *Hymn to Ishtar* composed around 1600 B.C. for King Ammiditana[27] lists attributes of the goddess which may readily be compared with these of the Jewish heroine: both are beautiful and lovely,[28] both are the cause of wise and excellent decrees,[29] both are compassionate and friendly,[30] both preserve people in all walks of life,[31] both occupy a throne room and save the life of a king,[32] and, through this king, the whole world is subject to the orders of both.[33]

As for Mordecai, he commits acts in the story that rather connect him with Marduk. He rides through the city of Susa in the early summer, dressed in the king's robes, an act which one might connect with Marduk's role in bringing plenteousness to the earth.[34] In the Greek addition to Esther, Mordecai is said to have had a dream in which he took part in a battle as a dragon, defeating Haman, also a dragon. In the same dream Esther was represented by a river.[35] When one finds all these correspondences between Babylonian literature and the Old Testament book, between the characterization of the goddess Ishtar and the person of Esther, and between Perso-Babylonian history and the story of Esther, how can the Biblical book be said *not* to have a Babylonian parent?

It is hard to imagine a Jewish writer of that very patriotic time, the second half of the second century B.C., making up a story whose characters could be so easily identified with pagan gods. On the other hand, it is not so difficult to imagine him using already existing pagan

---

[25] Esth. 1. 11.

[26] Esth. i. 1—ii. 18.

[27] "Hymn to Ishtar," *A.N.E.T.*, 383.

[28] *Ibid.*, 5–12; cf. Esth. ii. 7, 9, 17; v. 2.

[29] *Ibid.*, 21–4; cf. Esth. viii. 4, ix. 13, 25, 29, 31.

[30] *Ibid.*, 17–20; cf. Esth. iv. 4 ff; viii. 3 ff.

[31] *Ibid.*, 33–40; cf. Esth. ii. 17.

[32] *Ibid.*, 45–8; cf. Esth. ii. 22–3 (Ahasoueros) ; vii. 1 ff. (Mordecai, who at viii. 15 assumes royal dress) .

[33] *Ibid.*, 49–52; cf. Esth. viii. 2 ff. (Mordecai becomes vizier of the Persian Empire through the agency of Esther) .

[34] Esth. vi. 7–11. Date is 23rd Sivan (Esth. viii. 9) . H. I. Frankfort, *Kingship and the Gods* (1948) , 330–1.

[35] Esth. x. 4–7; xi. 2–11.

literature that he could recast for a definite purpose. It is certain that in the second century and later, the Jews deliberately remodelled pagan literature, more or less completely, for their own ends. Such was the case with at least some of the prophecies in Daniel, which were erected on Persian and Babylonian foundations. The whole body of Jewish Sibylline literature had both Greek and Oriental prototypes. 1 Enoch, Ahiqar, Ecclesiastes, and the Wisdom of Solomon all show unmistakable signs of gentile ideas, in matters both secular and religious.[36] From the Jewish point of view, there were sound reasons why this half-gentile literature should be put into circulation. This was a period in which the Maccabean Jewish state was competing with the Hellenistic powers; it was a period during which the Jews began for the first time seriously and diligently to seek converts on a wide scale. It was a time, too, when the Diaspora played an increasingly important role in determinining the course of Jewish thought, producing a Greek translation of the scriptures as well as making its own unique contributions to what we know as the Apocrypha and Pseudepigrapha. Many of the persons in the Diaspora were by no means as committed to a single-minded, hyper-Jewish nationalism as were zealots in Palestine. They were much more susceptible, on the whole, to pagan influence than were the people of Judah.

Along these lines it is understandable how Esther could have been used by Jews during the second century B.C. As a propaganda work designed to show gentiles the extraordinary successes of the Jews against pagans and the invincible righteousness of their cause, Esther would have had greater effect if it resembled gentile literature. To do this, as in the case of the proselytising Sibylline Oracles, Esther would have to be drawn from some pagan source. To use ideas already current among pagans meant that the Jews would have an audience partially prepared by familiarity to accept them.

How Ishtar passed over to her new Jewish name and nationality is difficult to say with certainty. It was most likely in a period when both Jews and Babylonians fought a common enemy. This condition was satisfied when both peoples were subject to the Hellenizing policy of Antiochos IV in the second quarter of the second century B.C. There may be evidence of contact between the hierarchy of Marduk and the hierarchy of Yahweh. E. T. Newell has noticed a curious resemblance between the Babylonian lion-staters of Seleukid times and the Jewish

---

[36] Gentile influence on Hellenistic Jewish literature is discussed by R. H. Pfeiffer, *History of New Testament Times* (1949), 224–30; W. F. Albright, *From the Stone Age to Christianity* (Anchor ed., 1957), 20, 345–57.

shekels of the First Revolt.[37] Be that as it may, the earliest evidence
we have of the celebration of Purim, and the purpose of the book was
to persuade persons to celebrate it, comes from the year 166 B.C. This
was about the time that the Palestinian Jews were making merry over
their defeat of Antiochos' general Nikanor. This was only two years
after the *chaldaioi* had shown violence to the friends of this same
Antiochos who wished to place "unsuitable images" in the sanctuary
of Marduk. Furthermore, there is a resemblance between Antiochos IV and Xerxes, both kings thinking of eliminating a stiff-necked
and independent people by proscription.[38] From this date we may infer
that Proto-Esther passed into Palestine during Antiochos' reign
through the agency of the Mesopotamian Jews, who of course would
have had an excellent opportunity to know Babylonian propaganda.
It is likely that Esther was transmitted orally to Palestine perhaps in
165, about the same time that our canonical Daniel came into circulation. From Palestine it later reached the Jewish community in Egypt.[39]
Only by postulating oral transmission can one explain the existence
of our rather different Esther texts, one Hebrew and two Greek versions, all derived from a lost Aramaic tale. This is shown by the numerous Aramaisms in the versions, and the fact that Hebrew Esther is
not an accurate translation of the older Greek Esther which has 107
verses more than the Hebrew.[40]

Proto-Esther, then, was a mythic interpretation of the conflict of
Antiochos IV and the priests of Marduk, based on the earlier crisis
between them and Xerxes. Marduk is threatened with death by the
foreign god Humman—the unsuitable image—who attempts to persuade Antiochos IV to carry out a proscription of Marduk's people in
Babylon. That meant the creation of the Greek *polis* was a threat. But

[37] E. T. Newell, *The Coinage of the Eastern Seleucid Mints* (1938), 106, n. 14.
Newell says concerning the Babylonian coins: "The somewhat daring thought occurs
to the writer that these lion staters may possibly have had some connection with the
great temple of Babylon and its vast hierarchy of priests. Could they, by any chance,
have represented some sort of temple money, in which case any over-careful ad-
justing of their weights may not have been so necessary? It is curious—or is it mere
coincidence—that the Jewish shekels of the First Revolt, whose coinage must also
have been more or less connected with the hierarchy at Jerusalem, should three and
a half centuries later so greatly resemble these lion staters in general form and
fabric."

[38] Esth. iii. 8–15; cf. 1 Macc. i. 41–50; iii. 34–6. B. W. Anderson, *op. cit.*, iii. 827.

[39] Esth. xi. 1; R. H. Pfeiffer, *I.O.T.* (2nd ed., 1948), 740–1; E. J. Bickerman, "The
Colophon of the Greek Book of Esther," *JBL* 63 (1944), 339–62.

[40] L. B. Paton, *op. cit.*, 63–5; C. C. Torrey, "The Older Book of Esther," *HTR* 37
(1944), 2–6, 9, 24–7.

Ishtar marries Antiochos[41] and through him succeeds eventually in thwarting Humman's evil plan. This was a hope. Marduk is restored and regains control of the world, becoming vizier of the king, and the Babylonians are saved from disaster. This pathetically optimistic propaganda and the riot in the temple were the result of the Hellenizing policy of the Seleukid king in Babylon. The "unsuitable images" were probably removed after Antiochos' death. What little evidence we have from E-sagila shows that the cult of Marduk seems to have functioned normally in Parthian times. How he regained undisputed possession we do not know.

Turning now to other countries, there was also resistance and propaganda in Elam, although the immediate causes here were somewhat different. Antiochos IV setting out in 165 to begin his long-expected campaign against Persis and Parthia stopped in Elam at the Temple of Nanaia. Polybios, Diodoros, and the author of 1 Maccabees say that he desired to confiscate money from the temple treasure, but it is possible that there were other motives as well. The priests of the goddess and the Elamites of the region, as well as some of the Greek townsmen, resisted an attack that Antiochos made, so that he was forced to desist. According to a tradition recorded by Polybios, Diodoros, and Appian, Antiochos died of a heaven-sent wasting disease as a result of this wanton assault.[42] This false interpretation of the death of Antiochos probably goes back to Greco-Elamite propaganda. The Greek worshippers of Nanaia at Susa could easily have carried the propaganda westwards. The tradition could not come from a pro-Seleukid source. Furthermore, a Jewish tradition of Antiochos' death connects it indirectly with his adventures in Elam. In 1 Maccabees he is said to have been stricken as a result of hearing of victories won by Jews over his own forces. This mortal illness comes immediately, however, after his withdrawal from the attack on the temple at Elymaïs. The Jewish writer obviously could not give Nanaia credit for striking the king down. Therefore it appears that 1 Maccabees used the same tradition that was known to the Greek historians.[43] Thus, Polybios,

---

[41] He married Syrian Atargatis: Granius Licinianus 5 (ed. Flemisch); he intended to marry Elamite Nanaia: 2 Macc. i. 14.

[42] Polyb. xxxi. 9. 1–4; 1 Macc. vi. 1–3; Diod. xxxi. 18a. 1; App. *Syr.* xi. 66. Townsmen: 1 Macc., *loc. cit.*; they were certainly interested in Nanaia at this time; dedications of hierodules to the goddess were made in 142/1 and 131 B.C. = *S.E.G.* vii. 22, 25.

[43] 1 Macc. vi. 1–3. The text says "Elymaïs in Persis," but this is a case of geographical misunderstanding; see p. 138, n. 9, above. Jos. *Ant.* xii. 354–8, misunder-

PLATE V

Relief and inscription depicting a fight between a god and a monster. It comes from the entrance of the temple of the god Ninurta at Nimrud in Mesopotamia, and was carved in the ninth century B.C. It is now in the British Museum. The line drawing below more clearly delineates the scene.

Since the inscription is an invocation of the god Ninurta, and since the relief was found in the ruins of his temple, the figure on the right must be Ninurta himself. On the left a monster half turns with a roar to confront him. This monster is clearly not Tiamat, a goddess, but some Babylonian form of the Death Demon. He, like the Persian monster, has a horned head, and forepaws and body of a lion, and is feathered and winged. His tail differs in that it is like a bird's instead of a scorpion's. One Persepolitan monster, however, is shown without the scorpion's sting; it has a feathered bird's tail somewhat different from the one shown here. The over-all similarity of these nightmare beasts is so great, however, that it cannot be fortuitous. Thus, this plate and Plate III show the very great dependence of Persian concepts on the earlier Babylonian.

Plate V also illustrates the Babylonians' belief in the warlike and saving powers of their high gods, whom their kings represented and acted for. Here Ninurta rushes forth to protect his Black Headed People, and he brandishes two lightning bolts in his hands to strike the demon a death blow. Heroic Ninurta was a benevolent warrior god similar to Enlil, Asshur, and Marduk, who not only slew monsters, but also caused a mountain (Hursag) to bring forth trees and sheep, silver and gold, wine and honey (S. N. Kramer, *Sumerian Mythology* [1944,] 79–82) . (Photographs supplied by the Trustees of the British Museum.)

PLATE V. BABYLONIAN GODS: THEIR COSMIC ROLE

PLATE VI. THE GODDESS ISHTAR

PLATE VI

Figurine of the Babylonian goddess Ishtar, now in the British Museum (No. 91822). It was made about 1700 B.C., so that it is roughly contemporaneous with the *Hymn to Ishtar* of Ammiditana. It serves to illustrate my remarks about Ishtar and ultimately about Esther.

Ishtar is shown here as the goddess of life, love, and fecundity, "laden with vitality, charm, and voluptuousness," as Ammiditana said. But she was also a goddess of righteous anger and powerful rule, as Ammiditana also knew. In Babylonian legend, Ishtar rescued the god Tammuz from death in the Netherworld, the dark domain of Ereshkigal. To get there she had to pass through seven gates, at each of which a gatekeeper forced her to remove a garment, so that she finally stood before Ereshkigal and her vizier in all her naked glory. She begged for the life of Tammuz, and it was granted her. This life-giving function of Ishtar was long believed in, and in late Assyrian omen-texts she is guarantor of the safety of the Assyrian kings, who beg her to avert the dangers that threaten them. Therefore, it may be significant that in the book of Esther, when Haman begs for his life to be spared, he approaches Esther and not King Ahasoueros (vii. 7).

The sexuality of Ishtar is underlined in the story of the gate-keepers, and it is shown in the figurine in no uncertain terms: clothed only in strings of beads of costly lapis lazuli, she offers her breasts. The sexuality of Esther is rather broadly hinted at in the Old Testament (Esth. ii. 16–17), and it is by means of this that she is able to in-fluence Ahasoueros. (Photograph supplied by the Trustees of the British Museum.)

1 Maccabees, Diodoros, and Appian would all represent the same
original tradition. Probably about the same time too there was opposition to Antiochos at a temple in Shami. This town was located south-
east of Susa in Susiana. Whether it was actually in a district inhabited
by Elamites is uncertain. The town may have been settled during
the reign of Antiochos, since almost all the artifacts excavated come
from the immediately following Parthian period. A fine bronze statue
of Antiochos belonging to a temple there was smashed. Since Antiochos was God Manifest, this attack on his image can be interpreted as
an act of religious defiance. Precisely who was responsible we do not
know.[44] Within the next twenty years Elam became an independent
state, and a man named Tigraios took the title "king." Nothing more
is known of him. Perhaps if Elamite traditional forms still had force
the priests of Bel and Nanaia had something to do with this. In early
times the kings of Elam were apparently subordinate to prophets of
the gods, spokesmen called *sukkals*.[45]

Antiochos' policy also aroused a native god in Kilikia. We know of
this mainly through archaeological and numismatic evidence. At Tarsos, the usual type on the autonomous coinage down to 160 B.C. was
a Greek Tyche or civic goddess. The reverse usually showed a bow that
scholars have taken to be a symbol of the local god Sandon Hellenized
as Herakles. The legend read *Antiocheōn tōn pros tōi Kydnōi*. Tarsos
had thus been renamed at least as early as 250 B.C. in the reign of
Antiochos II Theos. Tarsos reacted violently against Antiochos IV.
She and the town of Mallos revolted about 170–65 B.C. The information comes from 2 Maccabees, whose author placed these events in the
time of the high priest Menelaos, who took office in 172. The reason
given for the revolt is that the cities were given to Antiochis, the
king's mistress, as a present. The real reason is unknown. The revolt
evidently was successful, for the coinage struck from around 164 to

---

stood 1 Macc., so that he expresses concern over the supposed inaccuracy of Polybios. 2 Macc. i. 13–6; ix. 1–3 is badly confused, containing elements of the two traditions of attacks on Susa: that of Antiochos III and the present one. See E. R. Bevan,
The House of Seleucus (1902) , ii. 120, 160; J. C. Dancy, *A Commentary on I Maccabees* (1954) , 111.

J. A. Fischel, *The First Book of Maccabees* (1948) , 54–5, commenting on 1 Macc.
vi. 12, says that the priests of Nanaia claimed that their goddess was responsible for
the retribution inflicted on Antiochos, but doesn't say why he thinks so.

[44] R. Ghirshman, *Iran* (1954) , 236, 278–9; Pl. 29a; L. Vanden Berghe, *L'archéologie
de l'Iran ancien* (1959) , 64–5; Pl. 94c.

[45] Tigraios: E. T. Newell, *The Coinage of the Eastern Seleucid Mints* (1938) , 140,
n. 38. *Sukkals:* C. J. Gadd, *Ideas of Divine Rule in the Ancient East* (1948) , 40.
Independence: R. Ghirshman, *Iran* (1954) , 245–6.

135 B.C. has the same obverse, but on the reverse shows sometimes Zeus seated and sometimes Sandon himself, bravely riding on the back of an animal in original, non-Greek form. The legend now reads *Tarseōn*, indicating at least partial independence and withdrawal from Seleukid allegiance. The reverse types of the period 135–95 B.C. are the pyre of Sandon or the god on his animal; Zeus has disappeared. At the same time that Sandon ousted his Greek colleague from the mint there was the beginning of a production of clay plaques showing Sandon mounted on a winged lion between altars wreathed and garlanded. These cheap, lower-class, obviously Oriental decorations continued to be made for the next century.[46] The evidence is conclusive that Tarsos resisted the Seleukid kings under the aegis of her Kilikian god.

This religiously patriotic movement had overtones of class war. One Lysias, Epicurean philosopher and *stephanophoros* of Herakles-Sandon—all things to all men he—late in the second century made himself tyrant of the city. He appeared in public wearing a purple tunic and a gold crown, so that he must have considered himself a king. A part of his program was to take money and goods from the rich and give them to the poor. Those who did not cooperate were killed. Tarsos seems to have had a long history of lower-class discontent, for around A.D. 100 it was probably necessary to own a property valued at 500 drachms to qualify for citizenship. There was also a group of linen-workers without civic rights whom the wealthier people of Hellenic descent accused of being a useless rabble responsible for the tumult and disorder that then existed. It is quite possible that a similar group of propertyless workingmen of Kilikian extraction without the franchise were involved in Sandon's rise in 160 B.C. It is tempting to speculate further about this incident. Was there a memory of earlier Hellenic aggression that made the Oriental Tarsians hostile? There certainly was an invasion of Kilikia by Ionians about 700 B.C. It was repulsed by the Assyrian King Sennacherib, who commemorated the event by building a columned temple at Tarsos and embellishing the city in the style of Babylon. He was said to have even diverted the Kydnos to do this. Certainly something of these monuments still

---

[46] Tarsos became Antiocheia in 250, not in 175 B.C.: A. H. M. Jones, *The Cities of the Eastern Roman Provinces* (1937), 217; 436, n. 13. The Revolt: 2 Macc. iv. 30–1. Coinage: H. Goldman, *Excavations at Gözlü-Tepe, Tarsus* (1950), i.: series 1: Nos. 110–28, pp. 68–9, Fig. 88; series 2: Nos. 129–45, pp. 69–70, Fig. 88; series 3: Nos. 146–69, pp. 70–1, Fig. 88–9. The plaques: *ibid.*, i. 337–8. Information on Sandon in Dio Chrys. *Or.* xxxiii; H. Goldman, "The Sandon Monument of Tarsus," *JAOS* 60 (1940), 544–5.

existed in 160 B.C. to keep alive the memory of the defeat of earlier Greeks.[47]

About the same time that Tarsos threw off Seleukid control there was a movement for independence in the temple-state of Olbe. After 160 B.C. the whole region of Kilikia gradually became more and more disorganized owing to the wars between rival members of the House of Seleukos. A general named Tryphon was for a time king—the first to have no connection with the legitimate royal family. In 146 B.C. much of Kilikia was in revolt against Alexander Balas. Taking advantage of this condition Olbe became autonomous, possibly at times completely independent, under its high priests of Tarku. Tarku, however, had been Hellenized by this time, and both god and priests went by the Greek name Teuker. Consequently it is difficult to say whether Olbe acted out of hatred for Hellenism or simply out of a desire to be free of higher control in those unhappy times. These temple states in Syria and Kilikia could not, however, take advantage of the feelings of an oppressed lower class as Sandon did at Tarsos because they themselves were slaveowners on a large scale.[48]

There was little if any resistance to Antiochos IV in Syria. The legends on the autonomous coinage of Phoenician cities began to be written in Aramaic alongside the Greek but this occurred even under Antiochos. In the period after 150 B.C., some towns and tribes, particularly those on the fringes of the desert, were able to gain or regain a measure of autonomy. But to call this Oriental resistance to Hellenism itself seems to go too far. The breaking away of these communities in a well-Hellenized area took place under auspices that show little trace of intensely national inspiration. Their autonomy came more from the weakening of the central power than from resurgence of the old culture. Syria for a long time retained a feeling of loyalty to the Makedonian regime, and the cities there hailed Demetrios II "Nikator" for his defeats of the Parthians in 140 B.C.[49]

[47] Lysias: Athen. v. 215 BC; he is not in *R.E.* The linen-workers of A.D. 100: Dio Chrys. *Or.* xxxiv. 21, 23. Sennacherib: Eusebios, *Chron.* 14, 17–8 (ed. Karst); D. D. Luckenbill, *Ancient Records of Assyria and Babylonia* (1927), ii. §§ 286–8, pp. 137–8; A. H. M. Jones, *The Cities of the Eastern Roman Provinces* (1937), 193–5.
The Greeks of Tarsos claimed to be descendants of colonists led variously by Argives: Strabo xiv. 5. 12 (673); Perseus: Lucan, *Phar.* iii. 225; and Herakles: Dio Chrys. *Or.* xxxiii. 1, 47. Does this indicate Greek factions?

[48] Tryphon and Seleukids: A. R. Bellinger, "The End of the Seleucids," *Transactions of the Connecticut Academy of Arts and Sciences* 38 (1949), 56–8. Revolt: 1 Macc. xi. 14. Olbe: Strabo xiv. 5. 10 (673); D. Magie, *Roman Rule in Asia Minor* (1950), ii. 1143–4, n. 23.

[49] Coinage: P. Gardner, *B.M.C. Seleucid Kings of Syria* (1878), Nos. 50–6, p. 39. Autonomy in general: E. R. Bevan, *The House of Seleucus* (1902), ii. 153, 156; M. I. Rostovtzeff in *C.A.H.* vii. 190. "Nikator": App. *Syr.* x. 67.

Antiochos' program of Hellenic urbanization collapsed with his death. His successors were unwilling to carry on a policy that generated such widespread resistance in the East. His plans had won him also the nickname "Madman" (*Epimanēs*) from Greeks. The Seleukids attempted to conciliate their disaffected subjects, and the coinage reflected the change. Timarchos, a Milesian satrap of Media, made alliance with Artaxias of Armenia and revolted against Seleukid Demetrios I Soter in 162 B.C. He issued coins inscribed with the Oriental title "Great King"—*Basileōs megalou Timarchou.* His revolt was quashed, and numerous coins of his conqueror Demetrios showed a Tyche seated on a throne supported by a winged female monster, which may have represented the Mesopotamian goddess of chaos, Tiamat. Demetrios may thus have identified his victory over Timarchos and his other enemies as victory over Chaos and sought to explain this to his Asiatic subjects.[50]

All over western Asia the age following the death of Antiochos Epiphanes was a time of troubles. Elam became independent, but had to fight to preserve her sovereignty from the advancing Parthians. Within the Seleukid dynasty there was constant intrigue that led to the murder of more than one king and much fighting over the succession. These intestine conflicts were duplicated in Greek cities in Syria and northern Mesopotamia, where rival parties backed one or the other of the Seleukid claimants. In these circumstances, the advance of the Parthians was much facilitated, so that around 140 B.C. Mithradates I captured Babylonia. During the next few years the region changed hands several times as the Seleukids sought to retake and hold this important country. There is no evidence, however, that the priests of Marduk or any other Babylonians assisted the Parthians, their recent opposition to Antiochos IV notwithstanding. Parthian rule was unrewarding for the old gods. At Uruk, the Temple of Anu had been destroyed, probably by accident, soon after its reconstruction by Anu-uballit II. In the Parthian period it was not restored. People erected only little huts in the ruins, and in the court of the Anu-Antum sanctuary a small Parthian shrine. In E-sagila, Marduk was still enthroned, and tablets written by his clergy show that they accepted Parthian occupation without comment, as they did the earlier Makedonian occupation. Attempts on the part of Demetrios II and

---

[50] Timarchos and his revolt: Diod. xxxi. 27a. 1; App. *Syr.* ix. 45–7; *R.E.*, R. II, vi. 1, Nu. 5, S. 1237–8. His coinage: P. Gardner, *B.M.C. Seleucid Kings of Syria* (1878), Nos. 2–4, p. 50; Pl. xxviii. 6; xv. 3. Demetrios' coinage, *loc. cit.*, Nos. 6–35, pp. 45–7, Pl. xiv. 1–2. See, too, R. H. McDowell, *Stamped and Inscribed Objects from Seleucia on the Tigris* (1935), 218–20; *Coins from Seleucia on the Tigris* (1935), 55–6.

Antiochos VII to regain Babylon were chronicled in a flat style that showed no emotion for or against either the victories or the defeats of the Seleukid kings. On the other hand, neither does the Seleukid coinage of this period show that the dynasty advertised their phil-Orientalism to mollify their old Mesopotamian subjects and compete for their allegiance. Only a few coins of Demetrios II show a male figure bearded in Asiatic fashion and wearing Parthian dress. But even this figure grasps the hand of a Greek city goddess who advances holding a cornucopia.[51] Both the Parthians and the Makedonians fought for Babylonia without much thought for Babylonian sympathies and without any real Babylonian support. The spirit of Babylonia was dying, and if the Marduk clergy passively accepted the Parthians it was because Marduk himself was faltering through lack of support and would soon be but a memory. Elam, however, resisted the Arsakids as strongly as they had sought to drive out the Makedonians. When Demetrios II Nikator fought the Parthians he was assisted by an Elamite contingent, but not by Babylonians. Justin, probably thinking of Persis and Elam, says that the "Eastern people" hated Arsakid cruelty and deemed the Makedonians more worthy of kingship. Several years later Antiochos VII attacked the Parthians and received the help of the small eastern dynasts. But presently there was, as we have seen, an Oriental reaction against him; he was forced to retire to the West.[52]

During the century between the death of Antiochos IV and the advent of the Romans under Pompey in 63 B.C., there was no sudden change in favor of revived Orientalism in areas for which there is evidence. Where the Western Asians did not try firmly to re-establish their old institutions and cultural ideals they could hardly have attacked Hellenism strongly. It is true that at the end of the first century B.C. there was racial rioting in Seleukeia-on-Tigris, on the one hand by Jews and Syrians against Greeks, but on the other by Greeks and Syrians against Jews. The archaeological evidence shows that Seleukeia in the early Parthian period remained a Greek city. Figurines show a very slow shift away from Hellenistic motifs towards Oriental types and styles.[53] But this shift was so gradual that it must have been

---

[51] Uruk: F. Wetzel, *Das Babylon der Spätzeit* (1957), 30. Tablets: T. G. Pinches, *Historical Records and Legends of Assyria and Babylonia* (1st ed., 1902), 481–2; A. T. Olmstead, "Cuneiform Texts and Hellenistic Chronology," *CPh* 32 (1937), 12–3. Demetrios' coins: R. Gardner, *B.M.C. Seleucid Kings of Syria* (1878), Nos. 24–5, p. 78, Pl. xxi. 8.

[52] Just. xxxvi. 1; xxxviii. 10.

[53] Riots: Jos. *Ant.* xviii. 374–9. General shift: W. van Ingen, *Figurines from Seleucia on the Tigris* (1939), 8, 18–9, 23.

the result of the natural numerical decline of Greeks, who dwelt after all in an ocean of Babylonians. Plutarch says that Seleukeia-on-Tigris and Babylon were always hostile to the Parthians. The Greeks in this region did appeal to Demetrios II to rescue them from the Parthians. But after his defeat we hear of no more appeals. There are literary references to the Seleukeians' maintaining their Greek way of life intact for a long time. At Babylon in 111 B.C. Greek athletic games and Greek ephebic training continued under the control of a Greek *gymnasiarchos*. But with such stylish Hellenic institutions gradual decline also soon began. When Amphikrates the Rhetorician visited Seleukeia around 85 B.C. he treated the education of the Greeks with contempt. They asked him to lecture; he retorted that a stewpan could not hold a dolphin, and departed for Armenia.[54]

Between 140 and 100 B.C. conditions of life in lower Babylonia were terribly confusing and uncertain, owing to the military vicissitudes of states and dynasts and the political and economic whirl that afflicted individual men. For these times, however, there is no evidence that an anti-Hellenic policy was anywhere invoked. Instead, kings and dynasts followed a policy of opportunity. An Iranian ex-satrap of the Seleukid Empire named Hyspaosines occupied and rebuilt an old Greek town named Charax about 140 B.C., and he began to build up the little kingdom of Charakene around it. He relied on the support of both Greek and Babylonian notables, one of the latter named Itti-marduk-balatu.[55] Hyspaosines had to fight against the Hyrkanian Greek Himeros, governor of Babylonia for the Parthian King Phraates II (*c.* 138–*c.* 128 B.C.). Himeros' regime was relentless. He carried out executions among the magnates of both Seleukeia and Babylon, perhaps because these persons supported the invasion of Seleukid Antiochos VII into Mesopotamia. There was violence in Babylon; part of the market and some temples were burned and Babylonians sold into slavery in Media. Some of these persons must have been Greek. At the same time, however, Himeros was a friend of the man Lysimachos of Babylon. Himeros may have rebelled against Phraates; he did issue a currency stamped with Dionysos tricked out as an

[54] Plut. *Cras.* vii. 4. Appeal: Jos. *Ant.* xiii. 184–6. Greek life: Livy xxxvii. 54. 18; Pliny, *N.H.* vi. 122; Tac. *Ann.* vi. 42. Livy directly contradicts himself at xxxviii. 17. 11. Babylon: B. Haussoullier, "Inscriptions grecques de Babylone," *Klio* 9 (1909), 352–63; his readings emended by C. B. Welles and M. I. Rostovtzeff, *op. cit.*, 40–1. Amphikrates: Plut. *Luc.* xxii. 5.

[55] Pliny, *N.H.* vi. 139; Loukianos, *Makrobios* 16; W. W. Tarn in *C.A.H.* ix. 578, 584; E. T. Newell, "Mithradates of Parthia and Hyspaosines of Charax," *NNM* 25 (1925); R. H. McDowell, *The Coins of Seleucia on the Tigris* (1935), 202–3, 219; A. R. Bellinger, "Hyspaosines of Charax," *YClS* 8 (1942), 51–67.

Asiatic. About the same time another Parthian governor of Akkad duly performed sacrifices at E-sagila, and the Marduk clergy duly uttered prayers for the long life and prosperity of the Arsakid monarchs. Temple tablets mention simultaneous incursions of "Elamites" into Babylonia. The Babylonians probably respected the power of the Parthians to protect them and hoped that they could soon establish order.

About 130 or 125 B.C. Hyspaosines was at war with Elymaïs. We do not know the result. Unfortunately for the independence of Chara-kene, the district was conquered by Parthian Mithradates II around 122, about the same time that he reconquered Babylon.[56] A wealthy Babylonian named Hadad-nadin-akhi about 100 B.C. restored an old palace at Tello and fitted up a museum with ancient artifacts. This was a safe form of nonpolitical activity. In none of this was anti-Hellenism apparent. The Parthians did not even garrison Seleukeia. And, on the other hand, for the period after 129 there is no evidence that the Seleukeians tried to revolt against the Parthians.[57]

A dynasty subordinate to the Parthians now ruled in Charakene. The princes claimed Seleukid succession and continued a coinage deeply influenced by Seleukid prototypes. Its usual type was Herakles. In the reign of Tiraios I (c. 90 B.C.) workmanship became less Greek; in the reign of Tiraios II (c. 60 B.C.) the coin legends were written in Aramaic alongside the Greek. By the end of the first century A.D. both types and legends were exclusively Aramaic.[58]

In Elam, too, Hellenism remained for a while an influence under the native dynasts, the Kamnaskirids. Greek ways continued in Seleu-keia-on-Eulaios, where about 75 B.C. Nikolaos was gymnasiarch. Hellenism does not seem to have touched the countryside, however. After the end of Seleukid kingship the Kamnaskirids were plagued by considerable brigandage which they were unable to control. Strabo implies that its source was the hill people, who had never really been conquered by the Seleukids, and that it was directed against settled

---

[56] Himeros: Diod. xxxiv. 21; Poseidonios, *Histories* xvi = Athen. xi. 466 BC; Just. xlii–xliii. E. T. Newell, "A Parthian Hoard," *NC* 5th Ser., 4 (1924), 174–7; A. R. Bellinger, "Hyspaosines of Charax," *YClS* 8 (1942), 59–61. N. C. Debevoise, *A Political History of Parthia* (1938), 38–40. Marduk: T. G. Pinches, *Historical Records and Legends of Assyria and Babylonia* (1st ed., 1902), 483–4.

[57] Tello: A. R. Bellinger, "Hyspaosines of Charax," *YClS* 8 (1942), 54–5. Seleukeia: Strabo xvi. 1. 16 (743); R. H. McDowell, *The Coins of Seleucia on the Tigris* (1935), 216–22.

[58] G. F. Hill, *B.M.C. Arabia, Mesopotamia, and Persia* (1922), cxciv–cxcviii; J. de Morgan, *T.M.G.R.* (1935), iii. 494, 517–9; Nos. 1–11, pp. 527–30, Pl. xl. 1–7; W. W. Tarn in *C.A.H.* ix. 578.

farmers and the cities. Whether these *barbaroi* had had anything to do with defending Nanaia against Antiochos IV is unknown. Since Hellenism was known only in the cities, it is likely that in Elam there was a union of the dominant Elamite notables and the Hellenized commercial people for mutual cooperation. Hellenism was valuable to the Elamite princes, who had to defend their precarious independence from the Arsakids. Around 140 B.C. Mithradates I raided Elam and relieved the Temple of Nanaia of about ten thousand talents because Elamites had supported Demetrios II in a war against the Parthians. On account of these ever-present dangers the dynasty relied upon Greeks who could supply the technical accompaniments for Kamnaskirid autonomy. The coinage of the founder of the dynasty, Kamnaskires I Nikephoros, was executed in very fine Hellenic style, the portraiture even modelled on that of Antiochos IV, would-be plunderer of the Nanaia temple. The reverses displayed a very fine Apollo. The currency retained its European flavor throughout the first century B.C., but after the Arsakids captured Elam about 35 B.C., the issues of Kamnaskires IV and V began to show influence from Parthia.[59]

As the Seleukid Empire broke up, in Syria there was a mad scramble for political authority by all manner of competing people. There is no evidence, however, that Hellenism per se was attacked. A Kingdom of Edessa arose in northern Syria under an Arab dynasty. We know virtually nothing of its history in Hellenistic times. Along the fringes of the southern Syrian desert a Nabataian Arab state came into existence at the beginning of the first century B.C. After the defeat and death of the Seleukid Antiochos XII, its king Aretas was asked by the people of Damaskos to rule them with the city as capital. They deemed the Itouraian Arabs a worse threat. The latter lived in Lebanon and were a people devoted to robbing and pillaging. About 115 B.C. they developed a loosely organized state and founded a reli-

[59] Gymnasiarch: *S.E.G.* vii. 3. Brigands: Strabo xv. 3. 12 (732) ; xvi. 1. 17–8 (744) ; W. W. Tarn in *C.A.H.* ix. 578; J. de Morgan, *T.M.G.R.* (1935) , iii. 420–7. Parthian threat: Strabo xvi. 1. 18 (744–5) ; Just. xli. 6; xlii. 1; W. W. Tarn in *C.A.H.* ix. 579–80. Parthian capture and social history: *S.E.G.* vii. 1; F. Cumont, "Une lettre du roi Artabanus III à la ville de Suse," *CRAI* (1932) , 238–60; A. G. Roos, "Bemerkungen zu einer griechischen Inschrift aus Susa," *Mnemosyne* 3rd Ser., 1 (1934) , 106–12; C. B. Welles, *The Royal Correspondence of the Hellenistic Period* (1934) , No. 75, pp. 299–306; M. Engers, "The Letter from the Parthian King Artabanus III to the Town of Susa," *Mnemosyne* 3rd Ser., 7 (1939) , 136–41.

Kamnaskirid coinage: G. F. Hill, *B.M.C. Arabia, Mesopotamia, and Persia* (1922) , pp. clxxxvi–clviii; 245–52; Pl. liii. 6; xxxviii. 1–xxxix. 11; J. de Morgan, *T.M.G.R.* (1935) , iii. 456–8, Nos. 1–8; pp. 465–8, Pl. xxxv. 1, 3–10; the Apollo coin is No. 1; W. W. Tarn, *The Greeks in Bactria and India* (2nd ed., 1951) , 465–6.

gious center at Ba'albek where a priest-tetrarch presided. The first two
of them were the Hellenized Mennaios and Ptolemy, the latter being
the threat to Damaskos. Aretas not only dealt with him but also
made successful war on the Jews to the south. Aretas' coinage was
copied from the issues of the last Seleukid kings. Further to the south
another Nabataian state came into being around Petra. These Arabs
quickly identified their Arabian gods with Greek: Dusares was Dionysos. They learned the arts of sculpture and architecture and techniques of engineering and long-distance trading from Greeks or
Hellenized Orientals and presently produced a remarkable blend of
these elements adapted to the peculiar geographical conditions of
the country. These Nabataians also were involved in wars with the
Jews; about 100 B.C. Obedas I roundly defeated Alexander Iannaios.[60]

The Seleukids, torn by their own dynastic wars, were utterly unable
to keep order, and in the scramble to fill the vacuum Edessans and
Itouraians, Seleukids, both legitimate kings and aggressive pretenders,
and Nabataians indulged in a bewildering whirl of wars and alliances
with one another. If the Arab peoples escaped from Seleukid control
so did the Greek cities. By the beginning of the first century, Antioch,
Seleukeia-in-Pieria, Laodikeia, and Apamea were all autonomous.
The Seleukid kings were unable to cope with the brigandage that
made life miserable. At Kyrrhestike a band of robbers established
itself around the Herakleion and carried out serious raids in the
country round about until the Romans stopped them in 63. Bandits
actually overran Byblos and Berytos. These bands of robbers were
made up of people of all cultures; they were not simple Arabs. Because
of this dreadful chaos neither the Syrians in the country nor the
Greeks in the cities wished to dissipate their resources by being
dragged along in the train of the feeble Seleukids; safety could be won
only by their own efforts. The idea of secession naturally led to faction
in the cities, but faction that knew no cultural boundaries. Nisibis,
formally Antiocheia-in-Mygdonia, reverted to its old name, and a regime of Hellenic and Syrian notables led by Kallimachos governed
the place. In Antioch itself, the old capital of Nikator, parties of
Greeks arose, one favoring Armenian Tigranes, another Pontian
Mithradates, and a third loyal to the *ancien régime*. All these persons

[60] Edessa: G. F. Hill, *B.M.C. Arabia, Mesopotamia, and Persia* (1922), xciv–xcv;
W. W. Tarn in *C.A.H.* ix. 586. Damaskos: G. F. Hill, *op. cit.*, xi–xiii, 1–3, Pl. i. 1–5;
Jos. *War* 103, 115; *Ant.* xiii. 392. Itouraians: Jos., *locs. cit.*; Strabo xvi. 2. 10 (753);
A. H. M. Jones, *The Cities of the Eastern Roman Provinces* (1937), 255–6. Petra
Nabataians: Strabo xvi. 4. 21–3 (779–80); N. Glueck, *Rivers in the Desert* (1959),
193–230; Obedas: Jos. *Ant.* xiii. 375–6.

were looking for security in this time of heavy troubles. In such a time an anti-Hellenic religious policy would have been a foolish luxury for anyone. Justin says that the people of Syria, exhausted by these wars and raids, looked eagerly for help from any strong king that could save them: they finally accepted the Romans.[61]

In Kilikia the declining Seleukids lost control of the whole country. Seleukos, son of Antiochos VIII, was killed in Kilikia when the people of Mopsouhestia burned him to death in the gymnasium of the city. Chaos replaced empire, and the region had a taste of Syria's bitter experience. Well might Dionysos of Tarsos say in his epitaph: "I never married and I wish my father never had." Late in the second century B.C., an independent state came into being here too, and it became particularly active after 90 B.C. raiding Greek temples by sea. The Kilikians struck at shrines located at Klaros, Didyma, Samothrake, Hermione, Epidauros, Corinth, Tainaron, Kalauria, Aktion, Samos, Argos, and Lakinion. According to Plutarch, moreover, these pirates introduced the cult of the god Mithra to the Mediterranean world, and also offered strange sacrifices of their own to some other god or gods.[62] This was not, however, anti-Hellenism.

As for the attacks on temples, while we know little about the personnel aboard the Kilikian ships, there is no reason to believe that they were exclusively, or even preponderantly, Asiatic. The state seems to have come into existence to fill the post-Seleukid vacuum of power in Kilikia, and its population therefore crossed cultural and ethnic boundaries. Looting Greek temples, however widespread and far afield it may have been, was done simply to acquire wealth and does not reflect any Mithraic hostility to Hellenic gods. The pirates' field of operations was determined for them: they were a sea power and struck therefore at temples near the coast, particularly temples that were weakly defended, as indeed many Greek temples were during these sad times.

As for Mithra, this god actually arrived in Asia Minor in the fourth century or earlier, and his cult flourished especially in Kappadokia and Pontos, aside from Kilikia. In coming this far west, Mithra lost some of

---

[61] Autonomous cities: A. R. Bellinger, *The Excavations at Dura-Europos* vi: *The Coins* (ed. M. I. Rostovtzeff *et al.*, 1949), 73–86; D. B. Waage, *Antioch-on-the-Orontes*, IV, 2: *Greek, Roman, Byzantine and Crusader's Coins* (1952), 69–70. Kyrrhestike, Byblos, and Berytos: Strabo xvi. 2. 8 (751); xvi. 2. 18 (755). Nisibis: Plut. *Luc.* xxxi. 3–5. Antioch: Just. xl. 1; Plut. *Luc.* xxi. 2. Justin: xl. 2. General conditions in Syria: M. I. Rostovtzeff in *C.A.H.* vii. 164; *S.E.H.H.W.* i. 427–8.

[62] Mopsouhestia: App. *Syr.* xi. 69. The Kilikian "Pirates": Strabo xiv. 5. 2 (668–9); App. *Mith.* viii. 56; ix. 63; Plut. *Pom.* xxiv. 1–5; xxviii. 1–4.

his native Persian characteristics and added Babylonian, Anatolian, and even Greek traits. But for these changes Mithras might have been an ideal god to inspire opposition to Hellenism, for in Iran he had been originally a god of truth and integrity, a foe of lying and broken contracts, an enemy of evil spirits, hateful towards the wicked, the spiritually impure, and the godless. But there is simply no evidence that Mithras was used in Asia Minor to further anti-Hellenism. The cult could not be used in this way because it was adopted by people of Greek background on a very large scale. The ethics, moreover, of the new Greco-Iranian god called for an ascetic way of life and a renunciation of the pleasures of this world. Mithras became a savior and giver of life.[63]

In summary, then, our survey of Oriental religious resistance to Hellenism in Western Asia has found little determined hostility. There was no deep-seated, widespread, consistently emphatic resistance to Makedonian rule and Hellenic society such as there was in Persis. This must be explained.

Oriental resistance always proceeded from an ideology established before the coming of the Europeans. Persian resistance was an effort to recover world rule for Ahura Mazdāh. There was no such thing as a tradition of world rule in Syria, Elam, or Kilikia. Syria had never even been united under home rule, but rather was a collection of temple-states or city-states. Syria's only unity came when she was included in the empire of some outside power. Much the same had been true of Kilikia. This was not quite true of Elam, for around 1200 B.C. a vigorous state had existed, and it had even carried fire and sword into Mesopotamia. Babylon was sacked and the famous stele with the Code of Hammurapi was taken off to Susa, the capital of Elam. But the memory of glory was already nine hundred years old in the Greek period, and does not seem to have inspired resistance. Elam certainly defended herself more successfully than Syria or even Babylonia, espe-

---

[63] In Asia Minor: A. D. Nock, *Conversion* (1933), 41–2; F. Cumont, "Mithra en Asie Mineure," *Anatolian Studies Presented to William Hepburn Butler* (1939), 67–76; M. J. Vermaseren, *Corpus Inscriptionum et Monumentorum Religionis Mithriacaei* (1956), 44.

His Persian origins: *Mithra Yasht*, translation and commentary in I. Gershevitch, *The Avestan Hymn to Mithra* (1959); Xen. *Kyro.* vii. 5. 53; Douris, *Histories* vii = Athen. x. 434 EF; Loukianos, *Menippos* 16.

Mithrism: F. Cumont, *The Mysteries of Mithra* (1903), esp. 3–12, 20–31, 137–46, 175; W. J. Phythian-Adams, *Mithraism* (1915), esp. 9–17; A. D. Nock, "Behn, Das Mithrasheiligtum zu Dieburg" (review), *Gnomon* 6 (1930), 30–5; *Conversion* (1933), 44, 75; M. J. Vermaseren, *op. cit.*, and A. D. Nock's review in *Gnomon* 30 (1958), 291–5.

cially when threatened with Hellenization by Antiochos III and IV. But she had the advantage of being a hill country far removed from the main body of Greeks and Makedonians in the plains of Babylonia and Syria. Opposition to the Seleukid dynasty, outside of Babylonia proper, came only from scattered, local areas, and was motivated by local, *ad hoc,* political or economic expediency. An example of this was Tarsos, which insisted on independence when forced to undertake a closer relationship to the empire of Antiochos IV.

But if one can explain the lack of real hostility to Hellenism in the fringe areas of Babylonian culture, one is still faced with the problem of explaining the lack of determined opposition in Mesopotamia itself. Here was indeed a great imperial tradition of fairly recent times centered around the name of the illustrious Nebuchadnezzar. His memory had animated the Babylonians to revolt against their Persian masters between 522 and 482 B.C.

But Babylonian revolts against the Achaemenids were confined to the early period of Persian Empire, and there was no military opposition after the reign of Xerxes. There was even increasing collaboration, and the Persian court was influenced by Babylonian culture. After 450 B.C. and on into the Makedonian period, hatred of foreign powers cooled. The Babylonian resistance literature was essentially passive, and as we know it, only once prophesied destruction for the Greeks. The Persian apocalypses, on the other hand, looked forward optimistically and aggressively to the violent overthrow of the Seleukids. The "Semiramis" and "Nebuchadnezzar Legends" brooded about the vanished past, and their archaism and choice of a heroine instead of a hero were alarming symptoms of decay. The approaching end of Babylonians' allegiance to native traditions and institutions was advertised by the lack of vigor in these poor phantasies. Semiramis was made merely to copy first a Persian and then a Makedonian. While the Babylonian gods were still worshipped in the first century B.C., and still attracted Greeks to their service,[64] nonetheless they were fading in popular esteem as surely as the culture as a whole was failing. The last cuneiform tablet we have dates from 7 B.C. An atmosphere of impotence pervaded Mesopotamia and stifled Babylonian resistance. An atmosphere of faith ran through Persis, and Persian culture would undergo a renaissance in the Sassanid period.

For a long time before Alexander the men of Babylonia had been in the grip of despondency and despair, and this deep-seated pessimism had in fact touched some souls deeply even in the days of glory. It

[64] W. W. Tarn in *C.A.H.* ix. 596–7.

only received impetus when the Chaldean Empire rattled down. Highly placed Babylonians long before the Greek period had decided subconsciously that life was ephemeral and human achievement vainglory. Thorkild Jacobsen has remarked that if a Babylonian of the old days could be revived and could accompany a modern expedition first to Egypt to behold the still-abiding granite pyramids, and then to Iraq to observe the broken mud remains of his once-imposing, now perished ziggurats, he could only feel that his ancient beliefs had been fully justified by time. The folk hero Gilgamesh had once said, with great feeling, "As for mankind, numbered are their days; whatever they achieve is but the wind."[65]

The Babylonian attitude towards being conquered is well expressed in the *Lamentation over the Destruction of Ur.* In the wake of the victory of Elamites and Subarians, a Sumerian poet of the twentieth century B.C. bleated piteously that he had been deserted by his gods:

> Enlil has abandoned Nippur, his sheepfold has been delivered to the wind;
> His wife Ninlil has abandoned her stable, her sheepfold has been delivered to the wind;
> The Queen of Kish has abandoned her stable, her sheepfold has been delivered to the wind;
> Ninmah has abandoned their house Kesh, her sheepfold has been delivered to the wind;
> She who is of Isin has abandoned her stable, her sheepfold has been delivered to the wind;
> Ninisinna has abandoned the Shrine Egalmah, her sheepfold has been delivered to the wind. . . .

and so on through a list of eighteen gods and goddesses. After this enumeration, the poem begins its lamentation:

> O city, a bitter lament, set up as thy lament;
> Thy lament which is bitter—O city, set up thy lament.
> His righteous city which has been destroyed—bitter is its lament;
> His Ur which has been destroyed—bitter is its lament;
> Thy lament which is bitter—O city, set up thy lament;
> His Ur which has been destroyed—bitter is its lament.
> Thy lament which is bitter—how long will it grieve thy weeping lord?

[65] Jacobsen: in H. I. Frankfort *et al., The Intellectual Adventure of Ancient Man* (1946), 125; Gilgamesh: in "The Gilgamesh Epic," *A.N.E.T.*, iii. 4. 7–8, 79.

Thy lament which is bitter—how long will it grieve the weeping Nanna?[66]

Here Nanna, god of Ur, like King Richard II, sits upon the ground and cries. If Babylonian gods wept impotently, what of Babylonian man?

Such an attitude of defeat was part and parcel of the concept of human nature. Human beings were thought to have been made of a mixture of river mud and the blood of a wicked god Kingu, who had been the consort of the personification of Evil Tiamat. The Babylonian was, therefore, bewitched by a sense of his own worthlessness and sin and bemused by the conviction of his own weakness and frailty. Even proud Esarhaddon, king of Assyria and scourge of mankind, in his secret heart of hearts constantly sought to relieve himself of terror and to win the reassurance of his familiar and tutelary spirits, who as constantly comforted him, "King of Assyria, fear not!"[67] This same Esarhaddon in his public texts boasted that he had wounded Pharaoh Tirhaka five times with his mighty bow and had slain King Inib-Teshub in personal combat.

When the Babylonian was afflicted he bowed his head and waited for relief from the outside. This attitude is well illustrated by the Sumero-Babylonian penitential psalms, as well as the interesting document *I Will Praise the Lord of Wisdom,* wherein a righteous sufferer after enduring patiently is saved by Marduk's intervention.[68] A feeling of the helplessness and uselessness of human existence is expressed with great feeling in the later Babylonian *Dialogue about Human Misery* and the *Dialogue between Master and Servant.* The latter says that there is really nothing either good or bad, and that everything happens as the result of chance.[69] An expression of the pathos in the Babylonian mind occurred in the episode in the *Akitu*-festival wherein the King of Sumer and Akkad and the Four World Quarters was struck by the Priest of Marduk. The king's face was anxiously regarded. If he wept, all was well, the coming year would be auspicious. If he did not cry, "The god Marduk is angry; the enemy will rise up

---

[66] "Lamentation over the Destruction of Ur," *A.N.E.T.*, 11. 4–20, 40–7, pp. 455–6. The gods cowered like dogs during the flood, fearful of the violence of Enlil's storm.

[67] "Oracles Concerning Esarhaddon," *A.N.E.T.*, 449–50.

[68] Examples of penitential psalms, *ibid.*, 383 ff.; "I Will Praise the Lord of Wisdom," *ibid.*, 434–7.

[69] "Dialogue about Human Misery," *A.N.E.T.*, 438–40. "A Pessimistic Dialogue between Master and Servant," *ibid.*, 437–8.

and bring about his (the king's) downfall."[70] Safety lies in tears.
The Babylonian penchant for withdrawal from crisis was sensed by
certain Greeks of the Hellenistic period. They thought Babylonians
womanly hedonists and expressed their contempt in stories about
Sardanapalos, a legendary king of the Assyrians. He was supposed to
have summed up his ideals in the famous sentence, "Eat, drink, and
be merry, because all things else are not worth a snap of the fingers."
He was said to have dressed like a woman among the concubines of
his harem.[71] While this was a judgment passed by foreigners, it was
nonetheless echoed in native literature. When the Babylonians created
legends around which patriotic spirits might rally, they once chose
the figure of the Queen Semiramis. Under similar circumstances the
Egyptians remembered their conquering king Sesostris, the Hebrews
David. The Greeks thought of the Syrians in similar vein, and considered them to be the superstitious votaries of an Asiatic goddess who
had forbidden them to eat fish, from which they abstained without
question.[72]

The feelings of helplessness which the Mesopotamians felt in themselves they of course transferred to the gods, and this explains why
Marduk and the rest of the pantheon never inspired the violent literature which Ahura Mazdāh, Yahweh, and Re did. According to the
Creation Epic, *Enuma elish,* the dread goddess Tiamat prepared to
fight these gods with a battle array of monster serpents, sharp of
tooth and unsparing of fang, warring dragons clothed with terror, the
viper, the horrible sphinx, the great lion, the mad dog, the scorpion
men. She proceeded to declare war against the good gods. Then Anu
their chief could not face her and abjectly reported that he was too
weak to prevail. The gods stared dumbly at the ground, for they did
not think themselves capable of fighting Tiamat and surviving. So
fragile was the pantheon. When a champion was finally found in shin-
ing Marduk, he was able to blackmail the others into making him
their ruler as the price of fighting Tiamat. Similarly, at the time of
the Deluge, the gods were appalled at their handiwork, and cowered
like dogs in the highest corner of heaven.[73]

With such a pantheon how could Babylonians be inspired to resist?

[70] "Temple Program for the New Year's Festival at Babylon," *A.N.E.T.*, 331–4.
The quotation is lines 445–55. This text comes from the Greek period.

[71] Strabo xiv. 5. 9 (672) ; he also quotes the poet Choirilos who used the same
story; Chrysippos = Athen. viii. 335 F–336 B. See, further, n. 12, p. 106 above.

[72] Antipater of Tarsos, *On Superstition* iv = Athen. viii. 346 CD; Mnesias, *On Asia*
ii = Athen. viii. 347 DE.

[73] Tiamat: "The Creation Epic," *A.N.E.T.*, iii. 15–iv. 121, pp. 64–9. The Flood:
"Gilgamesh Epic," *ibid.*, xi. 11–6, p. 94.

The gods fixed the destinies of men and states, and the gods were most of them cowards. There was no escape from their pusillanimous decree. It was believed, moreover, that once the bird god Zu had stolen Marduk's tablets on which were engraved the destinies for the year. With these in his control Zu threw the entire cosmos into confusion.[74] Therefore even Marduk was vulnerable. And thus the Babylonians lived in an uncertain environment always vaguely threatened with disaster.

That this feeling of sin, helplessness, and despair existed in the Hellenistic period can be seen in a penitential psalm dated to 287/6 B.C., copied from a tablet obviously much older:

> For the misfortunes of Uruk, for the misfortunes of Agade, I am stricken.
> The Lady of Uruk wept, that departed was her might;
> The Lady of Agade wept that departed was her glory.
>
> .....
>
> The Lady of Dunna wept, Who has a resting place, who has leave to go forth?
> Whose is it to defeat the enemy, with the exits cut off?
>
> .....
>
> Weep for Uruk, ravaging and shame has she received.
>
> .....
>
> The throne of my glory has been caused to pass away from me;
> The bridegroom, the husband of my well-being, Marduk has been taken from me.[75]

The state of Babylonian culture in this last age of its existence is portrayed symbolically in the *Ninos Romance.* It is extant in Greek on a papyrus from the end of the first century B.C. or the beginning of the first century of the Christian era. Ninos at one time had been thought of as the militant founder of the Kingdom of Assyria. But in the romance he is only a lover—he wins a chaste young woman by his own virtue and purity. He makes war on Armenia, but he employs Greek and Karian mercenaries to do his fighting for him.[76] This is the Babylonian of the Hellenistic period, passive, relying on inaction, dependent on his Greek contemporaries.

It is true that Hellenism in the East itself eventually faltered and

---

[74] "The Myth of Zu," *A.N.E.T.,* 111–3.

[75] T. G. Pinches, *Historical Records and Legends of Assyria and Babylonia* (1st ed., 1902) , 477–8.

[76] *Ninos Romance* (ed. S. Gaselee) in *Parthenius* (Loeb Classical Library, 1935) , 382–99.

died, overcome by a revival of the Orient. But it should be noted that the traditional culture of Babylonians died earlier on its own native ground. Their wish to retreat into the past was unavailing, for there is always only the present to live in and the future to prepare for. Babylonia died even while Strabo wrote, "The Babylonians bewail their dead and bury them in honey, first smearing them with wax."[77]

[77] Strabo xvi. 1. 21 (746).

Chapter VII

The Anatolians

The Greco-Makedonian conquest and occupation of Anatolia north-west of the Tauros Mountains did not result in native anti-Hellenic religious resistance. In this chapter I shall be principally concerned with explaining why it did not occur, and with examining the warlike movements of Aristonikos and Mithradates VI to show that these men did not act as they did out of a hatred for the institutions of Hellenic civilization.

There were a good many reasons why indigenous peoples of Asia Minor did not show hostility to Hellenism. One was that by the middle of the fourth century Anatolia was already partially penetrated by Hellenism; consequently the highly placed people in a position to resist, like the priests of Marduk or the supporters of the Achaemenids, were already familiar with the ideas and methods of the Greeks when Alexander and the succeeding generations of Hellenic immigration came upon them. This early Hellenization had occurred naturally, on account of the close proximity of Hellas itself. Priests and dynasts in Asia Minor had gradually become acquainted with Hellenism as early as the sixth century, and it undoubtedly attracted them. Kroisos of Lydia maintained relations with the Delphic oracle. The ruling classes of Asia Minor imported Hellenism themselves, and this way of life was therefore not a set of strange institutions that a swaggering, victorious Makedonian government fastened on a conquered state. Alexander's conquest meant little more than an exchange of kings, that is, the expulsion of the alien Achaemenids and the acceptance of the Hellenized Makedonians.

The religious resistance in Persis was founded on the interruption of Persian cosmic kingship. Such was not the case in Hellenistic Asia Minor. There was no abolition of native imperial rule anywhere in Anatolia. The last strong state to exist there was the Lydian Empire of philhellenic Kroisos, and that state had been shattered in the sixth century B.C. by the Persian Kyros. The burning of the temples in

Persian-occupied Sardeis by the Greeks in 499 B.C. seems to have left behind no memory of cultural animosity, and in the fifth century the Temple of Kybele at Sardeis was rebuilt on the Greek pattern. The Lydian notables here subsequently had themselves buried under stelae with their names engraved in Greek, and in the fourth century the goddess accepted a dedication in the Hellenic tongue. When the Makedonian army was approaching in 334, the most important of the Sardeians and the Persian garrison commander hastened seventy stades from the city to surrender. Alexander carefully made proclamation that the Lydians were free to follow ancestral law and custom. He gave them funds to build a Temple of Zeus and wished to locate it on a fortified height in the town. Thunder and lightning unexpectedly fell, and this phenomenon was interpreted to be Zeus' sign that he desired his new house built near the palace of the ancient Lydian kings. Sardeis settled down to be a city on the Greek model, and her business men busied themselves in commerce with the Greek towns in Ionia.[1] No evidence of resentment here.

A second reason why anti-Hellenism did not exist was that Asia Minor was not culturally homogeneous. As in Parthia, the territory was shared among many different groups of people. In addition to Greek settlements around the coasts of the peninsula, there was a variety of ethnic and linguistic groups in the interior. Among them were remnants of the aboriginal people and the persons brought in by successive waves of migration: Hittites, Karians, Lykians, Kimmerians, Phrygians, and Lydians. Anatolia, more than any other region in the ancient world, except possibly Syria, was a patchwork of differing cultural groups. There were even small colonies of former eastern empire-builders and merchants, Persians and Babylonians, to add to the babel.[2] The heterogeneity of the multitude of districts never permitted the people of any one of them to have the feeling that they could prevail over the others. They had no sense in Hellenistic times that they were great enough to challenge Makedonian imperialism. Rebellion always comes from some solid bloc of people, either culturally or ideologically united. Cultural unity did not exist.

It is true that there were independent kings in Asia Minor that might have taken the lead in opposing the new rulers. But experience shows that they did not do so, because the kingdoms that they managed

[1] Funeral stelae: W. H. Buckler and D. M. Robinson, *Sardis: Greek and Latin Inscriptions* (1932), Nos. 102–3. Artemis: *loc. cit.*, No. 85. Alexander: Arr. *Anab.* i. 17. 3–6; Strabo xiii. 4. 8 (627). Commerce: Ditt. *Syll.*³, No. 273.

[2] F. Justi, "Geschichte Irans," *Grundriss der iranischen Philologie* (1904), ii. 479; A. T. Olmstead, *H.P.E.* (1948), 378, 412, 414, 422, 502.

were weak themselves. This was true even of the state of Kappadokia, which came into existence partly because survivors of the Achaemenid army defeated in the Battle of Issos retreated into this territory. Probably supported by these forces, a Persian named Ariarathes became the independent dynast here, ruling from 331 to 322 B.C. He began in defiance, minting coins depicting an Oriental gryphon devouring a Greek stag.[3] The difficulties that the Makedonians had in controlling the inner areas of Asia Minor are well illustrated by this chapter in the history of Kappadokia. After the death of Alexander, the Makedonians attacked Ariarathes. Perdikkas fell upon his army reputedly 45,000 strong, which shows it contained native troops. Perdikkas won and killed Ariarathes. The area then came under the control of the Greek Eumenes of Kardia. For a time this new regime was supported by some of the local military aristocracy, as the mixed nationalities in Eumenes' army indicate. Perhaps these persons were glad to be rid of the moribund Achaemenids. Perhaps they would be glad, too, to be rid of Eumenes so that they could live in peace. The shifting fortunes of the Wars of the Successors did in fact force Eumenes to quit Kappadokia, though not because of a native push. These wars then lasted throughout the two last decades of the fourth century. A nobleman named Mithradates, apparently a distant descendant of the Achaemenid dynasty, took advantage of this, and eluded defeat by Antigonos the One-Eyed. He established himself in Kappadokia and founded a dynasty that was to endure until 63 B.C.[4] But, probably profiting by the example of Ariarathes, he was cautious. He did not wish to lose his throne to the powerful Seleukids or to Lysimachos. There is no evidence that he tried to eliminate these states or to encourage others to do so in any way.

Under similar circumstances other dynasts arose in other parts of Asia Minor, making Pisidia, Bithynia, and Pontos independent. These small powers were not centralized, thoroughly organized states of the usual Hellenistic kind. The mountainous terrain that made it difficult for the armies of the Makedonian Successors to exercise authority also made it difficult for these dynasts to control all the area nominally

---

[3] Alexander: App. *Mith.* ii. 8; Arr. *Anab.* ii. 4. 2; Curt. iii. 1. 24; 4. 1; Plut. *Alex.* xviii. 3. Ariarathes: Diod. xvii. 48. 7; Strabo xii. 1. 2, 4 (534); xvi. 2. 30 (759); Arr. *Anab.* ii. 25. 4; 26. 1–27; Curt. iv. 6. 7. His coins: W. Wroth, *B.M.C. Pontus*, . . . (1889), xii, n. 5; E. Babelon, *T.M.G.R.* (1935), ii. Nos. 17–9, pp. 431–9.
[4] End of Ariarathes: Diod. xviii. 16. 1–2; 19. 3–5; App. *Mith.* ii. 8; Plut. *Eum.* iii. 6–7; Just. xiii. 6. Eumenes' army: Diod. xviii. 30. 1, 5; xix. 40. 2; Plut. *Eum.* iii. 2; iv. 2–3; vii. 1; xii. 3. Mithradates: Diod. xxxi. 19. 1–8; App. *Mith.* ii. 9–10; Plut. *Dem.* iv. 1–4.

subject to them. In Phrygia and Kappadokia, for example, the territory was subdivided into clan or tribal areas subject to some aristocratic baron or into temple states ruled by hereditary priest-kings. The resulting mixture of local religious practices, social customs, and political procedures made the task of governing very difficult for the petty kings. It was impossible, and even undesirable, therefore, for any of these dynasts to try to create a state policy favoring any single culture. In Kappadokia, for example, in the third century the dynasty of Mithradates had to deal with independent hill people, Greeks living in Mazakene, no fewer than ten hieratic centers, and a number of landed, secular magnates.[5]

The social and political structure became somewhat more confused early in the third century B.C. when the Gauls, savage barbarians in the eyes of all the previously settled communities, succeeded in penetrating into Phrygia and creating a tribal-state there. Their frequent raids wrought havoc in the more civilized and wealthier areas, and the problem of dealing with the Gallic tribes served to bring about cooperation between various dynasts and kings in Anatolia. Antiochos I was hailed *Soter* for his victory over them in 275 B.C. Ziailas, an early king of independent Bithynia, was killed attempting to prevent the Gauls from extending their hold on Asia Minor. Attalos I of Pergamon fought them later; his victory was accounted a gain for civilization.[6]

If the dynasts did not hate the Greeks, neither did the Seleukid and Pergamene kingdoms, which between them ruled the southwestern part of Anatolia, hate the dynasts. These royal governments, while they sought to further Hellenism within their boundaries, never adopted a culturally intolerant policy. As we shall see below in some detail, the Attalids of Pergamon repeatedly cooperated with the Phrygians and other local peoples. If Hellenism was accepted by the people of Anatolia, the reverse was true as well. The Greeks in Asia Minor were respectful of culture here—an attitude that began at least as early as Thales—since they had learned and taken so much from it. The Greeks on the local level did not regard the natives of Anatolia with the same hauteur with which, say, a Ptolemaic bureau-

---

[5] Hill people: Plut. *Dem.* xlvii. 4; Greeks: Strabo xii. 2. 9 (539); temple states: *ibid.*, xii. 2. 3 (535). On the importance of the landed families see M. I. Rostovtzeff in *C.A.H.* ix. 213–4; A. H. M. Jones, *The Cities of the Eastern Roman Provinces* (1937), 38–40; 91–5; W. M. Ramsay, *The Social Basis of Roman Power in Asia Minor* (1941), 3–4, and *passim*.

[6] Gauls: Strabo xii. 8. 7 (574); iv. 4. 2 (195–6); Polyb. ii. 20. 7; Paus. i. 4. 5–6; x. 30. 9; 32. 4. Ziailas: Phylarchos = Athen. ii. 58 C.

crat looked at the natives of Egypt. The Hellenes lived on ground they felt was their own by right of long occupation. Anatolia was not "spear-won" in quite the same sense that the rest of the East was. The long tradition of Greco-Oriental joint occupation was fortified by the children of much intermarriage.

Very well. In Asia Minor there were a number of areas of distinctive culture, and these regions cooperated with the Greek dynasties; this cooperation was reciprocated. Added to this, there was a common bond all rulers shared. In Asia Minor, the social organization showed no cultural cleavage as it did in Ptolemaic Egypt. In the latter country, the Greeks generally occupied the luxurious and well-paid positions, while the Egyptians were the hewers of wood. They noticed this. Such was not the case in Asia Minor, and the Makedonians and native dynasts alike lorded it over their subjects. Possibly more important was the fact that the rigid control of these men was borne by both Greeks and Anatolians alike. The history of the Pergamene state is a relatively well-documented example of this. It was a Greek who called the Attalid kings purple welts on the backs of whipped slaves. Both Greeks and Anatolians rose against the ruling class of this kingdom in the class war of Aristonikos in 133 B.C.[7]

This Pergamene kingdom was a tightly knit entity designed along Ptolemaic lines to produce revenues and goods for the Attalids so that they might be able to maintain the existence of their second-class power in the highly competitive state-system of the Hellenistic world. Land was owned by both small farmers and the holders of large estates, but particularly by the kings, the greatest landowners of all. Royal land was let in allotments to settlers in return for military service; many, if not most, of these colonists were non-Greek. The control of agriculture, as well as the control of trade and manufacturing, was well organized by the government. Under this system certain magnates who held property of their own and also were officers of the king became extremely wealthy. The laboring people, both Greek and Anatolian, in state-owned factories or on state-owned land, were often viciously treated and extremely poor. Thus, the channels of hate flowed towards eventual class war and not towards anti-Hellenism. Close supervision and control of the population was carried out by royal police and royal gendarmerie. The flavor of this dynasty was mostly Hellenic, but not entirely so. The cults in the capital included

[7] A summary sketch of Hellenism in Asia Minor is in D. Magie, *Roman Rule in Asia Minor* (1950), i. 119–21; ii. 970–5. Aristonikos is discussed below, pp. 177–178. Attalid welts: Strabo xiv. 1. 39 (647).

veneration of Zeus Soter, Athena Polias, Dionysos, Herakles, and Hermes; alongside these rites there was an Anatolian cult Hellenized as the worship of Demeter and Kore, and the important religion of the Anatolian Great Mother.[8]

The Hellenizing program of the Attalids was maintained throughout the existence of the dynasty. Its founder, half-Paphlagonian Philetairos, protected the Greek cities of Mysia against attacks of hill people. Later, the Ionian League of ancient Greek cities publicly praised Eumenes II for having made himself a benefactor of the Greeks by carrying on many and great struggles against the barbarians in their behalf.[9] This policy of the dynasty was vividly portrayed in the great sculptures adorning the Altar of Zeus at Pergamon. The massive, deeply undercut reliefs showed the gods of the old Hellenic mythology engaged in victorious combat with barbarous earth deities who suffer at their feet. The evidence shows that although Pergamon had a part-Oriental dynasty, it was a propagator of Hellenism. These kings and the Greek cities of Asia Minor, some old and some newly founded by the Seleukids and the Attalids, were the chief agencies by which Hellenism took deeper and deeper root in Anatolia. This process, begun long before the time of Alexander, was greatly forwarded in the Hellenistic period and brought to completion in the time of the Roman Empire. It did not result in Asia Minor's adoption of the ideas and institutions of the classical Greek period, for Hellenism itself was changing in Hellenistic times. It did result in Anatolia's accepting a good deal of Greek culture, especially the language, and thus was created that solid base on which the Greek Christian Byzantine state would one day rise.

During the Hellenistic period there was increasing cooperation between Pergamon and the more nearly Asiatic ruling families of the lesser dynastic states, for the dynasts did not hold aloof from either the Attalids or the devices of Hellenism. Eumenes II married Stratonike, the Hellenized daughter of the Ariarathids of Kappadokia. Indeed, all the royal families of the smaller powers were intermarried with the great Makedonian dynasties. Seleukid Antiochos III gave his daughter Antiochis to Ariarathes, and the groom in turn supplied a contingent of horse to Antiochos during his war against Rome in

[8] For Pergamon see M. I. Rostovtzeff in *C.A.H.* viii. 594–5; *S.E.H.H.W.* i. 553–65; E. V. Hansen, *The Attalids of Pergamum* (1947), 169–71; W. W. Tarn, *H.C.* (3rd ed., 1952), 163–70.

[9] Philetairos: M. I. Rostovtzeff in *C.A.H.* viii. 590–1; *S.E.H.H.W.* i. 178–9; Eumenes II: *Milet: Ergebnisse der Ausgrabungen* (1914), i, No. 306.

190 B.C. Ariarathes was himself the son of the daughter of Antiochos II. He was loyal to the new alliance until the Seleukids had been hopelessly defeated. Kappadokia had been one of the less Hellenized areas; it was a stronghold of Persian religious ideas.[10] The dynasts could not afford a policy that sought to arouse resistance to Hellenism. They, like the Parthians, required the assistance of Greek technicians, for they were never strong enough to feel completely safe from some form of foreign domination. One of the Ariarathids of Kappadokia, for example, was deposed in 159 B.C. by Seleukid Demetrios I, who made Orophernes king in his stead.[11] But such cases of interference were rare. The Seleukids and Attalids required the dynasts as allies, too. Perhaps the absence of dynastic propaganda against the Greco-Makedonians was due to the fact that no feeling of frustrated independence such as existed in Persis or Babylonia was present among the dynasts, since they were independent in fact.

The kings of Kappadokia, Pontos, and Bithynia were actual Hellenizers, partly, perhaps, because they deemed it expedient, but partly, too, because Hellenism was fascinating. Polybios' account of Orophernes describes a philhellene; we have also an inscription of this king commending the loyalty of Priene to him and making it a gift of a statue valued at three thousand drachms. Later he deposited four hundred talents of his funds for safekeeping in Athena's temple there. About 240 B.C. Ziailas of Bithynia recognized the inviolability of the Asklepeion at Kos, and the dynasty sought to identify itself with descent from a European people, the Thrakians. The royal coinage honored the Thrakian Ares and was consistently Hellenic in style and types. King Prousias of Bithynia in 156 B.C. as thanksgiving for victory over Pergamon, conducted magnificent rites in honor of the Hellenic savior Asklepios.[12]

---

[10] Eumenes II: Strabo xiii. 4. 1–3 (623–5). Ariarathes: App. *Syr.* i. 5; vi. 32; vii. 42; Diod. xxxi. 19. 6. Kappadokia: J. H. Moulton, *Early Zoroastrianism* (1913), 431; W. W. Tarn, *H.C.* (3rd ed., 1952), 170 and literature and sources cited there.

[11] App. *Syr.* viii. 47; Just. xxxv. 1.

[12] Orophernes: Polyb. xxxii. 11. 1; xxxiii. 6. 2; Diod. xxxi. 32. 1; C. B. Welles, *Royal Correspondence of the Hellenistic Period* (1934), No. 63, pp. 255–9. Ziailas: *ibid.*, No. 25, pp. 118–25. Thrakian legends: Strabo xii. 3. 3 (541). Coinage: W. Wroth, *B.M.C.* Pontus, . . . (1889), xxxviii–xxxix; 208–15. Prousias: Polyb. xxxii. 15. 1; Diod. xxxi. 35. 1.

Prousias is also pilloried by Polybios' accusations of numerous moral shortcomings, including the sack of several Greek temples. This means nothing; he also sacked the Temple of Artemis Persika at Hiera Kome. The same thing had shortly before been done by Philip V of Makedonia.

The political practice and even religion of Greece were well understood and appreciated by dynasts and notables. Amestris, queen of
Pontos, daughter of King Oxyathres, niece of Dareios III, founded the
Greek *polis* of Amastris by *synoikismos* of four native villages. In Lydia
there was a continuing trend towards Greek institutions. The chief
goddess here was the Anatolian Kybele; in the Persian period she
was identified with Anahita; in the fourth century she was assimilated
to Grecian Artemis. Third- and second-century restorations of her
temple were carried out in Greek style. Temple personnel were both
Lydian and Greek or Hellenized Lydian, as shown by personal names.
Sardeis had a *boulē* and *ekklesia* in the second century, and her Hellenic or Hellenized moneyers issued a coinage that venerated Apollo,
Herakles, Dionysos, and the Lydian Zeus. Analysis of Lydian inscriptions honoring various gods shows that Hellenism began slowly
to penetrate even the countryside after Alexander. While the Anatolian Great Mother remained most popular, nonetheless the growing
acceptance of European religion was a fact.[13] In Lykia Hellenism
took root at Xanthos in the sixth century and was firmly established
by the end of the fourth. There were also remnants of Iranian influence there, as seen from the names of some Hellenistic landlords:
Pharnabazos and Mithradates. Interculturation went on throughout
the peninsula, strongest in the west, as in Lydia, or along the coast,
as in Lykia, but also in the more Asiatic central and eastern parts. At
Themisonion in Phrygia the native god Sozon was affiliated with
Herakles; at Laodikeia Aseis with Zeus; at Eumeneia Men with Apollo
and Zeus. In Kommagene part-Iranian Antiochos I Epiphanes in the
first century B.C. claimed descent from both Alexander and Dareios III,
and showed in his public inscriptions that his religion was a blend
of Persian, Babylonian, and Hellenic beliefs. At the same time that
this part-Persian king honored Greek gods, Attalos III of Pergamon
guaranteed the inviolability of the much-ravaged shrine of Persian
Anahita at Hiera Kome, and introduced the cult of Anatolian Zeus
Sabazios into his capital. In Kappadokia, the Ariarathids, who had
begun to rule in defiance of the Seleukids, became ardent Grecophiles.
Ariarathes IV, husband of Seleukid Antiochis, had his children Holophernes and Mithradates educated in Ionia; the latter became king

---

[13] Amastris: Strabo xii. 3. 10 (544). Sardeis: H. C. Butler, *Sardis: The Temple of
Artemis* (1925), 103–5, 140–2. Personnel: W. H. Buckler and D. M. Robinson,
Sardis: Greek and Latin Inscriptions (1932), Nos. 3, 90–1. *Boulē: ibid.*, No. 4. Coins:
H. W. Bell, *Sardis: Coins* i (1916), Nos. 240–61; pp. 25–7. Lydian inscriptions: W. W.
Tarn, *H.C.* (3rd ed., 1952), 344.

as Ariarathes V, a man gripped by Greek philosophy, a student of Karneades and an honorary citizen of Athens.[14]

The foregoing shows how complicated the ethnic and cultural milieu of Anatolia was. Its complexity was a powerful reason why no native religious resistance appeared. No single ethnic or religious group was numerous enough to feel that its culture could prevail, or even ought to prevail. The dynasts were well Hellenized, and the religion of the peninsula was hopelessly Balkanized. Ethnic confusion was compounded with social disunity within the various regions. The economic systems of Asia Minor brought about a sharp distinction between the owning, ruling class and the working, propertyless class. Thus there was in no district the identity of interest between the intellectual, governing class and the numbers of simple folk who might have supported their rebellious feelings. Therefore, there would have been little basis for armed resistance. The dynasts, the Attalids, and the Seleukids all had to depend on a landowning aristocracy for support. All over Anatolia, much land was in the hands of such a military class, which had existed long before the advent of Alexander. In view of the shortage of manpower competent to continue to govern the land locally, the Makedonians did not replace the native lords with their own nationals, but simply continued the system. It is true that in some cases a Greek government confiscated some estates, turned out the hereditary owners, and substituted Makedonians or Greeks, as Eumenes did in Kappadokia. But this seldom happened. The remainder of the local nobility, now aware that their holdings could be similarly disposed of, might tend more willingly to cooperate with the regime. Others might more cordially resent it. But these barons had to depend on royal support, since they did not always enjoy the confidence of their agricultural laborers, the native serfs who dwelt in squalid villages in the neighborhood of the fortified manor houses.[15] The class consciousness of this rural proletariat finally

[14] Lykia: E. R. Bevan, *The House of Seleucus* (1902), i. 85–90; P. Demargne, "Les étapes de l'hellénisation à Xanthos de Lycie," *RÉG* 67 (1954), 14–5. Phrygia: W. M. Ramsay, *The Cities and Bishoprics of Phrygia* (1895), i. 32–3, 260–3; ii. 356–74. Kommagene: M. J. Vermaseren, *Corpus Inscriptionum et Monumentorum Religionis Mithriacaei* (1956), Nos. 28–32. Attalos III: C. B. Welles, *Royal Correspondence of the Hellenistic Period* (1934), Nos. 67–8. Ariarathids: Diod. xxxi. 19. 6–8; Diog. Laer. iv. 9, 65. For a general study of syncretism here see J. B. McMinn, "Fusion of the Gods: A Religio-Astrological Study of the Interpenetration of the East and the West in Asia Minor," *JNES* 15 (1956), 201–13.

[15] Plut. *Eum.* viii. 3, 5; Strabo xii. 2. 6 (537); M. I. Rostovtzeff in *C.A.H.* ix. 213–4; *S.E.H.H.W.* i. 465–7, 507–9; E. V. Hansen, *The Attalids of Pergamum* (1947), 169–71.

exploded in the conflicts in western and central Anatolia in 90 B.C. Along with land held by the mixed-blooded nobility, there was also a good deal in the possession of Hellenized cities. They also functioned to preserve order. We know the names of more than thirty new Seleukid military colonies in central Asia Minor alone; these, along with the older coastal *poleis,* were essentially loyal to Hellenism. The countryside around them was not necessarily so loyal. Philhellenic Selge had to resist numerous attempts of the Tauric Pisidians to capture it, and succeeded, Strabo says, because of the orderliness of the citizens.[16]

There was a third form of social and economic organization. This was the autonomous temple-state, a most important institution in the life of Asia Minor, and one which on first sight might be thought capable of heading up resistance to the Greeks. But this did not happen. These entities existed within the various kingdoms, but were not completely a part of them, since they had a good deal of self-government. Such a state was that belonging to the goddess Ma at Komana in Kataonia. This temple had a considerable settlement around it, populated by a small group of divinely inspired prophets and a large number of temple slaves. Strabo says that while the people here were nominally subject to the king of Kappadokia, nonetheless they were really ruled by the king-priests of Ma. The temple slaves numbered about six thousand men and women. They worked considerable land, and its revenues belonged to the high priest. Other temple states existed in the rest of Asia Minor. Many of them were large and important with similar royal rights. Ma of Pontic Komana and Men at Kabeira had estates about as large as Ma of Kataonian Komana. Somewhat smaller ones were at Zela, Venasa, Dastarkon, and Phrygian Antiocheia.[17]

Both the Seleukid and Pergamene dynasties cooperated with these states. Such collaboration was often reciprocated and some states became thoroughly Hellenized. Some did not. Occasionally we hear of part of their lands being confiscated by the Seleukids and secular-

[16] Colonies: M. I. Rostovtzeff in *C.A.H.* vii. 171–2, 180; D. Magie, *Roman Rule in Asia Minor* (1950), 111–6. Selge: Strabo xii. 7. 2–3; A. H. M. Jones, *The Cities of the Eastern Roman Provinces* (1937), 126; W. W. Tarn, *H.C.* (3rd ed., 1952), 130. The Greeks rejected Selge's claim to have been founded long before by Hellenes.

[17] Kataonian Komana: Strabo xii. 2. 3 (535); Pontic Komana: *ibid.,* xii. 3. 32–6 (557–9); 8. 9 (574–5); Kabeira: *ibid.,* xii. 3. 31 (557); Anahita of Zela: *ibid.,* xii. 3. 37 (559–60); Zeus of Venasa: *ibid.,* xii. 2. 5–6 (537); Dastarkon: *ibid.,* xii. 2. 6 (537); Men of Phrygian Antioch: *ibid.,* xii. 8. 14 (577). See, too, E. V. Hansen, *The Attalids of Pergamum* (1947), 165–8.

ized, perhaps to provide territory for a military colony. In all cases, however, the temple retained enough land to keep it self-sufficient. The Seleukids, nonetheless, respected the religion of these communities and left them undisturbed as far as possible. Much the same policy was followed by the Attalids.[18]

We have a good deal of information concerning the temple-state of Kybele at Pessinous, the greatest of them all. According to Strabo the priests had once been strong and independent dynasts, but in the Hellenistic period retained only a little of their old power. The history of the relationship between these priests and the Attalids shows a great deal of mutual cooperation. The kings built up the wealth of the precinct and embellished it with a sanctuary and porticoes of white marble. The high priest Attis sacrificed for the safety of Eumenes II. Such a degree of collaboration existed that Attalos II was able to obtain a black stone image of the goddess from her clergy for export to Rome at the end of the third century B.C. Eumenes II in 163 B.C. lent troops to reconquer an area near Pessinous held by Gallic plunderers. The correspondence of Attis with Eumenes was carried on in an atmosphere of cordiality.[19] There is not the slightest indication that Pessinous ever resisted or opposed Hellenism at all.

It paid the priests of the temple-states of Anatolia well to cooperate with the Hellenic kings. Both the royal houses and the priestly houses enjoyed a great amount of political power and social prestige. By standing together for mutual support, they were able to continue to enjoy their high positions. For the priests to have attacked Hellenism would have called forth a Hellenic counter attack which almost certainly would have unseated whatever high priest dared to raise his head. These men were interested in perpetuating the dynasty, and they collaborated with whatever state dominated the territory around them. The soldiers in the victorious Roman armies of Sulla and Lucullus were taught the worship of the Great Mother of the Gods Ma in Kappadokia.[20] There was, too, a subconscious factor at work.

---

[18] M. I. Rostovtzeff, *S.E.H.H.W.* i. 504–7; W. W. Tarn, *H.C.* (3rd ed., 1952), 140–1; T. R. S. Broughton, "New Evidence on the Temple Estates in Asia Minor," *Studies in Roman Social and Economic History* (1951), 236–50. For a grant of *asylia* and tax exemption by Seleukos I see C. B. Welles, *Royal Correspondence of the Hellenistic Period* (1934), No. 9, pp. 54–60.

[19] Diod. iii. 58, 1–59. 8; Strabo xii. 5. 3 (567). Eumenes and Attis: C. B. Welles, *Royal Correspondence of the Hellenistic Period* (1934), Nos. 55–60, pp. 242–5; E. V. Hansen, *The Attalids of Pergamum* (1947), 49–51, 119; D. Magie, *Roman Rule in Asia Minor* (1950), i. 25–6; ii. 769–70.

[20] Plut. *Sul.* ix. 4.

Most of the states officially worshipped the Great Mother, a goddess of birth and of becoming, not one of militance and pugnacity. It was her function to further life and not to take it.

What propaganda these states generated was entirely in behalf of their reputation as centers of holy religion. When Strabo visited the Ploutonion, a temple-state at Hierapolis, he was shown a sizeable grotto in the earth with vapor steaming from it. The priests first threw various animals into the fissure or near it, and these were overcome by the gases. Then the clergy themselves descended into the chasm and emerged unharmed. The rationalist Strabo decided that they probably held their breath and speculated that their being emasculated might make them immune.[21] The feat was, of course, a proof of the power of the god and goddess, who could make their devotees secure from danger. Perhaps, in view of the pillaging by brigands that went on around these places, such propaganda was aimed at instilling awe into the unhappy, poverty-stricken people of the countryside.

While there is no evidence that native religion was used against the Greek regimes by the native states, there is evidence that Persian anti-Hellenic prophecies circulated in Anatolia.[22] A good many Persians still dwelt in Asia Minor, and they were undoubtedly saddened to think that they no longer belonged to the dominant group. Persians lived in places like Dareiou Kōmē and Kyrou Pedion, colonies sent out from Persis in the sixth century. Iranian settlers meant the

[21] Strabo xiii. 4. 14 (629). Lucretius (On the Nature of Things ii. 608–30) describes the propaganda of Kybele in republican Rome.

[22] There is no evidence of Phrygian religious resistance, although the country had in the eighth century been the seat of a powerful and wealthy kingdom. The old capital at Gordion seems, too, to have associated religion with the idea of political domination of Asia, as shown by the episode of Alexander and the knot (Plut. Alex. xviii. 1; Arr. Anab. ii. 3. 1–6; Curt. iii. 1. 11–6; Just. xi. 7; W. W. Tarn, Alexander the Great [1948], i. 21–3; [1950], ii. 262–5). There are signs, too, of Persian influence in Phrygia. At Gordion there was sacrifice of horses at royal funerals and a carving has been found of a bull attacked by a lion similar to the Persepolis reliefs (R. S. Young, "The Campaign of 1955 at Gordion," AJA 60 [1956], 266; "Gordion 1956," AJA 61 [1957], 326–30; Pl. 91, Fig. 18). At Phrygian Hiera Polis there was an important cult of Apollo (W. M. Ramsay, Cities and Bishoprics of Phrygia [1895], i. 84–107). Nearby at Kalletebos was the place where Xerxes found his so-beautiful tree (Herod. vii. 31). Not far away at Kelainai Pythios lived in the fifth century (ibid., viii. 99). Livy called it the "caput Phrygiae," (xxxviii. 13. 5), whatever that means. Close by was an Apameia with priests called Asiarchs (Dio Chrys. Or. xxxv. 10). But there is no evidence that these places influenced the Phrygians. The country's legendary King Manes (Herod. i. 94; iv. 45) was talked about as a wonder-worker, in Hellenistic times, but nothing in the legends about him indicates that he opposed or hated or prophesied against any Greek (Dion. Hal. i. 27. 1; Plut. Isis and Osiris 24 [360 B]; M. Braun, History and Romance in Graeco-Oriental Literature [1938], 5–6).

settlement of Iranian gods and goddesses, and therefore of the *magoi,* without whom sacrifice was unlawful. Persians dwelling in the valley of the river Hermos lived in villages around a Temple of Anahita. Most of these settlers were nobles of the military sort. How numerous the Persians and their Iranian allies were in respect to the Anatolians as a whole is, in the absence of anything like complete information, impossible to say. In 319 B.C., the army of a certain satrap Arrhidaios attacking Kyzikos included a contingent of five hundred Persian bowmen, but whether these were locally recruited or enrolled from the wreckage of the Great King's armies is unknown.[23] We do know of many places where Persians were settled: Sardeis, Kelainas, Daskyleion, Hiera Kome, Hypaipa, Kastabala, Ephesos, and throughout Kappadokia.[24] Greek cities in eastern Anatolia occasionally struck coins honoring Persian deities, probably in behalf of Iranians living in the town. Mithra and Anahita were honored by Amastris in Paphlagonia, whose issues, however, were mostly typed with Hellenic gods. There is also evidence of the settlement of Chaldeans and of *chaldaioi* in Asia Minor.[25] But it was, in all probability, from a Persian temple that Aemilius Sura learned of the Persian prophecy of the progression of empire in the first quarter of the second century B.C.

There is evidence that the Persian propaganda was combatted by Greeks in Anatolia. Plutarch says that when Alexander was near Xanthos in Lykia a spring miraculously cast up a bronze tablet inscribed in ancient letters, predicting that the world empire of the Persians would fall to Alexander.[26] Of course this did not happen. Nor was the story made up, apparently, until sometime in the third cen-

[23] Dareiou Kōmē: *R.E.* iv. 2212; Kyrou Pedion: Strabo xiii. 4. 13 (629). Hermos: Polyb. xvi. 1. 6–7; xxxii. 15. 1–6; Paus. vii. 6. 6. Settlers: Polyb. xxxi. 1–4; Nepos, *Datames* iv. 1–3; Strabo xv. 3. 14–5 (733); E. R. Bevan, *The House of Seleucus* (1902), i. 78–9; A. D. Nock, *Conversion* (1933), 42–3; E. V. Hansen, *The Attalids of Pergamum* (1947), 167. Bowmen: Diod. xviii. 51. 1.

[24] Sardeis: Seals from tombs, as well as decorative motifs around the Temple of Artemis, with opposed, winged, human-headed lion-sphinxes, paws touching, eight-petalled rosettes surmounted by crenellated walls as on Persian fire-temples, and the crowned hero fighting a monster all in Persepolis style, show that Persians had settled in this important provincial capital. This information from H. C. Butler, *Sardis: The Excavations* (1922), i. 87, 121–2, 143; Fig. 131, 158.

Kelainas: Xen. *Anab.* i. 2. 7, 9; Pergamos: *ibid.,* vii. 8. 9–16; Daskyleion: Xen. *Hell.* iv. 1. 15; Hiera Kome: Paus. v. 27. 5; Tac. *Ann.* iii. 62; Hypaipa: Paus. v. 27. 5; Kastabala: Strabo xii. 2. 7 (537); Ephesos: Thuk. viii. 109; Strabo xiv. 1. 22–3 (640–1); Kappadokia: *ibid.* xi. 8. 4 (512); xv. 3. 14–5 (733).

[25] Amastris: W. Wroth, *B.M.C. Pontus,* . . . (1889), xv; Amastris Nos. 1–3, p. 84; Pl. xix. 3. *Chaldaioi:* Plut. *Luc.* xiv. 3; xix. 2; F. Cumont, "La fin du monde selon les mages occidentaux," *RHR* 103 (1931), 29–30.

[26] Plut. *Alex.* xvii. 2.

tury, after the *Bahman Yasht* was in existence. Since this story does not appear in the accounts of Curtius or Arrian, it was probably not in the memoirs left by Aristoboulos or Ptolemy, both of whom wrote shortly before 280 B.C. Therefore, the story in Plutarch must be third- or second-century counterpropaganda. The Persian apocalypses predicted divine intervention to overthrow the Makedonian regime. Plutarch's story shows that someone wanted people to believe, on the other hand, that the gods had predicted Alexander's victory, and that therefore by inference they supported it. Consequently, it would seem that in some quarters of Asia Minor the Persian prophecies were taken seriously. The Persian Sibylline Oracle predicting Alexander's death probably came from the *magoi* in the Temple of Ephesos about 325. This also, I think, caused some Greeks to respond with counterpropaganda directly aimed against the Ephesian *magoi*. Hegesias of Magnesia preserves an inaccurate tale that must have been in existence only by 275 or so, since he lived between 300 and 250 B.C. The story was that the Temple of Ephesos burned down at the very time that Alexander was born. The reason he gives is that Artemis-Anahita was busy in Pella supervising the birth of the new world-ruler. The magian priests in Ephesos that day rushed about in the midst of flaming disaster crying aloud that great calamity for Asia had come to pass.[27] The *magoi*, who disliked Alexander's fiery likeness, are thus poetically singed by it. So far from their prophecy of Alexander's fall coming true, they actually predicted their own fall. Artemis-Anahita did not protect the Persian Empire: she actually protected the king of Makedonia.

It is likely that by 100 B.C. the *Oracle of Hystaspes* was also circulating in Asia Minor. Around 80 or 90 B.C. Phrygian Apameia was heavily damaged by an earthquake. The Greek Strabo's account of the disaster is merely that it occurred and that Mithradates VI restored the city with a grant of one hundred talents. But a fragment of the *History* of the Hellenized Syrian Nikolaos of Damaskos gives a good deal more information obviously laid over with supernatural details. He says that the earthquake brought into existence lakes that had never existed before and that rivers and springs were also opened by the upheaval. From these, brackish and bluish ($\pi\iota\kappa\rho\grave{o}\nu$ $\tau\epsilon$ $\kappa\alpha\acute{\iota}$ $\gamma\lambda\alpha\acute{\nu}\kappa o\nu$) water gushed forth. Simultaneously the old sources of fresh water dried up. The region was filled with shellfish and other sea creatures, although it was a great distance from the ocean. This account is apocalyptic; it

[27] Hegesias' tale: Plut. *Alex.* iii. 3–4. His date: L. Pearson, *The Lost Histories of Alexander* (1960), 247.

is not entirely a description of natural phenomena. These phenomena sound like the conditions prophesied to precede the end of the old world political order in the *Oracle*. Apameia was a region where Persian kings had taken an interest in local trees and so on.[28] The earthquake happened when Mithradates was preparing to fight the Romans or had actually begun to; the times were exciting and the air was filled with his extraordinary prophecies. Since Mithradates probably used the *Oracle* himself, it should occasion no surprise to find it circulating and being used to interpret a disastrous natural calamity. Its use at this late time, however, would not mean that it was being given an anti-Hellenic interpretation. The Romans were just across the Phrygian frontier and were showing signs of expansiveness, and the extant fragments of the *Oracle* show anti-Romanism.

The last things we must investigate for signs of anti-Hellenism are two important Anatolian revolutionary movements which employed religious propaganda. These were the rebellion of Aristonikos and that widespread movement set on foot by the part-Greek, part-Iranian king of Pontos, Mithradates VI Eupator. Aristonikos, a bastard of the Pergamene dynasty, in 133/32 B.C. organized an extraordinary revolution, which broke out shortly after the death of the last king of Pergamon, Attalos III. This king had willed the state to the Roman Republic. When this occurred, Aristonikos united persons of the rural laboring class, slaves from the cities, and broken, discouraged, and outcast elements drawn from all nationalities and fell upon the cities of western Asia Minor. He called his people *Heliopolitai*, "Citizens of Sun-City," and it has been suggested that this involved the use of Oriental religious ideas. Sun-gods had always been important in the East, and had usually been connected intimately with the quality of justice. While all this may have been true of Aristonikos, his movement was also strongly motivated by secular Greek utopian ideals. Equal property for all was an idea of the Hellenic propagandists Iamboulos and Alexarchos of the third century.[29] Therefore,

---

[28] Strabo: xii. 8. 18 (578). Nikolaos: *Histories* civ = Athen. viii. 332 F–333 A. *Oracle of Hystaspes* frag. 14 = Lac. *Div. Inst.* vii. 16. Apameia and Persian influence in region: see n. 22, p. 174 above.

[29] Aristonikos' revolt: Diod. xxxiv. 2. 26; Strabo xiv. 1. 38 (646); Florus i. 35. 4–7; Just. xxxvi. 4–6; xxxvii. 1; M. I. Rostovtzeff, *S.E.H.H.W.* ii. 807, 1106; iii. 1521–2, n. 76; E. V. Hansen, *The Attalids of Pergamum* (1947), 142–8; D. Magie, *Roman Rule in Asia Minor* (1950), i. 148–54; ii. 1034–42; W. W. Tarn, *H.C.* (3rd ed., 1952), 41–2, 125; T. R. S. Broughton, "Stratonicea and Aristonicus," *CPh* 29 (1934), 252–4.
  Oriental sun cults: J. Bidez, *La cité du soleil chez les stoïciens* (1932), 32–4. Alexarchos: W. W. Tarn, *Alexander the Great and the Unity of Mankind* (1933), 21–3; 38, nn. 108 ff. Iamboulos: Diod. ii. 55. 1–60. 3; W. W. Tarn, *op. cit.*, 9–10.

Aristonikos, whom we know to have been advised by the Greek Cynic
Blossios of Kumai, was a leader of the widespread class war tran-
scending national or cultural frontiers, which convulsed the Mediterranean in the late second century b.c. Slave revolutions or class violence broke out in southern Italy, Sicily, Attica, Delos, Syria, and
Kilikia. This same Blossios had been an advisor of the reformer
Tiberius Gracchus at Rome, and after his death went to Asia to join
Aristonikos. In view of this and the fact that wealthy Anatolians in
Pergamon opposed Aristonikos, it is impossible to see this rebellion
as evidence of Oriental religious resistance to Hellenism. Revolts
similar to Aristonikos', which were the despairing attempts of brigands to deal with their upper-class exploiters, occurred in Thrake,
the Chersonnesos, and Mysia both just before and soon after this
period.[30]

This brings us to the consideration of Mithradates VI of Pontos,
who did use religious propaganda to further his policy of expansion.
The population of Pontos included many people of Iranian blood.
Ahura Mazdāh was the god who protected the dynasty. This line of
kings, as noted above, had been founded by Mithradates Ktistes
around 310 b.c. during the Makedonians' involvement in the Wars
of the Successors. The region adopted its own Era of Pontos beginning
from 297 b.c. Mithradates VI claimed to be a descendant of the old
Achaemenid kings Kyros and Dareios.[31] In view of this was Mithradates an embodiment of anti-Hellenism?

No, for Justin also says that he claimed to be descended from Alexander and the Seleukids. Mithradates' background was simply an
expression of the Greco-Oriental culture of Asia Minor in the first
century b.c. His religious propaganda was directed entirely against
Latin expansion into the interior of Anatolia. After Rome suppressed
Aristonikos, she organized Pergamon into the province of Asia and
in 102 also occupied Kilikia. Those who had eyes to see could easily
predict that Roman aggressiveness would soon carry her on deeper
into Asia Minor. Mithradates posed as the spokesman for all Asia,
denouncing the Romans as the enemy in common of all mankind.

[30] Slave wars: Diod. xxxiv. 2. 1–48; xxxvi. 7. 1–11. 3; Athen. vi. 272 E–273 A; W. W.
Tarn, H.C. (3rd ed., 1952), 122–5, 264–6. Blossios: Plut. Tib. Grac. viii. 4–5; xx. 3–4.
Thrake and the Chersonnesos: T. R. S. Broughton, "Stratonicea and Aristonicus,"
CPh 29 (1934), 253. Mysia: Cic. To Quintus i. 1. 25.

[31] Iranians in Pontos: pp. 174–175, above; M. I. Rostovtzeff, S.E.H.H.W. i.
573–7; W. W. Tarn, H.C. (3rd ed., 1952), 170. The dynasty: Polyb. v. 43. 2; Diod.
xxxi. 19. 1; Strabo xii. 3. 41 (562); Just. xxxviii. 7; App. Mith. xvi. 112; M. I.
Rostovtzeff in C.A.H. ix. 214–9; P. Waltz, La question d'Orient dans l'antiquité
(1942), 239–40.

According to Athenion, one of his numerous Greek supporters, Mithradates' coming victories over Rome were everywhere foretold by oracles. One such prediction is extant in Greek in the *Sibylline Oracles* in the form of a six-line denunciation of Rome. She will be requited three times over for what she has stolen from Asia and will give up twenty times as many people to be slaves as she has carried off from Asia.[32] This prophecy has been influenced by the idea spread by the Persian apocalypses that world dominion will return to Asia. Of course two texts anticipated the coming of a savior, and none appears in the *Sibylline Oracle*. Mithradates, however, advertised his possession of supernatural qualities so that he may have been understood to play the savior's part. Justin says that a comet appeared to signal his birth. The *Bahman Yasht* predicts the same sign, which, incidentally, reminds one of the legend of the birth of Jesus in the Gospel according to St. Matthew. Justin also says he was supposed to be unconquerable; some Persians tried but failed to kill him in infancy. This motif is not in either Persian apocalypse, but the same one appears in Matthew, where Jesus' parents save him from the designs of Herod. Mithradates also was alleged to be immune to poison and to be able to run down on foot and overwhelm wild beasts. In short, he was invincible.[33]

But while the propaganda had roots in Persian ideology, it cannot be understood as anti-Hellenic. It is patently anti-Roman, hoping to turn to Mithradates' advantage the hatred inspired by Rome's methods of governing western Anatolia, an occupation more harsh, more unjust, more merciless than Greek rule had ever been. Roman methods of tax collection were truly shocking, depending as they did on enterprising, rapacious *publicani*. By 100 B.C. some communities were being rapidly reduced to penury. Orientals and Greeks shared the hardships of Roman domination. Actually, Ionian Greek propaganda existed alongside the Mithradatic. Hellenic anti-Romanism had begun at the time of the Third Makedonian War, when oracles

---

[32] Justin: xxxviii. 4, 7. Common spokesman: C. B. Welles, *Royal Correspondence in the Hellenistic Period* (1934), No. 74, pp. 295–6. Athenion: Poseidonios = Athen. v. 213 B.

The oracle is *Sib. Or.* iii. 350–5, as follows:

For all the wealth that Rome took from tribute-paying Asia,
Three times as much Asia shall take back from Rome,
And shall repay her for her deadly arrogance.
And for those Asians enslaved in Italian homes,
Twenty times as many Italians shall toil for Asia
In poverty, and shall be held for debts a thousandfold.

[33] Just. xxxvii. 1–2.

were uttered predicting that Athena would bring dread war to Italy
or that Zeus would devastate Italian lands in revenge for the suffering
Hellas underwent at Roman hands.[34] There was, therefore, a blending
of anti-Roman Greek with anti-Roman Mithradatic propaganda.
About this time or a little later the *Oracle of Hystaspes* was translated
into Greek and its anti-Makedonism altered to anti-Romanism. Much
of Mithradates' propaganda was published, after all, in Greek, in
order to attract Hellenes in Anatolia to his side. He sought to unify
as many persons as possible into a common front, much as Antiochos IV had tried to do. Mithradates, far from following an anti-
Greek policy, actually created a Greco-Iranian state. Its currency was
minted on the Attic standard, designed in Hellenic style, and orna-
mented by Greek gods like Zeus, Athena, Nike, Hermes, and Tyche.
At the same time, the coins depicted undoubtedly Persian elements
of dress and decoration. Some of the *poleis* he controlled were allowed
to begin a semiautonomous coinage of their own, a right they had not
enjoyed earlier.[35] He made a show of his philhellenism. He gave some
of his children Greek names, some Iranian names. Two of his wives,
Berenike and Monime, came from the ancient Greek cities of Miletos
and Chios. At Delos he named an Athenian the "Most Honored Com-
panion of the King." He dedicated his armor at Nemea and at Delphi.
Appian says that he cultivated Greek learning on a wide scale, and
was well acquainted with Greek forms of religion.[36]

His propaganda and his anti-Romanism helped to win him an
extraordinary amount of cooperation from the Greeks of Anatolia.
The military expert Dorylaos, the sophist Athenion, and the philosopher Metrodoros threw in their lot with him and were given high
positions in the government. The overwhelming number of military
commanders, naval officers, ambassadors, and even some priests and
royal secretaries, were persons of Hellenic background and culture.
The infantry of the army was partly Asiatic and partly Greek; it used

[34] Ionian propaganda: *Sib. Or.* iii. 464–9, which is satisfaction over the self-
inflicted wounds of Italy during the Social War, 90–88 B.C. Earlier Greek oracles
in Pflegon, *Amazing Stories,* 3.

[35] Coinage: W. Wroth, *B.M.C. Pontus,* . . . (1889), Mithradates VI: pp. xiii–xvi,
xxiv. Amaseia: No. 2, p. 6, Pl. i. 13; Amisos: Nos. 30–6, p. 16; Pl. iii. 3; Kabeira: No. 1,
p. 25; Komana: No. 1, p. 28, Pl. v. 5. Cities with the new right to coin included
Gaizoura, Laodikeia, Pharnakia, Pimolisa, Taulara, and Chabakta; *ibid.,* pp. 30–9.
For policy towards cities see App. *Mith.* xi. 78; Strabo xii. 3. 30 (556).

[36] Wives: Plut. *Luc.* xviii. 2–3; App. *Mith.* iii. 21. Other relatives are named here
and there in Appian, *loc. cit.,* especially chapter ii; the *Lucullus,* especially chapter
xviii, and in Justin xxxviii. 3. Honors: C. B. Welles and M. I. Rostovtzeff, *op. cit.,*
54; App. *Mith.* xvi. 112.

Greek tactics and Greek weapons, but was clothed more in Median fashion.[37] When Mithradates finally fell on the unsuspecting Italians in Asia one day in 88 B.C., perhaps eighty thousand were slain in a sort of "Anatolian Vespers." Many Greek cities all over the Aegean area came over to his side. While a few held aloof and even resisted his forces, many received the king gladly; these included such old centers of Hellenism as Ephesos, Mitylene, and Athens. These places and Sinope were honored by Mithradates; and Amisos, at least, received funds for temple-building.[38]

In view of the foregoing there is no reason to think that Mithradates Eupator pursued an anti-Hellenic policy. Indeed the growing together of Greeks and Orientals in the first century B.C. was a phenomenon occurring throughout Anatolia. A similar process will be noted towards the close of the history of the Ptolemaic dynasty. When Roman occupation and annexation threatened at the end of the last century B.C., there was cooperation of Greek and Egyptian to prevent it.

This fusion was a most important development in the relations of East and West in the ancient world. The *homonoia* that Alexander prayed for at Opis here and there became a fact. In this milieu religion underwent natural syncretism; the eventual result was the blending of cultural patterns on that large scale which made possible the acceptance of Christianity, the greatest of the Greco-Oriental mystery religions. The working of this process can be seen in Mithradates' cult of Zeus Stratios. F. Cumont says that this god was probably Karian in origin, but widely known by 100 B.C. He had been worshipped by Eumenes of Kardia, and probably was a member of the royal pantheon of Bithynia. As Appian makes quite clear in his description of Mithradates' practice of the cult, it was a rite to which many Achaemenid religious ideas had become attached.[39]

Another important aspect of Mithradates' program was the emphasis he placed on correcting, or pretending to correct, the unfortu-

---

[37] Dorylaos: Strabo xii. 3. 33 (557); Athenion: Poseidonios = Athen. v. 212 A; Metrodoros: Strabo xiii. 1. 55 (609); Plut. *Luc.* xxii. 2. The personnel of the government and armed forces are named throughout Plutarch's biography of Sulla, Appian's account of the Mithradatic Wars, and here and there in Strabo. A complete list would be much too long to include here.

[38] The slaying: Val. Max. ix. 2. 4; Plut. *Sul.* xxiv. 4; App. *Mith.* iv. 22–3. Ephesos: App. *Mith.* iv. 23; Mitylene: *ibid.,* iv. 23; Plut. *Luc.* iv. 2; Athens: App. *Mith.* v. 28. Sinope and Amisos: Strabo xii. 3. 11 (545), 14 (547). For cities in Hellas supporting Mithradates see Plut. *Sul.* xii. 1.

[39] The sources for this cult are Herod. v. 119; Strabo xiv. 2. 23 (659); App. *Mith.* ix. 66; Plut. *Eum.* xvii. 4; M. I. Rostovtzeff in *C.A.H.* ix. 223–5; F. Cumont, "Le Zeus Stratios de Mithradate," *RHR* 43 (1901), 47–57.

nate economic injustices of Anatolia. Aristonikos had pursued a similar course. Both men took advantage of the demand voiced by certain people in the lower classes for a more equitable distribution of property and the cancellation of debts. This old desire was coming to have the support of religion, and the effect was beginning to be felt. The older religions had been pretty much the monopoly of the wealthy classes, but now there were people convinced that the low and oppressed counted for as much in the eyes of gods as the mighty and the rich.[40]

On this note we may close this chapter. It is a notable fact that the region could show no indigenous program of hostility to Hellenism; nonetheless, it was important as the place where anti-Hellenic prophecies came to be turned against Rome. Asia Minor, like Syria and Sicily, originated little culture of its own in ancient times. But in spite of this, its importance was immense, for it was a region in which cross-fertilization of differing cultures occurred. And presently a Greco-Oriental civilization arose in Asia Minor that bloomed as the Byzantine Empire, whose existence was to dominate this portion of the *oikoumene* for a thousand years.

[40] The effectiveness of Mithradates' program in attracting slaves in Asia Minor in App. *Mith.* iv. 22; Agatharchides, *History* xxxv = Athen. xii. 527 F–528 A; Nikolaos of Damaskos and Poseidonios = Athen. vi. 266 EF. In Sicily in 134 and 104 B.C. the slave leaders of the great rebellions claimed to be in intimate contact with gods and goddesses (Diod. xxxiv. 2. 5–7; xxxvi. 4. 4) .

Chapter VIII

The Jews to 166 B.C.

Our records of Jewish religious resistance to Hellenism are more numerous than those of any other people in the East, and we can, therefore, obtain a more intimate and detailed knowledge of the different reactions of Jewish people to Greco-Makedonian occupation. Yet there are certain obstacles to a complete understanding of this phase of Jewish history, for Jewish writers of the third and second centuries often wrote anonymously and made few exact references to historical events of their day. They were more concerned with interpreting the history of their times as illustrating the ageless, unchanging value of Israel's covenant with God. To do this, furthermore, they made growing use of apocalyptic idiom, so that the scholar's task of solving problems of date, authorship, and meaning of a document is often difficult. The study of Hellenistic Judaism is virtually a separate field in itself, and I do not, therefore, intend to deal exhaustively with matters of textual criticism. I shall rely on the work that has already been done on this period, and shall refer the reader in the notes to more extended treatments of literary problems.

The Greeks knew nothing of the Jews, so far as our literary sources show, before the Makedonian conquest. The vague remarks in Herodotos concerning the "Syrians of Palestine" probably do not refer to the Jews. Nor is there any substance to the story that Aristotle once met and conversed with a Jew in Asia Minor.[1] Consequently, it is impossible to show that fourth-century Greeks scorned the Jews as some had the Persians or the Babylonians. Of course it is safe to assume that certain Greeks would regard the religious concepts of the Jews with scant respect, given the fact that Hellenes generally felt superior to Asiatics.

On the Jewish side there was previous knowledge of Greeks. The

---

[1] Herod. ii. 104; vii. 89; rejected by W. Jaeger, "Greeks and Jews," *JR* 18 (1938), 127, n. 1. The story of Aristotle in Jos. *A. Ap.* i. 176–82; see W. Jaeger, *op. cit.,* 128–32.

Jews said that the Greeks were descended from Japheth; therefore they were rather far removed from the center of creation and the ebb and flow of divine history. They were aware that the people of Ionia did not know Yahweh or his glory, and that they were retailers of bronzeware and dealers in the slave trade. In the fourth century Attic tetradrachms were already circulating on a large scale in Jewish Palestine, and it was a little earlier than this time that the writer of Joel condemned Tyre and Sidon for selling Jewish slaves to the far distant Greeks.[2]

This rather inconsiderable evidence is not grounds for assuming that the Jews of 300 B.C. were prepared to hate Hellenes as a matter of course. One may believe, however, that the Jews would feel superior to the pagan Greeks, for the former were the Chosen People of Yahweh, exclusive partners in the divine covenant. The feeling of uniqueness had been growing in the period of Persian rule, and the Jews had been occasionally restless subjects. But attempts of firebrands to revolt had been quashed either by conservative Jews in the community or by the agents of the Great King. Not all Jews of this period had been narrowly patriotic. Rather, Judaism in the sixth and fifth centuries showed a general tendency towards universalism. After Kyros the Great had allowed those Jews exiled by Nebuchadnezzar to return to Palestine, he facilitated the reconstruction of the badly damaged Temple of Solomon. Artaxerxes showed favor to Ezra and Nehemiah. This tolerance was reciprocated by Jews interested in the world-wide allegiance of all mankind to Judaism, an attitude seen in the authors of Ruth and Jonah, although first expressed by Deutero-Isaiah.[3] But as the Persian period progressed, feelings of exclusive superiority tended to dominate these other ideas, as Ezra forced the Hebrews to rid themselves of their foreign wives. Many Jews continued to be parochial during the Hellenistic period, and this feeling was an important facet of opinion confronting the European conquerors of Palestine.

After the death of Alexander the Great, Judah for over a century was a part of the Ptolemaic Empire. After 285 B.C., the assimilation of Palestine into this imperial system was rapid and must have been completed in the reign of Ptolemy II Philadelphos. The victory of Antiochos III in the Battle of Paneion transferred her to Seleukid control in

    [2] Gen. x. 1; Is. lxvi. 19; Ezek. xxvii. 13. Coins: S. W. Baron, *S.R.H.J.* (2nd ed., 1952), i. 184. Slaves: Joel iii. 6–8.
    [3] Rebelliousness: Haggai; Malachi; Jos. *Ant.* xi. 297–301; A. T. Olmstead, *H.P.E.* (1948), 304, 398; R. Ghirshman, *Iran* (1954), 142. Cooperation: Ezra; Nehemiah; A. T. Olmstead, *op. cit.*, 145–6, 304–8, 313–7; R. Ghirshman, *op. cit.*, 195. Allegiance: Is. xlii. 6–7; xlv. 14–7, 23–4; xlix. 6, 22–3; lv. 5; lx. 1–12.

200 B.C. The third century thus formed a unified period in which a large part of Jewish history was determined by the Ptolemies' establishment of their system of state-capitalism. The Jews' reaction to this was varied: some liked it and more hated it. The hostile reaction grew out of the sense of the peculiar relationship of the Jews to Yahweh that was becoming more pronounced at this time. Scholars generally agree that 1 and 2 Chronicles, Ezra, and Nehemiah received their present form at the hands of an anonymous editor and compiler of priestly rank, whom we designate the Chronicler, early in the third century. These books were an ecclesiastical history of the Jews which covered the period from the earliest times, especially from the founding of the Temple, to the Persian era. It was not specifically anti-Hellenic, for the Greeks are passed by with no more than a reference to their having been descendants of Japheth. But the Chronicler does show evidence of increasing parochialism. This history is written to glorify a chosen people; it is made to exalt Judah. The Temple, its clergy, and its service are given prominent place, and the sins of Judah and its greatest royal hero, David, are either minimized or omitted. R. H. Pfeiffer has called this work an apologia for Judaism constructed out of history, for the Chronicler interpreted human events as culminating in the temple-state of Yahweh.[4] It is antiquarian and its ethos somewhat similar to that of the Babylonian Semiramis and Nebuchadnezzar legends.

A contemporary book was Proverbs, a compilation made from divers sources. Some sections go back to rather remote times, a few verses even to wisdom literature of pharaonic Egypt. Only chapters 1–9 seem to be a collection gathered for the first time in the third century. This section shows no traces of anti-Hellenism. Indeed the author shows little consciousness of Jewish national life and never uses the terms "Judah" or "Israel." He has instead a wide, international outlook, and may have lived in the society of the upper classes.[5]

While these currents were prevalent in studious circles in Judah, a

[4] G. H. Box, *Judaism in the Greek Period* (1932), 116; J. A. Bewer, *The Literature of the Old Testament* (rev. ed., 1933), 287–8; O. Eissfeldt, *E.A.T.* (1934), 612–3; R. H. Pfeiffer, *I.O.T.* (2nd ed., 1948), 811–2; H. H. Rowley, *G.O.T.* (1950), 162–5; A. Bentzen, *I.O.T.* (2nd ed., 1952), ii. 215; M. Burrows, "Ancient Israel," *The Idea of History in the Ancient Near East* (ed. R. C. Dentan, 1955), 125–6.

[5] G. H. Box, *Judaism in the Greek Period* (1932), 135; J. A. Bewer, *The Literature of the Old Testament* (rev. ed., 1933), 309; R. H. Pfeiffer, *I.O.T.* (2nd ed., 1948), 645; H. H. Rowley, *G.O.T.* (1950), 140; A. Bentzen, *I.O.T.* (2nd ed., 1952), ii. 171–2.

The reference to a "strange woman" in Prov. vi. 24 is not a reference to Hellenism but to sin in general.

handful of scholarly Greeks were recording the peculiar customs of the
Jews. On the whole they were impressed. Hekataios, court historian of
the Ptolemies, wrote a monograph on Jewish life about 300 B.C. and
was favorably inclined toward it. He said the Jews lived under laws
given long ago by Moses. They were now administered not by a king
but by a high priest noteworthy for the excellence of his wisdom and
the eminence of his morality. The Jews were faithful to this law even
unto death. It inculcated bravery, endurance, and self-discipline. The
result has been to make these people philosophical. Their religion is
free from idolatry while also abstract and spiritual. God is *ouranos*.
That diligent recorder of facts Theophrastos wrote out similar opinions, being guided by what he read in Hekataios.[6]

These four literary men—two Jews and two Greeks—lived well
removed from the experience of everyday life. While they were writing
their moderate opinions, practical men of affairs were consolidating
the Ptolemies' organization of Palestine, and other men were beginning to resent it. Hekataios did observe that the Jews were being
widely slandered by various people. Some Greeks regarded them as
unimportant hillbillies; Hieronymos of Kardia did not mention them
in his book about the history of the *Diadochoi*.[7] This was not anti-
Semitism; it was the attitude of certain Greeks that Asiatics existed to
be exploited. The Chosen People resented this bitterly, and in the
second half of the third century condemnation of the Hellenes began
with a series of oracles now contained in Isaiah. Like the Old Testament as a whole, this book is really a library, a collection of prophecies,
psalms, bits of prose history, proverbs, and descriptions of apocalyptic
visions. These come from the prophet Isaiah himself, a man of the
eighth century, and from a number of men of subsequent generations.
The most important of these is Deutero-Isaiah, the exiled Jew in
Babylon responsible for most of chapters 40–56. The first thirty-nine
chapters contain all the late material. This section shows undoubted
patchwork, with frequent alternation of passages of prose and verse,
and constantly changing style and content. The diversity of conditions
and things described makes a series of vignettes depicting the Assyrian,
Chaldean, Persian, and Greek eras.

One part of Isaiah, chapters 24–27, belongs to the Ptolemaic period.
This section is itself a collection of ten separate apocalytic oracles,[8]
some in prose but most in verse. The poetic sections are as follows.

6 Hekataios = Diod. xl. 3. 5; Jos. *A. Ap.* i. 190–1. Theophrastos = Porphyry, *On
Abstinence* ii. 26. For both, see W. Jaeger, "Greeks and Jews," *JR* 18 (1938), 130–42.

7 Jos. *A. Ap.* i. 191, 214.

8 E. Meyer, *Ursprung und Anfänge des Christentums* (1921), ii. 5–8; J. A. Bewer,
The Literature of the Old Testament (rev. ed., 1933), 399; O. Eissfeldt, *E.A.T.*

xxiv. 1–23 is a description of the twisting the earth will undergo when Yahweh scatters all its inhabitants. The people have violated the covenant. Therefore the god will punish the kings of this world, and at the end of time will reign in glory as Judah's rightful king.

xxv. 1–5 is a joyful hymn, praising Yahweh for destroying a city full of aliens. The poor and downtrodden find refuge in his victory.

xxvi. 1–6 is a hymn to be sung by the faithful on That Day, the day of judgment. Yahweh attacks a lofty, proud city and razes it to the ground, so that the feet of the poor can walk through its dust.

xxvi. 7–21 expresses the yearning of a psalmist for salvation. The evil flourish and do not know the commandments of God. May fire consume them. But the Lord has saved and sustained the nation in the past, and soon his wrath will fall upon the people of the earth.

xxvii. 2–5 is another Judgment Day song; Yahweh threatens those who threaten his righteous people.

xxvii. 6 is a very short aggressive prediction that in the future a world-wide population will come from the seed of Jacob and Israel.

xxvii. 7–11 is a lament for the desolate plight of Judah. It has come about because of the people, who forsake the law for the sake of idols. God will show them neither mercy nor compassion.

In these verse oracles no certain identification of people or places or events can be made. Nor can such identification be made in closely associated prose passages. Isaiah xxv. 6–12 is a hopeful vision of a transfigured world with abundance of things to eat. Death is no more and neither is sorrow or sadness. The faithful turn to their god with gladness while he presses down a foreign power into a dung-pit. Although the nation is called Moab, it is possible that Egypt was really meant. Chapter xxvii. 1 is a short prophecy of the coming victory of Yahweh over Leviathan, the fleeing serpent, and over Tannim, the sea dragon. This is an apocalyptic allusion to the two world powers, the Ptolemaic and Seleukid states. The image comes from the old myth of the New Year enthronement of Yahweh, victorious over the powers of evil. The oracle in xxvii. 12–13 looks forward to the return of the Jews outside Palestine to worship at the holy mountain of Zion.

The evidence of Isaiah 24–27 is that in the third century Ptolemaic economic activity and government in Palestine were beginning to make a bad impression on Jewish society. The protest was against the changing social conditions and religious ideas that the regime brought about. In xxiv. 1–23 death is wished to city-dwellers, slaves

(1934), 363–8; R. H. Pfeiffer, *I.O.T.* (2nd ed., 1948), 420, 441–8; H. H. Rowley, *G.O.T.* (1950), 91–3; A. Bentzen, *I.O.T.* (2nd ed., 1952), ii. 114–5. On early Jewish apocalyptic literature see S. B. Frost, *Old Testament Apocalyptic* (1952).

and their masters, buyers and sellers, lenders and borrowers, who are all violators of the Mosaic law. This sounds like a complaint against the rich class resulting from the introduction of a more intense form of money economy than the Jews were accustomed to. The oracle xxv. 1–5 denounces Palestinian cities for their wickedness: it looks forward to the release of the poor from foreign exploiters. This is an obvious protest against the growing management of the country by Greek and Hellenized native elements. In fact, the cry of the peasant against the landlord in the city is a motif running throughout Isaiah 24–27 and into the literature of the following century.

The book of Zechariah contains a good deal of material similar to the above. This is found in chapters 9–14, which belong to the third century. The section cannot be dated precisely, since allusions to persons and events are quite general. These chapters were once separate pieces, but were later collected to form part of a single book. The superscription "An Oracle" occurs twice in 9–14; furthermore, there is alternation between prose and verse within the six chapters, as well as significant changes in subject. There are six distinct oracles in the collection, and since they are longer than the oracles in Isaiah 24–27, they may represent a more developed and later form of the same apocalyptic style of literature.[9]

ix. 1–10 is the voice of Yahweh. He states that the cities of the Levant from Damaskos to Gaza belong to Him as much as does Jerusalem. But Tyre has heaped up silver like the dust, and gold like the dirt of the streets. These will be taken away, for the pagans have not practiced true religion. Only a remnant will survive the onslaught of his triumphant king-savior. Perhaps hatred for the Greeks' military operations in Palestine lies behind the militant denunciations of this prophet. The five Syrian Wars of the third century used Palestine at least as a base of operations when not as a battlefield. The consequent destruction or confiscation of property or the necessity of quartering and supplying large armies of the Ptolemies may have led to this peasant Jew's prediction that God would send an humble savior-king whose triumph would be to command peace to the nations.[10]

---

[9] G. H. Box, *Judaism in the Greek Period* (1932), 88–106; J. A. Bewer, *The Literature of the Old Testament* (rev. ed., 1933), 407, 419–24; O. Eissfeldt, *E.A.T.* (1934), 489–92; R. H. Pfeiffer, *I.O.T.* (2nd ed., 1948), 607–11; H. H. Rowley, *G.O.T.* (1950), 121–2; A. Bentzen, *I.O.T.* (2nd ed., 1952), ii. 158–60; S. B. Frost, *Old Testament Apocalyptic* (1952), 125.

[10] For an account of warfare in Palestine during the Hellenistic Period see I. Abrahams, *Campaigns in Palestine from Alexander the Great* (1927). Peasant: L. Finkelstein, *The Pharisees* (1938), ii. 518, 528–34.

ix. 11–17 is another oracle spoken by Yahweh. After condemning the world of the Greeks for selling and buying slaves, he prophesies that the Jews will defeat the Greeks in battle with his own active help, and when he has slain them all, his people will drink a victory toast in blood. Then nature will be transformed supernaturally, and happiness will be established forever. Since the seer predicts that in the new age grain will make the young men flourish and new wine the maidens, the hate that provoked the oracle may have been outrage at food shortages in Judah for which the Greeks were held responsible.

x. 1–xi. 3 is a hot outburst against the kings of the world, both in Egypt (the Lagids) and in Assyria (the Seleukids). This oracle is a war cry, an angry call to battle. The power of God will defeat the vain calvary of the foe. The poem ends with the overthrow of the Greeks and the despair of their kings. The inspiration of the oracle is abhorrence for the general conditions imposed by the Ptolemies and for the religious apostasy perpetrated by diviners and dream interpreters. Because of the latter, people reject the covenant of Yahweh. The king does not act like a shepherd, for he does not remove such people from the community. According to Jewish ideas, it was a prime duty of a king to protect true religion, as Josiah had done in the seventh century. Thus, the prophet condemns the Makedonians for not increasing the authority of Yahweh.

xi. 4–17 and xiii. 7–9 is a single, confusing, curious, and textually corrupt prose prophecy. As it begins, it seems to be the voice of the Lord. But as it proceeds, a human speaker intervenes, and the whole meaning of the passage becomes obscure. Like Joel, the prophet denounces trade in Hebrew slaves and the harsh treatment they must bear. As a result of this and other evils, two-thirds of the inhabitants of Palestine will be consumed in fire.

xii. 1–xiii. 6 is a prediction by a man living in Jerusalem of Israel's glorious future. When the Makedonian armies are smitten with madness by God, Judah will be exalted and the destruction of idol worship and false prophets assured.

xiv. 1–21 is a similar prediction by a plebeian of future glory and ultimate triumph, except that its tone is far more vicious. The gentiles will disgorge their silver and gold and fine clothes for the use of the Chosen People. The enemies of Judah will suffer from plague, thirst, and dry rot. The Ptolemies are threatened with pestilence and other punishments if they do not submit to the true king, Yahweh of Jerusalem.

Thus, the general impression that one obtains from the prophets who composed these six oracles is a hatred of Ptolemaic kingship, on the grounds that it has led to the interposition of a human king between Yahweh and his people, and that this, in turn, has led to the introduction of false religion into Palestine. And in agreement with Isaiah 24–27, the prophets condemn the suffering and hardship that Jews have to undergo to provide comfort for alien merchants, landlords, and slave dealers. Deutero-Zechariah, then, is concerned with the impact of Makedonian kingship in both economic and theological terms.

More anti-Hellenic literature of the third century was contained in the stories about Daniel, in chapters 1–6 of the book.[11] They were concerned with the problem of Greek kingship. Was it a worthy agent of divine rule? Some of the ideas in these chapters were brought into Palestine from Persia, being passed along by the Jewish community in Babylonia, perhaps from Babylon itself, or from Seleukeia or the new city of Doura.[12] The Jewish prophet was sure that Greek kingship was evil. Nebuchadnezzar stands for the Hellenistic kings, and it is shown again and again that his religion is idolatrous. He is attacked for not supporting the religion of the one true god. In Daniel 4 he is smitten with madness for worshipping idols and is then returned to his senses and converted. There is a denunciation of the Hellenistic cult of kings, an institution of both Ptolemies and Seleukids.[13] This kingship did not lead to safety for Jewish religion, and the prophet therefore foretells in Daniel 2 that Makedonian kingship is coming to an end. Yahweh will intervene, and a divine fifth monarchy will make the Jewish people dominate Asia. In the cataclysm

[11] The evidence for a Persian source behind Daniel 2, 4, and 7 is given on pp. 20–25, above. The dating and analysis of the various chapters in Daniel is still a matter of discussion. The grouping of Daniel into a third-century section made up of chapters 1–6 and a second-century section of chapters 7–12 is uncertain. A grouping of 1–7 and 8–12 is alternatively possible. There are also some important scholars who argue for complete unity of the whole book. For this view see H. H. Rowley, "The Unity of the Book of Daniel," *The Servant of the Lord* (1954), 237–68.

Several dates have been proposed for the first section, varying between 250 and 175 B.C.: G. H. Box, *Judaism in the Greek Period* (1932), 207–9; O. Eissfeldt, *E.A.T.* (1934), 574–6; R. H. Pfeiffer, *I.O.T.* (2nd ed., 1948), 760–2; A. Bentzen, *I.O.T.* (2nd ed., 1952), ii. 195–6; J. C. Dancy, *A Commentary on I Maccabees* (1954), 25. Here, I have followed the analysis of J. A. Montgomery, *A Critical and Exegetical Commentary on the Book of Daniel* (1927), 90–9, and H. L. Ginsberg, *Studies in Daniel* (1948), 6–30.

[12] Dan. iii. 1.

[13] Dan. iii. 1–7.

towards which human history is relentlessly moving only persons faithful to Judaism will be preserved.

This cycle of encouraging stories was a contribution of the Diaspora, which in the third century began to influence the development of Jewish religion, culture, and society as a whole. The Dispersion could make a more universal-minded contribution than could narrow-minded, parochial persons in Palestine. The Jews in Egypt or Mesopotamia were much more intimate with the gentile world than their cousins in Judah. Through continual contact many became more willing to accept at least certain alien ideas, like those in the *Bahman Yasht,* than the very straitly ritualled members of the Palestinian community. This was the case with Tobit, an apocryphal book never admitted to the Jerusalem canon. Tobit was written in Aramaic around 200 B.C. or maybe a little later in Mesopotamia.[14] Persian influence is apparent in the angel Asmodeus and in the Median locale of the story. These details were of secondary importance; the purpose of the writer was to confirm the Diaspora in its faithfulness to Judaism. He also looked forward to the conversion of the gentiles and the peacefulness of the subsequent age. If C. C. Torrey is right in identifying the Nineveh of the story with the Seleukeia of Mesopotamia, the writer of Tobit equated the Seleukids' eastern capital with the source of evil and evil kingship.[15]

There are two principal complaints that run through all these third-century oracles: hatred for foreign kingship and loathing for the hard conditions faced by poverty-ridden people in Judah. The fate of the downtrodden was blamed on the evil inherent in the kingship itself, because of Hebrew conceptions of the proper duties of a king. These ideas had been developed as early as the eleventh and tenth centuries B.C., during the time that the Davidic monarchy came into being. They came, however, not only from the kings and the

---

[14] O. Eissfeldt, *E.A.T.* (1934), 640–1; C. C. Torrey, "Nineveh in the Book of Tobit," *JBL* 41 (1922), 237–45; *The Apocryphal Literature* (1945), 85; R. H. Pfeiffer, *History of New Testament Times* (1949), 265–74; A. Bentzen, *I.O.T.* (2nd ed., 1952), ii. 224–5; F. Zimmermann, *The Book of Tobit* (1958), 16–27, argues for a second-century date and composition in the Jewish community of Antioch. G. Widengren, "Quelques rapports entre juifs et iraniens à l'époque des Parthes," Suppl. to *Vetus Testamentum* 4 (1956), 216–7, argues for an ultimate origin in the wisdom literature of Babylonia and Sumeria. The original language was almost certainly Aramaic, so F. Zimmermann, *op. cit.;* J. M. Allegro, *The Dead Sea Scrolls* (1956), 119; M. Burrows, *More Light on the Dead Sea Scrolls* (1958), 117–8; and F. M. Cross, *The Ancient Library of Qumran* (1958), 34.

[15] Tob. i. 10–2, 17–20; xiii. 11–4; xiv. 6–7.

circle around them, but also from an exceedingly important party which opposed the kings and sought to inculcate ideas of true and righteous rule. This party claimed prophetic inspiration, and the men in it were fearless critics of certain practices of the monarchy. Samuel condemned the institution from the beginning, predicting that the professional standing army the kings would keep would be a sorrowful burden for the people and that the kings would act as interpreters of Yahweh's will. Only a prophet could do that; the kings would therefore sinfully stand between the god and his people. Royal theories of eminent domain would curtail individual rights, and Nathan exposed David for the crime of sending soldier Uriah to his death so that he could lay grasping hands on Bathsheba. Elijah opposed Ahab to his face not only for confiscating the vineyard of a free man but principally because this king permitted the worship of Ba'al and kept a number of that no-god's prophets in his palace.

Out of this struggle emerged the traditional Hebrew prophetic concept of kingship. The true king was Yahweh, the source of law, the fount of power, the lord of nature, the giver of the covenant. His human king was only the mortal administrator of divine justice; the commander of the troops; the reliever of the distressed, the helpless, and the unprotected; the obedient protector and enthusiastic upholder of the covenant. The human king was still a most important person, and his good behavior was necessary for the existence of the state itself. If he overlooked the covenant or thirsted after foreign gods, Judah itself was in danger. To check his evil inclinations, the prophets interpreted the king's actions for him in terms of the law, and they pronounced the will of Yahweh concerning his activity.[16]

Now, the prophecies in Isaiah 24–27 are not as overtly concerned with the problem of kingship as those in Daniel and Zechariah. But all agreed basically that the Ptolemaic kings were evil because they did not dispense Yahweh's justice; they did not protect the helpless and poor, and they above all did not protect and encourage the worship of Yahweh. They were aliens who allowed Greek law to be enforced, who permitted Jews to be enslaved or pompous rich landowners to lord it over the poor, and who above all tolerated the existence of cults of Ba'al, Zeus, Isis, and themselves. The old standard of judgment showed through quite clearly in Zechariah. Just as in 1

---

[16] Two scholars who have recently discussed Hebrew kingship are S. Mowinckel, *He That Cometh* (1955), see especially p. 68, and A. R. Johnson, *Sacral Kingship in Ancient Israel* (1955), especially pp. 3–6, 22–7, 129–31; "Hebrew Conceptions of Kingship," *Myth, Ritual and Kingship* (ed. S. H. Hooke, 1958), 204–35.

Kings xvii. 1 the sins of Ahab were said to have caused a drought lasting three years in Israel, so in Zechariah xiv. 17 the people who do not go up to Jerusalem to worship Yahweh the King will have to live without rain.

The third-century prophets were not unanimous as to how God would finally vindicate the covenant and drive out the enemy; would it be with the agency of a human king or without? Some men thought of direct and drastic divine intervention. But Zechariah ix. 1–10 looked forward to the coming of a human king and prophesied that his dominion would be "from Sea to Sea, and from the River to the ends of the earth." This was the exact terminology of an old royal psalm written before the exile and the death of the last king of David's line.[17] This new Jewish king would be "humble and riding upon an ass." This may be tinged with irony, a satire on Ptolemy IV who rode into the Battle of Raphia on top of an elephant, but what was really meant was that any new monarch would have to be covenant-abiding. The differences among these men was an old ambivalence of Jewish society. The pressure of events in the second half of the third century was such that some men longed for a return of a human monarchy —let us settle with these Greeks with our own royal army—God will strengthen our arms. "I will brandish your sons, O Zion, over your sons, O Greece."[18] Others clove to the stricter tradition that Yahweh was king and needed no human representative but the high priest in Jerusalem. Human kingship remained popular with a minority, but with an influential and important minority, and in the second century the institution would be revived.

Turning from these partly theoretical considerations of the prophets to the problem of the lower classes, here there was stern denunciation of the conditions existing in Palestine under Ptolemaic administration. The denunciations of the prophets were as much against Hellenized Jews as against Greeks themselves, and oracles in the Isaian and Zecharian collections were confident that half of native Jerusalem would be consumed along with the aliens in the city. This feeling resulted from the nature of the administrative and propertied classes dominating Palestine, and it is to a consideration of this Greco-Oriental group that we must now turn. In the third century there was a great reorganization of trade routes and other forms of economic life in Palestine, owing less to the overthrow of the Persian Empire than to the close connection the Lagids developed

---

[17] Zech. ix. 10c = Ps. lxxii. 8. This apparently is a Babylonian phrase.
[18] Zech. ix. 13.

between Judah and Egypt and the large influx of Greeks interested in making their fortunes in this fabled land. Ptolemy I and II developed institutions designed efficiently to exploit the resources of the countries subject to them. Jews were inevitably involved in this activity, and many found their way into Egypt for one reason or another. There is a story that Ptolemy I conscripted 100,000 Jews for service with his army. There had been a Jewish mercenary garrison in Egypt on Persian service, and Soter may have thought these hill people from Palestine first-class fighting men. I am certain that the story is exaggerated, since Hekataios says that many voluntarily accompanied him. By 300 B.C. Ptolemy was obviously a success and therefore a good master to serve. Many civilians also went to Egypt. These included an *archieireus* named Ezekias and the others who accompanied him to escape certain unspecified disturbances in Palestine. Perhaps some were driven to leave by an excess of population living on too little land.[19] At any rate, there were many Jews in Egypt by 250. Some were soldiers and some were royal peasants or other kinds of rural workmen —shepherds, vine-keepers, field guards. Some went into business. Little settlements sprang up and organized "houses of prayer" for themselves from Alexandria to Upper Egypt. Disputes broke out between Judaeans and Samaritans as to whether sacrifices sent to the old country should be made at Zion or Gerizim. The majority of these persons learned Greek and took Greek names; a few of them took Egyptian names.[20] This was the beginning of Hellenization for the Jews in the Dispersion. With some it stopped with learning the language; with others it went a good deal further.

The evidence of personal names shows that Jews identified themselves much more closely with the Greeks in Egypt than with the natives. On the whole they had higher status than Egyptians did in their own country, since some Jews were soldiers in the Ptolemaic forces from the beginning and Egyptians were not until 218 B.C. This must have been a particularly acid dose, coming as it did after the Makedonian conquest exchanged Alexander for Dareios III. The Egyptians had repeatedly tried, and with some success, to be independent of the Persian Empire, a state which had also employed Jewish soldiers to keep the country down. Now, these former servants of the

[19] Soldiers: (Pseudo-) Aristeas, 4, 12–4, 19; Jos. *Ant.* xii. 7; Hekataios = Jos. *A.Ap.* i. 186. Ezekias: *ibid.*, i. 186–7. Overpopulation: V. Tcherikover, *Hellenistic Civilization and the Jews* (1959), 209–10.

[20] Soldiers: *C.P.J.*, 18–32; peasants: *ibid.*, 9, 12–4; wool business: *ibid.*, 38. Houses of prayer: *O.G.I.S.*, 129, 726; *S.B.* 8939; *C.P.J.*, 129. Disputes: Jos. *Ant.* xii. 10. Greek names: *C.P.J.*, pp. 27–8; Nos. 30, 126; Egyptian: *ibid.*, No. 46. See, too, V. Tcherikover, *Hellenistic Civilization and the Jews* (1959), 347; 524, n. 8.

Great King were soldiers still. How dishonorable for Egypt! And I suppose that when Jews and Egyptians were able to talk to one another, the Egyptians were told that their gods were no-gods, that only Yahweh of Hosts ruled in heaven, and that the Jewish god had killed a pharaoh during the Exodus. All this was the beginning of Egyptian hatred for the Jews. This primitive anti-Semitism must willy-nilly have helped curtail Jewish anti-Hellenism. One cannot be hateful both to God and to his enemies. Around 275 B.C. the Egyptian priest Manethon made a formal attack on the Jews. He identified them with the historical Hyksos, and accused them of having invaded and conquered the Valley of the Nile under the leadership of the leprosy-ridden renegade Egyptian Osarsiph, who changed his name to Moses. They razed cities and temples, forced priests to roast the sacred animals, and treated the population with utmost ferocity, killing some and enslaving others. They were ultimately expelled from the country by the XVIIIth and XIXth dynasties. Much later, Manethon continued inaccurately, Pharaoh Nechon captured Jerusalem and carried off King Ioachaz to Egypt. To an Egyptian this was pleasant to hear, for little incidents kept the fires of Egyptian hatred burning. In 218 B.C. a wool merchant named Harmyysis was cheated by the Jew Seos. In 210 B.C. three swashbuckling Jewish soldiers raided a vineyard to see what they could steal and severely mauled and injured the Egyptian guard Horus, who tried to stop them. On the other hand the government scribe Marres seems illegally to have raised the rent of the peasant Judas, who had to appeal to higher authority for redress.[21]

Jews in Egypt rapidly forgot Hebrew and Aramaic and took to Greek. The Septuagint translation of the Old Testament was begun in the third century. They even acquired a taste for Alexandrian literature, and towards the end of the third century the Jew Demetrios wrote a book *On the Kings of Iudaia* in Greek. Its meticulous scholarship and attention to details of chronology were in the best tradition of Hellenistic historiography.[22] Perhaps this book was mainly intended for Jewish readers who wanted to be assured that Manethon was wrong.

While the Diaspora along the Nile gradually adopted a veneer of Greek culture, it maintained its contacts with Palestine, and in the process no doubt helped bring Hellenism into Palestine. In the third

---

[21] Jews' invasion: Manethon, *Egyptiaka*, frag. 42 (Waddell) = Jos. *A.Ap.* i. 73–92; frag. 54 = *ibid.*, i. 227–87. Nechon: Manethon, *op. cit.*, frag. 68, 69 A and B (Waddell) = Syncellus, pp. 141, 143; Eusebios, *Chronicle* (Armenian) i. p. 104. Wool: *C.P.J.*, 38. Soldiers three: *ibid.*, 21. Marres: *ibid.*, 43 (150 B.C.) .

[22] R. H. Pfeiffer, *History of New Testament Times* (1949) , 200–1; M. Hadas, *Hellenistic Culture* (1959) , 94–5.

century one Solymios travelled from Judah into Alexandria to marry
his daughter to a Jew of high rank there. The wealthy Palestinian
Joseph bar Tobias deposited his money in the metropolis under the
care of his own *oikonomos*.[23] At the same time Greeks, and their
Syrian and Arab dependents, involved in the economic management
of the Lagid Empire, made contacts in Palestine, an area valuable for
its supply of slaves, beasts of burden, and other commodities. There
was a natural identity of interest between men of business. Zenon,
agent of the powerful royal *dioiketes* Apollonios, was sent to Palestine
to develop his master's business there. In 259 B.C. he bought a slave
girl and met Nikanor, a man in the service of the wealthy Jewish
sheikh Tobias. The contact ripened and in 257 Tobias sent presents
to Apollonios, a eunuch and four slaves. His covering letter included
the Greek formula "many thanks to the gods," showing that a form of
Hellenization other than linguistic was taking root.[24] This slave
traffic was roundly denounced in Isaiah xxiv. 1–23 and Zechariah
ix. 11–17.

This Tobias became a petty factor in the Ptolemaic imperial system,
holding a fortress in the Jordan Valley for the king against wandering
Nabataians of Transjordan. If prophets hated Tobias for a slave-deal-
ing Jew paying court to pagan gods, they overlooked the undoubted
service he performed protecting Judah from raids. His son Joseph
carried the family further along the road towards Hellenization and
oppression of the poor. Since he was the nephew of the high priest
Onias, he had extremely influential connections and much prestige,
and did not scruple to use bribes to pervert justice and secure his ends.
Aside from enjoying a large income derived from land, he was able to
grow extremely rich from being a farmer of revenues for Ptolemy IV
in Koile Syria. Much of the great wealth the Tobiads accumulated
went for the private use of the family, as shown by the massive
foundation blocks of their mausoleum surviving near the Jordan, a
building originally decorated with Greek akanthos patterns and
Corinthian columns.[25]

[23] Solymios: Jos. *Ant.* xii. 187. Joseph: *ibid.*, xii. 200.

[24] *C.P.J.*, 1 and 4. The selling of slaves in Palestine was not without regulation
by the government. *S.B.* 8008 says that slaves could be sold only publicly under
government auspices, and that freemen were *not* to be enslaved. What was an
effort on Ptolemy's part to protect people probably resulted in his being blamed
by the prophets for allowing this ancient institution to continue to sell Jews to
gentiles.

[25] Tobias: V. Tcherikover in *C.P.J.*, 116–7. On Joseph: Jos. *Ant.* xii. 160–87;
P. Cairo Zenon 59037; M. I. Rostovtzeff, *S.E.H.H.W.* i. 338; V. Tcherikover, *Hellenistic Civilization and the Jews* (1959), 70–2, 133–4. Bribery: Jos. *Ant.* xii. 185;

The financial and commercial activity of men like Joseph and his brothers was not entirely new, nor was the peasant resentment that it provoked. The rural poor whose labor helped to make the entrepreneurs rich were rather despised by the upper classes, who about this time were making the phrase '*am ha-arez,* "people of the soil," into the equivalent of the American English term "peasants." Resentment among the peasants was based on the religious tradition which held that land was inalienable. A man could not buy a neighbor's land in perpetuity, although he could rent it. The original holder or his kinsmen had an absolute theoretical right to recovery at any time; and, in any case, the new owner had to hand back the fields in the Year of Jubilee. In no circumstances could the common land of a village be sold. These regulations were intended to prevent the accumulation of large estates in the hands of a few. But they were difficult to enforce, and the rich were continually attacked for their malpractice. Around 615 B.C. Zephaniah execrated rich landowners along with wealthy men in Jerusalem's countinghouses. Later on Nehemiah forced the gentry to return property that had been mortgaged to them so that the original owners could pay their taxes.[26] Of course the rich either ignored the legal theories of Leviticus and Numbers or found ways to circumvent them. Judges could be bribed. There are recollections of their self-justifications among the Proverbs. Wealth, they said, was a positive protection against unforeseen disaster. The poor were lazy, the rich diligent; let the poor therefore be put to labor while the enterprising ruled them. The response of the poor was sometimes meek and sometimes malicious. Let the rich have their revenues; honest, unaffecting righteousness is better. Or, "He who trusts in his riches will wither, but the righteous will flourish like a green leaf." It was from the religious tradition respecting the rights of the peasants on the land that the protests of Isaiah and Zechariah came. The city of the alien Greek and his Jewish cohort would be brought low and cast into the dust. "The foot tramples it, the feet of the poor, the steps of the needy."[27]

The struggle of rich and poor was complicated by the new conditions of Hellenistic Palestine, which led to the rise of new men. Their

---

cf. Eccl. v. 8. Mausoleum: Jos. *Ant.* xii. 230–3; W. F. Albright, *The Archeology of Palestine* (1949) , 149–50; A. Reifenberg, *Ancient Hebrew Arts* (1950) , 53.

[26] The phrase: L. Finkelstein, *The Pharisees* (1938) , i. 25–6. Regulations: Lev. xxv. 10, 13–7, 23–8, 31, 34; Num. xxvi. 52–6; cf. Hekataios = Diod. xl. 3. 7. Zeph. i. 13, 18. Neh. v. 1–13.

[27] Justification of wealth: Prov. x. 15; x. 4; xii. 24. Comfort for the poor: Prov. xvi. 8; ix. 28. The last quotation is Is. xxvi. 6.

eager desire to acquire money led to bickering in the holiest institution of Judah. Ptolemaic taxes in Palestine were farmed, and the official responsible for this activity was none other than the high priest. Joseph, son of Tobias, heartily desired to become collector, and he consequently charged his uncle Onias, the high priest, with fiscal misconduct, demanding he surrender his supervision of taxes. Sad to say he was right. But either the great importance of tax collecting or the high priest's lack of piety led him to suggest that he give up his priestly office instead, in order to devote himself more fully to his secular duties. Joseph resorted to pressures; he harangued the notables of Jerusalem and ultimately created so much discontent against Onias that he gained permission to go to Alexandria and buy the collectorship from Ptolemy. For twenty-two years thereafter he farmed the royal revenues. And these taxes were resented. The Ptolemies may have instituted special imposts over and above the ancient charge on land. There was riot and government repression. Ecclesiastes complained of government spies who looked for signs of disloyalty everywhere. Joseph was one of those persons whose silver and gold would not save him on That Day.[28]

Oppression of peasants and urban poor by landlord and tax farmer was not the only issue. A greater threat was the influx of Europeans bringing their laws, their culture, and their gods. Hellenism had undoubted appeal for the urban youth of Jewish towns, particularly those whose leisure gave them the opportunity to cultivate it. Samaria was prosperous in the third century, a fortified place boasting much money and importing goods from Rhodes. Greeks and Hellenized Jews bought statuettes of goddesses and the hero Herakles, and temples dedicated to Kore and to Isis and Sarapis were built. At Marisa in Judah, a colony of "Sidonians" was founded by a certain Apollophanes about 250 B.C. These persons had themselves buried in stylish rock-cut tombs inscribed with Greek epitaphs, which implies Greek funeral rites, and in the town itself practiced the arts of magic in the Greek tongue. Hellenism was imported especially by the rich, the wellborn, and the powerful, but it came in, too, with the ordinary Greek soldiers and settlers in Syria and Palestine who took wives from among the local women. Children of culturally mixed marriages tend to worship several gods.[29]

[28] Joseph as tax-farmer: Jos. *Ant.* xii. 161–78; V. Tcherikover, *Hellenistic Civilization and the Jews* (1959), 126. Taxes: Jos. *Ant.* 155, 158–9; M. I. Rostovtzeff, *S.E.H.H.W.* i. 341–9; W. W. Tarn, *H.C.* (3rd ed., 1952), 182. Spies: Eccl. x. 20.

[29] Samaria: J. W. Crowfoot, *et al.*, *Samaria-Sebaste* i (1942), 24–27, 65; iii. (1957), 4–5, 71, 83, 235–81. Kore Temple: i. 65–6; iii. 5. Isis-Sarapis: Inscription No. 13;

People of this more nearly universal turn of mind did not have as great a resentment of Makedonian rule or the new spirit of the age. There is evidence that some Jews accepted a few Greek philosophical ideas and withdrew from a strict interpretation of the law. Ecclesiastes, generally considered to have been written not long before 200 B.C., is a book that faintly shows this. It was a text of wisdom, and as such had religious overtones. It was not accepted as a religious book until after a good deal of grumbling and editing by more orthodox persons much later. The writer, let us call him Qoheleth, lived among the upper classes of Palestine, probably in Jerusalem, during the last years of the Ptolemaic regime. He had a pessimistic view of life, and advocated the enjoyment of pleasure, a good in itself. Do not be overweening in zeal for the law. "Be not righteous overmuch." Whether this was due to contact with Hellenism is difficult to say. The appearance of Greek precepts and loan words in his book does show the author knew Greek ideas. He does not appear, however, to have known any more of the Hellenism of the philosophical schools than he might have picked up second- or third-hand as proverbs in the market place. As for the Hellenic ruling class, its king and his supporters, Qoheleth sighs over the uselessness of their vain and luxurious life. But it is only a sigh, it is not denunciation. He sees oppression in Palestine and concludes that while the oppressed are unhappy, so are the oppressors.[30]

Real Hellenic philosophical influence was apparent in the life of Antigonos of Socho, who flourished around 225 B.C. This teacher with a Greek name has left a saying that performance of one's duty should be without hope of reward, an idea that shows contact with Stoicism.[31] The acceptance of foreign ideas by these men was only the beginning

---

iii. 37. Marisa: W. F. Albright, *The Archeology of Palestine* (1949), 147–9, 152–3. Cf. Zech. x. 2–3. Greek soldiers: *S.B.* 8008 (261 B.C.). Mixed marriage: *P. Cairo Zenon* 59009.

[30] Ecclesiastes generally: G. H. Box, *Judaism in the Greek Period* (1932), 148–9; J. A. Bewer, *The Literature of the Old Testament* (rev. ed., 1933), 330; O. Eissfeldt, *E.A.T.* (1934), 556–7; R. H. Pfeiffer, *I.O.T.* (2nd ed., 1948), 729–31; H. H. Rowley, *G.O.T.* (1950), 139, 153–4; A. Bentzen, *I.O.T.* (2nd ed., 1952), ii. 190; W. F. Albright, *From the Stone Age to Christianity* (Anchor ed., 1957), 20, 352; F. M. Cross, "The Oldest Manuscripts from Qumran," *JBL* 74 (1955), 147–72; *The Ancient Library of Qumran* (1958), 121–2. Greek ideas: Eccl. ii. 14; iii. 12, 19; v. 18; xii. 7. Hellenic class: Eccl. iv. 1, 13–6; v. 18.

[31] *Pirkhe Aboth* i. 3; H. H. Rowley, *G.O.T.* (1950), 139; A. Bentzen, *I.O.T.* (2nd ed., 1952), ii. 190; W. F. Albright, *From the Stone Age to Christianity* (Anchor ed., 1957), 351, 354.

of the serious inroads which Greco-Oriental culture was to make in
Judah by 170 B.C.

While Antigonos was scarcely a man to withdraw from the law of
the fathers, there were men who did withdraw, and these included
supporters of the Ptolemies. The pro-Ptolemaic faction had to fight
the anti-Lagid oracles and the secular propaganda that also circulated.
This last was responsible for the story that Ptolemy Soter had taken
Jerusalem by treachery, coming to the city with simulated peaceful
intent as if to sacrifice, but once inside laying violent hands on the
city. His subsequent rule was harsh and he enslaved many. This story
grew until in the Christian era it said that the king had actually
destroyed the city. But the friends of the king retorted that Ptolemy
had released Jews from slavery in Egypt, and had made them into
soldiers so that they could inspire fear in the Egyptians.[32]

It is obvious that by the end of the third century there were persons
entirely hostile to the Ptolemies. Prophecy foretold divine intervention
and the fire of heaven; and practical politics noted that the Seleukids
had been trying to win Koile Syria during four unsuccessful Syrian
Wars. The kings of the North might be more lenient than the efficient
Lagids. About 201 B.C. the Fifth Syrian War began, and the forces of
Antiochos III drove south into Palestine to avenge their defeat at
Raphia in 217. During these hectic times there was an uprising in Jerusalem. Polybios says that the common people of Koile Syria favored
the Lagids, but this statement could be only a generalization covering the region from Gaza to Damaskos during the period 300–150 B.C.
The evidence of the oracles in Isaiah and Zechariah shows that there
were numerous common people in Judah who hated the Ptolemies.
No doubt the rising was in part an affair led by upper-class men. A
change in the imperial regime could confer two benefits for these
people. First, it was no doubt known that the Seleukid Empire allowed
more autonomy to its constituent peoples than the Ptolemaic. That

---

[32] Anti-Ptolemy: Jos. *Ant.* xii. 3–4, 7. Some of this information was spread by the
anti-Semite Agatharchides (*ibid.,* xii. 4–7), but this does not make the story more
nearly true. The great exaggeration of the destruction of the city in App. *Syr.*
viii. 50. Pro-Ptolemaic propaganda in Jos. *Ant.* xii. 8, 11, 45, based on the tradition
in the *Letter of Aristeas.*

The Jewish soldiers in Egypt (see G. Lefebvre, "Inscriptions grecques d'Égypte,"
BCH 26 [1902], No. 16, p. 454; *P. Hibeh* 96) seem to have interested a good
many Palestinian Jews. Their existence may explain the martial verses in Zech.
ix. 11–3, which follow immediately the thought of the return of captives from a
waterless land. They predict that the sons of Zion will be brandished over the sons
of Greece. Apocalyptic writers may have thought that this body of Jews would
wage God's battle on earth on That Day.

was a good for the diligent. Second, it would make possible fresh opportunities in Jerusalem. Would a Joseph, a wealthy official of the Ptolemies, be able to maintain his position? Would an Onias, having lost such a position, be able to gain revenge? Would hitherto unknowns be able to profit? The history of the ruling circle was the aggrandizement of one noble or priestly faction at the expense of another. And while aristocrats cautiously maneuvered for position, persons inspired by prophecy tried drastic measures. The writer of Daniel 11 says of this exciting time, "The men of violence among your own people shall lift themselves up, in order to fulfill the vision." But Ptolemy's general Skopas suppressed the insurrection, only to be defeated at the Battle of Paneion a few months later in 200 B.C. Judah passed out of the hands of the Lagids into those of Antiochos III.[33]

There is evidence that the change of government was welcome. Josephos says that the Jews of "Koile Syria and Samaria" greeted the victorious Seleukid troops after the battle and provisioned the army generously. Of course conquerors have to be made to feel wanted; otherwise they may be harsh. But aside from appreciating this help, Antiochos may have been prepared to look upon the Jews favorably by reason of the experience his dynasty had had with the Dispersion. Jews in Babylonia and Asia Minor in the third century had shown themselves not entirely hostile to Hellenism, and Antiochos' opinions of the Jews would certainly have been strongly colored by his knowledge of the Diaspora, much more so than by what he may have known of Judah itself.[34] Perhaps with this in mind and because of the support given after the battle, Antiochos rewarded the Jews with exemptions and privileges. This sort of magnanimity, too, was usual for a conqueror. He gave animals, wine, oil, and frank-incense for the Temple services, and ordered that timber used for the building's maintenance be admitted free of tolls. Local government would conform to ancestral law and custom. The priests and elders would be exempt from certain imposts, and the inhabitants of Jerusalem from all taxes for three years. The *phoros* itself would thereafter be two-thirds of the Ptolemaic. The sanctity of the Temple was guaranteed by special royal enactment. Antiochos also ar-

[33] The uprising and Skopas: Jos. *Ant.* xii. 129–36; Polyb. v. 86. 10; xvi. 39. 1. The maneuverings of the *aristoi:* Jos. *Ant.* xii. 158–60; V. Tcherikover, *Hellenistic Civilization and the Jews* (1959), 127–30. Daniel xi. 14. In general: W. W. Tarn, *H.C.* (2nd ed., 1952), 213.

[34] For Hellenizing Jews in the Diaspora see W. W. Tarn, *H.C.* (2nd ed., 1952), 219, 224–5.

202   THE KING IS DEAD

ranged to send a party of two thousand Jewish families from Babylonia
to be military settlers in Lydia and Phrygia to keep those provinces
quiet. They would be given exemption from taxation for ten years
in their new homes.[35] It may have been about this time, too, that
Jews living in Ionia and Syria and in Antioch were given privileges
and legal recognition—*politeuma* organization—by Antiochos.[36] On
the whole, therefore, the Jews gained by the change in regime.

The new Seleukid government was, of course, rather similar to the
Ptolemaic. It is a matter of debate how much of the former administration was continued, or whether the Seleukids introduced changes
more in keeping with the older and looser Persian organization of the
district. We know that after the reign of Antiochos III the Jews
paid taxes on salt, a head tax, a crown tax, and certain tolls on commerce. The scale of taxation does not appear to have been too
heavy to bear; it did, at any rate, work for some years without of
itself arousing protest. What so often made taxation intolerable in the
ancient world was the method of collection by farming out the duty
to private capitalists like the Tobiads. It is likely that the collection
of taxes in the first two or three decades of the Seleukid regime was
more honest than it had been for some time; such a condition often
followed a thorough change of regime in ancient times.[37]

The literature that came from the first twenty-five years of the
Seleukid period shows that the bitterness of the oracles in Isaiah,
Zechariah, and Daniel was somewhat dissipated. These prophecies
must still have been known, but the writers of the new period have

[35] Antiochos made three decrees in all, the first granting privileges to Jerusalem = Jos. *Ant.* xii. 138–44; the second protecting the Temple = *ibid.*, xii. 145–6;
the third creating the military settlement = *ibid.*, xii. 148–53. There has been much
controversy concerning their authenticity, which is now generally accepted, although some minor points in them are rejected as forged additions. Criticism of
these passages and literature on the subject in R. Marcus, *Josephos* (Loeb Classical
Library, 1943), vii. 743–66; V. Tcherikover, *Hellenistic Civilization and the Jews*
(1959), 82–8.

Josephos says (*ibid.*, xii. 129–30) that the campaign of Paneion caused hardship in
Judah, on account of devastation of fields by the armies, so that no matter which
Greek king won, the Jews lost. This, I think, is his own much later judgment
(A.D. 90), one that is exaggerated to win sympathy for the Jews of his own day.
While some devastation no doubt occurred, still, Antiochos' "Seleukid Charter of
Jerusalem" was a positive gain.

[36] Jos. *Ant.* xii. 119, 125 refers these privileges to the time of Seleukos I and
Antiochos II. Most scholars, however, if they do not reject these statements as
Jewish lies, refer them to the period of Antiochos III. See R. Marcus, *op. cit.*,
vii. 737–42.

[37] 1 Macc. x. 29–42; E. Bickermann, *Der Gott der Makkabäer* (1937), 55–7; M. I.
Rostovtzeff, *S.E.H.H.W.* i. 346, 467–70; ii. 999–1001.

altogether a milder tone. This may have been due to three causes. First, a growing sense of acceptance of the inevitability of continuing gentile rule. Jerusalem had not been independent since 586 B.C., and its latest rising had been suppressed. Second, the nature of the new regime itself, which may have convinced many Jews that it was more amiable than the older Ptolemaic. And third, there was growing admiration for Hellenism and the life of a Hellenistic city by the Jewish upper classes. These persons had the opportunity to see Hellenism at close range, and were in a position to exert considerable influence, to set standards for the society.

Among the literature of this period was the Book of Noah, now lost, but preserved in fragments in the Books of Jubilees and 1 Enoch.[38] The message of this work is passive rejection of the works of the heathen. To observe the covenant and be loyal to Yahweh are to escape destruction. Not to do these things is to be wicked, and were not the deaths of the unrighteous compassed by the Great Flood? The book is much concerned with morality, denouncing as illicit various exceptional sexual relations. While this was no doubt in opposition to Greek customs, the book should not be entirely construed in this sense. Judaism was always concerned with refining beliefs within itself and attacking Phoenician or Jewish secular or religious practice, as this work attacks magic and astrology. The writer of Noah was certainly more concerned with sinners in Jewish society than with Greeks, who are not specifically mentioned in the fragments.

The Wisdom of Jesus ben-Sirach was written by a teacher, ideologically an early kind of Sadducee, around 180 B.C. He wrote in Hebrew, and his work was translated into Greek around 132 B.C. by his grandson, and thereby achieved wide popularity and circulation, in the Egyptian Diaspora especially.[39] He was a man who enjoyed life as much as he could within the precepts of the law and outside the notice of a nagging wife. He loved to eat well, but not so well as would cause him to lie awake nights gasping heavily. He loved to drink—indeed, life without wine was no life at all—but not so much wine as to make him forget who he was. Dignified, wise through hours

---

[38] R. H. Charles in *Apocrypha and Pseudepigrapha of the Old Testament* (1913), ii. 168–70; O. Eissfeldt, *E.A.T.* (1934), 674; A. Bentzen, *I.O.T.* (2nd ed., 1952), ii. 242–3. The fragments are in 1 Enoch vi–xi; xxxix. 1–2a; liv. 7–lv. 2; lx; lxvi. 1–lxix. 25; cvi–cvii; Jubilees vii. 20–39; x. 1–15; xxi. 10.

[39] G. H. Box. *Judaism in the Greek Period* (1932), 160–2; O. Eissfeldt, *E.A.T.* (1934), 653; C. C. Torrey, *The Apocryphal Literature* (1945), 93–4; R. H. Pfeiffer, *History of New Testament Times* (1949), 364; A. Bentzen, *I.O.T.* (2nd ed., 1952), ii. 233.

of study and meditation, travelled, a respected scribe, in his old age he set down the precepts that he felt constituted the righteous life. His wisdom admonished the rising generation of somewhat Hellenized young men. Sirach thought of the conflict of cultural ideals in terms of the loyalty that Jews must continue to show to Yahweh through allegiance to the high priest at Jerusalem. The section in praise of famous men like David, Solomon, and the Prophets culminates in an encomium on Simon II. It was his very important office to offer sacrifice, to make atonement for the community, and to teach the law. These ideals of Sirach show the importance loyal Jews attached to the Temple. This attitude is significant, since the high priesthood was shortly to become the prize of the Hellenizing circle in Jerusalem. Sirach also denounced the rich of his time, whose oppression of widows and orphans threatened to bring God's wrath upon them.[40] He denounced those who sought to take on the ways, religious or other, of aliens, and he advised the men of his generation to maintain the customs of their fathers by adherence to the law. This was true wisdom, and was found at the gate of the Temple. Israel was ruled directly by Yahweh. The gentile states had merely human kings. Israel was comparable to David, small but made strong by God; the heathen were like towering, unholy Goliath. Thus Judah could sustain her unique religion and society even though she was surrounded by a sea of enemies.[41] The conviction that religious rectitude was absolutely necessary for the continuity of Judaism runs through all the literature of this period; it is symptomatic of the deep determination of numerous Jews to preserve their society by preserving the legal code that sanctioned their behavior. The message of Sirach, while warning the Jews of the danger of foreign influence and showing them how to resist passively, does not call for overt resistance as Deutero-Zechariah had done. Like Qoheleth, he feared the secret police.[42] Neither Sirach nor the writer of the Book of Noah had the prophetic fervor of the third century.

Other men were making decisions outside Judah, however, that would presently make conditions intolerable for obedient upholders of the law. The severe beating that the Romans gave Antiochos III eventually had its repercussions in Palestine. Seleukos IV Philopator

---

[40] David to Simon: Ecclus. xliv. 1—l. 21. Wealth and poverty: ii. 10; iv. 1–10; v. 4; vii. 10, 20, 32; xi. 21–8; xiii. 18–9, 24; xiv. 6–16; xxviii. 10; xxix. 1–14; xxxi. 1–5; xxxiii. 24–31; xxxv. 12–22.

[41] Ecclus. xlvii. 4–7; cf. xvi. 7–10; xxxvi. 1–17.

[42] Passive rejection: Ecclus. xii. 4–16; x. 6–8. Secret police: xii. 11, 16; xiii. 11–6; xxviii. 14.

(187–175) about the middle of his reign sent an officer to collect bullion from the Temple of Yahweh in Jerusalem. The hard-driven Seleukid king probably had more than the one motive of raising money for the Roman indemnity. The second motive arose from the continuing disputes among the Jewish notables. Now the Temple was not only a holy place, it was also a bank, and the magnates of Judah deposited their wealth in it. The Tobiads, still wealthy and influential, were included among the depositors. About 188 or 187 B.C. they fought a duel to see who of Joseph's six sons should become the dominant one. The old tax farmer was now quite aged and unable to prevent the family from falling into factions. This division also involved the supporters of these patricians, that is, certain ordinary men in Judah, some taking one side, others the other. There came to be an actual skirmish between them, son Hyrkanos fighting with the other five, actually his half-brothers. Hyrkanos won, killing two of them, and the three survivors retired into Jerusalem with Joseph, where they received the support of the high priest Simon. Thereby Hyrkanos lost the sympathy of the capital, so that he established himself in the family stronghold near the Jordan and levied tribute on the Arab people around about. At this point Seleukos IV became king. When some Arabs refused to pay Hyrkanos, he went to war with them. Seleukos obviously could not tolerate this turbulent and independent spirit, and since Hyrkanos had deposits in the Temple, Seleukos probably intended to discipline him by confiscating his money. Let the empire's troublemakers pay the empire's indemnity.[43]

When Seleukos became king, he had more immediate problems to deal with than Hyrkanos: there was the affair of the death of his father at the Temple of Bel in Elam. There was danger all along the eastern frontier, not only in Elam, but in Persis as well. It was some time, therefore, before he could quell Hyrkanos, and above all else, he had to deal with him without resort to force, since Hyrkanos had a stronghold and Seleukos few available soldiers. Therefore, in the attempt on Hyrkanos' treasure in Jerusalem, perhaps around 180 B.C., Heliodoros, Seleukos' minister, failed to get the money, why we do not know. Perhaps the new high priest, Onias III, explained to him that removing the money would be interpreted as a violation of the sanctity of Yahweh's house instead of as a secular punishment

---

[43] Seleukos and Heliodoros: 2 Macc. iii. 1–13. Dan. xi. 20. 2 Macc. gives no motive to Seleukos except, by inference, royal greed. The struggle within the Tobiads from Jos. *Ant.* xii. 221–9. V. Tcherikover, *Hellenistic Civilization and the Jews* (1959), 137–9. Hyrkanos' deposit: 2 Macc. iii. 10–1.

of Hyrkanos. It would certainly be construed as a violation of the
autonomy of Jerusalem. About this time Onias himself was under fire
by a man named Simon, who had made complaint about the high
priest's conduct of the city market to Apollonios, the Seleukid governor
of Koile Syria. If the money was confiscated and Onias lost face,
would Simon be able to upset the balance of factions in Jerusalem
by making capital of this truckling to a gentile? We do not know
what happened, but Heliodoros went away without the money. Certain it is, however, that at once propaganda tales were made up
about the incident. 2 Maccabees relates two of them, telling that
Heliodoros was repulsed by divine intervention. According to one
version, a dreadful horse and rider suddenly appeared, and the horse
knocked the royal emissary down by striking at him with his forefeet.
The pagan had to be carried away on a stretcher. The second said
that two beautiful young men miraculously appeared; they knocked
the minister down and flogged him with whips, so that he nearly
died. Onias saved him by praying to God for his mercy. The second
version sounds like propaganda of Onias' clique. It is interesting to
note, with E. Bikerman, that the first version has Hellenic motifs in
it: it combines a Greek narrative theme of a divine epiphany with
the frequently employed Greek iconology of a horseman felling an
enemy.[44] Perhaps this first version was propaganda of the Hellenizing
party which wanted to oust Onias from the priesthood.

    After this incident, Simon still maintained pressure on Onias, both
accusing him of complicity in the Seleukid plot to steal the money of
"widows and orphans" and committing murders among Onias' supporters. Then Seleukos died, and was succeeded by his younger
brother Antiochos IV in 175 B.C.[45] Almost at once Judah was made to
feel the effects of this king's policy of Hellenization, urbanization and
closer imperial unity. In 174 B.C. the brother of the high priest, a
man called Jesus, involved himself against Onias in the struggle for
the office. He decided to take advantage of Antiochos' wishes in order
to use the authority of the king to make himself high priest. He approached Antiochos, proposing partially to Hellenize Jerusalem and
to raise the taxes to the approximate level they had been under the
Ptolemies. In return, he asked the king's intervention to depose Onias

[44] Heliodoros before the Temple: 2 Macc. iii. 23–36; E. Bikerman, "Heliodore au
temple de Jerusalem," *AIPhO* 7 (1939–44), 5–40. Version I: 2 Macc. iii. 24–5, 27–8,
30. Version II: 2 Macc. iii. 26, 29, 31–6. The agitation of Simon: 2 Macc. iii. 4–5.

[45] Activity of Simon: 2 Macc. iv. 1–6. Accession of Antiochos: J. C. Dancy, *A Commentary on I Maccabees* (1954), 56–8; J. Schaumberger, "Die neue Seleukiden-
Liste BM 35603 und die makkabäische Chronologie," *Bib.* 36 (1955), 423–35.

and to make him, Jesus, high priest. Antiochos agreed. The king's motives are nowhere stated accurately; we can probably safely say that what he gained by the transaction was a furthering of his imperial policy and the riddance of Onias, a man who had not delivered up the treasure of Hyrkanos to Heliodoros, a man who was also unable to maintain order in Jerusalem.

The changes took place. Onias retired to Antioch and Jesus, now named Jason, became high priest. A part of Jerusalem was constituted as the *polis* of Antiocheia. Citizens were created, probably with a census rating, so that only the wealthy belonged. They appeared in the streets wearing strange Greek hats, and they exercised naked in the newly built gymnasium. Many of these men must have been relieved to have escaped the superstitious rigors of the law. A class of ephebes was enrolled. These institutions—gymnasium and ephebate—were exceedingly important Hellenizing forces, being nothing less than the usual means whereby higher education was imparted in Hellenistic cities.[46] There was, therefore, now the possibility of systematic Hellenization for the upper classes. The Temple was still itself untouched, although its high priest was responsible for institutionalizing a competing way of life. Would other people now conform to Jason's ways?

Strict obedience to the covenant was now abandoned in the high priestly circle. An embassy of the new Antiochenes was dispatched by Jason to Tyre to take part in the Quinquennial Games in honor of Melkart, the god against whom Elijah and Elisha had struggled so successfully. The embassy, however, could not quite bring itself to partake in the pagan rite, and gave over the money they had brought the god for the purpose of fitting out royal warships. Jason's control of the high priesthood, however, was precarious. This highly lucrative and influential dignity was well worth having, and the notables of Judah watched its new holder narrowly. The alignment of the magnates was never secure, and if one man could use the strength of the Greek king, so could others. About this time, moreover, Antiochos succeeded in ridding the empire of one of its petty malefactors. Hyrkanos, at

[46] Jason-Antiochos: Dan. xi. 23; 1 Macc. i. 1–15; 2 Macc. iv. 7–11; Jos. *Ant.* xii. 237; S. W. Baron, *S.R.H.J.* (2nd ed., 1952), i. 397–9; J. C. Dancy, *A Commentary on I Maccabees* (1954), 46, 58–60. The status that Jerusalem had is disputed. Some scholars contend it was only a *politeuma*: E. Bickermann, *Der Gott der Makkabäer* (1937), 59–62; J. C. Dancy, *op. cit.*, 60. I have followed the view that it was a *polis*: W. O. E. Oesterly, *A History of Israel* (1932), ii. 217–20; V. Tcherikover, *Hellenistic Civilization and the Jews* (1959), 161–9, 404–9.

For the importance of Hellenistic gymnasia and ephebates: H. I. Marrou, *A History of Education in Antiquity* (1956), 95–228.

war with the Arabs over by Jordan, committed suicide out of fear of the king's reprisals. Antiochos certainly was one to use force if necessary to keep the state under reign, and he probably made sounds that indicated his intention to lay Hyrkanos low. The king now confiscated his property. The end of Hyrkanos upset the balance among the aristocratic parties, and freed the three surviving Tobiads of the necessity of watching their half brother. They themselves had been expelled from Jerusalem by Onias, and the opportunity of aggrandizing themselves at the expense of his brother and successor Jason now seemed good, since the Oniads were in faction themselves.[47]

About 172, Jason sent a man named Menelaos to take the taxes of the year to the king. Menelaos was the brother of that Simon who had attempted to remove Onias III from the Temple. In the transactions that followed, these two were supported by the Tobiads. Menelaos told the king that he was one of the foremost Hellenizers in Jerusalem, and perhaps Antiochos took his name as an earnest of his pro-Greek intentions. The king was preparing a war against the Parthians, and had not Homeric Menelaos helped lead the Achaeans against eastern Troy? Menelaos offered to increase the tax paid by Judah, and succeeded thereby in outbidding Jason by three hundred talents. Antiochos agreed. Increased revenues were welcome, and the empire was growing prosperous; at Samaria three times as many coins per year have been found for Antiochos' reign as for the whole Ptolemaic period. Jason's men had not gone through with the sacrifice to Melkart-Herakles at Tyre. There was obviously much opposition to him in Jerusalem. The order went out, Menelaos became high priest, and Jason was deposed.[48]

Menelaos' first acts were aimed at making himself secure against a fresh alignment of old factions. He drove Jason from the city; the latter fled to Ammon and bode his time waiting for an opportunity to return. Onias III he had killed in or near Antioch by an agent.[49] All this was most dangerous in view of Jewish sensitivities regarding the high priesthood. The man was a representative of Yahweh on earth, and his deposition was tantamount to the deposition of a Persian or Babylonian king. The one who was deposing him, moreover, was a gentile. The gentile, of course, thought that his procedure was entirely legal, since as Seleukid king he was in charge ultimately

[47] Tyre: 2 Macc. iv. 12–20. Hyrkanos: Jos. *Ant.* xii. 236. Tobiads: Jos. *War* i. 31.
[48] Menelaos-Antiochos: 2 Macc. iv. 23–6; Jos. *Ant.* xii. 229, 240–1. Tobiads: Jos. *Ant.* xii. 241. Simon: 2 Macc. iv. 23. Samaria: J. W. Crowfoot *et al., Samaria-Sebaste* iii (1957), pp. 45–6.
[49] 2 Macc. iv. 26, 33–7.

of cults within the state. But Antiochos was scarcely worthy to be a king—where was respect for Yahweh's covenant? Here were rising taxes—where was care for Yahweh's people?

The high priesthood was now in the hands of the wealthy class of the Judahite hill state, persons grown wealthy through commercial prowess or tax contracting. What effects the increased taxation had in Judah cannot be measured exactly, for data is lacking. But since high taxation had been a frequent complaint in the third century, and since real consciousness of taxation appears in 1 Maccabees, it was a definite cause of hostility to the new regime. The wealthy Hellenizing people began to ape the manners and customs of the Greek court at Antioch, and some, we are assured, even including priests, not only exercised nude in the new gymnasium, but had themselves de-circumcised. Life in Antiocheia-Jerusalem was now becoming more and more influenced by the activities of these part-Greeks, who had property and high position in the society only because of their connections with the royal party. Some such men could be extremely rich. There was a Makedonian of Antioch the capital, Dionysios, *epistolographos* under Antiochos IV, who owned at least a thousand slaves and at least a thousand pieces of silver plate, each of a thousand drachms weight. Dionysios probably was able to amass this amazing capital through the opportunities that state service afforded, as the high priests Jason and Menelaos did. These wealthy persons led a kind of life that was condemned by all the prophets and wisdom teachers of the past, from Amos to Zechariah. Poseidonios' description of the doings of the idle rich in the Syrian cities of the first century B.C. probably holds true in general for Jerusalem around 170 B.C. These men, relieved of any necessity to work by their holdings in land, spent their time in a continual whirl of social activities, leisurely bathing at the gymnasium, anointing themselves with expensive imported oils and aromatics, dawdling for hours over rich dinners, gorging themselves with rare foods and abundant wine. The cities were filled from end to end with the sound of harps. The cost of this gracious living was borne ultimately by the peasants and little shopkeepers.[50]

In the midst of these growing economic and religious tensions,

---

[50] Taxation: A. Mittwoch, "Tribute and Land Tax in Seleucid Judea," *Bib.* 36 (1955), 352–61. Exercises: 1 Macc. i. 12–5; 2 Macc. iv. 13–7. Dionysios: Polyb. xxx. 125. 16. Syrian city life: Poseidonios = Athen. xii. 527 EF; xv. 692 C; cf. Is. iii.
Objection to gracious living of just this sort appears in the Talmud (*Ta'anith* 1. 4. 64a), where a Jew confesses to four sins: attending the theater, engaging *heterai*, enjoying the public baths, and making merry with lewd music and dances. See, too, S. Lieberman, *Greek in Jewish Palestine* (1942), 31–2.

affairs were suddenly and inordinately complicated by events in
Egypt. Here the minor Ptolemy VI was king, and he was being advised by his amateur regents Eulaios and Lennaios to avenge Paneion
and recover Koile Syria. The Lagid state pressed its preparations in
171 and 170. Antiochos found out about them—they could scarcely
be kept secret—and realizing that his eastern plans were in jeopardy,
determined to fight a preventive war. Each side appealed to the
Roman Senate—its victory at Magnesia made it advisable—to see the
justice of its cause, but since Rome was fully engaged in the Third
Makedonian War (171–168 B.C.), neither seems to have worried un-
duly about the Senate's reaction. Egypt may actually have declared war
first, but Antiochos attacked first, and in 169 he carried all before him,
taking Pelousion and Memphis, and even capturing Ptolemy VI. He
seems next to have established some sort of protectorate over Egypt
and to have then withdrawn to Asia. About this time, too, Antiochos
assumed the title *Theos Epiphanes,* "God Manifest."[51]

About the time the war started Menelaos and his supporters, including a man named Lysimachos, sold some of the Temple plate,
probably to raise money to pay off the three hundred talents Menelaos
had promised the king. For the first time there was determined
opposition to the Hellenizing faction. In 169 there was a riot in
Jerusalem against the sale, and Lysimachos attempted to put it down
by a straightforward application of force; he called up three thousand
Jewish militia, possibly the citizens and ephebes. The force was
beaten by the common people and Lysimachos was killed. Jerusalem is
said to have had a population of 120,000 people about this time,
although this number may be too high. But the people were fighting
on their own ground; Lysimachos' commander was old and foolish,
according to 2 Maccabees, and superior numbers always made things
difficult for even professional troops fighting inside a town. Hence, the
militia lost. The *gerousia* of Jerusalem made complaint against
Menelaos to the king, indicating that some of the notables at least
were on the side of the people. Menelaos was able to escape from this
difficult situation by bribing the king's councillors to take his side;

---

[51] Egypt: Diod. xxix. 29. 1; xxx. 2. 1; 15. 1. Campaign of 169: 1 Macc. i. 16–9;
Dan. xi. 25–7. Title: D. B. Waage, *Antioch-on-the-Orontes,* IV, 2. *Greek, Roman,
Byzantine, and Crusader's Coins* (1952), Antiochos IV: Series II, p. 11.

For events in 170, 169, and 168 see E. R. Bevan in *C.A.H.* viii. 505–7; E. Bickerman,
The Maccabees (1947); W. W. Tarn, *H.C.* (3rd ed., 1952), 33–4, 214–6; E. Bikerman,
"Sur la chronologie de la sixième guerre de Syrie," *CÉ* (1952), 396–403; J. C.
Dancy, *A Commentary on I Maccabees* (1954), 26–7, 62–6.

the affair was smoothed over from Antiochos' point of view and
Menelaos remained in power.[52]

During the winter of 169/8 the Greeks behind the Ptolemaic
government found a new king in Ptolemy VII and prepared to resume war if necessary to end Seleukid influence. Antiochos, therefore,
in 168 returned to the attack and captured Alexandria against negli-
gible opposition. He had himself crowned king, perhaps in June, 168,
and set about reorganizing the administration. But on June 22, the
Romans defeated Perseus of Makedonia at Pydna, and there soon
appeared a Roman embassy to intervene in Egypt. The Romans
feared that a united Ptolemaic-Seleukid state would completely overthrow the favorable position they had just established, and therefore
curtly ordered Antiochos to withdraw forthwith from Egypt. He, fear-
ing a repetition of the disaster of Magnesia, prepared to obey. Rumors
about the king's defeat flew, and in Jerusalem one said that he was
dead. News, too, came from Babylon speaking of revolt against him
there, and from Tarsos. Deposed Jason came over from Ammon with
his partisans, took control of the city, and slaughtered the followers of
Menelaos who could not find a refuge. At this point Antiochos, having
retreated from Egypt, reappeared. He was naturally in a furious state
of mind, and he interpreted Jason's *coup* as a revolt. His troops
retook the city from Jason after a fight, which inevitably touched
neutral townsfolk as well as Jason's adherents. Antiochos found Jews
who favored Ptolemaic victory and executed them as traitors. Finally,
to punish this rebellious state and principally to satisfy his government's ever-present need for money, Antiochos confiscated 1,800 talents
from the Temple, including holy furniture and vessels made of gold
and silver. And having finally restored Menelaos, Antiochos withdrew, and the eventful year 168 came to an end.[53]

Thoroughly determined to complete the centralization of his Hel-
lenically oriented *poleis* so that the Roman menace might be faced,
and also to create a solid basis for his still projected invasion of
Parthia, Antiochos in 167 B.C. undertook to repress the recalcitrant

[52] The affair is in 2 Macc. iv. 39–50; date from v. 1. Population of Jerusalem:
Hekataios = Diod. xl. 3. 8; V. Tcherikover, *Hellenistic Civilization and the Jews*
(1959), 119.

[53] Antiochos: Dan. xi. 29–30; 2 Macc. v. 1–21; 1 Macc. i. 21–4; Jos. *Ant.* xii. 239;
War i. 31–2; *A.Ap.* ii. 84. For secondary accounts, see those listed in n. 51, especially
J. C. Dancy, *op. cit.*, pp. 70–1.

There is no literary evidence that rumors of revolt came from Babylon and
Tarsos. Both did revolt, and it is difficult to see how the Jews could have failed
to know of it.

Jewish nation, whose people were so troublesome. He therefore proscribed Judaism, though only in Judah, and in the Temple installed a
religion more nearly like the Greco-Oriental religions of other cities
in the empire. As E. Bickermann has shown, this was not a worship
of the Greek Zeus Olympios, but rather a cult of Ba'al Shamim, the
old high-god of the Canaanites. This rite was instituted in the Temple
of Antiocheia-Jerusalem, and so was that of Dusares, a Syrian god
whose service may have included ritual prostitution. Pigs were sacrificed on Yahweh's altar. Judaism was simultaneously forbidden and
confiscation of the holy books proceeded. The observance of Jewish
rites was punishable by death, and agents of the government went
around Judah to compel even the peasants to perform the new sacrifices. A fortified citadel for Seleukid troops was built in Antiocheia-
Jerusalem, and a racially mixed force of mercenaries—including
Jews—occupied it to enforce the royal decrees.[54]

Thus, the king forced a new religion on the suffering peasantry
whose labors supported the Hellenizing party in their luxuries. Simultaneously, the increased taxes contracted for by Jason and Menelaos
had wiped out the gains accruing from the privileges granted by
Antiochos III, so that conditions reverted to those unhappy ones so
heatedly denounced by the prophets of the previous generation.
Traditional Jewish society was threatened, and this situation was an
abomination that the devout could not bear; faithful and determined
elements prepared to resist to the death.

[54] Dan. xi. 31–9; 1 Macc. i. 29–59; 2 Macc. v. 22—vi. 11; Jos. *Ant.* xii. 362–3; E.
Bickermann, *Der Gott der Makkabäer* (1954), 72–4, 81; V. Tcherikover, *Hellenistic
Civilization and the Jews* (1959), 175–203.

Chapter IX

The Jews under the Hasmoneans

To appreciate fully the situation in Palestine between 167 and 164 B.C., while Judaism was forbidden, it is necessary to remember that the people in Judah were not the only persons in the world who were Jewish. When Antiochos forbade the practice of the religion he did not threaten to abolish it, because his decree did not apply to Jews everywhere. There is no evidence that it was invoked against the Diaspora, and there is evidence that it did not apply to the Jews of Samaria. In 167/6 B.C. they wrote to the king to enquire whether the decree was in force against them. They averred that while they kept the Sabbath, their god was called Zeus Xenios, meaning that Yahweh here had received a new name. Antiochos replied that his measures were not in force against them.[1] Hence, practicing the Jewish religion was not proscribed everywhere; it was forbidden only in Judah. Now S. W. Baron thinks that three-quarters of all the Jews living about the beginning of the Christian era were outside of Judah.[2] Therefore, since the proportion could not have been very different in the second century B.C., only a minority was affected, and the continuity of Judaism was not threatened. Antiochos did not, from his point of view, carry out a religious persecution—he took action that was political. He behaved as the Spartans had towards Athens in 404: they abolished the democracy which had fought them by abolishing its constitution. Thus a new democracy could not arise to fight them again. They did not destroy the people themselves; instead they arranged to have Athens governed by an oligarchy with a new set of laws. Antiochos did not care about abolishing Yahweh or his people. He intended to abolish the corpus of law that was followed by a group of rebels, including the ex-high priest Jason. With

[1] Diaspora: 2 Macc. vi. 8; J. C. Dancy, *A Commentary on I Maccabees* (1954), 73–4. Samaria: Jos. *Ant.* xii. 257–63; the name of the god here is corrected from 2 Macc. vi. 2; E. Bikerman, "Un document relatif à la persécution d'Antiochos Epiphane," *RHR* 115 (1937), 188–223; J. C. Dancy, *op. cit.*, 83.

[2] S. W. Baron, *S.H.R.J.* (2nd ed., 1952), i. 168–70.

this done, the group would be broken up, and the Hellenizing party could gradually gain ground.

To return to events, in the summer of 166 the king held a grand review of the imperial troops at Daphne near Antioch. A powerful army of fifty thousand men paraded, including no fewer than thirty thousand heavy infantry. These hoplites were almost twice the force that his father had been able to deploy at Magnesia against Scipio; they were the fruits of Antiochos' policy of Hellenization. Having thus impressed the world that the state was strong and Rome's past humiliations counted for little, Antiochos marched east to begin the conquest of the lost Iranian provinces and those foes of civilization, the Parthians. Towards winter, at Modein in the hill country of Judah, a priest of Yahweh, Mattathias, while watching an official persuade a Jew to sacrifice to Ba'al and to break the law of God, killed the king's subject and the king's officer. Mattathias had committed an act of unmistakable defiance, and a revolt against the minions of the king began.[3]

What manner of man was Mattathias, and what were his motives? The scanty evidence is interpreted usually to show a priest full of holy wrath fearlessly fighting for religious freedom, or a pious man defending the commandments of God against the orders of men, championing the revealed law of the kingdom of Yahweh against arbitrary earthly power.[4] Actually, I do not think that he was very important in the revolt, except as its ostensible leader. He was the father of the Hasmonean family, and therefore ought to have been the leader of his five sons, especially since the sons are depicted as heroes faithful to the law by the principal literary sources, 1 and 2 Maccabees. The sons could do little else, therefore, than "honor their father" according to the Commandment. But in fact Mattathias died almost as soon as the resistance began, so that when the royal officer was killed he must have been rather old, or perhaps ill, or both. His death made no difference at all to the course of events. The opposition continued unabated, led by his vigorous sons, first Judas, then Jonathan, and finally Simon. They must have been the real force behind the movement, or at least as important as their old father. Hence, the problem of finding out what motivated Mattathias is not really as important as finding out what intentions the Hasmo-

³ Chronology: J. Schaumberger, "Die neue Seleukiden-Liste BM 35603 und die makkabäische Chronologie," *Bib.* 36 (1955), 434–5. Antiochos' army: Polyb. xxx. 25; his father's army: Livy xxxvii. 40; App. *Syr.* vi. 31–2. Mattathias: 1 Macc. ii. 15–25.

⁴ Holy wrath and freedom: W. O. E. Oesterley, *A History of Israel* (1932), ii. 225–7; defender and champion: E. Bickerman, *The Maccabees* (1947), 17.

nean family had and what their contemporaries thought of them. Now these men undoubtedly risked their lives for the law of Moses, and this does show a measure of religious motivation; at the same time, I think, they wanted very badly to improve their position in respect to the other priestly families of Judah, or, in other words, to become high priests. This is what actually happened, and there is no reason for thinking that it was not a motive from the beginning. Their piety was tempered with ambition.

Mattathias and his sons were descendants of a man named Joarib, or Jehoarib. In the fifth century his family did not have priestly rank; in the fourth century it did; by the third it was reckoned among the leading clans with priestly status. Such a rise was certainly not unique. In the fifth and fourth centuries the family of Hakkoz was forbidden a place in the priesthood because its name could not be found among the proper genealogies; but in the third century it was enrolled in seventh place among the twenty-four courses. Mattathias' immediate ancestors, therefore, included aggressive men who wished, like Tobias, or Joseph or Hyrkanos or Jesus-Jason or Onias-Menelaos, to see the fortunes of the clan increase. The evidence is that in 167 B.C. the Hasmoneans were not humble, rural priests, but a family on the rise. They lived in Jerusalem and owned an estate near Modein. No doubt, therefore, they had adherents. A royal messenger is made to address Mattathias at Modein as "leading man, great and distinguished in this place." We have explicit statements that they had property around the village, but that they normally lived in the city. When the revolt began, father and sons had only left Jerusalem for Modein to escape possible unpleasant consequences of Antiochos' interdict.[5]

If the family were acting out of ambition would they have risked fighting Antiochos as they did? It is certainly possible. Jason had done so. In the first place, success would go a long way towards justifying them in the king's eyes. There is no evidence that the people's victory over Lysimachos' ineffectual militia led to immediate reprisals by the king; on the other hand Jason's abortive coup did. As events were to show, victorious Judas did win amnesty from Antiochos in 164.

[5] Rise of the Hasmoneans: Ez. ii. 36 = Neh. vii. 39; fourth century: 1 Chron. ix. 10; third: 1 Chron. xxiv. 7; L. Finkelstein, *The Pharisees* (1938), ii. 706, n. 19. Rise of Hakkoz: Ez. ii. 61–2; 1 Chron. xxiv. 10. Mattathias was a descendant of Joarib (Jehoarib) : 1 Macc. ii. 1; Jos. *Ant.* xii. 265.

Messenger: 1 Macc. ii. 17. Property: *ibid.*, ii. 28; Jos. *Ant.* xii. 271. Jerusalemite: 1 Macc. ii. 1; 2 Macc. v. 27; Jos. *Ant.* xii. 265; J. C. Dancy, *A Commentary on I Maccabees* (1954) , 84.

In the second place, there is no warrant for assuming that Antiochos meant a war to the knife in Judah, or that he intended to forbid Judaism forever. We look at the movement through the haze of interpretation given by Daniel and 1 and 2 Maccabees, who see the struggle as between one Greek man and his minions and no less a one than God and his holy followers. This puts the whole affair in the perspective of eternity. But on earth Antiochos actually may have intended to enforce his decree for only a few years. Let these people apostatize for a bit and become loyal; then they can taste our royal magnanimity. This intention may have been known. In the third place, I think that the chances for success looked good to the Hasmoneans. Opposition to the king and his Jewish friends in 166 was more widespread than ever before. No one had tried to oppose Jason in 174 when a part of Jerusalem was made a *polis*. A few of the gentry demurred when he presently proposed a sacrifice to Melkart. More of the gentry and many of the common people opposed Menelaos and Lysimachos around 170 when these intense Hellenizers tried to sell the Temple furniture. Now the proscription was the best and most clear-cut issue of all. The three thousand militia had been unable to stop the mob from killing Lysimachos. Jason had almost taken Jerusalem from Menelaos, and had been stopped only because of the appearance of the king with the first-line troops. The hoplites were now months away from Judah in the East. There is no reason to suppose that Menelaos had very many more troops in 166 than the same three thousand he had about 170. Judas shortly after Modein raised six thousand men from the neighborhood.[6] We must suppose that he and his brothers knew a good deal about loyalties to themselves in the country around Modein. The chances for success—forcing the distant king to rescind his decree and perhaps to depose Menelaos—were not perfect, but they were far from impossible.

If the Hasmoneans had really been fighting simply on the issue of religious freedom, they would not have proceeded as they did. Josephos says that Mattathias was joined at once by many ($\pi o\lambda\lambda\hat{\omega}\nu$) of the common people. No doubt he was joined by some. But the fact is plain that he and his sons had to use compulsion and fear against people hostile to them in the countryside, let alone in Antiocheia-Jerusalem. There was a particularly unhappy period in the hill country when Mattathias and his sons attacked "sinners and those who disobeyed the law." Many actually fled from the rural districts into Jerusalem to gain the protection of the Hellenizers and their citadel called

[6] 2 Macc. viii. 1.

Akra.[7] I find it hard to believe that a man fighting simply for the religious constitution of Judah would have had such trouble. Whose side were the Jews really on?

This opinion that many opposed the Hasmoneans does not militate against the one previously stated that the Hasmoneans could count on finding armed force to support them. They did not need anything like a majority of Jews on their side. An armed minority would be sufficient. It is plain that some of the men fighting with the Hasmoneans were not Jews: Judas' army included soldiers who wore amulets picturing the pagan gods of Iamneia. That town was only some sixteen miles distant in an air line from Modein. Furthermore, when Judas' army was besieging some fortifications, the beleaguered troops offered bribes to his generals to let them go: the generals accepted them and the soldiers escaped. Of course Judas punished these men, but from these facts showing through the Jewish histories, it emerges that the earliest Maccabean forces included men who were not Jews, and Jews who were opportunists. As for Menelaos' troops in Jerusalem, men who were also willing to risk their lives, or the troops that were sent down from Syria by the government, these included Jews, not only Samaritans, but Judahites as well.[8] Certainly not all these men were "rich Hellenizers." Therefore, the war of liberation in 165 must have had strong overtones of a civil war for the high priesthood, and while the Hasmoneans fought for the law, they fought also for personal power. In the latter motive, they were no different from Jason or Menelaos.

There were persons fighting Antiochos who were undoubtedly motivated much more than Mattathias and his sons by purely religious considerations. These included the Hasidim, the "Pietists," who were scribes and interpreters of the nation's religious law. These people came mostly from the lower classes. They belonged neither to the priestly houses nor to the secular families of the gentry, but were much more identified with the simple people. Victory would bring them little or no tangible reward. This group probably began to exist in the 180's or 170's, when Hellenization and neglect of the law were being felt seriously for the first time in Jerusalem. No doubt many of these people were sincerely religious, and not only loved their god and his law, but also the common people of Judah. Their

---

[7] Josephos: *War* i. 37. Attacks on "sinners": 1 Macc. ii. 44; 2 Macc. viii. 6; Jos. *Ant.* xii. 278.

[8] Amulets: 2 Macc. xii. 40. Generals: *ibid.*, x. 18–22. Seleukid forces: 1 Macc. iii. 10, 15; 2 Macc. viii. 9; Jos. *Ant.* xii. 288–9, 299.

ideological forebears were responsible for the oracles in Isaiah and
Zechariah denouncing the rich and their administrative colleagues of
the third century. In 165 the Hasidim made common cause with the
Hasmoneans, but they were not heart and soul with them, and they
presently rejected them. In 164 Antiochos rescinded his decree against
Judaism; the same year Judas captured the Temple. In 163/2 Menelaos was deposed as high priest by Antiochos V, and a man of priestly
rank, Alkimos, was appointed. But Judas fought on. He must therefore have fought for more than religious freedom. In 160 the Hasidim
accepted Alkimos and broke with Judas and his brothers.[9] The religiously motivated Jews also included that remarkable group of one
thousand persons who allowed Menelaos' forces to kill them without
attempting resistance, for the day was the Sabbath and to have defended themselves would have been to transgress the law they fought
for. These persons may have been Hasidim, but they may have been
an even more pious group which had little in common with the
Hasidim of the cities and still less with Judas.[10]

That the Hasmoneans fought for more than Temple and law is
clearly shown by what happened in 164 B.C. By that time their revolt
had had great success, first against the police reprisals that Menelaos
sent out against Mattathias, and then against the second-line troops
that came down from Antioch. The first-line troops were with Antiochos in the East, and only this fact saved the rebellion from probable
extinction. In 165/4 Antiochos IV authorized his minister Lysias to begin negotiations with Judas. These went on during the winter. They
are not mentioned by 1 Maccabees, which glorifies the Hasmoneans, because the upshot was so disgraceful to their memory. Antiochos offered
Judas an end of the interdict against Judaism in Judah and an
amnesty for the rebels. Judas on his part would have to stop fighting;
the Akra would continue to exist in Jerusalem-Antiocheia; and Menelaos would continue to be high priest. Judas accepted these terms,
probably in spring or early summer, 164. Late in the fall, however,
news arrived that Antiochos was dead in Elam. Like Jason, Judas

---

[9] Origins of the Hasidim: 1 Macc. ii. 42 is earliest reference in time to them;
L. Finkelstein, *The Pharisees* (1938), ii. 573, 592–5; J. C. Dancy, *A Commentary on
1 Maccabees* (1954), 86; V. Tcherikover, *Hellenistic Civilization and the Jews*
(1959), 125, 196–8. For connections with earlier prophetic literature: L. Finkelstein,
op. cit., ii. 518, 528–34.

Hasids at war: 1 Macc. ii. 42; 2 Macc. xiv. 6. Break with Hasmoneans: 1 Macc.
vii. 13–4; J. C. Dancy, *op. cit.*, 122.

[10] 1 Macc. ii. 31–8. For possible identification of this group see L. Rabinowitz,
"The First Essenes," *JSS* 4 (1959), 358–61.

felt that now was the time. Hastening into Jerusalem in November, he seized the Temple by force, and in December reconsecrated it to Yahweh. Menelaos, however, continued to be high priest. Therefore, in 163 Judas attacked but failed to take the Akra, and spent the rest of the year retrieving his military reputation by fighting in Idoumaia, Ammon, Gilead, and Galilee.[11] This course led up to the break with the Hasidim. During the year he fought with great violence against paganism, not only plundering towns and villages, but also over-throwing pagan altars and statues.[12] These acts made him seem zealous for Yahweh.

While the Hasmoneans were thus fighting, a violent, anti-Seleukid propaganda came into being. Some may have originated in Maccabean circles, but most did not. It was written in Hebrew, now revived as the language of revelation. It had been partly supplanted by Aramaic in the third century. Like its language, the resulting literature was extremely nationalistic, and it must have been intended to inflame the Jews with zeal for their law.

Probably the earliest pieces of anti-Seleukid propaganda were psalms originating as patriotic hymns. The canonical Psalter does not, however, contain any psalms of Maccabean date. Recent Old Testament scholarship has almost unanimously interpreted the Psalms as belonging to several types of cultic ritual originating in the monarchical period. S. Mowinckel has even categorically affirmed that only Psalm 137 was composed after the Exile of 586, a view quite different from the one held even thirty years ago, that most of these hymns were post-Exilic. Emphasis is now placed on reading the Psalter against the background of our increasingly rich knowledge of psalmody in other Near Eastern societies, principally the Ugaritic, Sumerian, and Akkadian. The Jews made several collections of psalms before our canonical collection was put together, and afterwards fresh series were written as, for example, in the first century B.C. by the

---

[11] The chronology: A. J. Sachs and D. J. Wiseman, "A Babylonian King List of the Hellenistic Period," *Iraq* 16 (1954), 202–12; J. Schaumberger, "Die neue Seleukiden-Liste BM 35603 und die makkabäische Chronologie," *Bib.* 36 (1955), 423–34. Antiochos' negotiations: 2 Macc. xi; the four letters there given are our only contemporary secular documents; E. Bikerman, "Un document relatif à la persécution d'Antiochos Epiphane," *RHR* 115 (1937), 218–9; J. C. Dancy, *A Commentary on I Maccabees* (1954), 19–21, 97–9.

Antiochos' amnesty: 2 Macc. xi. 27–33. Judas' capture of the Temple: 1 Macc. iv. 37–61; J. C. Dancy, *op. cit.,* 99–102. Judas' wars of 163: 1 Macc. v. 1–54; Jos. *Ant.* xii. 327–9.

[12] 1 Macc. v. 65, 68.

anonymous author of the Psalms of Solomon. There is no psalm in
the Psalter which can be assigned a Maccabean date. The evidence,
particularly linguistic, is entirely against it.[13]

But there is a possibility that alterations were made in the existing
Psalter. The content of Psalm 30 was admirably suited to celebrate
the victories of Judas Maccabaeus. The superscription, "A Song at
the Dedication of the Temple," was probably inserted in 164 B.C.
when Judas cleared the Temple of its pagan pollutions and resumed
services according to Mosaic law.[14]

Examples of psalms which definitely were composed in these times
include the hymn of penitence in Daniel ix. 4–19, which would appear from internal evidence to have been composed between 167 B.C.,
when the Temple was given over to the worship of Ba'al Shamim, and
164 B.C., when it was rededicated. If it achieved popularity, as seems
likely, at the time, this would readily explain how it came to be incorporated in the book of Daniel, which was collected and published
about 164 B.C. Psalms of lamentation for the desecration of the Temple
by Antiochos' officers were later incorporated in the prose text of 1
Maccabees.[15] A didactic hymn intended to accompany the restored
Yahwistic cult is in the text of 2 Maccabees. It teaches that true
kingship resides with Yahweh, and not with alien, human rulers. It
may have been a reaction against the Jews who offered sacrifice for
King Antiochos Epiphanes.[16] These nonmilitary psalms were composed, most likely, by persons directly concerned with the continuity
of the religion itself, and not by persons in the immediate Hasmonean
circle. Perhaps the Hasidim wrote them. On the other hand, from a
source close to the Maccabees came newly composed battle hymns

[13] R. H. Pfeiffer, *I.O.T.* (2nd ed., 1948), 628, 637–40, is the only recent important
scholar to insist on Maccabean dates for some of the canonical Psalms. H. H. Rowley,
G.O.T. (1950), 133, 166–70, is most skeptical of Maccabean originals, but says that
the final editor of the collection "may have incorporated a few."
For ancient backgrounds of the Hebrew Psalter see W. F. Albright, "The Psalm
of Habakkuk," *Studies in Old Testament Prophecy* (1950), 1–18; and for cultic
connections, A. R. Johnson, "Jonah II. 3–10: A Study in Cultic Phantasy," *ibid.*,
82–102. For the Book of Psalms, the position of contemporary scholarship is admirably summarized by A. R. Johnson, "The Psalms," *The Old Testament and
Modern Study* (1951), 162–209, and A. Bentzen, *I.O.T.* (2nd ed., 1952), i. 146–67.
See, too, F. M. Cross, *The Ancient Library of Qumran* (1958), 122.

[14] C. A. and E. G. Briggs, *The Book of Psalms* (1906), i. p. lxviii, 257; G. H. Box,
Judaism in the Greek Period (1932), 183; A. T. Olmstead, "Intertestamental
Studies," *JAOS* 56 (1936), 249; R. H. Pfeiffer, *I.O.T.* (2nd ed., 1948), 643.

[15] 1 Macc. i. 37–40; ii. 7–13; A. R. Johnson, "The Psalms," *The Old Testament and
Modern Study* (1951), 164; A. Bentzen, *I.O.T.* (2nd ed., 1952), i. 166.

[16] 2 Macc. i. 24–9. The burnt offering for Antiochos: 1 Macc. vii. 33.

for Judas' army.[17] Since these psalms survived to be incorporated in the later histories of those stirring times, it is evident that they were popular, and they must have inspired the Jewish soldiers to resist the armies that Lysias and other generals brought against them.

Alongside these early psalms, interpretative prose literature was written explaining how resistance fitted the relationship of the nation to Yahweh. The book of Daniel was completed and issued in its present form about 164 B.C. The new section, chapters 7–12, included fresh material drawn from the Mesopotamian version of the Persian *Bahman Yasht,* and is in chapter 7. This must have been mediated to the Palestinian community by the Babylonian Diaspora, who doubtless were in touch with events in Jerusalem, and who could not have failed to be familiar with the anti-Seleukid activities of the native Babylonians, who had in 168 B.C. attacked Antiochos' revised Marduk cult. Daniel 7 was a prophecy dealing with the overthrow of a fourth human monarchy, the Makedonian, which had followed the earlier Assyrian, Median, and Persian empires. It looked forward to the establishment of a divine monarchy under the kingship of a Yahweh-sent messiah. Daniel 9 predicted the destruction of the Hellenizing party. Daniel 10–12 contained a long, historically minded prophecy of the end of the Seleukid kingdom and Antiochos IV, detailing the history of the Makedonian monarchy from its foundation by Alexander the Great, who was therefore identified as the beginning of evil. In xii. 1 it is said that the Great Prince Michael will intervene against Antiochos. These prophecies look forward to divine intervention on analogy with older Hebrew interpretations of history, except that a figure distinct from but acting for Yahweh intervenes on earth.[18]

The work is otherwise thoroughly imbued with the normative Jewish interpretation of history. Faithfulness to the law brings divine

---

[17] 1 Macc. iv. 30–3; 2 Macc. xv. 22–4; A. Bentzen, *I.O.T.* (2nd ed., 1952), i. 166.

[18] It may be that "the Son of Man" in Daniel vii. 13 does not stand for a messiah, but rather for the nation itself; see S. Mowinckel, *He That Cometh* (1955), 349–50. "Michael, the Great Prince" (Dan. xii. 1), is probably an angel, a divine being acting for god; he is therefore not, strictly speaking, a messiah; but his functions are "messianic."

It is interesting to speculate about the horns that deck out the various Greek kings in Dan. viii–xii. Was this motif inspired by the Seleukid coinage, which frequently after 304 B.C. showed the kings with horns? The Persepolis mint issued such a series: E. T. Newell, *The Coinage of the Eastern Seleucid Mints* (1938), No. 413–27, pp. 154–7; Pl. xxxii. 1. The ram would, of course, point to Alexander's alleged descent from Zeus-Ammon.

reward in turn. Antiochos IV himself is not portrayed as a real, individualized human being, but rather is caricatured, explained as the rod of divine anger. This is the theological determinism of the Deuteronomists, who had similarly interpreted the victories of Canaanite or Assyrian kings in the books of Judges and Kings.[19] It shows that the living continuity of the prophetic tradition was maintained into the Hellenistic period; this tradition strongly distrusted the vision of the strong man armed, and in Daniel the Hasmoneans play little or no part. Whether the figure of the Son of Man in Daniel vii. 13 is messianic or symbolic of the nation as a whole, it has no reference to Judas. Nor does the angelic being of Daniel xii. 1. This book possibly was written by a man of the Hasid party, and it was certainly concerned with showing that the conflict of Antiochos with the Jews was only another chapter in the unfolding divine history of Yahweh and his people. It did not propose to make propaganda for the Hasmoneans; they are probably referred to in verse xi. 34a as the people who give a little help. The Hasids may be the people at Daniel xi. 33, the wise who are the first to fight and make the nation understand the evil force in the cosmic struggle.[20] If these considerations are true, they confirm the interpretation given above that the Hasmoneans were understood as persons motivated essentially by political considerations and not by religious faith.

The conclusion of the review of world history in Daniel xi. 45—xii. 1 is a prediction that the enemies of the Jews will be overthrown in the vicinity of Jerusalem, near the Holy Mountain. This prediction was based on earlier, similar prophecy in Joel, of the Persian period, and Zechariah 12 and 14, oracles of the third century.[21] The long life of the idea and the statement of Daniel xi. 14 concerning the uprising in Jerusalem in 200 B.C. show how consequential this sort of religious prophecy was.

Akin to the apocalyptic utterances in Daniel is the "Apocalypse of Weeks," contained in the pseudepigraph 1 Enoch. It is a résumé of

[19] On Daniel 7–12 see O. Eissfeldt, *E.A.T.* (1934), 574–6; H. H. Rowley, *Darius the Mede and the Four World Empires* (1935), 67–8, 94–5, 138–60; E. Bickermann, *Der Gott der Makkabäer* (1937), 13, 17, 26–7, 143–4. And on Daniel in general, J. A. Montgomery, *A Critical and Exegetical Commentary on the Book of Daniel* (1927); H. L. Ginsberg, *Studies in Daniel* (1948); R. H. Pfeiffer, *I.O.T.* (2nd ed., 1948), 755–68; A. Bentzen, *I.O.T.* (2nd ed., 1952), ii. 197–9; F. M. Cross, *The Ancient Library of Qumran* (1958), 33–4, 56 n., 123–4, 147–9.

[20] For the connection of the compiler of Daniel with the Hasids see L. Finkelstein, *The Pharisees* (1938), ii. 592; J. C. Dancy, *A Commentary on I Maccabees* (1954), 86, 122.

[21] Joel iii. 9–21; Zech. xii. 2–9; xiv. 2–21.

Jewish history from the age of the patriarch Enoch to the then present time, when the Temple has been rewon for Judaism and rebuilt by the victory of the righteous. It is now the eighth of the series of ten cosmic weeks. The last two are imminent, and will bring the conversion of humanity to Judaism, the judgment of the godless, and the final transfiguration of nature. Its date is therefore around 164–60 B.C.[22] Like Daniel, it is concerned with the religious issue raised by the Seleukid interdict.

While these oracles were being written, Lysias, now regent for the boy king Antiochos V, campaigned vigorously against the Jews. He finally realized that one of the obstacles to peace was Menelaos. Therefore this factor was deposed in late 163 or early 162 and subsequently put to death. In his stead Lysias installed a man named Alkimos as high priest and simultaneously issued a decree recognizing Jewish law a second time in the name of the king, and agreeing to the right of the orthodox Jews to control the Temple. Although Alkimos had a Greek name, his real name was Iachim or Eliachim, and he was undoubtedly of the legitimate line of Aaron. The Maccabean histories later called him "godless," but this was simply propaganda. His authority was also contemporaneously challenged by Judas and his circle. But the Jewish struggle for religion and the Temple was now won, and in 160 the Hasidim recognized the legitimacy of Alkimos and broke with the Hasmoneans. But for Judas the war had to continue, and he succeeded in making things so unpleasant for Alkimos that he fled to Antioch after the defeat of Nikanor in 160, dying a year later.[23] The high priesthood then stood vacant.

In the meantime the war had rolled on with new intensity. In 163 Judas took Bosora by storm, killed all the men of military age in it, and burned the city. He attacked Timotheus of Ammon and defeated his Arab mercenaries; to Karnaim the surviving soldiers fled and huddled in a precinct sacred to Atargatis. Judas burned it, burned them, and burned the nearby town. The author of 2 Maccabees says

[22] "The Apocalypse of Weeks" is 1 Enoch xciii. 1–10; xci. 12–7 (in that order). Its date: R. H. Charles, *Apocrypha and Pseudepigrapha of the Old Testament* (1913), ii. 171, and O. Eissfeldt, *E.Á.T.* (1934), 675, have argued for a date slightly earlier than Daniel's. But most scholars have preferred a slightly later date, as H. H. Rowley, *The Relevance of Apocalyptic* (2nd ed., 1946), 77–84; R. H. Pfeiffer, *History of New Testament Times* (1949), 77; and A. Bentzen, *I.O.T.* (2nd ed., 1952), ii. 242–3.

[23] Lysias' campaign: 1 Macc. vi. 18–63; his decree: 2 Macc. xi. 22–6. Menelaos-Alkimos: 2 Macc. xiii. 4; 1 Macc. vii. 9, 14, 20; Jos. *Ant.* xii. 235. Hasids: 1 Macc. vii. 13–4. On this period see J. C. Dancy, *A Commentary on I Maccabees* (1954), 118–23. End of Alkimos: 1 Macc. ix. 56.

that he killed twenty-five thousand people in that attack, a number
that is probably exaggerated. At Ephron he is said to have slaughtered
another twenty-five thousand. At Ashdod, when he penetrated the
walls, Judas had the altars torn down, the holy statues burned, and
the place plundered.[24] His army returned laden with booty.

   This bloody campaign was not entirely without provocation. About
the time it began there were outbreaks against the Jews living in
gentile communities in Gilead and Galilee, and in the towns of
Ptolemais, Tyre, and Sidon. Judas' movements were in part designed
to rescue his co-religionists from these cities. It is interesting to speculate why the gentiles' attacks on Jews should have occurred in far-off
Tyre and Sidon, since they were relatively distant from Judah. Perhaps when Judas sacked Ephron and Ashdod he may have acted in
the way of fulfilling the prophecy of Zechariah ix. 1–10, which marks
out a number of places from Gaza to Damaskos for destruction by
God. If the magistrates of Tyre and Sidon knew this third-century
oracle, which is entirely possible, then seeing two of the towns,
Ashdod and Ephron, actually going up in smoke, they may have
feared that they were next, for Tyre and Sidon had been similarly
proscribed. They could strike at least at potential traitors within their
walls. Judas may also have been avenging himself against the slave
dealers from the coastal cities who came up to Judah before the Battle
of Emmaus in 165, expecting to carry off the captives Seleukid Gorgias
was supposed to make. Ninety Jews for a talent of silver. Being sold
into slavery among gentiles was something that the Jewish prophets
of the third century had especially abhorred. Judas knew that they
were prepared to sell him, and he may have decided therefore to kill
them. Of course the gentiles had their grievances of long standing
against Judah, and it is impossible to say who started what. They had
suffered their most serious recent calamity in the third century from
vigorous action of Ptolemy's Jewish tax-farmer Joseph. He had
brought up two thousand soldiers to take action against Ascalon and
Skythopolis because their taxes were in arrears; he collected the money
and gave them a lesson for the future by executing the notables of
these towns.[25]

   At all events, therefore, the war was becoming much more than a

----

[24] Bosora: 1 Macc. v. 26; Jos. *Ant.* xii. 336. Karnaim: 1 Macc. v. 44; 2 Macc. xii.
26; Jos. *Ant.* xii. 343–4. Ephron: 1 Macc. v. 46–51; 2 Macc. xii. 27–8; Jos. *Ant.* xii.
346. Ashdod: 1 Macc. v. 68.

[25] Judas' motive: 1 Macc. v. 1–2, 9, 14–5. The case of Emmaus: 1 Macc. iii. 41;
2 Macc. viii. 10–11, 34. Joseph: Jos. *Ant.* xii. 180–5. On the anti-Jewish feeling in
Palestinian cities: J. C. Dancy, *A Commentary on I Maccabees* (1954), 102.

war against the Greek kings of Syria. It was becoming a war between
old enemies, one going back to the conflicts of Hebrew and Canaanite, and both sides were beginning to wage it on religious lines.
Gentiles attacked people because they believed in the Jewish god.
Jews retaliated against pagans and pagan gods. Judas' warfare, accompanied as it was by hymns and inspired as it was by oracles, was
really holy warfare, a *jihad*. The rank and file were religiously inspired at first to achieve a religious goal, the recovery of the law and
the Temple. Having won these objects, the war turned against paganism in the area immediately around Judah. The enthusiasm of
the Maccabean army of this period had something to do with inspiring
the writing of one of the Dead Sea Scrolls, the one called *The War
of the Sons of Light against the Sons of Darkness*. Although this
text was not published until after 50 B.C., there are certain resem-
blances between the conditions of religious warfare described in the
scroll and the actual behavior of the Maccabean army. In both cases
leadership is provided by men of priestly rank, the banners are inscribed with inspirational texts, and the armies sing hymns during
and after battle. There are, however, certain practices mentioned in
the text which show that the document as we have it—there are two
recensions of a lost earlier text in the Qumran scroll—is not entirely
a description of a real war. It describes military techniques that are
more nearly apocalyptic. The priests' trumpets are expected to have
magical effects when blown, and the troops are expected to throw
seven each of stones and javelins, all this in partial and mystical
imitation of the old stories about Joshua's capture of Jericho. The
text was seriously regarded, however, and was kept by the quietistic
Essenes because they thought it described the eschatological battle
at the end of time.[26] While Judas' troops were preparing this religious
legacy for a later day, Judas made a treaty of mutual friendship with
the Roman Senate. His ambassadors were the partially Hellenized
sons of an older generation: Eupolemos, son of John and Jason, son
of Eleazar.[27] Judas had to use them, for he could hardly employ men

---

[26] Parallels: 1 Macc. v. 67 and *The War* vii. 8—ix. 9; 1 Macc. iv. 24, v. 31–3; 2
Macc. xii. 36–7 and *The War* x. 1—xii. 18; 2 Macc. viii. 15, 23 and *The War* iii.
12—iv. 2. For criticism of the text and its date see A. Dupont-Sommer, *The Dead Sea
Scrolls* (1952), 61–2; H. H. Rowley, *The Zadokite Fragments and the Dead Sea
Scrolls* (1952), 45, 62–76; T. H. Gaster, *The Dead Sea Scriptures* (1956), 281–306,
315–21; M. Burrows, *More Light on the Dead Sea Scrolls* (1958), 194–200, which is
based on Y. Yadin's study.
[27] The treaty: 1 Macc. viii. 1–32; the ambassadors: 1 Macc. viii. 17; 2 Macc. iv. 11.
The alleged Maccabean treaty with Sparta, however, is undoubtedly a forgery:

who spoke nothing but Hebrew; there is no evidence that these two men were anything but orthodox. But this embassy was symbolic of what was to come. Judas and his brothers could not do without secular Hellenism.

About May, 160, Judas was killed by Seleukid forces in the Battle of Bereth, and the Hasmonean movement was taken over by his brother Jonathan, who remained its leader until his death at the end of 143 B.C. His policies were very similar to those of his brother Judas and his father Mattathias; the war against the Seleukids and their friends among the Jews continued, as did the struggle to advance the family. Hostilities with the Syrian cities around Judah and with the Arabs in the eastern and southern deserts grew somewhat more intense. The pro-Seleukid Jews attempted to rid themselves of Jonathan in 157 in concert with King Demetrios I. Their military plans miscarried, however. After 155 Jonathan began to make extraordinary headway against all his enemies, since the Seleukids were not only beginning to feel strong pressure from the Parthians along the Tigris front, but particularly because the dynasty began to fall perpetually into warfare among its members and even its generals. Demetrios had become king only after a battle and the murder of Lysias and the young Antiochos V. He himself presently had to contend with an attempt to overthrow him led by Alexander Balas. Since neither royal rival really controlled Judah's countryside, both appealed to Jonathan for assistance and support. In 152 Demetrios recognized him as Seleukid *stratēgos* and authorized him to raise an army, and Jonathan promptly occupied Jerusalem and commenced fortifications to check the Akra. Alexander then offered him the high priesthood, and he accepted with alacrity. In 152 he donned the holy vestments and became the successor of Alkimos. He thus realized his family's ambition thirteen years after Mattathias revolted. Jonathan therefore came down on Alexander's side, although his contribution was no more than moral support.[28]

This considerable victory brought about a new relationship between Hasmoneans and Seleukids. Alexander granted the high priest the title "First Friend" of the king. After Alexander had been violently

---

M. S. Ginsburg, "Sparta and Judea," *CPh* 29 (1934), 117–22. All that it shows is that there were Jews conversant with pagan history.

[28] Jonathan's wars against Syrians and Arabs: 1 Macc. ix. 35–42, 66–7; xii. 31; Jos. *Ant.* xiii. 10–21; 150–3; 192. The pro-Seleukid Jews' activity: 1 Macc. ix. 58–64; Jos. *Ant.* xiii. 23. Demetrios-Alexander-Jonathan: 1 Macc. x. 6, 18–20, 29–45; Jos. *Ant.* xiii. 37–45; J. C. Dancy, *A Commentary on I Maccabees* (1954), 146–7.

supplanted by Demetrios II, friendly relations continued, and Jonathan sent three thousand troops to Antioch in 143 to help the new king maintain his precarious control of the capital. One was treated to the spectacle of the successor of Mattathias helping the successor of Antiochos maintain his seat on the Seleukid throne.[29]

While these gains were being made, the war on paganism continued, Ashdod being put to the torch along with its Temple of Beth-dagon. 1 Maccabees reports that eight thousand persons were burned to death.[30] During this victorious period between the death of Judas and the winning of autonomy, there was continuing production of religious literature. To this period is assigned 1 Enoch 12–36, a description of the torment of the fallen angels, of the horrible punishments they have brought upon themselves for having sinned against God. Messianism is lacking here. The document is more concerned with the question of re-establishing Judaism and with punishing those Jews who had followed Jason and Menelaos than with instilling confidence in the ultimate victory of the Maccabean armies. This text is not so much opposed to Greeks proper as to Hellenizing Jews.[31] Its author had a taste for violence and an enjoyment of suffering which is rare in Judaism.

But the same thing can be seen in the apocryphal book of Judith, written about 150 B.C. for inspirational purposes.[32] It shows a sense of extreme nationalism, of unscrupulous fanaticism. In the story King Nebuchadnezzar, King of Assyria, who is worshipped as a god, decides to make war on the people in the Near East because they refused him help in a fight against the king of the Medes. He dispatches his general Holophernes to force their submission and take earth and water from them as a token of victory. The Assyrian army moves out, and all the people of Syria obsequiously surrender to his force of 120,000 men, all, that is, except the Jews. This sounds very much as though the story is modelled on Jewish traditions about Antiochos IV. He attacked the Parthians. He also demanded the empire become one people. All submitted to his will, all but the Jews.

[29] First Friend: 1 Macc. x. 65; Jos. *Ant.* xiii. 85. Demetrios II in Antioch: 1 Macc. xi. 44–52; Jos. *Ant.* xiii. 135–41.

[30] 1 Macc. x. 83—xi. 5.

[31] R. H. Charles, *Apocrypha and Pseudepigrapha of the Old Testament* (1913), ii. 170; O. Eissfeldt, *E.A.T.* (1934), 673–5; R. H. Pfeiffer, *History of New Testament Times* (1949), 75–9; A. Bentzen, *I.O.T.* (2nd ed., 1952), ii. 242–3.

[32] O. Eissfeldt, *E.A.T.* (1934), 643; C. C. Torrey, *The Apocryphal Literature* (1945), 91–3, dates the book to the first half of the first century B.C.; R. H. Pfeiffer, *History of New Testament Times* (1949), 291–7; A. Bentzen, *I.O.T.* (2nd ed., 1952), ii. 227–8.

Against them he therefore sent Lysias with 120,000 men. He was worshipped as a god.[33] For Holophernes to enter Judah, he must first capture Bethulia, and he blockades the town in such a way as to prevent its people from getting water. At this point, enter Judith the heroine. She is a widow, rich and beautiful, and she therefore gains the confidence of the Assyrian general. One day when he is asleep she cuts off his head with a carving knife, in a patriotic way. Bethulia is saved, Judah is saved, and Judith lives happily ever after, an object of admiration for the women of the country. Holophernes probably stands for the Seleukid Greeks. Jewish literature sometimes archaized and called them "Assyrians," since both Assyrian and Seleukid armies descended upon Judah from the north. To call the Greeks "Assyrians," furthermore, made a hopeful analogy between the present and the heroic old days when God and man in Judah opposed the host of Sennacherib.

The curious thing about the book of Judith is that it shows undoubted signs of Hellenic influence. Holophernes' siege of Bethulia reduces the town to a supply of water good for only five days. Uzziah, the chief man in the place, agrees to surrender to Holophernes, if help from God does not come within this period. It comes in the shape of Judith. A similar story was told by the Greek Lindian Chronicle. During the Persian Wars Datis the Mede besieged Lindos, and the town's water dwindled to a five-day supply. The Lindian magistrates made an agreement to surrender if help did not come within that period, whereupon Athena appeared to one of them and promised water from Zeus. It rained, and Datis was so astonished that he raised the siege. The Jewish story has further attributes of Hellenistic romance. It is full of exaggerations, like the sizes given cities and armies; the scene in Judith 2 where Nebuchadnezzar sends Holophernes against his enemies sounds as though it owed something to Herodotos' account of Xerxes' preparations, especially because both kings demand earth and water. The heroine herself has an eroticism about her like that of Hellenic heroines: she is a widow, rich, wise, beautiful, chaste, pure, pious, and extremely desirable. Plutarch knew of similar ladies.[34]

The Greek elements in the book show that the author belonged to the partially Hellenized segment of the Jewish population, although

[33] Whole Empire: Jth. i. 12; 1 Macc. 1. 41. The Syrians submit: Jth. ii. 21—iii. 8; 1 Macc. 1. 42. 120,000 men: Jth. i. 15; 1 Macc. vi. 30. Holophernes has 12,000 mounted archers over and above the 120,000 infantry and cavalry; but Lysias has 32 elephants over his 120,000 infantry and cavalry. Worship: Jth. iii. 8.

[34] I owe these parallels to M. Hadas, *Hellenistic Culture* (1959), 166–9.

he was undoubtedly a loyal Jew. This indicates, then, that by the time of Jonathan the Hellenizers were shifting away from the Seleukids and towards the Hasmoneans. Well they might, for the Greek kings of Syria were losing everywhere. Jonathan himself employed men with Greek educations: in 144 B.C. he sent to Rome ambassadors with the names Noumenios, son of Antiochos, and Antipater, son of Jason.[35] As the fathers' names indicate, these men belonged to the second generation of Hellenizers; the second of these two may have been the son of that Jason, son of Eleazar, whom Judas had used to negotiate his treaty with the Romans in 161.

Another work composed around 150 was the Book of Jubilees.[36] Its author did not exult in violence, but was a pietistic nationalist who gloried in Jewish law. It is a reinterpretation of Jewish history during the period covered by the canonical books of Genesis and Exodus, in which the law is given a much greater significance than it originally had. The patriarchs are idealized models of piety, who obey eternal Torah. Sinners, and the author was thinking of the Hellenizers and their Greek allies, the Kittim, are shown to come to destruction through nonobservance of the law. Such persons always incur the wrath of God. Intermarriage with gentiles is strongly condemned. The hope is expressed that eventually the Jews will dominate the aliens through the eventual coming of a messiah and his kingdom. Hellenism is rejected by this author almost entirely for theological reasons. He thought the Jews suffered before the Maccabean age because they forsook the regulations of Moses, and therefore became unclean and polluted. They amassed wealth and the wicked gentiles forthwith came among them. When Judah cried to God to be saved and returned to a life based on Torah, the defeat of the gentiles occurred, and times grew happy and prosperous once more.[37]

While all these things were going on in Judah, there was a rather different state of affairs in the Diaspora. In the second century these very numerous Jews became increasingly articulate, and began to

---

[35] 1 Macc. xii. 16.

[36] R. H. Pfeiffer, *History of New Testament Times* (1949), 70; H. H. Rowley, *The Relevance of Apocalyptic* (1946), 84–90; *The Zadokite Fragments and the Dead Sea Scrolls* (1952), 65, n. 1; 77; A. Bentzen, *I.O.T.* (2nd ed., 1952), ii. 237.

W. F. Albright, *From the Stone Age to Christianity* (Anchor ed., 1957), has now changed his date for this book from around 300 B.C. to 175 B.C.; O. Eissfeldt, *E.A.T.* (1934), 662–3, thinks it was written around 125 B.C.; R. H. Charles, *Apocrypha and Pseudepigrapha of the Old Testament* (1913), ii. 6–8, about 100 B.C.

[37] Messianic kingdom: Jub. vi; xii; xvi; xx. 6–10; xxv; xxvii. 10, 23; xxx. 7–17; xxxi. 18; xxxii. 11, 18–9. Interpretation of history: Jub. xxxii. 13–31.

make important contributions to Jewish thought. Some of their literary works became known in Palestine, and therefore the Dispersion had some influence on Judah's attitude towards Hellenism. While many Judahites of the generation from 160 to 120 B.C. tended to reject foreign influence completely, the Diaspora did not, and began to come to terms with certain facets of gentile culture. Oriental astrology, for example, became popular in Jewish circles in Mesopotamia, and these transmitted it eventually to Palestine, freed, of course, from Babylonian theology and conceptions of astral determinism. An astronomical treatise based partly on eastern speculative astrology was written by a Jewish author about 150 B.C. or a little later; it came to be incorporated in 1 Enoch. The Jewish redactor's main purpose was to explain the workings of the heavenly bodies so that his co-religionists would not worship them. As an afterthought, he added an appendix which depicted the astronomical details of the final age of the world. The similarity between this section and the *Bahman Yasht* and *Oracle of Hystaspes* is quite striking. All three include predictions of a shortened year, failure of rain, lack of crops, the darkening or disappearance of the moon, and irregular motions of the stars. The Jewish writer hopefully concluded, moreover, that because sinners worship the stars, they will all be destroyed in the Last Judgment.[38]

The most influential section of the Diaspora, however, lived in Egypt, and during the second half of the second century its importance grew large. There were persons here quite happy to be quit of the warfare and turmoil in Hasmonean Judah, and the attitude of part of the Egyptian Dispersion towards Hellenism was quite respectful. In 165 B.C., Onias, the son of the deposed high priest Onias III, fled Palestine to Egypt with a number of companions, and he was received and protected by Ptolemy VI Philometor, who had very definite uses for him. For one thing, generous treatment of Onias might win the Lagids Jewish sympathy in Koile Syria. Onias was therefore given land in the Leontopolis district and an abandoned temple, which he reconstructed along the lines of the one in Jerusalem. He became its priest. But he was also given a fortress to defend, and the tract granted him was extensive enough to support a large number of military settlers. Onias assumed command of these troops, and in

[38] Date: R. H. Charles, *Apocrypha and Pseudepigrapha* (1913), ii. 171, says only before 110 B.C.; O. Eissfeldt, *E.A.T.* (1934), 675; R. H. Pfeiffer, *History of New Testament Times* (1949), 76; A. Bentzen, *I.O.T.* (2nd ed., 1952), says about the middle of the century. Persian parallels: 1 Enoch lxxx. 2–8 with *Bahman Yasht* ii. 31, 43, and *Oracle of Hystaspes,* frag. 14 = Lac. *Div. Inst.* vii. 16.

return he became one of King Ptolemy's defenders. Ptolemy made this arrangement because the aftermath of Antiochos Epiphanes' withdrawal from Egypt in 168 was a violent revolutionary outbreak against the government, a movement in which both Greeks and Egyptians took part. Ptolemy, therefore, was bringing into being a new, well-concentrated ethnic group loyal to the dynasty, which needed well-armed defenders.[39]

In this way a real alliance grew up between many Greeks and the Jews in Egypt, and while Judah was suffering from the efforts of the Seleukids to repress Judas or of Jonathan to repress the Syrians, Onias and his men were waxing great in the Kingdom of the Lagids. Onias and a colleague named Dositheos commanded contingents of the royal forces which rescued Philometor's wife Kleopatra from a large and determined mob in Alexandria about 146 B.C. Unfortunately for them, however, Ptolemy VI was killed in a war with his successor Ptolemy VII Euergetes II (145–116 B.C.), and the victor took political revenge on the friends of the vanquished. But the Jews remained a force to be reckoned with, and in the struggles between Ptolemy VIII Lathyros (116–108/7 B.C.) and Ptolemy IX Alexander (108/7–88 B.C.) they took the side of the latter, with generals Chelkias and Ananias commanding some of the troops. When Ptolemy VIII returned to power (88–80 B.C.) there was another repression.[40]

Still, on the whole, the lot of the Jews in Ptolemaic Egypt was favorable. Some were clerks and minor officials in the government and others became prosperous through enterprise. Synagogues continued to be built and dedicated to the Lagid kings. These "houses of prayer" were no doubt important in combating the blandishments of Hellenism and keeping Jews loyal to Judaism, because in the Dispersion there was always a certain amount of slipping away from obedience to the law. The Jews in many localities lived in such close contact with Greeks that some people became out-and-out cultural converts, some because it was good business, others because of the freedom from superstition that paganism offered them. To Asia Minor, around 150 B.C., came one Niketas, son of Jason, from Jerusalem, and he donated a sum of a hundred drachms to a festival of Dionysios.

[39] Jos. *War* i. 33; vii. 421–31; *Ant.* xiii. 62–73; *O.G.I.S.*, 129. E. R. Bevan in *C.A.H.* viii. 517; W. W. Tarn, *H.C.* (3rd ed., 1952), 218; V. Tcherikover, *Hellenistic Civilization and the Jews* (1959), 277–83.
[40] Onias-Dositheos: Jos. *A.Ap.* ii. 49–52. Chelkias-Ananias: Jos. *Ant.* xiii. 349. On this period, and its lack of anti-Semitism from Greeks in Egypt, see H. I. Bell, "Anti-Semitism in Alexandria," *JHS* 31 (1941), 1–4.

There was also the case of the grateful Jews who thanked the god Pan of Thebes for deliverance from the perils of the sea. In the late third century Dositheos, son of Drimylos, had given up Judaism to become eponymous priest of Alexander and the deified Ptolemies. Giving up Judaism outside Judah was not even new then, for in Upper Egypt at the end of the fifth century Jewish soldiers serving at Elephantine had flirted with the gods of the place.[41]

The deepest impression that Hellenism made on the Dispersion was linguistic. The Jews learned the language of the dominant Greeks and speedily lost their command not only of Aramaic, the language of conversation, but of Hebrew, the language of worship. Consequently, the Septuagint translation of the scriptures was completed in Egypt in the last part of the second century B.C., so that the Jews could still know their holy books. This translation was an excellent and accurate piece of work and was an important weapon in the struggle to prevent Jews from immersing themselves in the literature of Greece. The Septuagint was not, however, intended to be a means for drawing converts from among the pagans, at least primarily, and there is no evidence that literate Greeks knew of its contents.[42] But the fact that the books of Moses, the psalms of David, and the wisdom of the prophets were now heard in Greek, the language of Homer and the other Greek poets, must have subtly created a slightly different meaning in the sacred literature and propagated a perhaps more tolerant opinion of the works of the heathen.

About 150 B.C. an Alexandrian Jew wrote the remarkable *Letter of Aristeas,* which not only explained how the newly completed translation had been made and how phenomenally accurate it was supposed to be, but also how Hellenism and Judaism were not mutually exclusive.[43] While Pseudo-Aristeas included an ardent panegyric upon

[41] Synagogues of the second and first centuries B.C.: *S.B.* 589, 5862, 7454; *C.P.J.,* 134 and 138; V. Tcherikover, *Hellenistic Civilization and the Jews* (1959), 349, discusses them.

Losses by Judaism: Niketas: *C.I.J.* 749; Pan of Thebes: *O.G.I.S.,* 73; Dositheos: *C.P.J.,* 138; 3 Macc. i. 3. Fifth century: *P. Aramaic Brook.,* 13; *P. Aramaic Elephan.,* 14, 22; discussion by E. G. Kraeling, *The Brooklyn Museum Aramaic Papyri* (1953), 84–7.

[42] On the Septuagint translation and its relation to other Jewish versions of scripture, as well as its excellence, see F. M. Cross, *The Ancient Library of Qumran* (1958), 128–45. On its lack of proselytizing influence: V. Tcherikover, "Jewish Apologetic Literature Reconsidered," *Eos* 48 (1956), 176–8.

[43] On the date of the *Letter of Aristeas* see E. Bickermann, "Zur Datierung des Briefs Aristeas," *ZNTW* 29 (1930), 280–96; O. Eissfeldt, *E.A.T.* (1934), 659–60; R. H. Pfeiffer, *History of New Testament Times* (1949), 224; A. Bentzen, *I.O.T.* (2nd ed., 1952), ii. 236–7; see, too, n. 44, below.

Judaism and its religious institutions, his work was shot through with Hellenistic ideas. V. Tcherikover thinks that the journey to Jerusalem described in the book was modelled upon Hellenistic utopian travel literature, which talked about wonderful journeys to ideal Never-Never Lands, to places of all virtue. The virtues that the pilgrim to Jerusalem found at his goal were, according to this book, Greek *sōphrosynē, dikaiosyne,* and *egkrateia.* Ptolemy II, in whose reign the Septuagint was falsely said to have been made, was painted in the colors of a man deeply interested in knowledge and in the customs and religion of the Jewish people. Greek philosophy was praised. Pseudo-Aristeas, therefore, was not seeking to make the Greeks of Egypt into Jews; he was hoping to lead the Jews of Egypt to understand and respect the Greeks.[44] The spirit of his ideology closely matched the well-being of Egyptian Jews of his time; they now were organized into a legally recognized *politeuma* in Alexandria, subject to their own *ēgoumenoi.* In the Ptolemaic administration they were *epistatai* and *stratēgoi.*[45] For some it was an era of good feelings.

In the two generations following Pseudo-Aristeas and Onias there was a good deal of Greek literature produced by the Egyptian Dispersion, little of it concerned with the conversion of gentiles.[46] It was really intended to reassure Greek-reading Jews that their great men and their past were as excellent as the epic heroes of the Achaeans or the brave history of the Athenians. It was apologetic literature only in the sense that it defended Jewish greatness for the benefit of Hellenized Jews. It did this by using the forms of Greek literary art, which had become popular among the Jews in Alexandria.

Of course all these pieces of literature did not exhibit the tolerance of Pseudo-Aristeas. About 150 or 125 B.C. Aristoboulos wrote an *Exegesis on the Law of Moses,* which amounted to a defense of the lawgiver against the charms of Greek mystics and the rationality of Greek philosophers. He claimed priority for Hebrew revelation against the wisdom of Hellas, and averred that the ideas of Homer, Hesiod, Orpheus, Pythagoras, Socrates, Plato, Aristotle, and Aratos were all copied from a translation of the law made long before the time of Alexander. He also called attention to the miracles in the Pentateuch,

---

[44] V. Tcherikover, "The Ideology of the Letter of Aristeas," *HTR* 51 (1958), 59–85; M. Hadas, *Hellenistic Culture* (1959), 93.

[45] *Ēgoumenoi: Letter of Aristeas,* 310. *Epistatēs: O.G.I.S.,* 96, *Stratēgos: C.P.J.,* 132.

[46] On this point see V. Tcherikover, "Jewish Apologetic Literature Reconsidered," *Eos* 48 (1956), 169–76.

and said that they showed how the god of the Hebrews had showered down benefits on mankind.[47] Presumably he defied anyone to make the same claim for the prodigies of Zeus.

Akin to Aristoboulos in his dislike of the Greeks was Jason of Kyrene, who wrote a history of Maccabean warfare. His work is lost, but an epitome was made of it around 125 or 100 B.C., and is known to us as 2 Maccabees. It was originally intended to be secular literature, however, and the Epitomator would have been astonished if someone had told him that someday his book would be considered revelation.[48] The picture of events is given in the overdecorated style of the florid school of Hellenistic historiography, like the histories of Douris or Kleitarchos. It exaggerates drastically, and teaches moral lessons. The Epitomator's purpose was to show that faith in God defeated the pagan Greeks. To do so he first wrung the reader's heart, making Antiochos IV kill or enslave eighty thousand persons in Jerusalem. This sort of thing fascinated him, and he went on with lurid descriptions of gore, blood, and suffering mixed with piety, giving an unpleasant account of the agonies of the martyrs of Antiochos' persecution. The agents of the cruel king set busily about attempting to stamp out articulate believers of true religion. The hot irons sizzle while old Eleazar bravely sermonizes. But God sustains him, for human beings are his tools. He had first prevented Heliodoros from taking money from the temple, but he allowed Antiochos to do so because of the Hellenizing sins of the Jews. He next gives Judas the victory in war, his small Jewish battalions smashing up and slaughtering whole armies of pagans. The Epitomator then exults: this victory could be extended to the whole world if God willed it.

[47] Fragments of Aristoboulos in Clem. Alex., *Strom.* i. 72, 150; v. 97; Euseb., *Prep. Evang.* viii. 8–10; ix. 6; xiii. 12; *Eccl. Hist.* vii. 32. For Aristoboulos see, too, R. H. Pfeiffer, *History of New Testament Times* (1949), 214–5; M. Hadas, *Hellenistic Culture* (1959), 101–3.

[48] Date: O. Eissfeldt, *E.A.T.* (1934), 637–8; E. Bickermann, *Der Gott der Makkabäer* (1937), 17, 146–50; C. C. Torrey, *The Apocryphal Literature* (1945), 78–9; R. H. Pfeiffer, *History of New Testament Times* (1949), 519–22; A. Bentzen, *I.O.T.* (2nd ed., 1952), ii. 222; J. C. Dancy, *A Commentary on I Maccabees* (1954), 12–5.

Secular: The Epitomator says (ii. 23–7), having briefly sketched the events that he is going to describe, "Since this has all been made clear by Jason of Kyrene in five books, we shall try to compress it into one. Looking over the flood of statistics and the plethora of material made for those who wish to plunge into historical literature, we have aimed more to attract those who like to be read to or those who like to memorize easy things, and to appeal to general readers. But for us who have undertaken this work, it is not easy, but takes sweat and sleepless nights. . . . Still, for the sake of the gratitude of many people, we shall gladly submit to this troublesome toil." He says, too, at the end (xv. 37) that he hopes he has done a good job and that his work is a good epitome; if it is a bad one, well, he did his best.

He hates the heathen and prays for their affliction. The book is the work of a vicious antigentile. It is partly based on lies; there is a forged letter and there are many discrepancies with the parallel accounts in 1 Maccabees. Of course the latter also distorts history favorably for the Jews, so that this quality in the Epitomator does not make 2 Maccabees consistently the poorer work.[49]

About the same time Eupolemos wrote another history, *On the Kings of Judah,* which informed its readers, among other things, that Moses was the first wise man in the world, that he had invented the alphabet, which had then been used by the Phoenicians and passed by them to the Greeks. The continuing insistence of most of these Alexandrian writers on the primacy and virtues of Moses is a little bit like the Babylonian insistence on the primacy and greatness of Semiramis and Nebuchadnezzar. But there are also significant differences. Moses was not a king; he had transmitted divine law to man, and this law was the basis for the organization of Jewish society. That was why both man and code were continually defended. Eupolemos was at pains to emphasize that the law came to the Jews long before any of the Greek lawgivers had given their human codes to their city-states. He also quoted from a corpus of forged letters purporting to have been exchanged by Solomon and Hiram, King of Tyre. These showed conclusively that the Hebrew king was extraordinarily wise and brilliant.[50]

Philo the Elder sometime in the second century wrote an epic poem *On the Kings of the Jews,* but only twenty-four verses survive. Theodotos, another epic poet, imitated Homer in eulogizing the adventures of Jacob in a poem *On Shechem.*[51] These literary efforts tended to glorify Judaism at the expense of the Greeks, but Alexandrian propaganda had other tasks to perform than this, since the

---

[49] Eighty thousand persons: v. 14; was Jerusalem's population as much as this? The Diaspora would scarcely know.
Martyrs: vi. 12–31; vii. 1–42. In the last-cited place Eleazar is made to sound a little bit like Socrates; as he is being put to torture he says that being ninety years old, he can hardly let people think now that he will foreswear the Law and go over to the heathen. The Epitomator then comments that his life was a pattern of nobility and a memorial to virtue.
Heliodoros: iii. 22–40; Antiochos IV: v. 17–8. Exulting: viii. 18. Afflict the Greeks: i. 24–9. Forgery: i. 10b—ii. 18; see J. C. Dancy, *A Commentary on I Maccabees* (1954), 15–6. Discrepancies: *ibid.,* 17–8.

[50] Fragments of Eupolemos in Euseb. *Prep. Evang.* ix. 31. 1—34. 19 (448 A–451 D); Josephos in *A.Ap.* i. 111 may be using Eupolemos as a source. See, too, M. Hadas, *Hellenistic Culture* (1959), 95–6.

[51] R. H. Pfeiffer, *History of New Testament Times* (1949), 211; M. Hadas, *Hellenistic Culture* (1959), 99.

highly sophisticated and scholarly Jews in Egypt never could escape the hostility of the Egyptians. Although by the second century Egyptians had finally acquired higher status and now could serve in the Ptolemaic army, still they had not surpassed the prestige of an Onias or Dositheos and they did not stop hating the Jews. Consequently, about the time that the above writers were acquainting their coreligionists with the glory of Judah in Greek, a Greek tragedy was written to celebrate the memory of past triumph over Egypt. Ezekielos dealt dramatically with the Exodus in his only known play, the *Exagoge*. In good Greek style Moses speaks a soliloquy describing his career down to his flight to Midian after having killed the servant of Pharaoh; he has a dialogue with God, who gives instructions concerning the miracles to be worked in Egypt; later, a messenger announces the destruction of Pharaoh and his host in the Red Sea. Ezekielos' language shows familiarity with the great Athenian dramatists, especially with Euripides.[52] The subject of this play must have comforted the Alexandrian Jews and vexed any Egyptians who knew of it. Artapanos, moreover, about 100 B.C. wrote a book answering the third-century charges of Manethon. His hero was Moses, of course, and Artapanos showed that Moses had not been an unclean and leprous renegade Egyptian at all, but rather that he was one of the greatest benefactors Egypt ever had. Moses becomes in his hands a romantic and intellectual figure, a sort of Hellenistic polymath, being skilled in statecraft, military science, religion, philosophy, and technology. Artapanos claimed for him nothing less than the invention of Egyptian civilization, and said that this had won him the respect of the Egyptian priests and the love of the common people. So far from having taken part in an invasion of Egypt, Moses had actually prevented the Arab King Rhagouel, his father-in-law, from carrying out his intention of placing Moses on Pharaoh's throne. The daughter of this man, Moses' wife, ultimately became the goddess Isis. Pharaoh Chenephres eventually turned ungrateful and persecuted Moses and the Jews, but God then struck him with leprosy, the first recorded instance of the disease.[53]

While all this literary activity in Alexandria helped to insulate some Hellenized Jews from the attractions of real Hellenism, it

[52] R. H. Pfeiffer, *History of New Testament Times* (1949), 211–2; M. Hadas, *Hellenistic Culture* (1959), 99–101. Who was the tragic hero—Pharaoh?

[53] Fragments of Artapanos in Euseb. *Prep. Evang.* ix. For commentary on them see M. Braun, *History and Romance in Graeco-Oriental Literature* (1938), 26–30; R. H. Pfeiffer, *History of New Testament Times* (1949), 201–2; M. Hadas, *Hellenistic Culture* (1959), 96–8.

couldn't help but spread knowledge of Greek philosophy and learning among others, and to soften the attitudes of many towards the greatness of the classical age. To argue that Plato was dependent on Moses was still to talk about Plato. This sort of thing helped chart the course that led up to the philosophical speculations of Philo of Alexandria and the historiography of Josephos. Philo loved Plato and respected Pythagoras and the Stoics. Josephos admired Thoukydides. None of these persons renounced Judaism. But the argumentative and rationalized Judaism of these writers was not the old-line hortatory religion of Judah, and it did not seek entirely to reject Hellenism, but rather to use it. The violence and hatred of the Hasmoneans and of literature contemporary with them was nowhere in evidence.[54]

The Diaspora, indeed, was well quit of the terrible struggles in Palestine, and its quietism was illustrated by its interest in wisdom literature, the soft-spoken, wise, and patient genre of ancient religious texts. It was noticeably less interested in eschatological visions. *The Wisdom of Solomon,* a work originally written in Greek in Alexandria about 50 B.C. shows this. The first of its two sections has a strong tendency towards pious eclecticism, combining the teaching of the Hebrew prophets with ethical conceptions drawn from Greek philosophy, particularly Stoicism. The second half of this composite work is not as gentle, for it denounces the rich and powerful people of first-century Ptolemaic Egypt.[55]

None of this implies that the Diaspora broke off contact with Palestine. Politically it did, but religiously it most emphatically did not; it rather maintained a close spiritual relation with Jerusalem. There was a difference in cast of mind, the Palestinians generally being more exclusive and less tolerant of paganism. But even in Palestine itself, wholly new attitudes towards Hellenism began to grow up after 140 B.C. They were apparent not only among the

---

[54] Philo: E. R. Goodenough, *By Light, Light: The Mystic Gospel of Hellenistic Judaism* (1935), especially pp. 265–305. Josephos: H. St. J. Thackerary, *Josephos* (Loeb Classical Library, 1926), i. pp. vii–xvi; (1930) iv. pp. vii–xvi. For Platonism's effects on the Jews, see, too, M. Hadas, *Hellenistic Culture* (1959), 72–82.

[55] The sections are chapters i–xi and xi–xix. Date and authorship: G. H. Box, *Judaism in the Greek Period* (1932), 172–80; O. Eissfeldt, *E.A.T.* (1934), 655–7; C. C. Torrey, *The Apocryphal Literature* (1945), 99–103; R. H. Pfeiffer, *History of New Testament Times* (1949), 320–7; A. Bentzen, *I.O.T.* (2nd ed., 1952), ii. 235–6, dates this work in the first century A.D.

Eclecticism: parallels with Greek philosophy listed by S. Holmes in *Aprocrypha and Pseudepigrapha of the Old Testament* (1913), i. 532–3, and in the notes to the translation; M. Hadas, *Hellenistic Culture* (1959), 72–82.

Hasmoneans, but also among the successors of the Hasidim, that is, the Pharisees. The former, now aiming towards human kingship vested in their own family, adopted one set of Greek values; the latter, aiming at preserving traditional Judaism in this new period, adopted another. The result was a fierce and violent collision. In late 143 B.C. Jonathan was treacherously killed by the Seleukid pretender-king Tryphon, and the fortunes of the Hasmoneans were taken over by Simon, the third of the brothers to rule in Judah. He at once made great gains against the Seleukid kings. In 142 he won freedom from taxation, and in the following year he captured the Akra, the stronghold of the alien kings in Jerusalem. Thus, Seleukid rule was effectively ended.[56]

From 141 until 63 B.C. the Jewish state was independent. During this time there was still occasional hostility towards the Seleukids; but on the whole it was much abated. The Hasmonean state had now to compete with other newly independent states that were coming into being out of the wreck of the Seleukid Empire, and the new little kingdoms that were growing up along the fringes of the sown-land in northwestern Arabia. This corner of the Mediterranean world grew increasingly wretched and unhappy as these many little princes and petty kings made alliances with one another or made war on one another, hoping to gain some small territory or city. In these circumstances the Hasmoneans found themselves at war continually, now against the Seleukids, then against the Nabataians, now attacking, then defending. Yesterday's enemy was tomorrow's ally.[57] The broken Seleukids ceased to be a threat, and the Hasmoneans began to create a state modelled on Hellenistic lines, that is, a centralized monarchy organized to maintain a strong army. I do not suppose that the creation of this military kingship was modelled solely on the example of the Seleukid and Ptolemaic states, or made necessary only by the rising power of the Nabataian kinglets. The old tradition of Jewish kingship, inspired by the memory of David's greatness, was still alive in Judah, and events were to show that there were men who willingly supported the royal ambitions of the Hasmoneans. But the detailed forms assumed by their kingship were borrowed from the Hellenistic prototypes around them.

Hellenistic monarchy was highly centralized, that is, the threads

[56] Jonathan's death: 1 Macc. xii. 48–xiii. 23; Jos. *Ant.* xiii. 191–209. Simon's gains: 1 Macc. xii. 23–52; Jos. *Ant.* xiii. 201–13.

[57] Narratives of these wars and shifting alliances are in Jos. *War* i. and *Ant.* xiii.

of all authority led up to the kings, who commanded the army, governed the state, administered the territory and revenues, and appointed the religious personnel. These tasks were accomplished with the aid of a complex bureaucracy. The great importance of the king was underscored in the eyes of a sullen but superstitious proletariat by an aura of mysticism created around the king. Simon took the first steps along this road by constructing a great monument for his family sometime between 140 and 135 B.C. He built the structure at Modein, where the ancestral estate was and where his father Mattathias had begun the war of liberation. The memorial was constructed on a monumental scale out of polished white marble, and was surrounded by pillared porticoes. There were seven pyramids, one each for Mattathias and his wife and the five brothers. The number must have reminded the beholder of the mystical Jewish respect for the number seven. The whole was decorated in Greek fashion with trophies, suits of armor, and prows of ships taken in the pomp and circumstance of glorious war. This glittering, towerlike building was a visible mark of the greatness and magnificence of the family, as were Alexander the Great's tomb in Alexandria and Philip's *tholos* at Olympia.[58] Simon did not, however, take the significant title "king."

The usual Hellenistic state also had a professional, paid army. This was vitally necessary, since volunteer forces were inadequate for the complicated warfare of the age. They were scarcely equipped for siege-operations, and they were likely to desert during long, sustained campaigns, either through indiscipline and terror or because of their absolute need to return home to attend to family affairs. Therefore, Simon took the very important step of arming and paying his soldiers from the resources of the state. One wonders whether this involved the acquisition of Greek instructors to train them. Perhaps not, since Hellenized Jews from Egypt or Asia Minor could have imparted the principles of military drill. But there was certainly Hellenistic influence around Simon: his son-in-law was named Ptolemaios.[59]

Hellenistic states also had to maintain complex relationships with foreign powers. We know something about these in the reign of Simon's son and successor, John Hyrkanos (134–104 B.C.). He maintained a number of ambassadors, men with Greek names like Apollonios, son of Alexander, and Diodoros, son of Jason. If this last-named man was a son of the Jason whom Judas had used to negotiate

[58] 1 Macc. xiii. 27–30; Jos. *Ant.* xiii. 210–1.
[59] Pay and equipment: 1 Macc. xiv. 32. Ptolemaios: Jos. *War* i. 54; *Ant.* xiii. 228.

with the Romans in 161, this would show the existence of a family whose primary function was to serve the Hasmoneans in their affairs with outside powers. Foreign policy frequently involved the use of money to bribe or subsidize possible opponents or friends of Judah into alliance or at least into neutrality. Thus, Hyrkanos sent three hundred talents to Antiochos VII Sidetes and four hundred talents to Ptolemy VIII Lathyros.[60]

The hard specie required for this activity made necessary a large income, which could come partly from tribute imposed on conquered communities, and we know that Hyrkanos both conquered and imposed. This money was insufficient, however, especially because foreign policy was supported in the last extremity by armed force. Hyrkanos' successor Alexander Iannaios (103–76 B.C.), a man with strong expansionist ambitions, had to keep a large professional army. He maintained not only Jewish troops, but also hired mercenaries from Pisidia and Kilikia. From the standpoint of the Jewish civilians this was dangerous, since it made the king partly independent of them, and in fact Iannaios twice used these mercenaries against them to keep himself in power. At one time he had at least one thousand mercenary cavalry and eight thousand paid infantry, in addition to ten thousand local troops, whom he also paid either in cash or with land allotted for service. The mercenary foot soldiers were an elite force called "Hundred Fighters," because they were organized in centuries and equipped with special weapons. This organization may have been suggested partly out of an archaizing respect for the formations of King David, but it was also undoubtedly founded on Hellenistic practice. The Hasmoneans also constructed a system of frontier fortresses, which were manned by these troops, some of whom had Greek names. The army included an engineering corps, competent to throw up extensive fieldworks involving entrenchments and palisades. This expensive military establishment remained a constant burden after the reign of Iannaios.[61]

The army as well as the subventions to foreign powers required a large and continuing outlay of money. Early in his reign Hyrkanos

[60] Ambassadors: Jos. *Ant.* xiii. 260. Josephos also mentions *loc. cit.* another such man with the more nearly Jewish name Simon, son of Dositheos. Sidetes: Jos. *War* i. 61; Ptolemy: *Ant.* xiii. 334–5.

[61] Hyrkanos' tribute: Jos. *War* i. 89; *Ant.* xiii. 374. Pisidian and Kilikian Mercenaries: Jos. *War* i. 88; *Ant.* xiii. 372–3. Numbers and "Hundred Fighters": Jos. *War* i. 93–4; *Ant.* xiii. 339. Josephos calls (*Ant.* xiii. 304) the troops in Aristoboulos' army "hoplites." David's example: 2 Sam. xviii. 1, 4; 1 Chron. xiii. 1. Fortresses: Jos. *Ant.* xiii. 417, 424. Engineering: Jos. *War* i. 99. After Iannaios: Jos. *War* i. 118, 120; *Ant.* xiii. 409.

was already hard pressed, and is said to have opened the tomb of David to get at the silver in it. This silver went partly to Antiochos VII and mostly to hire troops. But this could be only a temporary palliative, and Hyrkanos had to depend on a more constant source of income than tomb robbery and a more profitable means than the imposition of tribute to maintain his family, its troops, and its monuments. He seems to have organized some kind of bureaucracy to gather revenues from land taxes and customs duties; Josephos says that he "exploited" Judah in order to gain the money, and he uses the Greek verb καρπόω, a standard term used to describe the systematic development of profits from agricultural and commercial activity. Unfortunately details are lacking, but Josephos' statement and the military establishment clearly imply the existence of an administrative bureaucracy on the Hellenistic model to supervise the reaping of revenues. The results can still be seen in the surviving currency of these men, which began with Simon.[62]

The Hasmoneans kept the high priesthood during this whole period, so that they also dominated the religious institutions of Judah. Queen Alexandra (76–67 B.C.) could not, of course, be high priest; she therefore appointed her son Hyrkanos II to the office.[63]

Having thus provided themselves with the usual institutions of Hellenistic kingship, the Hasmoneans finally took the title outright. Hyrkanos may have had it; certainly his son Aristoboulos (104–103 B.C.) did. He also called himself "philhellene." This increasing Hellenization of the dynasty is faithfully shown by the coins. Simon inscribed his "For the Redemption of Zion" and decorated them with citron and palm branch. Under John Hyrkanos they were engraved "Jehochanan, the High Priest, and the Community of the Jews," in deliberately archaizing, nationalist Hebrew script. The obverse, however, carried a Hellenic wreath of laurel and the reverse a double cornucopia. Under Iannaios the coinage appeared with the Greek superscription "King Alexander" and was decorated with nothing less than a Seleukid anchor. On the reverse was a wheel and the Hebrew inscription "Jonathan the King." Both state and money were now the king's: like an Anatolian or Kyrenaikan dynast, Iannaios bequeathed the community of the Jews to his wife Salome Alexandra.[64]

[62] The tomb: Jos. *War* i. 61; *Ant.* xiii. 249. "Exploitation": Jos. *Ant.* xiii. 273; s.v. καρπόω in Liddell and Scott. Coinage: see n. 64, below.

[63] Jos. *War* i. 109; *Ant.* xiii. 408.

[64] Coinage: A. Reiffenberg, *Ancient Hebrew Arts* (1950), 68–70. S. W. Baron, *S.R.H.J.* (2nd ed., 1952), i. 401, n. 31. Bequest: Jos. *War* i. 107.

The new dynasty was supported like the Ptolemaic or Seleukid by literary propaganda, which for the benefit of Jews lukewarm to the family, attacked devilish foreigners and glorified pious Hasmoneans. Such was 1 Maccabees, a book written in revived national literary Hebrew during the reign of Hyrkanos.[65] It does not seem to have been intended to be read as an inspired book, since it insisted that the age of prophecy was past. Nor did its author take part in the theological issues of the day. He made no reference to the rather new belief in a happy afterlife as a reward for good people. Contemporary scholars consider him a Sadducee. This is certainly possible, although he may have been merely a rather worldly person whose task was to idealize the Hasmonean house. His accounts of battles and politics show that he was a highly placed man of affairs. He was certainly close to the Maccabean rulers, for he devotes several passages to fulsome praise of Judas, Jonathan, and Simon. The last-named, whom he probably knew firsthand, he considered the greatest of the brothers. He was obviously close to Hasmonean sources of information, for he quoted both genuine and spurious diplomatic correspondence. He interpreted the Hasmonean-Seleukid struggle as the battle of a righteous people led by the sons of Mattathias against an evil, lawless people led by wicked Antiochos and his successors. The Jews of the Maccabean age were zealous for the law and faithful to the covenant; God therefore intervened and protected them. This was the normal interpretation of traditional Hebrew historiography, a form of writing that the author was certainly familiar with.[66]

So far as the Makedonians and Greeks were concerned, 1 Maccabees says that evil came to Judah in the body of Alexander the Great. The foreign king was a despoiler, a vain man with an overly exalted human heart. His successors were similar, and they did much evil on the earth. The most sinful of all was wicked Antiochos Epiphanes, and in dealing with him hatred for the Seleukids reaches its crescendo. Mattathias is made to call on his faithful, law-abiding followers to pay back the heathen in full for what they have done.

[65] G. H. Box, *Judaism in the Greek Period* (1932), 222–3; O. Eissfeldt, *E.A.T.* (1934), 635–6; E. Bickermann, *Der Gott der Makkabäer* (1937), 17, 29–31, 145–50; C. C. Torrey, *The Apocryphal Literature* (1945), 72–3; R. H. Pfeiffer, *History of New Testament Times* (1949), 483–4; A. Bentzen, *I.O.T.* (2nd ed., 1952), ii. 221–2; J. C. Dancy, *A Commentary on I Maccabees* (1954), 3, 8–9.

[66] Age of Prophecy: 1 Macc. iv. 46; xiv. 41; cf. Zech. xiii. 3–5. Praise: Judas: iii. 3–9; ix. 20–2; Jonathan: xii. 52; xiii. 26; Simon: xiv. 4–15. Correspondence: spurious: i. 41–2; genuine but paraphrased: i. 44–50; see J. C. Dancy, *A Commentary on I Maccabees* (1954), 76. Normal interpretation: 1 Macc. ii. 24–6; cf. Num. xxv. 10–3. Divine intervention: iv. 8–11, 25, 30–3; vii. 38. There are other cases.

Judas is a relentless avenger, ruthlessly stamping out Hellenizing Jews and Greeks alike. To emphasize the virtues of these vigorous defenders of the Torah, 1 Maccabees omits some dishonorable moments, like Judas' rapid negotiation and breaking of the Peace of Lysias. He also exaggerates the strength of the Greek armies in order to show that God sustained the small but righteous band led by the Hasmoneans.[67]

Outside of dynastic circles there still appeared anti-Hellenic literature, too. Esther was one of the last examples to lust after Grecian gore in the blood-curdling style of Judith. This fictional story, based on a Babylonian plot, began to circulate among the Jews about 125 B.C.[68] It glorified the heroine's saving the Chosen People from an imaginary persecution said to have been planned to ferret them out over the whole of the civilized world. It thus plays in an exaggerated way on the proscription of Antiochos Epiphanes, made after living memory of it had almost died. At the end of the book the enemies of the Jews are slaughtered in grand style. Esther therefore advocates drastic action against pagan enemies of Judaism, like the fierce reprisals that the Hasmonean brothers had inflicted on gentile towns and sanctuaries around Judah. It urges celebration of a national holiday consecrated to the memory of the heroine's imaginary triumph. But this sort of anti-Hellenism was definitely on the wane. The Epistle of Jeremiah, an Aramaic document composed in Mesopotamia around 100 B.C., simply condemned religion involving idol worship.[69] It was intended, moreover, to discredit not only Hellenism but the paganism of Parthian-ruled Babylonia, and to persuade Jews against trafficking with false religion. In Palestine, expansion and collection of older messianic anti-Hellenic oracles was undertaken, resulting in the completion of 1 Enoch early in the first century.[70] The late sections of this work begin to show a concern for the relationship of the patriotic, orthodox religious party in Palestine, the Pharisees, with the Hasmonean kings, for their assumption of the royal dignity strongly aroused the feelings of these men, who still believed the prophetic tradition that Yahweh was true king.

[67] Alexander: i. 3. Successors: i. 9. Antiochos IV: i. 10. Mattathias: ii. 68; Judas: iii. 4–9. Omission of Peace of Lysias: n. 11, p. 219, above. Exaggerations: iii. 38–9; cf. 2 Macc. viii. 9; 1 Macc. ii. 28; death of Antiochos narrated at 1 Macc. vii. 11; see p. 145, n. 43, above. Lysias with 120,000 men (vi. 30) is impossible.

[68] See p. 137, n. 8, above.

[69] O. Eissfeldt, *E.A.T.* (1934), 651–2; C. C. Torrey, *The Apocryphal Literature* (1945), 65–7; R. H. Pfeiffer, *History of New Testament Times* (1949), 428–30; A. Bentzen, *I.O.T.* (2nd ed., 1952), ii. 232–3.

[70] For 1 Enoch see n. 22, p. 223, n. 31, p. 227, and n. 38, p. 230, above.

The trend in this Hasmonean literature was symptomatic of the problems of Judaism. By the last years of the second century narrow particularism, the total rejection of Hellenic culture, could not be in Judah, for the Jews now had other states to fight than the Seleukid, and other religious enemies than the Ba'al Shamim of Antiochos. Greek ways were highly valuable in combatting these foes. For official people, Hellenic administrative ideas helped to organize the state for defense. For religious people philosophical and logical systems could be used to build a fence around the Torah to defend it from competing cults and ways of life. Or Alexandrian scholarship could defend the Jewish past against the attacks of a Manethon. Dramatic forms were useful for presenting ideas in the popular new ways. For upper-class people closely associated with the Hellenizing dynasty, especially after the reign of Aristoboulos, Hellenism had many ways to beguile a leisure hour, and the patricians could hardly be expected to work themselves into that frame of mind necessary for rejecting them. The sophisticated folk in Judah saw little danger in accepting Hellenistic culture as long as the religious content was properly censored. Urban Jews, both in Judah and in Egypt, were more inclined to look tolerantly on Greek ideas than country people, who through ignorance were more inclined to reject foreign ways. Many of them identified aliens with evil customs and heavy taxes—the works of sinners and publicans—because they were not conversant with the high politics and the needs of the state, let alone with Hellenism. They did not know Greek; they did not even know many Greeks. The city people, on the other hand, had a more intimate contact with the Europeans, and therefore better understood what Greek culture was. Even among the cultural extremists in Judaism there is no evidence that Hellenism was ever attacked with the intention of totally blotting it out. The rabbis of the period knew and taught the Greek language; there is only a single case of their banning the learning of Greek, and that was a wartime measure of the Roman period.[71]

While the descendants of Mattathias were founding Hellenistic kingship in Judah, there were important religious developments taking place in city and country. Definite religious sects within Judaism began to take form, and these were more or less imbued with Hellenism, and more or less faithful to ancient tradition. The most impor-

[71] *Megillah* i. 8; *Sotah* 49a; N. Bentwich, *Hellenism* (1920), 253–87; S. Liebermann, *Greek in Jewish Palestine* (1942); E. Wiesenberg, "Related Prohibitions: Swine Breeding and the Study of Greek," *HUCA* 27 (1956), 213–33.

tant, historically speaking, were the Pharisees. They were the spiritual heirs of the faithful and patriotic Hasidim. "Pharisee" itself means "Separated One," the idea being that this group kept apart from defilement and impurity through obedience to the law. By the last years of the second century they were in being, and among them were influential scholars and students of the law, a group devoted to the defense of the practices and principles of Judaism. The Pharisees, in distinction to the Sadducees, another important sect, accepted the whole Palestinian canon of literature as inspired. This included not only the books of the law, but the books of the prophets. This group, therefore, continued to uphold the ancient traditions concerning kingship much more than the Sadducees. The Pharisees were numerous, especially since they drew support generally from the lower classes, the peasants in the countryside, and the artisans of Jerusalem, the people who were compelled financially to support the new monarchy.[72]

The patriotic Pharisees came to terms with Hellenism by adopting Greek dialectical and logical methods. This scholarly group could use these valuable tools in their efforts to extend the Torah to cover new conditions faced by Jews in the Hellenistic period, conditions which had not been contemplated during Israel's more agrarian past. Greek polemic technique was extremely valuable, too, for defending Judaism against pagan philosophical and historical attacks.[73] Greek logic and methods of debate could be applied also to the study of Torah and to the new process of legal cross-examination. The question had become, for the Pharisees as for the Hasmoneans, not whether Hellenic influence should be rejected, but rather what should be taken from it and what neglected. Judaism accepted Greek culture because it was not strong enough to make its way alone in the last century of the pre-Christian era. Hellenism had much to contribute because of its extraordinary way of life, its diversity, and its creativity.

[72] For the rising sectarianism in Judaism see Jos. *Ant.* xiii; E. R. Bevan, *Jerusalem under the High Priests* (1904), 125–6; in *C.A.H.* viii. 520–33; M. Radin, *The Jews among the Greeks and Romans* (1915); M. I. Rostovtzeff, *S.E.H.H.W.*, ii. 1018; W. O. E. Oesterley, *A History of Israel* (1932), ii. 281–316.

For the Pharisees: L. Finkelstein, *The Pharisees* (1938), i. 73–81; ii. 609–10; S. W. Baron, "The Pharisees: . . . by Louis Finkelstein" (review), *JBL* 59 (1940), 60–7.

[73] E. Bickerman, *The Maccabees* (1947), 77–118; W. F. Albright, *From the Stone Age to Christianity* (Anchor ed., 1957), 354–7. For early Jewish apologetics see Josephos, *Against Apion*. This is a surviving example of the kind of literature begun by Aristoboulos and Jason of Kyrene.

A second group was the Sadducees, a sect that religiously speaking was very conservative. They admitted that only the law had come directly from God, and rejected belief in the inspiration of the books of the prophets. They also rejected some of the new ideas which the Pharisees accepted, such as the belief in rewards and punishments hereafter. They were rather closely identified with the landed gentry of Palestine, and with the professional priestly families in Jerusalem. Their numbers included many Hellenized persons, that is, persons whose Hellenism was purely secular.[74] They were the Jewish upper classes around the Hasmonean monarchy, people rather envious of the ways of their social opposite numbers in the Greek *poleis* in the Levant. They did not, however, undertake to introduce formal Hellenic institutions leading to the establishment of another Antioch in Jerusalem, having learned from the Maccabean experience that an indirect approach was preferable to direct antagonism.

Late in the reign of John Hyrkanos, when it had become fully apparent that he was creating a strong, Hellenistic monarchy, Pharisee and Hasmonean collided over this issue. In the style of an ancient prophet opposing the will of an overweening king, the Pharisee Eleazar demanded that Hyrkanos give up the high priesthood if he intended to be governor as well. In doing this, the Pharisees were motivated by the old tradition hostile to strong human kingship, the tradition that went back through the prophets Elijah and Nathan to Samuel. No doubt, too, they hated the threat of Hyrkanos' standing army and the burdens imposed by his taxes. A Sadducee named Jonathan, a friend of Hyrkanos, gave the high priest and Ethnarch comfort, and advised him to break with the Pharisaic party and expel them from court. There resulted considerable ferment in Judah, for Josephos says that the masses at this time were on the side of the Pharisees, and the wealthy on that of the Sadducees.[75] The growing kingship must have seemed admirable to the gentry and the rich men of the cities, many of whom were in state service as ambassadors, generals, tax-farmers, and priests. It was attacked by the little people, who supplied the state with blood and taxes; these men gained the least obvious and tangible rewards from its existence. But Hyrkanos broke with the Pharisees, and therefore definite, organized opposition, inspired by a religious party, commenced against the Hellenized Hasmoneans.

[74] L. Finkelstein, *The Pharisees*, i. 73–81, 251; S. W. Baron's review, 61–3, and the literature cited in n. 72, p. 245, above.
[75] Jos. *Ant.* xiii. 293–8.

Within a few years this opposition reached fever heat against Alexander Iannaios, the man who held outright the title of king and brought to completion the institutionalization of the monarchy. Two revolts against him were led by the Pharisaic party. Thus, some sixty years after the rising of the Hasidim against Antiochos IV, the Pharisees rebelled against a great-grandson of Mattathias. In their eyes a man could not be both high priest and king; he could not make new law at the expense of the divinely sanctioned law and its traditional, prophetic interpretation. He could not be king on the Hellenistic model. Iannaios was, however, able to suppress these revolts, although in the case of the second it was a near-run thing. He fought it with Greek mercenaries with great success at first, so that the Jewish rebels called for help from Demetrios III, the Seleukid king. He appeared with an army including Jewish soldiers in its ranks. But when this alien began to press Iannaios heavily, many of the rebels rallied behind their king, so that Demetrios was compelled to withdraw. Iannaios then had much less difficulty in suppressing the insurrection. He ultimately massacred its Pharisaic leaders to the number of eight hundred. Whereupon, eight thousand Jews went into voluntary exile. Fortunately for the peace of Judah, Iannaios' successor and wife Alexandra abandoned the Sadducaic party and went over to the Pharisees.[76] The force of religious tradition was strong.

The appalling helter-skelter of life in Jerusalem, punctuated by riot, insurrection, and crucifixion, triumph, defeat, and lamentation was too much for some persons. It was about this time that the Essenes came into being, a sect noteworthy for its regard for the law, its extreme piety, and its quietism. Possibly for a time they cooperated politically with the Pharisees; one of them named Judas prophesied the murder of King Antigonos (104–103 B.C.). But probably during the early years of Iannaios' unhappy reign one group of them withdrew from city life and established itself at Qumran near the solitude of the Dead Sea. Here, about 100 B.C., they built themselves living quarters and a scriptorium, and devoted themselves to a holy life made secure by regulation and the study of the scriptures.[77] This

---

[76] Iannaios and the revolt: Jos. *War* i. 97–8; *Ant.* xiii. 376–83. Alexandra: *War* i. 110–1, 113–4; *Ant.* xiii. 401–6; 410–1.

[77] Judas the Essene: Jos. *War* i. 78–80. On the Essenes in general, their relation to the Qumran community, and the history of the sect itself see A. Dupont-Sommer, *The Dead Sea Scrolls* (1952); H. H. Rowley, *The Zadokite Fragments and the Dead Sea Scrolls* (1952); M. Burrows, *The Dead Sea Scrolls* (1955); *More Light on the Dead Sea Scrolls* (1958); J. M. Allegro, *The Dead Sea Scrolls* (1956); F. M. Cross, *The Ancient Library of Qumran* (1958). The regulations governing the sect are in

scholarly and worshipful withdrawal of the Qumran sect, however, did not keep its members from impotently hating both Jewish and Greek kingship. The *Genesis Apocryphon* (Lamech Scroll) retells the old story of Abraham, Sarah, and Pharaoh. It calls Pharaoh's *voyeur,* the man who reports the beauty of Sarah to his master and so titillates his id, "Hyrkanos." This same scroll makes God promise a large territory to Abraham, that is, to the Jews, for eventual owner- ship. It is to extend "from the river of Egypt to Lebanon and Senir, and from the Great Sea to Hauran and all the land of Gebal to Kadesh, and all the Great Desert east of Hauran and Senir to the Euphrates." This land, much of it in the hands of Greek cities and Syrian principalities, was considerably larger than the territory prom- ised Abraham in canonical Genesis. In similar nationalist vein a fragment of a commentary on Isaiah says that a descendant of King David would someday rule over all nations.[78]

These Essenes also hated the Greek kings Antiochos IV and De- metrios III, and they identified the latter's opponent Iannaios with a lion tearing flesh for its lioness and cubs. They were comforted to know the lion would be destroyed, since the comparison was made on the basis of a passage in Nahum, a book which originally execrated the bloody warfare of the Assyrians. The community actually lived in hope of the last apocalyptic catastrophe, and was organized like an army in hundreds, fifties, and tens for "the war to subdue nations." The campaigns would be fought not only against the surrounding people in Syria and Transjordan, but also against the remnant of the Seleukids. Therefore they studied the text called *The War of the Sons of Light against the Sons of Darkness,* to see how eschatological war- fare should be waged.[79]

The Pharisees and Essenes shared a deep interest in eschatology, in

---

the scroll called *The Manual of Discipline* and in the so-called Zadokite documents. Translations of these are in Burrows, *op. cit.,* and T. H. Gaster, *The Dead Sea Scriptures* (1956), 39–86.

Date of the buildings: J. M. Allegro, *op. cit.,* 84–5; M. Burrows, *More Light on the Dead Sea Scrolls* (1958), 21–2.

[78] Abraham-Hyrkanos: *Genesis Apocryphon,* col. xx; the territory: col. xxi. (translation in M. Burrows, *More Light on the Dead Sea Scrolls* [1958], 389–91). The canonical passage is Gen. xv. 18–21.

David: *Isaiah Commentary* in M. Burrows, *op. cit.,* 351.

[79] Antiochos, Demetrios, and Iannaios are the figures in the *Nahum Commentary,* only a fragment dealing with Nah. ii. 11–3 being preserved. For identifications of the figures with these kings see T. H. Gaster, *op. cit.,* 263; J. M. Allegro, *op. cit.,* 96, and M. Burrows, *More Light on the Dead Sea Scrolls* (1958), 201–2.

Organization: *Rule of the Congregation,* i. 14, 21. Opponents: *The War,* i. 1–17.

the doctrines concerning the last things, and in the prophetic and apocalyptic portions of the Old Testament. Both drew comfort from messianic hopes. Expectation of a savior was not their own exclusively, for it was a wish that from time to time touched many persons. It had become important in the third century, with prophecies of coming kings in Zechariah, and had reappeared more strongly in the second century during the dangerous struggle against Antiochos. Daniel 7, if the Son of Man figure stood for a messiah, was an early instance of the predicted intervention of a divine figure sent by God. Daniel 12, which looked forward to the advent of the Great Prince Michael, was another. Jubilees 31 prophesied the coming of another. So did sections of 1 Enoch. These saviors all were expected to exercise the historic functions of Hebrew kingship: they would destroy foreign powers; they would act as righteous judges of good and evil people; they would intercede between God and the people; they would bring natural blessings. In short, the messianic savior would establish the glorious kingdom of God to exist at the end of earthly time. The undoubted royal inspiration behind these messianic visions is shown, too, by the saviors being made to speak in the "I-style" of the ancient Near Eastern royal inscriptions.[80] Many Pharisees and Essenes, despairing of the ability of men to found a goodly monarchy in the tradition of the prophets, looked forward to the appearance of a divine figure, whose attributes and powers were partly to be based on the old conception of human kingship but partly on superhuman righteousness. Other men than they still had faith in human institutions, so that the rift that was growing up between Pharisee and Sadducee had one important cause in the dispute over monarchy. This rift widened and deepened from other causes as well, and grew up throughout Judaism. Sectarianism was not exactly a new thing in the Hellenistic period, for Judaism had never been completely united even in its earliest days. But during the Maccabean struggle, which was directed against the Jewish Hellenizers as much as against the Seleukids, the division of the people into competing camps tended to become more widespread and more intense, and the groups better organized and less compromising with one another. The Pharisees themselves tended ultimately to divide into lesser sects, mostly over the issue of the policy to be followed against royal governments of gentile occupying powers. This led in the Roman period to the splitting off of the Zealots, who looked forward to the renewal of violent measures

[80] For the functions of these messiahs see S. Mowinckel, *He That Cometh* (1955), 311–21; 416–7.

against the government, and eventually to an even more extremist party, the *Sicarii*, cloak-and-dagger assassins of the first century of the Christian era.

Nor were all Essenes ever exactly alike. The *Therapeutai* of Egypt followed the ideal of the contemplative life, but with differences as compared with the Qumran people. All these currents led to the great upsurge of sectarianism which Judaism was experiencing in the time of Jesus. It occurred in part from the great crisis of loyalties produced by the Maccabean wars, and this crisis was due to the stimulation Judaism received, and kept on receiving, from Hellenism.

The uncompromising hostility of the early Hasmoneans and many contemporary writers, down to about 125 B.C., towards pagans and paganism had sometimes led to massacres of gentiles and destruction of their temples. Judas and his immediate followers had, moreover, sought to bring Jewish people back from Galilee and Gilead into Judah to remove them from pagan reprisals and possibly from pagan influence. But this defensive scheme was supplanted by an offensive spirit, which was a special concern to begin the conversion of the gentiles to Judaism. This was not entirely a fresh idea, since early prophets had foretold it would someday happen. But only in the second century B.C. did Jewish people begin consciously and purposefully to take an interest in conversion. Mattathias and his sons had forcibly circumcized the children of Hellenizing Jews.[81] That was only a faint beginning. The new departure was to aim at converting gentiles. This religious response to the Hellenistic world became a widespread phenomenon and far overshadowed the efforts of Persian *magoi* to win enthusiasm for their view of the divine intervention of Ahura Mazdāh in behalf of the defunct empire of the Achaemenids. Conversion to Judaism involved a fresh orientation of the convert towards much of daily life, including law and the sources of authority. In this sense, Jewish proselytism was a unique reaction to the challenge of Hellenic imperialism. On one view it was nothing less than spiritual counter-imperialism.

Proselytizing was carried on both in Palestine and in the Dispersion. In Judah, the Hasmoneans in the last quarter of the second century set out forcibly to convert the heathen of the Dekapolis and Idoumaia. They may have done this partly to secure their control of these strategically important areas, but they did it as well to win converts. Hyrkanos compelled the people of Idoumaia to become

81 1 Macc. ii. 45–6; Jos. *Ant.* xii. 278.

Jews in the fullest sense of the word, and forced them to undergo circumcision. Aristoboulos, the "philhellene," did the same thing in Itouraia. Alexander Iannaios tried to do it around Pella, but the inhabitants resisted, so that he demolished the city.[82] This activity was accompanied by war on competing forms of religion. Hyrkanos attacked the Samaritan Jews, and about 108 or 107 B.C., his army, commanded by his sons, succeeded in starving the city into surrender. The inhabitants were sold into slavery, and the city was destroyed with such ferocity that modern excavation has failed to discover a coherent plan of the town's ruins. Alexander Iannaios attacked and captured Gaza with the help of traitors within; he first looted and then destroyed the city, desecrating the Temple of Apollo by killing five hundred of the councilmen in it; this massacre must have included the local priests.[83] This sort of thing eventually had repercussions.

In the Dispersion, in places where the Hasmonean armies could not reach, but also in Palestine, more humane methods were used. There was a literary propaganda for conversion, and Pharisees and other Jews were active in their efforts to bring over pagans to Judaism. Around 140 B.C. an Alexandrian Jew published a collection of gentile and Jewish prophecy as material for proselytizing. These now form part of our corpus of *Sibylline Oracles,* and they were published in Greek hexameters.[84] The poems included résumés of world history. Past experience was made to show that only the people who had followed the Jewish law were holy and worthy of salvation. The good lived; the wicked perished. In the poems many Greek cities were threatened with destruction. V. Tcherikover has suggested that the oracles were made simply to give expression to Jewish hopes for the ruin and death of Israel's foes, or to encourage the Jews to wait a little longer for the coming of the now-imminent messiah. He has said that they were not intended to be used as propaganda, and one of his reasons is that these poems do not seem to be quoted in classical

[82] Hyrkanos: Jos. *Ant.* xiii. 257–8; Strabo xvi. 2. 34 (760). Aristoboulos: Jos. *Ant.* xiii. 318–9 (which also cites Timagenes and Strabo as authorities). Iannaios: Jos. *Ant.* xiii. 397. Forcible circumcision was practiced by certain Jews down to the destruction of the Second Temple: see Jos. *Life,* 23 (113); *War* ii. 454.

[83] Samaria: Jos. *War* i. 64–6; *Ant.* xiii. 275–81; J. W. Crowfoot *et al., Samaria-Sebaste* i (1942), 30; iii (1957), 4. Gaza: Jos. *Ant.* xiii. 358–64.

[84] *Sib. Or.* iii. 97–end. H. C. O. Lanchester, "The Sibylline Oracles," *Apocrypha and Pseudepigrapha of the Old Testament* (1913), ii. 370–2; H. N. Bate, *The Sibylline Oracles* (1918), 22–3, 49; R. H. Pfeiffer, *History of New Testament Times* (1949), 227–9; A. Kurfess, *Sibyllinische Weissagungen* (1951), 288–9; A. Bentzen, *I.O.T.* (2nd ed., 1952), ii. 241–2.

literature. Hence they were not known; hence they were not pushed on pagans.[85] But I do not think that the Jewish missionaries were as interested in converting men like Tacitus and Horace as they were in converting the ordinary citizens. Nor would Tacitus or Horace have been impressed by these vaporings, and the *Sibylline Oracles* were not intended for educated, classical readers. They were written in poetry for commoners, so that proselytizers could memorize them and recite them as occasion demanded. This kind of approach was certainly popular among Christian missionaries, and the appeal to alleged prophecy of past events was one they often used to prove the truth of what they said. I agree that Tcherikover was right in wanting to de-emphasize the interpretation that most Jewish literature in Greek was propaganda for conversion. But the inclusion of gentile oracles in this collection[86] is evidence that the collection was not written by a Jew simply "to pour out his heart in patriotic poetry," but was composed with the design of using already familiar Greek and Oriental material for its persuasive effect. Certainly the highly literate and sophisticated Jews must have written something to further their proselytizing; if the *Sibylline Oracles* were not a part of this literature, none has survived.

From the beginning of the first century B.C. until the second century of the Christian era, Judaism made a determined effort to find proselytes, and enjoyed no small measure of success. Jewish synagogues admitted to partial fellowship pagans who did not wish to submit to circumcision or to obey the dietary restrictions of the Pentateuch. Jewish communities with proselytes among them are known to have existed in many places, among them Syria, Anatolia, the Crimea, Greece, and even Italy in the West. The great interest many Pharisees took in conversion was well shown by that testy remark of Jesus to one of his interlocutors, "You scour land and sea to make one convert. . . ."[87]

This urge to convert must be understood against the fact of cul-

---

[85] In "Jewish Apologetic Literature Reconsidered," *Eos* 48 (1956) , 176.

[86] *Sib. Or.* iii. 381–475.

[87] There is abundant evidence of Jewish proselytizing, assembled in N. Bentwich, *Hellenism* (1920) ; F. M. Derwacter, *Preparing the Way for Paul* (1930) ; B. D. Mazur, *Studies on Jewry in Greece* (1935) ; W. G. Braude, *Jewish Proselytizing* (1940) . See, too, the remarks of A. D. Nock, *Conversion* (1933) , 78–9, and the enthusiastic interpretations of S. W. Baron, *S.R.H.J.* (2nd ed., 1952) , i. 171–83; 224–5.

For Jewish literature in the first century A.D. see F. C. Burkitt, *Jewish and Christian Apocalypses* (1914) , 35, in addition to the above works. Converts in the various places in the text are mentioned in Acts ii. 5, 10; vi. 5; xiii. 17, 43. Jesus' remark from Mt. xxiii. 15.

tural competition between Jews and gentiles, particularly Hellenized gentiles. Hellenism had gained converts from Israel. Thus, Jewish proselytism began as an effort to combat conversion from Judaism. It became an effort to win the world to Yahweh. This may seem fanatically impractical to us now, but to the Jew of the wildly passionate first century B.C. it did not seem impractical or even impossible. Had not the conversion of mankind been prophesied long ago by Isaiah?[88] Jews in this age gloried in the victories of the puny Maccabean guerillas against the armed might of the great Seleukid Empire, and they interpreted their military victories as demonstrations of the holy power of their god. In this climate of opinion the idea that the world could be persuaded to obey the law of Moses through God's continuing help was entirely believable. Of course the response of gentiles was not nearly as universal as was hoped, and the Jewish leaders had to create a special category for those Greeks—the "devout"— who were enough attracted to Judaism to attend the local synagogue and listen to sermons in Greek, but who were shy of taking upon themselves all the obligations enjoined by Torah. Nonetheless, the results of this missionary enterprise were noticeable, and numbers of inscriptions and numerous literary references from the end of the first century on attest the conversion of gentiles. These successes in part explain the repressive measures of the Roman government against Jewish proselytizing. The fact that the missionary spirit had an anti-Hellenic flavor, a desire to abolish the "foolishness of the Greeks,"[89] accounts in part for the antiphilosophical attitude of some of the early Fathers of the Church. For Christianity inherited the ideal of conversion from Judaism, as it also inherited the numbers of Greeks sympathetic to Judaism that the predecessors of Paul had won in the cities of the East. In the aftermath of the conflict of Judaism and Hellenism there was a strong current of cultural assimilation, and a significant number of Judaeo-Greeks and Helleno-Jews came into being, and from these persons flowed the victory of Christianity.

The message of hope and of escape from sin and the world held out to gentiles was pretty generally taught in a context of the messianic expectations of Hellenistic Judaism, which saw the world as about to undergo its final, awful cataclysm, followed by the supernatural transformation of nature and the last relentless judgment of a wicked generation. This tendency to think in apocalyptic and eschatological terms was another legacy of the Maccabean age to Judaism, a tendency

[88] Is. xlii. 67; xlv. 23–4; xlix. 6; lvi. 6–7; lx. 1–10. See, too, Ps. xcvi.
[89] 1 Cor. i. 23.

which was simultaneously at work in Persis. It was the necessary response of a people who could not overcome the Greek by force alone, hard as they might try. Divine intervention was something beaten Greeks knew about and believed in too, for they had their moments of despair and their own Sibylline literature. Much of Judaism taught that conversion *now* was of critical importance before the imminent last act of the divine drama unfolded. Judaism counselled perfection for this last age, and the believer, born Jewish or converted, must keep himself unspotted from the world, like the solitary, contemplative Essene. The Judgment was to separate the good from evil men, and all the torments that distracted minds could conjure up were promised to the evil. The good man who would be saved on this view could hardly be too good. There was, therefore, an intense interest in high morality, a morality which in some instances tended towards virtual withdrawal of the body from activity in this world and fastening the mind upon the unseen world of God. Jewish and Greek asceticism were drawing close together, as were parallel developments in the mystery religions. At the same time, of course, some Jews may have insisted on strict ethical behavior because of the trial by arms with other states. Jewish numbers could be preserved if all obstacles to cooperation within their society could be removed. On the whole, however, these high ethics were the response of despairing people in a war-torn world; human institutions seemed to be a failure; prepare ye then the way of the Lord![90]

[90] For the new ethical emphasis and asceticism in Judaism see the literature cited for the Essenes, n. 77, p. 247, above. It is also well illustrated in the collection of texts called *The Testaments of the Twelve Patriarchs*. The date of this work is still a matter of debate. Usual opinion had favored a date in the second century B.C., as F. C. Burkitt, *Jewish and Christian Apocalypses* (1914), 34–5; O. Eissfeldt, *E.A.T.* (1934), 689–90; and R. H. Pfeiffer, *History of New Testament Times* (1949), 65–6. C. C. Torrey, *The Apocryphal Literature* (1945), 131, on the other hand, defended a date in the first Christian century. Since then, M. de Jonge has ably argued that it should be dated around 200 A.D., and that as it now stands it comes from Christian hands: *The Testaments of the Twelve Patriarchs* (1953).

Down to 1958, no manuscript of the *Testaments* had been found at Qumran, except variant recensions of our older text, embodying, however, only two of the twelve sections in the book: the testaments of Levi and Naphtali: M. Burrows, *More Light on the Dead Sea Scrolls* (1958), 179–80; F. M. Cross, *The Ancient Library of Qumran* (1958), 150, n. 7. De Jonge had said that he felt there were early prototypes of these two testaments, and so far this has been archaeologically supported, along with his principal contention, therefore, concerning the date of the whole collection. There certainly should be no a priori assumption that all twelve of the testaments were written at the same time. I have, consequently, regarded only Levi and Naphtali as existing in the Hellenistic period.

An appreciation of the ethical teaching of Judaism in this period, based partly on *The Testaments of the Twelve Patriarchs*, is in R. H. Charles, *Religious Development between the Old and New Testaments* (1914), 133–58.

Gentle and loving though Jewish ethics sometimes were, the gentile world did not always love the Jews in return. The warm mien of a Hillel was only one face of Judaism; the martial glare of an Iannaios was another. Many persons learned to hate the Jews with willing fervor. Jewish missionaries threatened gentiles with hellfire and the worm, and assured them that their gods and institutions were leading them to fiery death. Only the law of Moses was true. Only Yahweh was god. Apollo, Zeus, Athena—those symbols of a venerable tradition—were actually demoniac and foul. The Greek kings were wicked. What had Jerusalem to do with the *oikoumene?* The Jews lived under their exclusive law, in separate groups, with customs unique among mankind. Some defended these usages to the death, and said that they alone were right. Many pagans, too, experienced at first hand beatings and rapings from Jewish soldiers in Egypt and in Syria. The Jew seemed to like this—did not some of them celebrate Nikanor's Day? Worst of all, many people underwent the always horrible and sometimes fatal experience of involuntary circumcision. To the Greeks this was unspeakable. Were the Jews really righteous and full of loving-kindness? To many it did not seem so, and out of Egypt and Syria, about the time that Pharisaic persuasion and Hasmonean compulsion were being applied, came evidence of a new and abiding, irrational and vicious hatred of the Jews and all their works. The sinister forms of anti-Semitism appeared.[91]

About 140 or 130 a story came into being from some Seleukid source. It described Antiochos Epiphanes' forcible entry into the Temple in 168. It said that inside he found a Greek prepared for immolation. The world shuddered. It is reported that Antiochos VII Sidetes (139/8–129 B.C.) was advised to wipe out the Jews because they lived apart from the rest of mankind. This charge of *amixia,* "apartness," certainly seemed justified in view of how the name "Pharisee" could be understood. Antiochos was a genuinely philhellenic king, a man who attempted to rescue Babylonian Seleukeia from the occupation of the Parthians. He may therefore have hated being told of pogroms the Hasmoneans occasionally inflicted on conquered communities. Of course Jews had suffered from Antiochos' proscription. But that had been intended as a legal reprisal to punish rebels. How far back did the chain of incidents lead? That was really unimportant now. Greek and Jew were engaged in a campaign

91 General literature on ancient anti-Semitism includes N. W. Goldstein, "Cultivated Pagans and Ancient Antisemitism," *JR* 19 (1939), 346–64; H. I. Bell, "Anti-Semitism in Alexandria," *JRS* 31 (1941), 1–18; R. Marcus, "Antisemitism in the Hellenistic World," *Essays on Antisemitism* (ed. K. S. Pinson, 2nd ed., 1946), 61–78.

of mutual hatred, a campaign that kept the hatred glowing. Some workman toiling for the Hasmonean Simon scratched on a building block, "May fire consume Simon's palace." Somebody in Egypt in the first half of the first century wrote a letter; only a piece has survived. It includes the phrase, "You know that they hate the Jews."[92]

Before the end of the second century an anti-Semitic literature came into being. Agatharchides wrote that Ptolemy I had been able to capture Jerusalem easily because of the superstitions of the Jews, that is, their refusal to fight on the Sabbath. This opinion—it was no fact— was based, according to Josephos, on the experience pagans had in the revolt of 166/5. Poseidonios in the first century said that the Jews were descended from the Egyptians. Moses had left the country because he was discontented with conditions there, and moved to Palestine. He gave the Jews righteous and pious precepts, and said that the Greeks were wrong to worship gods in human form. Poseidonios approved of that much. After Moses' death, his immediate successors were good and behaved as Moses would have wanted, but they eventually degenerated into superstitious and tyrannous men, bands of deadly robbers. This came about because they abstained from meat and practiced circumcision.[93]

The sustained output of anti-Semitic literature purposefully distorting the history and customs and religion of the Jews did not begin until after the capture of Palestine by the Romans in 63 B.C. After this time a number of men like Mnaseas of Patara, Lysimachos, Molon, and Apion in Egypt denounced the Jews irrationally for being misanthropic, cowardly, reckless, insane, witless people, who contributed nothing to the common civilization of the ancient world. Their Jewish enemies responded in kind: may the fire of heaven fall![94]

Thus in the last century of the pre-Christian era, Judaism, as a result of its great encounter with Hellenism, was looking two ways. It looked in upon itself and with hate in its heart cursed the gentile. It looked out upon the world and called the nations into its Temple to worship its Lord. These were two legacies of a profound experience.

---

[92] Antiochos IV: E. Bickermann, "Ritualmord und Eselkult," *MGWJ* 71 (1921), 171–87; 255–64; S. W. Baron, *S.R.H.J.* (2nd ed., 1952), i. 192–3; 382, n. 33. Antiochos VII: Jos. *Ant.* xiii. 245; cf. Diod. xxxiv. 1. Workman: R. A. S. Macalister, *The Excavation of Gezer* (1912), i. 210–1. Egyptian letter: *C.P.J.*, 141.

[93] Agatharchides = Jos. *Ant.* xii. 5; *A.Ap.* i. 205, 209–11. Poseidonios = Strabo xvi. 2. 34–7 (760–1).

[94] These four men in Josephos, *A.Ap.*: Mnaseas: ii. 112–4; Lysimachos: i. 304–11; ii. 145; Molon: ii. 79, 145; Apion: *passim*.

Chapter X

The Egyptians

The religious reaction of the Egyptians to Greco-Makedonian imperialism included a series of rebellions whose strength was sustained over a long period of time. The violence of the revolts bears comparison with the Maccabean wars, and they were almost more remarkable, for while the Hasmoneans were successful in breaking away from the disintegrating Seleukid Empire, the Egyptians could not free themselves from the Lagid state, which survived longer than any other Hellenistic monarchy. But the men of Egypt rebelled and fought until the end. Mutual hatred of Greek and Egyptian grew intense, in part because numerous Greek immigrants to this curious land were prepared to hold the natives in contempt. During the three centuries of Ptolemaic control, scarcely any of these Hellenes ever acquired a real knowledge of Egyptian culture, and few troubled to learn the language.[1]

Greek knowledge of Egypt before Alexander's time was quite limited, coming mostly from the experience of occasional travellers like Herodotos, traders, and numerous mercenary soldiers who saw service in Egypt between 640 and 340 b.c. One thing these visitors learned was that Egyptians liked to communicate a feeling of the primacy of their own culture over the Greek. Herodotos was told such things, and he dutifully reported them upon his return. He began by stating that the Egyptians considered themselves the most ancient of mankind, and regarded all other people as barbarians. They thought their institutions absolutely unique, and they shunned Greek and all other foreign customs, even refusing, strangely enough, to eat beef. They practiced circumcision, an unfit and ugly religious rite. They always drank from washed bronze cups, wore newly cleaned

---

[1] Lack of knowledge of Egypt by Greeks in J. G. Milne, "Egyptian Nationalism under Greek and Roman Rule," *JEA* 14 (1928), 226–34, and by P. Jouguet, "Les destinées de l'hellénisme dans l'Égypte gréco-romaine," *CÉ* 19 (1935), 89–108; 201–12.

linen, and, in short, were fastidious beyond moderation. No Egyptian, he continued, either man or woman, would kiss a Greek, or use his knife or any of his eating utensils. The Egyptians thought the Greeks unclean, and sold them the heads of sacrificed animals that had been ritually cursed as scapegoats. Later Greeks than Herodotos looked upon these strange people with suspicion, and did not always know what to think about them. Diodoros was astonished at their worship of living animals and their fetish of burial customs. Panyassis had dark tales to tell of human sacrifice.[2]

The attitude of Plato was quite ambivalent. On the one hand he respected the antiquity and lack of variability about Egyptian wisdom, and particularly the permanence and formalism of their art; but on the other hand he objected to their dislike of foreigners and their strange religious ceremonies. He also felt that the Egyptian system of property developed a greed for money and had been responsible for creating the rigid class system of the country. Aristotle thought that the pharaohs had built the pyramids in order to force the people to work so that they would be too busy to think about revolt. Herodotos had said that the peasantry was a docile group, unable to escape being worked to death by their kings. He reported that Nechon caused the death of 120,000 men when he built the ancient version of the Suez Canal.[3]

During the fourth century, Greek contact with Egypt became more intimate than it had been before, through the repeated expeditions of Greek mercenary forces hired by Egyptian kings. Hellene and Egyptian had a common interest in defeating the armies of the Persian Great King. But the sojourns of these Greeks were generally unhappy on account of the confusing political struggles going on among the Egyptians themselves at the same time that the Persian hammered at the frontiers. Furthermore, many Egyptians strongly disliked these troops hired to fight their battles for them. The service of the Spartan king Agesilaos was a case in point. Soon after Pharaoh Tachos engaged him to fight the Persians, the nobleman Nektanebo revolted against Tachos. Agesilaos chose to support Nektanebo on the grounds that Tachos was anti-Hellenic. In the war that followed Nektanebo was successful, and with the support of Agesilaos' men became pharaoh. But almost at once, the Spartan had to defend him

[2] Herod. ii. 2, 35–41, 91, 158, 196. Diod.: i. 83. 1; 84. 1; 86. 1; 91. 1. Panyassis = Athen. iv. 172 D; *R.E.* xviii. 3 (2e Reihe), Nu. 1, S. 872–3.

[3] Plato: *Tim.* 21 E–24 B; *Laws* ii. 656 D–657 B; v. 747 D; xii. 953 E. Aristotle: *Pol.* v. 11 (1313 A). Herodotos: ii. 158.

against a new rebellion. Such episodes made the Greeks realize that Egyptian politics were quite instable and their kings incompetent. The Athenian general Chabrias had also spent a term in Tachos' service. Chabrias saw how far a competent, well-armed foreigner could press the Egyptians. He was able, rather easily, apparently, to extort money from the Egyptian priesthoods to support his operations. He was able to persuade the aristocracy to contribute a portion of their property. Topping this, he finally made a requisition of all uncoined gold and silver.[4] The experience of numerous Greeks, then, for all this was witnessed by the rank and file of the mercenary soldiers, was that Egypt was split into quarreling factions, was weak, incompetent, cowardly; their religion and their customs were strange, uncivilized, definitely inferior. The odd traditionalism and lack of vigor stood in strong contrast to the storm and stress of dynamic fourth-century Hellas.

This contemptuous attitude showed itself in comedies written in the middle of the fourth century. These plays publicized Greek experience with Egypt and made it much more widely known than it would have been if simply written in the books of historians and philosophers. The prolific and popular Athenian comedian Euboulos had one of his characters swear an oath by the god Ammon of Egyptian Mendes—that he was drunk. Mendes was the town that the pharaohs of the XXIXth Dynasty came from. Antiphanes mocked Egyptian animal worship. He slyly observed that Egyptians thought eels were gods—indeed, the most valuable of the gods. "For merely by offering prayers," he said, "we may reach the gods, but to get just a *smell* of eels we must spend at least a dozen drachms or more. It is altogether a sacred beast." Timokles scorned the impotence of the Egyptians. What possible help, he appealed to his audience, could an ibis-god, a dog-god, or a pussy-cat-god be to a man? The popular Rhodian poet Anaxandrides waxed eloquent on his dislike of the Egyptians. He said he could not possibly be their ally since his beliefs and their customs were so different. The Egyptians worshipped cows, which were allowed to wander untouched about the streets; they were great gods. Anaxandrides sacrificed and ate them. They held the eel to be a mighty deity; he relished it as a great delicacy. Egyptians wouldn't eat pork, and they worshipped dogs and, of all things,

---

[4] Agesilaos: Xen., *Ages.* ii. 30–1; xxxvii. 3—xl. 1. Chabrias: (Ps.-) Aristot., *Economica* ii. 2. 25. This text was a handbook for the early Hellenistic period explaining how a state can extort money; it was well enough regarded to be eventually included in the Aristotelean corpus.

field mice. Worse, their priests were castrated, a custom that always shocked. There were other references in literature pointing up the Greeks' contempt. Hipparchos late in the fourth century parodied Homer's *Iliad* with his *Egyptian Iliad,* in which he laughed at the hard-working Egyptian peasant who had to spend his days cleaning slimy birds for the market.[5]

To the Greeks, the docile Egyptian *fellahin* seemed created to serve as the working force of confident and vital Greek entrepreneurs. The writer of an early third-century tract on economic policies and theory thought that the best laborers came from the races of mankind which were neither bold enough to revolt nor too weak to work. Such a population would be ideal for the Greeks to manipulate, for as a result of their own experience in the fourth century, they were beginning vigorously to exploit natural resources and were seeking new ways to produce raw materials and revenues from agriculture, metallurgy, forestry and mining, and both local and long distance commerce.[6]

The notion that Greeks were superior to Egyptians was maintained long after Alexander's conquest. Of course not all the Greeks who came to Egypt despised the natives. Polybios thought those in Alexandria quite keen and civilized. But Strabo rejected them as hot-tempered and unpolitical, determined in their hostility to foreigners. He thought Egyptian architecture ugly, a vain and megalomaniac display. Apollodoros repeated stories that the Egyptians sacrificed foreigners to their own outlandish gods. An unknown writer, a fragment of whose work is in Athenaios, was not so harsh; he thought the Egyptians merely drunkards.[7]

Now, the Greek opinion that they were the better men was exactly opposite to the attitude of the Egyptians, who were convinced of their excellence long before Alexander's time, and had learned to hate the Greeks. Strabo says that the pharaohs of the XXVIth Dynasty (640–525 B.C.) had become prejudiced against all seafarers, particularly Ionians, because they ravaged the Egyptian coast. Diodoros visited

[5] Euboulos: frag. 126 (T. Kock, *Comicorum Atticorum Fragmenta* ii. 209) = Athen. i. 23 AB; his date and popularity: *R.E.* vi. Nu. 14, S. 877–8. Antiphanes: frag. 147 (Kock, ii. 71) = Athen. vii. 299 E; *R.E.* i. Nu. 15, S. 2518–21. Timokles: frag. 1 (Kock, ii. 300) = Athen. vii. 300 AB; *R.E.* vi. 1 (2. Reihe), Nu. 3, S. 1260–2. Anaxandrides: frag. 39 (Kock, ii. 150) = Athen. vii. 299 E–300 A; *R.E.* i. Nu. 1, S. 2078–9. Hipparchos, *The Egyptian Iliad* = Athen. ix. 393 E; *R.E.* viii. Nu. 13, S. 1665.

[6] These views on the labor force and economic expansion from (Ps.-) Aristot., *Economica* 5. 5; ii. 1. 7.

[7] Polybios: xxxiv. 14. 2–3. Strabo: xvii. 1. 12–28 (797–806). Apollodoros: ii. 5. 11. Unknown writer: Athen. i. 33 F–34 C.

Egypt around 60 B.C. and heard a legend about King Psammetichos. When he put Greek mercenaries in the post of honor in his army, the native contingents deserted in disgust. In truth, this king was philhellenic, and so was Amasis, the last great pharaoh of the XXVIth Dynasty. Perhaps this is why he left a memory of harsh rule, unjust punishments, and illegal confiscations among the Egyptians. When an Ethiopian king invaded Egypt, it was said, many of Amasis' subjects voluntarily went over to the Nubian. None of this was literally true; there were contrary traditions of Amasis' excellence as king.[8] The Egyptians had been convinced of their own superiority from exceedingly ancient times. Around 2200 B.C. the Olympian author of *The Admonitions of Ipuwer* observed that Asiatics then invading and settling in Egypt were in process of becoming people. The Carnarvon Tablet, which discusses Egypt's enemies of 1600 B.C., makes Pharaoh Kamose refer to the Nubians as "niggers." Many of the inscriptions coming from kings of the XVIIIth and XIXth Dynasties gloat over Egyptian domination of Asiatics, whose name is frequently accompanied by the standard epithet "wretched." The continuity of this attitude in the Hellenistic period is shown by remarks in Strabo, who was shown the royal obelisks at Thebes. His priestly guides falsely informed him that the hieroglyphs on the monuments proved that Egypt had once held empire over the Skythians, Baktrians, Indians, and Greeks.[9]

During most of the period from 525 to 332 B.C. Egypt was a province of the Persian Empire, and the history of this period shows Egyptian nationalism in action. The country was conquered by Kambyses, whose rule Greek historians generally agreed was harshly cruel. But contemporary monumental and epigraphic evidence from Egypt contradicts the accounts of Herodotos and Diodoros. Moreover, there is a complete contrast between their versions of what happened and

---

[8] XXVIth Dynasty: Strabo xvii. 1. 6 (792). Psammetichos legend: Diod. i. 67. 3–7; cf. Herod. ii. 30; this king's philhellenic works from Diod. i. 67. 8–9; see, too, É. Drioton and J. Vandier, *L'Égypte* (3rd ed., 1952), 578–82.
Amasis: stories of his harshness in Herod. ii. 172–3 and Diod. i. 60. 1–5. His philhellenism in Herod. ii. 178–81. Favorable judgments on his reign in Herod. ii. 161–2, 177 and Diod. i. 68. 5–6; 95. 1–3. There was a hostile Egyptian folk tale about him, recounting his wine bibbing and dallying with women, his wondrous great hangover, and his apparent cure by a common sailor. It is written on the reverse of a Demotic papyrus, published by W. Spiegelberg, *Die sogenannte demotische Chronik* (1914), 23–8.
For a summary statement of pre-Hellenistic Greco-Egyptian animosity see S. Davis, *Race Relations in Ancient Egypt* (1951), 1–21.
[9] "The Admonitions of Ipuwer" i. 1, in *A.N.E.T.*, 441. Carnarvon Tablet 3, *ibid.*, 232. Examples of gloating texts, *ibid.*, 234–56. Strabo xvii. 1. 46 (876).

what Ktesias, who knew the Persian side of the story, had to say. The latter reported merely that Kambyses took Egypt with the help of a treasonable Egyptian, and that the defeated pharaoh was taken away to Susa in a dignified manner along with six thousand picked companions. Nothing was said of the horrors of war or of occupation. On the other hand, Diodoros and Herodotos talked of little else. Hence, what these three Greeks were doing was unwittingly to retail Persian and Egyptian propaganda. So far as the Egyptian versions were concerned, they omitted to say that the priest Udjahorresnet had been a traitor and had become an advisor to Kambyses, and had even helped direct his policy towards the temples along the Nile. What the priests of these temples told Herodotos was that Kambyses was mad and that he killed the Apis Bull, the manifestation of the god Ptah on earth. When the native priests protested against this senseless sacrilege, Kambyses had them executed and stopped the celebration of Egyptian religious festivals. Actually, Kambyses did not kill but did bury the Apis with magnificent ceremony; what else he did was to confiscate the revenues of many of the temples, possibly to improve the economic condition of priest-ridden Egypt. The clergy of these places therefore attacked his memory, so that Herodotos was told that he desecrated tombs, mocked statues of Ptah, and burned images of the other gods. According to stories in Diodoros, he carried off the gold, silver, and ivory fittings of the Temple of Ammon at Thebes, and burned the other temples of Egypt. One notes that in the four centuries intervening between the Egyptian visits of Herodotos and Diodoros, local traditions about the atrocities of Kambyses had become rather inflated.[10]

Herodotos also was given a story that Kambyses sent a military force to capture the priests of the Temple of Ammon, but that this detachment of fifty thousand men was destroyed by a divine sandstorm. The same Egyptian propaganda exalting the protective power of the native gods appeared in Justin. Diodoros was told that Kambyses constructed his monumental palaces at Susa and Persepolis

---

[10] Ktesias' account in his *Persika*, Epit. 9. The Egyptian stories are in Herod. iii. 25–37; Diod. i. 46. 4; 49. 6 and Just. i. 9. Reconstruction of the historical course of events in A. T. Olmstead, *H.P.E.* (1948), 89–92; É. Drioton and J. Vandier, *L'Égypte* (3rd ed., 1952), 600–2; and E. G. Kraeling, *The Brooklyn Museum Aramaic Papyri* (1953), 28. These scholars cite contemporary, unquestionable Egyptian evidence refuting the notion that Kambyses tried to destroy Egyptian religion. One piece is the inscription of Udjahorresnet in E. Otto, *Die biographischen Inschriften der ägyptischen Spätzeit* (1954), No. 30, pp. 169–73. What Kambyses did do, aside from what is mentioned in the text, was to carry out a conquest per se in Egypt. That was sufficient grounds for hate.

with artisans and workmen abducted from Egypt.[11] This was obvious Egyptian propaganda calculated to take credit for Persian architecture: the palaces at Susa and Persepolis were built neither by Kambyses nor by Egyptian labor.

As time went on, Egyptians' hatred for the ancient Persian conquest waxed strong, and their paranoia attributed to the Persians greater and greater wrongs. Strabo was told that Kambyses had destroyed all the temples at Heliopolis and all the sacred obelisks, and that in the Thebaid he had mutilated and destroyed the temples and reduced this once populous district to a collection of poor villages. By the end of the seventh Christian century, the account of the Egyptian John of Nikiu attained the realm of pure phantasy. After Kambyses had overcome the righteous Egyptians, John recorded, he destroyed the capital at Saïs, plundered and burned all the other cities, destroying the houses and slaying all the animals and men. He cut down trees and laid waste plantations throughout the country so that the whole land became a desert. Fifty thousand Egyptians were deported.[12] These horror tales show how neurotic and unrealistic Egyptian hatred of alien conquest was. Foreigners, as Ipuwer had said, were not even people.

The reign of Kambyses' successor Dareios seems to have been a time of growing stress. We know that he carried out a reform, probably along liberalizing lines, of the legal system of Egypt and restored the revenues of certain temples. Nonetheless, at the end of his reign a great revolt broke out to re-establish native rule. Xerxes ultimately suppressed it with great brutality. A new and more oppressive Persian regime was put into effect. Egypt now was made to pay a tribute of seven hundred talents and bore the expense of a large Persian garrison maintained in the venerable and holy capital of Memphis. The new governor Achaemenes, brother of the king, was subsequently assassinated by an Egyptian patriot.[13]

Within a generation of this unsuccessful revolt, the Egyptians rose again around 461. A Libyan and an Egyptian prince made common

[11] Ammon: Herod. iii. 26; Just. i. 9. Workmen: Diod. i. 49. 6.

[12] Strabo: xvii. 1. 27 (805); 1. 46 (816). John of Nikiu: in R. H. Charles, *The Chronicle of John of Nikiu* (1916), pp. 21–40.

[13] The legal reforms of Dareios are known from a Demotic papyrus in W. Spiegelberg, *Die sogennante demotische Chronik* (1914); Diodoros (i. 95. 4–5) reports a late Egyptian tradition that Dareios gained his legal knowledge through having studied theology with Egyptian priests! Rebellion *c.* 486: Herod. vii. 1–7; A. T. Olmstead, *H.P.E.* (1948), 227–8, 235; R. Ghirshman, *Iran* (1954), 151, 190. The character of the new regime: Herod. vii. 7; iii. 91.

cause to drive out the hated government of Artaxerxes I. That this revolt was an attempt to re-establish the native kingship is proved by Inaros' giving out that he was the son of Psammetichos III, the last native pharaoh before Kambyses. The revolt had large initial success, and within a short time only Memphis itself was still held by Persian troops and Egyptians loyal to the regime. The Egyptian aristocracy suffered, as did all other Oriental noble classes, from divided loyalty and faction. Despite intervention by the Greek Delian League on Inaros' side, the Persians were able subsequently to reconquer the rebellious province after some twelve or thirteen years of fighting.[14]

Towards the end of the fifth century, a third great insurrection took place and spread gradually over all Egypt, aiming at the expulsion of all foreign groups. Not only were the Persians attacked, but a Temple of Yahu belonging to a colony of Jewish mercenary soldiers on Persian service at Elephantine was destroyed. The revolt was ultimately completely successful, and its leader, Amyrtaios, became pharaoh, ruling as the XXVIIIth Dynasty (404–398 B.C.) at Saïs.[15]

The priesthoods of Egypt played an important part in these transactions and in the subsequent period of Egyptian independence. The clergy of the Temple of Khnum led the attack on Yahu's temple, since they loathed the influence of this foreign god. In fact, the kings of the XXVIth Dynasty, perhaps inspired by the priests, had earlier dropped the worship of the Syrian deities that their predecessors had sometimes known. On the other hand, Psammetichos I had taken steps to diminish the authority of the priests of Ammon of Thebes. In the period of restored independence, however, the clergy remained very influential, and seem to have played a part in controlling the selection of the pharaohs of the XXIXth and XXXth Dynasties. The *Demotic Chronicle* claims that because Pharaoh Nepherites (398–393 B.C.) did what he did, his son was deposed "for many sins after a short time." On the other hand, Pharaoh Hakoris (391–378 B.C.) was not deposed for some time, it was said, for he was generous to the temples. The following XXXth Dynasty was, in fact, rather liberally inclined towards the temples; constructions of Nektanebo I (378–360 B.C.) are known from Edfou, Memphis, Hammamat, Koptos, Philai, El Kab, Medinet Habu, Karnak, Dendera, Abydos, Hermopolis, Letopolis, Damanhur, and Maskhuta. He also granted increased

[14] Herod. vii. 236; Ktes. *Persika*, Epit. 32–7; A. T. Olmstead, *H.P.E.* (1948), 303, 308; É. Drioton and J. Vandier, *L'Égypte* (3rd ed., 1952), 603–4.

[15] *Demotic Chronicle* iii. 18–9; A. T. Olmstead, *H.P.E.* (1948), 364–6, 373–4; E. G. Kraeling, *The Brooklyn Museum Aramaic Papyri* (1953), 111–3; R. Ghirshman, *Iran* (1954), 197–8.

income to the goddess Neith at Saïs. All this shows the close association of pharaoh and priest. Egyptian independence continued until around 340 B.C. During these years Greek mercenaries were employed, as in the cases of Agesilaos and Chabrias, to repulse the continuing efforts of the Persians to reconquer their province. But at the same time that the pharaohs brought in foreign soldiers, they were most careful to maintain the good will of the priesthoods; Nektanebo II (359–340 B.C.) secured their loyalty by means of extensive building operations in the temples.[16]

In 343 B.C., however, the Persian King Artaxerxes III began his reconquest of Egypt. Nektanebo's lack of sound military experience, and his lack of good native Egyptian generals—the wages of having employed Agesilaos and Chabrias—led to his losing Pelousion to the enemy and his subsequent flight to Ethiopia, where he died. The defeat of this king was very important for subsequent developments in Hellenistic Egypt. Some Egyptians hated to think of his having been defeated by an unclean foreigner, so that according to rather late reports appearing in Greek histories, the Persian reoccupation was called punitive and heavy-handed. Diodoros says Artaxerxes dismantled cities, profaned temples, carried off a great deal of gold and silver, and stole the sacred writings in the temples. Be this as it may, the Persian victory was followed almost at once by a revolt against their new king Dareios III. The dynast Khabbash maintained a precarious independence in the marshland of the delta, and was recognized by priests in Memphis as sovereign king. There were revolts and riots in Upper Egypt, so that the Persians did not really succeed in pacifying the country until a year or two before the conquest of Alexander.[17]

Years after this last experience with Persian government, Egyptians still told Greek and Roman visitors that they had revolted against Persia because of her harsh rule and lack of respect for the gods of Egypt. Artaxerxes was said to have killed the Apis and then deified an ass, an animal especially abominated in Egypt. He even,

[16] Priests of Khnum: *P. Aramaic Elephan.* 30; E. G. Kraeling, *The Brooklyn Museum Aramaic Papyri* (1953), 102–8. XXVIth Dynasty: É. Drioton and J. Vandier, *L'Égypte* (3rd ed., 1952), 588; Psammetichos: *ibid.*, 579–81. Nepherites–Hakoris: *Demotic Chronicle* iii. 20–1; iv. 9–10; É. Drioton and J. Vandier, *op. cit.*, 606–7. Nektanebo I: A. T. Olmstead, *H.P.E.* (1948), 402–4; É. Drioton and J. Vandier, *op. cit.*, 609–11. Nektanebo II: A. T. Olmstead, *H.P.E.* (1948), 430–1. For the wars of these pharaohs and Greek mercenaries: P. G. Elgood, *The Later Dynasties of Egypt* (1952).
[17] Diod. xvi. 49. 2; 51. 1–2; A. T. Olmstead, *H.P.E.* (1948), 438–41, 492–3; É. Drioton and J. Vandier, *L'Égypte* (3rd ed., 1952), 612–4; R. Ghirshman, *Iran* (1954), 201.

they said, ate the Apis and put many Egyptians to death.[18] These stories are important, for they show that after the Makedonian conquest traditional hatred for foreigners continued. What would the Egyptians think of the Ptolemies?

Egyptian resistance to Persia was essentially religious, for they believed that the state, even the whole world, was ruled by a god incarnate in a man, the Egyptian pharaoh. They identified him sometimes with their god Horus, sometimes with the universal sun, Re, and sometimes with both these and several other gods. The king was expected to rule in accordance with Ma'at, that is, with respect for the right physical order of the natural world and the social stratification of Egypt, tempered by Egyptian ideals of social justice. Under the XXIXth Dynasty, pharaohs who did not rule in accordance with this Ma'at, the law mentioned in the *Demotic Chronicle,* were deposed. This principle of right rulership had old roots. Pharaoh Akhnaton of the XVIIIth Dynasty had ruled Egypt with peculiar conceptions of the natural order of things. After his death, his reform program was overthrown by the clergy of Ammon-Re, and official inscriptions always referred to him as "that criminal of Akhetaton," and never by his name. The *Demotic Chronicle,* too, says that Pharaoh Psemut (392–391 B.C.) "was not; he was not in the way of God; he was not permitted to rule long."[19] The Persians had not ruled Egypt properly either. For one thing, they were in Egyptian eyes second-class people of a foreign culture and tradition. On the realistic level they could not carry on the detailed administration of this large and complex state without breaking laws and customs unknown to them, even if they tried not to. They had carried off a considerable annual tribute, and this the Egyptians deemed simple robbery. They had not shown the traditional respect due the gods by embellishing the temples. Therefore, they were guilty of abolishing true kingship. When Inaros revolted against them, he pretended to be a true king, the son of the legitimate Psammetichos III. The reasons Diodoros and Curtius gave to account for Egyptian revolt were simply that the Persians had ruled harshly, and that they had been guilty of a lack of respect for Egyptian religion. These two statements came to much the same thing, and meant a good deal more than that the Achaemenids rifled a few temples. What was meant was that they

[18] General reasons: Diod. i. 44. 3; Curt. iv. 7. 1. Artaxerxes and the Apis: Deinon = Plut. *Isis and Osiris* 31 (363 C) ; Plut. *ibid.,* 11 (355 C) ; Aelian, *Char. Anim.* x. 28.

[19] Reign of Akhnaton: J. A. Wilson, *The Burden of Egypt* (1951) , 206–35; his conception of the natural order: R. Anthes, *Die Maat des Echnatons von Amarna,* Suppl. 14, *JAOS* (1952) . Psemut: *Demotic Chronicle* iv. 7–8.

offended the basic ideas of Egyptian divine rule. They did not support Ma'at; they did not support the establishments of the Egyptian gods on the scale the latter expected; but they did supplant native kings and native law. Such an offence against the Egyptian state was an offence against its gods, and it imperilled the whole relationship of man to society, both to other men and to the gods, and even of man to nature.[20]

These extremely old beliefs continued to command loyalty in the Ptolemaic period. The inscriptions of the Lagids show that the old ideas still existed, somewhat modified it is true, but essentially in their ancient forms. The old *Sed*-festival was a rite which supernaturally renewed every thirty years the power of the king to rule; in the Rosetta Stone Ptolemy V is called "Lord of the Thirty-Year Periods." The much venerated Pharaohs Sesostris, Ramesses, and Amenophis of the second millennium B.C. were still happily remembered, and at Ammon's Temple in Karnak priests in the third century copied a hieroglyphic list of conquests made by Tuthmosis III in the fifteenth. Aside from the ideology of kingship, other facets of Egyptian culture drew out their extraordinary longevity. *Papyrus Insinger,* a wisdom-text of the first century A.D., still advised persons to keep silence in cemeteries, to be content with their station in life, and to remember that the gods would judge the goodness of people with traditional weights and balances. The canons of ancient art forms were still respected, and statues were still inscribed with prayers to beautiful Osiris, humbly requesting he give the worshipper a beatified life in the Land of the West beyond the grave.[21] In 332 B.C. Egyptian culture was still very much alive, because many people still believed in its value.

In that year Alexander the Great, leading his Greco-Makedonian forces, burst into Egypt and, helped by the extreme hatred for the Persians there, overcame the Achaemenid regime almost without

[20] For Egyptian ideas of divine rule and its importance to society, see J. A. Wilson, "Egypt," *The Intellectual Adventure of Ancient Man* (1946), 62–91; *The Burden of Egypt* (1951), *s.v.* "King" in index; H. I. Frankfort, *Kingship and the Gods* (1948), 15–212; H. W. Fairman, "The Kingship Rituals of Egypt," *Myth, Ritual and Kingship* (ed. S. H. Hooke, 1958), 74–104.

[21] On the longevity of these ideas in Hellenistic times see E. Otto, *Die biographischen Inschriften der ägyptischen Spätzeit* (1954), 102–18; H. W. Fairman, "The Kingship Rituals of Egypt," *Myth, Ritual and Kingship* (1958), 76, n. 3; 83–4. List of Tuthmosis: J. Simons, *Handbook for the Study of Egyptian Topographical Lists* (1937), 41–4, 127. *P. Insinger:* F. Lexa, *Papyrus Insinger* (1926), ii. 86–100. Art: H. Gauthier, "Un groupe ptolémaïque d'Héliopolis," *Revue égyptiologique* 2 (1924), 1–12; H. Ranke, "A Late Ptolemaic Statue of Hathor from Her Temple at Dendereh," *JAOS* 65 (1945), 238–48.

striking a blow. His retinue had included an Egyptian named Smatu-tefnakht of Herakleopolis, and Alexander was now careful to make his peace with the priesthoods. He not only journeyed to Siwah to consult the clergy of Ammon-Re, but he also consulted them else-where, probably at Memphis. While it was put about that Ammon claimed him as his son, whether the priesthood really accepted his divinity will probably never be known. We only know that after these consultations Alexander began to publish the idea that he was the son of Ammon. According to Plutarch, the priest Psammon told Alexander that the Egyptians were under the kingship of a god, and that since he had got the rule and mastery of Egypt he was therefore a god. This is certainly possible; Psammon may have wished to ingratiate himself with the conqueror. Alexander's becoming god-king of Egypt was part of his program, as Curtius later said, of preserving as much as possible of native custom.[22]

Alexander's regime, however, turned out almost at once to upset the established order of things, at least in Lower Egypt. His founding of Alexandria by the Nile delta resulted in time in this extraordinary city's dominating the social and economic life of all Egypt, and thus effecting large changes. Its foundation, too, involved the painful re-location of a considerable native population from surrounding villages in Alexandria in order to supply its Greek ruling class with a laboring force. But at the time that seemed unimportant. Birds were said to have appeared when the city was being laid out and to have eaten the grains of barley being used to mark the boundaries of the streets. This was interpreted as a good omen: the city would grow to great size and would become a storehouse of abundance to many lands and peoples.[23] We shall see subsequently what it became to Egyptian prophets, and what they said about it.

A certain Kleomenes became satrap of Egypt and showed how a foreigner could violate the principles of native justice. He acted as though he was well aware of previous experience of Greeks in Egypt. He removed the market established at Egyptian Kanobos to the new city of Alexandria, informing the Egyptian clergy and other notables at Kanobos that he must remove them too. Since these men wished to remain where they were, Kleomenes accepted a sizeable bribe to

[22] Smatu-tefnakht: É. Drioton and J. Vandier, *L'Égypte* (3rd ed., 1952), 614. For Alexander's possible knowledge of Egypt before 332 B.C.: Curt. iv. 10. 1–6. Siwah: Strabo xvii. 1. 43 (813–4); Curt. iv. 7. 25–6; Plut. *Alex.* xxvii. 1–5; Arr. *Anab.* ii. 4. 4–5. Psammon: Plut. *Alex.* xvii. 5–6; Plutarch calls the man *philosophos*, which I am sure should really have been *'iereus.* Curtius' general remark: iv. 7. 5.

[23] Strabo xvii. 1. 6 (792); Curt. iv. 8. 5–6; Plut. *Alex.* xxvi. 6. (Ps.-) Kall. i. 32. 4.

allow them to stay. He had no idea, however, of giving up his original idea; and having extorted as much money as he thought he safely could, he forced the Egyptians to move anyway. Kanobos eventually became a sort of Riviera for the wealthy Hellenes in Egypt. Kleomenes, like so many other Greeks, seems to have thought that the weakling native population might be readily exploited for private purposes. During the great famine of 330–326 B.C. he used his official position to gain personal control of most of the grain supply of the country, and he exploited this monopoly for his own enrichment. On another occasion he threatened to close certain temples, and then accepted bribes from their priests not to do so. Kleomenes was eventually removed,[24] but much mischief was done, and it can only be that Kleomenes' administration made a most unhappy impression on exactly those Egyptians—clergy and notables—who had the position and influence to resist. Kleomenes' regime was illegitimate in their eyes. To impress persons of high rank, to extort monies from them, to use the produce of Egypt for one's own purposes, and to insult the priests was not to rule in accordance with justice and law.

Another satrap of Egypt, Euaises, who was probably the predecessor of Kleomenes, was no better. Learning that rebellion was meditated, he arrested and hanged the suspects, sending word to their relatives that he would release his prisoners if a certain sum was paid for each. When he collected the money, he forwarded their corpses.[25]

Despite the actions of Kleomenes and Euaises, the former ruling classes of Egypt did not overtly oppose their new masters. No doubt they realized that to retain what still favorable positions remained to them they would have to cooperate with the new world power. Hence, when Alexander consulted the oracle of Ammon as to whether it would be lawful to worship his dead friend Hephaistion, the priests replied that it would. And Alexander was later remembered in the *Chronicle* of John of Nikiu as simply the *Pantarchos*, the "All-ruler," who had slain the last of the dreadful Persians. There was no universal hatred of Alexander, then, nor of the first Ptolemies. There was some assistance and cooperation. The high priest Petosiris of

---

[24] (Ps.-) Aristot., *Economica* ii. 2. 33; Curt. iv. 8. 5; Arr. *Anab.* vii. 23. 6; (Ps.-) Dem., *Against Dionysodoros* 7–8.

[25] (Ps.-) Aristot., *Economica* ii. 2. 32. This Euaises, called a Syrian in this reference, is not listed in Pauly-Wissowa. Since Ptolemy succeeded Kleomenes as satrap after June, 323 B.C. and then became king so that the title lapsed, Euaises must have preceded Kleomenes. *P. Insinger* (xiv. 14) says that a ruler does badly when he establishes a bad man in office, and counsels that a ruler should not permit the wicked and dishonorable to govern (xv. 1).

Hermopolis was appointed to advise King Ptolemy [I?], he boasted, and received a gold ring as a reward. The scribe who wrote P. *Insinger* advised respect for royal affairs, and commanded his readers not to scorn or oppose the king's decrees. But on the other hand, there was some hatred. There is a variant tradition in Arrian, coming from certain unnamed Greek writers, that Ammon really refused to recognize the propriety of Hephaistion's projected cult.[26]

In the years following Alexander's death, the Makedonian kingdom of the Ptolemies was organized, and Egypt became the goal of thousands of Greek immigrants seeking to escape the poor land of Hellas or the war-driven Greek communities of Asia Minor. Many of these Greeks came to Egypt to seek their fortunes, and some must have conceived of the Egyptians as they were represented by the comic poets of the fourth century. While the Ptolemies did not wish to inflict a harsh regime upon the Egyptians, certain Greeks didn't care, and the Ptolemies could not be everywhere at once to control them. Hellenistic Greek poets described Egypt in terms that attracted Greeks who wanted to get rich quick. Herodes spoke of the extraordinary wealth at the disposal of right good Ptolemy, of Egypt's beautiful climate, its spectacles, its extensive playgrounds, its gold, wine, and women; all these good things could belong to a Greek who made his way in Egypt. Theokritos, subsidized by the government, sang that Egypt was the most bountiful of all the countries of the world; no land could rival it for its splendid cities, its fertile fields, or its lavish wealth; whatever Greek, he said, sought for a paternal and a generous master, he should come to serve King Ptolemy. And come they did, seeking escape from the Greece of the *Diadochoi*, and found it in the lush Arsinoïte nome. Strabo later praised its luxuriant olive groves, vineyards, grain fields, plants of all sorts, activity of all kinds. Numerous papyri of the third century show the great diversity of the Greek immigrants, who included scientists, poets, politicians, soldiers, capitalists, and day laborers and workingmen of all descriptions. These immigrants were by no means always high-class persons. Polybios said that the Greeks of Alexandria were a mongrel race, who behaved little better than barbarians. Livy said they degenerated into Egyptians after they had been there for some time. Strabo had a good

---

[26] Ammon's permission: Arr. *Anab.* vii. 23. 6–7; Plut. *Alex.* lxxii. 2. John of Nikiu: *Chronicle*, li. 62. Petosiris: his funerary inscription in E. Otto, *Die biographischen Inschriften der ägyptischen Spätzeit* (1954), No. 46, pp. 112–3, 174–5, 180–3. P. *Insinger*: iv. 4; xxiii. 25; xxxiii. 1. Negative tradition about Ammon in Arr. *Anab.* vii. 14. 7. This did not come from Ptolemy or Aristoboulos, but from "some other writers."

deal to say about the licentiousness of the rich Alexandrians frolicking in their pleasure domes at Kanobos.[27]

Immoral or irresponsible Greeks lived in contradiction to what Egyptians taught was godly behavior. *Papyrus Dodgson,* written in Demotic at some native shrine around 200 or 150 B.C, still upheld the old ideals of the good, quiet life of the Middle Kingdom. The papyrus contains three oracles uttered by the gods of Syene, as the Greeks called old Elephantine. One accused the Egyptian Ptr', son of Pshenpwer, of having drunk wine in a precinct sacred to one of the old pharaohs; he was condemned as loathsome to Osiris, judge of the dead, and his consort Isis. Ptr' has also consorted with moneylenders, probably Greeks, and has led other Egyptians along the same path. They have been, as a result, pursued by foreigners. For all this he has been found guilty by the god Khnum. Another Egyptian, Patei, son of Espmeti, was denounced by the gods for having committed wrongs against the people of the district. These involved oppressions of some sort. The divine will was that he be excommunicated from the fellowship of the Egyptian gods. This document shows the old norms of Egyptian culture still being followed in the Hellenistic period—foreigners are not named, they must not be one's companions, there must be no oppression of one's fellows, there must be no disrespect shown the gods. To commit wrongs, in the usual Egyptian view, was to dare the torments of Apophis in the underworld. Either the Egyptian modelled his life according to regulation or he faced condemnation by the gods. On the other hand, obedience to moral concepts of social justice, cultivation of quietness and humility, and the acceptance of the place designated for oneself would bring reward when after death the Egyptian attained bliss in the Land of the West.[28]

Egyptian religious resistance to Hellenism was based on two concepts: insistence on the continuity of divine kingship by a native Pharaoh, and insistence on the maintenance of justice and morality

[27] Herodes i. 23–35. Theokritos xiv. 59, 65–8; xvii. 79–86, 95–9. Arsinoïte nome: Strabo xxvii. 1. 35 (809). Immigrants: C. Préaux, *Les Grecs en Égypte d'après les archives de Zenon* (1947). Polybios' opinion: xxxiv. 14. 5–6; Livy's: xxxviii. 17. 11; Strabo's: xvii. 1. 17 (801). This would seem to have been a constant in Greek Alexandria. See the remarks of the Emperor Claudius in *P. London* 1912 and of Dio Chrys., *Or.* xxxii.

[28] *Papyrus Dodgson:* F. L. Griffith, "Papyrus Dodgson," *PSBA* 31 (1909), 100–9. Morality: see the "Protestation of Guiltlessness," a document listing 42 mortal sins in *A.N.E.T.*, 34–6; H. I. Frankfort, *Ancient Egyptian Religion* (1948), 59–123; J. Cerny, *Ancient Egyptian Religion* (1952), 67–96; J. A. Wilson, *The Burden of Egypt* (1951), *passim.*

in this world. While this was no more than men wanted elsewhere, one must understand that Egyptian rebels demanded Egyptian institutions—their opposition was closely akin to modern nationalist agitation. The resistance took several forms, including the passive creation of the myth that Egyptian religion, culture, and civilization were better than Greek religion, culture, and civilization. Second, legends circulated exalting the old god-kings of the Middle and New Kingdoms. Third, there was the dissemination of violent messianic prophecies foretelling the overthrow of the Makedonian government by a divine Egyptian king. And last, there were numerous revolts against the Ptolemaic regime, risings which were wars of religion and for religion, holy wars like the Maccabean.

The Egyptians claimed that Egypt was the place of origin of all things, of humanity itself, of government, law, and the arts, of crafts, and of knowledge—in short, of civilization. These claims were not an invention of the Hellenistic period; Herodotos had known them. But information in later Greek writings shows that Egyptian propaganda along this line was expanded and embellished. It is possible, however, that some of the legends of the excellence of Egyptian kingship were actually Ptolemaic propaganda disseminated for the benefit of the Greek cities of southern Anatolia, the Aegean islands, and Hellas itself, as well as for the general consumption of the Hellenistic world. But the sum of the stories in Diodoros alone is so basically anti-Hellenic that they could not possibly all come from Greek sources. The stories essentially deny the uniqueness of Hellenism, a quality Greeks loved to think about. Many or all of the stories must have been invented by Egyptians, probably priests, whom foreign travellers were fond of consulting when they visited the monuments of the Nile valley. In fact, Diodoros explicitly says that many items of his information came from Egyptians to whom he talked during his tour of the country. Some Egyptian priests certainly knew both the Greek language and Greek literature as early as 275 B.C., when Manethon made criticisms of Herodotos. This priestly knowledge was used consciously to refute the idea of Hellenic excellence. Greek civilization was said to have come from Egypt. Thereby Egyptian ideals were exalted, for they still retained true value. This kind of anti-Hellenism attempted, like Jewish veneration of the Mosaic law, to preserve from attack concepts that were the essence of native society.

It was averred that human beings had been first spontaneously generated in Egypt, and proof was offered from the supposed spontaneous generation of mice in the Thebaïd when the Nile flood

receded. The earliest Egyptians were the first men to look in the sky
and to conceive that there were gods, and in connection with this
discovery to develop religion itself.[29] It may have been that there was
a touch of the missionary in this: the Greek should take note of these
origins, take cognizance of the old Egyptian view—the essentially true
view of the cosmos. He would then cease to be a Greek and become
more nearly Egyptian. Greeks found the Egyptian cults attractive—as
will be noticed below—and a considerable class of Greco-Egyptian
half-breeds grew up in the course of time. But if proselytism existed it
cannot be proved.

   This technique of anti-Hellenism was directed particularly at Greek
gods, whom the Egyptians seemed to have thought contemptible imita-
tions of the world's true gods. An Egyptian origin was found for the
popular cult of Dionysos. Egyptians claimed that the worship had
been brought to Hellas by Orpheus after his initiation into the rites
along the Nile. This story may again have been meant to suggest
that Greeks adopt Egyptian forms of cult. As Orpheus, so now you.
Perhaps this priests' tale was responsible for a statement about
Dionysos' early life made by the Greek writer Phylarchos: Dionysos,
said he, was the first to bring bulls from India to Egypt. There were
two of them—named Apis and Osiris. This certainly sounds anti-
Egyptian. Greeks had reason to counterattack, because Egyptians went
on finding Egyptian nationality for the favorite heroes of Hellas.
Herakles, that exemplar of Hellenic culture, was said to have been
born in the Nile valley. He was even said to have visited the rest of
the inhabited world before he went to Greece. There was proof of
this. Greek legend said that Herakles had fought for the Olympian
gods only a thousand years ago at the beginning of Greek history.
Yet the Egyptian records showed that time began ten thousand years
ago. The primitive date of Herakles was shown by his crude accoutrements, his club and lionskin. This was a sophisticated argument. Egyptians also claimed that Perseus was a native, that Hera
was modelled on their goddess Isis as demonstrated by the association
of both with cows, and that Greek Apollo was none other than

---

[29] Manethon: fragment 88 (Waddell) from his *Against Herodotos*. The origin of
mankind in Egypt: Diod. i. 10. 1–7; Just. ii. 1–2. This proposition was also known to
Herodotos, who also knew (ii. 2) Greek counterclaims. On this point see W. W. How
and J. Wells, *A Commentary on Herodotos* (1912), i. 156. The mice cited in Diodoros as having appeared spontaneously remind one of the miraculous mice the
Egyptians reported as having eaten the bowstrings of Sennacherib's advancing Assyrian host (Herod. ii. 141). The first conception of the gods: Diod. i. 11. 5–6; cf.
Herod. ii. 4.

Egyptian Horus. Other stories claimed that the ancient battle between the Giants and the Olympian gods had been won for the
latter by Osiris. In Egyptian mythology he was after all the first king
on earth after the gods. All these claims were old, for Herodotos
had known similar Egyptian arguments for the priority of their religion. But the evidence of Diodoros is that during the Hellenistic
period the idea of the priority and originality of Egyptian religion
was much elaborated.[30]

Diodoros says that the Egyptian priests could prove from written
records that they had been visited by many of the great Greek religious
thinkers like Orpheus, Mousaios, Daidalos, Melampos, Homer,
Lykourgos, Plato, Pythagoras, Eudoxos, Oinopides, and Demokritos.
The Egyptians claimed that in each case these Greeks had copied
ideas from Egyptian sources. So, too, Herodotos had been told that
Hellenes had learned the art of divination, the organization of religious processions, and the meaning of holy ceremonies from Egyptian
prototypes. But his list of copied items was much shorter than
Diodoros'.[31]

If the Egyptians claimed priority for their religion, they also
claimed priority for many other facets of human culture. Isis, they said,
discovered agriculture. Osiris forced men to give up cannibalism and
turn to law and justice. The idea that the gods of Egypt were responsible for establishing right dealing among men was stressed in Hellenistic Egyptian religious thought. It was probably a pathetic,
ironic protest against the hard conditions Ptolemaic state capitalism
sometimes created. It was certainly a continuation of the older Ma'at
concept. Diodoros says that Isis had come to ask for love and respect
from the whole world, and to teach it. Thoth, whom the Egyptians
equated with Greek Hermes, was said to have invented the alphabet,
astronomy, music, and the dance, and to have taught all arts in
Greece in times long past. Greek philosophy itself, according to
the Egyptians, was invented by Thoth, son of the River Nile,
exactly 48,863 years before the coming of Alexander of Makedon.[32]

The Egyptians even claimed that all mankind had learned law and
human culture from Egyptian colonies sent all over the world, to
Babylon, to Kolchis, even to Judah, and finally to Hellas, led by the

[30] Osiris and Herakles: Diod. i. 23. 8–25. 7; cf. Herod. ii. 43. Phylarchos = Plut.,
Isis and Osiris 29 (362 C) .
[31] Diod. i. 29. 2; 96. 2–98. 5; cf. Herod. ii. 49–50, 58.
[32] Diod. i. 14. 1, 3; 15. 8; 20. 1–2; 25. 2–6; 16. 1–2; 69. 5; Diog. Laer. *proem*. 2.

hero Danaos, a settler at Argos. Athens was said to have been founded by Egyptians from Saïs; Erechtheus brought grain from Egypt and introduced the Eleusinian worship in honor of Demeter. Athens, Sikyon, and Argos were none of them very old; Thebes in Egypt existed long before Kekrops and divine Phoroneus built these places. Other Egyptians said that their King Menes invented the alphabet some fifteen thousand years before Phoroneus' time. This did slightly conflict with the tradition that Thoth had invented it, but the Egyptians were not necessarily united, for their temples sometimes competed with one another's tales of primacy and lordship. But one thing various Egyptians did agree upon was that all human culture came from Egyptian gods and Egyptian kings, and that these excellent institutions had been changed for the worse by the Makedonians, the conquerors and destroyers of civilization.[33]

This idea of the superiority of Egyptian creativity over Hellenic barbarism became as fixed and rooted in Egyptian minds as their earlier idea that all Egypt had been destroyed by Kambyses. Around A.D. 100, three or four generations after the end of the Ptolemaic Dynasty, similar anti-Hellenic stories were still being told. An Egyptian priest attacked the Homeric poems, complaining that they showed the Greeks knew nothing of most things, that they were vainglorious, that they felt superior to others when they were actually most inferior, that Greeks had been struck blind by the gods for their lies, that they were pleasure-lovers, and that, above all, they had undertaken the conquest of the world merely so that they might plunder all Asia.[34]

This rejection of Hellenic culture was paralleled by rejection of the Greco-Egyptian god Sarapis. Ptolemy I Soter had this deity artificially made by synthesis of Greek and native religious ideas and ceremonies. Egypt contributed the Memphian god Osorapis, himself a blend of the Egyptian deities Osiris and Ptah manifest in the Apis Bull. These ingredients were mixed with concepts drawn from Greek mystery-religion and brought to Egypt by the Eleusinian exegete Timotheus, who worked with Manethon to complete the whole. Many

[33] Colonies: Diod. i. 28. 1–29. 3. Thebes: Pliny, *N.H.* vii. 194. Menes: *ibid.*, vii. 193. Judgment on Makedon: Diod. i. 95. 6.

[34] Dio Chrys. *Or.* xi. 37–43, 56, 59–65. In the third century A.D. there was a changed Egyptian interpretation of Homer: he was said to be an Egyptian well versed in Egyptian knowledge. He came from Thebes and his father was Thoth. The sweetness of his poetry proved his Egyptian temperament. Thus Heliodoros, a Phoenician of Emesa, in his *Ethiopica* iii. 13. 3; 14. 1–4.

scholars agree that Ptolemy's purpose was to create a religious institution common to both Greeks and Egyptians, a worship in which imperial unity could be found.[35]

The Makedonian government outfitted the new worship with impressive temples. Near Memphis, a great Sarapeon was built in connection with the burial sanctuary of the Apis Bulls. An even greater center was established at Alexandria, where the Sarapeon reached magnificent and sumptuous proportions. By the middle of the third century numerous Greeks in Egypt had adopted this worship, and Sarapis began to develop as a *Kosmokratōr*—a ruler of the whole world, a master of fate itself, a savior to all mankind. From Egypt the cult spread to Hellas, where occasionally it found enthusiastic acceptance, so that Sarapis was worshipped in numerous Greek cities from Kypros and Halikarnassos in the east, to Athens and Chaironeia in the west, and even in the Bosporos in the north.[36] But Egyptians themselves took virtually no interest at all in the new god. The numerous dedications to him were made almost entirely by Greeks. After the great native rebellions at the end of the third century Sarapis lost favor even with the Greek population of Egypt, and in the eyes of the Ptolemaic government no longer appeared to be its most honored god. The cult of Sarapis was, therefore, predominately Greek; as a means of uniting the peoples along the Nile, the Egyptians made it a miserable failure. There was probably Egyptian propaganda against it; the Egyptian temples were always sensitive to competition, as their own pre-Hellenistic history had shown, and one can readily

---

[35] For the establishment of the cult of Sarapis see W. Otto, *Priester und Tempel im hellenistischen Ägypten* (1908), i. 12–6; ii. 267–73; P. Jouguet, *L'Égypte ptolémaïque* (1933), iii. 39–40; H. I. Bell, *Egypt from Alexander to the Arab Conquest* (1948), 38–9; E. Kiessling, "La genèse du culte de Sarapis à Alexandrie," *CÉ* 48 (1949), 117–23.

A. D. Nock is not so sure that ethnic unity was the purpose behind the creation of the god. He thinks ("The Roman Army and the Roman Religious Year," *HTR* 45 [1952], 208–9) that "if any special appeal was intended, it was as Nilsson argued, one directed to the Greek-speaking world as a whole and not to Egypt. Ptolemy I, as J. Kaerst remarked, aimed at ruling more than the land of the Nile, and in his account of Alexander he included propaganda for Sarapis." It is true that Sarapis was used as propaganda for the Ptolemies outside Egypt, but I do not think that this purpose and the imperial unity purpose are mutually exclusive.

[36] Sarapis Temples: E. R. Bevan, *A History of Egypt* (1927), 41–7; H. I. Bell, *Egypt from Alexander the Great to the Arab Conquest* (1948), 38–40. Sarapean theology: A. D. Nock, *Conversion* (1933), 102; P. Hombert, "Sarapis Kosmokrator et Isis Kosmokrateirea," *AC* 14 (1945), 319–29. Acceptance by Greeks in Egypt: T. A. Brady, *The Reception of the Egyptian Cults by the Greeks* (1935), 13–6; by Greeks outside: *loc. cit.;* P. Perdrizet, "Voyage dans la Macédoine première," *BCH* 18 (1894), 416–45, and especially p. 418.

imagine the priests of, say, Ptah in Memphis looking askance at the favored creation of the king.[37]

The failure of this official policy was paralleled by declining Greek interest in Greek gods along the Nile valley. Beginning with the third century, and on a growing scale thereafter, one notes increasing worship of Egyptian gods by Greeks, and a corresponding decline in the numbers of dedications to Hellenic gods. It must be emphasized that this trend was gradual and never achieved completeness, but it did serve to bring about a slow reorientation of religious and cultural loyalties. One of the deities to become popular was Isis, whose acceptance by Greeks, however, involved her becoming much Hellenized. But Isis at the same time retained many native characteristics. By the end of the first century b.c. her cult had become so widespread that she was regarded as one of the few universal saviors of all humanity, not only in Egypt, but in the eastern Mediterranean, in Greece, and even in faraway Roman Italy.[38] This is good evidence of the toughness of the native Egyptian religious tradition.

The Egyptians seem to have been discriminating in choosing what European gods to reject. There is the interesting case of the Thrakian war-god Heron, who was imported into the Fayum by mercenary soldiers. The Greeks scarcely adopted his worship, but the Egyptians in the area became strongly attached to it around the middle of the second century, and by 100 b.c., Heron's Temple was as wealthy as many native establishments.[39]

After the beginning of Sarapis' decline, Ptolemy IV Philopator seems to have made one more effort to create a Greco-Egyptian imperial god, this time from Hellenic Dionysos. This policy was implemented soon after the outbreak of the Egyptian rebellions that marked Philopator's reign. The coinage for the first time showed the king as Dionysos, diademed with ivy and with the thyrsus behind his shoulder. If the official Dionysos cult was a new imperial, cross-cul-

---

[37] Rejection of Sarapis: J. G. Milne, "Egyptian Nationalism under Greek and Roman Rule," *JEA* 14 (1928), 226–34; T. A. Brady, *The Reception of the Egyptian Cults by the Greeks* (1935), 26–9; M. I. Rostovtzeff in *C.A.H.* vii. 115, 146.

[38] The rise of native gods and the decline of Hellenic among Greeks: T. A. Brady, *The Reception of the Egyptian Cults by the Greeks* (1935), 9, 26, 34; H. I. Bell, "Popular Religion in Graeco-Roman Egypt," *JEA* 34 (1948), 82–97; H. I. Bell, "Graeco-Egyptian Religion," *Mus. Hel.* 10 (1953), 222–37. W. W. Tarn, *H.C.* (3rd ed., 1952), 337–8. Rise and cult of Isis: A. D. Nock, *Conversion* (1933), 38–40; T. A. Brady, *op. cit.*, 39–41; P. Hombert, "Sarapis Kosmokrator et Isis Kosmokrateirea," *AC* 14 (1945), 319–20. Her importance in Roman Egypt: V. Chapot, *L'Égypte romaine* (1933), iii. 350.

[39] T. A. Brady, *The Reception of the Egyptian Cults by the Greeks* (1935), 34.

tural worship, and if Philopator took steps firmly to encourage his subjects to accept it, this might explain the legend in 3 Maccabees, an apocryphal story of an attempt of this king to persecute the Jews of Egypt for their religious exclusiveness. Whatever the situation was, Dionysos did not become a symbol of faith to the natives any more than Sarapis had been.[40]

After 200 B.C., the acceptance of Oriental religious ideas by Greeks grew at a slightly faster pace. This occurred at the expense of the old Greek image of the incompetence and cowardice of the Egyptians. That notion died when Egyptians fought so successfully in the phalanx at the Battle of Raphia in 217 B.C. and with such astonishing tenacity in their revolt which immediately followed. Also, there was by then a century-long association of Greeks and Makedonians with the native institutions and ideas that still survived. For when these immigrants saw the magnificent pyramids, many of them must have been impressed with the idea of Egypt's enduring force—of her sheer permanence. And when they saw the statues of Egypt's gods and kings, some must have felt a sense of Egypt's immortality. There were the extraordinarily large and richly decorated temples with ornate and striking rites and processions and their promises of afterlife. All this must have worked on the minds of the Greeks, and helped to lead some persons to respect for Egypt's gods. In this milieu the acceptance of the Oriental deities went forward. Indeed, the period around 200 B.C. was generally a time of mounting religious excitement in Egypt. Then the cults of Dionysos and Sarapis struggled for acceptance. Apocalyptic Egyptian prophecies circulated in the countryside. Even Buddhist missionaries from the far-off India of Asoka appeared. He actually sent religious emissaries to convert Makedonian kings of the third century, probably Antigonos Gonatas, Antiochos II, and Ptolemy II. Some Buddhists really did arrive in Alexandria.[41]

[40] Reorganization of Dionysos' cult: P. Berlin 11774. Coins: R. S. Poole, B.M.C., The Ptolemies (1883), 63, Nos. 16–20, Pl. xiv. 6–7. The interpretation of this evidence in P. Roussel, "Un édit de Ptolémée Philopator relatif au culte de Dionysos," CRAI 47 (1919), 237–43; R. Reitzenstein, "Zur Religionspolitik der Ptolemäer," ARW 19 (1919), 191–4; E. R. Bevan, A History of Egypt (1927), 234; M. I. Rostovtzeff in C.A.H. vii. 145, 151–2; P. Jouguet, L'Égypte ptolémaïque (1933), iii. 62; F. Jesi, "Notes sur l'édit dionysiaque de Ptolémée IV Philopator," JNES 15 (1956), 236–40.

3 Maccabees: R. Roussel, La Grèce et l'Orient (1928), 473, 507; M. Hadas, The Third and Fourth Books of Maccabees (1953).

[41] Asoka: his second and thirteenth rock inscriptions are quoted by A. D. Nock, Conversion (1933), 45–6 and the thirteenth by E. R. Bevan, The House of Seleucus (1902), i. 298, n. 3. Indians and Buddhists in Egypt: W. Simpson, " 'The Buddhist Praying Wheel' " JRAS (1898), 874–5; H. I. Bell, Egypt from Alexander to the Arab Conquest (1948), 53; W. W. Tarn, H.C. (3rd ed., 1952), 248.

This was a time when propaganda about Alexander himself circulated, alleging that he actually was not Makedonian, but part Makedonian and part Egyptian. Some said he was the son of the god Ammon, others that he was the son of Pharaoh Nektanebo II, the last god-king of the XXXth Dynasty. The idea appears in Plutarch's biography, on the authority of Eratosthenes of the third century B.C. Plutarch's story is certainly not Makedonian propaganda, as an included denial explicitly indicates. The story was that Philip II, Alexander's father and predecessor in Makedonia, sent an ambassador to Delphian Apollo, and this man returned with the message that Ammon should be reverenced, for the god shared the bed of Olympias, mother-to-be of Alexander. It is hard to imagine Alexander originating this, for he always insisted on his being the legitimate son of Philip. Neither Alexander nor the Ptolemies especially reverenced Ammon, and such respect is what Plutarch's story preaches. Rather, then, this is Egyptian propaganda. Priests of Ammon may have spread the story, although this cannot be conclusively demonstrated, among the Greek population of Egypt, from whom it found its way into Plutarch through some Hellenistic writer. There was precedent for this. Egyptians had earlier insisted that their Persian conqueror Kambyses had had an Egyptian parent, the princess Neitetis, daughter of Pharaoh Apries, and that story turned up in Herodotos' account of Egypt. There was also an old tradition in Egypt that Ammon had miraculously intervened to select one of the pharaohs of the New Kingdom, and it was still known as late as 600 B.C. This same tradition apparently turns up again in this legend.[42] I do not deny that Alexander claimed to be the son of Ammon; he did, but the Makedonian story was that the god elected Alexander at Siwah in 332. The Egyptian story was that his sonship was imparted at conception in 356. Alexander thought of being deified because of his achievements, the Egyptians in terms of his Egyptian divine fatherhood being the cause of his achievements.

A variant and later form of this propaganda concerning Alexander's birth occurs in Pseudo-Kallisthenes. The story is as follows. The last native pharaoh, Nektanebo II, when he saw the Persians would

---

[42] Plut. *Alex.* iii. 1–2. Neitetis: Herod. iii. 2; Deinon, *Persian History* and Lykeas of Naukratis, *Egyptian History* iii = Athen. xiii. 560 F. Lykeas' date is unknown: *R.E.*, xiii. Nu. 3, S. 2266–7. For the pre-Hellenistic tradition see "The Divine Nomination of Thutmose III," *A.N.E.T.*, 446–7; "The Divine Nomination of an Ethiopian King," *A.N.E.T.*, 447–8.
The story of Nektanebo's visit to Pella is much elaborated in (Ps.-) Kall. i. 3. 3—8. 4.

overwhelm Egypt, went to Makedonia disguised as a soothsayer. While Philip was absent, Nektanebo appeared to Olympias, having first by magic transformed himself into a serpent. From this union came Alexander. Alexander was not crowned king of Makedonia at Pella, but rather Pharaoh of Egypt at Memphis.[43] This fairy tale reminds one of similar Persian propaganda claiming Alexander as the son of an Achaemenid princess and Philip.

This propaganda was not entirely hostile to the Makedonian. It even implied a certain measure of acceptance of his kingship, and it might, therefore, represent attempts of a pro-Ptolemaic faction of the Egyptian priesthoods to arrive at a theological *modus vivendi* with the problem of Makedonian occupation. Such a faction actually existed, as will be shown later. Many of these persons knew Greek, so that they could certainly have spread the story in a language Greeks could understand.

Egyptians also circulated patriotic legends on the order of the "Semiramis Legend" in Mesopotamia. They were, however, much more virile than the Babylonian. They were composed in order to show that Egypt had produced god-kings greater, more militant, and more law-abiding than Alexander. These legends were improvements on pre-Hellenistic versions, and we can determine what changes were made by comparing the accounts reported by Herodotos and Diodoros.

First, there was the "Sesostris Legend." "Sesostris" had been the name of several pharaohs of the Middle Kingdom, and they had in fact been great military figures. Tales about them were fused around the single name itself, and a Sesostris, much distorted, became a legendary hero. Egyptian priests told Herodotos that Sesostris had once fitted out a fleet on the Arabian Gulf, subdued the people along the Red Sea coast, returned to Egypt, gathered a vast army, invaded Asia, and subdued every nation there. Having disposed of the Asiatics, he invaded Europe, defeating the Skyths and Thrakians. After these victories, he planted an Egyptian colony at Kolchis and returned with numerous captives, whom he employed building temples and canals along the Nile. He was able, eventually, to defeat the Ethiopians.[44]

The Herodotean version of the exploits of Sesostris made up one chapter in the continuing history of Egyptian foreign propaganda. Its Sesostris was unhistorical, for none of the kings of the XIIth

---

[43] (Ps.-) Kall. i. 3. 3–8. 4. The story still appeared in the *Chronicle* of John of Nikiu, li. 61.

[44] Herod. ii. 102–10. For the origins of the "Sesostris Legend," its place in anti-Persian propaganda, and its subsequent literary development, see M. Braun, *History and Romance in Greco-Oriental Literature* (1938), 13–8.

Dynasty ever conquered Asia as the legendary Sesostris did, and never even approached Thrake or Skythia. This tissue of lies of about 450 B.C. shows the hero made in the image of the Persians Kyros and Dareios, historical conquerors of Asia, Thrake, and part of Skythia, and the latter ruler of Egypt as well. Both kings also established colonies in Anatolia, and Dareios carried on constructions in Egypt.

Now, during the Hellenistic period there was a good deal said about the exploits of Sesostris. Megasthenes, writing around 275 B.C., reported that while Sesostris had subdued most of Europe and Asia, he had not invaded India. This fragment of the legend shows that around 300 B.C. Sesostris was still functioning on anti-Persian lines, and had not yet switched his attack to the Makedonians by appropriating the deeds of Alexander. He did so, however, very soon, and Diodoros' version of his labors includes a conquest of India.

Diodoros says that Sesostris campaigned from Ethiopia to the Persian Gulf, to India, finally to victory over all Asia, as was proved by the numerous steles he left behind. He reached places never even visited by Alexander, including Skythia. His campaign lasted for nine years, the same length of time that Alexander took to conquer a smaller area. Sesostris' treatment of the conquered was gentle, and he bestowed many benefactions on his new subjects. But he still took more prisoners and booty than any other warrior, and his native Egyptians, therefore, were able to live carefree lives, enjoying the good things he had won for them. He constructed marvellous things—temples to the gods, many whole cities—had canals dug in Egypt and crops harvested, and, in short, organized the world. He also built a great ship, 280 cubits long, plated with gold and silver, and presented it to Ammon as an offering. While he allowed foreign kings to continue to rule, he made them subject to tribute. He finally committed suicide when he was wasted by natural diseases in old age.[45]

This unhistorical and fantastic Sesostris was modelled not only after Kyros and Dareios, but also on Alexander, the first kings of the Lagid dynasty, and finally on various Greek technicians and architects. The 280-cubit-long ship was inspired by the great ship, the *Syrakousia,* built in the last quarter of the third century by Hieron, tyrant of Syrakouse, and presented by him to the Lagids. Her size was so vast that Hellenistic harbors could scarcely take her, so that the ship was pulled up on the shore near Alexandria and made into a monument. The inclusion of the ship in Diodoros' account shows that the Hel-

---

[45] Megasthenes = Strabo xv. 1. 6 (686–7) ; xvi. 4. 4 (796) ; and Arr. *Ind.,* viii. 5. 5–7. Diodoros: i. 53. 1—58. 3.

lenistic recension of the "Sesostris Legend" went on growing in the
third century, for his version must not have been circulated until after
the *Syrakousia* was drawn up on the beach in Egypt. But a version
already based on Alexander had appeared earlier, around 270 B.C. or
so, since the Egyptian priest Manethon said that the imaginary king
had subdued all Asia and Europe as far as Thrake in nine years.
He added that the pharaoh was about seven feet tall and was esteemed
by the Egyptians next to the god Osiris himself.[46] Therefore, a first
anti-Alexandrian Hellenistic version was succeeded by a second, including the report on Sesostris' ship, actually the *Syrakousia*, and the
repeated appearance of the legend shows its importance. Its second
appearance between 225 and 200 B.C. coincides with the course of
the great native revolts which broke out in 217 B.C.

These tales about Sesostris did not go unchallenged by Greek
counterpropaganda. In the first century B.C. Pompeius Trogus wrote
about him and the epitome of his biography in Justin makes the
pharaoh a vainglorious military idiot. Trogus reported that he captured Pontos, which in Greek eyes was a pathetically weak state until
around 100 B.C., and then withdrew on the grounds that it was beneath
him to rule beaten men. He next declared war on the Skyths, but
fled when they advanced, abandoning not only his stores, but even
his whole army. This sounds more like the normal Greek view of
stupid and cowardly Egyptians, and it probably originated in the
early third century B.C., because Trogus said, like Megasthenes, that
Sesostris had not conquered India, although Alexander had.[47]

There was also a "Ramesses Legend." It came into being early,
for Diodoros reported an extract of it he took from the *History of
Egypt* written by Hekataios of Abdera around 300 B.C. He said that
Pharaoh Ramesses II established empire over Baktria on a campaign
employing 400,000 soldiers. This was not historical; it was based on
Alexander's invasion of Baktria. It was, therefore, propaganda of
apparently late-fourth-century date. It may be that Strabo much later
heard this legend in more embellished form. He says that when he
was in the Valley of the Kings at Thebes a priest pointed out inscriptions allegedly telling of Egypt's rule over Baktria, India,
Skythia, and Grecian Ionia, which had been taken with a force of one
million men.[48]

---

[46] *Syrakousia:* Athen. v. 207 ff. Manethon: frag. 34 and frag. 35 (Waddell).
[47] Just. i. 1–3.
[48] Hekataios = Diod. i. 46. 8–47. 6; Strabo xvii. 1. 46 (816). There is an Egyptian
folk tale concerned with a cure effected by an Egyptian god in Bekhtan, which may

An "Osiris Legend" was also created to prove that this god, the Judge of the Dead and mythic First King of the divine Egyptian state, was greater than Alexander, the son of Ammon. According to Diodoros, Osiris had visited the countries of the earth, and had taught all men agriculture, orderliness, the gentle way of life. This meant Ma'at. He was said to have discovered ivy, probably to make him compete with Greek Dionysos. This would tend to date the legend around 200 B.C., after the Dionysos cult in Egypt was reformed by Philopator. Osiris proceeded through all the nations of the world, but fought no battles with their peoples; they accepted his divinity because of the benefits he conferred on them. In Ethiopia he taught agriculture, built cities, and left behind him an orderly government. In Egypt he built dykes to regulate the Nile. In India, numerous benefactions led the Indians to claim him as their own. He visited the rest of Asia, leaving behind many monuments. In Europe he passed through Thrake, where he slew the barbarian Lykourgos. He became king of Makedonia, founded the city Maroneia, and then brought the art of agriculture to Attika. Finally he returned to Egypt, bringing presents from a grateful world, which conferred godhood upon him and established rites in his honor.[49]

Osiris was a likely god for the Egyptians to champion, for he was traditionally thought of as the First King of Egypt. He loved Ma'at, he judged the dead according to their morality, and he made the grain grow. He thus brought about all the things that Egypt wanted and did not have under Lagid rule. The "Sesostris Legend," the "Ramesses Legend," and the "Osiris Legend" had this in common: an Egyptian hero, a greater than Alexander, was true king because he ruled for the benefit of his subjects, and thereby fulfilled the Egyptian ideal of kingship emphasized from the Middle Kingdom onwards. These three kings, Osiris, Sesostris, and Ramesses, had all been historically deified and worshipped. Osiris had far outstripped the other two in importance, and had become one of the most important gods of Egypt. But Sesostris and Ramesses were gods too, and there was probably still a funerary cult in their honor in Hellenistic times, since pharaohs always established cults for their worship as one of their most important preparations for passage to the Hereafter. The translated, immortal, divine god-kings after death formed a sort of divine corporation, and they played their part in the kingship

---

or may not be identifiable with Baktria. The text dates from the fourth or third century B.C. See "The Legend of the Possessed Princess," *A.N.E.T.*, 29–31.

[49] Diod. i. 17. 1–20. 6.

rituals of pharaonic Egypt. Since these rituals were important for insuring the harmonious working of the cosmic Egyptian state, an association of men and gods, these Hellenistic legends exalting the deeds and benefactions of Osiris, Sesostris, and Ramesses expressed the firm conviction that Egypt's traditional culture and gods still lived on. They lived, they lived, they lived—despite whatever changes Ptolemaic society might effect.[50]

The mythic functions of Osiris were fully detailed in the *Bremner-Rhind Papyrus,* a ritual containing numerous magical spells collected about 310 B.C. by an Egyptian scribe in the Thebaïd. The compilation was entitled *The Book of Overthrowing Apophis.* Its beginning discussed Osiris as creator of the world, and then passed on to describe his victory over Apophis, who was hacked to bits and whose bits were then trampled. This particular text was not anti-Greek, since it included charms to protect Pharaoh Alexander and overthrow his enemies. But its contents showed how Osiris could be used against the Greeks. Some Egyptians identified the Greeks with Typhon, who was equated with Seth. The latter had stood for the wretched Asiatic enemies of Egypt in the past. Typhon, Seth, and Apophis were all symbols of chaos, the opposite of the creation, orderliness, and justice that Osiris and the native pharaohs guaranteed. From being the specific enemy of Apophis, Osiris was exalted to become one champion of the Egyptian religious reaction against the Typhonian Greeks.[51]

These three legends were, however, generally passive and concerned with the past; they did not prophesy a future overthrow of the Greeks. They appear to have been intended to inspire Egyptians to venerate the divine ancestors and so to keep themselves unspotted from the Hellenic world. But although these legends did not openly foretell the end of Lagid rule, there was such apocalyptic prophecy, and like the three archaizing legends, it arose out of traditional Egyptian concern for true kingship. Early in the Ptolemaic period someone prophesied that Nektanebo II would return to drive out Egypt's enemies.

Unfortunately, the only statement of this prediction to survive comes from a late source. Other evidence, however, shows that it must actually have been circulated rather early. The version of the prophecy which we have is a verse oracle in Pseudo-Kallisthenes,

[50] On the importance of the deified kings in ritual, see H. W. Fairman, "The Kingship Rituals of Egypt," *Myth, Ritual, and Kingship* (ed. S. H. Hooke, 1958), 104.

[51] *P. Bremner-Rhind:* R. O. Faulkner, "The Bremner-Rhind Papyrus I," *JEA* 22 (1936), 121–40. There is a more recent translation of part of it by J. A. Wilson, *A.N.E.T.,* 6. Identification of Seth and Typhon: Manetho, frag. 79 (Waddell). Greeks and Typhon: see pp. 292–294, below.

whose book was written about A.D. 300 but certainly based on earlier material, at least in part. The prediction made is that Nektanebo has fled Egypt, but when he has circled through the countries of the world, he will return youthful and conquer Egypt's foes. Although the enemies in this oracle are not named, they must have been the Makedonians and Greeks, at least at one time. This oracle seems to have been remade from an earlier one of around 340 B.C., for Pseudo-Kallisthenes also has a paraphrase of another prophecy, this in prose, that Nektanebo would return and would drive out specifically the Persians. Now, that the word "enemies" in the verse oracle at one time meant the Greeks is shown, I think, by several things. In the first place, Memphis had a long tradition of hatred of foreigners. These Nektaneban oracles were credited to Memphis, for Pseudo-Kallisthenes says that Alexander saw the prose version in the Temple of Hephaistos, that is, in the Temple of Ptah there. Long after Alexander's time, a Roman author reported that in this same Memphis there was a column—surely belonging to a temple—on which was written in letters of gold a prophecy that the Romans would be overthrown. Thus, there seems to have been a long-standing tradition here. In the second place, it is certain that anti-Persian ideas were made over into anti-Greek ideas. This occurred with the "Sesostris Legend"; it also occurred with the *Demotic Chronicle,* an oracle which will be discussed presently.[52]

Even though the verse oracle comes from a book written about A.D. 300, it contains two elements that are undoubtedly drawn from traditional Egyptian ideology. The one is that kingship is renewed. This was affected in pharaonic times by the state *Sed*-festival, an institution still known in Ptolemaic times, as already noted. The other is the idea that the king would defeat all the enemies of Egypt. In the pharaonic age the kings were said to beat and trample "The Nine Bows," who stood for all the foreign countries ringing Egypt; in Hellenistic times, Sesostris, Ramesses, and Osiris were said to have defeated enemies in Africa, Asia, and Europe, the three continents in the world. Therefore, the verse oracle was probably made to be anti-Makedonian.

[52] Verse oracle: (Ps.-) Kall. i. 3. 4, as follows:
    The strong, brave sire, who has fled Egypt,
    Monarch and king will he come again youthful.
    When he has put off his features old semblance,
    And has circled the world to Egypt's plain once more,
    He will give us conquest over all our enemies.
Prose oracle: *ibid.,* i. 34. 3. Anti-Roman oracle: *S.H.A., 30 Tyr.,* xxii. 13–4.

Moreover, as to the early date and anti-Hellenic nature of the oracle, Diodoros gave what must have been an Egyptian explanation for Nektanebo's defeat by Artaxerxes III. He said the reason was that Nektanebo was deserted by his Greek mercenaries. Diodoros did not believe it; he only reported it. In his opinion, the real reason was that the Egyptian troops, which were much more numerous than the Greek, lacked experience, and therefore Persian numbers overcame the defense. I think, too, that this is more nearly the true explanation. The Greeks actually did not come to terms with the Persians until the invaders had taken Pelousion. This fortified place was of critical importance, and the Greeks fought bravely here until Nektanebo himself withdrew to Memphis. Then the fall of the city was only a matter of time. With Pelousion in Persian hands, their communications with Phoenicia, whether by land or by sea, were secure, and in the long run they could bring up overwhelming numbers of troops. Since they also employed Greek mercenaries as the striking force of their army, the Greeks fighting for Egypt had to surrender. The fighting around Pelousion in 343 was somewhat like the Battle of Kounaxa in 401, in which the Greek ten thousand fought until the Oriental main body of Kyros' army surrendered. Then, alone in a foreign land, they made terms with the Persians. So, too, cut off in Pelousion they negotiated. Therefore Diodoros was right in rejecting the explanation that Nektanebo was ruined by Greek desertion. Rather, his own inability to maintain communication with Pelousion led to his defeat. The explanation that the Greeks were to blame was Egyptian propaganda seeking to exonerate the king at the expense of the Greeks.[53]

Now there was an Egyptian anti-Semitic legend which exalted the old Pharaoh Amenophis. M. Braun has shown that it was modelled on the actual experiences of Nektanebo II. That it already existed in 275 B.C. is shown by Manethon's having known it. Amenophis was said to have been beaten by treachery and by invasion; the renegade Egyptian Osarsiph-Moses and numbers of leprous Egyptians conspired to admit the Hyksos to Egypt. Amenophis could not withstand them and fled south to Ethiopia, as Nektanebo had actually done, so that Egypt was in the grip of the leprous Egyptian rebels and the unspeakable foreign Hyksos. In the twelfth year of this domination, which exactly conforms to the period of Persian rule, 343–332 B.C., Amenophis returned with his son from the south, drove out the foreigners, and expelled the renegades. Therefore, since this much

[53] Diod. xvi. 49. 1—50. 8.

seems clearly to have been drawn from the history of Nektanebo, there is no good reason to deny that the oracle predicting his return also was not known at this early date.[54] It would exactly match the notice in Pseudo-Kallisthenes predicting his return and his victory over the Persians. After 332 this was simply understood to mean the Greeks.

In fact there seems to have been Egyptian spiritual resistance from the beginning of Alexander's occupation. Since all the propaganda—archaizing or futuristic—drew on the theology of kingship or the facts of kingship as the means of expressing hatred for the Greeks, it would not be surprising to find Alexander attacked and the last native pharaoh used as the anti-Makedonian hero. The idea of the coming of a pharaoh from the south, from Ethiopia, the land of the sun, of the god Re, was not by any means a new one. The Middle Kingdom *Prophecy of Nefer-rohu* said that a king born in Nubia would come to restore order out of the dreadful, topsy-turvy chaos that foreign invaders and Egyptians living without Ma'at had made. Since this prophecy had been much used as a school exercise text, it may still have been known in the fourth century b.c. But was there contemporary hatred of Alexander? It would seem so. Besides Ammon's rejection of the cult of Hephaistion, mentioned above, Ptah in Memphis seems to have hated him. This priesthood is the one mentioned by Pseudo-Kallisthenes in connection with the prophecy of Nektanebo's return. The story is that when Ptolemy I brought Alexander's body to Memphis for temporary burial, the high priest there said that it should be taken to his own city of Alexandria. "For the place that his body is will never be quit of war and battle."[55] Alexander, in other words, was Typhonian.

The prophecy of Nektanebo's return was not believed by all the Egyptians. Certainly his failure eventually to return was an empirical test that could scarcely be gainsaid. Consequently, there was an Egyptian explanation of his defeat that said nothing at all about his return. It may even have existed from the beginning, for Nektanebo was not especially perfect for anti-Hellenic figures to rally around. Sesostris and Ramesses, if an old king must be chosen, were better. They had been, so legend related, consistently victorious. Nektanebo II had not; he had been defeated by Artaxerxes. This seems to have worried the

---

[54] Amenophis Legend: Manethon, frag. 54 (Waddell) = Jos. *A.Ap.* i. 227–87. M. Braun, *History and Romance in Greco-Oriental Literature* (1938), 19–21.
[55] "The Prophecy of Nefer-rohu," *A.N.E.T.*, 444–6. Alexander's body: (Ps.-) Kall. iii. 34. 5.

Egyptians, and we find Egyptian stories concerned with his defeat.
Pseudo-Kallisthenes preserves another bit of genuine tradition
about him: he was a great miracle-worker. Technically, of course,
all Egyptian kings were: they could make the Nile rise by supernatural
means. But Pseudo-Kallisthenes says that he was a great worker of
war magic; he did not have to mobilize armies, but dealt with his
enemies by modelling little ships and sailors out of wax, putting them
into a bronze cauldron, and reciting incantations over them. The
text does not say how the enemy was destroyed by this rite, but the
cauldron suggests the wax was melted in boiling water. This was good
sympathetic magic. As the figures were melted, so the flesh-and-blood
enemies of Egypt were dissolved and dispersed. This sort of thing
had long been practiced in pharaonic Egypt as an accompaniment
of real warfare. The kings of the late XIIth or XIIIth Dynasty are
known to have tried to annihilate their Asiatic enemies by writing
their names on pots, reciting incantatory execrations, and then
smashing the pots to bits. As the name broke up, so the foreign foe
went to pieces. Pseudo-Kallisthenes says, however, that Nektanebo
saw in the cauldron that the gods guided the Persians' ships, which
meant in some way the Persians would escape destruction, and that
the omens were against Egypt. Therefore he went to Makedonia to
sire Alexander. The sign in the cauldron was certainly not actually
this, because Nektanebo fought the Persians. Therefore, in this brief
story of Pseudo-Kallisthenes, there seems to be an old Egyptian tradition that Nektanebo for some unstated reason could not defend the
country and consequently had to leave it.[56]

There is another, somewhat similar tradition about Nektanebo
in one of the Sarapeon papyri of the second century B.C., five hundred
years older than Pseudo-Kallisthenes. According to it, when the Persians were attacking, Nektanebo arranged for himself to have a vision
to explain what was going to happen. The vision duly occurred, and
the king saw a boat coming downriver. It tied up at Memphis, and
he watched the war-god Onouris complain to Isis, the guardian of
Egypt, that his temple had not been completed. The vision over,
Nektanebo at once took steps to complete the temple, but here the
papyrus ends.[57] There are connections with Pseudo-Kallisthenes' tale:
in both Nektanebo arranges to have a vision concerning Persia; it is
an unfavorable one in which a boat or boats play a part; it is connected with Memphis. Perhaps this shows that there was once a

[56] (Ps.-) Kall. i. 1. 1–3; "The Execration of Asiatic Princes," *A.N.E.T.*, 328–9.
[57] *The Dream of Nektanebo* = *U.P.Z.* i. 81, pp. 369–74.

forthright explanation that Artaxerxes defeated the Pharaoh because he, who was responsible for the maintenance of the state cults, had not properly looked after them, and the gods had withdrawn their support. This was a normal, mythic explanation of political events in the native Egypt of the fourth century and even earlier. Ipuwer, at the time of the First Intermediate Period, explained to his pharaoh that Asiatics had succeeded in making a foothold for themselves in the Delta region because the king had not enforced Ma'at. The fourth-century *Demotic Chronicle,* which was certainly still known in Hellenistic times, explained that certain pharaohs of the XXVIIIth and XXIXth Dynasties had not been permitted to rule long or to have their sons succeed them because they neglected religious law. It has already been noted that the kings of the XXXth Dynasty had been much concerned with their relationship to the temples. Therefore, it would appear that this theological explanation of Nektanebo's defeat was created to explain how he was defeated: he could hardly rule after lapsing in his duty towards the Temple of Onouris and/or some other obligations.

Perhaps the Egyptians who created this myth were entirely hostile to the memory of Nektanebo. There certainly had been Egyptians who after his fall collaborated first with the Persians and then with the Makedonians. Perhaps these persons had something to do with making up the tale that Nektanebo went to Pella to become Alexander's father. In this way, in fact, the oracle of his return would be effectively answered: the young Nektanebo had returned not in his own body but in the body of his divine son Alexander, brave in the horns of Ammon. Makedonian rule was therefore divinely ordained.

To return to anti-Lagid propaganda, as time went on antagonistic religious literature became more violent, and more inclined to prophesy their overthrow. The "Sesostris Legend" seems originally to have had a little to do with feeding these hopes for the future, although its second edition was a bit less concerned with the past.

The stories of the extraordinary military exploits of Sesostris explicitly stated that his soldiers after their triumphs led a carefree life of luxury. This could easily have been turned into a hope, and therefore could have been connected with the violent anti-Hellenic revolts of the late third century. The statement sounds like an attempt to encourage Egyptians to rebel by holding up for their inspection the valor, success, and reward of their forefathers. They would be able, in effect, to enjoy the prosperous life Greek and Makedonian military colonists enjoyed in the countryside among them. The

"Sesostris Legend" did say that prophecies were made by Sesostris' daughter Athyrtis. She foretold from sacrifice and by astrology that her father would complete an easy conquest of the world. It was also said that Thoth appeared to Sesostris in a dream and similarly prophesied world conquest. And with an army of 600,000 foot and 24,000 horse he was gloriously successful.[58] Was, then, the nationalist author of the "Sesostris Legend" showing that in the past prophecies of victory had been followed by victory? Prophecies certainly were made in the late third century specifically foretelling the overthrow of Alexandria and the hated Makedonian regime. The "Sesostris Legend" would at least have supported these oracles. They seem to have taken effect, for Polybios said that when the Egyptian soldiers returned from their victory at Raphia, they were looking specifically for a leader to free them from foreign rule.[59] The result was the first great revolt.

The date of the second anti-Hellenic "Sesostris Legend," around 200 B.C., coincides closely with the dates assigned to the two anti-Greek apocalypses, the *Demotic Chronicle* and the *Oracle of the Potter,* and the outbreak of the native rebellions in 217 B.C. All these prophets and soldiers would seem to have worked together to attempt expulsion of the Ptolemaic government. In fact, Ptolemaic Egypt was on the verge of a whole series of native risings, long, hard-fought, and vicious, rather like the guerilla operations of the Maccabees, different only in that the Egyptians failed to achieve independence. Through them all, the Egyptians continued to believe in their gods, in their culture, and in their final victory, as shown by their continuing though unavailing efforts. Egypt's vital propaganda reflected her hopes.

The *Demotic Chronicle* has survived in Egyptian on a papyrus now held by the Bibliothèque Nationale in Paris. Unfortunately, both the beginning and the end of the document are lost. The papyrus is a palimpsest with both Greek and Demotic of the early Ptolemaic period, so that its date can be fixed with some accuracy either in the reign of Ptolemy II, or, more likely, in the reign of Ptolemy III Euergetes I (246–221 B.C.). Its provenance is not known with certainty, although it is said to have been found in the Nekropolis at Memphis. This would certainly have been a likely place for someone to have an anti-Makedonian text, because the prophecies of Nektanebo's return were connected with Memphis, and therefore they probably originated there. As for the *Demotic Chronicle,* however, it is quite likely on grounds of internal evidence that the original version of the

58 Diod. i. 53. 8—54. 4.
59 Polyb. v. 107. 1–3.

document came from Herakleopolis, from among the clergy of the gods worshipped there. Moreover, it is likely that it went through two recensions, a first produced in the Persian period, and a poorly revised second edition in the Ptolemaic period.[60]

The oracle would appear to be a revelation granted by the god Thoth. The prophecy is principally concerned with the re-establishment of the native kingship. It not only hopes for a king who-is-to-come; it is also concerned with the history of the pharaohs of the XXIXth Dynasty, whether they observed the law or not, and with the *Sed*-festival, the old coronation rite of the Egyptian kings.[61] This is an important consideration, since it shows that Egyptian prophecy, like Jewish or Persian, was concerned with the re-establishment of native kingship in a true and perfect form. The prophet looks forward to the time when a man of Herakleopolis will rule after the expulsion of the Ionians. His rule will bring copious bread, called the opening of hearths; plenteousness of cattle; resumption of true sacrifices to the gods; and true kingship. The man of Herakleopolis will appear with a force of Egyptian warriors. They will overcome the enemy, the man will be crowned pharaoh, and bread will be given to those who require it. Isis will rejoice, happiness will return to Egypt, and law and custom will be restored. The prophecy next summarizes the rule of six pharaohs of the XXVIIIth and XXIXth Dynasties, emphasizing their loyalty, or lack of it, to Ma'at, and point-

---

[60] The *Demotic Chronicle* is *P. Dem. Paris* 215. It is critically discussed and translated into German by W. Spiegelberg, *Die sogennante demotische Chronik* (1914). See, too, C. C. McCown, "Egyptian Apocalyptic Literature," *HTR* 18 (1925), 388; E. R. Bevan, *A History of Egypt* (1927), 240.

Internal evidence of provenance: *Dem. Chron.* ii. 14, 16, 24–5; iii. 1. These are references to Herakleopolis and its god Harsaphes.

Two recensions may be deduced from the following considerations. The present text admits it is a second edition when it refers to prior "tablets" (*ibid.*, i. 15; ii. 7, 19; iii. 6, 17; v. 14; vi. 13; vii. 1). This is not decisive; the author may have been trying for a stylistic effect. Second, the historical summary of the pharaohs runs to Tachos (361–359 B.C.) only, which would have made sense in a text of the Persian period, but which has an obvious lacuna in a text of the Hellenistic period. The historical summary (iii. 18—iv. 18), which incidentally has a doublet (ii. 2–4), is really out of context between the mystic, religious utterances of the second and third, and the fourth and fifth columns of the papyrus. This looks like clumsy editing. Third, and most important, there are inconsistencies in naming the enemies who ruin Egypt. They are called simply "foreigners" (ii. 21; vi. 15); "foreigners, who are Medes" (iii. 18; v. 15–6, 17); "Medes" (iv. 1, 3, 6, 7, 9, 11, 13, 20, 23); "foreigners and Ionians" (ii. 25); and simply "Ionians" (iii. 1; vi. 20). The effect of these indications is cumulative. It appears that there was a first recension around 340 B.C. and a second around 250 B.C., in which fresh material was added to a rearranged original, and the whole published.

[61] Thoth: *Dem. Chron.* ii. 4. Thoth was identified with the Greek Hermes. Thoth was the source of revelation in the *Corpus Hermeticum* of the Christian era. *Sed*-festival: ii. 65; H. I. Frankfort, *Kingship and the Gods* (1948), 79–88.

ing out that those were deposed who rejected the law. It then reverts to melancholy predictions of conquest by foreigners, lamenting and sighing over the booty these foreign dogs will make of Egypt.[62]

The objections of the *Demotic Chronicle* to foreign rulers are three: they have supplanted the national god-kings; they have interfered with the conduct of the normal religious festivals; and they have caused want and suffering through nonobservance of law. Because of these sins they will be defeated and expelled. Thus the basic complaints of the *Demotic Chronicle* closely parallel the basic thoughts of the legends about Sesostris and Osiris, heroes who had performed well and truly these three functions.

The second Egyptian apocalypse of roughly the same period is the *Oracle of the Potter*. It seems to have enjoyed a wider popularity than the *Demotic Chronicle,* both among Egyptians and Greeks, for it is extant in three slightly variant versions, all of them specimens of translation Greek of the first century B.C. or the third century of the Christian era. Scholars who have studied this text are agreed in assigning a date at the end of the third century B.C. as its time of composition. There is not sufficient internal evidence to date it more closely. There may be a reference to either Antiochos III or Antiochos IV in the line which mentions a king coming from Syria, but this is doubtful. This oracle is much in the style of both older and later examples of Egyptian prophecy, belonging to the tradition going back to the *Prophecy of Nefer-rohu* of Middle Kingdom date.[63]

The contents of the oracle are as follows. It opens with a description of wretched conditions in suffering Egypt; society and the order of nature are chaotically confused and drastically mixed up. It goes on to curse the city of the Greeks, the hated capital Alexandria, and to look forward to the time when it shall become a dank spot where fishermen dry their nets. The Greeks are Typhonians—wreckers and destroyers of the established order. It prophesies the resumption of

---

[62] Man of Herakleopolis: *Dem. Chron.* ii. 25. His rule: iii. 1–5. Isis and the law: iii. 6–16. Pharaohs: iii. 18—iv. 18. Conquest: iv. 22–3; v. 2, 23; vi. 2–3, 17–21.

[63] The versions of the Oracle exist in a very short and fragmentary Graf papyrus; in a Rainer Papyrus published by R. Reitzenstein and H. H. Schraeder in *Studien zum antiken Synkretismus aus Iran und Griechenland* (1926) ; and in Oxyrhynchus Papyrus 2332, published by E. Lobel and C. H. Roberts, *The Oxyrhynchus Papyri* 22 (1954) .

Its date: E. Lobel and H. H. Roberts, *op. cit.,* 92–3; W. W. Tarn, *H.C.* (3rd ed., 1952) , 207, 228; M. I. Rostovtzeff in *C.A.H.* vii. 115; C. Préaux, "Esquisse d'une histoire des révolutions égyptiennes sous les Lagids," *CE* 22 (1936) , 525; E. R. Bevan, *A History of Egypt* (1927) , 240; R. Reitzenstein and H. H. Schraeder, *op. cit.,* 38–9. Syrian King: *P. Rainer* i. 15–6; *P. Oxy.* i. 31–2.

Old tradition and later parallels; "The Prophecy of Nefer-rohu," *A.N.E.T.* 444–6; C. C. McCown, "Egyptian Apocalyptic Literature," *HTR* 18 (1925) , 357–411.

native holy rites and the coming of a king sent by Re and established by Isis. When he rules, the backward state of nature will be reversed again, and the seasons will come in their proper times. The sun formerly darkened will break forth, and the country will become so happy and prosperous that the people will wish that the dead might be resurrected in order to share the bountiful good things. The Rainer papyrus concludes with a colophon, missing in the Oxyrhynchus version, that the Potter, having delivered this revelation to Pharaoh Amenophis, died, and the king buried him in Heliopolis and preserved the oracle in the royal treasury.[64]

R. Reitzenstein has suggested that the *Oracle of the Potter* was somewhat influenced by the Persian *Bahman Yasht*. He finds evidence in the references in the Egyptian text to *Zōnophoroi*, "girdle-wearers," whom he identifies with the demons wearing leather girdles mentioned in the Persian text. The yasht did not, however, influence this oracle. As is shown in Appendix 1, the leathern-belted enemies of Iran are Turks of post-Sassanid date. It is likely that the term *Zōnophoroi* in the Egyptian text refers to the armored soldiers or policemen of the Greek regime. Such terminology would be analogous to a sixth-century B.C. Egyptian epithet for Karian mercenary soldiers, "the men of bronze," who rose out of the sea.[65]

The wording of this *Oracle*'s curse on Alexandria may reflect exact Egyptian knowledge of the religious rites which went on when the city was founded. The Greek seers foresaw that the city would become large and prosperous, a source of nourishment to many lands. The *Oracle* says these things in reverse: the all-nourishing city inhabited by many races of men would become a desolate place visited only by fisherfolk. This prediction seems to have made some Greeks anxious, for in Pseudo-Kallisthenes it is stated, unhistorically, that when Alexander was in Egypt he asked the god Sarapis if Alexandria would preserve his name, and received a reassuring reply.[66]

This oracle became rather well known, as seen from its preservation in three versions. It was translated or adapted from an Egyptian original into wretched Greek in the first century B.C., and it remained

[64] The text of the work is to be found in the works cited in n. 63, p. 292 above. The Rainer version is partially translated into English by E. R. Bevan in *A History of Egypt* (1927), 240, and almost entirely by C. C. McCown in "Egyptian Apocalyptic Literature," *HTR* 18 (1925), 398.

[65] R. Reitzenstein and H. H. Schraeder, *op. cit.*, 44–5. The *Zōnophoroi: P. Rainer* i. 13, 21, 29; ii. 16; *P. Oxy.* i. 26; ii. 43, 49, 55. Karians: Herod. ii. 152. *"Zōnophoroi"* as a circumlocution for "soldiers" also occurred to A. D. Nock in his review of Reitzenstein's book in *JHS* 49 (1929), 111–6.

[66] Greek seers: n. 23, p. 268, above. *Oracle of the Potter: P. Rainer* ii. 4–5; *P. Oxy.* ii. 61–2. Sarapis' reassurance: (Ps.-) Kall. i. 33. 1–3.

popular until at least the third century of the Christian era. This was a period in which Greek and native elements in Egypt made common cause against the government, largely because of the unhappy conditions that existed for the lower classes. The *Oracle of the Potter* was one source for the "Little Apocalypse," now contained in the *Corpus Hermeticum*, a collection of the third century A.D. It therefore went through a development similar to the *Oracle of Hystaspes*, beginning as an anti-Hellenic prophecy and becoming a Greco-Egyptian anti-Roman prophecy.[67]

Certain motifs in the oracle were known, of course, in Hellenistic Egypt, and even elsewhere. Diodoros preserves an Egyptian tradition that the sun-god, Re, from whom the savior was to come, had once been the king of Egypt. The king-to-be, therefore, is God's own son. The colophon attributing the prophecy's safekeeping to Amenophis is paralleled by remarks in Manethon. He says that Amenophis was a magician with full knowledge of the future. The long, secret preservation of the document reminds one of Daniel and the *Oracle of Hystaspes*. Typhon, whom the *Oracle of the Potter* names as the inspirer of all evil, is also said by Manethon to be the personification of all wickedness.[68]

The essential idea of the *Oracle of the Potter* is rather similar to the basic thought of the *Demotic Chronicle*, and the prophet hopes for the destruction of Greek rule in Egypt for similar reasons. He hates the interruption of the native dynasty, the dislocation of Egyptian religion caused by the foreigners, and the harsh social and economic conditions prevailing under the Lagids. Both predict the return of a native pharaoh to put an end to Egypt's suffering. Pharaoh had always been the agent that controlled the forces of nature, and one of his most important functions as head of the state religion had been the manipulation of natural forces by means of various religious devices. The two apocalypses lament the current state of apocalyptic confusion of nature: the Nile is always low, the crops always poor, and the seasons in backward order. Where was pharaoh, to set things right? The forces of Chaos, the Greek Typhonians, are in the ascendent, and there is no Egyptian king on Egypt's throne. The king is dead.[69]

[67] For the influence of the Oracle on the *Corpus Hermeticum*, see R. Reitzenstein and H. H. Schraeder, *op. cit.*, 44; A. D. Nock and A. J. Festugière, *Corpus Hermeticum* (1945), i. 1–7; ii. 275–6, 284–92.

[68] Re: Diod. i. 13. 2–3; 26. 1–2. Amenophis: Manethon, frag. 52, 53a, 54 (Waddell). Typhon: *ibid.*, frag. 49, 79, and 86 (Waddell). *Oracle of the Potter: P. Rainer* ii. 15; *P. Oxy.* i. 4, 9, 14–5; ii. 50.

[69] *Dem. Chron.* v. 1–3; vi. 8–14; *Oracle of the Potter: P. Rainer* i. 1–2; ii. 10–5; *P. Oxy.* i. 13, ii. 45; iii. 73–9. For the role of pharaoh in controlling nature, see the literature cited in n. 20, p. 267, above.

Chapter XI

Priest, Peasant, and Patrician in Hellenistic Egypt

We may now begin a more detailed investigation of the causes of the Egyptian resistance, and determine its relationship to the social classes along the Nile, so that something may be said about the people who were responsible for writing the oracles and composing the legends that were anti-Hellenic. Hatred of foreign rule, of course, was still a powerful emotion in many Egyptians, and it certainly lay behind all the literature. It seems to have affected all social classes, although in varying degree. In the *Egyptiaka* of the Hellenized priest Manethon it was at work, although his dislike for Hellenism was exceedingly mild and his acceptance of the Lagid Dynasty apparently complete. Manethon was a priest of Sebennytos during the reigns of Ptolemy I and II, and, as already noted, he assisted Soter in establishing the worship of Sarapis. His history of Egypt and other monographs were based on Egyptian sacred literature, and therefore were rather accurate, especially for the last few hundred years preceding his own day. His literary efforts apparently had the purpose of explaining the history and customs of Egypt to his Makedonian masters in a language they could understand, so that in a way he collaborated with them. But he did have the normal native view of the primacy and priority of Egyptian civilization, which began with the gods and demigods, and devolved ultimately on the pharaohs. He took pains to correct errors in Herodotos, and reverenced the memory of Ramesses, who, he pointed out, had once defeated his brother Harmais Danaos, whose name probably made him the founder of Argos, in battle. But these remarks were as far as his anti-Hellenism went, and his xenophobia was mostly expended on Asiatics. He discussed the occupation of Egypt by the Hyksos, an historical event of the second millennium B.C. He says that there were a polluted people who were given the city of Auaris to dwell in, a city associated by ancient tradition with

295

Typhon. These polluted people, by whom Manethon apparently meant the Jews, invited the Hyksos into Egypt, and when the latter attacked the country, they forced Pharaoh Amenophis to flee. Eventually he returned, and with his son Ramesses expelled both the polluted Egyptians and the Hyksos. The unflattering epithet which Manethon used for the Jews is similar to the name the *Demotic Chronicle* used for the Ionians. It called them "dogs," and Alexander the Great was apparently the "big dog."[1] If both Manethon and the prophet who wrote the *Chronicle* called foreigners these things, the Egyptian feeling that foreigners were unclean curs, which had so impressed Herodotos, was certainly still a strong force in the third century.

This hatred of rule by foreigners was an important cause of the impressive series of native risings against the Lagids. These revolts were astonishingly long-lived, widespread, and determined, and they were an important phenomenon of Egyptian anti-Hellenism.[2] For the rebellions were much more manifestations of religious passion than of national aspiration. The ancient Egyptian expressed his "nationalism" by means of his religion; it was not for him a secular emotion. The modern feeling of "nationalism" comes from consciousness of the historical development of a whole people, heirs of a common secular culture usually rooted in a single language. This feeling did not exist in the ancient world, for peoples then thought a great deal less in purely secular terms. The Egyptians thought their society was an eternal association of gods and men. Warfare to them was a religious act; it was a service performed for the gods and at the command of the gods. The Maccabean revolt was directly comparable with the Egyptian revolts. Both were inspired by a religious literature; both were fought to preserve a religion by restoring its god to his rightful throne. To accomplish that it was necessary to expel the foreigner by force. His military power was supporting a corrupting, antisocial government, polluting the land with false gods and nonobservance of the traditional religious ideas, and exploiting the native population. Since we admit religious inspiration in the Jewish wars, we must also grant religious inspiration for the Egyptian wars.

[1] Manethon: frag. 1, 3, 42, 50, 54, 88 in W. G. Waddell's edition in the Loeb Classical Library (1948). Dogs: *Dem. Chron.* vi. 20–1.

[2] Special literature on the native risings includes J. G. Milne, "Egyptian Nationalism under Greek and Roman Rule," *JEA* 14 (1928), 226–34; C. Préaux, "Esquisse d'une histoire des révolutions égyptiennes sous les Lagids," *CÉ* 22 (1936), 522–52; M. Alliot, "La Thebaïde en lutte contre les rois d'Alexandrie sous Philopator et Épiphane," *RBPh* 29 (1951), 421–43, and "La fin de la résistance égyptienne dans le sud sous Épiphane," *RÉA* 54 (1952), 18–26.

The first native revolt may have taken place in the reign of Ptolemy III Euergetes I about 245 B.C. This is by no means certain, for the sources call the outbreak of violence a "domestic sedition," whatever that may be. We know that there were famine conditions during Euergetes' first years, but if they were a cause we do not know. Nor do we know what people took part in the rising. It could have been a palace revolution, it could have been a revolt of the Greeks of Alexandria, it could have been an uprising of the Egyptians in the country, or any combination of these.[3]

In the reign of Ptolemy Philopator (221–205/4 B.C.) there was an outbreak of a serious, sustained, and vicious character. Ptolemy, having to make preparations to withstand an invasion of Egypt by his Seleukid rival Antiochos III, recruited twenty thousand Egyptians to serve as heavy infantry of the phalanx. These men played a substantial part in winning victory for the Lagids in the Battle of Raphia in 217 B.C. They returned to Egypt with new confidence in their military abilities against Greek soldiers. They also returned in a dangerous frame of mind. Polybios says that they were looking for a ruler, a leader who would bring about their independence. This sounds as if they might have been inspired by the *Demotic Chronicle,* which promised Egypt a human savior to lead a human army to expel the foreigner. Within six months of their return, they began a tremendous revolt in the Delta region which rapidly spread throughout Egypt. It became a long-drawn-out affair that blazed up here and there for more than thirty years. There were no pitched battles, scarcely any engagements worthy of note. But there was a long period of guerilla war against Lagid troops, and it eventually degenerated into a savage and lawless conflict. On the whole, it seemed a serious threat to Hellenism itself, so serious that both Philip V of Makedonia and Antiochos III offered aid to Philopator to suppress it.

It is likely that propaganda was used to excite these men, and, aside from the texts already mentioned, it is possible that it was composed of some curious stories in late Greek sources. Aelian says that certain Egyptian priests claimed the sacred crocodiles were endowed with prophetic ability, and that when one of the Ptolemies was trying to feed the tamest of them, the animal paid him no attention and refused to accept his food. The priests, he goes on, realized that the crocodile knew the Greek king's end was near, and for this reason did

[3] Just. xvii. 1; Polyainos viii. 50; C. Préaux, "Esquisse . . . ," *CÉ* 22 (1936) , 523–6. See, too, the remarks of W. W. Tarn in *C.A.H.* vii 717. Food shortage: Athen. v. 206 D, 209 AB.

not take from him. Unfortunately Aelian says he does not know which
Ptolemy this was, and refers his readers to the priests. It is possible that
it was Ptolemy IV, however, not only because of the likelihood of
prophecy against him, but also because Aelian tells a story which is
definitely about this king's religious troubles. He reports that when
Philopator returned from his victory at Raphia, he decided to sacrifice
four of his best war elephants to the Sun. After these victims had
been immolated, the king had a vision in which the Sun scolded him
for having made so strange and unusual an offering. Therefore
Ptolemy arose in fear of the god, and had four elephants made of
bronze offered to propitiate him.[4] The specific time assigned this event
coincides exactly with the post-Raphia rising. The story also says that
Ptolemy IV was in difficulties with the sun-god, that is Re. And this
was the god, according to the *Oracle of the Potter*, who was to send
the king to reign. The *Oracle* also accused the Greek regime generally
of tolerating "strange images" and upsetting the proper celebration of
Egyptian rites, so that Aelian's tradition must have historical origin
in the reign of Philopator, who was actually accused of monstrously
sacrificing elephants to Re. Elephants were never at all numerous in
Egypt, and had no place in Egyptian religion. Therefore, may we not
say that the crocodile's prediction that Ptolemy would die also probably referred to this king?

While Egyptian priests were telling tales about wicked foreign kings
and prophesying the advent of good Egyptian messiahs, the war rolled
on. Egyptian militia—the *machimoi*—deserted the Ptolemaic forces
and involved themselves on the side of the rebels. In Nubia, south of
Egypt, there was revolution, and the philhellenic king Ergamenes was
succeeded about the end of Philopator's reign by a nationalist king
named Asekh-Re-Ammon, who reversed his policy. He returned to the
old, unhellenized religion, and made common cause with the restored
Ammon clergy in his capital at Napata, and they in turn consecrated
him "King of Egypt." These Nubian persons seem to have made
contact with the Ammon clergy at Thebes in Egypt, and about
207/6 B.C., Nubian invaders assisted Egyptian rebels who occupied
the Temple of Edfou in the Thebaïd. Ptolemy III had restored this
temple, but he had not repaired and embellished Ammon's Temple at
Karnak or Luxor, so that perhaps the latter priests felt it was time to
invoke the law against him. The rebels around Edfou were led by a
man named Harmakhis, "King of Egypt, Living Forever, Beloved of
Isis, Beloved of Ammon-Re-Sonther, the Great God." The divine

---

[4] Crocodiles: Aelian, *Char. An.*, viii. 4. Elephants: *ibid.*, vii. 44.

name Ammon-Re may show the gods' priest assisted him. He reigned for six years in the Thebaïd, as shown by contracts written in Demotic found around Karnak and Luxor. A native king had come.[5]

As though this were not enough for Philopator's regime, there were also grave rumblings against him by Greeks in Egypt. Theodotos, his governor of Koile Syria, defected to Antiochos, and in Alexandria discontent mounted. Ptolemy IV did not live to see this problem solved, or the native revolt crushed. In 205/4 he died, and he was succeeded by his minor son, Ptolemy V Epiphanes. There was a violent antigovernment riot in Alexandria itself. The Greek disturbances and the native wars had a common cause in the harsh demands for revenues made by the authoritarian Lagids.[6] Of course, with Antiochos III preparing to invade Koile Syria again, the Lagid government could scarcely sit with hands folded. But despite their efforts to equip troops Syria went lost in 200.

The extreme gravity of these events led the government to make wide-sweeping changes of policy towards native Egyptians. There were concessions, military, religious, economic, and social. Egyptians began to appear in the Ptolemaic civil service. Privileges were granted to the clergy. Lighter taxes were levied. Amnesties were granted. All this was done to gain the support of the clerical and re-created military aristocracies of Egypt. The government granted only a morsel of what these classes wanted, that is, control over the destinies of Egypt, for while Ptolemy was determined to cooperate with these persons, he was still strong enough to demand their support in return. Hence, the concessions were limited.[7] Ptolemy seems to have wanted to buy off the

[5] On the rising of 217 see Polyb. v. 107. 1–3; xiv. 12. 3–5; xv. 33; *B.G.U.* 1215 (a fight around a police station). Modern interpretations of this evidence include those by P. Jouguet, *L'Égypte ptolémaïque*, iii. 118–9; C. Préaux, "Esquisse . . . ," *CÉ* 22 (1936), 526; E. R. Bevan, *A History of Egypt* (1927), 239–40; M. I. Rostovtzeff, *S.E.H.H.W.* ii. 709–10; W. W. Tarn, *H.C.* (3rd ed., 1952), 22–3. Pan-Hellenic aid: Polyb. xv. 20. 1; E. R. Bevan, *The House of Seleucus* (1902), ii. 30.

The promise of the *Dem. Chron.* is iii. 7–9. Desertion by the *machimoi: P. Teb.* 703, although this passage may refer instead to the events of 240; similar desertion is noted by *P. Cairo Zenon* 59590. The Rosetta Decree of Ptolemy V (*O.G.I.S.* 90, ll. 19–20) certainly offers *machimoi* and others amnesty, so that their desertion is certain for the period after 207.

Events in Nubia and the Thebaïd: M. Alliot, "La Thebaïde en lutte contre les rois d'Alexandrie sous Philopator et Épiphane," *RBPh* 29 (1951), 421–32.

[6] Theodotos: Polyb. v. 40. 1–3; 61. 4. Violence in Alexandria: *ibid.*, xv. 26. 8—33. 13. There is an apparently Hellenistic definition of kingship in Suidas, *s.v. Basilea* 3, which reminds kings that they do not own all the property of the world.

[7] The concessions are known from the Rosetta Decree: *O.G.I.S.* 90; see, too, E. R. Bevan, *A History of Egypt* (1927), 261–5; M. I. Rostovtzeff, *S.E.H.H.W.* ii. 707; W. W. Tarn, *H.C.* (3rd ed., 1952), 205–6.

native aristocrats, since members of the Egyptian noble class had no
doubt contributed leadership to the revolt. Considerable numbers of
peasants were involved, since the length of time the revolt lasted—
until 185—indicates that a sizeable fraction of the native population
provided manpower to feed and maintain the effort. With the native
ruling class won over, the revolt would lack direction by the old
notables and would therefore be easier to repress.

Significantly enough, then, the coronation of Ptolemy V took place
at the old Egyptian capital of Memphis according to native rubrics.
He took the title *Epiphanes Eucharistos,* whose hieroglyphic equiva-
lents signified "He Who Cometh Forth" and "Lord of Beauties."
These were sops to Egyptian theology. In the meantime, however, the
war continued. About 200 B.C. 'Ankhmakhis became King of Egypt in
the Thebaïd, and ruled for fourteen years. Like his predecessor, he
advertised himself as beloved of Ammon-Re-Sonther and Isis. Guerilla
outbreaks continued to flare up, and the rebels now had Greek de-
serters on their side. Peasants raided temples, guardposts, and the
offices and officials of the government. But the revolt was first gradually
fought down and then finally suppressed in 185 B.C., when Ptolemy V
captured the town of Lykopolis after a siege. The ultimate viciousness
of all this desperate fighting was symbolized by the dreadful treatment
he meted out to the surrendered rebel chiefs. He had them tied to
carts, dragged naked through the streets of the old capital at Saïs,
tortured, and finally put to death. After all, Diodoros said that this
revolt had nearly cost Ptolemy his throne.[8]

After winning the victory and after receiving the congratulations of
the loyal native clergy, the Makedonian government tried with quarter
measures to accommodate Egyptian opinion. In 175 B.C., the regents of
Ptolemy VI Philometor (181/0–145) were Orientals, although their
names, Eulaios and Lenaios, show they were Hellenized. The relations
of Greeks and Egyptians remained tense, however, so that when Seleukid Antiochos IV invaded Egypt in 169 B.C. he was able to play
upon their mutual hostility to simplify his conquest.[9] But when the

[8] Ptolemy's titles: A. D. Nock, "Notes on Ruler-Cult, I–IV," *JHS* 48 (1928), 39–40.
The war: Polyb. xxii. 17. 1–5; Diod. xxviii. 14. 1; *P. Teb.* 919, 920. P. Jouguet,
L'Égypte ptolémaïque (1933), iii. 120, 130–4; M. Holleaux in *C.A.H.* viii. 187–8;
C. Préaux, "Esquisse . . . ," *CÉ* 22 (1936), 531–3; M. I. Rostovtzeff *S.E.H.H.W.* ii.
715; M. Alliot, "La Thebaïde en lutte contre les rois d'Alexandrie sous Philopator et
Épiphane," *RBPh* 29 (1951), 431–46, and "La fin de la résistance égyptienne dans le
sud sous Épiphane," *RÉA* 54 (1952), 18–26.

[9] Diod. xxx. 14. 1—16. 1; J. W. Swain, "Antiochos Epiphanes and Egypt," *CPh* 39
(1944), 73–94; W. W. Tarn, *The Greeks in Bactria and India* (2nd ed., 1951), 193,
n. 4.

Romans quickly succeeded by threat of force in getting Antiochos out of the country again, the weakness of the battered Ptolemaic government was such that a new series of native rebellions broke out, led by a half-Greek, half-Egyptian named Dionysios-Petosarapis. The insurrection actually began among the Greek population, but it very rapidly spread to the Egyptians of the countryside. Like its predecessor, this revolt was bloody and was fought with great brutality and cruelty on both sides. It included risings in both Lower and Upper Egypt, and again Nubians were able to invade, or at least to raid, the Thebaïd. They may have held it for a certain number of years.[10]

After this rebellion was crushed, peasants continued to withhold their loyalty from the Lagids in a new way—by mass refusal to work. Sometimes they left their villages to take asylum in temples of Egyptian gods, and sometimes they fled outright to sparsely settled places. Royal peasants—those employed to cultivate state-owned land—in the neighborhood of Tebtunis, for example, refused to work on irrigation projects and withdrew from their village. A quartermaster reported to another official that Egyptians at Krokodilopolis had taken the roofs off their houses which were used by the government to quarter its troops. The peasants then walled up the doors and built altars in the rooms so that the buildings had the status of religious sanctuaries and could not, therefore, be occupied by soldiers.[11] Thus the gods of Egypt fought for Egypt.

In these circumstances, the Ptolemaic government continued gradually to take on the guise of a more nearly Egyptian kingship. From the revolt of Dionysios-Petosarapis onward, local copper currency lost some of its original Greek flavor, and began to appear instead with symbols of Egyptian gods. Already Ptolemy V had issued tetradrachms on which an ear of corn symbolic of Sarapis or Osiris appeared, but thereafter the symbols and portrait of the somewhat Hellenized Egyptian goddess Isis became exceedingly common.[12]

---

[10] Diod. xxxi. 15a. 1–4; 17b. 1; *P. Amherst* 30; *P. Teb.* 781. E. R. Bevan, *A History of Egypt* (1927), 290–3; C. Préaux, "Esquisse . . . ," *CÉ* 22 (1936), 538–42; M. I. Rostovtzeff, *S.E.H.H.W.* ii. 719–21, iii. 1496, n. 141.

[11] For examples of flight from work—*anachōrēsis*—see the list in M. I. Rostovtzeff, *S.E.H.H.W.*, ii. 899, and sources cited, and the remarks in W. W. Tarn, *H.C.* (3rd ed., 1952), 199. Tebtunis peasants: *P. Teb.* 707 (118 B.C.); Krokodilopolis: U. Wilcken, *Chrestomathie*, as quoted by W. S. Ferguson, *Greek Imperialism* (1913), 174–5.

[12] R. S. Poole, *B.M.C.*, *The Ptolemies* (1883), p. lviii. Ptolemy V: Nos. 52, 60, 62–8, pp. 72–4, Pl. xvii. 5. Copper currency: Ptolemy VI: Nos. 1–6, p. 78, Pl. xviii. 7; Nos. 9–12, p. 79, Pl. xviii, 9. Antiochos IV in Egypt: p. 81. Ptolemy VIII: Nos. 6–12, p. 89, Pl. xxi. 3; Nos. 67–77, p. 93, Pl. xxii. 5. Ptolemy X: Nos. 48–56, p. 107, Pl. xxvi. 11.

The small Egyptianizing policy of the Ptolemies was only partially successful, and native rebellions continued to be frequent, if not as widespread as previously. Unfortunately we are not as well informed about the later cases as we are about the earlier ones, but a rapid résumé will suffice to show that Egyptians remained militantly hostile to the foreign kings. In 143 B.C. police operated against brigands in the Fayum. In 130 B.C. there was a revolt of the Greeks of Alexandria, which was accompanied by disorders in the countryside; in the far south the region around Hermonthis was in revolt. Eight years later there were disturbances in the Thinite nome, and a rebellion about this time at Panopolis. Part of the Fayum rose in 114 B.C. In 111 B.C. the Thebaïd became restive again. By 90 B.C. this area was in headlong and determined rebellion, so that two years later this ancient Egyptian capital was destroyed by royal forces. In Lower Egypt there were disturbances at intervals, in 79 and in 64. In 58 B.C. a state of warfare existed around Herakleopolis, the city from which the savior of the *Demotic Chronicle* was to come.[13]

This long-continued warfare sapped the strength of the Lagids. It was not due to chance that the outbreak of the great series of native wars and the more frequent recourse to *anachōrēsis*—flight—by Egyptian peasants coincided with the loss of their Syrian and Palestinian possessions by the Lagids, as well as their Aegean Empire. From the point of view of the patriotic Egyptians, the rebellions achieved a partial success, for they served to further the Egyptianization of the government and of the Greek people in Egypt.[14] It must be emphasized that such revolts and unrest in the Hellenistic period had no real parallel in the pre-Greek periods of Egyptian history, with the single exception of the era of Persian domination. In pharaonic times revolts against the native kings were all but unknown. There can be no question, then, that the revolts were directed against a specifically foreign government by the Egyptians acting from a belief in their theology of divine kingship.

While flight, riot, and guerilla warfare had a religious motivation, they also had an economic cause within the context of religion. There was undoubted oppression of the *fellahin* by the governing European class—behavior contrary to Ma'at—so that in Egypt, as in Palestine, class warfare played its part in arousing opposition to the Lagids.

---

[13] Documentation of these risings in E. R. Bevan, *op. cit.*; M. I. Rostovtzeff, *S.E.H.H.W.* ii. 874–7 and notes; and C. Préaux, "Esquisse . . . ," *CÉ* 22 (1936), 542–9.

[14] On the decline of Hellenism in second-century Egypt see H. I. Bell, "Hellenic Culture in Egypt," *JEA* 8 (1922), 139–58.

Almost all the Egyptian anti-Hellenic religious literature mentions economic hardship as a grievance against the foreigners, either declaring that the pharaohs of the great age had carefully looked after their subjects, or predicting that the coming savior would put food in the mouths of the people of suffering Egypt.[15]

Hardship was one result of the system of state capitalism begun by Ptolemy I Soter and developed by Ptolemy II Philadelphos. Much of their system was actually taken from pharaonic practice, but it was improved upon and made more efficient by application of Greek ideas of government, administration, and the scientific control of agriculture and exploitation of natural resources. Greek insistence on strict organization of production seems merely to have been added to a rather completely worked out native scheme of economic management, so that it was the efficiency of the system that threatened to make the life of the lower classes—both Greek and Egyptian—intolerable, and did make the Ptolemies seem in the eyes of the *fellahin* to be "Occidental Despots." While the peasants were actually used to hardship in the modern meaning of the word, they seem not to have been accustomed to the extraordinary demands Lagid administration could occasionally inflict upon them. This is not to say that the system was always intolerable and unbearable. During much of the third century it seems not to have been, and the prosperity of the country in general was shared by the masses to some degree. But the increasing demands of warfare in the second half of the third century, and the increasingly sharp practices of Egyptian-hating royal officials, those with a colonial mentality, sometimes transformed the system of the Ptolemies into an unbearable burden. Our papyrological evidence—strike notices—shows that it was against corruption of the officials rather than against the system itself that peasants most frequently rebelled.[16] This too

---

[15] Exploitation of the poor by the mighty was condemned in the *Protests of the Eloquent Peasant,* a Middle Kingdom text in *A.N.E.T.,* 407–10. From the same period came a remarkable coffin text which averred that all men were created equal, *ibid.,* 7–8. Under the XIXth Dynasty, the gods had been the refuge of the poor against the rich: *ibid.,* 380. *P. Insinger* maintains the tradition in the first century A.D.: "If something has just become your property, give part of it to God, that is, a part to the poor" (xvi. 4) ; "He who gives nourishment to a poor man, God receives him in his infinite mercy" (xvi. 16) .

The anti-Hellenic texts are the "Sesostris Legend" in Diod. i. 17. 1, 5–6, 8; the "Osiris Legend," *ibid.,* i. 56. 1–6; *Dem. Chron.* iv. 22–3; vi. 8–11, 17–21; *Oracle of the Potter: P. Rainer* i. 8–9; ii. 8–10; *P. Oxy.* i. 19–20; iii. 66–72.

[16] On the Hellenization of the Egyptian economy and the role of the peasant in it consult C. Préaux, *L'économie royale des Lagids* (1939) ; M. I. Rostovtzeff, "Foundations of Social and Economic Life in Hellenistic Egypt," *JEA* 6 (1920) , 161–78; *S.E.H.H.W.* i. 263–73; ii. 1071–2; W. L. Westermann, "The Greek Exploitation of

PLATE VII

Courtyard of the Temple of Horus at Edfou, built by the Ptolemaic government for the god and the goddess Hathor. It is the best-preserved temple in Egypt. The temple proper, behind the columns in the lower picture, was begun in the reign of Ptolemy III Euergetes I and finished by Ptolemy IV Philopator in 212 B.C., except for details of the carvings. The courtyard was not completed until 57 B.C. Thus, the building of the temple coincided with the great native risings at the end of the third century, and it may have been carried out to put the priests of Horus in a good humor at this critical time.

The two pictures are taken from approximately the same spot in the court, which measures about 150 by 120 feet. The picture at the top shows the inside of the entrance pylon, which originally must have been even more splendid than it is now. The figures of the gods were then painted, and probably stood out sharply from the massive walls. Horus, the hawk-headed god, is shown in the lower row wearing the double crown of Egypt, for his principal function as god was to rule the Two Lands of Egypt. Hathor, goddess of plenty and sustainer of life, is shown with her cow horns. Her attributes were rather similar to Isis'.

In the bottom picture is the entrance to the forecourt of the temple proper, which extends a long distance beyond that. The whole complex of courtyard, forecourt, and temple is immense, measuring about 425 by 135 feet. (The Parthenon is about 350 by 100 feet.) The doorway is flanked by statues of Horus as a hawk wearing the crown of Egypt. Royal iconography and symbols of divine rule are everywhere apparent in this building. Thus it shows the concern of the Ptolomies for native religion and the Egyptian priesthoods, and it also gives us an impression of the grandeur of Egyptian religious architecture, expressive of great strength and permanence. (Photograph supplied by the Hirmer Verlag, Munich.)

PLATE VII. EGYPTIAN ARCHITECTURE AND EGYPTIAN KINGSHIP

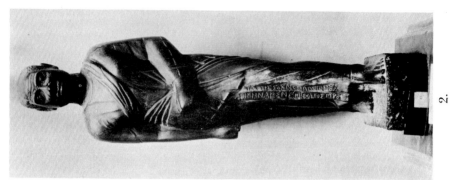

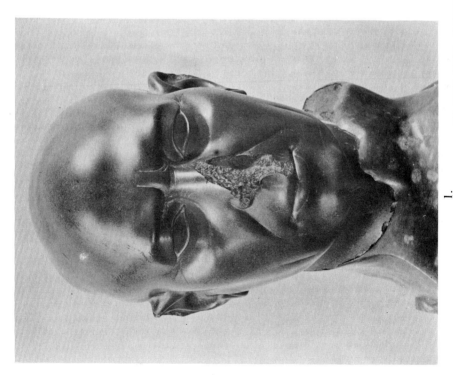

2.

1.

PLATE VIII. EGYPTIAN PRIESTS

PLATE VIII

1. Dark green basalt head of an Egyptian priest, probably from Memphis, of about 400–350 B.C. It is now in the Ehemals Staatliche Museen, Berlin (No. 12,500). This picture is intended to illustrate the strength and importance of the native Egyptian priesthoods, especially in the period before the reign of the Ptolemies. The priest is sculpted in traditional Egyptian style, and his character may be judged from the severity of the lines about the head: the firm mouth, the heavy nose, the slight frown and muscular look about the eyes, in short, the general air of forcefulness and decision. This head comes from the period during which the priesthoods intervened in the selection of the Pharaohs of the XXIXth Dynasty, as we know from the *Demotic Chronicle*. (Photograph supplied by the authorities of the Ehemals Staatliche Museen, Berlin.)

2. Black basalt statuette of the Priest Eirenaios, of the first century B.C. It is in the Musée Gréco-Romain, Alexandria (No. 3192). This figure shows the progress of Hellenism amongst the Egyptian clergy, some of whose members found it politically expedient to adopt a partly Hellenic way of life. The statuette shows mixed Greco-Egyptian styles. Eirenaios is posed in the native manner, his left foot stiffly forward, but his robe is nonetheless influenced by Greek ideas of drapery, and the votive inscription down the front of it is in Greek. The dedication is made to the great god Soknopaios, but the phrase is written only partly correctly in the dative and partly incorrectly in the genitive.

The expression on Eirenaios' face is nothing like that of the other priest; the former appears to be weak and self-indulgent, as no doubt many of the Greco-Egyptian clergy were. (Photograph supplied through the kindness of Dr. Henry Riad, Musée Gréco-Romain, Alexandria.)

would indicate that the Egyptians hated the foreignness of the administrators perhaps more than the administrative organization itself.

Greek occupation of Egypt was responsible for making rather profound changes in the old social structure, and this would have been regarded as an interruption of the normal order of things, a situation to be fought against. When the Greek city of Ptolemais was founded, for example, near the ancient capital of Thebes, the native town of Psoi was made away with to furnish the building site. The construction of Alexandria similarly compelled the moving of Egyptians from Kanobos and from the districts round about to form the working class of the new Greek capital. The Makedonians frankly ruled Egypt as "spear-won" territory, and felt that when necessity compelled them, they might undertake a rather total reorganization of some district for their own purposes.[17] The class on whom Greek rule fell hardest was the old secular aristocracy, for the Ptolemies broke up and destroyed the native Egyptian army. Between 312 B.C. and the campaign of Raphia no Egyptian was a first-line soldier. For the Ptolemies it was essential to maintain an efficient Greco-Makedonian force based on shock cavalry and a well-drilled, heavy-infantry phalanx. The Egyptians having no such military training or tradition were therefore useless. Consequently, in the third century only European personnel served in the Ptolemaic field army, and the old Egyptian military class became redundant. Even most of the policemen in the third century were Greeks, certainly in the higher grades; it was not until the second century that Egyptian police appeared in significant numbers. What happened to the old military aristocracy during this period we do not know exactly, but many families survived and retained some sort of standing, since in the second century Egyptians drawn from some such class appeared in the army and civil services. But absolute European control over the military and police functions in the third century gave the Greeks a monopoly on power and position. The Egyptian army in 343 B.C. is said to have numbered sixty thousand men, supported by

---

Egypt," *CW* 20 (1926), 3–6, 10–4; W. W. Tarn, "Ptolemy II," *JEA* 14 (1928), 246–59; *H.C.* (3rd ed., 1952), 177–209.

For the corruption of the bureaucracy and the effect of war: Polyb. xvi. 21. 1; *P. Teb.* 5; C. J. Kraemer, "Bureaucracy and Petty Graft in Ancient Egypt," *CW* 20 (1927), 163–8; M. I. Rostovtzeff, *S.E.H.H.W.,* i. 414; ii. 893–4, 912; W. W. Tarn, *H.C.* (3rd ed., 1952), 200–4.

17 For the foundation of these two cities see E. R. Bevan, *A History of Egypt* (1927), 8, 17, 97, 104–6; W. W. Tarn, *H.C.* (3rd ed., 1952), 178–9; and pp. 268–269, above.

Egyptian protest against Alexandria: *Oracle of the Potter: P. Rainer* ii. 2–5; *P. Oxy.* ii. 50–2, 59–60.

twenty thousand Libyans. Assuming that all these troops were commanded by Egyptians at the rate of one officer to a hundred men,
there would have been about a thousand Egyptian noblemen, used to
privilege and the enjoyment of it, great and distinguished men in
their country, who were forced to find some other outlet for their
energies. This was a serious matter, because for reasons known only
to God the military profession has always been deemed personally
honorable. It certainly had been in Egypt. It would be unreasonable
to deny, therefore, that the attitude of many native military aristocrats
was very hostile to the Greeks, and that it was translated into action
during the great revolts.[18]

Not only did the Hellenization of Egypt involve losses of rank and
privilege for Egyptians, it even created a profound cleavage between
them and the Makedonians and Greeks. People of Egyptian culture
were definitely second-class. The Makedonian military settlers enjoyed considerable freedom and an adequate income from the amount
of land allotted to them by their king. On the other hand, many of the
original inhabitants became peasants on state-owned land, and they
worked according to royal fiat for the benefit of the foreign king.
European settlers were permitted some choice in the crops the government wished him to grow, but the royal peasant none. Settlers paid
lighter taxes than Egyptians, in the case of wine a tenth instead of a
sixth of the crop. Greek and Makedonian settlers were often enabled
to work their land with *fellahin* labor arranged for by the state administration.[19]

The position of the Egyptian agricultural class was not enviable.
Peasants on royal land were registered in the local village and were
supposed to remain there, although they were not bound to the soil
like serfs. They did, therefore, occasionally move about. They paid a
rent, usually amounting to about fifty percent of a grain crop, for
cultivating ground belonging to Pharaoh Ptolemy. The royal quota
was a fixed weight, which was taken first at the annual threshing; in
case of a light yield owing to unfavorable weather or other conditions,
the cultivator had to bear the loss. The peasant also owed the state
numerous obligations. One of the most unpopular of these, one sub-

---

[18] Personnel in the Ptolemaic forces: Polyb. v. 65. 5–9; 79. 2–13; Diod. xix. 80. 4;
E. R. Bevan, *A History of Egypt* (1927), 163–6, 175; W. W. Tarn in *C.A.H.* vii. 729;
M. I. Rostovtzeff, *S.E.H.H.W.* i. 262–3.

Army of 343: Diod. xvi. 47. 6. Egyptian military honor: see the excerpts from the
autobiography of the officer Ahmose of el-Kab in *A.N.E.T.*, 233–4.

[19] Differences between European *klērouchoi* and Egyptian *laoi basilikoi* in M. I.
Rostovtzeff, *S.E.H.H.W.* i. 286, 327; W. W. Tarn, *H.C.* (3rd ed., 1952), 188.

ject to a great deal of abuse by government officials, was compulsory labor on irrigation canals or in the transport system. Another hated duty was service in the rural guard—particularly in demand in the second century—which involved the heavy and unhappy responsibility of preventing other peasants from escaping service by taking to flight. Egyptians tried hard to escape this burden.[20]

Consequently, the lot of the peasant was sometimes most unhappy. Not only did he have to work hard and long hours cultivating the ground, he had sometimes to go out on *corvée*. The *fellahin* also performed the most disagreeable and unpleasant work. It was they who were the porters, brickmakers, and swineherds, as Greeks almost never were, especially in the third century. And these unfortunate Egyptians were sometimes exploited by their landlords: the Egyptian Labois had to write to his, appealing for his salary. Another wrote: "I have nothing to wear and we are living in the open. Will you kindly, then, order them to give me four drachms that I may buy an old cloak." When officialdom was in league with the exploiter, *anachōrēsis* was the peasant's only remedy. When about 119 B.C. the village scribe Marres extorted money from the wives of some peasants at sword's point, the husbands deserted the village. No wonder the *Demotic Chronicle* and *Oracle of the Potter* promised good things to the suffering people.[21]

One outrightly inhuman institution of the state was the system of royal mines. Agatharchides has described the Nubian gold fields, which were worked with prisoners of war, slaves, and condemned criminals. Persons of both sexes and all ages were forced to work under appalling conditions by armed Nubian guards. They toiled in fetters, and were freely flogged. Agatharchides adds that when death finally came to them they welcomed it. Such working conditions, of course, hardly obtained throughout the whole Lagid economy. But life was hard in Ptolemaic Egypt. A study by M. Hombert and C. Préaux shows that the average life expectancy in Greek and Roman Egypt together was 23.18 years, whereas the average length of life in the ancient world as a whole was between 31 and 32 years.[22] This statistic does not necessarily mean that all Egyptian workmen were

[20] Obligations of peasants: M. I. Rostovtzeff, *S.E.H.H.W.* i. 275–9, 315–20; ii. 707–8; iii. 1382, n. 88; 1392, n. 117; W. W. Tarn, *H.C.* (3rd ed., 1952) , 187–91.

[21] On the status of Egyptian workingmen in the third century see A. Swiderek, "La société indigène en Égypte au iiie siècle avant notre ère d'après les archives de Zenon," *JJP* 7–8 (1953–4) , 231–84. Labois: *P. Mich. Zen.* 89; another: *P. Mich. Zen.* 90. Marres: *P. Teb.* 41.

[22] Agatharchides = Diod. iii. 12. 1–14. 5. M. Hombert and C. Préaux, "Note sur la durée de la vie dans l'Égypte gréco-romaine," *CÉ* 20 (1945) , 139–46.

overworked or undernourished, although it is certain that was occasionally true of some. It also means that infant mortality was high. But whatever the causes of the shortness of life, one must recall that the *Oracle of the Potter* laments the hunger and misery of the Egyptian countryside existing under the Ptolemies, and promises a paradisaical existence so pleasant when the new king comes, that people will wish the dead were alive again.

The Ptolemaic government was aware of the conditions that existed, particularly of the rapacious activities of the corrupt members of their bureaucracy, and they attempted to deal with them. Ptolemy VII Euergetes II tried hard to prevent dishonest and inhumane practices that had grown up by his day. The government always opposed the extension of slavery, and took strict measures against the enslavement of free persons of all kinds. Hence, there seems to have been little slavery in Egypt, only the king, his immediate officials, and the Egyptian clergy, be it noted, having slaves. In the three Greek cities in Egypt slavery existed, and some of the wealthiest Greeks in the countryside owned others. But in general, there was little slavery in either agriculture or industry in rural Egypt, a condition going back to the pharaonic age. W. L. Westermann has observed that this was one native institution which the Ptolemies were careful not to disturb. It is true that there were no protests against slavery in the anti-Hellenic literature. There was certainly no royal policy of wilful exploitation, and the kings tried to check it, but the government did have the Olympian attitude that it was competent and correct, and those who thought otherwise were wrong. This stultified efforts at reform. Towards the end of the third century, a *dioiketes* issued a set of instructions to a lesser official; it ended on the following note:

> Take care that no peculation or wrong takes place, for everyone resident in this country must clearly understand that all acts of this kind have been stopped and that they are freed from the bad conditions of the past, no one having a right to do what he likes, but everything being managed in the best way.

Such Jovian management sometimes worked not for the best but for the worst. An unpublished Zenon papyrus in the British Museum registers a complaint by peasants weary of blundering long-distance royal management of a plot of ground. They recommend that a native agricultural expert be put in charge of the project. Royal reform of officialdom did not always mitigate the system. The Egyptians therefore sometimes took affairs into their own hands, and in the course of native revolts burned up the archives which contained the records of taxes in arrears or obligations owed the state.[23]

In the field of industry there was close state regulation, peculation, and sometimes hardship. It should be noted, however, that the rules and unhappiness applied both to Greek and to Egyptian workingmen. This explains why the rebellions sometimes involved both nationalities simultaneously against the government. The work of artisans was restricted by royal monopolies. Private production of oil from plants was absolutely forbidden since it was the exclusive right of the king. Work of many other kinds was rigidly controlled.[24]

The new Greek management of Egypt included the use of coined money on a scale heretofore unknown. There were occasional drastic inflation and loss of revenue to the government, and therefore increased demands by the officials on the native classes of Egypt. This was one more burden the peasant had to bear as the result of new means of state administration and management.[25]

This picture of the Ptolemaic royal economy affords ample evidence that the system of state capitalism was one of the causes of the religious revolt of the Egyptians. Traditionally, Egyptian culture had insisted that public affairs be conducted humanely, or, rather, within the Egyptian conception of social justice. But the Ptolemaic exploitation of Egypt was sometimes carried out with scant regard for Egyptian principles; it was much more oriented towards meeting royal demands for production so that the dynasty could maintain itself in the competitive state system of the third and second centuries B.C. The economic exploitation of an inferior social class aroused the hatred of the Egyptians, and naturally led them to long for the destruction of the Greeks and the establishment of a native kingship.

There was another cause of religious resistance, and that was occasional disrespect for Egyptian religious foundations. This was a most serious matter, for the Egyptians' respect for their religious institu-

[23] Ptolemaic concern for harsh conditions explained by W. L. Westermann, "The Ptolemies and the Welfare of Their Subjects," *AHR* 43 (1938), 270–87. Decree of Ptolemy VII: *P. Teb.* 5. The quotation in the text from *P. Teb.* 703, ll. 222–32 (trans. A. S. Hunt and J. G. Smyly). On slavery see M. I. Rostovtzeff, *S.E.H.H.W.* i. 321–2; ii. 1262; iii. 1365; W. L. Westermann, *The Slave Systems of Greek and Roman Antiquity* (1955), 46–57. For the complaint of the peasants see H. I. Bell, *Egypt from Alexander to the Arab Conquest* (1948), 46, 138, n. 19. Burning records: P. Jouguet, *L'Égypte ptolémaïque* (1933), iii. 186; M. I. Rostovtzeff, *op. cit.,* i. 412–3.

[24] C. Préaux, "Restrictions de la liberté du travail dans l'Égypte grecque et romaine," *CÉ* 18 (1934), 338–45; M. I. Rostovtzeff, *S.E.H.H.W.* i. 304.

[25] For Ptolemaic fiscal operations see W. L. Westermann, "The Greek Exploitation of Egypt," *CW* 20 (1926), 3–6; 10–4; H. I. Bell, *Egypt from Alexander to the Arab Conquest* (1948), 59; W. W. Tarn, *H.C.* (3rd ed., 1952), 203–4.

tions was profound, as was keenly felt by some Greek and Roman visitors. Diodoros noted that every group of people in Egypt was at odds with its neighbor over some point in the observance of ritual or dietary restrictions.[26] What a Greek would consider trivial or ludicrous in Egyptian religion could be a thing of great importance in Egyptian eyes. Furthermore, Egyptian religion was not everywhere the same— doctrines and beliefs varied from place to place. How a Greek could unwittingly offend Egyptian religion may be illustrated by the following case. In the Fayum and around Thebes crocodiles were venerated as the sacred and inviolable manifestations of the god Sobkh. On the other hand, they were hunted and eaten like any animal by Egyptians at Syene. The satrap Kleomenes once went boating in the neighborhood of Krokodilopolis, and when one of the beasts carried off a slave of Kleomenes, the satrap organized a crocodile hunt. The nearby priests of Sobkh implored him to cancel it, and gave him what gold they had. From the point of view of the priests this was extortion compounded with atheism. From the point of view of the Greeks it might all have been a dreadful mistake. Cases of unknowing transgression of local religious rules did exist in Egypt, just as they exist in our modern Western history of imperialism. Of course there must have been deliberate cases too. What does one do if one is determined to show the king a profit, and the sacred crocodiles carry off one's pigs, as they sometimes did?[27]

There were enough differences in Greek and Egyptian religious customs to constitute a source of considerable animosity. Egyptian use of statues in certain rites differed somewhat from Greek techniques. Egyptian styles of temple architecture varied considerably from Greek. The creation of the god Sarapis, who resembled the old Egyptian deity Osiris-Hapi, excited the hatred of the Egyptians, and they totally rejected the new cult. Egyptians insisted on inhumation after mummification—Greeks sometimes cremated. The Egyptians were horrified by Greeks' exposure of infants and called it a crime against the gods.[28]

Greek religious sin was referred to in the Egyptian propaganda.

[26] Diod. i. 89. 6; 83. 8–9. Herodotos (ii. 18) had noted the same thing in the fifth century. Tacitus (*Hist.* i. 11) later observed that the superstitions of the Egyptians were a source of trouble to the Roman government. See, too, A. D. Nock, *Conversion* (1933), 293.

[27] Status of crocodiles: Herod. ii. 69; Diod. i. 35. 6. Kleomenes' hunt: (Ps.-) Aristot. *Economica* ii. 2. 33. Pigs and crocodiles: *P. Cairo Zen.* 59379.

[28] Differences between Greek and Egyptian cultic custom in E. Kiessling, "La genèse du culte de Sarapis à Alexandrie," *CÉ* 48 (1949), 317–23. Burial customs: A. D. Nock, "Cremation and Burial in the Roman Empire," *HTR* 25 (1932), 321–59. Infant exposure: Diod. i. 80. 3.

There may be a reference to the cult of Sarapis in the *Oracle of the Potter,* wherein the return of holy things removed from Memphis and taken to Alexandria is prophesied; this may mean that the cult of Osiris-Hapi has been illegally carried off to an infidel city. There is also a remark in the Oxyrhynchus version about a strange image made in Alexandria. This might refer to the cult of Sarapis or of the deified Ptolemies, or of the deified Alexander. Certainly some religious event the Egyptians hated happened at Alexandria. There is also the curious notice in Pseudo-Kallisthenes that when the city was being built a serpent appeared and Alexander killed it. The Greeks built a sacred enclosure on the spot, buried the snake in it, and worshipped it as Agathos Daimon.

I confess that I do not know exactly what to make of this late story. It could be simply Greek, for the snake was an important religious symbol to them, more important, perhaps, than to the Egyptians. On the other hand, Agathos Daimon was identified with the Egyptian god of good luck, Sai, and the story can be interpreted to make Alexander out a killer. Did the foundation of Alexandria and the introduction of Sarapis' cult here overshadow Sai and his consort Ernutet in such a way that the Egyptians claimed they had been killed? Ptolemy I was certainly at pains to show that snakes loved and protected Alexander. He says that during the king's march to Siwah the army was guided by two snakes who uttered human speech. This is absolutely unique among Greek accounts of this affair, for the other writers said that the army had been escorted by ravens. There is the general accusation by the Potter that the Greeks were irreligious in his eyes, that they were Typhonians. Typhon was Seth to the Egyptians, and Seth killed Osiris. Since Osiris was the god of everlasting life, and since the Greeks thought snakes were immortal, the snake in Pseudo-Kallisthenes might stand for Osiris-Hapi, who was "killed" when made over into Sarapis. These details are all most unclear. All that is certain is that the Greeks were said to have interfered with the holy rites of Egypt.

This same charge was hinted at by the "Sesostris Legend" and the "Osiris Legend," which stressed the pious attitudes of their heroes towards the temples of Egypt. This can probably be taken to refer to the lack of Ptolemaic respect for the Egyptian temples, at least in the sense that the Egyptians responsible for the legends considered the Ptolemies guilty of a lack of respect and generosity. In the third century revenues were diverted from the old gods to the new Makedonian goddess, the deified Arsinoe. Ammon at Karnak did not have his temple restored by Ptolemy III when this king was rebuilding the temple at Philai. Ammon at Siwah was similarly neglected. Strabo says that by the end of the first century B.C. the shrine there was almost abandoned.[29]

Along with un-Egyptian religious practice, the Makedonians and Greeks brought their own concepts of law to Egypt. It is hard to imagine how its use could not have excited Egyptian feelings. There was a tendency for Greek judges to replace native judges, and it is certain that the use of Greek law in the country in time partly supplanted Egyptian law. There were instances, however, of Egyptian concepts influencing Greek usage. Diodoros says that the Egyptians had great zeal for the maintenance of native law since they regarded it as the foundation of their social organization,[30] by which he meant that the most patriotic Egyptians hated to have native customs supplanted, since this process would destroy the old society. Thus the anti-Hellenic literature and the rebellions of the Egyptians were attempts to prevent the establishment of a new order of society in Egypt. The representatives of the new order, the Greeks, enjoyed rights and privileges which were barred to non-Hellenized Egyptians, and many natives became Hellenized in order to share in the privileges of the ruling caste. It was another case of cultural conflict, and since Egyptian culture was thought of in religious terms, as a part of the whole cosmos of gods and men, the response to the challenge of Hellenism was expressed in religious terms. The conservative Egyptian fought to preserve his own way of life much as the Persian and Jew had fought.

There resulted deep animosity between Greeks and Egyptians, a profound hatred. The conflict was not one of race, but one of culture. It was fought by persons with divergent views of life and differing cosmologies, and was made much more fierce by the fact that the antagonists occupied opposite positions in the social order. Egyptian society was dominated by Hellenes and Hellenized Egyptians, who held the high posts in government, had a monopoly over the army

[29] *Oracle of the Potter: P. Rainer* ii. 3–4; *P. Oxy.* i. 32–3. (Ps.-) Kall. i. 32. 6–7. Identification of Agathos Daimon and Sai: W. W. Tarn, "The Hellenistic Ruler Cult and the Daemon," *JHS* 48 (1928), 218. Snakes: Ptol. = Arr. *Anab.* iii. 3. 5; ravens: Kallisthenes = Strabo xvii. 1. 43 (814); Aristoboulos = Arr. *Anab.* iii. 3. 6. Arrian says this was the majority opinion. Arsinoe: *P. Revenue Laws*, xxxvi. Ammon: Strabo xvii. 1. 43 (813–4).

[30] Diod. i. 75. 1–2. For developments in legal affairs see R. Taubenschlag, *The Law of Greco-Roman Egypt in the Light of the Papyri* (2nd ed., 1955), especially the historical summary in pp. 1–55 and the extensive literature cited in the footnotes.

and navy, lived in the most pleasant and productive parts of the country, and generally set the standard of life socially, economically, politically, and religiously. In the third century there was a nearly complete
lack of integration of Greeks and Egyptians in Egypt, although thereafter gradual mixing occurred. But on the whole Greeks dominated
Egypt, and they sometimes took shocking advantage of the indigenous
people. The Greek dastard Nikias appropriated a she-ass belonging to
the Egyptian widow Senchons. The rather well-to-do hundred-arourai-
holder Ptolemaios set upon the peasant Pnepheros for some reason,
and during the struggle one of the farmer's cows was eaten by a
crocodile. Stratonike seized the house of Petesouchos in Oxyrhynchia.
Pyrrhichos with an armed gang of toughs raided peasants' houses
around Tebtunis looking for plunder. Lykos dammed up a royal irrigation ditch and peasant Pasis had his water cut off. In the courts
Egyptian witnesses were intimidated by a Greek, and prevented from
giving testimony in favor of an Egyptian woman. In 141 B.C. a royal
peasant made formal complaint that he had been tortured. There
were other cases of illegal torture of Egyptians held in prison. In a
Temple of Anubis Greeks highhandedly installed a government police
station and attached a jail to it, as well as quarters for a representative
of the governor of Memphite nome. An Egyptian with Hellenic status
complained that he had been insulted by Greeks of the blood. One
native—perhaps he was an Arab—protested to a Greek official that
Greeks looked down on him because he was non-Hellenic. He asked
the Greek to order them to pay him what was owed, so that he would
not starve to death "because I do not know how to act the Hellene."
After all, Greeks frequently referred to non-Hellenes as *egchōrioi*, a
word approximately equivalent to the modern English "native."[31] In

---

[31] On the matter of Greek status in general see W. L. Westermann, "The Ptolemies
and the Welfare of Their Subjects," *AHR* 43 (1938), 270–87; C. Préaux, "Politique
du race ou politique royale?" *CÉ* 21 (1936), 111–38.

Senchons: *P. Mich. Zen.* 29 (256 B.C.). Pnepheros: *P. Teb.* 793 (183 B.C.). Petesouchos: *P. Teb.* 771 (*c.* 150 B.C.). Tebtunis peasants: *P. Teb.* 45–7 (113 B.C.). Pasis:
P. Teb. 50 (*c.* 113 B.C.). Intimidated witnesses: *P. Enteuxeis* 86. Resignation was always a possible response to such injustice: *P. Insinger* (xxiii. 14) says that violent
people always go to an unhappy death. The tortured Egyptian: *P. Teb.* 78; *P.
Insinger:* "Time passed in misery does not disturb the man of God" (xxi. 2). The
Temple of Anubis from E. R. Bevan, *A History of Egypt* (1927), 41; this was very
serious: *P. Insinger* (xxiii. 10) says that when a temple is without calm the gods
abandon it. The insulted Hellenic Egyptian: *P. Enteuxeis* 79.

The ignorant Egyptian (or Arab): *P. Col. Zen.* ii. 66. Greek contempt for Egyptians also expressed in Theokritos xv. 50. The attitude scarcely died out, as shown by
third century A.D. *P. Oxy.* 1681.

this environment some Egyptians went Hellenic if they could to escape.[32]

This state of affairs does not seem to have been due to a conscious policy of the Lagids; rather, there were many Europeans in Egypt, completely undistinguished common people, who felt nothing but contempt for the hard-working peasants. It was they who created this attitude in much the same way as their modern opposite numbers in areas of Western imperialism have made Africans and Asiatics bear the weight of the White Man's Burden. No doubt the image of Egypt which the Greeks had was brought with them as immigrants, and popular notions such as were expressed by the comic poets of the fourth century had a good deal to do with making many petty tyrants. The Egyptian sometimes reacted violently and revengefully. Ptolemaios, a Makedonian worshipping in the Memphite Sarapeon, was attacked in 163 B.C. by Egyptian priests for the sole reason that he was a European.[33] Modern Harlem and ancient Egypt! The Lagids made little effort, however, except possibly in the case of the disastrous Sarapis cult, to bring about a fusion of Greeks and Egyptians. The Greek cities, Alexandria, Naukratis, and Ptolemais, even banned intermarriage. Mixed marriages did take place, however, although they occurred only in the countryside, and only from about the middle of the third century onward.[34]

Thus the reasons for conflict were numerous and deep, and involved all parts of Egyptian society. The actual warfare that sometimes existed shows that hostility was to be found in all parts of the country and in all ranks of society. While all classes had a hand in it, no single class of Egyptians was entirely responsible for it.

The priesthoods of Egypt had something to do with organizing and leading the resistance, in both its literary and militant aspects. Only some sort of unity of plan, determination, and organization made possible the sudden, widespread outbreaks in 217 and 163 B.C. The subsequent conciliation of the priesthoods by the government probably indicates that some members of the clergy, which did have ready-made unity of doctrine and of organization, took part in the resistance. The clergy lost a good deal through the Greek occupation. The clerical ideal, not only in the Pharaonic past but still

[32] On conversion to Hellenism see P. Jouguet, *L'Égypte ptolémaïque* (1933), iii. 173–5.

[33] Ptolemaios: *U.P.Z.* 7.

[34] On intermarriage and regulation thereof: M. I. Rostovtzeff, *S.E.H.H.W.* ii. 883–4, 1072, 1088–94; S. Davis, *Race Relations in Ancient Egypt* (1951), *passim*.

in the Hellenistic period, was to cooperate closely with the dynasty on an almost equal footing. But this they were not allowed to do. Attempts of the Lagids to change or modify Egyptian religion in any way without consulting the priesthoods and cooperating with them must have fed the hatred of the clergy.[35]

The Europeans certainly did not always conform to the Egyptian ideal, as the examples of Kleomenes and the Sarapis cult show. But at the same time the Ptolemies did make some effort to cooperate with the clerical *ancien régime*. Most temples remained rather wealthy throughout the period, and although temple land was taxed by the government, the establishments remained essentially autonomous and in control of their own land. In some cases the Ptolemies diverted old temple revenues to new state cults, as happened in the Arsinoïte nome. Such acts would explain why Strabo found a few of the old temples in poor condition at the end of the first century. At Heliopolis, for example, he visited large shrines and the houses where the priests had formerly lived, but the personnel themselves had disappeared. On the whole, however, what neglect there was was not great. Probably the economic decline of old Egyptian commercial centers like Memphis and Thebes was a more important reason for this than royal religious policy.[36] But for whatever reason decline took place, the priesthood would blame and hate the royal government, whose responsibility they said it was to nourish and protect the shrines of the gods.

The temples were the principal repositories of the Egyptian civilization, and the priesthoods seem in the Greek period to have been the spokesmen for it. It was they who explained the history and customs of the country to men like Herodotos, Plato, Diodoros, and Strabo. The priesthoods were often held by hereditary right in aristocratic families, so that they had memories of past greatness. These persons had a common tradition of ideology and leadership necessary for undertaking resistance. They had also an impressive hierarchical organization. Within each temple priests held grades of rank, and in the country as a whole, certain temples outranked and

[35] For pre-Hellenistic relationship of king and priest see J. A. Wilson, *The Burden of Egypt* (1951), especially pages 88–9, 175, 184–6, 206–35, 288; *Dem. Chron.* iii. 18—iv. 18. For the Hellenistic period: Diod. i. 73. 2–3; Strabo xvii. 1. 3–5 (787–90).

[36] The status of Egyptian temples under the Ptolemies in W. Otto, *Priester und Tempel im hellenischtischen Ägypten* (1908), i. 262–399; E. R. Bevan, *A History of Egypt* (1927), 183–5; M. I. Rostovtzeff, *S.E.H.H.W.* i. 281–2. In the Arsinoïte nome old priestly revenues were diverted to the state's cult of the deified Arsinoe: *P. Revenue Laws*, col. xxxvi. Heliopolis: Strabo xvii. 1. 27–9 (805–6); Memphis: *ibid.*, xvii. 1. 32 (808).

had greater prestige than others. Synods of priests drawn from all Egypt met periodically, although under royal auspices. There was, therefore, undoubtedly the possibility at least of the temple organizations forming the framework for national resistance. Furthermore, these temples commanded the allegiance of Egyptian *machimoi;* about 120 B.C. numbers of Egyptian soldiers holding only seven-arourai plots dedicated an area of 130 arourai to the "great, great god Soknebtunis" at Tebtunis.[37] While there is no direct evidence that the synods did function as breeding grounds for conspiracies to rebel, it is possible to imagine the clergy of Egypt brought together from all over the Nile valley making plans to revolt, returning to their districts with a set scheme, and then putting it into effect among the *machimoi* more or less simultaneously everywhere.

The only evidence of clerical participation is indirect. Presumably the Sesostris and Osiris legends and the prophecies had priestly authors, for priests knew the traditions. Whoever worked out the attacks on Greek gods, poets, and philosophers were educated men, and therefore probably priests. Aelian says the priests of Sobkh prophesied the death of a king, probably Ptolemy IV. It is just possible that the *Demotic Chronicle* was written by the priesthood of Harsaphes at Herakleopolis, for it mentions this god and a man of Herakleopolis who were to save Egypt. This city had once furnished dynasties in Lower Egypt—the IXth and Xth (2150–2050 B.C.). This memory was still green and growing in the Hellenistic period, for Manethon reported that these dynasties had once ruled all Egypt. It is also possible that clergy at Memphis were implicated in the Egyptian opposition. The *Oracle of the Potter* specifically mentions a grievance of Memphis: Alexandria had gained ground at her expense. The papyrus with the *Demotic Chronicle* written on it is said to have come from this city; Memphis is also connected with the prophecy of the return of Nektanebo. If this old Egyptian capital had been implicated, this might explain the decline of her temples as Ptolemaic reprisals.[38]

---

[37] The priestly families are discussed by C. Préaux in "Les Égyptiens dans la civilisation hellénistique," *CÉ* 35 (1943), 148–60; W. Otto, *Priester und Tempel im hellenischtischen Ägypten* (1908), i. 200–2; E. R. Bevan, *A History of Egypt* (1927), 177–9; H. I. Bell, *Egypt from Alexander to the Arab Conquest* (1948), 37–8.

Hierarchical organization in W. Otto, *op. cit.,* i. 23–43; M. I. Rostovtzeff in *C.A.H.* vii. 149; *P. Merton Dem.* 1; S. R. K. Glanville, "The Admission of a Priest of Soknebtynis in the Second Century B.C.," *JEA* 19 (1933), 34–41. Soknebtunis: *P. Teb.* 60. But see the comments of the editors, *The Tebtunis Papyri* (1902), i. 543, 552–3.

[38] Sobkh: Aelianus, *Char. An.,* viii. 4. Herakleopolis: The real history of the IXth and Xth Dynasties in J. A. Wilson, *The Burden of Egypt* (1951), 105–7; the Hellen-

The god Khnum of Elephantine may very well have taken part, and his clergy may have been responsible for writing the *Oracle of the Potter*. Khnum's chief temple was here, and it was in a region that was certainly in the hands of rebels or Nubians during the great revolt of 217–185 B.C. According to *Papyrus Dodgson*, Khnum about 150 B.C. was concerned with the integrity of Egyptian religion. The priests of Khnum seem also to have had some sort of title-deed grievance against the Ptolemies or to have tried to extort land from the Ptolemies; in either case their hostility to the regime is indicated. The evidence of this is an inscription carved on a large rock on the island of Siheil near the First Cataract. It purports to memorialize a grant of fertile territory along both banks of the Nile given to the priests of Khnum by Pharaoh Djoser of the IIIrd Dynasty (2700–2650 B.C.). The inscription actually was cut, however, only in the second century and it was almost certainly a forgery. Was it done to establish a case for their occupying the territory mentioned? The text also says that the land was given by Djoser after Khnum had brought to an end a famine of seven long years. Famine was a complaint prominently mentioned in the Potter's oracle. As for the Potter himself, he may have been understood to represent Khnum, for this god was the one who created mankind by turning out a mannikin on his potter's wheel. Hence, the *Oracle* might be saying that the Creator Khnum is still concerned that his creations have full stomachs, and the rock inscription would be other evidence of the god's solicitude for them. The latter document certainly awards the god's town of Elephantine an important place in the world: "It is the Beginning of the Beginning, the Beginning Nome . . . the Primeval Hillock of Earth, the Throne of Re." This sort of consciousness was a part of resistance almost everywhere, the Persians of Persepolis, the Jews of Jerusalem, the Babylonians of Babylon all feeling that their particular place was the capital of the world. If Elephantine was deemed the throne of Re, and if Re sent the king promised by the Potter to come and relieve famine, might this not connect the authors of the text with Khnum of Elephantine? Furthermore, Khnum here was ram-headed, and the *Oracle* generally resembles a later Egyptian apocalypse written in the reign of Augustus, which a lamb allegedly delivered in the reign

istic interpretation in Manethon, frag. 27–9 (Waddell). On Harsaphes and the man of Herakleopolis, see *Dem. Chron.* ii. 24–5.

Memphis: *Oracle of the Potter: P. Rainer* ii. 3; provenance of *Demotic Chronicle:* n. 60, p. 291, above; Nektanebo: n. 52, p. 285, above. Decline: Strabo xvii. 1. 32 (808).

of Pharaoh Bokchoris. Rams were also connected with the idea of rule, for the god of Mendes was a ram and Mendes had been the capital of the XXIXth Dynasty. It seems at that time to have made common cause with Khnum of Elephantine, because when Amyrtaios was rebelling against Persia, the priests of Khnum helped to attack the Jewish mercenaries hired by the Great King.[39] Interesting as this circumstantial evidence may be, I do not find it decisive, and the question of Khnum's implication had best be left open. It is half probable, but not proved.

It is also possible to make a very slight case that Heliopolis was responsible for the *Oracle of the Potter*. It predicts that Re will send a king; Heliopolis was the chief seat of Re's worship, a place with a tradition of meddling with rulership in Egypt.[40]

What role the priests of Ammon-Re at Thebes played is impossible to say in the absence of direct evidence. They had, of course, been quite important historically, and may have been influential at the time of the troubles in the Thebaïd in 208/7 B.C. The destruction of Thebes by royal forces in 88 B.C. may be significant along these lines.[41]

But all this is inconclusive. While there is enough indirect evidence to establish a case in favor of clerical participation in the resistance, the exact role the priests played, and what priests played it, is impossible to determine. Many must have cooperated with Alexandria, or at least have remained neutral, for the Ptolemies cooperated with the clergy to the extent of building temples in honor of the gods and of endowing them. They also made grants of sanctity and inviolability, and made some of the temples *asylia*. Following older tradition, they invested Egyptian priests themselves, and they gave them sums of money in the style of the ancient pharaohs. Ptolemy I loaned fifty talents to bury an Apis Bull; Ptolemy II gave the equivalent of

[39] Rock inscription: date: J. A. Wilson in *A.N.E.T.*, 31; É. Drioton and J. Vandier, *L'Égypte* (3rd ed., 1952), 168–9; W. F. Albright, *From the Stone Age to Christianity* (Anchor ed., 1957), 78. J. A. Wilson translates the text in *A.N.E.T.*, 31–2, and he and Drioton and Vandier briefly discuss the possibilities of forgery, *loc. cit.* The quotation is line 18.

A potter as author of the *Oracle of the Potter: P. Rainer,* colophon. Mendes, its connection with Elephantine, and Khnum's hatred of the Jews discussed by E. G. Kraeling, *The Brooklyn Museum Aramaic Papyri* (1953), 102–8, 113, 283. Bokchoris: C. C. McCown, "Egyptian Apocalyptic Literature," *HTR* 18 (1925), 357–411.

[40] Heliopolis: J. A. Wilson, *The Burden of Egypt* (1951), 88, 185, 208–9, 222–3, 228, 270.

[41] Thebes: 208/7 B.C.: see n. 5, p. 299, above. For subsequent history and remarks in general: A. Bataille, "Thèbes, gréco-romaine," *CÉ* 52 (1951), 325–53.

three thousand talents outright to the temples.[42] It was, therefore, rather to the advantage of the temples to collaborate with the Lagids, particularly since the priests were dependent on the regime for their rights, privileges, and incomes.

There was a large amount of support for the government. The prima facie evidence of the trilingual Pithon Decree, written in traditional Egyptian style by one of the synods of clergy on the eve of the great revolt of 217 B.C., is that the clergy were loyal to the government. It celebrated the mighty Pharaoh Ptolemy IV for his victory over Antiochos III. Philopator on his part stated his concern for the well-being of the temples, and awarded them new income. On another occasion the clergy of Ammon in the Fayum publicly declared its loyalty in a papyrus. The Rosetta Decree of 196 B.C., a document written after the rising of 217 had become war and the Nubians had entered the Thebaïd, was much more oriented towards royal praise of the priesthoods and guarantees of their rights than earlier decrees. Ptolemy V says how well disposed towards the native gods he is, how he has dedicated new revenues to the temples and remitted or lightened their taxes. On the other hand his statue was to be prominently displayed in each temple. He promises to defend the temples against rebels. It is noteworthy that this synod met at Egyptian Memphis and not at Greek Kanobos, as had happened earlier. This, like Ptolemy V's coronation at Memphis, was indicative of a new royal orientation towards the Egyptian temples, but also of the willingness of the priests to cooperate in return.[43]

The Ptolemies and many priests actually drew close together. Continuing grants of property to the temples and, after 118 B.C., a grant of immunity from most forms of taxation greatly increased their wealth, and therefore their stake in the continuity of the royal government. This wealth attracted temple robbers, so that the temples had to depend on the king for protection. This growing together of altar and throne was part, of course, of the larger blending of Egyptian and Greek all along the line. In the political sphere Egyptian Paos was both "Kinsman" of the king and general in the Thebaïd, where he suppressed a native revolt in 131/30 B.C.[44]

[42] Diod. i. 84. 1; E. R. Bevan, *A History of Egypt* (1927), 183–5; W. W. Tarn, *H.C.* (3rd ed., 1952), 201, 206–7.

[43] Pithon stele: E. R. Bevan, *A History of Egypt* (1927), 388–92; C. Préaux, "Esquisse . . . ," *CÉ* 22 (1936), 527–8. Ammon clergy: *P. Teb.* 781. Rosetta Decree: *O.G.I.S.* 90.

[44] Grants to temples: *P. Teb.* 5, lines 57–82; E. R. Bevan, *A History of Egypt* (1927), 182–6; M. I. Rostovtzeff, *S.E.H.H.W.* i. 265–6; ii. 884–5. Paos: *P. Louvre* 10595.

There was one excellent reason for the priesthoods to collaborate, because their temples were sometimes attacked during the disorders of the second century. Some Egyptian peasants put them in the same category, apparently, as Greek police stations or the state oil factories which they liked to rob. In 164 B.C., for example, a shrine in the Ammon Temple at Moeris was plundered for the building materials in it. About the same time an Egyptian priest was killed by brigands in the Arsinoïte nome. A little later persons in the village of Oxyrhynchos extorted money from the clergy of Arsinoe. Ptolemy VII was compelled to decree again the inviolability of the temples, but nonetheless raids continued to be made against them on into the first century.[45]

Numbers of the clergy must have become pro-Ptolemaic because of such acts, particularly during the period after 164 B.C. The increasing wealth of the temples derived in large part from the labor of their own peasants, who were as badly off as the royal peasants, so that some priests seemed to be oppressors too. Perhaps the growing division within the ranks of the Egyptians themselves explains why almost all of the anti-Hellenic literature we have noted was written in the first century and a half of Greek rule. The Egyptian upper class was becoming Hellenized, and the priesthoods began to include Greeks. In the reign of Ptolemy VI, Herodes, a native of Pergamon, held the priestly rank of Prophet of Khnum. There had always been priests willing to get along with the Greek regime, and even in the reign of Ptolemy I the priest Petosiris of Hermopolis, he who received a gold ring from the king, constructed a tomb for himself in eclectic Greco-Egyptian style. Manethon was another example, and so was the Egyptian Apollonios, who led the worship of Sarapis on the Greek island of Delos; these latter two men were active as early as 275 B.C. In the first century B.C. Pshereni-Ptah, high priest of Ptah at Memphis, left behind a sepulchral inscription boasting of his greatness, his wealth, his harem, all won by loyal service to the government. Egyptian law, incidentally, forbade the clergy to practice polygamy. His favorite wife Taim-hotep recorded similar sentiments, glad to recall that she was personally known to Ptolemy XI. Statues of other priests of this period show some dressed in Egyptian clothes,

---

[45] Attacks on temples: C. Préaux, "Esquisse . . . ," *CÉ* 22 (1936), 529–30, 545, 549; T. A. Brady, *The Reception of the Egyptian Cults by the Greeks* (1935), 37–40: M. I. Rostovtzeff, *S.E.H.H.W.*, ii. 724, 901–2.
   Thefts from oil factories: *P. Teb.* 703, ll. 140–1. Moeris: *P. Teb.* 781. Slain priest: *P. Amherst* 30. Extortion: *P. Teb.* 790. Decrees: *P. Teb.* 5 and 6.

some in Greek clothes. Many such persons at that time had their tomb inscriptions written in Greek.[46]

Summing up all this evidence, it would appear that there were both loyal and disloyal members of the priesthoods. Since we have so very little, however, we are forced to take refuge in broad generalizations. It would seem, then, that the elite of the clergy, socially and economically speaking, tended to support the Ptolemies, whereas the lower ranks tended to support the peasants and their leaders in the rebellions. We are reminded of the similar attitudes of the French priests on the eve of the Revolution in 1789. After all, the high priests of Egypt had much to lose by attacking the government. The lower ranks of the clergy, on the other hand, while they had something to lose, also had a good deal to gain. Perhaps the best evidence that the clergy as an organization were involved in the revolutions in Egypt is that the Romans in 30 B.C. took steps to control them and to bring them under continuing close surveillance. They rigorously diminished the number of asylum rights granted, and ended the synods.[47]

Thus it would appear from this survey of the social classes in Egypt that the anti-Hellenic movement was recruited by certain priests and by remnants of the old military aristocracy, from part of the Egyptian laboring class. The movement in time also was paralleled by Greek hostility, for some Hellenes came to hate Alexandria and its regime almost as much as the natives did. There was a strong flavor of class war in all this, as the literature, the strikes, the flight of peasants, and the rebellions show. Of course loyalty to the regime was also to be found in all these social classes.

The Egyptian religious reaction sought more to rally its own people than to recruit foreigners, as Hebrew missionaries had done. There is no evidence of conscious proselytizing of Greeks by the Egyptian clergy. Greeks did become devotees of the native gods, but this seems to have been due to a natural process—adoption by people of the locally established gods, or as the result of intermarriage —than to a program of purposeful conversion. We have obvious propaganda produced only for the cults of Sarapis and Isis. These two gods were successfully established in Roman Italy before the end of

[46] Pro-Ptolemaic attitudes of the clergy in general in M. I. Rostovtzeff, *S.E.H.H.W.* ii. 886–7. Apollonios: *I.G.* xi. 4. 1299. Herodes, Petosiris, and Pshereni-Ptah: E. R. Bevan, *A History of Egypt* (1927), 81, 294–5, 347–9. Taim-hotep: E. Otto, *Die biographischen Inschriften der ägyptischen Spätzeit* (1954), No. 57, pp. 190–4. Ban on polygamy: Diod. i. 80. 3. Statues of priests: M. I. Rostovtzeff, *op. cit.*, Pl. C, 1, 3.

[47] V. Chapot, *L'Égypte romaine* (1933), iii. 339–40.

the first century B.C. Their propaganda was disseminated by means of inspiring religious processions and other ceremonies, and also by speakers and by books extolling the healing miracles of these gods who alleviated the miseries of long-suffering humanity.[48]

These two cults were not, however, really manifestations of the Egyptian spirit. Their personnel was mostly Greek. The Isis cult spread to Greece, brought not only by Egyptian priests, who were its ritual specialists, but also by retired European mercenaries and merchants. In the third century Greek clergy actually predominated outside of Egypt, and only in the Christian era did Egyptian priests become important numerically. What little we know of the ceremony and other aspects of these two worships shows that while they were built on an Egyptian foundation, this was much overbuilt with an Hellenic veneer, so that the deities were really Greco-Egyptian.[49]

The worshippers of Isis included both Greeks and Egyptians. Her devotees often formed a cult society, and normally it was organized, even in Egypt, along Greek lines. These were not priestly associations, but rather fellowships of persons drawn from some common profession for the worship not only of Isis but sometimes of some other god. These included Greek as well as Egyptian gods, and sometimes the king. The societies therefore were Greco-Egyptian.[50]

The mixing inside these religious gilds was symptomatic of the growth of a half-breed Greco-Egyptian class. This came about after years of intermarriage on a gradually increasing scale in the rural areas of Egypt. The city governments could not prohibit intermarriage in the numerous villages. This class brought about real cooperation in the first century B.C. between some Greeks and some Egyptians. A statue of the man Amphiomis was carved in Egyptian style, but with unmistakable traces of Hellenic influence. He was both priest and royal *stratēgos* in the Mendesian nome. His son Pelaias followed his

---

48 For an overview of Greco-Egyptian religious syncretism see H. I. Bell, "Graeco-Egyptian Religion," *Mus. Hel.* 10 (1953), 222–37. For the propaganda: A. D. Nock, *Conversion* (1933), 80–91, and the sources cited on pp. 286–8. For proselytizing: T. Zielinski, *La Sibylle* (1924), 85, 94; P. Jouguet, *L'Égypte ptolémaïque* (1933), iii. 230, and A. D. Nock, *loc. cit.*

49 E. Kiessling, "La genèse du culte de Sarapis à Alexandrie," *CÉ* 48 (1949), 323; P. Perdrizet, "Voyage dans la Macédoine première," *BCH* 18 (1894), 418–9; A. D. Nock, *Conversion* (1933), 38–40, 48–56, 89–91, 131–5; T. A. Brady, *The Reception of the Egyptian Cults by the Greeks* (1935), 9–32.

50 Greco-Egyptian cult societies in W. Otto, *Priester und Tempel im hellenisch-tischen Ägypten* (1908); M. I. Rostovtzeff, *S.E.H.H.W.,* ii. 1062–5; iii. 1388–9, n. 105; A. D. Nock, T. O. Skeat, and C. Roberts, "The Gild of Zeus Hypsistos," *HTR* 29 (1936), 39–87; A. E. R. Boak, "The Organization of Gilds in Graeco-Roman Egypt," *TAPA* 68 (1937), 212–20.

career as commander of troops for Ptolemy. A man with the Greek
name Lysimachos wrote to his sister with the Egyptian name Taarmiu-
sis that he had received a revelation from the mighty god Soknebtunis.
The bureaucracy included a collector of revenues named Horus, and
he was the son of a man named Diogenes. In 48 B.C. the Egyptian
Pothinos was a high minister in the Ptolemaic state and tutor to the
young Ptolemy. The commander-in-chief of the military forces was
another Hellenized Egyptian named Achillas.[51]

Finally, in this milieu, in the last decade of its existence, the
Ptolemaic state tried to become publicly Greco-Egyptian. This was an
effort to rally all groups possible for the defense of the Nile valley
against the approaching power of the aggressive Roman republic.
In 40 B.C., Ptolemaic Egypt was the sole survivor of the Hellenistic
monarchies, and had seen all its sister powers overwhelmed by the
rising power of the Parthians or other Oriental peoples, or annexed
into the rising empire of the Romans. Kleopatra and Antony en-
deavored to organize what remained of the Greek East, and consciously played to win the support of non-Hellenic persons. In the
celebrated public festivities underscoring the Donations of Alexandria,
Kleopatra the Makedonian queen appeared in the regalia of the
goddess Isis, and Antony the Roman was decked out as king and consort Osiris. Their children played the roles of the divine Sun and
Moon. In Kilikia, the pair masqueraded as Astarte and Dionysos-
Tammuz. Kleopatra, incidentally, was able to speak many Oriental
tongues, including Egyptian. The Orientalism of the two rulers was
apparent to all, and in Rome Antony's opponent Octavian claimed
that Antony was attempting to subvert the *Romanitas* of the eastern
provinces.[52]

[51] On the rise of the Greco-Egyptian class see V. Chapot, *L'Égypte romaine*
(1933), iii. 266–7; M. I. Rostovtzeff in *C.A.H.* vii. 150–1; P. Jouguet, "Les destinées
de l'hellénisme dans l'Égypte gréco-romaine," *CÉ* 19 (1935), 89–108; 201–12.
Amphiomis and Pelaias: H. Ranke, "The Statue of a Ptolemaic Στρατηγός of the
Mendesian Nome," *JAOS* 73 (1953), 193–8. Lysimachos: *P. Teb.* 284. Horus: *P. Oxford* 1 in E. P. Wegener, *Some Oxford Papyri* (1941), 1–2. Pothinos: Plut. *Pom.*
lxxvii. 2; *Caes.* xlviii. 5; Caesar, *Civ. War*, iii. 108. Achillas: Plut. *Pom.* lxxvii. 2;
lxxviii. 3; Caesar, *Civ. War*, iii. 104.
Early connections between the Ptolemies themselves and the native aristocracy
in W. W. Tarn, "Queen Ptolemais and Apama," *CQ* 23 (1929), 138–41; "Two
Notes on Ptolemaic History," *JHS* 53 (1933), 57–68. Egyptian noblemen in Ptolemaic service in third and second centuries in E. Otto, *Die biographischen Inschrift-
en der ägyptischen Spätzeit* (1954), No. 48, pp. 184–6; No. 49, pp. 186–7; No. 55,
p. 109; and No. 60, p. 93.
[52] The Donations described by Plut. *Ant.* xxxvi. 1—xxxvii. 4; liv. 4–6. See, too,
P. Jouguet, *L'Égypte ptolémaïque* (1933), iii. 229–30. Kilikia: Plut. *Ant.* xxvi. 3–4.
Roman counterpropaganda: K. Scott, "Octavian's Propaganda and Antony's *de Sua
Ebrietate*," *CPh* 24 (1929), 133–41.

This Ptolemaic government disseminated oracular propaganda to support this program and cement the unity of Greek and Egyptian. Motifs drawn from Egyptian mythology, as known from the Greco-Egyptian Isis-hymns, appeared in an oracle which was ultimately added to the Sibylline collection. Kleopatra claimed to be the Sun, as well as Isis. Since her son was called Alexander Helios, it is even possible that she was attempting to turn the *Oracle of the Potter* to her own advantage, for that document foretold that the coming savior-king would be sent by the Sun-god and would rule under the auspices of Isis. Of Kleopatra, the Sibylline Oracle prophesied that she would overthrow European Rome, but raise her up again, and so inaugurate a new age of peace and *homonoia* between West and East.[53]

Thus, with the last Makedonian monarch on the throne of the Ptolemies, one came to an expression of that ideal unity which Alexander at Opis had prayed for. This was the union of minds, this was *homonoia*, which one hoped would unite Europe and Asia in common brotherhood. Kleopatra had come round full circle. But lack of unity and like-mindedness had been, not only in Egypt but elsewhere as well, the usual thing and a primary cause of Oriental hatred for the Greek. At last, three centuries too late, Kleopatra prayed for it again. But her prayers availed her naught. The future of the sullen East was not to be determined by Hellenic kings, but by emperors of Rome and kings of Parthia.

[53] The oracle is *Sib. Or.* iii. 350–61, 367–76, 378, 377, 379–80 (in that order). It is thoroughly discussed by W. W. Tarn, "Alexander Helios and the Golden Age," *JHS* 22 (1932), 135–60. See, too, K. W. Meiklejohn, "Alexander Helios and Caesarion," *JRS* 24 (1934), 191–5.

Chapter XII

General Considerations

In previous chapters I have described the reaction of each major region of the Ancient Near East to Greco-Makedonian imperialism. The response of each was unique. Some, for example, began to rebel and revolt early, while others scarcely reacted at all. Yet while the countries differed in their anti-Hellenism, nonetheless when opposition did occur, it took forms that were generally similar. Egypt, Persis, and Judah all prophesied the downfall of the Greek regime, and all three fought with weapons against it to make this dream come true. There ought, therefore, to be some general consideration of the areas that did resist and comparison with those that did not resist, so that the whole problem of Oriental religious resistance to Hellenism may be better understood, and the course of the spiritual and military opposition seen as a part of the history of the ancient world as a whole.

There were three chief causes of the resistance. The first was the overthrow or continuing suppression of native kingship by a foreign dynasty. This, in turn, endangered the positions, prestige, and authority of the indigenous aristocracy, and of native law and custom. So far as kingship itself was concerned, resistance came almost exclusively from the old established capitals of the Near East, places which had once been the centers of prosperous and aggressive kingdoms or empires. This was true in Egypt so far as we may be able to identify the places that led the opposition, in Jerusalem of Judah, and in Persis. It was consistently true that those regions which did not have an imperial tradition and a former aristocracy conscious of its loss of empire did not undertake determined resistance. Examples of the more passive cultures would be Israel, Syria, the various Anatolian states like Bithynia and Kappadokia, and those parts of Iran like Parthia and Baktria, which had never been the heartland of a strong empire.

A few regions lay halfway between the two ends of this spectrum.

Media, for example, had once been crowned with empire, but this had been wrested from her by the Persians two centuries before Alexander. Her resistance to the Greeks, as imperfectly known from the unrest in Greater Media and the establishment of independent Media Atropatene, was greater than Baktria's, but far less than Persis'. Much the same could be said of Elam. Similarly, in Asia Minor there was no real native opposition to Hellenism—Aristonikos' rebellion against the Attalid regime late in the second century and Mithradates' onslaught on Rome in the early first were not anti-Hellenic. The only strong recent Anatolian state was the Lydian Empire, another kingdom abolished by the Persians. In fact, relief at liberation from Persia felt by many persons of the East probably delayed development of anti-Hellenism in some places. What resistance there was to Hellenism in Asia Minor was actually closely linked to the remnants of the old Persian nobility there. In the East as a whole, therefore, anti-Hellenism had as one major purpose the restoration of the kingship of an old imperial, or at least simply a strong independent, native dynasty. Hatred of the invader came from the aristocracies of these regions, both the warrior class, which was dishonored by defeat and its subsequent loss of dominance, and the priestly class, whose high god was sullied or his legal system put in jeopardy. The peasantry were in many places generally unaware of or indifferent to their alien conquerors, except some of them in Egypt and in Judah. But even in these two places when they rose they were led by representatives of the upper classes. Things had always been so.

The experience of Judah in Hellenistic times deserves special consideration, as those remarkable people the Jews always seem to. Here the resistance was not always the work of the aristocrats. While Judas, a Hasmonean of priestly rank, rebelled, so did the Hasidim, who had scarcely any rank at all. The sources of opposition in Judah were therefore unique. Among the Jews there was a persistent tradition that the peasant should remain free from overexploitation, and that as prophet, like Amos the shepherd, he might talk back to his would-be oppressors. This tradition did not exist in Hellenistic Babylonia or Iran or Asia Minor. It may have in Egypt. But most peasants in these places were simple serfs, with greater or lesser obligations to their feudal or commercial landlords. But not so in Judah: men of slight social standing took an important part in resistance to the Greek kings. These were men like the authors of Zechariah 9–14, the compiler of Daniel, and Eleazar the Essene. On the other hand, aristocrats like the Hasmoneans and the writer of 1 Maccabees did play an important part, like the Egyptians Harmakhis, 'Ankhmakhis, and the priestly author of the *Demotic Chronicle*.

Kingship was the primary concern of these persons, both rebels and prophets, and they had always explained the kingship of their society in religious terms. Therefore both the militant and the literary reaction to the different Makedonian dynasties was always conceived in a theological setting. The defense of the memory of a deposed kingship was important in determining that there would be a new emphasis on messianism in the East, for the various messiahs, Persian, Jewish, and Egyptian, were really mythical figures perfectly fulfilling the old concepts of cosmic kingship. During the first years of rapid and astonishing Hasmonean success, the prophet responsible for one of the sections in 1 Enoch predicted that the messiah would come from the tribe of Levi, to which the Hasmoneans themselves belonged. This was counter to the usual tradition that the messiah would come from the tribe of Judah, which had included amongst its members the Dynasty of David, deposed by the Babylonians in 586. This switch, and the subsequent switch back to Davidic hopes when the Hasmoneans had turned evil in prophetic eyes, shows conclusively how important old or living dynasties were, and how their existence or their memory deeply colored prophetic thinking in Judah. In like manner, the *Bahman Yasht* thought of the advent of Peshyotanu, who was called son of Hystaspes, and therefore was a scion of the Achaemenid line. In Egypt, the tradition of divine descent of the king from Re was maintained, and it is likely that the *Demotic Chronicle* was considering a resumption of rule by a Herakleopolitan noble family, in memory of the IXth and Xth Dynasties.

There was a partial exception to the rule that resistance was strong in former imperial centers. This was not the case in Babylon, which in the long history of the Ancient Near East had frequently been the capital of a powerful, expansive state. Nor did any of the other *ci-devant* imperial cities of Mesopotamia start down the path of stern hostility to Hellenism. The reason for this, as explained above, was that the will to rule in Babylonia had been well-nigh totally crushed out, first by Assyrian atrocities and then by the savage Persian repression of the Babylonian revolts, so that in Hellenistic times desire for world dominion was dead and wishes for even native rule were flagging.

Looked at in another way, the desire of the imperial centers to continue to dominate the East came from their sense that they had once and could again prevail. The Babylonians no longer thought they could. Nor did the peoples of Anatolia. The sense that old victories would be renewed continued in the messianic hopes of Persis, Judah, and Egypt. The Persians even hoped that loyalty to the coming savior would be as widespread as the former state had been or at least as the present Dispersion was. Therefore, an important reason that made some people willing to risk resistance was that a large population gave them hope. Without numbers there could be no sensation or feeling that victory could come. The lack of religious resistance in the numerous, small principalities of Anatolia confirms this conclusion. Egypt and Persis, on the other hand, were two areas where persons enjoying a common language were thickly settled, and therefore were conscious of their own strength. Judaism was no exception to this. Jews in Palestine were considerably more militant than elsewhere, for in Judah they outnumbered the local gentiles overwhelmingly. In other parts of the Orient they were more inclined to passivity, for there they were dispersed among Greek and Egyptian or Mesopotamian populations. Looked at in the sum, there were actually a large number of Jews in the ancient world, when one considers both Palestine and the Diaspora together. One might note parenthetically too that the Jews in Egypt were more concerned with their relation to Hellenism than the Jews of the Dispersion elsewhere, which may show that they were consciously or subconsciously influenced by the militance of Egyptians around them. The Diaspora in passive Mesopotamia was more a simple channel of communication than a source of fresh ideas.

Ultimately, the common denominator in all this was that the large population which had once been the basis for the original imperial expansion now continued to give confidence in final triumph. Of course the exception to this rule was still populous Mesopotamia. But one should remember that the population there had usually created empires at its own expense, that the empire of Babylon, for example, had been established over kindred states in Borsippa, Ur, and Uruk. Hence, most Babylonians may have thought of empire as something inflicted on themselves and not as something they took from others. Babylonians simply did not prevail—they were prevailed against, and they seem to have been subconsciously prepared to accept first the Seleukids and later the Arsakids. One cannot completely and convincingly explain Babylonia's lack of enthusiasm for itself. It was a case of what anthropologists call "cultural fatigue," and this must be explained in psychological terms, which I cannot do. It may be noted, however, that the three determined societies, the Jewish, Egyptian, and Persian, each had a religion teaching belief in future reward or future punishment. The Babylonian did not. When men died, all came to the same end. The enthusiastic religions thought in terms of failure and success. The Babylonians thought the fate of all men was much the same. So did passive Qoheleth.

Aside from the struggle over traditional kingship, there was a second significant cause of religious resistance, and that was the economic exploitation and social degradation of Orientals at Greek hands. An important aspect of this was the partial supplanting of old aristocratic families by Greek and Makedonian immigrants. Much has been said about the participation of the military and priestly aristocracies in the anti-Hellenic movements, and while in all societies these classes were never united in their loyalty to the *ancien régime,* nonetheless numbers of them consistently opposed the Makedonian regimes. They fought for their own continuity as the leaders of the ancient state. They called it a struggle to preserve ancient law.

In the religious literature consciousness of economic exploitation is sometimes rather marked. The intensity of this feeling can be measured fairly well, and the most vigorous anti-Hellenism along these lines was in Egypt and Judah. Persis was an exception. Why this should have been so is difficult to say. We know very little of social and economic conditions there, but since the Seleukid regime was generally much less intensively organized for the economic benefit of Greek conquerors than was the Ptolemaic in either Egypt or Judah, it is quite possible that Persian economic grievances were minor. There was a greater tendency in Seleukid areas for the native economy and local entrepreneurs to survive and flourish. In Egypt, on the other hand, the old order was swept aside by Greek immigrants, who came to occupy the choicest positions in the commercial and political elite of this country. In Judah, Hellenized Jews and Syrians had similar high prestige. The protests of the prophets were against both the Greco-Makedonian and the Hellenized Jewish commercial and administrative class. The causes of religious resistance in some places, therefore, sometimes included class warfare by a dispossessed proletariat fighting for its particular existence, as well as warfare by aristocrats fighting for their own form of existence. Occasionally these ends must have conflicted, as they did in Judah before and after the Hasmonean rising, but more often they coincided, and peasant and patrician made common cause, as they did in Egypt and in Judah, against the foreign king. To win control of the kingship would have made it possible in theory to alleviate the life of the suffering peasantry, so that motives leading to class warfare and motives leading to war for the kingship often supplemented each other. Such was the case in second-century Palestine and Egypt. Both motives could be expressed, also, in religious terms, since both the concepts of divine rule and the concepts of right law and dealing were similarly derived from God.

As was said, Persis was less conscious of local economic loss. Apparently the economy of the region remained largely in the hands of the Iranian aristocracy. The *Bahman Yasht* and the *Oracle of Hystaspes* scarcely protested against class oppression. Their aristocratic authors hated the Greeks because Persis lost the great prize of the empire of the Orient to Alexander. Egypt's and Judah's loss of native control over economic life was more immediate to the commonalty of their people. Neither country had lost an empire; both had been themselves provinces of the Achaemenid Great King.

It should also be noted that ideas of social justice were more highly developed in Judah and Egypt, both these societies having been highly developed, partly urbanized, and rendered quite complex before Alexander's coming. This was less so in agrarian Persis. Zarathushtra showed in his Gathas that he knew something of social justice, but he was not as concerned with this question as were prophets in Egypt and Judah. The royal inscriptions of the Achaemenids were more concerned with listing imperial achievements and the provinces that owed them loyalty than with praising their own concern for the masses, as Mesopotamian and Egyptian kings sometimes did. Society and therefore morality were more complex outside of Persis, and so were better equipped to resist in more complicated ways the policies of the Hellenic kings. Egypt and Judah had earlier faced the problem of social justice, for they had earlier made cities, slums, and rural proletariats. Persis as a whole had not, and was still too unsophisticated in 300 B.C. to have faced these complex problems.

Opposition to the Greek king, then, sometimes came from economic motives, but sometimes, too, from the belief that he was simply a foreign interloper. This was particularly true in two of the three very militant areas, Judah and Egypt. It was less true in Persis. Egyptians and Jews, more than any others, insisted that they were select peoples. Of course to a certain extent this was true of the Babylonians and Persians as well, but to nothing like the same degree. Were not the Jews Yahweh's Own Particularly Chosen? Were not the Egyptians the creators of human civilization and holy religion? So they said.

No doubt this feeling was an important symptom of the will to resist. Although the Persians resisted as manfully and successfully as the Jews, there is no evidence that they were in as withering, blighting, and hateful a grip of particularism as were either the Jews or the Egyptians. Perhaps this seems so to us only because particularist feelings had not excited as many members of Persian society as it had the other two more sophisticated ones. Persian aristocrats who were taught the manly arts of horsemanship, archery, and truth-telling may have been very unpleasant to deal with, and the institution of the Seven Very Noble Families may have been a hotbed of "nationalism." Still, their hopes for the recovery of Ahura Mazdāh's empire were expressed, I think, in highly mystical ways, more as a universalist theology and less as a loyalty to a particular culture, a chosen race, or a unique religion. Mysticism in Persia, from the scarcely intelligible hymns of Zarathushtra to the lush musings and fantastic images of al-Rumi, has always been highly theoretical, difficult for Westerners to appreciate, and, if I may say so, removed from reality. Yet, Magian insistence that Ahura Mazdāh had selected the Achaemenids to be his kings, and that on them the lordship of Asia would one day devolve again, is not more remarkable than the equal Jewish insistence that David's line would come again in the person of God's own messiah. All these persons—Jews, Egyptians, Persians—badly wanted native kings to defend native law and native religion from the threatening innovations of the kings of Makedon.

Thus we come to the conclusion that there were three main motives for the religious resistance, and that these were interlocking. First, there was the effort to regain native rule as an end in itself. Second, there was the effort to regain native rule as a means of ending social upheaval and economic exploitation. Third, there was the effort to regain native rule to protect law and religion. The master institution of the Ancient Near East had been kingship. The master hope of the Hellenistic period was for a return of native kingship. When the three reasons operated together, resistance was the most intense, taking the form not only of religious propaganda, but of violent warfare as well.

Returning to the occurrence of class warfare, this did not always break out, and the existence of sizeable cities, as in Mesopotamia or Syria, did not always act to create grounds for hatred. Actually, there are indications that in regions where Greek city life was introduced on a large scale the force of resistance was often diminished. The most intensely urbanized regions of the Orient were Seleukid Meso-

potamia, Syria, and Anatolia, and Greco-Baktrian Baktria. Here resistance was slight. Egypt, Judah, and Persis were not provided with
Greek *poleis* on any large scale. It would appear, therefore, that
anti-Hellenism in areas without Greek cities was partly due to the
lack of just these institutions. In practical terms, this meant fewer
opportunities for the native people to assimilate themselves to Hellenism. They could not become Greco-Oriental because they could
scarcely find out how to do so. Of course where *poleis* existed but
refused to admit Orientals to membership, as in Egypt, there was anti-
Hellenic reaction. But in the half-Oriental Seleukid or Baktrian
poleis this was not true. The existence of civic institutions meant
that dominant, aggressive, or adventurous people from the Oriental
population had an opportunity to win rank and privilege at the expense of Greeks, to gain compensation for their losses, real or
imaginary, and to become merchants, entrepreneurs, soldiers, astrono-
mers, or philosophers. These possibilities did not really exist in
Judah, Egypt, or Persis, and persons there with no outlet for their
hostile energies could only rebel against the regime to win high
status. It is impossible, however, with the small evidence available
to correlate these considerations with conclusions drawn above concerning the lack of will to prevail in Mesopotamia. Pergamon seems
also to have been a partial exception.

A well-known case was Jerusalem-Antioch. The Jewish community
there was led by a Hellenized native group to take on more and
more of the institutions of Hellenism. Actually, the rebellion led by
the Maccabees does not seem to have been entirely a reaction to Hellenism per se, but a reaction to the acceleration of the process, which
under Antiochos proceeded more rapidly than many Jews were willing to go. The Maccabees were supported primarily by rural people,
those least touched by Hellenism. During the wars some Hellenized
Jewish communities opposed the Maccabees, and the latter sometimes
took violent revenge on these places which were unwilling to revert to
old-line Judaism. Hellenization of the towns had been proceeding
down to the reign of Antiochos IV without arousing undue hostility.
After the reign of Antiochos, Hellenism was again accepted and
proceeded to make a permanent impression on Jewish society.

Exactly the same situation occurred at Tarsos and Babylon in the
time of Antiochos. Both cities reacted violently to his policy; but
after the relaxation of pressure both accepted Hellenism again,
Babylon retaining her civic institutions, Tarsos even becoming an
important center of Hellenistic philosophy.

There have been parallels to this in the history of modern imperialism, for violent resistance has broken out usually in the countryside where Westernization proceeded rapidly and completely at the expense of nativism. Where there has been a more permissive attitude, resistance has not been so violent. So in ancient times there were numerous instances of natives going Greek without compulsion. This was the case especially in urbanized western Asia Minor. The Seleukid administration of the region seems to have allowed a good deal more local control than the later Pergamene regime, which tended to model itself on the Ptolemaic system of rigid control of the population. The society the Attalids ruled created resentment which began to accumulate after 200 B.C., when the dynasty became once and for all independent of the Seleukids. The pressure ultimately blew off in the savage revolt of the pretender Aristonikos. The effect of a sudden end to gradualism is shown by comparison of the Ptolemaic and Seleukid experiences with Judah. The Ptolemaic regime of the third century provoked more oracles antagonistic to it than did the easy Seleukid regime of Antiochos III between 200 and 175 B.C. After this generation of peace, resistance quickly flared up and became violent when Antiochos IV and his friends applied heavy pressure.

The effects produced by the Makedonian dynasties' stepping up their demands can be seen, too, in the over-all history of anti-Hellenism. The rivalries of the Hellenistic states grew in intensity towards the end of the third century, as each began to shape its foreign and military policy to deliver or to ward off a knockout blow. There was consequent tightening of political and economic control over the Orientals to wring from them the revenues necessary to sustain the new program. There was an increase in native resistance, and all over the East in the last two decades of the third century growing restiveness. Propaganda circulated from Persis to the Aegean, in Egypt, and in Jerusalem, and revolts broke out in Judah, Egypt, and the eastern provinces of the Seleukid Empire.

This tendency continued into the second century, so that by 175 B.C., the eastern revolt was in full swing. Egypt was in the grip of a whole series of rebellions and desertions by peasants. The Jews raised a bloody and successful rebellion under Judas the Hammer. The Iranian provinces and Elam escaped from their Seleukid suzerains. Persian propaganda circulated throughout Asia, turning up in Anatolia and in Judah, and even a few Babylonians were stimulated to reject the Hellenizing policy of Antiochos IV and to mediate legends of native heroines and Iranian messiahs to the peoples of the fertile crescent. The pressure of increased political and economic control hit very sensitive nerves in the Oriental civilizations. With the relaxation of Hellenic pressure after 140 B.C., the reaction to Hellenism waned, and with the advent of the Romans and Parthians, real cooperation developed between Greeks and Orientals.

Of course the intensity of resistance stemmed from the nature of the Greek regime as well as from the character of the Orientals under it. The content of Oriental culture had a great deal to do with determining the course of resistance. In the cases of Egypt, Judah, and Persis, there were two things that these regions had in common which other places—Mesopotamia, Syria, and Asia Minor—did not. In the first three societies religion had a rather high ethical content, and there was insistence on proper behavior as a means of securing a divine reward at life's end. The religions differentiating sharply between good and evil reacted more drastically to harsh Greek treatment. The Egyptian and the Jew and the Persian had optimistic hope for their eventual bliss, much more than the Babylonian, whose gods were fickle and not overly interested in ethical behavior.

The second common characteristic of these three cultures was some sort of ecclesiastical organization, whereas there was no corresponding organization in Mesopotamia, Syria, or Anatolia. The existence of organization, no doubt, is symptomatic of a deeper sense of unity, present in Judah or Egypt, lacking in Mesopotamia. Organization helped create that sense of numbers mentioned above.

In the final analysis Oriental resistance was an effort to maintain a native way of life whose continuity was threatened by Hellenism. The reaction was directed only at those Greek institutions which were actually in action against Oriental institutions. There was no opposition to Hellenism in its totality, and there was no effort made by anybody to destroy Hellenism entirely. One does not find hatred expressed in the literature against the rationality of Hellenism, or its scientific or philosophical achievements. These were facets of culture rather lacking among the Orientals, and they therefore did not feel threatened by them. The Orient fought to get or keep something it already knew.

There is no evidence that people in any Oriental society, except a handful in the Jewish Dispersion, thought of themselves as a City of God besieged by a City of Men. There is no evidence that Persians or Egyptians or most Jews were shocked because a Euripides had made one of his characters say, "There are no gods in heaven; no, not one!"

They do not seem to have minded Aristotle's interesting opinions about First Causes or Epikouros' notion that the gods were remote, beautiful, and ineffable, unconcerned with the affairs of men, happy only to converse with one another in the most perfect of all languages, Greek. In general, the Orientals did not know that Euripides or Aristotle or Epikouros had existed. Neither, for that matter, did many of the Hellenistic Greeks, or if they did, these names were as vague and empty of meaning to them as Shakespeare, Kant, or Voltaire to most people today. Certainly the people dwelling along the Congo or Zambesi or Ganges do not hate the West because of these men. They hate the gunboats and plantation overseers. So too the Orientals did not feel threatened by these Greek geniuses.

The few Oriental people who did become acquainted with the monuments of the Hellenic mind, the Alexandrian Jews and a few Egyptian priests, do not seem to have been terribly upset by what they found. On the contrary, they were impressed. The Egyptians hastened to say that they had really invented many of these things, and the Jews to say that these men had plagiarized their ideas from the scriptures. Ezekielos the Dramatist may have disliked some of the more exciting insights of Euripides, but he also copied his style. So it was with Stoic ethics, and if Antigonos of Socho didn't like to think of God as Reason, he didn't say so, so far as we know, but used Zeno's dictum that acts are done without hope of reward simply because it is one's duty to be responsible. The Pharisees equipped themselves with Greek logic, and Jewish historians with the techniques of Alexandrian scholarship.

The serious struggle in the East was the fight against the Makedonian kings, and against their economic and military agents. Everywhere parts of Greek culture, economic innovations, bureaucratic organizations, the methods and styles of artists, even certain religious ideas, were borrowed by the Orient and made a part of its various cultures. Whether the Oriental fought to maintain an imperial tradition or whether he fought to maintain his social standing and economic integrity, he ultimately fought only to maintain a way of living. For Hellenism was efficient, wonderful, and fascinating, sometimes quite seductive. Anti-Hellenism on one view was only an expression of the widespread human hostility to change.

The Orientals themselves were not conscious of pan-Easternism, except possibly in Persis, as some Greeks like Euthydemos or Antiochos III or IV were conscious of pan-Hellenism. In Western Asia there was some effort made by the Persians to win over Mesopotamians and Anatolians, but more, I think, to gain manpower than to preach "Asia for the Asiatics" sincerely. In Judaism there was a loose sort of unity between Judah proper and the Diaspora. But Egypt fought her battle all alone. And in no case did contacts between the various Oriental civilizations play a really important part in the anti-Hellenic movement.

The East frequently had to respond to Greco-Makedonian imperialism with spiritual weapons as well as by warfare. This was due to two reasons. First, kingship was explained in theological terms. This was simply a fact of Eastern culture. But spiritual resistance was also necessary because Eastern societies at first could not stand up to Greek armies. The usual suppression of revolt in Asia and Egypt shows this. Even Persis did not become finally independent until around 160 B.C., when it had received considerable indirect help from the growth of the Parthian state, which so sapped the strength of the then-divided Seleukid Empire. But generally, the Greeks were able to put down Oriental risings until well into the second century B.C. Therefore the Oriental could express his hatred of the Greek only in a spiritual way, and hence there was created the oracular opposition. It is no coincidence that most of our propaganda comes from the third century and the fourth, and that most of our militant resistance comes from the second and first centuries. By the later time the East was learning how to fight Greek-style.

Resort to prophecy is a universal response of beaten men. The Greek himself took refuge in it. In periods of threatening military defeat at the hands of Gauls in the third century the Hellenes called upon their gods for salvation. Against Roman occupation in the second they prophesied the intervention of Zeus.[1] Religion is a means of salvation when ordinary human means fail. In the East, religious resistance against alien domination was not new in 334 B.C., and the reaction of Babylonians or Egyptians to their Persian overlords was the prototype of the resistance offered their Hellenic conquerors. There was no break in the continuity of behavior.

There were four basic kinds of resistance: passive, militant, messianic, and proselytic. Passive resistance was the use of legends venerat-

[1] For Greek appeal to the gods at the time of the Gallic invasion see Paus. x. 15. 3; 30. 9; 32. 4. For oracles invoking the power of Zeus or Athena against Rome: Phlegon, *Amazing Stories*, 3. The *Alexandra* of Lykophron of the early third century is a prototype of this sort of literature. In Egypt in the early fifth century B.C., the Greek gods of Naukratis had protected their votaries (A. D. Nock, *Conversion* [1933], 19–20).

For the religious response of Greece to the Roman occupation following 146 B.C. see R. Fuchs, *Der geistige Widerstand gegen Rom in der antiken Welt* (1938), *passim;* W. W. Tarn, *H.C.* (3rd ed., 1952), 39–40.

ing ancient heroes. This was symptomatic of the archaism running
through so much of the East in the Hellenistic period. The Oriental
faced with the prospect of Hellenization recalled his old ideals, his
old social customs, his old victories, and sought to indoctrinate his
immediate group with them, so that it would have some frame of
reference in the struggle with Hellenism. This was passive in that it
neither sought nor advocated overthrow of the Hellenizing people, but
only provided an antidote to them. This form of resistance was common to all cultures that resisted. Some of it came from the part of the
aristocracy willing to temporize with Greek occupation, either because
they admired certain aspects of Hellenism or because they wished partially to cooperate with the Greek regime.

The second type of resistance, the militant, showed up in wars of
religion. We see it best in Palestine and Egypt. Something like it may
have occurred in Persis, but details are lacking. This was a defense of
the native culture seen as the defense of its gods, and it was aggressively
directed against the Makedonian institution of kingship. The movement sought to install a native god-king, in Egypt pharaoh, in Judah
Yahweh. Militance was in all cases accompanied by its spiritual cousin,
messianic prophecy.

This was yearning for a messiah, a god or a person associated with
a god who would appear miraculously for the salvation of his people.
Salvation was the expulsion of the dominating Greek class as well
as bringing a new moral order or life eternal. Messianism was a
phenomenon known only in the most vigorous cultures, for it came
from a wish-image of ends usually gained by ordinary human
violence. Messiahs were consistently conceived of as idealized kings
of the older pattern.

The exact nature of each messiah was determined by the nature of
the particular society which longed for him. The messiah was a
spiritualization of previous historic kingship. This was plainly the case
in Egypt. In the pharaonic period kings were held to be the source
of good, even of life itself. Ramesses IV was hailed at his accession
as the bringer of joy to heaven and earth. Persons who had fled in
terror returned to their places. The hungry were fed, the thirsty
made drunken, the naked clothed, and the imprisoned set free. The
Nile became full, and the harvest was abundant.[2] The parallel between this hymn and the *Oracle of the Potter* is unmistakable. The
latter prophesied that the king to come would drive out Chaos and
re-establish order in Egypt's religion and Egypt's agriculture. The peo-

[2] J. A. Wilson, "Joy at the Accession of Ramses IV," *A.N.E.T.*, 378–9.

ple of Egypt would be so happy that they would wish the dead could return to share the good things.

In like manner, the messiahs of Judaism were to be protectors of the Jews, of Judaism, of the whole society. They would defend the poor from oppression, drive away foreign tormentors, and protect religion from enemies both within and without. These activities traditionally had been the functions of historic Jewish kings, whether they had fulfilled them in the eyes of the Deuteronomic historians or not. In the Hellenistic period it was confidently hoped that the messiahs of Yahweh would finally bring to pass all that had been royal duty in the past.

The fact that in ancient theology kingship included power over physical nature explains why the Hellenistic saviors were to transform nature upon their arrival. Such had been a traditional function of kingship. And, too, the restoration of the actual landscape from the point of view of the Hellenistic Oriental had some foundation in reality. To a demoted clergy, a dispossessed aristocracy, or an oppressed and exploited peasantry, nature had indeed been reversed by the Hellenes. To the Egyptian starving in his ancient village-slum the Typhonian Ptolemy had interrupted nature, for the peasant's stomach was as empty as it would have been if the Nile had sunk to a little trickle. Imaginary conditions like these were used by the Jewish prophets as a contrast for the description of the New Jerusalem. Foretelling the restoration or transfiguration of nature should be understood in part as a restoration of the normal channels of distribution, that is, that the economic organization of the Greeks would be put to purposes other than the support of a foreign army and foreign wars directed towards an alien world. Egyptians, Jews, and Persians hated their helplessness before the advance of the remorseless phalanx of the Greeks. And so deeply impressed became this hatred of the foreign king and his assistant demons of the Race of Wrath that the galloping horses and bounding chariots of Assyrian and Chaldean kings, which had been so bloodily described by ancient prophecy, came to stand for the enemy army that the king-who-is-to-come would destory at a mythologized Armageddon. Our king is dead? Long live the king-messiah!

Peshyotanu the Persian was to exercise this function of expelling the enemies of Ahura Mazdāh from Persis as the Achaemenid Great Kings had dealt with the Lie in the past. He would bring about a restoration of the good religion. A chief difference between the Hellenistic savior and the flesh-and-blood king of the past lay in the

notion that the savior would be perfect, whereas the old kings had
often failed properly to perform their duties. In fact the failure of
certain kings to rule according to Ma'at or to fulfill the commandment
of the Annunaki or to obey the Law of Yahweh had tended before
Alexander to discredit the idea of kingship.[3] In conceiving the king-
who-is-to-come to be morally perfect, the Hellenistic Orient was un-
consciously attempting to solve the old moral dilemma of the presence of evil in a world whose Creator and whose agents were supposed
to be good.

For all these prophecies identified evil with the Greeks. The Egyptians poetically called them Typhonians, the bringers of Chaos and
Unright. The Persians called them Demons with Dishevelled Hair,
and exaggeratedly claimed that their rule had brought the near collapse of society and real disorder to nature. One Hebrew writer, more
humanistically inclined, simply said that trouble in Asia began with
Alexander and culminated in Antiochos Epiphanes. Other Jews
likened the Greeks to dreadful monsters.

All these considerations are of some importance in explaining both
the nature of the messiahship of Jesus and his acceptance as the
Christ in countries which otherwise rejected Judaism. Anti-Hellenism helped prepare the ground for him. In Egypt, famous for its
anti-Semitism, Christianity nonetheless made marvellous headway,
partly because the messiahs of the *Demotic Chronicle* and the *Oracle
of the Potter* had had attributes—true kingship, true priesthood, love
for the poor and downtrodden—which were similar to the ones that
the apostles claimed for Jesus.

It seemed necessary to the Oriental prophets to make the messiahs
advocate conditions in which all the human members of the society
could unite against the Greeks. This required the Orientals to treat
one another benevolently, and one finds, therefore, that there is
an emphasis, seen particularly in the Jewish experience, on morals

---

[3] See the remarks of Sumerian scribes in the *Sumerian King List* vii. 1–7 (in T.
Jacobsen, *The Sumerian King List* [1939]) on military chaos and in the inscription
describing the fall of Uru-kagina, the good social reformer overthrown by bad King
Lugal-zaggesi (in G. A. Barton, *The Royal Inscriptions of Sumer and Akkad*
[1928], 75–91). See, too, the remarks about serving or rebelling against kings in the
Pessimistic Dialogue between Master and Servant (*A.N.E.T.*, 437–8), especially sections 1, 9, and 10. This text is remarkable for its moral lassitude.

For Egypt, there are the *Admonitions of Ipuwer* (*A.N.E.T.*, 441–4), which advise
a Pharaoh that his failure to follow Ma'at is responsible for the supreme crisis
confronting state and society. For Persia, there are the bitter remarks in the
Gathas: Yasnas xxxii. 9–12; xliv. 20; xlvi. 1–2, 11; xlviii. 5. For Judah, the numerous
criticisms in 1 and 2 Kings.

leading to greater cooperation and love. The Persian, Jewish, and Egyptian prophets say that as a result of the Makedonian occupation, fathers hate sons, brothers hate brothers, or simply that people enslave and despise one another, and the insistence on generous behavior in the age to come was evidence of the human desire to escape from the round of hate and revenge for hating that so often accompanied the social revolution of the Hellenistic age.

Usually the prophecies excluded the Greeks from attainment of future bliss in the messianic age and condemned them to death or to eternal fire. Alexander and his successors, the Persian hoped, would flee to hell. Alexandria and the Ptolemies, the Egyptian hoped, would be destroyed. Dead Greek soldiers, the Jew once hoped, would furnish the means for drinking a victory toast of blood. Occasionally, however, Judaism also held out hope for the conversion of the Greeks. But their salvation had to be by practice of Jewish religion so that they therefore ceased to be Greek. Thus the anti-Hellenic religious movement of the Near East served to maintain or widen the gulf between Hellene and "barbarian" that some Greeks and Orientals had created. This was a legacy of the Hellenistic world to the Roman Empire.

The fourth type of resistance, proselytism, the development of the will to force acceptance of the new messianic, moral theology on nonbelievers, was seen in only two societies, the Persian and the Jewish. In the widespread mission of conversion that became a part of Judaism after the experience of the Maccabees all this is apparent. It was a form of religious resistance that was aggressive, and sought to go beyond the messianic expulsion of the Greek and to take him into a new world-wide system. It was an expression of older imperialism, now conceived as a spiritual instead of a military conquest.

The results of the religious resistance were impressive, and the Oriental movements played a most important role in undermining the Makedonian kingdoms. Scholars like W. W. Tarn and M. I. Rostovtzeff have minimized the role that religion played in the Oriental reaction to Hellenism, and rightly point out that the various dynasties did a great deal to make their regime palatable to religious groups in the East. The kings' record of noninterference with the temples, while not perfect, was nevertheless respectable, and the amount of rebuilding and restoration of Eastern temples was impressive. Hence, the question becomes an issue of terms. The motives for resistance were political or economic only from our point of view. Secular economic and political motives constitute valid grounds for war nowadays, although religious motives do not. But the ancient Oriental, when he lost his independence, did not form an underground "People's Liberation Army" or prepare manifestoes on the natural rights of man or other "self-evident" truths. When he suffered under the yoke of the tax-farmer he did not organize cells of revolutionaries indoctrinated on Marxist lines or trained in a School of Economics. There were political motives, no doubt, and no doubt economic motives as well, but the Orient formulated its ideas and carried them out in the spirit of theology and divinely inspired law. Its response came from a world of religious thinking and speculative thought. It was not rational or empiric. The reaction, judging by the enthusiastic violence of Egyptian and Jew, when it came made full use of the passions and feelings of persons aroused by the irrational impulse to hate and to kill for the sake of either a god and his church or a people and its nation.

The four types of resistance were all of them normal human responses to domination by an alien culture which threatens to end or modify the old. The messianic response was, in essence, the outpouring of humanity's desire to escape from bloody conflict through substituting intervention by a superhuman hero, for society itself feared it was unable to prevail over its enemies by force. Similar responses have been made in recent times. The reaction of the American Indian, for example, to American imperialism was the same. The Indians suffered loss of independence, economic hardship, and the breakdown of their order of society, and they experienced nativistic revivals passively advocating continued belief in Indian culture by Indians, undertook militant wars of religion like that led by the Prophet and Tecumseh, believed in messianic movements emphasizing high morality, like those in the Pacific Northwest, and even began proselytism among themselves, as in the case of Indian Shakerism or the Peyote cult.[4]

Similar reactions took place also during the Mahdist movements in Asia and Africa in the nineteenth century, and in the rise of Baha'ism and its expansion in the nineteenth and twentieth centuries. In modern Africa, violent resistance propped up by revived belief in native cult and witchcraft is going on among the Mau Mau in Kenya, and in Northern Rhodesia a messiah is still expected to come to drive out the white man.

[4] For Indian reactions see the short survey of F. Voget, "The American Indian in Transition: Reformation and Status Innovations," *American Journal of Sociology* 62 (1957), 369–78, and the literature cited in the footnotes.

The result of Oriental religious resistance in the larger history of the ancient world was to bring about a weakening of the Hellenistic monarchies at a most inopportune time. The revolts in Iran and in Western Asia and in Egypt, and the strikes and general refusal to cooperate with the regime in Judah and in Egypt, occurred at the same time that these states were assailed from without by the Parthians from the East and especially by the Roman Republic from the West. Disloyalty from within hindered resistance to these outside powers. From the point of view of the Jews and the Egyptians this was ultimately unfortunate, since the Roman regime was much more harsh than the Greek had been. The Hasmoneans liberated Judah; the men who revolted in A.D. 66, A.D. 115, and A.D. 132 did not, but the Jewish state was utterly broken up. In Egypt, from the first century of the common era on there were rounds of revolts and particularly of strikes and flights from villages by Egyptian peasants that contributed so much to making Egypt a horrid place to live. One of the questions frequently asked oracles in the third century A.D. was "Shall I live?"

While the Oriental resistance undoubtedly fought against real oppression inflicted by the Greeks, it also fought against real benefits that the Greeks brought. One can easily compile a list of complaints against Greek governors from the papyri; we even have a published collection of such. But how can one compile a list of thanks to them? People rarely offer their congratulations. They mostly obsequify to kings but spurn Mozart or Shaw. But Hellenism did confer great benefits on the East. As Plutarch said, Alexander spread civilization amongst the Oriental peoples, and established Greek cities in these foreign nations. Such cities could have been a means by which ignorant and downtrodden peoples could have learned self-respect and responsibility through the functioning of democratic Greek magistracies. The East, Plutarch said, was taught to respect marriage, to support its parents, to marry persons other than brothers or mothers, and to learn Homer, Euripides, and Sophokles.[5] Plutarch was wrong: this didn't happen. But it might have.

The East, after all, had known centuries of self-inflicted oppression, and nothing that the Greek kings did along such lines was new. In fact, in the free, rational atmosphere of numerous Hellenic *poleis* there was some release from the irrational past, and one can hardly blame those Orientals who converted themselves to it, like Jason or Menelaos, for thinking that city air makes a man free. If the op-

[5] Plut. *Fort. Alex.* 70 (328 A–329 A).

position in Egypt had succeeded in repulsing the Greeks as early as 275 B.C., the world never would have known the work of Eratosthenes, of Straton of Lampsakos, or of Aristarchos. If it was necessary to oppress some peasants in Egypt in order to know the things such men discovered, it was better that the peasants be oppressed than that they hound Aristarchos out of Alexandria and give the Museum over to fisherfolk, as the Potter hoped. The Orient had much to learn from Hellas, and more respect was owed to Alexandria or to Antiocheia-Jerusalem than was given it. As for those Persians, Egyptians, and Jews who clapped hand to sword and prepared to make blood flow—"He who ruleth his spirit is greater than he who taketh a city."

Appendix

The following translation of the *Bahman Yasht*, adapted from that of E. W. West, *Pahlevi Texts* i. pp. 1–lix; 189–235, in *Sacred Books of the East* v, is an attempt to approximate the original version of Hellenistic date. I have excised material of late origin, and have indicated the grounds for doing so in the footnotes. The numbers of the chapters and verses are those of West's edition.

That the original underwent extensive alteration is proved by the fact that the *Bahman Yasht* as it now stands is a compilation drawn from several other works. The text names three commentaries used, those on the *Vohuman, Harvadad,* and *Astad Yashts.*[1] Since the first verse of the present edition is a paraphrase of the *Studgar Nask,*[2] there must be at least four written documents behind the extant text.

Aside from these named sources, much other material was added, as shown by the extensive glosses of successive editors. In iii. 19, for example, seven homelands of the army of the avenging savior who restores Iran are named.[3] Five locations are listed for the apocalyptic battle.[4] This accumulation of geographical data shows how the prophecy was continually altered to keep it abreast of the fluctuating political situation in Iran over a long period of time. Five distinct saviors are named; three of them are mythical figures, Peshyotanu, Saoshyans, and Hushedar.[5] Two of them are Sassanid kings, Bahram V and Shapur.[6] This in itself shows at least five sucessive alterations, the earliest at least of the fifth century of our era. Peshyotanu was the original militant messiah of the prophecy, but when other names were added, he was relegated to the position of supernatural high priest of restored Zoroastrianism.[7]

Hence, we are justified in thinking that beginning in Sassanid times the original four-monarch prophecy underwent revision on at least four occasions, becoming a seven-monarch prophecy in the process. Alteration continued until approximately the thirteenth century, as shown by E. W. West,[8] being made necessary by the Muslim and Turkish invasions of Iran.

---

[1] *Bahman Yasht* i. 6.

[2] *Ibid.,* i. 1.

[3] Sagastan, Pars, Khurasan, the Lake of Padashkhvargar, Hiratis, Kihistan, and Taparistan.

[4] *Ibid.,* iii. 21.

[5] *Ibid.,* iii. 25 ff.; 43 ff.; 62.

[6] *Ibid.,* iii. 14, 39–40.

[7] Peshyotanu is born of a father of Kayan race (iii. 14), Hystaspes (iii. 52), and he drives out the enemy and restores Iran (iii. 25 ff.). But Hushedar also restores Iran (iii. 44 ff.), and it is said (iii. 52) that Peshyotanu because of Hushedar becomes priest and primate of the world.

[8] E. W. West, *Pahlevi Texts* i. pp. liii–lvi.

THE BAHMAN YASHT

i. 1. . . . [When][9] Zarathushtra asked for immortality from Ahura Mazdāh, then Ahura Mazdāh displayed the omniscient wisdom to Zarathushtra, and through it he beheld the root of a tree,[10] on which were four branches, one golden, one of silver, one of bronze[11] and one was clay[12] mixed up with iron. 2. Thereupon he reflected in this way, that this was seen in a dream, and when he arose from sleep, Zarathushtra spoke thus: "Lord of the Spirits and Earthly Existences! It appears that I saw the root of a tree, on which were four branches."[13]

3. Ahura Mazdāh spoke to Zarathushtra Spitama thus: "That root of a tree which thou sawest, and those four branches, are the four periods which will come.[14] 4. That of gold is when I and thou converse, and King Hystaspes shall accept the religion, and shall demolish the figures of the demons, but they themselves remain for . . .[15] concealed proceedings. 5. And that of silver is the reign of [Artaxerxes],[16] the Kayan king,[17] and that of [bronze][18] is the reign of the glorified . . . ,[19] and that which

---

[9] Omitting editorial beginning, "As it is declared by the *Studgar Nask* that," and supplying "when" as demanded by sense of the sentence.

[10] Cf. *Sib. Or.* iii. 396–7; Dan. iv. 10–15, 20–6.

[11] The text actually reads "steel." I have substituted "bronze" for two reasons. First, in the late doublet on this passage at ii. 14–22, the metal following silver is bronze; steel is the sixth metal there, immediately preceding the mixed with clay, as it appears here. Second, since the king identified with the steel is called glorified (i. 5), a more noble metal than ferrous would be indicated. Third, steel would not so likely appear in a Hellenistic text, it being still uncommon, although bronze would, as being plentiful.

[12] A word is missing from the text; "clay" supplied from Dan. ii. 34, 41.

[13] This section of Chapter i dealing with the vision of the tree root, and not the doublet in ii. 14–22, is the original of the prophecy. First, the tree of i. 2 comes from a nask, and not from a commentary on a yasht. Second, the tree of ii. 14 has seven branches, not four roots. The larger number in all likelihood indicates a later version, made necessary by the coming of the Arsakid, Sassanid, and Muslim periods in Iran following the Makedonian. This is quite late as shown by the sequence of these periods. Ardakhshir, Shapur, and Bahram, kings of the Sassanids, are named in ii. 18, 20. But ii. 19 mentions the Arsakid ("Askanian") dynasty and Alexander ("Akandgar"), whom the Arsakids destroyed. This disorder of historical data is certain evidence of late date. Consequently, the doublet ii. 14–22 is younger than its parallel text i. 1–5.

[14] Cf. Dan. ii. 36–40; iv. 19–23. A similar progression of metals is given in 1 Enoch lii. 2, 6–8, where the person to whom revelation is given sees seven mountains represented by iron, copper, gold, silver, soft metal, lead, and tin.

[15] A word is missing from the manuscripts.

[16] The text reads, "Ardakhshir," but it is likely that it originally read, "Ardakhshir, the Kayan, whom they call Vohuman the son of Spendad," as in ii. 17, where such is the name of the second monarch. Both E. W. West (*Pahlevi Texts* i. 198, n. 5) and A. V. W. Jackson ("Die iranische Religion," *Grundriss der iranischen Philologie* ii. 691; *Zoroaster, the Prophet of Ancient Iran*, 160) identify this monarch with Artaxerxes I or II.

[17] The Kayan kings were mythical, legendary kings of Iran to the writers of the Sassanid period, ancestors of the Achaemenid Dynasty. See *Dinkard* viii. 13, 24; *Bahman Yasht* iii. 26.

[18] See n. 11, above.

[19] The text has "Khusro, son of Kevad," who reigned in the sixth century of our era, and whose name is therefore suppressed.

was [clay]²⁰ mixed with iron is the evil sovereignty of the demons with dishevelled hair of the Race of Wrath, and when it is the end of the tenth hundreth winter of thy millennium, O Zarathushtra Spitama." . . .²¹

ii. 23. Zarathushtra said thus: "Creator of the material world! O Propitious Spirit! What token would you give of the tenth hundreth winter?"

24. Ahura Mazdāh spoke thus: "Righteous Zarathushtra! I will make it clear: the token that it is the end of thy millennium, and (that) the most evil period is coming, is that a hundred kinds, a thousand kinds, a myriad kinds of demons with dishevelled hair, of the Race of Wrath, rush into the country of Iran . . . .

25. . . .²² O Zarathushtra Spitama! The Race of Wrath is miscreated, and its origin is not manifest. 26. Through witchcraft they rush into these countries of Iran which I, Ahura Mazdāh, created, since they burn and damage many things;²³ and the house of the house-owner, the land of the land-digger, prosperity, nobility, sovereignty, religion, truth, agreement, security, enjoyment, and every characteristic which I, Ahura Mazdāh, created. . . .²⁴ 27. And that which is a great district will become a town; that which is a great town, a village; that which is a great village, a family; and that which is a great family, a single threshold. 28. O Zarathushtra Spitama! They will lead these Iranian countries of Ahura Mazdāh into a desire for evil, into tyranny and misgovernment, those demons with dishevelled hair who are deceivers, so that what they say, they do not do; and they are of a vile religion, so that what they do not say, they do. . . .²⁵

30. "And at that time, O Zarathushtra Spitama, all men will become deceivers, great friends will become of different parties,²⁶ and respect, affection, hope, and regard for the soul will depart from the world; the affection of the father will depart from the son; and that of the brother from his brother; the son-in-law

---

²⁰ See p. 344, n. 12, above.

²¹ The section i. 6—ii. 22 is omitted as of Sassanid date.

i. 6–8 is stated to be from the commentaries on the *Vohuman Yasht, Horvadad Yasht,* and *Astad Yasht;* it is implied in i. 7–8 that this comes from the time of Khusro.

ii. 1–22 is a unity, partly dependent on the *Vohuman Yasht* (ii. 1). But it contains material postdating the Muslim occupation, for native sovereighty in Iran is lost (ii. 22), after the rule of the Sassanids (ii. 18, 20).

²² Omitting from v. 24, "from the direction of the East, which has an inferior race and Race of Wrath," as a rewriting of the section introducing the Race of Wrath to fit an invasion other than the Greek. E. W. West (*Pahlevi Texts* i. 202, n. 1) suggests the Turks.

The first part of v. 25 is also omitted, as a gloss, detailing the appearance of the invaders: "They have uplifted banners, they slay those living in the world, they have their hair dishevelled on the back, and they are mostly a small and inferior race, forward in destroying the strong doer."

²³ Persepolis? Cf. *Dinkard* iii. 3–5; iv. 24.

²⁴ Omitting from v. 26, "this pure religion of the Mazdayasnians, and the fire of Bahram, which is set in the appointed place, encounter annihilation, and the direst destruction and trouble will come into notice."

Religion was mentioned a few words before the phrase on the "pure religion of the Mazdayasnians," so that the phrase is redundant, particularly because it, and the rest of the verse, follow the typical closing phrase, "which I, Ahura Mazdāh, created." This destruction of the religion, including the fire of Sassanid Bahram, does not fit the actions of the Greeks as it does the Muslims; the fire worship in Hellenistic Persis was continued, as proved by coins.

²⁵ Omitting ii. 29, which is an editorial summary of what has gone before.

²⁶ Cf. Mt. xxiv. 10. There is a striking similarity between this section of the *Bahman Yasht* and the apocalypse of the Gospels.

will become a beggar from his father-in-law, and the mother will be parted and estranged from the daughter.[27]

31. "When it is the end of thy tenth hundreth winter, O Zarathushtra Spitama, the sun is more unseen and more spotted;[28] the year, month, and day are shorter;[29] and the earth of Spendarmad is more barren, and fuller of highwaymen;[30] and the crop will not yield the seed, so that of the crop of the corn fields in ten cases, seven will diminish and three will increase, and that which increases does not become ripe; and vegetation, trees, and shrubs will diminish; when one shall take a hundred, ninety will diminish and ten will increase, and that which increases gives no pleasure and flavor.[31] 32. And men are born smaller, and their skill and strength are less; they become more deceitful, and more given to vile practices; they have no gratitude and respect for bread and salt, and they have no affection for their country. . . .[32]

42. "And a dark cloud makes the whole sky night, and the hot wind and the cold wind arrive, and bring along fruit and seed of corn, and even the rain in its proper time; and it does not rain . . . ;[33] and the water of the springs and rivers will diminish, and there will be no increase. 43. And the beast of burden and ox and sheep bring forth more painfully and awkwardly, and acquire less fruitfulness; and their hair is coarser and skin thinner; the milk does not increase and has less cream; the strength of the laboring ox is less, and the agility of the swift horse is less, and it carries less in a race.

44. "And on the men in that perplexing time, O Zarathushtra Spitama, who wear the sacred thread-girdle on the waist, the evil seeking of misgovernment and much of its false judgment . . .[34] come as a wind in which their living is not possible, and they seek death as a boon; and youths and children will be apprehensive, and gossiping chitchat and gladness of heart do not arise among them. 45. And they practice the appointed feasts of their ancestors, the propitiation of angels, and the prayers and ceremonies of the season festivals and guardian spirits, in various places, yet that which they practice they do not believe unhesitatingly; they do not give rewards lawfully, and bestow no gifts and alms and even those they bestow they repent of again. 46. And even those men of the good religion . . .[35] of the Mazdayasnians proceed in conformity with those ways and customs, and do not believe their own religion. 47. And the noble, great, and charitable who are the virtuous of their own country and locality will depart from their own original place and family as idolatrous; through want they beg something from the ignoble and vile, and come to poverty and helplessness; through them nine in ten of these men will perish in the northern quarter. . . .[36]

---

[27] Cf. Mk. xiii. 12; Lk. xxi. 16.

[28] Cf. Mt. xxiv. 29; Mk. xiii. 24; Lk. xxi. 25.

[29] Cf. Mt. xxiv. 22; Mk. xiii. 20.

[30] Or "tax-collectors" (E. W. West, *Pahlevi Texts* i. 204, n. 1) .

[31] Cf. Mt. xxiv. 40–1.

[32] The section ii. 33–41 is omitted here, because it is a denunciation of Islam, its burial customs and the hypocrisy of its practitioners' words on good works. The section was written by a person who knew that the veneration of the Fire of Bahram was almost wholly gone (ii. 37) , having begun to die out as a result of the conversion of Iran by the Muslims. The original resumes at ii. 42 with more tokens of the last age, as requested by Zarathushtra.

[33] Omitting "and that which rains also rains more noxious creatures than water," as inconsistent in the context.

[34] Omitting "have," a copyist's slip.

[35] Omitting the gloss, "who have reverenced the good religion."

[36] The remainder of chapter ii is omitted.

vv. 48–52 is a continuation from ii. 30, detailing the subject of tyranny and mis-

iii. 1.[37] Zarathushtra [spoke] to Ahura Mazdāh thus: "O Ahura Mazdāh, Propitious Spirit! Creator of the material world! Righteous One! . . .[38] 2. O grant me death, and grant my favored ones death, that they may not live in that perplexing time; grant them exemplary living, that they may not prepare wickedness and the way to hell!"

3. Ahura Mazdāh spoke thus: ". . .[39]

12. Zarathushtra enquired of Ahura Mazdāh thus: "O Ahura Mazdāh, Propitious Spirit! Creator of the material world! Righteous One! When they (the Race of Wrath) are so many in number, by what means will they be able to perish?"

---

rule to which Iran will be subject. It is a late doublet (cf. ii. 26 and ii. 48, 51), for the source of the tyranny and misrule is ascribed to the Byzantines (ii. 49) and particularly the Turks (*ibid.*).

v. 53 is an extension of ii. 31, 42, even contradicting them. v. 53 says that the night will be brighter, and that the year, month, and day become shorter by one-third.

v. 54 is out of place in this chapter. It probably comes from chapter iii.

vv. 55–64 make up a late exordium closing the section dealing with the calamities of the last period. It is certainly Sassanid or later, since it implies the existence of an impressive religious literature with commentaries (ii. 55) in the hands of a well-organized priesthood (*ibid.*), and an impressive and detailed ritual, all of which is being lost (ii. 56–61). This is manifestly post-Sassanid. Also, there is mention of a 9,000-year period (ii. 62), which contradicts the 1,000-year period of i. 5. The invading army is described as a cavalry force, which cannot be the army of Alexander with its phalanx. Since this army destroys the religion of Iran, and carries away its power (ii. 63–4), it is probably a Muslim force.

[37] Chapter iii is very much disordered as a result of an editor's having to include the exploits of no less than five avenging saviors accumulated over a long period of time. The editor arranged his material more or less biographically, but sometimes also under subject heads like birth of the savior, the gathering of the army, defeat of the enemy, and restoration of Iran. Consequently, whole sections are out of place, and the narrative concerning any one savior must be carefully separated from the others, for it to make sense.

[38] The very first verse shows that an editor has disturbed the original wording. The text has Zarathushtra ask a question, "Whence do they restore the good religion of the Mazdayasnians? And by what means will they destroy these demons with dishevelled hair of the Race of Wrath?" which is here omitted, because a similar question appears later at iii. 12, and so seems unnecessary here. This is especially so, because in the dialogue Zarathushtra does not wait for an answer, but states that he gives up his request for immortality, with which the prophecy began (i. 1), so as not to witness the horrors in store for Iran. Omitting the question here, then, I have also emended the verb, changing it from "enquired," to "spoke."

[39] It would seem that some rejoinder to Zarathushtra's statement is called for, but none is given in any part of our Pahlevi version.

The following section, iii. 3–11, is omitted. It describes a battle between fresh invaders of Iran and the Race of Wrath. It is most difficult to understand what transpires, as even the Pahlevi redactor knew. He worked numerous glosses into his text attempting to identify the actors in the battle. Since the invaders come from Armenia (iii. 3; *Bundahishn* xx. 12), the army is probably a Christian Byzantine force, but it might be a Crusader force. In iii. 7, however, it is also called Turk, and in iii. 9 the Arabs are mentioned. Whatever the section means, it is certainly much later than Hellenistic date, and has grown out of the confusion of an editor who knew an already existing *Bahman Yasht,* and experienced another foreign conquest.

13. Ahura Mazdāh spoke thus: "O Zarathushtra Spitama! When the demon with dishevelled hair of the Race of Wrath comes into notice, . . .[40] (ii. 54) that wicked evil spirit, when it shall be necessary for him to perish, becomes more oppressive and more tyrannical.[41] (iii. 13). First a black [night as][42] token becomes manifest, and . . . (14.) . . . [in the East][43] a prince is born. It is his father [Hystaspes],[44] a prince of the Kayan race, (who) approaches the women, and a religious prince is born to him; he calls his name [Peshyotanu].[45] 15. That a sign may come to the earth, the night when that prince is born a star falls to the earth . . . .[46] 16. . . . .[47] They rear him with the damsels of the king, and a woman becomes ruler.[48]

17. "That prince when he is thirty years old[49] . . .[50] comes with innumerable banners and divers armies[51] [of the East][52] having exalted banners and having exalted weapons; they hasten up with speed as far as the [Oxus?][53] river . . . ,[54]

[40] Omitting "in the eastern quarter," an editorial insertion to make the prophecy fit the Turks. See n. 22, above.

[41] Inserting here ii. 54, except for its words "Ahura Mazdāh said to Zarathushtra Spitama: 'This is what I foretell:'" as redundant. The verse is inserted here on analogy with the *Oracle of Hystaspes*, frag. 15, where an otherwise similar course of events is described.

[42] The reading "a black token" hardly makes sense. I have added these words on the authority of verse 15.

[43] Omitting "Hushedar, son of Zarathushtra, is born on Lake Frazdan. 14. It is when he comes to his conference with me, Ahura Mazdāh, O Zarathushtra Spitama, that in the direction of Kinistan, it is said, some have said among the Hindus." Hushedar plays no part in the sections immediately to follow, although towards the end of the yasht he does, his birth being mentioned again, to occur 1,600 years after the creation (iii. 44). This is an instance of an editor making notable births coincide in verses 13–4.

"In the East," is substituted for the proper names, which reflect post-Hellenistic terminology. The phrase "in the East" is supplied on analogy with verse 22.

[44] The name "Hystaspes" is inserted here. Hystaspes is named as the father of the Kayan Peshyotanu in iii. 51.

[45] The text actually reads, "Bahram the Vargavand, some have said Shapur." These two Sassanid kings hardly were named in the original. Since Hushedar is born 1,600 years after the creation (iii. 44), it must be that the original name was Peshyotanu.

[46] Cf. Mt. ii. 2, 9–10; the second half of this verse, "when the prince is born the star shows a signal," is omitted as a gloss.

[47] The first part of this verse is a Sassanid gloss: "It is Dad-Ahura-Mazdāh who said that the month Avan and the day Vad is his father's end." Cf. Mt. xxiv. 36; Acts i. 6–7.

[48] In the Gospel accounts, Jesus' father Joseph is a member of the royal Davidic dynasty (Mt. i. 1–16; Lk. iii. 23–37). He quickly drops out of the story altogether, so that Jesus grows up with Mary, belonging to the blood royal by marriage. Cf. Mt. ii. 11.

[49] Cf. Lk. iii. 23.

[50] Omitting "some have told the time." Cf. Mt. xxiv. 36.

[51] Cf. Mk. viii. 38. Mt. xxvi. 53.

[52] Omitting the late glosses, "Hindu and Kini, having uplifted banners, for they set up their banners." The phrase "of the East" substituted; see n. 43, above.

[53] The text reads "Veh"; this is a half-mythical river in northeast Iran; the restoration "Oxus" is conjectural. See E. W. West, *Pahlevi Texts* i. 77–8, n. 7 on *Bundahishn* xx. 9.

[54] Omitting the glosses, ". . . some have said the country of Bambo, as far as Bukhar and the Bukharans within its bank."

O Zarathushtra Spitama. 18. When the star Jupiter comes up to its culminating point and casts Venus down, the sovereignty comes to the prince. 19. Quite innumerable are the champions, furnished with arms and with banners displayed from . . . Persis;[55] and from that direction every supplicant for a child[56] comes into view. 20. . . .[57] They . . .[58] slay an excessive number in companionship and under the same banner (of Peshyotanu) for these countries of Iran.

21. Those of the Race of Wrath and the extensive army of [the East][59] wage [a][60] battle . . . in Persis.[61] 22. For the support of the countries of Iran is the innumerable army of the East; . . .[62] innumerable are the mounted troops, and they ride up to the lurking holes of the demons (with dishevelled hair of the Race of Wrath); they . . . slay so (many) that afterwards a thousand women can afterwards see and kiss but one man.

23. "When it is the end of the time,[63] O Zarathushtra Spitama, those enemies will be as much destroyed as the root of a shrub[64] when it is in the night on which a cold winter arrives, and in this night it sheds its leaves; and they . . . reinstate these countries of Iran which I, Ahura Mazdāh, created. . . .[65]

---

[55] The text actually reads, ". . . some have said from Sagastan, Pars, and Khurusan, some have said from the Lake of Padashkhvargar, some have said from the Hiratis and Kihistan, some have said from Taparistan." The original, then, had a single homeland, and working from the Hellenistic origin of the text, Pars (Persis) is the most logical.

[56] The meaning is every man capable of bearing arms (E. W. West, *Pahlevi Texts* i. 222, n. 5).

[57] The first part of verse 20 is obviously an editorial gloss.

[58] Omitting "will" as a scribal error; the remainder of the prophecy is written in the present.

[59] "Of the East" substituted for "of Shedaspih." See p. 348, n. 43, above.

[60] The text has "three battles." But the glosses, here omitted, indicate that originally only one battle was contemplated: "one in Sped-razur and one in the plain of Nisanak; some have said it was on the Lake of the Three Races, some have said it was in Maruv the brilliant."

[61] Retaining "Pars" from the list, here rendered "Persis."

[62] This part of the verse is a gloss explaining the meaning of the army's banners.

[63] Cf. Dan. xii. 7; Rev. xii. 14.

[64] Cf. Mt. xxiv. 32–3.

[65] The remainder of the yasht is of late date.

vv. 24–38 is a revision and expansion of the victory of Peshyotanu over the evil demons, with some detail of his restoration of Iran included.

vv. 39–40 describe the coming and work of Bahram.

vv. 41–2 belong with vv. 24–38, as part of the revised prophecy concerning Peshyotanu.

vv. 43–49, 52–4 describe the exploits of Hushedar, which occur 600 years after the end of the millennium of Zarathushtra.

vv. 50–1 belong to the Peshyotanu prophecies.

vv. 55–62 are undoubtedly of ancient origin, describing a conflict between one Sam and Azi-dahak, and the savior Soshyans. But it could not have stood in the original *Bahman Yasht,* since it would have been redundant.

v. 63 is a standard colophon.

Bibliography

I. ANCIENT SOURCES

1. Literary

(a) Persian

The *Bahman Yasht* (Pahlevi version) in E. W. West, *Pahlevi Texts* i (Sacred Books of the East v), Oxford, 1880.

The *Bahman Yasht* (Persian version) in J. Darmesteter, *The Zend-Avesta* ii (Sacred Books of the East xxiii), Oxford, 1883.

The *Dinkard* in E. W. West, *Pahlevi Texts* iv (Sacred Books of the East xxxvii), Oxford, 1892.

The Gathas in J. Duchesne-Guillemin, *The Hymns of Zarathustra* (tr. M. Hennings), London, 1952.

The *Oracle of Hystaspes* in F. Cumont and J. Bidez, *Les mages hellénisés* ii, Paris, 1938.

The *Shah nameh,* Book xviii in A. G. Warner and E. Warner, *The Shahnameh of Firdausi* vi, London, 1912.

T M 393 (Manichean-Sogdian fragment) in W. B. Henning, "The Murder of the Magi," *Journal of the Royal Asiatic Society* (1944), 133–44.

The *Videvdād* in J. Darmesteter, *The Zend-Avesta* i (Sacred Books of the East iv), Oxford, 1880.

(b) Jewish

The Old Testament (Revised Standard Version, New York, 1952; An American Translation, Chicago, 1951).

Haggai; Malachi; Jonah; Joel; Ezra; Nehemiah; 1 Chronicles; 2 Chronicles; Proverbs; Psalms; Isaiah; Zechariah; Daniel; Esther.

The Apocrypha (An American Translation, Chicago, 1951).

The Septuagint: *The Old Testament in Greek* (ed. H. B. Swete), ii–iii, Cambridge, 1912–22.

The Pseudepigrapha, in R. H. Charles (ed.), *The Apocrypha and Pseudepigrapha of the Old Testament* i–ii, London, 1913.

Jubilees; Letter of Aristeas; 1 Enoch; The Testaments of the Twelve Patriarchs; 3 Maccabees; Psalms of Solomon; Pirkhe Aboth; Sibylline Oracles.

For the text of the Sibylline Oracles:

    Bate, H. N., *The Sibylline Oracles, Books III–V*, London, 1918.

    Geffcken, J., *Die Oracula Sibyllina* in *Die griechischen christlichen Schriftsteller* xxviii, Leipzig, 1902.

    Kurfess, A., *Sibyllinische Weissagungen*, Munich, 1951.

For (Pseudo-) Aristeas:

    Aristeae ad Philocratem Epistula (ed. P. Wendland, Teubner), Leipzig, 1900.

The Dead Sea Scrolls (translations only):

    M. Burrows, *The Dead Sea Scrolls*, New York, 1955; *More Light on the Dead Sea Scrolls*, New York, 1958.

Gaster, T. H., *The Dead Sea Scriptures in English Translation*, Garden City, 1956.

Josephos, *The Life; Against Apion; The Jewish War; The Antiquities* (ed. H. St. J. Thackerary and R. Marcus, Loeb), London and New York, 1926–43.

Philo, *On the Contemplative Life* (ed. F. H. Colson, Loeb), London and Cambridge, 1941.

(c) Egyptian

The *Book of Overthrowing Apophis* (*P. Bremner-Rhind*) in R. O. Faulkner, "The Bremner Rhind Papyrus—I," *Journal of Egyptian Archeology* 22 (1936), 121–40 and subsequent to 24 (1938), 41–53.

The *Demotic Chronicle* in W. Spiegelberg, *Die sogenannte demotische Chronik*, Leipzig, 1914.

The *Dream of Nektanebo* (*Somnium Nectanebi*) in *Urkunden des Ptolemäerzeit*, *ältere Funde* i (ed. U. Wilcken), Berlin, 1922.

John of Nikiu, *Chronicle* in R. H. Charles, *The Chronicle of John of Nikiu*, London, 1916.

Manethon, fragments (ed. W. G. Waddell, Loeb), London and Cambridge, 1948.

The *Oracle of the Potter* in R. Reitzenstein and H. H. Schraeder, *Studien zum antiken Synkretismus aus Iran und Griechenland*, Leipzig, 1926; and *P. Oxyrhynchus* 2332 in E. Lobel and C. H. Roberts, *The Oxyrhynchus Papyri* xxii, London, 1954.

Papyrus Insinger in F. Lexa, *Papyrus Insinger. Les enseignements moraux d'un scribe égyptien du premier siècle après J.-C.*, Paris, 1926.

(d) Greek and Latin
(i) Collections

Clemen, C., *Die griechischen und lateinischen Nachrichten über die persische Religion*, Giessen, 1920.

Jacoby, F., *Die Fragmenta der griechischen Historiker*, Berlin, 1923– .

Kock, T., *Comicorum Atticorum Fragmenta*, Leipzig, 1880.

(ii) Individual Authors

Aelianus, *On the Characteristics of Animals* (ed. A. F. Scholfield, Loeb), London and Cambridge, 1957– .

Aischylos, *Persians* (ed. H. W. Smyth, Loeb), Cambridge and New York, 1946.

Ammianus Marcellinus, *History* (ed. J. C. Rolfe, Loeb), London and Cambridge, 1937.

Apollordorus, *The Library: Apollodori Bibliotheca* (ed. R. Wagner, Teubner), Leipzig, 1926.

Appianos, *Mithradatika; Syriaka* (ed. H. White, Loeb), London and New York, 1921.

Aristophanes, *Wasps* (ed. B. B. Rogers, Loeb), London and New York, 1924.

Aristotle, *Nichomachean Ethics* (ed. H. Rackham, Loeb), London and Cambridge, 1939; *Politics: Aristotelis Politica* (ed. W. D. Ross, Oxford), Oxford, 1957.

(Pseudo-) Aristotle, *Economica* (ed. G. C. Armstrong, Loeb), London and New York, 1935.

Arrianos, *Anabasis of Alexander; Indika* (ed. E. I. Robson, Loeb), London and Cambridge, 1929–33.

Athenaios, *Savants at Dinner* (ed. C. B. Gulick, Loeb), London and New York, 1927–41.

Caesar, *The Civil War* (ed. A. G. Peskett, Loeb), London and Cambridge, 1951.

Cicero, *On Divination* (ed. W. A. Falconer, Loeb), London and New York, 1923.

Clement of Alexandria, *Protreptikos; Stromata* (ed. O. Stahlin) in *Die griechischen christlichen Schriftsteller* i–iii, Leipzig, 1905–6.

Corpus Hermeticum (ed. A. D. Nock and A. J. Festugière), Paris, 1945–54.

Q. Curtius Rufus, *History of Alexander the Great* (ed. J. C. Rolfe, Loeb), London and Cambridge, 1946.

Demosthenes, *Against Timokrates* (ed. J. H. Vince, Loeb), London and Cambridge, 1935.

Dion Chrysostomos, *Orations* (ed. J. W. Cohoon and H. L. Crosby, Loeb), London and Cambridge, 1932–51.

Diodoros Sikoulos, *Library of History: Diodori Bibliotheca Historica* (ed. C. T. Fischer, Teubner) , Leipzig, 1906.

Diogenes Laertius, *On the Lives and Opinions of Eminent Philosophers* (ed. R. D. Hicks, Loeb) , London and Cambridge, 1950.

Euripides, *Hekouba; Medea; Troades* (ed. G. Murray, Oxford) , London, 1901–25.

Eusebios, *Preparation for the Gospel* (ed. K. Mras) , in *Die griechischen christlichen Schriftsteller* xliii. 1–2, Berlin, 1954.

Florus, *Epitome of Roman History* (ed. E. S. Forster, Loeb) , London and Cambridge, 1947.

Frontinus, *Strategems* (ed. C. E. Bennett, Loeb) , London and New York, 1925.

Heliodoros, *Ethiopika* (ed. R. M. Rattenbury and T. W. Lamb) , Paris, 1935–8. This book has been translated into English by M. Hadas, *Heliodorus*, Ann Arbor, 1957.

Herodes, *Works* (ed. A. D. Knox, Loeb) , London and Cambridge, 1946.

Herodotos, *The Histories* (ed. A. D. Godley, Loeb) , London and New York, 1920–4.

Hippokrates, *Airs, Waters, and Places* (ed. W. H. S. Jones, Loeb) , London and New York, 1923.

Justin, *Epitome of the History of Pompeius Trogus: Epitoma Historiarum Philippicarum Pompei Trogi* (ed. M. Galdi) , Turin, 1921.

(Pseudo-) Kallisthenes, *History of Alexander the Great: Historia Alexandri Magni* (ed. W. Kroll) , Berlin, 1926. This has been translated into English by E. H. Haight, *The Life of Alexander of Macedon by Pseudo-Callisthenes*, New York, 1955.

Ktesias, *Persika; Indika: La Perse, L'Inde: Les sommaires de Photius* (ed. R. Henry) , Brussels, 1947.

Lactantius, *The Divine Institutes* (ed. S. Brandt and G. Laubman) , in *Corpus Scriptorum Ecclesiastorum Latinorum* xix, Leipzig, 1890.

Livy, *From the Founding of the City* (ed. B. O. Foster *et al.*, Loeb) , London and New York, 1919– .

Loukianos, *Works: Luciani Samosatensis Opera* (ed. C. Jacobitz, Teubner) , Leipzig, 1897.

Lucanus, *Pharsalia* (ed. J. D. Duff, Loeb) , London and New York, 1928.

Lucretius, *On the Nature of Things* (ed. W. H. D. Rouse, Loeb) , London and Cambridge, 1937.

Lykophron, *Alexandra* (ed. A. W. Mair, Loeb) , London and New York, 1921.

Malalas, *Chronicle* (ed. B. G. Niebuhr) in *Corpus Scriptorum Historiae Byzantinae* xv, Bonn, 1881.

Nepos, *On the Great Generals of Foreign Nations* (ed. J. C. Rolfe, Loeb) , London and Cambridge, 1947.

The Ninos Romance (ed. S. Gaselee, Loeb) , London and Cambridge, 1935.

Pausanias, *Description of Greece* (ed. W. H. S. Jones, Loeb) , London and New York, 1918–35.

Plato, *Alkibiades I* (ed. R. M. Lamb, Loeb) , London and New York, 1927; *Laws* (ed. R. G. Bury, Loeb) , London and New York, 1926; *Timaios* (ed. R. G. Bury, Loeb) , London and New York, 1929.

Pliny, *Natural History* (ed. H. Rackham, Loeb) , London and Cambridge, 1938– .

Plutarch, *Moralia* (ed. F. C. Babbitt *et al.*, Loeb) , London and New York, 1927– ; *The Lives: Agesilaos; Alexander; Antony; Artaxerxes; Caesar; Crassus; Demetrios; Eumenes; Lucullus; Pompey; Sulla; Themistokles* (ed. B. Perrin, Loeb) , London and New York, 1916–26.

Polyainos, *Generalship* (ed. E. Woelffin, Teubner) , Leipzig, 1887.

Polybios, *The Histories* (ed. W. R. Paton, Loeb) , London and New York, 1922–7.

Strabon, *Geography*, Books xi–xvii (ed. H. L. Jones, Loeb) , London and Cambridge, 1928–32.

Tacitus, *The Annals* (ed. J. Jackson, Loeb), London and Cambridge, 1931–7; *The Histories* (ed. C. H. Moore, Loeb), London and Cambridge, 1925–31.

Theokritos, *Idylls* (ed. J. M. Edmonds, Loeb), London and New York, 1912.

Thoukydides, *The Peloponnesian War* (ed. C. F. Smith, Loeb), London and New York, 1919–23.

Xenophon, *Agesilaos* (ed. E. C. Marchant, Loeb), London and Cambridge, 1925; *Anabasis* (ed. C. L. Brownson, Loeb), London and Cambridge, 1921–2; *Hellenika* (ed. C. L. Brownson, Loeb), London and Cambridge, 1918–22; *Kyropaideia* (ed. W. Miller, Loeb), London and Cambridge, 1914.

2. Catalogues of Coins

Babelon, E. (ed.), *Traité des monnaies grecques et romaines*, ii–iii, Paris, 1935.

Bell, H. W., *Sardis—The Coins, Part I, 1910–1914* (Publications of the American Society for the Excavation of Sardis xi), Leiden, 1916.

Bellinger, A. R., *The Excavations at Dura-Europos: The Coins* (ed. M. I. Rostovtzeff et al.), New Haven, 1949.

Gardner, P., *Catalogue of Greek Coins: The Seleucid Kings of Syria* (British Museum Catalogue), London, 1878.

Hill, G. F., *Catalogue of the Greek Coins of Arabia, Mesopotamia, and Persia* (British Museum Catalogue), London, 1922.

Markoff, A. de, *Catalogue des monnaies Arsacides, Subarsacides, Sassanides, Dab-weihides*, St. Petersburg, 1889.

McDowell, R. H., *Coins from Seleucia on the Tigris*, Ann Arbor, 1935.

Miles, G. C., *Excavation Coins from the Persepolis Region* (Numismatic Notes and Monographs 143), New York, 1959.

Newell, E. T., *The Coinage of the Eastern Seleucid Mints* (Numismatic Studies 1), New York, 1938.

Poole, R. S., *The Ptolemies, Kings of Egypt* (British Museum Catalogue), London, 1883.

Waage, D. B., *Antioch-on-the-Orontes IV, 2: Greek, Roman, Byzantine, and Crusaders' Coins*, Princeton, 1952.

Wroth, W., *Catalogue of the Coins of Parthia* (British Museum Catalogue), London, 1903.

———, *Catalogue of Greek Coins: Pontus, Paphlagonia, Bithynia and the Kingdom of Bosporus* (British Museum Catalogue), London, 1889.

3. Inscriptions and Inscribed Objects

Ancient Near Eastern Texts Relating to the Old Testament (ed. J. B. Pritchard), Princeton, 1950.

Buckler, W. H., and Robinson, D. M., *Sardis—VII. 1: Greek and Latin Inscriptions* (Publications of the American Society for the Excavation of Sardis), Leiden, 1932.

Cameron, G. G., *Persepolis Treasury Tablets* (Oriental Institute Publications 65), Chicago, 1948.

———, "Persepolis Treasury Tablets Old and New," *Journal of Near Eastern Studies* 17 (1958), 161–76.

Clay, A. T., *Babylonian Records in the Library of J. Pierpont Morgan. Part II: Legal Documents from Erech*, New York, 1913.

Corpus Inscriptionum et Monumentorum Religionis Mithriacae (ed. M. J. Verma-seren), The Hague, 1956.

Cumont, F., "Deux inscriptions de Suse," *Comptes rendues à l'academie des inscriptions et belles lettres* (1933), 260–8.

———, "Inscriptions grecques de Suse," *ibid.*, (1931), 233–50; 278–92.

———, "Nouvelles inscriptions grecques de Suse," *ibid.*, (1930), 208–20.

———, "Nouvelles inscriptions grecques de Suse," *ibid.*, (1932), 271–86.

Cumont, F., "Une lettre du roi Artabanus III à la ville de Suse," *ibid.*, (1932), 238–60.

Epping, J. and Strassmeier, J. N., "Babylonische Mondbeobachtungen aus den Jahren 38 und 79 der Seleuciden Ära," *Zeitschrift für Assyriologie* 7 (1892), 220–54.

Hausoullier, B., "Inscriptions grecques de Babylone," *Klio* 9 (1909), 352–63.

——, "Notes sur les inscriptions grecques des fouilles de Suse," *Comptes rendues à l'academie des inscriptions et belles lettres* (1927), 220.

Johansen, K. F., "Tonbullen der Seleukidenzeit aus Warka," *Acta Archeologica* 1 (1930), 41–54.

Kent, R. G., *Old Persian: Grammar, Texts, Lexicon* (2nd ed.), New Haven, 1953.

Lefebvre, G., "Inscriptions grecques d'Égypte," *Bulletin de correspondance hellénique* 26 (1902), 440–66.

McDowell, R. H., *Stamped and Inscribed Objects from Seleucia on the Tigris*, Ann Arbor, 1935.

Orientis Graecae Inscriptiones Selectae (ed. W. Dittenberger), Leipzig, 1903–5.

Otto, E., *Die biographischen Inschriften der ägyptischen Spätzeit* (Probleme der Ägyptologie 2), Leiden, 1954.

Perdrizet, P., "Voyage dans la Macédoine première," *Bulletin de correspondance hellénique* 18 (1894), 416–45.

Sachs, A. J. and Wiseman, D. J., "A Babylonian King List of the Hellenistic Period," *Iraq* 16 (1954), 202–12.

Smith, Sidney, *Babylonian Historical Texts*, London, 1924.

Strassmeier, J. N., "Einige kleinere babylonische Keilschrifttexte aus dem British Museum," *Actes de Huitième Congrès Internationale de Orientalistes*," 2eme Partie, 279–83.

Supplementum Epigraphicum Graecum, iv–xiv, 1929–57.

Thureau-Dangin, A., *Tablettes d'Uruk à l'usage des prêtres du temple d'Anu au temps des séleucides* (Tablettes du Louvre vi), Paris, 1926.

Welles, C. B., *Royal Correspondence in the Hellenistic Period*, New Haven, 1934.

4. Papyri and Parchments

B.G.U.: Aegyptische Urkunden aus den Koniglichen Museen zu Berlin, Griechischen Urkunden, Berlin, 1892–1932.

P. Amherst: The Amherst Papyri (ed. B. P. Grenfell and A. S. Hunt), London, 1900–1.

P. Aram. Elephan.: A. Cowley, *Aramaic Papyri of the Fifth Century* B.C., London, 1923.

P. Aram. Brook.: E. G. Kraeling, *The Brooklyn Museum Aramaic Papyri*, New Haven, 1953.

P. Cairo Zen.: Zenon Papyri (ed. C. C. Edgar), Cairo, 1925–31.

P. Col. Zen.: Columbia Papyri, Greek Series, Nos. 3–4 (ed. W. L. Westermann), New York, 1934–40.

Corpus Papyrorum Judaicarum (ed. V. A. Tcherikover and A. Fuks), Cambridge, 1957– .

Cowley, A., "The Pahlevi Document from Avroman," *Journal of the Royal Asiatic Society* (1919), 147–54.

P. Enteuxeis: O. Gueraud, Ἐντεύξεις, *Requêtes et plaintes addressées au Roi d'Égypte au IIIe siècle avant J.-C.*, Cairo, 1931–2.

Griffith, F. L., "Papyrus Dodgson," *Proceedings of the Society for Biblical Archeology* 31 (1909), 100–9.

P. Hibeh: The Hibeh Papyri (ed. B. P. Grenfell and A. S. Hunt), London, 1906.

P. Mich. Zen.: Zenon Papyri in the University of Michigan Collection (ed. C. C. Edgar), Ann Arbor, 1931.

Minns, E. H., "Parchments of the Parthian Period from Avroman in Kurdistan," *Journal of Hellenic Studies* 35 (1915), 22–65.

P. *Oxford: Some Oxford Papyri* (ed. E. P. Wegener) , Leiden, 1941.
P. *Oxy.: The Oxyrhynchus Papyri* (ed. B. P. Grenfell, A. S. Hunt, E. Lobel, and C. H. Roberts) , London, 1898– .
P. *Paris: Notices et Extraits des Manuscrits Grecs de la Bibliothèque Impériale* xviii (ed. W. Burnet de Presle) , Paris, 1865.
Rostovtzeff, M. I., and Welles, C. B., "A Parchment Contract of Loan from Dura-Europos on the Euphrates," *Yale Classical Studies* 2 (1931) , 1–78.
Sammelbuch Griechischer Urkunden aus Ägypten (ed. F. Preisigke *et al.*) , Berlin, 1913– .
P. *Teb.: The Tebtunis Papyri* (ed. B. P. Grenfell, J. G. Smyly, and E. J. Goodspeed) , London, 1902– .
U.P.Z.: Urkunden des Ptolemäerzeit, ältere Funde (ed. U. Wilcken) , Berlin, 1922–7.
Welles, C. B., Fink, R. O., and Gilliam, J. F., *The Excavations at Dura-Europos V: The Parchments and Papyri,* New Haven, 1959.

II. MODERN WORKS
1. General

Albright, W. F., *From the Stone Age to Christianity* (Anchor ed.) , Garden City, 1957.
Baron, S. W., *A Social and Religious History of the Jews* (2nd ed.) , New York, 1952.
Bevan, E. R., *A History of Egypt under the Ptolemaic Dynasty,* London, 1927.
———, *The House of Seleucus,* London, 1902.
Bouché-Leclerq, A., *Histoire des séleucides,* Paris, 1913.
Cambridge Ancient History, vii–ix, Cambridge, 1928–32.
Delaporte, L., *Le Proche-Orient Asiatique* (3rd ed.) , Paris, 1948.
Drioton, É., and Vandier, J., *L'Égypte* (3rd ed.) , Paris, 1952.
Geiger, W., and Kuhn, E., *Grundriss der iranischen Philologie,* Strassburg, 1904.
Ghirshman, R., *Iran, from the Earliest Times to the Islamic Conquest,* Harmondsworth, 1954.
Hadas, M., *Hellenistic Culture,* New York, 1959.
Hanotaux, G. (ed.) , *Histoire de la nation égyptienne* iii, Paris, 1933.
Hansen, E. V., *The Attalids of Pergamum,* Ithaca, 1947.
Jouguet, P., *L'Égypte ptolémaïque:* see Hanotaux, G., above.
Olmstead, A. T., *History of the Persian Empire,* Chicago, 1948.
Pauly-Wissowa-Kroll, *Realencyclopädie der classischen Altertumswissenschaft,* Stuttgart, 1894– .
Rostovtzeff, M. I., *The Social and Economic History of the Hellenistic World,* London, 1941.
Roussel, P., *La Grèce et l'Orient,* Paris, 1928.
Tarn, W. W., and Griffith, G. T., *Hellenistic Civilization* (3rd ed.) , London, 1952.
Tcherikover, V., *Hellenistic Civilization and the Jews,* Philadelphia, 1959.
Waltz, P., *La question d'Orient dans l'antiquité,* Paris, 1942.
Wilson, J. A., *The Burden of Egypt,* Chicago, 1951.

2. Special

Abrahams, I., *Campaigns in Palestine from Alexander the Great* (Schweich Lectures, 1922) , Oxford, 1927.
Albright, W. F., *The Archeology of Palestine,* Harmondsworth, 1949.
———, "The Psalm of Habakkuk," *Studies in Old Testament Prophecy* (ed. H. H. Rowley) , Edinburgh, 1950, 1–18.
Allegro, J. M., *The Dead Sea Scrolls,* Baltimore, 1956.
Alliot, M., "La Thebaïde en lutte contre les rois d'Alexandrie sous Philopator et Épiphane (216–184) ," *Revue Belge de philologie et d'histoire* 29 (1951) , 421–43.

Alliot, M., "La fin de la résistance égyptienne dans le sud sous Épiphane," *Revue des études anciennes* 54 (1952) , 18–26.

Allotte de la Fuye, "L'oiseau légendaire des monnaies de la Perside," *Arethuse* (1926) , 103–6.

——, "Monnaie inédite de Xerxes, roi d'Arsamosate, provenant des fouilles de Suse," *Revue numismatique* 30 (1927) , 144–54.

Allouche-Le Page, M. T., *L'art monétaire des royaumes bactriens. Essai d'interpretation de la symbolique religeuse gréco-orientale du iiie au ier siècle av. J. C.*, Paris, 1956.

Altheim, F., "Awestische Textgeschichte," *Hallische Monographien* 9 (1949) .

Anderson, A. R., *Alexander's Gate, Gog and Magog, and the Inclosed Nations*, Cambridge, Mass., 1932.

Anderson, B. W., "The Book of Esther," *The Interpreter's Bible* iii, New York, 1954.

Anthes, R., *Die Maat des Echnatons von Amarna*, Supplement 14 to the *Journal of the American Oriental Society*, Baltimore, 1952.

Aymard, A., "De nouveau sur Antiochos III d'après une inscription grecque d'Iran," *Revue des études anciennes* 51 (1949) , 327–45.

——, "De nouveau sur la chronologie des Séleucides," *Revue des études anciennes* 57 (1955) , 102–12.

——, "Une ville de la Babylonie séleucide," *Revue des études anciennes* 40 (1938) , 5–42.

Bailey, H. W., "Iranian Studies," *Bulletin of the School of Oriental and African Studies* 6 (1930–32) , 945–55.

——, "Iranica," *Bulletin of the School of Oriental and African Studies* 11 (1943–6) , 1–5.

Baron, S. W., "The Pharisees: The Sociological Background of Their Faith, by Louis Finkelstein," (review) *Journal of Biblical Literature* 59 (1940) , 60–7.

Bataille, "Thèbes, gréco-romaine," *Chronique d'Égypte* 52 (1951) , 325–53.

Bell, H. I., "Anti-Semitism in Alexandria," *Journal of Roman Studies* 31 (1941) , 1–18.

——, "Graeco-Egyptian Religion," *Museum Helveticum* 10 (1953) , 222–37.

——, "Hellenic Culture in Egypt," *Journal of Egyptian Archeology* 8 (1922) , 139–55.

——, "Popular Religion in Graeco-Roman Egypt," *Journal of Egyptian Archeology* 34 (1948) , 82–97.

Bellinger, A. R., "Hyspaosines of Charax," *Yale Classical Studies* 8 (1942) , 51–67.

——, "The End of the Seleucids," *Transactions of the Connecticut Academy of Arts and Sciences* 38 (1949) , 51–102.

Bentwich, N., *Hellenism*, Philadelphia, 1920.

Bentzen, A., *Introduction to the Old Testament* (2nd ed.) , Copenhagen, 1952.

Bertholet, A., "Der Schutzengel Persiens," *Oriental Studies in Honour of Cursetji Erachji Pavry* (ed. J. D. C. Pavry) , London, 1933, 34–40.

Bevan, E. R., *Jerusalem under the High Priests*, London, 1904.

——, *Sibyls and Seers*, London, 1928.

Bewer, J. A., *The Literature of the Old Testament* (rev. ed.) , New York, 1933.

Bickerman, E. J., "Notes on Seleucid and Parthian Chronology," *Berytus* 8, fasc. 2 (1944) , 73–83.

——, "The Colophon of the Greek Book of Esther," *Journal of Biblical Literature* 63 (1944) , 339–62.

——, *The Maccabees*, New York, 1947.

Bickermann, E., *Der Gott der Makkabäer*, Berlin, 1937.

——, "Ritualmord und Eselkult," *Monatsschrift für Geschichte und Wissenschaft des Judentums* 71 (1921) , 171–87; 255–64.

——, "Zur Datierung des Pseudo-Aristeas," *Zeitschrift für die Neutestamentliche Wissenschaft* 29 (1930) , 280–92.

Bikerman, E., "Heliodore au temple de Jerusalem," *Annuaire de l'Institute de Philologie et d'Histoire Orientales et Slaves* 7 (1939–44) , 5–40.

——, "Sur la Chronologie de la Sixième Guerre de Syrie," *Chronique d'Égypte* 54 (1952) , 396–403.

——, "Un document relatif à la persécution d'Antiochos IV Épiphane," *Revue de l'Histoire des Religions* 115 (1937) , 188–223.

Bidez, J., *La cité du soleil chez les Stoiciëns*, Brussels, 1932.

Boak, A. E. R., "The Organization of Gilds in Greco-Roman Egypt," *Transactions of the American Philosophical Association* 68 (1937) , 212–20.

Bousset, W., "Oracula Sibyllina," *Zeitschrift für die Neutestamentliche Wissenschaft* 3 (1902) , 22–5.

Box, G. H., *Judaism in the Greek Period* (The Clarendon Bible v) , Oxford, 1932.

Boyce, M., "Some Reflections on Zurvanism," *Bulletin of the School of Oriental and African Studies* 19 (1957) , 304–16.

Brady, T. A., *The Reception of the Egyptian Cults by the Greeks (330–30 B.C.)* , Columbia, 1935.

Braidwood, R. J., *Mounds in the Plain of Antioch: An Archeological Survey*, Chicago, 1937.

Braude, W. G., *Jewish Proselytizing*, Providence, 1940.

Braun, M., *History and Romance in Greco-Oriental Literature*, Oxford, 1938.

Briggs, C. A., and Briggs, E. G., *The Book of Psalms*, New York, 1906–7.

Broughton, T. R. S., "Cleopatra and the Treasure of the Ptolemies," *American Journal of Philology* 63 (1942) , 328–32.

——, "New Evidence on Temple Estates in Asia Minor," *Studies in Honor of A. C. Johnson* (ed. P. R. Coleman-Norton) , Princeton, 1951, 236–50.

——, "Stratonicea and Aristonicus," *Classical Philology* 29 (1934) , 252–4.

Brown, F. E., "The Temple of Zeus Olympios at Dura and the Religious Policy of the Seleucids," *American Journal of Archeology* 45 (1941) , 94.

Browne, E. G., *A Literary History of Persia* (2nd ed.) , Cambridge, 1951.

Burkitt, F. C., *Jewish and Christian Apocalypses* (Schweich Lectures, 1913) , London, 1914.

Burrows, M., *More Light on the Dead Sea Scrolls*, New York, 1958.

——, *The Dead Sea Scrolls*, New York, 1955.

Butler, H. C., *Sardis* i, *The Excavations*, Leyden, 1922; ii, *The Temple of Artemis*, Leyden, 1925 (Publications of the American Society for the Excavation of Sardis) .

Calder, W. M., and Keil, J., *Anatolian Studies Presented to William Hepburn Buckler*, Manchester, 1939.

Cameron, G. G., "Darius and Xerxes in Babylonia," *American Journal of Semitic Languages* 58 (1941) , 314–25.

Cerny, J., *Ancient Egyptian Religion*, London, 1952.

Charles, R. H., *Religious Developments between the Old and the New Testaments*, London, 1914.

Charlesworth, M. P., "Some Fragments of the Propaganda of Marc Anthony," *Classical Quarterly* 27 (1933) , 172–7.

Christensen, A., *Études sur le Zoroastrianisme de la perse antique*, Copenhagen, 1928.

Cook, S. A., *An Introduction to the Bible*, Harmondsworth, 1945.

Cross, F. M., *The Ancient Library of Qumran and Modern Biblical Studies* (Haskell Lectures, 1956–57) , New York, 1958.

——, "The Oldest Manuscripts from Qumran," *Journal of Biblical Literature* 74 (1955) , 147–72.

Crowfoot, J. W., *et al.*, *Samaria-Sebaste: Reports of the Work of the Joint Expedition in 1931–33 and of the British Expedition in 1935*: i, *The Buildings at Samaria*, London, 1942; III, *The Objects from Samaria*, London, 1957.

Cumont, F., *Fouilles de Doura Europos* i, Paris, 1926.

Cumont, F., "Le fin du monde selon les mages occidentaux," *Revue de l'Histoire des Religions* 103 (1931) , 29–96.

———, "Le Zeus Stratios de Mithradate," *Revue de l'Histoire des Religions* 43 (1901) , 47–57.

———, "Mithra en Asie Mineur," *Anatolian Studies Presented to William Hepburn Buckler*, Manchester, 1939, 67–76.

———, "Portrait de une reine parthe trouvé a Suse," *Comptes rendues à l'academie des inscriptions et belles lettres* (1939) , 330–41.

———, *The Mysteries of Mithra* (tr. T. J. McCormack) , Chicago, 1903.

Dancy, J. C., *A Commentary on I Maccabees*, Oxford, 1954.

Davis, S., *Race Relations in Ancient Egypt*, London, 1951.

Dayet, M., "Un tétradrachm arsacide inédit," *Arethuse* (1925) , 63–6.

Debevoise, N., *A Political History of Parthia*, Chicago, 1938.

———, "When Greek and Oriental Cultures Met at Seleucia," *Asia* 38 (1938) , 746–51.

Demargne, P., "Les étapes de l'hellénisme à Xanthos de Lycie," *Revue des études grecques* 67 (1954) , 14–5.

Dentan, R. C. (ed.) , *The Idea of History in the Ancient Near East*, New Haven, 1955.

Derwacter, F. M., *Preparing the Way for Paul*, New York, 1930.

Dhalla, M. N., *History of Zoroastrianism*, New York, 1938.

———, *Zoroastrian Civilization*, New York, 1922.

Dix, G. H., "The Influence of Babylonian Ideas on Jewish Messianism," *Journal of Theological Studies* 26 (1925) , 241–56.

Duchesne-Guillemin, J., "Notes on Zervanism in the Light of Zaehner's *Zurvan*, with Additional References," *Journal of Near Eastern Studies* 15 (1956) , 108–12.

———, *Ormazd et Ahriman. L'Aventure dualiste dans l'antiquité*, Paris, 1953.

———, *The Western Response to Zoroaster* (Ratanbai Katrak Lectures, 1956) , Oxford, 1958.

Dupont-Sommer, A., *The Dead Sea Scrolls* (tr. E. M. Rowley) , Oxford, 1952.

Ehtécham, M., *L'Iran sous les Achéménides. Contribution à l'étude de l'organisation sociale et politique du premier Empire des Perses*, Fribourg, 1946.

Eissfeldt, O., *Einleitung in das Alte Testament*, Tubingen, 1934.

Elgood, P. G., *The Later Dynasties of Egypt*, New York, 1952.

Engers, M., "The Letter from the Parthian King Artabanus III to the Town of Susa," *Mnemosyne* 7 (1939) , 136–41.

Engnell, I., *Studies in Divine Kingship in the Ancient Near East*, Uppsala, 1943.

Fairman, H. W., "The Kingship Rituals of Egypt," *Myth, Ritual, and Kingship* (ed. S. H. Hooke) , Oxford, 1958.

Farmer, W. R., *Maccabees, Zealots, and Josephos. An Inquiry into Jewish Nationalism in the Greco-Roman Period*, New York, 1956.

Ferguson, W. S., *Greek Imperialism*, Boston, 1913.

Finkelstein, L., *The Pharisees: The Sociological Background of Their Faith*, Philadelphia, 1938.

Fischel, H. A., *The First Book of Maccabees*, New York, 1948.

Foakes-Jackson, F. J., "The Influence of Iran upon Early Judaism and Christianity," *Oriental Studies in Honour of Cursetji Erachji Pavry* (ed. J. D. C. Pavry) , London, 1933.

Frankfort, H. I., *Ancient Egyptian Religion*, New York, 1948.

———, *Kingship and the Gods*, Chicago, 1948.

——— et al., *The Intellectual Adventure of Ancient Man*, Chicago, 1946.

Frazer, J. G., *The Golden Bough* ii, xi, New York, 1900.

Frost, S. B., *Old Testament Apocalyptic* (Fernley-Hartley Lectures, 1952) , London, 1952.

Frye, R. N., *Notes on the Early Coinage of Transoxania* (Numismatic Notes and Monographs 113) , New York, 1949.

Fuchs, R., *Der geistige Widerstand gegen Rom in der antiken Welt*, Berlin, 1938.

Gadd, C. J., *Ideas of Divine Rule in the Ancient East* (Schweich Lectures, 1945) , London, 1948.

Gardiner, A. H., "New Literary Works from Ancient Egypt," *Journal of Egyptian Archeology* 1 (1914) , 100–6.

Gauthier, H., "Un groupe ptolémaïque d'Héliopolis," *Revue égyptologique* 2 (1924) , 1–12.

Gershevitch, I., *The Avestan Hymn to Mithra*, Cambridge, 1959.

Ghirshman, R., *Village Perse-Achéménide* (Mémoires de la Mission Archeologique en Iran xxxvi) , Paris, 1954.

Ginsberg, H. L., *Studies in Daniel*, New York, 1948.

Ginsburg, M. S., "Sparta and Judaea," *Classical Philology* 29 (1934) , 117–22.

Glanville, S. R. K., "The Admission of a Priest of Soknebtynis in the Second Century B.C.," *Journal of Egyptian Archeology* 19 (1933) , 34–41.

Glueck, N., *Rivers in the Desert. A History of the Negev*, New York, 1959.

Godard, A., "L'Art de l'Époque Séleucide et Parthe," *Le Civilisation Iranienne*, Paris, 1952, 111–5.

Goldman, H., *Excavations at Gözlü Tepe, Tarsus*, i: *The Hellenistic and Roman Periods*, Princeton, 1950.

———, "The Sandon Monument of Tarsus," *Journal of the American Oriental Society* 60 (1940) , 544–53.

Goldstein, N. W., "Cultivated Pagans and Ancient Antisemitism," *Journal of Religion* 19 (1939) , 346–64.

Goodenough, E. R., *By Light, Light: The Mystic Gospel of Hellenistic Judaism*, New Haven, 1935.

Gow, A. S. F., "Notes on the *Persae* of Aeschylus," *Journal of Hellenic Studies* 48 (1928) , 133–58.

Gressman, H., "Das Gebet des Kyriakos," *Zeitschrift für die Neutestamentliche Wissenschaft* 20 (1921) , 23–35.

———, "Foreign Influences in Hebrew Prophecy," *Journal of Theological Studies* 27 (1926) , 241–54.

Gunkel, H., *Schöpfung und Chaos*, Gottingen, 1895.

Hadas, M., *The Third and Fourth Books of Maccabees*, New York, 1953.

Hallock, R. T., "New Light from Persepolis," *Journal of Near Eastern Studies* 9 (1950) , 237–52.

Haug, M., *Essays on the Religion of the Parsis* (3rd ed.) , London, 1884.

Haupt, P., *Purim,* Leipzig, 1906.

Henning, W. B., "The Disintegration of the Avestic Studies," *Transactions of the Philological Society* (1942) , 40–56.

———, "The Murder of the Magi," *Journal of the Royal Asiatic Society* (1944) , 133–44.

Herzfeld, E. E., *Archeological History of Iran* (Schweich Lectures, 1934) , London, 1935.

———, "Notes of the Quarter: Recent Discoveries at Persepolis," *Journal of the Royal Asiatic Society* (1934) , 226–32.

———, *Zoroaster and His World*, Princeton, 1947.

Herzog, I., "The Outlook of Greek Culture upon Judaism," *Hibbert Journal* 29 (1931) , 49–60.

Hill, G. F., "Alexander the Great and the Persian Lion-Gryphon," *Journal of Hellenic Studies,* 43 (1923) , 156–61.

Hombert, M., and Préaux, C., "Note sur la durée de la vie dans l'Égypte gréco-romaine," *Chronique d'Égypte* 20 (1945) , 139–60.

Hombert, P., "Sarapis Kosmokrator et Isis Kosmokrateirea," *Antiquité classique* 14 (1945), 319–29.

Hooke, S. H., *Babylonian and Assyrian Religion*, London, 1953.

——— (ed.), *Myth, Ritual, and Kingship*, Oxford, 1958.

How, W. W., and Wells, J., *A Commentary on Herodotus*, Oxford, 1912.

Jackson, A. V. W., *Zoroastrian Studies*, New York, 1928.

Jaeger, W., "Greeks and Jews," *Journal of Religion* 18 (1938), 127–43.

Jeffery, A., "Daniel," *Interpreter's Bible* vi, New York, 1956, 341–54.

Jensen, P., "Elamitische Eigennamen," *Wiener Zeitschrift für die Kunde des Morgenlandes* 6 (1892), 47–9, 209–11.

Jesi, F., "Notes sur l'édit dionysiaque de Ptolémée IV Philopator," *Journal of Near Eastern Studies* 15 (1956), 236–40.

Johnson, A. R., "Hebrew Conceptions of Kingship," *Myth, Ritual, and Kingship* (ed. S. H. Hooke), Oxford, 1958, 204–35.

———, "Jonah II. 3–10: A Study in Cultic Phantasy," *Studies in Old Testament Prophecy* (ed. H. H. Rowley), Edinburgh, 1950, 82–102.

———, *Sacral Kingship in Ancient Israel*, Cardiff, 1955.

———, "The Psalms," *The Old Testament and Modern Study* (ed. H. H. Rowley), London, 1951, 162–207.

Jones, A. H. M., *The Cities of the Eastern Roman Provinces*, Oxford, 1937.

———, *The Greek City from Alexander to Justinian*, Oxford, 1940.

de Jonge, M., *The Testaments of the Twelve Patriarchs*, Leiden, 1953.

Jouguet, P., "Les destinées de l'hellénisme dans l'Égypte gréco-romaine," *Chronique d'Égypte* 19 (1935), 89–108.

———, *Macedonian Imperialism*, London, 1928.

Kiessling, E., "La genèse du culte de Sarapis à Alexandrie," *Chronique d'Égypte* 48 (1949), 317–23.

Kincaid, C. A., "A Persian Prince—Antiochus Epiphanes," *Oriental Studies in Honour of Cursetji Erachji Pavry* (ed. J. D. C. Pavry), London, 1933, 209–19.

Koldewey, R., "Ausgrabungberichte aus Babylon," *Mitteilungen der Deutschen Orient-Gesellschaft* 32 (1906), 3–7.

Kornemann, E., "Zur Geschwisterehe im Altertum," *Klio* 19 (1925), 355–61.

Kraeling, C. H. (ed.), *Gerasa, City of the Decapolis*, New Haven, 1938.

———, *The Excavations at Dura-Europos* VIII, i. *The Synagogue*, New Haven, 1956.

Kraeling, E. G. H., "Some Babylonian and Iranian Mythology in the Seventh Chapter of Daniel," *Oriental Studies in Honour of Cursetji Erachji Pavry* (ed. J. D. C. Pavry), London, 1933, 228–31.

Langdon, S., "The Babylonian and Persian Sacaea," *Journal of the Royal Asiatic Society* (1924), 65–72.

Lattimore, R., "Portents and Prophecies," *Classical Journal* 29 (1934), 441–9.

Lehmann, C. F., "Noch einmal *Kassu: Kissioi*, nicht *Kossioi*," *Zeitschrift für Assyriologie* 7 (1892), 328–34.

Lenzen, H., *Vorläufiger Bericht über die von dem Deutschen Archäologischen Institut und der Deutschen-Orient-Gesellschaft aus Mitteln der Deutschen Forschungsgemeinschaft unternommen Ausgrabungen in Uruk-Warka*, Berlin, 1956.

Levy, H., "Aristotle and the Jewish Sage according to Clearchos of Soli," *Harvard Theological Review* 31 (1938), 205–35.

Lieberman, S., *Greek in Jewish Palestine*, New York, 1942.

Lozinski, B. P., *The Original Homeland of the Parthians*, The Hague, 1959.

Macalister, R. A. S., *The Excavation of Gezer*, London, 1912.

Magie, D., *Roman Rule in Asia Minor*, Princeton, 1950.

Mahaffey, J. P., *The Progress of Hellenism in Alexander's Empire*, Chicago, 1905

Mazur, B. D., *Studies on Jewry in Greece*, Athens, 1935.

McCown, C. C., "Egyptian Apocalyptic Literature," *Harvard Theological Review* 18 (1925), 357–411.

McMinn, J. B., "Fusion of the Gods: A Religio-Astrological Study of the Interpenetration of the East and the West in Asia Minor," *Journal of Near Eastern Studies* 15 (1956), 201–13.

Meiklejohn, K. W., "Alexander Helios and Caesarion," *Journal of Roman Studies* 24 (1934), 191–5.

Meissner, B., "Zur Entstehungsgeschichte des Purimfestes," *Zeitschrift der deutsche Morgenlands-Gesellschaft* 50 (1896), 296–8.

Meyer, E., *Ursprung und Anfänge des Christentums* ii, Berlin, 1921.

Milne, J. G., "Egyptian Nationalism under Greek and Roman Rule," *Journal of Egyptian Archeology* 14 (1928), 226–34.

Mittwoch, A., "Tribute and Land Tax in Seleucid Judaea," *Biblica* 36 (1955), 352–61.

Montgomery, J. A., *A Critical and Exegetical Commentary on the Book of Daniel*, New York, 1927.

Moore, G. F., *Judaism in the First Three Centuries of the Christian Era* i, Cambridge, Mass., 1927.

Moulton, J. H., *Early Zoroastrianism* (Hibbert Lectures, 1912), London, 1913.

Mowinckel, S., *He That Cometh* (tr. G. W. Anderson), New York, 1955.

Newell, E. T., "A Parthian Hoard," *Numismatic Chronicle* 4 (1924), 141–80.

———, *Mithradates of Parthia and Hyspaosines of Charax: A Numismatic Palimpsest* (Numismatic Notes and Monographs 26), New York, 1925.

Nock, A. D., "A Vision of Mandulis Aion," *Harvard Theological Review* 27 (1934), 53–104.

———, "Behn, Das Mithrasheiligtum zu Dieburg" (review), *Gnomon* 6 (1930), 30–5.

———, *Conversion*, Oxford, 1933.

———, "Cremation and Burial in the Roman Empire," *Harvard Theological Review* 25 (1932), 321–59.

———, "M. J. Vermaseren: Corpus Inscriptionum et Monumentorum Religionis Mithriacae" (review), *Gnomon* 30 (1958), 291–5.

———, "Notes on Ruler-Cult, I–IV," *Journal of Hellenic Studies* 48 (1928), 21–43.

———, "Studien zum antiken Synkretismus aus Iran und Griechenland" (review), *Journal of Hellenic Studies* 49 (1929), 111–6.

———, "Taylor: The Divinity of the Roman Emperor" (review), *Gnomon* 8 (1932), 513–8.

———, "The Problem of Zoroaster," *American Journal of Archeology* 59 (1949), 272–85.

———, "The Roman Army and the Roman Religious Year," *Harvard Theological Review* 45 (1952), 187–252.

———, Skeat, T. C., and Roberts, C., "The Gild of Zeus Hypsistos," *Harvard Theological Review* 29 (1936), 39–87.

Nyberg, H. S., *Die Religionen des alten Iran* (tr. into German by H. S. Schraeder), Leipzig, 1938.

Oesterley, W. O. E., *The Books of the Apocrypha*, London, 1915.

———, *The Jews and Judaism in the Greek Period*, New York, 1941.

———, and Box, G. H., *A Short Survey of the Literature of Rabbinical and Medieval Judaism*, London, 1920.

———, and Robinson, T. H., *A History of Israel* ii, London, 1932.

Olmstead, A. T., "Ahura Mazda in Assyrian," *Oriental Studies in Honour of Cursetji Erachji Pavry* (ed. J. D. C. Pavry), London, 1933, 366–72.

———, "Cuneiform Texts and Hellenistic Chronology," *Classical Philology* 32 (1937), 1–14.

Olmstead, A. T., "Intertestamental Studies," *Journal of the American Oriental Society* 56 (1936), 242–57.

Otto, W., *Priester und Tempel im hellenischtischen Ägypten*, Leipzig, 1908.

Paton, L. B., *A Critical and Exegetical Commentary on the Book of Esther*, New York, 1916.

Pearson, L., *The Lost Histories of Alexander the Great*, New York, 1960.

Peek, W., *Der Isishymnus von Andros und verwandte Texte*, Berlin, 1930.

Pfeiffer, R. H., "Hebrews and Greeks before Alexander," *Journal of Biblical Literature* 56 (1937), 91–101.

———, *History of New Testament Times*, New York, 1949.

———, *Introduction to the Old Testament* (2nd ed.), New York, 1948.

Phythian-Adams, W. J., *Mithraism*, Chicago, 1915.

Pinches, T. G., *The Old Testament in the Light of the Historical Records and Legends of Assyria and Babylonia* (1st ed.), London, 1902; (2nd ed.), London, 1903.

Pinson, K. S. (ed.), *Essays on Antisemitism* (2nd ed.), New York, 1946.

Pope, A. U., "Persepolis as a Ritual City," *Archeology* 10 (1957), 123–30.

Porada, E., "Greek Influence on a Seal-Cutter from Ur," *American Journal of Archeology* 59 (1955), 173.

Préaux, C., "Esquisse d'une histoire des révolutions égyptiennes sous les Lagids," *Chronique d'Égypte* 22 (1936), 522–52.

———, *L'economie royale des Lagids*, Brussels, 1939.

———, "Les Égyptien dans la civilisation hellénistique d'Égypte," *Chronique d'Égypte* 35 (1943), 148–60.

———, *Les Grecs en Égypte d'après les archives de Zenon*, Brussels, 1947.

———, "Politique du race ou politique royale," *Chronique d'Égypte* 21 (1936), 111–38.

———, "Restrictions de la liberté du travail dans l'Égypte grecque et romaine," *Chronique d'Égypte* 18 (1934), 338–45.

Pritchard, J. B. (ed.), *The Ancient Near East in Pictures Relating to the Old Testament*, Princeton, 1954.

Rabinowitz, L., "The First Essenes," *Journal of Semitic Studies* 4 (1959), 358–61.

Radin, M., *The Jews among the Greeks and Romans*, Philadelphia, 1915.

Ramsay, W. M., *The Cities and Bishoprics of Phrygia*, Oxford, 1895–7.

———, *The Social Basis of Roman Power in Asia Minor*, Aberdeen, 1941.

Ranke, H., "A Late Ptolemaic Statue of Hathor from Her Temple at Dendereh," *Journal of the American Oriental Society* 65 (1945), 238–48.

———, "The Statue of a Ptolemaic Στρατηγός of the Mendesian Nome in the Cleveland Museum of Art," *Journal of the American Oriental Society* 73 (1953), 193–8.

Rehm, A. (ed.), *Milet: Ergebnisse des Ausgrabungs und Untersuchungen* i, Berlin, 1914.

Reiss, E., "Religious Gleanings from the Magical Papyri," *Classical Weekly* 28 (1935), 105–11.

Reitzenstein, R., "Zur Religionspolitik der Ptolemäer," *Archiv für Religionswissenschaft* 19 (1918), 191–4.

———, and Schraeder, H. H., *Studien zum antiken Synkretismus aus Iran und Griechenland*, Leipzig, 1926.

Robinson, D. M., "A Graeco-Parthian Portrait Head of Mithradates I," *American Journal of Archeology* 31 (1927), 338–44.

Roos, A. C., "Bemerkungen zu einer griechischen Inschrift aus Susa," *Mnemosyne* 1 (1934), 106–12.

Rostovtzeff, M. I., "Dura and the Problem of Parthian Art," *Yale Classical Studies* 5 (1935), 155–304.

Rostovtzeff, M. I., "Foundations of Social and Economic Life in Egypt in Hellenistic Times," *Journal of Egyptian Archeology* 6 (1920), 161–78.

———, "Le Gad de Doura et Séleucus Nicator," *Mélanges Syriens offerts à Monsieur René Dussaud* i, Paris, 1939, 281–95.

———, "Seleucid Babylonia," *Yale Classical Studies* 3 (1932), 3–114.

———, Brown, F. E., and Welles, C. B., *The Excavations at Dura-Europos: Preliminary Report of the Seventh and Eighth Seasons*, New Haven, 1939.

Roussel, P., "Un édit de Ptolémée Philopator relatif au culte de Dionysos," *Comptes rendues à l'Academie des inscriptions et belles lettres* (1919), 237–43.

———, "Un nouvel hymne à Isis," *Revue des études grecques* 42 (1929), 137–68.

Rowley, H. H., *Darius the Mede and the Four World Empires in the Book of Daniel*, Cardiff, 1935.

———, *The Growth of the Old Testament*, London, 1950.

———, *The Relevance of Apocalyptic* (rev. ed.), New York, 1946.

———, "The Unity of the Book of Daniel," *The Servant of the Lord and Other Essays on the Old Testament* (ed. H. H. Rowley), London, 1954, 237–68.

———, *The Zadokite Fragments and the Dead Sea Scrolls*, Oxford, 1952.

Sarre, F., and Herzfeld, H., *Iranische Felsreliefs*, Berlin, 1910.

Schaumberger, J., "Die neue Seleukiden-Liste BM 35603 und die makkabäische Chronologie," *Biblica* 36 (1955), 423–35.

Schmidt, E. F., *Persepolis* i (1953); ii (1957), Chicago, 1953–7.

———, *The Treasury of Persepolis and Other Discoveries in the Homeland of the Achaemenians*, Chicago, 1939.

Schnabel, P., *Berossos*, Leipzig, 1923.

Scott, K., "Octavian's Propaganda and Antony's *de Sua Ebrietate*," *Classical Philology* 24 (1929), 133–41.

Simon, J., *Handbook for the Study of Egyptian Topographical Lists Relating to Western Asia*, Leiden, 1937.

Simpson, W., " 'The Buddhist Praying Wheel,' " *Journal of the Royal Asiatic Society* (1898), 873–5.

Smith, Sidney, "Notes on 'The Assyrian Tree,' " *Bulletin of the School of Oriental and African Studies* 4 (1926), 69–76.

Stillwell, R. (ed.), *Antioch-on-the-Orontes* ii. *The Excavations 1933–36*, Princeton, 1938.

Swain, J. W., "Antiochos Epiphanes and Egypt," *Classical Philology* 39 (1944), 73–94.

———, "The Theory of the Four Monarchies: Opposition History under the Roman Empire," *Classical Philology* 35 (1940), 1–21.

Swiderek, A., "La Société indigène en Égypte au iiie Siècle avant notre ère d'après les archives de Zenon," *Journal of Juristic Papyrology* 7–8 (1953–4), 231–84.

Tarn, W. W., "Alexander Helios and the Golden Age," *Journal of Roman Studies* 22 (1932), 135–60.

———, *Alexander the Great*, Cambridge, 1948–50.

———, *Alexander the Great and the Unity of Mankind*, London, 1933.

———, "Notes on Hellenism in Bactria and India," *Journal of Hellenic Studies* 22 (1902), 268–93.

———, "Ptolemy II," *Journal of Egyptian Archeology* 14 (1928), 246–59.

———, *Seleucid-Parthian Studies*, London, 1930.

———, *The Greeks in Bactria and India* (2nd ed.), Cambridge, 1951.

———, "The Hellenistic Ruler Cult and the Daemon," *Journal of Hellenic Studies* 48 (1928), 206–19.

———, "Two Notes on Ptolemaic History," *Journal of Hellenic Studies* 53 (1933), 57–68.

Taubenschlag, R., "Das Babylonische Recht in den Griechischen Papyri," *Journal of Juristic Papyrology* 7/8 (1953–4), 169–85.

Faubenschlag, R., "Keilschriftrecht im Rechte der Papyri der römischen und byzantinischen Zeit," *Akten des VIII. Internationalen Kongresses für Papyrologie,* Vienna, 1956.

————, *The Law of Greco-Roman Egypt in the Light of the Papyri* (2nd ed.), Warsaw, 1955.

Taylor, L. R., "The Daimon of the Persian King," *Journal of Hellenic Studies* 48 (1928), 6.

————, "The 'Proskynesis' and the Hellenistic Ruler Cult," *Journal of Hellenic Studies* 47 (1927), 53–62.

Tcherikover, V., "Jewish Apologetic Literature Reconsidered," *Eos* 48 (1957), 169–93.

————, "The Ideology of the Letter of Aristeas," *Harvard Theological Review* 51 (1958), 59–85.

Terry, M. S., *The Sibylline Oracles,* New York, 1890.

Torrey, C. C., " 'Medes and Persians,' " *Journal of the American Oriental Society* 66 (1946), 1–15.

————, "Nineveh in the Book of Tobit," *Journal of Biblical Literature* 41 (1922), 237–45.

————, "Notes on the Aramaic Parts of Daniel," *Transactions of the Connecticut Academy of Arts and Sciences* 15 (1909), 241–82.

————, *The Apocryphal Literature,* New Haven, 1945.

————, "The Older Book of Esther," *Harvard Theological Review* 37 (1944), 1–40.

————, " 'Yāwān' and 'Hellas' as Designations of the Seleucid Empire," *Journal of the American Oriental Society* 25 (1904), 302–11.

Ungnad, A., "Keilinschriftliche Beiträge zum Buch Esra und Ester," *Zeitschrift für die Alttestamentliche Wissenschaft* 58 (1940–41), 240–4; 59 (1942–43), 219.

Unvala, J. M., "Notes de numismatique (fouilles de Suse, 1934)," *Revue numismatique* 38 (1935), 155–62.

van Ingen, W., *Figurines from Seleucia on the Tigris,* Ann Arbor, 1939.

Vanden Berghe, L., *Archéologie de l'Iran ancien,* Leiden, 1959.

Voget, F., "The American Indian in Transition: Reformation and Status Innovations," *American Journal of Sociology* 62 (1957), 368–78.

Ward, W. H., *The Seal Cylinders of Western Asia,* Washington, 1910.

Waterman, L., *Preliminary Report upon the Excavations at Tel Umar, Iraq,* Ann Arbor, 1931.

————, *Second Preliminary Report upon the Excavations at Tel Umar, Iraq,* Ann Arbor, 1932.

Welles, C. B., "The Population of Roman Dura," *Studies in Honor of A. C. Johnson* (ed. P. R. Coleman-Norton), Princeton, 1951, 251–74.

Westermann, W. L., "The Greek Exploitation of Egypt," *Classical Weekly* 20 (1926), 3–6, 10–4.

————, *The Slave Systems of Greek and Roman Antiquity,* Philadelphia, 1955.

————, "The Ptolemies and the Welfare of Their Subjects," *American Historical Review* 43 (1938), 270–87.

Wetzel, F., Schmidt, E., and Mallwitz, A., *Das Babylon der Spätzeit* (Ausgrabungen der deutschen Orient-Gesellschaft in Babylon 8), Berlin, 1957.

Widengren, G., "Quelques rapports entre juifs et iraniens à l'époque des Parthes," Supplement to *Vetus Testamentum* 4 (1956), 197–241.

————, *The King and the Tree of Life in Ancient Near Eastern Religion* (= King and Saviour IV), Uppsala, 1951.

Wiesenberg, E., "Related Prohibitions: Swine Breeding and the Study of Greek," *Hebrew Union College Annual* 27 (1956), 213–33.

Windisch, H., *Die Orakel des Hystaspes,* Amsterdam, 1929.

Young, R. S., "Gordion 1956: Preliminary Report," *American Journal of Archeology* 61 (1957), 319–31.

————, "The Campaign of 1955 at Gordion: Preliminary Report," *American Journal of Archeology* 60 (1956), 249–66.

Zaehner, R. C., *Zurvan: A Zoroastrian Dilemma*, Oxford, 1955.

————, *The Teachings of the Magi. A Compendium of Zoroastrian Beliefs*, London, 1956.

Zielinski, T., *La Sibylle*, Paris, 1924.

Zimmermann, F., *The Book of Tobit*, New York, 1958.

Zimmern, H., "Zur Frage nach dem Ursprung des Purimfestes," *Zeitschrift für die Alttestamentliche Wissenschaft* 11 (1891), 157–9.

Zotenberg, H., "Geschichte Daniels. Ein Apokryph," *Archiv für wissenschaftliche Erforschung des Alten Testaments* 1 (1867–69), 385–427.

Index

The index includes references to the map as well as to the text. Map references are in parentheses. For example, the letter and number in parentheses following the first entry indicate that Abydos may be found on the map at coordinates C and 3.

Acknowledgements

I should like to render thanks to three very able scholars who read the manuscript of this book at an early stage in its development and who commented upon it. They are Professors A. E. R. Boak and George E. Mendenhall of the University of Michigan, and A. D. Nock of Harvard University. They have been sources of much useful information and advice which prevented blunders being made. The present version of the manuscript has also benefited from the suggestions of Professors Clark Hopkins of Michigan and C. Bradford Welles of Yale University. My thanks are also due to them. I ought to say, however, that the conclusions expressed in this book are my own.

My gratitude is also due to the staffs of the libraries of the University of Michigan and of the University of Nebraska for their assistance in finding books and for obtaining loans of books from other libraries. For the latter chore, I am particularly in the debt of Margaret Cooper of Nebraska.

Permission has been given by several presses to quote passages from their published works. I wish, therefore, to acknowledge the kindness of the Harvard University Press for the quotation from A. D. Nock's "The Roman Army and the Roman Religious Year," which appeared in the *Harvard Theological Review;* of the American Numismatic Society for the passage from E. T. Newell's *The Coinage of the Eastern Seleucid Mints;* of the Cambridge University Press for material from Ilya Gershevitch's *The Avestan Hymn to Mithra;* of the University of California Press for the sentences from *Tebtunis Papyrus* 703; of the American Oriental Society for the Old Persian texts translated in R. G. Kent's *Old Persian;* and, finally, of the Princeton University Press, publishers of that excellent compendium *Ancient Near Eastern Texts.*

Photographs and permission to reproduce them here have been supplied by a number of museums. I am indebted to Oberkonservator Dr. R. Lullies of the Glyptothek in Munich; the Museo Nazionale in Naples; the Oriental Institute of the University of Chicago; the Trustees of the British Museum; the Hirmer Verlag, Munich; to Herr

Dr. Greifenhagen, Director of the Ehemals Staatliche Museen in West Berlin; and to Dr. Henry Riad, Director of the Musée Gréco–Romain at Alexandria in the United Arab Republic.

S. K. E.

Lincoln, August 20, 1960.

A Note About the Author

SAMUEL K. EDDY was born in St. Louis, Missouri, in 1926. He has studied at Washington University (St. Louis) from which he holds an A.B. (1950) and an A.M. (1951), and at the University of Michigan (Ph.D., 1958). From 1955 to 1961 he was a member of the Department of History, University of Nebraska, holding the rank of Assistant Professor, and served as Research Associate in Classical Archeology in the University of Nebraska State Museum. He is now a member of the Department of History at the University of California, Santa Barbara. THE KING IS DEAD is his first book.